Thomas Robinson

Suggestive Commentary on St. Paul's Epistle to the Romans

Vol.II.: With Critical and Homiletical Notes

Thomas Robinson

Suggestive Commentary on St. Paul's Epistle to the Romans
Vol.II.: With Critical and Homiletical Notes

ISBN/EAN: 9783744779319

Printed in Europe, USA, Canada, Australia, Japan

Cover: Foto ©Lupo / pixelio.de

More available books at **www.hansebooks.com**

A SUGGESTIVE COMMENTARY

ON

ST. PAUL'S EPISTLE

TO THE

ROMANS,

WITH CRITICAL AND HOMILETICAL NOTES.

BY

REV. THOMAS ROBINSON,
AUTHOR OF "THE EVANGELISTS AND THE MISHNA."

VOL. II.

Second Thousand.

'Ο λύχνος αὐτῆς τὸ 'Αρνίον.—Rev. xxi. 23.

LONDON:
R. D. DICKINSON, 73 FARRINGDON STREET.
1878.

TO

DAVID A. WALLACE, D.D.,

PRESIDENT OF MONMOUTH COLLEGE, ILLINOIS, U.S.,

AS A SLIGHT ACKNOWLEDGMENT OF HIS

KINDNESS AND COURTESY

EXPERIENCED PERSONALLY AND IN RELATION TO THE PRESENT WORK,

These Volumes

ARE GRATEFULLY AND RESPECTFULLY INSCRIBED

BY

THE AUTHOR.

PREFACE TO SECOND VOLUME.

THE reader is already aware that, whatever merit may attach to the plan of the present work, it belongs, not to the Author of the Commentary, but to the projector of the scheme, the Rev. Dr Van Doren of America. It was Dr V.'s object, in the present undertaking, to popularise the Bible, and to provide for teachers of Sabbath Schools, conductors of Bible Classes, and preachers who might lack time and opportunity for greater preparation, a concise, ready, and, at the same time, interesting help in their important labours. The rule and characteristic feature of the work was to be rigid *condensation.* " It is surprising how many words can be left out, and yet the sense remain plain." The work was to be a kind of imitation of Bengel's Gnomon,—as Tholuck expresses it,

"Every pointing of the finger a sunbeam, and each hint a gleam of lightning."

The present Commentary, like the rest in the series, was to consist of two parts; the first, practical and homiletical, intended for ordinary readers; the second, critical, and designed especially for scholars. The first part was to contain only what might be introduced in a weekly Lecture or Bible Class of young persons. The critical notes, on the other hand, were to embrace, along with the nicer shades of meaning conveyed in the original, and the state of the Greek text itself according to the best authorities, a bird's-eye view of the sanctified wisdom of the Church from the earliest period to the present day, as brought to bear upon each passage, clause, and word in question. To this part of the work, also, were to be assigned illustrations from all sources, classical, Rabbinical and ecclesiastical; as well as all allusions, whether of a historical, scientific, or archæological nature. Thus were to be presented, for example, in their proper place and in the same condensed style, a sketch of the history, condition, and character of the Grecian states, both in their civil and social, moral and religious aspects; the history and character of Roman legislation; the hypocrisy and arrogant pretensions of Pharisaical and Rabbinical Judaism; the nature and moral influence of heathenism, especially among the Greeks and Romans, the principal arguments of Natural Theology in proving and illustrating the existence and perfections of God; and finally, the history of the leading doctrines taught in the Epistle, from the age succeeding that of the apostles to the present time.

While acknowledging how far short he has come of the high ideal placed before him by the projector of the work, the Author is conscious of having spared no pains to attain to it. The wide sweep intended to be taken in the Commentary was not, indeed, presented to him at the time of his undertaking the work; or else it is possible he might have shrunk from a task which, had there even been a consciousness of ability, might have involved more time and labour than he might have been able to expend upon it. Circumstances in divine providence, however, have enabled him to give much more time to the work than he could at first have calculated upon; while, by his residence abroad, partly in and near a city long celebrated as a seat of theological learning, and partly in Egypt and the Holy Land, he has obtained aids and facilities for prosecuting the work which he could not otherwise have enjoyed.

The works consulted, and the sources from which materials have been drawn, have been necessarily numerous and multifarious. In the critical notes the names are uniformly given; while in the practical part of the work this is done only in exceptional cases. Various and opposite opinions are of course cited in the notes, while in the body of the work itself the Author has given his own views, though sometimes exhibiting more senses of the text than one, and for these alone he is responsible.

Through the kindness of a friend, the Rev. G. Wilson of Glenluce, most of the sheets, after leaving the printer, have undergone a double examination, with verification of the numerous Scripture references. It is therefore hoped that, besides the errata noted at the end of Vol. I., but few corrections may require to be made. In a work, however, like the present—so abounding in references, it is almost unavoidable that, after the utmost care has been exercised in correcting the proofs, some typographical errors or mistakes in transcribing will still remain.

In conclusion, while conscious of the many imperfections cleaving to the work, the Author cannot forbear expressing his gratification at the favourable opinion given in various periodicals, and by many competent judges, regarding that part of it which has been already in the hands of readers. His prayer is, that the same gracious Spirit who presented the Church with this glorious Epistle, and who has aided him in his feeble attempts to unfold its precious contents for the benefit of his brethren and fellow-men, may also accompany the reader of these pages with His divine light and power, affording him as much pleasure and profit in the perusal of the work as he himself has experienced in the preparation of it; and to God only wise, of whom, and through whom, and to whom, are all things, be all the glory, through Jesus Christ, Amen.

T. R.

MORPETH, *July* 27, 1871.

SUGGESTIVE COMMENTARY.

EPISTLE TO THE ROMANS.

CHAPTER IX.

1. *I say the truth in Christ, I lie not, my conscience also bearing me witness in the Holy Ghost.*

I say the truth. Speaks deliberately in what he is about to say.
The doctrine finished, he applies it to the case of his countrymen.
A free gospel apparently opposed to their position as God's people.
Jews placed by justification through faith on a level with Gentiles.
This doctrine a stumbling-block to the Jews, 1 Cor. i. 23 ; 1 Pet. ii. 8.
A gospel without circumcision the ground of persecution, Gal. vi. 12.
Gentiles, as such, being made God's people, offensive to Jewish pride.
Apparently inconsistent with God's past dealings and promises.
Involving Israel's rejection as God's peculiar people.
This divine procedure in harmony with Scripture.
Explained and defended by various arguments.
Answers given to various objections on the part of the Jews.
A delicate subject, yet to be thoroughly dealt with and set at rest.
Paul first bespeaks his countrymen's calm and candid attention.
Solemnly assures them of the depth and sincerity of his love.
Rendered necessary by his doctrine and assumed position.
Paul appeared an antagonist of Judaism and the Jewish people.
Important to preachers to win confidence and disarm prejudice.

VOL. II. A

Hearers must be assured of the preacher sincerity and affection.
Preachers to be careful in all their statements to speak the truth.
In Christ. Paul not only spoke the truth, but spoke it in Christ—
1. As one united to Christ, belonging to Him and serving Him;
2. As in His sight and in constant fellowship with Him.
What he speaks is spoken—1. By Him whose member he is; 2. Under a consciousness of the most intimate union and communion with Him; 3. In virtue of that union and communion.
Paul conscious that what he speaks agrees with the mind of Christ.
Christ the element in which his soul ever moved.
To speak in Christ the fullest proof of sincerity and uprightness.
Not an oath, but a solemn averment resembling one.
Made by him—1. As a Christian; 2. As an apostle.
The matter being—1. Important; 2. Likely to be doubted.
All our words to be spoken in Christ—1. In union with Him; 2. In His sight.
Lie not. Truth and sincerity to mark our intercourse with each other, Col. iii. 9.
Professions of regard often hollow and insincere.
Only what is truthfully spoken is spoken in Christ.
Christ the enemy of all falsehood and deceit, Prov. xii. 22.
Himself the Faithful and True Witness, Rev. iii. 14.
My conscience. Conscientiousness to be constantly cultivated.
A tender and enlightened conscience a new covenant blessing.
Conscience only troublesome to the guilty and insincere.
To be kept void of offence toward God and toward men, Acts xxiv. 16.
Believers always to speak and act in all good conscience, Acts xxiii. 1.
Expensive to keep a conscience, damning to cast it away, 1 Tim. i. 19.
Bearing me witness. Precious testimony of a good conscience, 2 Cor. i. 12.
Conscience usually speaks the truth whether *we* do so or not.
A man carries his own witness within him, for or against.
In the Holy Ghost. Conscience accompanied by the Holy Spirit.
Each man has a conscience, the believer has the Holy Ghost besides.
The believer's conscience purified and enlightened by the Spirit, 1 Tim. iii. 9.
Conscience may be—1. Defiled, Titus i. 15; 2. Seared, 1 Tim. iv. 2.
Paul's statement made as in the presence of the Holy Ghost.

The Spirit a divine person and witness of our words and actions, Acts v. 3.
All insincerity and hypocrisy hateful to the Spirit of truth, Acts v. 9.
Fruit of the Spirit is in all goodness and righteousness and truth, Eph. v. 9.
To speak in the Holy Ghost a sufficient guarantee of sincerity.
Paul conscious of the Holy Spirit's presence and operation.
The Spirit the element in which he lived and acted.
A believer's privilege to speak and act in the Holy Ghost.
Our bodies the temples of the Holy Ghost who dwells in us, 1 Cor. iii. 16; vi. 19.

Ἐν Χριστῷ, by Christ, His Spirit guiding my tongue. *Beza.* In Christ, *i.e.*, even as Christ is true. *J. Cap.* By Christ; ἐν for νη, a form of swearing. *Pisc.*, *Ferme*, *Beng.*, *Flatt*, *Bloomf.* As I wish to be His apostle and to please Him. *Mor.* Before Christ as witness and Judge. *Melv.* According to Christ, *i.e.*, in virtue of fellowship with Him; as is right for a person to do who worships and fears Christ. *De Wette*, *Thol.*, *Meyer*, *Rück*. Agreeably to what becomes one who is in Christ; not an oath, but a solemn declaration such as Christ suggests and prompts. *Stuart.* Indicates perfect intimacy and fellowship. *Phil.*—Συμμαρτυρούσης, testifying along with me. *Eras.* Attesting at the same time. *Beza, Pisc.*—Ἐν πνεύματι ἁγίῳ, by the Holy Spirit, who is our witness. *Ferme.* Internal testimony of the Holy Ghost enlightening and confirming conscience. *Beng.* I who am moved by or am in the Holy Ghost. *Stuart.* Through or in conformity with the Holy Ghost. *De Wette.* Appeal to Christ and the Holy Spirit as Judge of the conscience a proof of their divinity and personality, *Leslie.*

---

2. *That I have great heaviness and continual sorrow in my heart.*

Great heaviness. Consistent with habitual joy, 2 Cor. vi. 10; 1 Pet. i. 6.
The apostle's heaviness was on account of others, not himself.
The greater our love to others the more heaviness on their account.
Paul comes down from his song of triumph to a wail of sorrow.
A believer's life a paradox. Great sorrow in the bosom of joy.
Sensibility not diminished but increased by spirituality.
In a world of sin and misery sensibility increases sorrow.
Paul wept while he warned the Church of false professors, Phil. iii. 18.
The Spirit of Jesus is a spirit of deep compassion for others, Luke xix. 41.
Continual sorrow. His heaviness not only great but constant.
The present and future state of his brethren daily upon his heart.

In the kingdom of grace on earth sorrow is as becoming as joy.
Only in the kingdom of glory are all tears wiped away.
Sowing time a time of weeping; joy comes in harvest, Ps. cxxvi. 5, 6.
Paul's sorrow was a generous, unselfish, Christ-like sorrow.
Had learned to weep like his Master over Christless souls, Luke xix. 41.
For three years warned the Ephesians night and day with tears, Acts xx. 31.
In Paul the highest knowledge was mingled with the deepest love.
The Christian's song of triumph is sung in the valley of tears.
In my heart. Therefore—1. A deep; 2. A sincere sorrow.
The renewed heart is enlarged and Christ-like. Room in it for a dying world.

Λυπη, grief, *i.e.*, for his brethren mentioned just after ver. 3—for them and their lost state. *Bloomf.* This verse to be connected with ὑπερ τ. ἀδελφων in ver. 3, the intermediate clause being a parenthesis.—'Οδυνη, the most vehement pain, as of a woman in childbirth. *Melv.* Anguish, keen and harassing pain. *Ellicot.*—Τῃ καρδιᾳ μου, not in the countenance and external, but in the heart, therefore vehement and sincere. *Ferme.*

---

3. *For I could wish that myself were accursed from Christ for my brethren, my kinsmen according to the flesh.*

For. Probably begins a parenthetical clause ending with "Christ." Gives either—1. A reason for his sorrow; or, 2. A proof of his love. The former, if read affirmatively, "I wished;" the latter, if potentially, "could wish."
Could wish. *Gr.*, Was wishing. Similar expression in Acts xxv. 22.
The wish either—1. One that actually existed, viz., before conversion;
Or, 2. One that would now exist, were it lawful or possible.
In the former case, describes his own former opposition to Christ;
In the latter, his fervent love to his brethren still in such opposition.
Paul once wished to be what his brethren were now, separate from Christ;
Could wish it even now, could he thereby win them to the gospel.
Frequently referred to his former unbelief, Acts xxii. 3, &c.; xxvi. 4; 1 Tim. i. 13.
Once as determined an enemy of the Nazarene as they were now.

Had seen the sin and experienced the misery of such a state.
Hence deeply concerned for his brethren in that condition.
"Brethren, be ye as I am, for I [was] as ye [are]," Gal. iv. 12.
Yet for their sakes could even now wish to change places with them.
Such a wish not to be entertained—1. Because its fulfilment impossible ;
2. Because no legitimate means appointed for their salvation.
Those delivered from the horrible pit (Ps. xl. 2) are concerned for friends still there.
Might wish again to experience its horrors, could it save them out of it.
Myself. Who am now so attached to Christ and His service.
When a standard-bearer in Satan's army submits, others may.
Those once guilty themselves cannot glory over but grieve for others.
Having tasted the wormwood and the gall, we can sympathise with others.
If read potentially, "I myself for or instead of my brethren."
Christ's love to His brethren seen in giving Himself for them.
Paul, in his measure, could have wished by His grace to do the same.
Accursed. 1. Separated ; 2. Devoted to destruction.
Paul once ignorantly wished to be in this condition.
Every sinner who keeps from Christ virtually wishes the same.
Away from and without Christ there is nothing but the curse.
Christ became a curse for His brethren to save them from it, Gal. iii. 13.
His Spirit in Paul would have made him willing to do the same.
From Christ. The only source of life and light and joy.
Wretched choice a sinner makes in keeping from Christ.
A Christless state of all others the most miserable.
The more precious Christ is to *us* the more we feel for those who are Christless.
Paul could wish for a time to be separated *from* Christ to bring others *to* Him.
For my brethren. Probably connected with ver. 2. His grief for his brethren.
The great body of the Jews still in unbelief and then likely to remain so.
The more grace in believers the more grief for unbelievers.
Believers, like Jesus, weep—1. With those who weep, John xi. 35 ;
2. For those who will not weep for themselves, Luke xix. 41.
In Christ's kingdom sorrow is exalted to a priestly feeling.

Grace sanctifies our passions. Sorrow for others a holy sorrow. Paul still calls the Jews by the endearing name of brethren. All of them his brethren by nature, only a few by grace. Grace consecrates, not cancels, natural affection. A Christian is a philanthropist, without ceasing to be a patriot. Paul loved the Jews all the more because a Christian. Love has degrees. Country and kin should lie nearest our heart. Our kindred should reap the advantage of our Christianity—
1. In greater love; 2. By our prayers; 3. Example; 4. Efforts for their good.

My kinsmen. A term more definite and nearer than "brethren." Paul wishes the Jews to recognise him as one of themselves. Never forgot, and did not wish to forget, that he was a Jew. Grace makes us neither ashamed nor forgetful of kinsmen. Family and national ties are of God's own institution, Ps. lxviii. 6. Such ties to be improved to His glory and the good of mankind.
According to the flesh. Natural descent from Abraham. An honour to be related to the Jews according to the flesh. Abraham the friend of God. Jesus the Son of God, a Jew. A still greater honour to be related according to the Spirit. A twofold relationship among men—1. By nature; 2. By grace. Fleshly kinship to the highest is less than spiritual to the lowest. Paul concerned for others, especially his kinsmen after the flesh. Deeply moved—1. By their present unbelief; 2. Their future ruin. Sufficient causes for his sorrow:—a rejected Saviour; a ruined temple; a desolated city; a dispersed nation; an undone eternity, Matt. viii. 11, 12; xxi. 40-44; Luke xix. 42-44; 1 Thess. ii. 15, 16.

Γαρ, indicates the greatness of His love. *Von Hofm.*—Ηὐχόμην, I wished or was wishing (optabam). *Vulg., Syr., Luth., De Wette.* I wish (opto). *Vat.* Could wish (optarem). *Eras., Pag., Beza, Pisc., Cas., Est.* Imperfect indicative, used for optative, like Gal. iv. 20; Acts xxv. 22. *Photius, Grot.* For potential. *Est.* For εὐχοίμην ἄν. *Beza.* So the most of interpreters from Origen downwards. I should gladly wish. *Dutch Bible, Flatt.* Could wish, were it possible. *Chrys.* Were it allowable. *Beng., Doddr., Whitby, Rückert, Thol., Hodge, Ellicot.* Was wishing or had almost wished. *Bloomf.* Others, with the *Syr.* and *Vulg.*, read the verb as simply indicative, and referring either to the time of unbelief (so *Cyprian, Ambrose, Jerome, Anselm*), or as *Bucer*, to the time when his grief was strongest; or, 'I wished if the thing were possible.' *Phil.* I not only wished (ἠβουλόμην), but prayed (ηὐχόμην). *Theod.* Had once or sometime prayed (aliquando orasse). *Bucer.* In this case ποτε required. *Thol.*— Αὐτὸς ἐγώ, placed after ἀνάθεμα in Codd. Sin. and Vat. I who but just now said, Nothing could separate us from Christ's love. *Theod.* I the same Paul who must utter the following judgment against Israel. *Lange.* The very person who writes this and is known to you. *Alford.* I who have laboured so much not to be separated from Christ. *Thol.* I my:'f instead of my brethren. *De Wette.* I myself now so devotedly attached to Chri:t. *Hald.*—'Ἀνάθεμα (ἀνά, apart, and τίθημι, to place ; to set apart or put away), distinguished from ἀνάθημα, an offering, Luke xxi. 5. Something offered to justice or devoted to destruction as a matter of justice. Κατάρα = קְלָלָה, Gal. iii. 10, more than ἀνάθεμα, which = חֵרֶם; the latter relative, the former absolute. *Beng.* According to Hebrew use חֵרֶם (= ἀνάθεμα) the separation of men, animals, cities, &c., for the Lord to be destroyed ; hence הֶחֱרִים, utterly to destroy, Jer. l. 21; Isa. xi. 15. LXX. ἀναθεματίζειν, ἐξολοθρεύειν. *Schütt.* So אִישׁ חֶרְמִי, the man of my curse, 1 Kings xx. 42. According to modern use among the Jews, חֵרֶם is the second of the three degrees of excommunication, viz.—1. נִדּוּי, removal from all domestic society to the distance of four yards for a month ; 2. חֵרֶם, exclusion from the synagogue-worship and social intercourse ; 3. שַׁמָּתָא (= μαράν-αθά, Maranatha, the Lord cometh), involving separation from God's worship and fellowship for ever. 'Ἀνάθ. = חֵרֶם—1. Devoted inalienably to God ; 2. Given up to destruction, Deut. vii. 25, 26 ; Isa. xxxiv. 2. *Mint.* 'Ἀνάθεμα εἶναι ἀπὸ Χριστοῦ, to forego the kingdom with its unspeakable glory and suffer all dreadful things. *Chrys.* Separated from the company around Christ ; not from His love, but from His glory and the enjoyment of it. *Theod.* Separated from Christ. *l'ag., Beza, Pisc., Vor., Mar., Ham., Taylor, Mackn. Whitby.* Anathema, or separated, not *to* but *from* Christ, Joshua vi. 18. *Ferme.* To be a devoted and execrable person,— to redeem them if it were possible by his own destruction. *Melv.* Anathema, cut off from Christ. *Diod.* From communion with Him. *Dickson, Per., Vat., Est.* From church fellowship. *Vat., Grot., Ham., Selden.* An execration from Christ, separated from His Church and the benefits He bestows on it. *Schött.* Forsaken by Christ for a time. *Beng.* Made an anathema after the example of Jesus Christ. *Waterland, Doddr.* Be given up to destruction, devoted to death for his country. *Tucker, Parkh., Flatt.* Indicates temporal judgments. *T. Edwards.* Banishment from Christ, and so from Christ's people. *Lange.* Be an outcast from Christ and excluded from the benefits of His religion. *Bloomf.* Bodily and spiritual destruction. *De Wette.* Cast out from Christ as an accursed thing. *Con. & Hows., Meyer.* Paul did not reckon his spiritual life too great a price if it might purchase their salvation. *Alford.* Counted his happiness nothing in comparison with his brethren's. *Hodge, Calv.* Ready to rescue his people at any price. *De Wette.* To die for them as David for Absalom. *Krebs.* Like the prayer of Moses, Exod. xxxii. 32. *Or., Bucer, Beng., Ferme.* Shut out from fellowship with Christ. *Von Hofm.* Words spoken hyperbolically. *Cyrill.* Spoken out of the warmth of his heart without any exact calculation or perhaps definite conception as to their meaning. *Calv.* Heroic love. *Beng.* 'Ἀνάθεμα = ἐπάρατος, ἀνακοινώνητος. *Hes.* Τὸ εἰς ἀφανισμὸν ἐσόμενον. *Suidas.*—Ἀπὸ Χριστοῦ. Some read ὑπὸ X. From Christ. *Most interpreters.* By Christ. *Gom., Flatt, Cobbin., Brown.* According to, or after the example of, Christ, as 2 Tim. i. 3. *Waterland.* Some connect ἀπὸ Χρ. with ηὐχόμην. *A. Clark, Elsner.* —Ὑπὲρ τ. ἀδελφῶν μου, for the benefit of my brethren. *Thol., Meyer.* Instead of my brethren. *Beng., De Wette, Brown.* Rabbins : ' Lo, I am his atonement ; I am in his place to bear his iniquities.' *Baal Aruch.* Among the Greeks καθάρμα and περίψημα (1 Cor. iv. 13), used for one devoting himself to death for the good of his country, as a public atonement or propitiatory sacrifice to the infernal gods in the time of public distress, as in pestilence. *Mint.* So Codrus and Menœceus ; and among the Romans, Curtius and the Decii.

4. *Who are Israelites : to whom pertaineth the adoption, and the glory, and the covenants, and the giving of the law, and the service of God, and the promises.*

Who are. Describes his brethren by their nationality and privileges.

Special reason for his concern and sorrow at their unbelief.
The more favoured they had been, the more calamitous their rejection.

Israelites. Their nationality. The descendants of Jacob or Israel.
"Israel," a name given by God himself to Jacob on a memorable occasion, Gen. xxxii. 28.
Meaning God's prince or champion; wrestled with God and prevailed, Hosea xii. 4.
The most honourable title a creature could bear. Heaven's heraldry.
Earthly dignities often won by victories over fellow-men.
A true Israelite one who prevails with God by prayer, John i. 47.
Even to be descended from Jehovah's champion no small honour
So regarded by the apostle himself, 2 Cor. xi. 22; Phil. iii. 5.
Israelite a name "above all Greek, above all Roman fame."

Pertaineth. Paul enumerates their privileges and prerogatives.
Infinitely surpassed those of every other nation.
No minstrel of his country's fame furnished with such topics.

Adoption. Sonship. Israel called God's son and first-born, Exod. iv. 22, 23; Hosea xi. 1.
The adoption was—1. National; 2. External; 3. Typical.
The type and figure of the adoption of believers in Jesus Christ.
The typical and national such as might lead to the personal.
Many among the national Israel God's true spiritual children.
The Israelites God's children as no other nation ever was.
As individuals, many of them not God's children but the devil's, John viii. 42, 44.

Glory. The Shekinah or visible presence of God dwelling among them.
A supernatural splendour in the Holy of holies, Exod. xxv. 22; Lev. ix. 6; Ezek. i. 28.
First in the tabernacle, Exod. xl. 34; Lev. xvi. 2; then in the temple, 1 Kings viii. 10; 2 Chron. v. 13.
The ark, on which it rested, hence called "the glory," 1 Sam. iv. 21; Ps. lxxviii. 61.
Not in the second temple. The symbol superseded by the reality, Hag. ii. 7.
The glory or symbol of the indwelling Godhead realised—
1. In Christ, John i. 14; Col. ii. 9; 2. In His members, 1 Cor. iii. 16; vi. 19; 2 Cor. vi. 16; Eph. ii. 21, 22.
God himself the glory of His people, Ps. cvi. 20; Jer. ii. 11; Isa. lx. 19; Deut. iv. 7.

A glory pertained to Israel unexampled among the nations.

Covenants. 1. Solemn engagements; here those made by God.
Repeatedly made with the patriarchs, Gen. xv. 18; xvii. 4, &c.; xxvi. 3, 4; xxviii. 13, 14.
Made with Israel—1. At Sinai, Exod. xxiv. 8; 2. In the land of Moab, Deut. xxix. 1, &c.; xxx. 1, &c.
Gracious promises on God's part their principal feature.
Made with the patriarchs unconditionally, with Israel conditionally.
Obedience to God's laws the condition enjoined on their part.
2. Covenants also ministrations, dispensations, economies.
To Israel the old covenant was given and the new promised, Jer. xxxi. 31, 32.
The first contained the promise, the second the fulfilment.
Both different modes of dispensing the grace of redemption.
The first preparatory and introductory to the second, Heb. vii. 18, 19; viii. 6, 7.
The first the type, the second the antitype, Heb. ix. 9–15; x. 1.
Together enveloped the spiritual destinies of the human race.

Giving of the law. 1. The act as described, Exod. xx. 18; Deut. iv. 32, &c.
2. The law itself. System of laws given, Deut. iv. 5–8; Ps. cxlvii. 19, 20.
A distinction exalting Israel above every other nation.
Served—1. For instruction; 2. For restraint; 3. For conviction.
Prepared the way for the promised Saviour, Gal. iii. 21.
Its observance brought national blessings in its train.

Service of God. 1. Worship of God as appointed by Himself.
The mode of acceptable worship prescribed to Israel.
Consisted in symbols and types. Sacrifices, washings, priesthood.
Establishment of God's true worship a people's highest privilege.
2. Service of God in daily personal life, Acts xxvi. 7; 2 Tim. i. 3.
Israel's highest honour to be servants of God, Neh. ii. 20; Isa. xliv. 2.

Promises. 1. Of blessings in general, Lev. xxvi. 4, &c.; Deut. xxviii. 1–14.
2. Of the Messiah in particular, Gal. iii. 16; Rom. xv. 8; Heb. xi. 17.
Given at various times and in various ways, Heb. i. 1. See chap. i. 2.
Some already fulfilled in Christ's first coming, Acts iii. 18, 22–26.
Others yet to be fulfilled in Israel's experience, Ezek. xxxvii.; Isa. lxvi.

All the promises of God Yea and Amen in Christ, 2 Cor. i. 20.
Gentiles by faith made fellow-heirs of the promises, Eph. iii. 6; Gal. iii. 29.
Promises all fulfilled at Christ's second appearing, chap. xi. 26; Acts i. 6; iii. 19-21.
Mentioned last as the transition to Christ himself.

'Ισραηλῖται, descendants of Israel, so called from שַׂר, a prince, and אֵל, God; יִשְׂרִי עִם אֱלֹהִים, as a prince thou hast had power with God, Gen. xxxii 28.—Υἱοθεσία, adoption; election to be God's peculiar people. *Ferme.* Family of God. *D. Brown.* With special relation to Canaan. *Bowyer, Bloomf.*—Δόξα, illustrious miracles. *Theod.* Israel's dignity as a people. *Est., Dick.* God himself the glory of His people. *Cam.* The ark. *Beza, Pisc., Calv., Drus, Grot., Ham.* Shekinah. *Con. & Hows., Niel.* Majesty. *Frit.* Elliptical for 'the glory of God,' as Rabbinical שכינתא, the Shekinah, lit. 'the inhabitation, = "כְּבוֹד, the glory of the Lord. *Stuart.* Presence of God which accompanied Israel through the wilderness and rested over the ark as the pillar of fire and cloud. *Reiche, De Wette, Ols., Rück.* Rabbins: 'The Shekinah dwells not out of the land of Israel.'—Διαθῆκαι (διά and τίθημι, to arrange, dispose), old and new covenants. *Theod.* Plural for singular = ἡ διαθήκη. *Vat.* Testament. *Vulg., Eth.* Testaments. *Eras., Mor., Cas., Vat.* Compacts or leagues (pacta s. foedera). *Pisc., Beza, Pag.* Two tables of the law. *Par., Tol., Melv.* Moral law. *Ferme.* Dispensations. *Beng.* Arrangements or constitutions in regard to Israel as a people. *Brown.* Compacts with the patriarchs and nation. *Cobbin.* 'Covenants of promise' (Eph. ii. 12); the one covenant with Abraham in its successive renewals (Gal. iii. 16, 17). *D. Brown.* Accommodation to Jewish mode of speaking; each renewal of the one covenant with Adam, as with Noah, Abraham, Isaac, &c., being regarded as a *new* covenant. *Bloomf.* = συνωμοσία. *Hes.* Heb. בְּרִית.—Νομοθεσία (νόμος and τίθημι), giving of the law from Mount Sinai. *Bloomf.* And possession of it afterward. *D. Brown.* More especially the judicial law. *Ferme, Melv.*—Λατρεία (λάτρις, a hired servant). Ministry. *Syr.* Religion. *Arab.* The true religion. *Tir.* Worship (cultus). *Eras., Pisc., Beza, Cas.* The ceremonial law. *Ferme, Melv.* Rites of the temple, priesthood. *Stuart.* Levitical service or worship, forming part of the νομοθεσία. *Ferme, Bloomf.* Service of the temple. *Con. & Hows.* Service of God or of the sanctuary, the whole divinely instituted religious service. *D. Brown.* Heb. עֲבֹדָה.—Ἐπαγγελίαι, promises; that of the Messiah variously repeated, the foundation of all special promises; or this general promise with many other special ones. *Melv.* The word of faith and of the covenant of grace, promised to Israel in divers manners (Heb. i. 1), and at length fully made manifest in the Gospel. *Ferme.* Various divine promises respecting the possession of Palestine and especially the Messiah. *Bloomf.* Equivalent to ἡ ἐπαγγελία, the promise, viz., of the Messiah. *De Wette.* Of blessings. *Con. & Hows.* The great Abrahamic promises successively unfolded and only fulfilled in Christ. *D. Brown.*

---

5. *Whose are the fathers, and of whom, as concerning the flesh, Christ came, who is over all, God blessed for ever. Amen.*

Whose. Israel distinguished by persons as well as things. A nation's privilege to call noble men of God their own.

Fathers. Patriarchs; the fathers and founders of the nation.
Illustrious men of whom God declared Himself to be their God.
Jews distinguished for their high and honoured ancestry.
The blood in Israel's veins was that of Abraham, Isaac, and Jacob.
A noble and holy stock, though a disobedient and gainsaying people.
Planted a noble vine, wholly a right seed, Jer. ii. 21.
Flesh. His human nature; therefore having also a divine one, chap. i. 3.
Not from Israel, but from God, as to His higher and divine nature, Micah v. 2.
The apostle careful to distinguish the two natures of Christ.
Christ came. The climax of Israel's lofty privileges.
Christ or Messiah the Saviour promised in Eden, Gen. iii. 15.
The high honour conferred on Abraham was to be His ancestor;
On the Jews, to be His brethren according to the flesh.
Christ's coming was the ground—1. Of the calling of Abraham;
2. Of the separation of Israel as the people of God.
Jews ought to be dear to Christians—1. For Christ's sake; 2. The Gospel's.
The prepared reservoir for the water of life destined for all lands.
Over all. Paul cannot mention Christ without magnifying Him.
Christ is *of* the Jews according to His human nature;
Over the Jews, and over all, in virtue of His divine nature.
Universal rule and supremacy ascribed to Him, Eph. i. 21.
Not merely given to Him as Mediator, as Matt. xxviii. 18; 1 Pet. iii. 22;
But properly belonging to Him as God, Isa. ix. 6, 7; Rev. i. 8.
This supremacy and power displayed when upon earth.
Over spirits, Matt. viii. 16; over nature, ver. 26; xvii. 27; over man, John ii. 14, 16; xviii. 6.
Christ the world's Creator, John i. 3; Col. i. 16; and Preserver, ver. 17; Heb. i. 3.
David's Son, and yet David's Lord, Ps. cx. 1; Matt. xxii. 42, 43; Rev. xxii. 16.
A Saviour needed who is over all, Isa. xlv. 21-25; John vi. 68; Heb. vii. 25.
God. Christ here expressly called God. So John i. 1; Acts xx. 28; Eph. v. 5.
The great God, Titus ii. 13; mighty God, Isa. ix. 6; true God, 1 John v. 20.
God manifest in the flesh, 1 Tim. iii. 16; God with us, Matt. i. 23.

In the form of God and equal with God, Phil. ii. 6.
Image of the invisible God, Col. i. 15 ; 2 Cor. iv. 4. One with the Father, John x. 30 ; xiv. 9.
Brightness of the Father's glory and express image of His person, Heb. i. 3.
Divine attributes ascribed to Christ by Paul and elsewhere :—
Eternity, Col. i. 15, 17 ; John i. 1 ; Rev. i. 8, 11 ; xxii. 13 ; Micah v. 2.
Omnipresence, Eph. i. 23 ; iv. 10 ; Matt. xviii. 20 ; xxviii. 20 ; Rev. ii. 2.
Omniscience, John ii. 24, 25 ; xxi. 17 ; Matt. ix. 4 ; Acts i. 24 ; Rev. ii. 23.
Omnipotence, Rev. i. 8 ; unchangeableness, Heb. xiii. 8 ; Rev. i. 8, 17, 18.
Divine operations attributed to Him :—
Creation and preservation of the world, Col. i. 16, 17 ; Heb. i. 2, 3.
Judgment of the world, Rom. ii. 16 ; xiv. 10 ; 2 Cor. v. 10 ; 2 Thess. i. 7-10.
Divine worship rendered Him, chap. x. 13 ; Acts vii. 60 ; Phil. ii. 10, 11 ; Rev. v. 12, 13.
His making Himself equal with God was the cause of the Jews' hatred, John v. 18 ; x. 33.
Cause of joy that Christ's Godhead is so fully and expressly declared.
The Saviour of man behoved to be God himself, Isa. xlv. 21.
The divinity of His person constitutes the value of Christ's atonement.
Makes His incarnation the highest lesson of condescension and love, Phil. ii. 3-8 ; 2 Cor. viii. 9.
Blessed for ever. 1. Worthy to be eternally praised, Rev. v. 12 ; vii. 10.
2. Actually so praised. Christ praised with the Father, Rev. v. 13 ; vii. 10.
God thus usually spoken of by the Jews, Rom. i. 25 ; 2 Cor. xi. 31.
The expression applied to no other without blasphemy.
The Godhead of Christ thus emphatically declared.
Early Christians sang praises to Him as God. *Pliny's Letter to Trajan.*
Though others blaspheme Him, we bless Him as God. *Chrysostom.*
Christ not to be named without feelings of adoration and love.

Amen. Verily; be it so. Added for solemn confirmation. The ascription of divine glory to Christ deliberately made. The apostle's whole soul goes out in this ascription. The enlightened and grateful believer will unite in this hearty Amen.

To κατα σαρκα, as to His human nature. Emphatical, alluding to His other and divine nature. *Bloomf.*—Ὁ ὢν ἐπι παντων Θεος, &c. Three interpretations according to punctuation—1. All referring to Christ and declaring His divinity; the view of the ancient church and the prevailing one of modern times; accepted by *Thol., Ols., Scholz*, &c. 2. Part referring to Christ and part to God. *Eras., Locke, Clarke, Ammon, Stolz, Frit., Meyer.* 3. All referring to God and not to Christ. Held by some few Fathers, the Rationalists, and some others. *Whiston, Wetstein, Semler, Glöckler, Reiche.* From Col. i. 15-18, Rückert in doubt between the first and the third. The third view possible. *Eras.* Θεος (God), omitted by the Syriac, Cyprian, Chrys., Hilary, Grotius; Cyprian and Hilary, however, quoting the passage in proof of Christ's divinity. Omitted per incuriam. *Par., Beza, Tol.* The Artemonites (early Unitarians) read ὢν ὁ ἐπι π. Θ., making thus another privilege of the Father. *Phil.* Not here a doxology, so much as a declaration of the divine nature of Christ as the antithesis of το κ. σαρκα; a doxology requiring εὐλογητος ὁ Θεος, as in each of the examples in the New Testament, Rom. i. 25; 2 Cor. xi. 31; 1 Pet. i. 3; Luke i. 68; 2 Cor. i. 3; Eph. i. 3. *Middleton.* Θεος εὐλ. follows ἐπι παντ. as a second predicate; σαρξ and Θεος contrasted as יְשׁ and אֵל, Isa. xxxi. 3. *Von Hofm.* A doxology here unmeaning and frigid in the extreme. *Alford.* A testimony to the identity of Christ's Deity with that of the Father. *Bp. Pearson.* Views of early Christians in reference to Christ's divinity clear. In the Fathers the intimate connection between His divine and human natures alluded to, though the relation not exactly defined, nor the part each takes in His person philosophically determined. Fathers careful on the one hand to avoid the error of the Ebionites and Artemonites who considered Jesus only as the son of Joseph and Mary, and on the other that of the Docetæ who rejected the true humanity of Christ. Opposed also the opinion of Cerinthus and Basilides, that the Logos (Christ) had descended on the man Jesus at His baptism, and that of Valentinus, that Christ was indeed born of Mary, but that He only used her as a channel by which to enter the world. Clement of Alexandria thought the body of Jesus not subject to the accidents of the external world, or the same physical necessity as other human bodies. According to Origen, it could appear to different persons under different forms. The Christians of Smyrna, in their account of the martyrdom of Polycarp, say that Christ alone is the object of their worship as the Son of God. Irenæus, a disciple of Polycarp, says, Every knee shall bow to Him us to the one Lord and God, one Saviour and King. Arius, a presbyter of Alexandria, maintaining that the Son was a creation of the Father, condemned by the First General Council held at Nice (325), which decided that the Son is of the same essence (ὁμοουσιος) as the Father, but sustains to Him the relation of one begotten to one begetting. The term ὁμοουσιος objected to by Eusebius, Bishop of Nicomedia, and others, but defended by Athanasius of Alexandria. A second General Council held at Constantinople (381) confirmed the decision of that of Nice. Semi-Arians, headed by Basil of Ancyra and Georgius of Laodicæa, with Cyril of Jerusalem and Eusebius of Cæsarea, abstained from using the term ὁμοουσιος, maintaining that Christ was of *like* essence with the Father (ὁμοιουσιος), in opposition to the strict Arians, the followers of Aetius, Bishop of

Antioch, Eunomius of Cyricum, and Acacius of Cæsarea in Palestine. Marcellus, Bishop of Ancyra, and still more Photinus of Sirmium, his disciple, went into the opposite extreme of Sabellianism, but modifying it by drawing a line between the Logos and the Son of God. Eusebius says, All the psalms and hymns of the brethren from the beginning celebrate the praises of the Word of God, and ascribe divinity to Him. Apollinaris, Bishop of Laodicæa, taught that the fulness of the Godhead dwelt bodily in Christ, and that the Logos supplied the place of the higher reason, which was therefore unnecessary in Him. His view opposed by Athanasius and the two Gregories, and condemned by the Council of Constantinople (381), which decided that Christ possessed a perfect human nature, consisting of a body and a rational soul, together with His divine nature. Theologians of the Alexandrian school asserted strongly the unity of the natures, while those of Antioch, Diodore of Tarsus, and Theodore of Mopsuestia, made a strict distinction between the two. The phrase Θεοτόκος (mother of God) brought into use by the increasing homage paid to the Virgin. Opposed first by Anastasius, a presbyter of Alexandria (428). Disapproved by Nestorius, patriarch of Constantinople and disciple of Theodore. Nestorius opposed by Cyril, patriarch of Alexandria, and by Celestius, Bishop of Rome ; but supported by John of Antioch and the Eastern bishops in general. Condemned by the Council of Ephesus (431), overruled by Cyril. The Nestorian party separating from the Church became known afterwards as Chaldean Christians, or Christians of St Thomas. Eutychus, Archimandrite or Abbot of Constantinople, maintained the doctrine of one nature alone in Christ. Dioscurus, the successor of Cyril, wishing to force it on the Eastern Church, was condemned by the Council of Chalcedon (451), which decided that the two natures were neither to be separated nor confounded. Eutychus himself deposed by a Synod held at Constantinople (449), charged with reviving Valentinian and Apollinarian errors. The admission of a new clause into the creed of the Fifth General Council (553), viz., that one of the divine persons had been crucified, gave the Monophysites an ascendency in the Church. Peter Fullo, or the Fuller, first introduced the clause Θεὸς ἐσταυρώθη (God was crucified) into the Trisagion, but was banished by an imperial decree (470). Justinian, in 533, pronounced the phrase 'unum crucifixum esse ex sancta et consubstantiali Trinitate.' to be orthodox, in accordance with John II., Bishop of Rome, but in opposition to his predecessor Hormisdas. The attempt of Heraclius to unite the Monophysites with the Church led to the controversy respecting the two wills of Christ. The emperor, in accordance with Cyrus, patriarch of Alexandria, adopted the doctrine of one divine energy and one divine will in Christ. Sophronius, patriarch of Jerusalem (635), opposed the doctrine ; and the Sixth General Council, held at Constantinople (680), decided that there existed in Christ two wills and two energies. The adoption-interpretation of the Sonship of Christ advanced by several Spanish bishops, as Elipand of Toledo and Felix of Urzella, but successfully combated by Alcuin, and condemned by the Synod of Frankfort (794). After the execution of Michael Servetus in Geneva (1553), a sect of Anti-Trinitarians formed themselves, professing the highest esteem for the man Jesus. Through Lelius Socinus, and especially his nephew Faustus, these were united into a distinct body under the name of Socinians, containing the germs of later Rationalism (negatively), and of external biblical Supranaturalism (positively). A difference of opinion between the Lutherans and the Reformed on the communicatio idiomatum (communication of the properties), and the unio personalis (personal union) in Christ, arose in connection with the controversy on the Sacrament ; the Calvinists maintaining the doctrine of two natures in one person, and so confining the human nature of Christ to heaven, the Lutherans that of a real transition of one nature into the other, and hence the ubiquity of Christ's body. That Christ is not now on earth according to His human nature was maintained in the Heidelberg Catechism, and in the Helvetic, Gallic, Anglican, and Belgic Confessions. *Hagenbach*.

6. *Not as though the word of God hath taken none effect: for they are not all Israel which are of Israel.*

Not as though, &c. Alluding to the grounds of his sorrow in ver. 2.
Israel's rejection by God not yet expressly mentioned.
Notwithstanding his grief for them, that rejection not absolute.
God's gracious promises had not fallen to the ground.
Israel's rejection consistent with God's faithfulness.
Opposed only to the Jewish view concerning all Israel's salvation.
This view supposed to be necessitated by God's veracity.
Word of God. God's promises. To Israel pertained the promises, ver. 4.
God's Word largely made up of great and precious promises, 2 Pet. i. 4.
Special promises made to Israel in the Old Testament.
Many of these already fulfilled; others yet to be so, Ezek. xxxvi. 26, &c.; xxxvii. 1, &c.
Taken none effect. Failed of its accomplishment.
Gr., Hath fallen; *i.e.*, to the ground, as in 1 Sam. iii. 19; Luke xvi. 17, *Gr.*
Israel's rejection an apparent, not real, breach of promise.
Individuals of them *now* saved; afterwards, the whole nation, chap. xi. 26.
Promises made to the patriarchs a splendid reversion for their race.
God's Word always fulfilled one way or another, Jer. xxxii. 42.
Promises true, though men refuse the blessing. *Theodoret.*
For. Proves the consistency of the promises with Israel's rejection;
1. From the nature of the promises (6–13); 2. From God's sovereignty (14–24); 3. From the prediction of that very rejection (25–29); 4. From the cause of it in their unbelief (30–33).
Not all Israel. The true Israel to whom the promises belonged.
All descended carnally from Israel are not the Israel of God.
Selection or choice made in the patriarch's posterity.
Many of Abraham's natural are not his spiritual seed, John viii. 39.
Nathaniel an Israelite indeed, John i. 47. Believers are God's Israel, Gal. vi. 16.
Those only Jews who are so inwardly, chap. ii. 28, 29. Described, Phil. iii. 3.
All are not Christians who belong to the Christian Church.
Grace often runs in the line though not in the blood, John i. 13.
Paul here enters on the deep and mysterious subject of election.
1. Election of nations to privileges; 2. Of individuals to salvation.

Οὐχ οἷον δὲ ὅτι, I do not say such a thing as that the word of God, &c. *Luth.*, *Winer.* It is not possible that. *Hes., Beza, Ferme, Ewald.* Like οὐχ ὅτι, with λέγω supplied before οἷον. *Meyer.* Denies this to be the reason of the wish. *Von Hofm.* Οἷον for ὡς, as 2 Thess. ii. 2 ; what I have said does not imply that, &c. *Bloomf.* Meets a tacit objection, God's promises appearing to fail if Israel is rejected ; distinguishes between the real and nominal seed of Abraham. *Melv.*—Ἐπέπτωκεν, has been void, as נָפַל, Jos. xxi. 43 ; 1 Sam. iii. 19. *Grot.* Fallen ineffectual to the ground. *Doddr., Con. & Hows.* Failed, been frustrated. *Stuart.*—Οὐ γὰρ πάντες οἱ ἐξ Ἰσ., for not all they which are of Israel are Israel. *D. Brown.* Of Israel as their father. *Ferme.* Rabbins : 'All Israel have a portion in the world to come except apostates and heretics.' *Pirke Aboth.* 'Only the disciples of the wise are called man and Israel.' *Zohar.*

---

7. *Neither, because they are the seed of Abraham, are they all children: but, In Isaac shall thy seed be called.*

Seed of Abraham—*i.e.*, By natural descent, according to the flesh. All that have come from Abraham's loins not his true children.
Are they—*i.e.*, Are they reckoned, regarded, intended ; are really.
Children—*i.e.*, Of Abraham in a spiritual sense ; or according to the promise.
All Abraham's children not included in the promise, Gen. xii. 7 ; xv. 5–18.
Ishmael and Abraham's children by Keturah excluded, Gen. xxv. 1–4.
The natural seed not those of whom the promises were made.
Thus election began even in the family of Abraham.
Abraham's true children are those who have Abraham's faith, chap. iv. 11, 13 ; Gal. iii. 9.
Thus many of the Jews were not Abraham's children, John viii. 39.
In Isaac, &c. Gen. xxi. 12. Isaac = Laughter. Reason given, Gen. xvii. 17 ; xxi. 6.
God's promises to be received with joy, Acts ii. 41 ; viii. 39 ; xvi. 31 ; 1 Thess. i. 6.
Holy laughter when the promises are fulfilled, Ps. cxxvi. 2 ; Luke vi. 21.
Exemplified in Abraham as highest worship, Gen. xvii. 17.
Isaac a type of Christ—1. Given by promise ; 2. His birth supernatural ; 3. Attended with joy, Luke ii. 10, 11, &c. ; 4. Isaac persecuted by Ishmael, Gen. xxi. 9 ; Gal. iv. 22 ; 5. Inherited all his father's possessions, Gen. xxiv. 36 ; Heb. i. 2 ; 6. Given up as a sacrifice ; 7. Received again as from the dead, Heb. xi. 19.
Be called. 1. Accounted as the seed referred to in the promise ; 2. Called into existence, as chap. iv. 17 ; 3. Chosen, as Isa. xlix. 1.

God's sovereign election indicated. Isaac, not Ishmael, the seed. Mere natural descent gives no claim to the promises.

Οὐδ' ὅτι, &c., sovereignty in excluding Abraham's children from the Church, except Isaac's seed. *Cobbin.*—Ἐν Ἰσαακ, &c., after Isaac. *Gesenius.* Through Isaac. *Frit., Meyer.* The true election such of Abraham's seed as God unconditionally chooses, as seen in the promise, 'In Isaac,' &c. *D. Brown.*—Κληθήσεται, be named, and obtain celebrity. *Bloomf.* Have its continuation with the blessings promised. *Delitzsch.* Rabbins : 'The seed of Abraham began with Isaac ; as it is said, In Isaac shall thy seed be called ; whence one of the wise men says : In Isaac, and not even in *all* Isaac ; thereby excluding Esau.' *Manasseh ben Israel.*

---

8. *That is, They which are the children of the flesh, these are not the children of God : but the children of the promise are counted for the seed.*

Children of the flesh. Children by mere natural generation, viz. : 1. Ishmael and his descendants ; 2. Abraham's sons by Keturah and their posterity ; 3. The natural descendants of Abraham in general.
Unbelieving Jews mere children of the flesh as truly as was Ishmael.
Children of God. 1. Children in God's esteem ; 2. By God's appointment ; 3. Those to whom He will be a God as He was to Abraham, Gen. xvii. 7.
Children of the flesh also distinguished from children of God, John i. 13.
Children of the promise. Born entirely in virtue of a promise, viz. :—1. Isaac ; 2. Believers, whether Jews or Gentiles, Rom. iv. 11, 16, 17 ; Gal. iii. 29.
Isaac a type of believers—1. As born according to divine promise ; 2. By supernatural power, Gen. xvii. 5 ; Isa. liii. 10-12 ; John i. 13 ; v. 25 ; vi. 44, 45, 65.
Born not according to nature's laws; but the power of a promise. *Chrysostom.*
Counted for the seed. Regarded as those called the seed.
A promised seed alone inherits promised blessings.
No claim from mere birth. Some Jews believed, and some not, Acts xxviii. 24.
Believing Jews and Gentiles counted Abraham's true seed, Gal. iii. 7, 9.
Christ the seed, including all believers as His members, Gal. iii. 29.

Τέκνα τ. Θεοῦ, those to whom pertained the adoption according to inward grace. *Ferme.*—Τέκνα τ. ἐπαγγελίας, for τέκνα ἐπαγγελμένα ; those to whom pertained the felicity promised to Abraham. *Bloomf.* Those born by the power of the promise, or 'born of God' (John i. 13), as Isaac from Sarah; contrasted with those born by the power of nature (τέκνα τ. σαρκός), or of flesh and blood (John i. 13), as was Ishmael from Hagar. *Ferme.* The patriarchal-theocratic privileges not to be enjoyed according to the claims of fleshly descent, nor even of certain *works* (10-13), but solely according to the purpose of God, independent of all human conditions. *Thol.* The same divine law in the completion as in the commencement of God's Church, viz., that its destined membership is not dependent on anything in man, but is solely a thing of God's free will. *Hofm.*—Λογίζεται εἰς for νομίζεται εἶναι. *Bloomf.*

---

9. *For this is the word of promise, At this time will I come, and Sarah shall have a son.*

Word of promise. 1. The terms; 2. The account of the promise. Quoted from Gen. xviii. 10, 14, *Gr.* Abridged, but main part exactly given.

Passages sometimes referred to without being exactly or entirely quoted.

Only so much quoted as suits the purpose in hand.

Literal exactness not always absolutely necessary.

At this time. Or, as in the passage quoted, "according to the time of life," Gen. xviii. 10, 14.

Also, "at the appointed time," ver. 14.

Greek translation followed rather than the Hebrew.

Time for its fulfilment often given along with the promise.

So the captivity in Babylon, Jer. xxv. 11, 12; coming of Messiah, Dan. ix. 24-26.

Faith expected the fulfilment at the appointed time, Dan. ix. 2; Luke ii. 25, 38.

Fulfilment of promises to be patiently and believingly waited for, Hab. ii. 3.

Will I come. God "comes" in remarkable acts of providence, Rev. ii. 5.

So He "visits" individuals and peoples, 1 Sam. ii. 21; Exod. iv. 31; Ruth i. 6.

Christ's birth like Isaac's, from a divine visitation, Luke i. 68.

God a living Agent in the events of life and of history.

Common blessings sweetened as coming from a covenant God.

Sarah. Means "princess." Abraham's wife and half-sister, Gen. xx. 12.

Name changed from Sarai, Gen. xvii. 15; reason of the change, ver. 16.

Connection with the godly brings both honour and advantage.

Names often changed by God on the occasion of special blessing.
So Jacob to Israel, Gen. xxxii. 28; Oshea to Jehoshua or Joshua, Num. xiii. 16.
Jehovah's own name often prefixed for honour and comfort.
Names sometimes changed by God to indicate His displeasure.
Jeconiah made Coniah, God's name withdrawn, Jer. xxii. 24, 28; xxiv. 1.
Christ writes on His victorious people God's name and His own, Rev. iii. 12.
Sarah accompanied Abraham from Chaldæa at God's command.
Fell into the hands of Pharaoh (Gen. xii. 15) and of Abimelech (xx. 2), yet preserved.
Impatient for children, gave Hagar her maid to Abraham as a concubine.
Died at Hebron and buried in the cave of Machpelah, Gen. xxiii. 19.
Sarah honourably mentioned in the New Testament as an example to wives, 1 Pet. iii. 5, 6.

Κατα τ. καιρον τουτον, at this (very) time; marking Isaac as a child of promise. *Ferme.* This time; reckoning the conception of the child from hence. *Doddr.* According to the usual time from conception to birth, nine months hence. *Guyse.* Καιρον (from καιρω, to run, curro), suitable time, season. Heb. מוֹעֵד עֵת. In Gen. xviii. 10, the Septuagint has κατα τ. καιρον τουτον εἰς ὡρας, reading חיה, instead of ה׳ת, in the present text, and adding εἰς ὡρ., from ver. 14, for Heb. כָּעֵת, 'at the appointed time.' According to Heb., 'the living time,' *i.e.*, the current, present time; so *Soph. Trach.* Χρονῳ τῳ ζωντι και παροντι. *Frit.* When the present time is repeated, I will return; כ in כָּעֵת indicating comparison, and so the duality. *Nielson.*—'Ελευσομαι, I will come, in the grant of my mercy, and by a supernatural operation of my providence. *Guyse.* Heb. אָשׁוּב, I will return.

---

10. *And not only this; but when Rebekah also had conceived by one, even by our father Isaac.*

Not only this. Election still further shown in Abraham's family.
Not even all Isaac's posterity counted for the seed.
Rebekah. Daughter of Bethuel, of Mesopotamia or Padanaram.
Chosen by God as a wife for Isaac, and remarkably pointed out, Gen. xxiv. 14, 50, 51.
Election even more manifest in Isaac's than in Abraham's children.
1. The distinction now made between sons of the same mother;
2. That mother a free woman and Isaac's lawful wife;
3. The sons twins, but the distinction in favour of the younger.
One. The children had both the same father and mother.

God's sovereignty rendered increasingly conspicuous.
Our father. The term applied to Abraham, Isaac, and Jacob, ver. 5.
To gain the Jews, Paul spoke and acted as a Jew, 1 Cor. ix. 20.
Always speaks honourably of his Hebrew ancestors, Phil. iii. 5.
This gain of ancestry counted loss for Christ, Phil. iii. 7.
Godly forefathers a blessing as engaging us to follow them.

Οὐ μόνον δέ. Not only he, but Rebekah also experienced this. *Ferme.* This distinction made not only between the immediate offspring of Abraham. *Guyse.* A like distinction made among the legitimate descendants of the 'son of promise,' showing God's right also to choose, justify, and glorify those who are κλητοί, called according to His purpose in respect to the heavenly inheritance. *Stuart.* An anacolouthon in Ρεβέκκα —ἐρρήθη αὐτῇ. *Bloomf.*—Κοίτην ἔχουσα, when she had conceived. *Pag., Beza, Per., Eras.* Uterum ferens. *Cas.* Κοίτην, used by LXX. for משכב, in Lev. xviii. 20, &c. Hebrew idioms naturally and appropriately abound in this chapter. *Beng.* Κ. ἔχουσα, by *metalepsis,* for συλλαβοῦσα. *Bloomf.* Κοίτην, by metonymy, for offspring; antecedent for the consequent. *Thol.*—'Εξ ἑνός, by one, in opposition to many husbands. *Niel.*

---

11. *For the children being not yet born, neither having done any good or evil, that the purpose of God according to election might stand, not of works, but of Him that calleth.*

Children. Those of Isaac and Rebekah, viz., Jacob and Esau.
Being not yet born. Mentioned to show God's free election.
Not a mere prediction in regard to them, but a purpose.
Neither having done. God's election not determined by works.
Works viewed not only as not existing, but as not foreseen.
Superior place given to Jacob without regard to superior merit.
Good or evil. So as to make the one more worthy than the other.
Election not grounded on good works existing or foreseen.
Believers created in Christ Jesus *unto* good works, not because of them, Eph. ii. 10.
That. Reason why the distinction was declared before the birth.
A wise reason for what God does, and for the time when He does it.
Here, to show the absolute sovereignty of God's election.
Purpose of God. 1. In respect to the two brothers, Jacob and Esau;
2. Generally, in respect to nations and individuals.
What God does in time, He purposes in eternity.
God's purposes respect—1. The universe; 2. Nations; 3. Men, Eph. i. 11.
His purposes universal, from the connection of events with each other.
Formed—1. Before He gave existence to the world, Eph. i. 4;

2. For His own glory and the good of His creatures, Rev. iv. 11; Ps. cxlv. 9.
3. In infinite wisdom, justice, holiness, and love.
Executed in His providence and government of the universe.
Their execution not contingent but certain, Ps. xxxiii. 11; Isa. xlvi. 10.
Include believers' predestination, calling, and salvation, chap. viii. 28; Eph. i. 11; 2 Tim. i. 9.
According to election. Respecting His election—1. Of Jacob; 2. Generally.
The purpose of God in regard to men rests on His own free choice.
Special favour to some involves no injustice to others.
All receive more benefits than they deserve, none less.
God claims the right to bestow His favours freely, Matt. xx. 15.
Absence of merit makes absence of complaint. "I do thee no wrong."
Stand. 1. Continue still to exist in God's dealings;
2. Remain secure, unaffected by man's doings.
God's object to display the sovereignty of His electing purpose.
Sovereignty a divine attribute, and to be glorified like the rest.
Manifested in His dealings both with angels and men.
Free election a standing feature in the divine government.
Not of works. Not as the reward of works, actual or foreseen.
God's election, not man's works, the ground of special favour.
Good works the result of God's purpose, not the ground of it, Eph. ii. 10.
All good in man the effect of grace in God, chap. vii. 14, 18; 1 Cor. iv. 7; xv. 10; Isa. lxiv. 6; Luke xvii. 10.
Of Him that calleth. God's purpose grounded in Himself, not man.
Jacob's call to supremacy unconditioned by Jacob's works.
The calling of God contrasted with the conduct of man.
The ground of preference in the caller, not the called.
Things that are not are called by God as though they were, chap. iv. 17; 1 Cor. i. 26-28.
Paul justifies God's choosing and calling the Gentiles to salvation.
That election sovereign and in harmony with His previous procedure.

Μηδε πραξαντων, &c. Strong intimation against the pre-existence of souls. *Guyse.*
—Κακον. Codd. Sin., Vat., and Alex. have φαυλον. Reference to Esau's profaneness, Heb. xii. 16. *Koppe.*—Κατ' εκλογην, according to election. *Eras., Cam., Mor.* By election. *Cas.* Elective, entirely free and unconditional. *Dick.*—Ἡ κατ' ἐκλ. τ.

Θεου. God's elective purpose; purpose resting alone on the most free election. *Beng.* God's free kindness. *Schött., Ernesti.* In respect to Jacob. *Theoph., Thol., Ols., Guyse.* The grace shown to Jacob, and his adoption; the cause put for the effect. *Ferme.* Taken generally, Jacob's case showing God's election of grace to be unmerited. *Meyer, De Wette.* Reference to right of primogeniture. *Beck.* To occupancy of Canaan. *Thol.* Election of nations represented by their respective founders to the privileges of God's chosen people. *Whitby, Taylor, Mackn.* The favour—1. Of visible Church membership and privileges given to some and not to other nations; 2. Of effectual grace given to some individuals and not to others. *Henry.* The bestowment of blessings according to a sovereign election of individuals one great standing characteristic feature of the divine government. *Brown.* Allusion to chap. viii. 28-40; hence the purpose here not merely in respect to nations chosen and called to external privileges, but also to certain persons chosen out of those nations to saving and external benefits. *Guyse.* A purpose which proceeds from free choice, moved by *internal*, not *external*, causes or motives; God's reasons for His counsels being not *arbitrary* or *ungrounded*, but only not disclosed, and pertaining to Himself alone. *Stuart.* Προθεσις for προαιρεσις. *Bloomf.* Rabbins: 'The tribe of Levi was always more beloved by God than all the rest, 1 Sam. ii. 28. God created many things in the world and chose one of them to Himself.' *Bammidbar Rabba.*—Μενῃ, might remain. *Eras., Tir.* Be firm. *Vat., Tol., Est.* Remain firm and established. *Cas., Pisc., Fer.* = קם, Isa. xlvi. 10, 'My counsel shall stand.' *Beza.* Be unchangeably established and fulfilled. *Guyse.* Stand firm, יצב, be a convincing argument. *Bloomf.* Continually remain in force; μενῃ, and not μεινῃ, indicating that the purpose had not respect merely to the two brothers. *Hofm.* The predicate includes the words that follow. *Flatt., Rück., Glöck.* Μενῃ alone the predicate. *Hofm.*—'Εκ καλουντος, of Him that calleth Jacob the superior, Esau the servant. *Beng.* Freely chose, and so called and blessed Jacob. *Ferme.* From the divine calling, and so from God's eternal counsel. *Melv.* Dependent on the will of the caller, chooser, or bestower. *Bloomf.* The election made of free-will, the grounds being not in the elected, but the elector. *Hofm.*

---

12. *It was said to her, The elder shall serve the younger.*

It was said. By God himself. The occasion related, Gen. xxv. 22, 23.

A divine declaration made for a sufficient object.

That object the giving prominence to the divine sovereignty.

The elder. Esau, who came first out of the womb, Gen. xxv. 25.

Special rights and privileges belonged to the first-born—

1. A double portion of the inheritance, 1 Chron. v. 1;
2. The priesthood among his brethren, Num. iii. 12; viii. 18; xviii. 15;
3. A respect bordering on parental authority, Exod. xii. 29; 2 Chron. xxi. 3.

So Christ is the first-born among many brethren, chap. viii. 29.

Shall serve. Be inferior and under subjection to.

Involving the transfer—1. Of the birthright; 2. Of the paternal blessing.

CHAP. IX.]   ST. PAUL'S EPISTLE TO THE ROMANS.   23

Yet this loss voluntary on the part of Esau, Gen. xxv. 32–34.
Incurred by his own sinful carnality and indifference, Heb. xii. 16.
God's free election consistent with man's free action.
Divine purpose usually accomplished through human agency.
The transfer of the blessing brought about by Rebekah's and Jacob's
   deceit.
God abhors man's sin, yet makes it subserve His own purpose.
The younger. Jacob, who thus had no claim to superiority.
From his own character less likely to obtain it, Gen. xxv. 27, 28.
The subjection seen more in their posterity than themselves :—
1. The Edomites, Esau's race, servants to the Israelites.
2. Israel chosen as the people of the Lord, not the Edomites.
3. The promised land inherited not by the Edomites but by Israel.
Edomites subdued by David, 2 Sam. viii. 14. Freed themselves
   under Joram, 2 Kings viii. 20. Subjugated again by Amaziah
   and Uzziah, 2 Kings xiv. 7, 22. Under Ahaz once more independent, 2 Kings xvi. 6. Continued so until entirely conquered by John Hyrcanus. Were then incorporated into the
   Jewish state.
Jacob's and Esau's personal character and eternal destiny not in
   view.
Their case introduced as a specimen of sovereign election.
God's purposes determined not by men's works but by His own will.

'Ο μειζων, the elder, like major natu. *Bloomf.* Heb. בר, the great or greater one, *i.e.*, in years.—Δουλευσει, shall serve ; involving loss of birthright and the paternal blessing, and consequently separation from the theocratic family and its spiritual blessings ; in their example unconditional election made clear. *De Wette, Alford.* The theocratic subjection of Esau. *Niel.* Fulfilled also in the political history of both races : the eternal destiny of the brothers not here expressly in view. *Brown.* The case introduced as a figure of the spiritual election. *Henry.* Refers to the posterity of the brothers,— 'two *nations* are in thy womb.' *Bloomf.* Fulfilled in a *spiritual* and *mystical* sense in their own persons, the birthright and its spiritual blessings being transferred from Esau to Jacob, Esau being thus cut off from God's covenant, and Jacob continued in it with the possession of Canaan, the type of heaven ; also in a *literal* sense in respect to their posterity. *Guyse.* To 'serve' need not be understood of political servitude, but must be referred to a state of spiritual dependence, the effect of casting away the birthright : the predictions refer to *posterity* and were fulfilled in them, but the unconditional choice of the one *individual* rather than the other that on which the apostle reasons. *D. Brown.*

----

13. *As it is written, Jacob have I loved, but Esau have I hated.*

Written. Mal. i. 2, 3. The same difference existing in the prophet's day.

The races therefore especially in view in the election.
The individuals regarded more by the apostle; the races, by the prophet.
The brothers and their respective posterities viewed as one.
Jacob. Means the supplanter; or, he that takes by the heel.
Origin of the name, Gen. xxv. 26. The act prophetical.
A figurative application made of the name by Esau, Gen. xxvii. 36.
Jacob born when Isaac was fifty-nine years old, probably at Lahai-roi.
Led a pastoral life, a plain man dwelling in tents, Gen. xxv. 27.
Bought the birthright from his brother with a mess of pottage, ver. 31–34.
Acquired the blessing by a fraud, at Rebekah's instigation, Gen. xxvii. 8, &c.
In his seventy-eighth year leaves his father's home to avoid Esau's wrath.
Marries his cousins Leah and Rachel in Padanaram.
After twenty-one years returns with his two wives and twelve children.
His name changed to Israel after wrestling with the angel at Peniel.
Obtained reconciliation with Esau in answer to prayer.
Lost his beloved Rachel, who died near Bethlehem on the way from Bethel.
Went to Joseph in Egypt when above 130 years of age.
Was presented to Pharaoh, and lived seventeen years in Rameses and Goshen.
Died in his 147th year; was embalmed in Egypt and buried at Hebron.
Much in Jacob's character we cannot admire.
His name too often verified by his conduct.
His experience, for the most part, a painful and sorrowful one.
His own testimony, "Few and evil have been the years of my pilgrimage."
An example of the truth, Whom the Lord loveth He chasteneth, Heb. xii. 6.
Jacob's sorrows generally such as to remind him of his sin.
His case a proof of the sovereignty of divine election.
Loved for nothing lovable in himself. So his posterity, Deut. vii. 6, 7.
His life a commentary on the text, The way of transgressors is hard, Prov. xiii. 15.

The gifts and calling of God, however, without repentance on his part, chap. xi. 29.
His faithfulness not overthrown by His people's fall.
He forgives them though He takes vengeance on their inventions, Ps. xcix. 8.
The voice from the ladder one of sovereign and unchanging mercy, Gen. xxviii. 13.

Loved. Regarded and treated with special favour.
Seen throughout Jacob's personal history—1. In the promise made before his birth ; 2. The vision at Bethel, Gen. xxviii. 12, &c. ; 3. The blessing given in Padanaram, Gen. xxxi. 5, 9 ; 4. The vision there, ver. 11–13 ; 5. The command given to Laban concerning him, ver. 24 ; 6. The blessing given at Peniel, Gen. xxxii. 28, 29 ; 7. The command to go to Bethel and the vision there, Gen. xxxv. 1, 9–11.
Same special favour seen in regard to his posterity, Deut. xxxiii. 26–29.

Esau. Isaac's eldest son. Esau=hairy. Reason of the name, Gen. xxv. 25.
His robust frame and rough aspect the type of his character.
Wild and daring, addicted to the chase. A son of the desert.
Sold his birthright when faint and hungry for a mess of pottage.
Married at the age of forty contrary to the wish of his parents.
His first wives Canaanites ; a grief to Isaac and Rebekah, Gen. xxvi. 34, 35.
Married also his cousin Mahalath, Ishmael's daughter, Gen. xxviii. 9.
Afterwards established himself in Mount Seir, Gen. xxxvi. 8.
Called Edom or "Red" from the pottage given him by Jacob, Gen. xxv. 29–34.
Mount Seir called afterwards by the same name, Gen. xxxii. 3 ; xxxvi. 16.
The inhabitants, Esau's descendants, called Edomites or Idumæans.
The original inhabitants Horites, from Hori, Seir's grandson.
The name supposed to denote "dwellers in caves,"—Troglodytes.
Edom entirely a rugged and mountainous country.
Everywhere caves and grottoes hewn out of the sandstone rocks.
Extended nearly from the Gulf of Elath to the Red Sea.
Its ancient capital Bozrah, now Buseirah, Isa. xxxiv. 6 ; lxiii. 1.
Selah or Petra (the Rock) its chief stronghold afterwards, 2 Kings xiv. 7.
Its extensive ruins often described by travellers.
"Looks like a vast pile asleep and ready to get up." *Laborde.*

Elath and Eziongeber the sea-ports of Edom, 2 Sam. viii. 14 ; 1 Kings ix. 26.
The whole province termed by Greek and Roman writers Idumæa.
Its inhabitants idolaters, 2 Chron. xxv. 14, 15, 20. Hostile to Israel, Num. xx. 18-21.
Hostility continued under the prophets, Amos i. 11, 12 ; Obad. 12, &c.
Were taken to Jerusalem and filled it with robbery and bloodshed.
Hated. 1. Comparatively, as loving less, Gen. xxix. 31 ; Matt. vi. 24 ; Luke xiv. 26 ;
2. Absolutely, the idea being that of rejection and abhorrence, Mal. i. 4.
Reference—1. To Esau himself ; 2. To his descendants after him.
Esau by nature a child of wrath as others, and so continued, Eph. ii. 3 ; Heb. xii. 16.
Jacob no less so, but visited with God's sovereign favour.
Reference to God's dealings rather than God's feelings.
Esau *left* by God what he was, Jacob *made* what he became.
God's dealings with their respective races corresponded.
Esau despised spiritual blessings and his posterity followed him.
God's dealings sovereign, but not unjust. Men have their wish.
Grace made Israel God's people ; justice left Edom aliens.
Grace gave Israel a revelation ; justice left Edom without one.
The difference—1. In temporal blessings ; 2. In spiritual privileges.
Israel as a people preserved for future mercy.
Edomites long ago disappeared as a nation.
The latter more likely to have been preserved than the former.
Edom rose earlier to power, and was more warlike in character.
Jews scattered by frequent captivities ; not so the Edomites.
Edom powerful and flourishing, while the Jews were exiles in Babylon.
Existed as a nation for 1700 years. Once thickly inhabited.
Traces of thirty cities within three days of the Dead Sea.
Yet the Edomites are no more, while Israel is in every land.
Edom not again to be inhabited, Isa. xxxiv. 5, &c. ; Jer. xlix. 7, &c.; Ezek. xxv. 13, &c.
Only savage and plundering Bedouins migrate through it.
Even Arabs afraid to enter or conduct others within its borders.
The country becoming one vast expanse of sand.
A nation's destiny often decided by one man's character.

Καθως γεγραπται. An example of the foregoing. *Bloomf.* Testimony accommodated to present purpose. *Guyse.*—'Ηγαπησα, have greatly preferred,—referring to the peculiar privileges and favours bestowed on Jacob's posterity. *Doddr.*, *Pyle*. To be understood comparatively. *Flatt*. Treated as peculiar favourites. *Brown*. Jacob's lordship from a free promise of divine love. *Melv*. Set my love on Jacob in a free and eternal choice of him for myself, to recover him from the ruins of the fall, and give him the spiritual as well as temporal blessings of the first-born. *Guyse*.—'Εμισησα, hated, repelled and rejected as a carnal seed. *Tol*. Eternal reprobation on account of foreseen works. *Chrys.*, *Theod*. Esteemed less, neglected, not bestowing singular benefits on his posterity. *Men*. Reprobated according to the divine free-will. *Aug.*, *Per*. Not loved, or had mercy on. *Fell*. Hated comparatively. *Thol*. Treated less kindly, withheld benefits given to the other. *Flatt*. Absolutely, implying hatred and abhorrence. *De Wette*, *Meyer*, *Haldane*. Neglected; different dispensations in relation to the two nations. *Brown*. Determined to leave him as others whom I justly abhor as sinners to his own free-will; will not favour him with recovering and saving mercy. *Guyse*. Servitude of the elder connected with God's hatred. *Melv*. The outward circumstances mentioned, Mal. i. 1, 2, to be viewed as expressions of the wrath of God, the persons being symbolical. *Ols.*, *D. Brown*. The ancestors themselves also to be understood under Esau and Jacob. *De Wette*. Both the individuals and the nations springing from them. *Hald*. In the case of Jacob and Esau and their posterity, temporal blessings referred to, but adduced to illustrate God's sovereignty as to eternal ones. *Stuart*. God's sovereign power and free election extend to every exercise of His mercy, temporal or spiritual, in providence or grace, national or individual. *Alford*. Predestination and reprobation both of God; but in the former the means as well as the end are His, in the latter the means are from men themselves. *Per*. The different fortunes of the two posterities are to be explained by the difference in God's conduct towards them, a difference lying beyond and earlier than the likeness existing between the two ancestors. *Von Hofm*.

---

14. *What shall we say then? Is there unrighteousness with God? God forbid.*

What shall we say then? Objection anticipated and answered.
Doctrine of God's sovereignty repugnant to fallen nature.
Ground of the wrath against Jesus at Nazareth, Luke iv. 25–29.
Cause of many disciples leaving Him afterwards, John vi. 37, 44, 45, 65, 66.
Is there unrighteousness with God?—*i.e.*, In making such distinction.
As if God must either treat all alike or be unjust.
In bestowing favours on some God is unjust to none, Matt. xx. 13–15.
No man but receives much more from God than he deserves.
Sufferings the consequence of sins, Lam. iii. 39. Man reaps as he sows, Gal. vi. 7.
God's sovereignty no interference with His justice, Gen. xviii. 25.
God forbid. God can only act in harmony with His attributes.
Righteous in all His ways, holy in all His works, Ps. cxlv. 17.
His procedure righteous, though not always explained, Job xxxiii. 13.
Not less righteous because free in dispensing His favours, Matt. xx. 15.
Where none are worthy none have right to complain.

Τί οὖν ἐροῦμεν ; Formula used in the Jewish schools ; employed by Paul as dealing with Jews. *Beng.* Customary formula of Paul in repelling doubt, objection, or calumnious interpretation. *Bloomf.*—Μὴ ἀδικία παρὰ τ. Θ. Objection implies absence of any consideration of foreseen good works or wickedness. *Guyse.* Unrighteousness in loving the one and hating the other without cause of difference in themselves. *Melv.* In choosing the posterity of Jacob for His people and not the other nations. *Bloomf.* In giving unequal things to those who are equal. *Ferme.* In choosing one and rejecting another, purely in the exercise of His own good pleasure ; the question without meaning except in reference to personal election and eternal salvation. *Ols., Hodge, D. Brown.*—Μὴ γένοιτο, far from it ; expresses abhorrence of the impious blasphemy. *Ferme.*

---

15. *For He saith to Moses, I will have mercy on whom I will have mercy, and I will have compassion on whom I will have compassion.*

For. God's sovereignty shown from His own words.
Leads to a further declaration and proof of it.
Saith. On the occasion of the people's idolatry, Exod. xxxiii. 19.
Moses. Under God the leader and legislator of Israel.
Son of Amram and Jochabed and great-grandson of Levi.
When three months old exposed on the Nile in a basket.
Found by Pharaoh's daughter and taken to the palace.
Name then given. Moses, in Egyptian, = "saved from the water."
Moses brought up in all the learning of the Egyptians.
Was eloquent and brave, "mighty in words and deeds," Acts vii. 22.
Resolved in his fortieth year to reclaim his nationality, Heb. xi. 24, &c.
Aimed also at delivering his oppressed countrymen, Acts vii. 23, &c.
Slays an Egyptian and seeks to reconcile two Israelites.
By the malignity of one of these is obliged to seek safety in flight.
Spends forty years in Midian in the neighbourhood of Sinai.
Lives in obscurity and seclusion as the keeper of Jethro's flocks.
Marries Zipporah, Jethro's daughter, and has two children.
Called by God at Horeb to be His prophet and the deliverer of Israel.
Along with his brother Aaron is sent back to Egypt for this end, B.C. 1491.
With his rod performs many miracles before Pharaoh and his people.
After the death of Egypt's first-born is allowed to lead Israel out.
Receives the law from Jehovah on Mount Sinai, Exod. xx. 1, &c.
Brings Israel, after forty years in the desert, to the borders of Canaan.
Died without entering it on the top of Pisgah, a part of Mount Nebo.
Buried by God himself, the place unknown, Deut. xxxiv. 1, 5, 6.

CHAP. IX.] ST. PAUL'S EPISTLE TO THE ROMANS. 29

Wrote first five books of the Bible, ninetieth Psalm, and, perhaps, the book of Job.
Distinguished for his meekness, faithfulness, and disinterestedness.
An illustrious type of Christ, Deut. xviii. 15, 18 ; Acts iii. 22 ; vii. 37 :—1. As a prophet from among his brethren ; 2. As a lawgiver, Matt. xxviii. 20 ; 3. As a leader, Isa. lv. 4 ; 4. As a mediator, Exod. xx. 19 ; 5. As an intercessor, Exod. xxxii. 32 ; 6. As an administrator of the covenant, Exod. xxiv. 6-8.
Contrasted with Christ—1. As a servant *in* the house, Christ a Son over it, Heb. iii. 5, 6 ;
2. As the messenger of the law, Christ of the gospel, John i. 17 ;
3. As the revealer of the shadow, Christ of the substance, Heb. x. 1 ;
4. As the administrator of the letter, Christ of the spirit, 2 Cor. iii. 6-9 ;
5. As the introducer of the temporary, Christ of the permanent, ver. 7, 11 ;
6. As leading only to the borders, Christ actually into Canaan, Heb. ii. 10.

Will have mercy. *Heb.*, Will be gracious, or show kindness.
Reference originally to those concerned in the golden calf.
The statement intended to have a general application.
Mercy a prominent attribute in Jehovah's character, Ps. cxlv. 8, 9.
Declared in the Decalogue, Exod. xx. 6. That in which He delights, Micah vii. 18.
Includes pity to the wretched and pardon to the guilty.
Shown to the guilty only through an atonement, chap. iii. 25, 26 ; Job xxxiii. 24.
Only to be exercised in harmony with justice and truth, Ps. lxxxv. 10, 11.
The ground of the incarnation and death of God's own Son, John iii. 16.

On whom I will, &c. Exercise of mercy free and voluntary.
Justice *must* be exercised by a ruler ; mercy *may*.
Where many are guilty mercy chooses its objects.
God's sovereignty in pardoning exercised in holy wisdom.
The grounds of His preference in Himself, not the sinner.
His own will the reason, His own glory the end.
Mercy provided a Saviour for men, not angels, Heb. ii. 16 ; 2 Pet. ii. 4.
Some sinners punished, others spared to profit by it. *Theodoret.*
In the Gospel mercy is exercised where the Surety is accepted.

All experience it who are willing to do so in God's own way. Where the gospel is preached, mercy offered to all without exception. Those only excluded who exclude themselves, Isa. lv. 1-7.
Sovereign grace draws the sinner to close with mercy's terms.
Gr., On whom I have mercy. God's mercy everlasting, Ps. cvii. 1. Loves to the end, John xiii. 1. Gifts and calling of God without repentance.
Objects of everlasting love are drawn, or have mercy still extended to them, Jer. xxxi. 3.
Will have compassion. Will both have and show pity.
Compassion more in the feeling, mercy in the action.
Compassion a father's feeling, Ps. ciii. 13. God full of it, Ps. cxlv. 8.
His compassion to men cost Him the death of His Son, Job xxxiii. 24. Not necessarily exercised on mere suffering. Angels passed by.
Praise comes to God from the smoke of Babylon's torments, Rev. xix. 3.
God as free in having compassion as in showing mercy.

Μωϋσῃ, from the Coptic *mo*, 'water,' and *ushe*, 'saved.' The idea also in the Heb. name משה, 'drawn.'—'Ελεήσω, refers originally to the favour bestowed on Moses of seeing God's face, but here generalised by the apostle. *Niel.* Properly to the mercy shown to Moses just then. *De Wette.* A general statement of God's showing mercy to each one who is the object of His mercy. *Meyer.* Indicates the unchangeableness and continuance of His mercy. *Beck.* Paul weakens the objection that God was unrighteous in having love and hatred ascribed to Him without any ground in the objects of it. *Hofm.* Answer adapted to the Jews, being taken from their own Scriptures. *Guyse.*— Ὅν ἄν ἐλεῶ, on whom I shall have shown mercy. *Ferme, Melv.* Sentences with the same verb in the same person before and after a relative, indicate that the doing or being has its ground in the actor, without being determined from without. *Hofm.*— Οἰκτειρήσω, Heb. רִחַמְתִּי. In the text, two properties of the benevolent will of God (εὐδοκία),—to be mercifully affected towards the wretched, and from mercy to confer grace as a remedy and means of deliverance : by hysterosis, the order of these reversed, חן, which stands first, being to show grace from mercy, רחם, to have compassion, as a mother towards her wretched children and therefore the cause of the former. So in Greek, ἐλεεῖν, 'to help,' or do good to any one from mercy (hence ἐλεημοσύνη, alms); οἰκτείρω, to be moved with maternal affection. *Ferme.* God shows mercy in promoting the salvation of those whom, from eternity, He purposed out of mere grace to elect; but the misery and guilt of men and God's mercy in justifying and sanctifying the elect in Christ coming between the eternal purpose and its execution in their salvation, no injustice can appear in saving them. *Melville.* The general sense, God acts in the distribution of His favours according to His own pleasure. *Bloomf.* The phrase in the text used either when we do not *choose*, though we *can* give reasons for the bestowment of favours on another, or when we wish to prevent the recipient from ascribing them to his own merit. *Koppe.* My showing mercy and pity is an act of my own good pleasure ; I will be gracious and compassionate to those of man's sinful race to whom I choose.

for reasons in myself not in them. *Guyse.* No injustice in making this distinction; as in speaking to Moses, God claims the right to do so. *D. Brown.*

---

16. *So then it is not of him that willeth, nor of him that runneth, but of God that showeth mercy.*

It. The preference shown, or the blessing bestowed.
Refers—1. To Jacob and Esau; 2. To Israel; 3. To men in general.
Willeth. As Isaac who willed to give Esau the blessing, Gen. xxvii. 1.
So Abraham's will was in favour of Ishmael, Gen. xvii. 18; xxi. 11.
God's children not born of the will of the flesh or of man, John i. 13.
God's will, not man's, the ground of His showing mercy.
Those who experience mercy made willing by divine grace, Ps. cx. 3.
Whosoever will, let him take the water of life freely, Rev. xxii. 17.
" Ye will not come to me that ye might have life," John v. 40.
Runneth. Allusion to Esau who ran for the blessing, Gen. xxvii. 1, &c.
Man's haste makes no speed when against God's will.
So Israel ran after righteousness but without success, ver. 31.
Only running according to God's will is successful, 2 Tim. ii. 5; Phil. ii. 12, 13; 1 Cor. xv. 58.
Running necessary, Heb. xii. 2; Phil. iii. 14. "So run, that ye may obtain," 1 Cor. ix. 24.
Running more than willing. *Strive* to enter in, Luke xiii. 24.
Many wish for the blessing who are unwilling to run for it, Prov. xiii. 4.
To will and to do in the matter of salvation both of God, Phil. ii. 13.
But of God. Of Him are all things. Works all in all. His counsel stands.
Divides to every man severally as He will, 1 Cor. xii. 6, 11.
God the source of all good *to* man and all grace *in* man.
The new birth, not of the will of the flesh or of man, but of God, John i. 13.
Man's endeavour necessary, yet dependent on God's grace.
Showeth mercy. God's free mercy the ground of all blessing.
That mercy sovereign yet shown to all who truly seek it, Ps. xxxiii. 18.
Right running the effect not the cause of God's mercy, Phil. ii. 12, 13.
Predestinating mercy precedes, not supersedes, man's endeavour.
The anterior part of the process is God's, the posterior part man's.

Ἄρα οὖν. Conclusive. *Bloomf.* Appears from hence. *Guyse.*—Οὐ τοῦ θέλοντος, viz., the work or success. *Cam.* The thing or matter. *Dickson, Hofm.* So *Arm. Vers.* Righteousness. *Vor.* Salvation. *Pisc.* Election. *Beza, Par., Est., J. Cap., Gom.* Purpose of God. *Guyse.* Experience of mercy. *Meyer, Phil.* Θελ., inward, strong desire; τρεχ., active, strenuous effort. *Bloomf., D. Brown.* Θελ., will, on the part of Isaac; τρεχ., effort, on that of Esau. *Guyse.* Θελ. and τρεχ.= to will and to do, Phil. ii. 13 ; both included in the grace of God who shows mercy. *Ferme.* Not only man's works and actions excluded, but even his efforts and desires. *Melv.*—Ἐλεοῦντος, shows mercy on us wretched. *Ferme.* Of God's own good pleasure, who determined in His free mercy to bestow the blessing on Jacob. *Guyse.* God's favours bestowed, not because first merited or acquired by effort either of strong desire or strenuous action, but because He has mercy on those who are the objects of His mercy. *Stuart.*

---

17. *For the Scripture saith unto Pharaoh, Even for this same purpose have I raised thee up, that I might show my power in thee, and that my name might be declared throughout all the earth.*

For. Further proof that God's procedure is sovereign. A case adduced in which not mercy but judgment was shown.

Scripture. God's words in the Scripture. Its testimony decisive, Isa. viii. 20.

Saith—*i.e.*, God saith in the Scripture. The Bible God's mouth to man.

Pharaoh. Common title of the ancient kings of Egypt. Signifies "the sun," its supposed representative being the king. Several Pharaohs mentioned in Scripture. The first, Gen. xii. 15, B.C. 2081 ; thought to be Salatis, one of the shepherd-kings who ruled Lower Egypt.

The Pharaoh of Joseph, perhaps Apophis of the same dynasty.

The Pharaoh of the Oppression, an Egyptian from Thebes, perhaps Amosis.

Began his reign of forty years shortly before the birth of Moses, B.C. 1732.

The Pharaoh from whom Moses fled, Thothmes I., reigned twenty-seven years.

The Pharaoh of the Exodus thought to be Thothmes II., by others Thothmes III.

The latter, when Moses was sent to him, had reigned four years.

An active, energetic, and enterprising sovereign.

His great aim to aggrandise himself and his country.

Took advantage of Israel's oppressed state and refused to let them go.

For this same purpose. A wise and holy purpose in all God's acts of providence.

That purpose first and supremely the manifestation of His own glory. All nations and creatures made to subserve God's designs, Rev. iv. 11. All things made for Himself, even the wicked for the day of evil, Pro. xvi. 4.
God's purposes executed in spotless holiness and justice.
Raised thee up. Called thee into being and spared thy life.
Exalted thee to power and raised thee to the throne.
Given thee an energetic disposition and roused it into action.
Kings as well as their subjects in God's hands, Prov. xxi. 1; viii. 15; Dan. ii. 21.
Pharaoh roused to greater rebellion by God's righteous demands.
Left to his own will. Means employed sufficient to convince him.
Divine purposes to be accomplished through his obduracy.
God under no obligation to bestow on him subduing grace.
Energetic disposition from God. Makes a great saint or great sinner.
Overruled by God in either case for His own glory.
Man alone responsible for the abuse of divine gifts.
Natural disposition and providential dealings to be accounted for.
Show my power. God's attributes glorified in His creatures.
His power exhibited in creation, providence, and grace.
In Pharaoh's case displayed—1. In the miracles wrought in Egypt; 2. In the passage of the Red Sea and destruction of Pharaoh's host.
Man's sin the occasion of the display of divine power—
1. In the resurrection of Christ; 2. The salvation of believers, Eph. i. 19.
In thee. Rather, through thee; not his person, but his conduct.
Pharaoh's obstinacy the occasion of the plagues in Egypt;
His malice that of the destruction of his army in the Red Sea.
Man's wrath made to contribute to Jehovah's praise, Ps. lxxvi. 10.
Name. Including existence, character, and attributes.
Declared. Made known, rendered conspicuous.
Realised at this very day. Always increasingly declared.
Tidings of the passage of the Red Sea, &c., early spread, Josh. ii. 10.
God thus glorified and mankind likely to be blessed.
By Pharaoh's punishment God brought benefit to many. *Theodoret.*
God's great object to make known and glorify His name, John xii. 28.
The object for which unbelievers are punished and believers saved, ver. 22, 23.
History a record of God using wicked men for gracious purposes.

The Spanish Armada the establishment of the Reformation in England.
The persecutions of the Puritans the evangelisation of America.

Γαρ, moreover. *Doddr.* Proves God's right to pass by those on whom He chooses not to show mercy. *Cobbin.* His right to refuse favours to some while bestowing them on others no more worthy. *Guyse.* Reprobation. *Melv.*—Φαραω, in Coptic, *ph-oura*, 'the king.' Corresponds in hieroglyphics to *ph-ra*, 'the sun.' What the sun was in the firmament, the king was thought to be in the state. According to Sir G. Wilkinson, the Pharaoh here meant was Thothmes III., not drowned, but overthrown in the Red Sea. Reigned twenty-five years after that event. So Jewish tradition. Carried on afterwards a vigorous war with the Northern nations. Sculptured records of his successes still preserved in the monuments he erected. Gave encouragement to the arts of peace. Founded numerous buildings in Upper and Lower Egypt, and in Ethiopia. Made extensive additions to the temples at Thebes. Improved Coptos, Memphis, and Heliopolis, by his taste for architecture. From caprice and love of change, made columns with reversed capitals at Karnak.—The last king of the nineteenth dynasty, Si Pta Menephtha, 'the light of the sun,' was not buried in his own tomb, and *may* have been this Pharaoh. Others say Thothmes II. Two astronomical notes of time on contemporary monuments of his successor Thothmes III., or Rameses the Great, show the accession of the latter, and consequent death of the former, to have taken place on the Egyptian day answering to May 4-5, B.C. 1515, or as astronomically verified, the 12th of the second spring moon, the Hebrew second month. *Stones crying out.*—'Εξηγειρα, provoked to opposition. *Aug., Tol., Per., Per., Frit., De Wette.* Preserved, after the Sept. *Chrys., Œcum., Vor., Ham., Von Hofm.* Made thee king, let thee advance. *Theod., Theoph.* Appointed. *Arab.* Brought into existence. *Beza, Pisc., Est., Tol., Gom., Dick.* Brought forward. *Est.* Appointed thee by my operation for this use, promoted thee for my glory. *Calv.* Raised thee up. *Diod.* To be powerful and illustrious. *Beng., Doddr., Flatt.* From sickness. *Von Hofm.* Preserved thee. *Mart.* In life. *Thol.* From the plague of the blains. *Taylor.* Supported during former plagues. *Shuckford.* Raised to the throne and continued in that station. *Guyse.* Preserved thee from the beginning, even from conception, that thou mightest be born, and endured thee with much long-suffering, while still acting wickedly after the many plagues I sent. *Ferme.* Brought thee into being as king of Egypt. *Bloomf.* The idea of the verb always that of arousing, exciting, urging to activity. *Stuart.* Often used for 'to rouse into action, or stir up,' as Ps. lvi. 8; lxxix. 2; Cant. iv. 16. *Alford.* Heb. הֶעֱמִיד, 'made to stand,' supposes the subject already in existence. *Beng.* — Appointed to an office, 1 Kings xii. 32; confirmed, 1 Kings xv. 4; stirred up, Dan. xi. 11; Neh. vi. 7. Διετηρηθης (LXX), 'hast been preserved to this day.' So the Chaldee of Jonathan, and the Syriac and Arabic versions. Refers to Pharaoh's preservation under the plagues: εξηγειρα, chosen by Paul to express God's raising him up as His instrument. *Nielson.* Raised up from a bed of affliction; gave respite from the plagues, according to Exod. ix. 15. *Brown.* —Δυναμιν, power in inflicting exemplary punishment: also used for εξουσια, 'authority,'—the uncontrollable prerogative and dominion exerted in those acts of power. *Guyse.*

---

18. *Therefore hath He mercy on whom He will have mercy, and whom He will He hardeneth.*

Mercy. Shown—1. In pitying; 2. In helping; 3. In pardoning.

Used with reference to *temporal* life, Phil. ii. 27 ; generally *eternal*, Jude 21.
To accept God's mercy in Christ is itself the fruit of mercy.
Repentance and faith among mercy's choicest gifts.
On whom He will. Mercy exercised according to sovereign will.
God's sovereignty thus again most explicitly declared.
Mercy dispensed in sovereignty, yet in wisdom and holiness.
Bestowed for wise reasons, known to God though not to us.
God under no obligation to bestow it on any sinner.
No regard had to anything in man as deserving mercy.
Hardeneth. Allusion—1. To Pharaoh ; 2. To Israel; 3. To the ungodly.
To "harden" the opposite of "having mercy ;" to treat with just severity.
When mercy does not soften, men harden of themselves.
Pharaoh hardened by God when abandoned to himself.
Hardening is—1. The natural effect ; 2. The just desert, of sin, Heb. iii. 7, 8.
God hardened Pharaoh's heart by leaving him to harden his own, Exod. vii. 3, 14 ; viii. 15.
Hardens men—1. By withholding grace ; 2. By ordering events.
God's patience and indulgence the occasion of Pharaoh's hardening, Exod. viii. 15.
His mercy celebrated even in His dealings with Pharaoh, Ps. cxxxvi. 15.
The grace that softens is God's, the sin that hardens men's own.
Men's repentance is of God, their hardening of themselves.
Providences, precepts, and promises, perverted by an impenitent heart.
Jews hardened under the prophets and under Jesus himself, Isa. vi. 9, 10.
Same process of hardening daily under God's providence.
Many undergoing it without being conscious of it.
God the author of the hardening providence, man of the sin.
God's hardening consistent with man's responsibility.
God as just and holy when He hardens as when He pardons.
In showing mercy God infuses good not already there ;
In hardening He leaves existing evil to its own operation.
Introduces no evil, but by His providence gives it shape.
None hardened by God who do not first harden themselves.
Softening grace refused to none who truly seek it.
God resists the proud, but giveth grace to the humble, 1 Pet. v. 5.

Σκληρύνει, hardens (indurat). Pharaoh's heart hardened by God *in fact* by His long-suffering and delay of punishment. *Or.*, *Basil*, *Theoph*. Suffers to be or grow hard, leaving to the exercise of free-will. *Œcum.* By not softening, and so leaving men's obstinacy to continue and increase. *Tor.*, *Est.* By presenting occasions of hardening. *Par.*, *Gom.* By giving them up to Satan and their own lusts. *Calv.*, *Will*. Passing by in the original and eternal act of reprobation, and, as its effect, abandoning on account of sin original and actual. *Tol.* Hardens in the execution of His decree of reprobation before He destroys; and that in justice, the act pre-supposing voluntary corruption and antecedent sin. *Melv.* Not to pity and soften. *Aug.* Treats with less kindness; the opposite of ἐλεεῖ; so Heb. הִקְשִׁיחַ, 'hardens herself against her young,' Job xxxix. 16. *Schött.* Does not show mercy. *Beng.* Treats severely, and that only in outward things. *Carpzov*, *Semler*, *Cramer*, *Ernesti*, *Beck*, *Flatt.* The expression founded on the popular mode of thinking and speaking. *Grot.* Passes by and leaves to the natural and chosen obstinacy of their own hearts, and finally, after patient trials, delivers up to a judicial hardness. *Guyse.* Reconcilable with the fact of men's responsibility. *Alford.* A hardening which has damnation as its consequence. *Phil.* Makes a man to be no longer a subject of divine mercy. *Meyer.* Indicates only what actually happened to Pharaoh, Exod. iv. 21. *Von Hofm.* Hardens in the ordinary sense; not making the vessels of wrath worse than they were, but is the cause that they resist in an evident manner, and do not enjoy the salvation which lies before their eyes. *Rückert.* Treats with severity, as Job xxxix. 16. *Brown.* Judicially abandons to the hardening influence of sin itself, and of the surrounding incentives to it. *D. Brown.* Rabbins: R. Phinehas says on Job xxxix. 13, 'God waits for the ungodly that they may repent, and they do not; even though they would do so afterwards, He takes away their heart that they may not repent. He bindeth them, shuts the door against them. So Pharaoh, &c.' *Shemoth Rabba.*

---

19. *Thou wilt say then unto me, Why doth He yet find fault ? for who hath resisted His will ?*

Thou wilt say. An objection anticipated and answered.
Then. If the case be so that all depends on God's will.
If men are just what He purposes and makes them to be.
Why. Man's natural tendency to cavil with God and His truth.
He—*i.e.*, God; the name here omitted out of angry displeasure.
Omitted by the Spouse from a very opposite feeling, Cant. i. 2.
Yet. Still; strongly expressive of sullen discontent.
Find fault—*i.e.*, With men who continue to sin.
Complain or be angry because they do not repent.
As if God had no right to blame where He does not give grace.
Men wish either—1. To be independent of God's sovereignty;
Or, 2. To be free from all personal responsibility.
The former is infidelity, the latter fatalism.
The former the offspring of pride, the latter of sloth.
God retains His right though man has cast away his ability.
To sin is man's own, to save from sin is God's.
Man is responsible for his acts, God sovereign in His gifts.

CHAP. IX.] ST. PAUL'S EPISTLE TO THE ROMANS. 37

Who hath resisted His will? A saying either good or bad, Gen. l. 19; 2 Chron. xx. 6.
Here a petulent question. God's will either—1. Preceptive; or, 2. Determinative.
Sinners constantly resist the first, the second as far they can.
His determinative will resisted in *purpose* though not in *fact*.
Glad of a pretext for sinning, men pretend submission to fate, Jer. vii. 9, 10.

Τι ἔτι; why still? 'Why then,' the true reading. *D. Brown.*—Μεμφεται, complain. *Eras., Vat., Zeg.* Blame. *Pisc., Grot.* Is angry. *Beza, Par., J. Cap., Ferme.* Condemn and destroy. *Melv.* Is offended; reprove, threaten, condemn. *Guyse.* Declare worthy of punishment. *Reiche.* Condemn and visit with punishment. *Krehl.* Blame or accuse. *Von Hofm.* Σκληροκαρδιας, understood. *Bloomf.* The doctrine objected to as incompatible with human responsibility; the doctrine, therefore, that of election and non-election to eternal salvation prior to any difference of personal character. *D. Brown.*—Ἀνθεστηκε, has resisted (obstitit). *Beza, Pisc.* Can resist; indicative for subjunctive, and preterite for indefinite, 'at any time.' *Grot., Glass.* Indicative perfect for optative aorist. *Thol.* Perfect for preterite; 'who has ever resisted?' *Glöck.* Resisteth. *D. Brown.* Objection: Does He make men bad and punish them for being so? *Rückert.*—Γαρ, omitted in the sentence by several MSS. and ancient versions; also by *Or., Chrys., Theod., Theoph.*, and the Latin fathers, but found in Codd. Sin. and Vat.

---

20. *Nay but, O man, who art thou that repliest against God? Shall the thing formed say to Him that formed it, Why hast Thou made me thus?*

Nay but. "Instead of that, I may rather ask, Who art thou," &c. God's sovereignty in His dealings with men not denied.
Paul's answer embraces—1. God's sovereign right over men, ver. 20, 21;
2. His not exercising that right even as He might, ver. 22.
O man. Implying the presumption and absurdity of the cavil.
Man, a being of such humble origin and limited powers, Gen. xviii. 27.
Man, the lowest in the class of intelligent creatures.
Incompetent to pass judgment on God's procedure.
Contrasted—1. With God: "Is a *man* to answer again to *God?*" *Theodoret;*
2. With other creatures; man already a proof of God's sovereignty.
Man visited with mercy while angels were passed by.
Man both limited in knowledge and feeble in judgment.

> " As if upon a full-proportioned dome,
> On swelling columns heaved, the pride of art,
> A critic fly, whose feeble ray scarce spreads

An inch around, with blind presumption bold,
Should dare to tax the structure of the whole." *Thomson.*

Who art thou? Man's primary duty is to know himself.
No creature's place to question the Creator's doings.
The very power to discern right and wrong the Creator's gift.
The objector's pride a contrast to Abraham's humility, Gen. xviii. 27.
Cavillers rather to be reprehended than reasoned with.
Repliest against God. Disputest against what He has done.
Man's place is not to bandy replies with his Creator.
When God speaks, man's wisdom and duty is to be silent.
The Creator not to be called to account by His creatures.
What He declares is to be believed, what He commands to be obeyed.
Man has not to do with God's decrees, but with His declarations.
The Creator not to be comprehended, but believed and obeyed.
Enough that God wills; its rectitude not to be questioned.
Paul says not, These things cannot be explained;
But only, They are not to be questioned or cavilled at. *Chrys.*
Many truths in the Bible we are unable to fathom;
Many problems in the universe we are unable to solve.
Now we know in part. Future light to the faithful, John xiii. 7;
1 Cor. xiii. 9, 10.
Shall the thing formed, &c. Reference to Isa. xxix. 16; xlv. 9.
The Jewish objector answered out of his own scriptures.
The objection answered rather by questions than direct statements.
The question implies God's absolute right over His creatures.
The "thing formed" applies equally to an archangel and an insect.
Why hast Thou made me thus? Parallel to the objector's cavil.
The parallel more in the spirit than in the expression.
The objection implied reflection on God as Creator and Ruler;
The answer implies the absurdity and wickedness of the cavil.
Man has neither right nor reason to ask such a question.
Man's arrogance answered by appeal to God's absolute character.
The reference not so much to creation as to predestination.
Man made upright, after God's own image, Eccles. vii. 29; Gen. i. 26.
Difference in character and destiny based on man's common fall.

Μενουνγε, same as μεν οὖν, but stronger; yea indeed, yea verily, Luke xi. 28; Rom. x. 18; Phil. iii. 8. *Robinson.* Has the force of a strong negation of anything with an affirmative of the contrary, 'Nay but.' *Bloomf.* Paul neither recalls his former conclusion, viz., 'that God hardens whom He will,' nor denies the antecedent of the foregoing enthymeme, viz., 'that no man can resist the will of God,' but denies the hypothetical proposition as most false and blasphemous, viz., 'that God is, therefore, unjustly angry.' *Ferme.* Marcionites and Manichæans charged Paul with inability to answer the objection.—'Ἄνθρωπε = Heb. אֱנוֹשׁ. *Par.* Three words in Heb. for man ; אָדָם (Adam), מאן simply as created by God out of the ground ; אִישׁ (ish), indicating His excellency ; אֱנוֹשׁ (enosh), implying weakness, disease, wretchedness as a fallen being. Wretch of a man (homuncio), whose little measure cannot take in the immensity of God. *Melv.* In direct antithesis with Θεῷ. *Bloomf.*—Ἀνταποκρινόμενος (ἀντί and ἀποκρίνομαι, to bandy replies against each other, as Judges v. 29 ; to reply against another, or contradict and refute by replying, as Job xiii. 22 ; xvi. 8 ; xxxii. 12 ; xxxiv. 36). Who answerest (respondeas). *Vulg.* Replies on the other side (ex adverso responsas). *Beza, Pisc.* Darest to reply. *Grot.* Arguest (disceptas). *Cast.* Disputest against God, and bandiest replies with Him. *Arab., Grot.* Enterest into a debate with God. *Doddr.* Ἀνταποκ. = to reply in a disputatious spirit. *Bloomf.* To dispute or altercate, Luke xiv. 6. *Schött.*—Πλάσμα, a potter's earthen vessel. *Grot.* The figure formed by the ὁ πλάσσων, or potter. So Aristophanes calls men πλάσματα πηλοῦ, in allusion to the fiction (borrowed from the Scriptures) of Prometheus forming of clay the first man and woman. *Bloomf.* Heb. יֵצֶר, a figure or figment.—Πλάσαντι (πλάσσω, from πηλός, clay ; used originally of potters), Him that formed it. God called ὁ πλάσσων by Plato. *Bloomf.* Heb. יָצַר, to form.—Ἐποίησας, refers not to God's creating man, but to His dispensations towards him, and disposal of him for happiness or misery in consequence of the fall. *Guyse.* Refers to the *destination*, not the moral quality, of the creature. *Von Hofm.* Heb. עָשָׂה, to make, Isa. xlv. 9.

---

21. *Hath not the potter power over the clay, of the same lump to make one vessel unto honour, and another unto dishonour ?*

Hath not, &c. Another question. Appeal to a well-known fact. God's absolute right over His creatures still further implied. The question has the force of a strong assertion. Sufficient to silence the objector, especially as found in his own Bible.

Potter. Reference to Jer. xviii. 1-6, in regard to Israel and the nations.

God compared to a potter also in Isa. xxix. 16 ; xlv. 9. As such He is—

1. The maker of their persons ; 2. The former of their destinies. The potter gives the clay its form and destines its use as he pleases.

Power. Right. No claim in the clay to this or that form or use. The potter has not only the *might* but the *right* over it. God had right as Creator—1. To make what creatures He chose ; 2. To assign to sinful creatures what destiny He pleased. God's power exercised only in harmony with goodness and justice. His power and right over man more than the potter's over the clay. His right over fallen sinners not exercised as it might.

Clay. The earthy material out of which vessels are made.

Not the creation of mere creatures, but the disposal of sinning ones here.

Same lump. The mass of clay when mixed and kneaded.
The substance of a uniform character throughout.
So mankind viewed as fallen in Adam, Eccles. vii. 29.
By nature children of wrath, because children of disobedience, Eph. ii. 3.
No claim with any to favour. All equally guilty and corrupt.
Make. The potter makes different vessels out of the same mass.
God may do the same out of the mass of fallen humanity.
Creatures formed with different natures and capacities.
Each has his place assigned and the purpose he shall serve.
No such thing as chance either in the world of mind or matter.
Of fallen hell-deserving sinners, a purpose designed for each.
Vessel. Vessels for use. So God's creatures, even sinners, Prov. xvi. 4.
Each has his position and significance in the universe of God.
Unto honour. Intended for an honourable purpose and use.
Vessels may be for use though not an honourable use.
Men's highest honour to be made kings and priests to God, Rev. i. 5.
The case of all who are joined to Christ and born of the Spirit, 1 Pet. ii. 4–9.
This honour refused by all who reject Christ and the Gospel, Luke vii. 30.
Dishonour. Dishonourable and meaner purposes.
All designed in one way or other to glorify God, Rev. iv. 11.
All things made for Himself, even the wicked for the day of evil, Prov. xvi. 4.
Sinners made to serve God's ends in a way to their own dishonour.
Thus Pharaoh, Sennacherib, Judas Iscariot, Pilate.
Purposes to be accomplished for which only bad men are fit, Acts ii. 23.
A vile use to betray Christ, but necessary to redemption.
Yet put into Judas's heart not by God but by Satan, John xiii. 2.
A vile use to persecute, yet the Church purged by it, Dan. xi. 35; xii. 10.
The evil that men willingly do God ordains and overrules for good.
Sinners used for the correction of saints. A vile but important use.
Sinners mean evil when God designs good, Gen. l. 20; Isa. x. 5–7.
Pharaoh's cruelty contributed to Israel's growth, Exod. i. 12.
Sinners made to shelter saints, Isa. xvi. 3. Chaff protects the wheat.

Moab God's washpot, Israel His royal diadem, Ps. lx. 8 ; Isa. lxii. 3.
God's purposes no interference with man's duties.
God works all, but in connection with man's free agency.
Human activity compatible with divine sovereignty.

Κεραμευς (κεω, to burn, ἑρα, earth), a potter. Heb. יֹצֵר, a former. Pottery one of the most common and ancient manufactures. Hebrews employed in it in Egypt, Ps. lxxxi. 6. Clay when dug was trodden by men's feet into a paste, Isa. xli. 25. Then placed by the potter on the wheel, beside which he sat and shaped the clay with his hands, Isa. xlv. 9 ; Jer. xviii. 3. The vessel then smoothed and coated with a glaze, and finally burned in a furnace. A royal establishment of potters formerly at Jerusalem, 1 Chron. iv. 23. Their employment, and perhaps the fragments cast away in the process, the origin of the Potters' Field, Matt. xxvii. 7 ; Isa. xxx. 14 ; Zech. xi. 13.—'Εξουσιαν, absolute power and authority. *Guyse.*—Πηλου (from παλασσω, to smear), over the clay : gen. after ἐξουσια, in the sense of *over*, also in Matt. x. 1 ; John xvii. 2 ; rarely in classic authors. *Bloomf.*—Φυραματος (φυραω, to mix, macerate ; properly a kneaded mass of meal ; the clay mixed with water), mass. Conspersio. *Aug.* Man as a mere creature. *Est., Gom., Beza.* As corrupt and fallen. *Par., Hodge.* As sinful creatures. *D. Brown.* Viewed—1. As creatures ; 2. As sinners ; not as yet to be brought into being, but as already existing. *Brown.* Not spoken of creation, but of character as formed out of the present mass of fallen humanity. *De Wette, Rück.* To be understood not of creating, but of *forming*, as in the case of the potter. *Meyer.* Nothing intended further than man's relation to God as his Creator. *Von Hofm.* We, the whole human race, are clay, and less than clay, in the hand of God, our Creator ; since He created us out of nothing, whilst the clay is something before it is formed by the potter. *Ferme.*—Σκευος, a general term applied to *vessels* or *utensils* of every description. *Bloomf.*—Εἰς τιμην—ἀτιμιαν, more or less honourable uses. *Melv.* The destiny assigned to each in consequence of the evil already existing. *De Wette.*

---

22. *What if God, willing to show His wrath, and to make His power known, endured with much long-suffering the vessels of wrath fitted to destruction ?*

What if, &c. A query rather than an express deliverance.
A truth intimated but not directly stated.
Paul's wisdom to be imitated in dealing with this subject.
Safely left with God to harmonise His own decrees.
Appeal made to the judgment of all sound-thinking men.
God has more reason to complain of men than men of God.
The case put in the form of a supposition, " what if," or " but if."
In such a case no possible room for just objection.
Willing. The objector's language taken up,—" His will," ver. 19.
God's will always—1. Holy ; 2. Wise ; 3. Just ; 4. Good.
His preceptive will revealed, His determinative will often secret.
With the first of these man has to do, not with the second.

His duty to obey the former, submit to and adore the latter, Deut. xxix. 29.

God's revealed will is that all men should repent and be saved, 1 Tim. ii. 4 ; 2 Pet. iii. 9.

To show. Demonstrate as already declared and known.

God's will the manifestation of Himself and all His attributes.

Man's slowness to apprehend necessitates sensible proofs.

Wrath. God's punitive justice as a holy and righteous Judge.

God's anger unchangeably and eternally against sin.

Manifested—1. In angels ; 2. In men ; 3. In His own Son.

" Wrath,"—not "riches of wrath" as "riches of mercy."

Wrath more sparingly spoken of. His strange act, Isa. xxviii. 21.

God willing to show His wrath, yet slow to execute it, Ps. ciii. 8.

Make known. In a conspicuous and illustrious manner.

God's character and attributes made known—1. By words ; 2. By works.

His power. *Gr.*, What He can do. Power an attribute of God.

Shown—1. In the miracles in Egypt ; 2. In the passage of the Red Sea.

God's power makes even man's sin contribute to His glory.

Seen in the vengeance He executes on the ungodly, Rev. xviii. 8 ; xix. 1, &c.

Displayed most of all in Christ and saved sinners, 1 Cor. i. 18, 24 ; Eph. i. 19.

God has done much to make His power known, more to make known His love, John iii. 16.

Endured. When He might justly have at once cast off.

God waits to be gracious, Isa. xxx. 18. Sentence not speedily executed, Eccles. viii. 11.

God's endurance glorifies both His justice and mercy.

Affords sinners both time and motive for repentance, chap. ii. 4 ; 2 Pet. iii. 9.

Sinning men endured ; not so sinning angels, 2 Pet. ii. 4.

Long-suffering. Seen in Pharaoh and sinners in general.

God only punishes men after much long-suffering.

Sovereignty and justice connected with goodness and patience.

God's justice vindicated by His great long-suffering.

Seen—1. In the multitude ; 2. In the magnitude, of men's sins.

Examples :—the old world ; Sodom and Gomorrha ; the Jews.

The world's continuance a proof of God's long-suffering.

Men's ruin their own act, not God's pleasure, Ezek. xviii. 23, 32.

Vessels of wrath. Men deserving of, and doomed to punishment.
Deserving of wrath, and therefore intended to display it.
Vessels into which deserved wrath shall be infused.
Objects of wrath, filling up the measure of their sins.
Examples :—Pharaoh ; the Canaanites, Gen. xv. 16 ; the Jews, Matt. xxiii. 32 ; 1 Thess. ii. 16.
God's wrath revealed against all unrighteousness of men, chap. i. 18.
God made men vessels of glory, Gen. i. 26 ; Prov. vii. 20.
Man makes himself a vessel of wrath, Hosea xiii. 9.
Believers by nature the children of wrath even as others, Eph. ii. 3.
Delivered by Christ from the wrath to come, 1 Thess. i. 10.
Sinners exhorted to flee to Christ for refuge from it, Zech. ix. 12 ; Heb. vi. 18.

Fitted for destruction. The dreadful consequence of sin.
Fitted, not prepared, as the vessels of mercy are for glory.
Self-fitted ; sinners not repenting fit themselves for destruction.
Ground bearing thorns and briars fit only to be burned, Heb. vi. 8.
Barren fig-tree, Luke xiii. 7 ; unfruitful vine-branches, John xv. 6.
God by His grace prepares men for glory ;
Sinners by their sin fit themselves for destruction.
God mentioned in the one case, not in the other.
God *dooms* sinners to destruction ; they *fit* themselves for it.
The *fall* fitted men for destruction, *impenitence* does so still further.
Sinners eagerly do what fits them for destruction, Eccles. viii. 11.
Destruction = perdition ; loss not of being, but of well-being.
Everlasting fire prepared for the devil and his angels, Matt. xxv. 41.
The second death, Rev. ii. 11 ; xx. 14. Everlasting punishment, Matt. xxv. 46.
Everlasting destruction from the presence of the Lord, 2 Thess. i. 9.

Εἰ δέ, for if. *Jer., Mor., Tol.* What if. *Vulg., Eth., Eras.* But if. *Syr., Trem.* But what if. *Beza, Pag., Pisc.* What, then, if ; what injustice is there if. &c. *Grot.* Supply, what shall we say, or what will you say. *Aug., Pisc., Vor., Par., Calv., Beza, Cam.* If, indeed. *Ferme.* But if, or since. *Beng.* How much less if. *Diod.* What is it if. *Mar.* What is it to thee, or, what right hast thou to find fault if. *Doddr.* What objection can there be against justice if. *Guyse.* But however if ; the first answer shows the incompetency of the objector to put such a question, the second, that God acts in conformity with His moral perfections. *Flatt.* If then, or, if now. *Stuart, Stier.* According to most interpreters, the sentence more or less imperfect. *Rück.* The antecedent member of a question indicated by εἰ δέ, with the consequent member not expressed but understood. *De Wette.* No consequent member found, ver. 23 not being adapted for such. *Von Hofm.* Though. *Phil., Meyer, Lange, Con. & Hows.* What if I bring to thy mind. *De Wette.* A possible case suggested. *Frit., Thol.* If God, &c. So also, He makes known the riches, &c. *Ols.* Some recent expositors would take εἰ interrogatively for *nonne ?* or supply, ἤν after θελων : better with the older commentators to suppose an *Anantapodoton* or *Anacoluthon*, supplying οὐκ ἔχει ἐξουσιαν. *Bloomf.*—Θελων, therefore when God wished, &c. *Luther, Flatt.* When He resolved. *Storr, Nösselt.* Resolving at last. *Doddr.* Purposing. *Bloomf., Ellicot.* Even the long-suffering intended to advance the judgment. *De Wette.* The long-suffering the main thought in the question. *Thol., Frit., Meyer, Phil.* Every thought of unrighteousness in God excluded by the connection of His will to show His wrath with His will to glorify the objects of His goodness. *Von Hofm.*—Ἐνδειξασθαι, to display, demonstrate as already known. *Beng.* Make it the more conspicuous and unexceptionable when the day of reckoning comes. *Guyse.*—Ὀργην, punitive justice, as chap. i. 18. *Stuart, Bloomf.* Righteousness. *De Wette.* Righteous sovereignty. *Guyse.*—Καὶ, omitted by Cod. Vat.—Γνωρισαι, make known ; special reference to Pharaoh. *Ferme.*—Τὸ δυνατον αὐτου, His power. *Vulg., Beza, Pisc.* What He could do (possibile) ; τὸ δυν., for δυναμις. *Grot., Pisc., Vor.* His might, what He could do ; not power or authority absolutely. *Alf.* His power in punishing rebellious men. *Pisc., Par.* In executing threatened judgments. *Grot.* In making even sin contribute to His glory. *Hald.*—Ἠνεγκε, endured, tolerated. *Pag., Beza, Pisc., Vat.* As Pharaoh. *Or., Chrys., Theod., Ambr.* Endured and cast them not at once away. *Con. & Hows.* Brought (attulit, adduxit), *i.e.*, to the end for which they were fitted, viz., destruction. *Aug., Est., Eras.* Bore with patience. *Theoph.*—Μακροθυμια, long-suffering, with a view to their improvement. *Thol.* Only a putting off of deserved punishment, as 1 Pet. iii. 20, compared with Gen. vi. 3, the object here being to show His wrath and make known His power. *Von Hofm., Ferme.*—Σκευη ὀργης, instruments or tools of wrath. *Calv, Beck, Reiche.* Vessels appointed for the reception of wrath. *Rück.* Objects of wrath. *De Wette, Thol., Lange.* Objects of His righteous punishment, or serious displeasure at evil. *Flatt.* Proper and deserving objects of His wrath. *Guyse.* Deserving of punishment. *Stuart.* Destined to, and deserving of, wrath. *Hodge.* Subject to punishment. *Brown.* Vessels full of divine wrath. *Meyer.* Pharaoh. *Paulus.* The Jews. *Klee, Bloomf.* Immediately Pharaoh, and, by way of parallel, the Jews. *Meyer.* Those who should serve for God to show His wrath on them. *Von Hofm.* Endured vessels of wrath ; without the article. *Ellicot.*—Κατηρτισμενα (κατα, and ἀρω, to fit ; hence ἀρτιος, complete, and ἀρτος, a joint or limb ; καταρτιζω, to set a dislocated limb ; or to work into consistency,—metaphor from clay. *Beza, Pisc.*). Fit (apta). *Vulg., Chrys.* Prepared. *Eras., Tir., Pisc.* Wrought (coagmentata). *Pag., Pisc., Melv.* (compacta), *Beza.* Have prepared themselves. *Chrys., Theoph.* By their own sin and impenitence. *Par., Vor., Tol.* — Ἑτοιμα, fit, ready. *Chrys., Tucker, Bloomf.* Taken in a middle or reciprocal sense, prepared themselves, as Acts xiii. 48, τεταγμενοι. *Schött.* Fitted or framed as planks in a fabric mutually fitted for each other ; indicates that predestination whereby, as vessels of wrath, they are destined for destruction to be effected by its own intermediate causes. *Ferme* = ןוכנ, fit, ready, from ןוכ, to prepare. *Grot.* Ripe, ready, suited. *Stuart.* Ready, or have fitted themselves. *Hodge, Guyss.* By their own sin and self-hardening. *Hald.* Brought by God into this condition. *Meyer.* An anterior, but not a creation-act of God ; the absolute and the moral, God's part and man's, mingled together. *De Wette.* Not arbitrary power, but riches of goodness, displayed even on vessels of wrath. *Alford.* Ripe for destruction ; the state for which they were formed, and for which they were suited. *Von Hofm.* Figure taken from the potter, that none might think the vessels of wrath are prepared merely by themselves. *Melville.*

23. *And that He might make known the riches of His glory on the vessels of mercy, which He had afore prepared unto glory.*

Make known. As that which has not yet been clearly revealed.
God glorifies Himself by making known His goodness and severity, chap. xi. 22.
Riches. Exceeding abundance. Favourite word with the apostle.
Not only glory, but riches of glory, beyond—1. All expectation ; 2. All conception.
Glory. Grace on earth preparatory to glory in heaven.
Riches of glory = riches of grace, Eph. i. 7. God's goodness His glory, Exod. xxxiii. 18, 19.
Riches of His glory = His glorious riches. Rich in mercy, chap. x. 12 ; Eph. ii. 4.
His superabounding goodness and grace in Christ, Eph. ii. 8.
Blessings of salvation. Unsearchable riches of Christ, Eph. iii. 8.
These riches revealed in the Gospel and bestowed on believers.
God's glorious grace in Christ, Paul's most delightful subject.
Vessels of mercy. Persons intended for and made subjects of mercy.
Mercy, not merit, that which distinguishes the saved.
Vessels of mercy, to show that all their salvation is of mercy.
Children of wrath by nature, vessels of mercy by grace.
Vessels of mercy filled out of Christ's fulness, John i. 16 ; Col. i. 19.
God's love in Christ poured into the heart by the Holy Ghost, chap. v. 5.
Afore. In relation to the glory to be enjoyed.
Grace here prepares for glory hereafter.
Prepared. Destined to and fitted for glory.
Heaven a prepared place for a prepared people, John xiv. 2 ; Col. i. 12.
Preparation of sinners for glory the work of God himself, 2 Cor. v. 5.
Those whom God chooses to salvation He sanctifies by grace, 2 Thess. ii. 13 ; 1 Pet. i. 2.
None admitted to glory who are not prepared by grace, Heb. xii. 14 ; Rev. xxi. 6-8.
Glory. Enjoyment of God and the blessedness of heaven, chap. ii. 10.
The glory to be revealed at the appearing of Jesus Christ, chap. viii. 18 ; Col. iii. 4.
The fruit and reward of the sufferings of Christ, 1 Pet. i. 11.

Glory and destruction, solemn contrast. Rich man and Lazarus, Luke xvi. 22, &c.

Καὶ, wanting in some copies. Appears to be redundant. *Melville.*—Ἵνα, to the end that. *Ellicot.*—Γνωριση, might show. *Grot.* Ἐνδεικ., applied to wrath as known before ; γνωρ., to grace as yet comparatively unknown.—T. πλουτον τ. δοξης αὐτ., God's glorious goodness as shown to Israel and still more to believers. *De Wette.* The universal preaching of the gospel and conversion of the heathen. *Lange.* The riches of divine goodness to the elect more conspicuous by the destruction of the ungodly. *Calv., Melv.* A Hebraism for 'His most abundant glory.' *Bloomf.* That 'glorious exuberance of divine mercy' manifested in choosing and eternally arranging for the salvation of sinners. *D. Brown.* Riches of His glorious grace. *Guyse.* Riches of the glory of God from mercy. *Ferme.*—Σκευη ἐλεους, objects of His goodness. *Flatt.* Subjects of mercy. *Lange, Brown.* Persons destined to receive mercy. *Hodge.* Mercifully *accepted* by God, with reference to the whole body of Christians, whether Jews or Gentiles. *Bloomf.* Ἔλεους, that love of which Jacob was the object (Mal. i. 2), the purpose of God or benevolent affection of His will (εὐδοκια), which belongs to all the children of God in common with him. *Ferme.* The vessels of mercy, with the article. *Ellicot.* —Προητοιμασεν (προ and ἑτοιμος, ready). Laid out, and fits beforehand. *Guyse.* Destined to and fitted for glory. *Brown.* Prepared before, *i.e.,* from eternity ; their predestination according to the good pleasure of His will. *Ferme.* Fore-ordained. *Bloomf.* Prepared, by election. *Vor., Par.* By effectual calling. *Vor., Cam.* A passive verb used in speaking of the 'vessels of wrath' (κατηρτισμενα, fitted to destruction) ; an active verb in speaking of the 'vessels of mercy,' προητοιμασε, whom He (God) prepared afore to glory : the former fitted by their own iniquity, the latter prepared by what God does upon them. *Guyse.*—Δοξαν, their glory, to be accomplished by its own intermediate causes. *Ferme.* Glory, commencing in this life and completed in the next. *Grot., Bloomf.* That of being made the Church and people of God ; glory of nations. *Mackn.* Δοξα = 1. The glorifying of Israel as the people of God ; 2. Glory, dignity, or salvation, brought to Christians. Compare Eph. ii. 10. *De Wette.* After δοξαν supply ἐκαλεσε. *Thol.* ; ἐλεησε. *Stuart.*

---

24. *Even us, whom He hath called, not of the Jews only, but also of the Gentiles.*

Even, &c. Gr., Whom also He hath called, even us, &c. So chap. viii. 30.
Not only "afore preparing," but in due time effectually calling.
Us. Paul himself and all true believers vessels of mercy.
Speaks not of nations but of individuals taken out of them.
Happy they who can thus rank themselves as vessels of mercy.
Called. Vessels of mercy known by their effectual calling.
Called—1. Outwardly by the Gospel ; 2. Inwardly by the Spirit.
God "endures" vessels of wrath ; "calls" vessels of mercy.
Every vessel of mercy called ; every called one a vessel of mercy.
Vessels of wrath called outwardly but refuse the call ;
Vessels of mercy called also inwardly and obey, John vi. 37 ; x. 16.

All who obeying the Gospel call come to Christ, are vessels of mercy.
Not of the Jews only. The leading thought in the whole section.
Gentiles are vessels of mercy, as well as Jews.
God's sovereignty in calling individuals out of both.
The calling of the Gentiles as such, the offence of the Jews.
Jewish pride wounded, Luke iv. 25-28. Hence persecution, 1 Thess.
ii. 15, 16.
Gentiles. Nations of the world. At that time all sunk in idolatry.
God's purpose to take out of them a people for His name, Acts xv. 14.
The multitude before the throne out of every nation, Rev. vii. 9.
Hence the commission to preach the Gospel to all nations, Matt.
xxviii. 19.

'Εκαλεσε, invited and brought over to obedience. *Grot.* Verbs of counsel and striving often so taken as to include the event. *Bloomf.* From God's eternal decree and secret will, the apostle comes down to the manifestation of it in calling men by the Gospel. *Melville.*

25. *As He saith also in Osee, I will call them my people, which were not my people; and her beloved, which was not beloved.*

As He saith. This calling of Gentiles matter of prophecy.
Osee, or Hosea, chap. ii. 23. First of the minor prophets.
Began his prophetic ministry in the reign of Uzziah.
Prophesied under Jeroboam II., king of Israel, and his successors.
Most of his prophecies written after that king's death, B.C. 783.
His ministry confined to the kingdom of Israel.
Probably continued fifty-nine years, from B.C. 784 to 725.
Subjects of his prophecies, Israel's sin, rejection, and restoration.
The Messiah foretold under the title of "David their king," Hosea
iii. 5.
Chap. xi. 1, quoted by Matthew as fulfilled in Jesus, Matt. ii. 15.
Chap. xiii. 14, applied by Paul to the saints' resurrection, 1 Cor. xv.
54, 55.
Chap. xiv. among the most precious passages of the Bible.
Chap. ii. 19, 20; vi. 1-3; xi. 8, 9; xiii. 9, also passages of great
beauty.
Call. What God calls men He makes them become.
Calls things that are not, as though they were, chap. iv. 17; 1 Cor.
i. 28.
My people. Title first applied to Israel in Egypt, Exod. iii. 7.

The highest distinction. Implies—1. Privilege ; 2. Honour ; 3. Happiness.
Involves responsibility. God's people—1. A happy ; 2. A holy, people.
Implies on God's part, protection, care, salvation ;
On their part, trust, obedience, loving devotedness.
God's covenant, "I will be their God, and they shall be my people," Heb. viii. 10.
Not my people. Applies—1. To the Ten Tribes after their rejection; 2. To the Gentiles who had never been adopted as God's people.
Applied by Peter to the elect scattered strangers, 1 Pet. ii. 10.
These strangers the "dispersed among the Gentiles," John vii. 35.
Israel to be many days without prince or sacrifice, Hosea iii. 4.
First invaded and made tributary by Pul, king of Assyria, under Menahem.
Cities taken and inhabitants carried away by Tiglath-Pileser under Pekah.
Invaded by Shalmanezer under their last king, Hoshea, 2 Kings xv. 19, 29 ; xvii. 3.
Samaria the capital taken after a siege of three years.
The inhabitants of the country taken captive to Assyria, 2 Kings xvii. 5, 6.
Distributed in the cities of Media and elsewhere.
Still continue in their dispersion. Greatly unknown.
Many of them supposed to be the Nestorian Christians in Chaldæa.
Many thought to have gone northwards and crossed over to America.
Known to be existing in the days of Christ and His apostles, Acts xxvi. 7.
Many of them had become believers in Jesus, James i. 1.
Israel (Ten Tribes) cast off and cast out on account of idolatry.
The same might happen to the Jews from rejection of Christ.
"Not a people" (1 Pet. ii. 10), descriptive of the state of the heathen world.
Not to be the people of God is to be no people.
Those who are God's people nationally may cease to be so.
Those who have been cast off may be graciously restored.
Those who have never been God's people may be made such.
Beloved. Israel as a people the spouse of Jehovah, Jer. ii. 2 ; iii. 14.
Solomon's Song understood by the Jews to represent this union.
Israel rejected for a time for adultery and whoredom, *i.e.*, idolatry.

The Lord free to choose whom He will for His spouse and beloved.
Believers among Jews and Gentiles now made such, Eph. v. 25.
Sinners everywhere espoused to Christ through the Gospel, 2 Cor xi. 2.
Christ became a sacrifice to be a Saviour, a Saviour to be a bridegroom, John iii. 29.
Not beloved. 1. Israel after their rejection; 2. The Gentiles.
Reference to God's dealings rather than to His feelings.
God's love an everlasting and unchanging love, Jer. xxxi. 3; Mal. iii. 6.
Rejected Israel was apparently and dispensationally "not beloved."
Gentile sinners without Christ and without God in the world, Eph. ii. 12.
Called through the great love wherewith God loved them, ver. 4.
Jews and Gentiles by nature and through sin the children of wrath, ver. 3.
Israel had sunk to the level of the heathen. Christless Jews and Gentiles alike.

Καλεσω, I will call, *i.e.*, I will make; not by an empty name, but by making what I name. *Est.*—Τον ου λαον μου. the idolatrous Ten Tribes, typical of the Gentiles. *Grot., Eras., Pisc., Est.* Gentiles, from the resemblance between both. *Par., Tol., Chrys.* Refers not only to the gathering again of the Israelites rejected in the carrying away by Shalmaneser, but also of the Gentiles rejected at the building of Babel; remnants elected from both. *Ferme.* Calling of the Gentiles. *Melv., Glück.* Originally referring to the restoration of the Jews, but properly accommodated to the calling of the Gentiles. *Doddr., Guyse.* Relates more immediately to the call of the Gentiles. *Horsley.* Israel sunk to the level of the Gentiles; an election from both intended. *D. Brown.* Reference to the names לֹא עַמִּי (Lo-ammi), and לֹא רֻחָמָה (Lo-Ruhamah), which the prophet was to give to his children, to indicate God's rejection of the kingdom of Israel: Israel alone in the view of the prophet. *Von Hofm.* Israel viewed by Paul as including the heathen. *Rückert.* The collective ingathered heathen viewed as an extension of the apostate Ten Tribes. *Phil.*—Ουκ ηγαπημενην, not beloved, *i.e.*, apparently and in men's judgment. *Vat.* Not spoken of God's eternal love, but the blessings and benefits which flow from it. *Est., Men.* Allusion to the marriage-relationship between God and Israel. *Flatt.*

---

26. *And it shall come to pass, that in the place where it was said unto them, Ye are not my people; there shall they be called the children of the living God.*

And, &c. Another quotation from the same prophet, Hosea i. 10.
In the place. 1. Of Israel's dispersion; 2. The lands of the Gentiles.
Lands of the heathen formerly regarded as outcast regions.

Only the land of Israel priestly consecrated ground, Dan. xi. 41, 45.
Admissibility of Gentiles as such into the Church long doubted.
The question only settled by a special vision, Acts x. 10, &c.
Special or exclusive sacredness of places to be abolished, John iv. 21.
In every place incense and a pure offering to be presented, Mal. i. 11.
Children. By regeneration and adoption in Christ, Eph. i. 5.
Believing Gentiles made members of the household of God, Eph. ii. 19.
God's amazing love, Jew and Gentile sinners made His sons, 1 John iii. 1.
Living God. 1. As alone having life and immortality in Himself, 1 Tim. vi. 16.
2. As the only source of life spiritual or temporal to others.
A living God must have living men for His people, Matt. xxii. 32.
God therefore to be worshipped only in spirit and in truth, John iv. 24.
The living God the ground of confidence and source of comfort, 1 Tim. vi. 17.

Ἐν τῷ τόπῳ οὗ, there where. *Diod.* Lands of the heathen; believers not required as proselytes to worship at Jerusalem. *Est.* The place where they should be found in their idolatry and unbelief; removal to Judæa not necessary, Zeph. ii. 11. *Beng., Thol.* Lands and places where the people for ages had not been in covenant with God. *Guyse.* Palestine, to which the people should be restored, and where it was long questioned whether the Gentiles were admissible to Christian fellowship. *Frit.* The Christian Church to which the Gentiles' admission was long doubtful. *De Wette.* In the prophet, the 'place' = Palestine; with the apostle, the lands of the heathen. *Lange, Nielson.* Reference to the restoration of Israel. *Horsley.* Not to be taken too strictly as referring to some particular locality; only gives greater emphasis to the change announced. *D. Brown.* In those nations. *Cobbin.* Ἐν τῷ τόπῳ, instead of its being said. *Hitzig, Ewald.*—Αὐτοῖς. Omitted in Cod. Vat.

---

27. *Esaias also crieth concerning Israel, Though the number of the children of Israel be as the sand of the sea, a remnant shall be saved.*

Esaias, or Isaiah. Prophesied in the kingdom of Judah.
His ministry commenced under Uzziah, king of Judah, B.C. 760.
Continued to be exercised for at least forty-eight years.
Is said to have been sawn asunder by order of Manasseh, Heb. xi. 37.
In this case must have exercised his office about sixty years.
Was contemporary with Amos, Hosea, Joel, and Micah.
His name descriptive of the character of his prophecies, The Lord's salvation.

CHAP. IX.]   ST. PAUL'S EPISTLE TO THE ROMANS.   51

Called, from his clear references to Christ, the Evangelical Prophet.
Chap. liii. reads more like a history than a prophecy.
Chap. lv. sounds like the invitations by Christ and His apostles.
More Jews converted by chap. liii. than any other part of Scripture.
Isaiah's writings the ideal of prophetic poetry.
A fountain of consolation to the Church in all ages.
Crieth. Lifts up his voice with boldness and without restraint.
Allusion to the earnest vehemence of his language in Isa. x. 20–23.
Repeats the word "remnant" a fourth time.
God's servants not to shrink from delivering unwelcome truth.
Attention to be earnestly called to Jehovah's message.
The speaker to be himself deeply affected with the message he bears.
Concerning. Or, "For." Mercy and judgment mingled in the messsage.
A remnant at all is mercy; *only* a remnant is judgment.
Israel. Sometimes used in a limited sense of the Ten Tribes.
Here taken generally of the whole covenant people.
Number. Judæa remarkable for its former populousness.
1,600,000 fighting men, not including Levi and Benjamin, 1 Chron. xxi. 5, 6.
The number of Israel a subject of divine promise, Gen. xv. 5.
The effect of divine blessing in fulfilment of it, Exod. i. 12; Lev. xxvi. 9.
Sand of the sea. Promised to be as the dust of the earth, Gen. xiii. 16.
According to another promise, as the stars of heaven, Gen. xv. 5.
A remnant. *Gr.*, The remnant; the remnant chosen to be saved.
A remnant saved according to the election of grace, chap. xi. 5.
Only a remnant. Rejection general but not total.
The great body of Israel to be destroyed or carried captive—
1. The Ten Tribes by Tiglath-Pileser and Shalmaneser, 2 Kings xvii. 6.
2. The two remaining tribes by Nebuchadnezzar, 2 Kings xxv. 1, &c.
3. The Jews by the Romans under the emperor Titus, A.D. 70.
This, called by themselves the Great Captivity, still continues.
1,100,000 perished in the war; 97,000 carried captive.
580,000 fell in the Jewish rebellion that followed.
Multitudes also perished by famine and by their own hand.
The captives too numerous to obtain purchasers.
Excision of Israel no violation of the divine promise.
Only a remnant saved from outward calamities;

So only a remnant from eternal destruction.
In both cases the salvation through faith, Heb. iv. 2.
Jews not therefore to wonder if few only believed in Jesus.
A saved remnant only promised by the prophet.
Saved. *Heb.,* Shall return—1. From outward captivity;
2. From the worse captivity of sin and Satan, Acts iii. 19.
The promise so important as to give name to Isaiah's son, Isa. vii. 3.
Temporal captivity a type of the spiritual, Isa. xxxv. 10.
Number of Jews at present from five to seven millions.
Scattered up and down among all the nations of the earth.
A distinct people and not reckoned among the nations, Num. xxiii. 9.
Retaining their own religion, language, and customs.
A standing testimony to the truth of the Word of God.
The cause of their dispersion not idolatry but unbelief.
That unbelief exhibited in the rejection and crucifixion of God's Son.
The cry, "His blood be on us and on our children," still verified.
Yet a remnant saved by that blood, and bye and bye the nation, chap. xi. 26.

Κραζει, cries; Jewish form of citation. *Schött., Wetstein.* Awakens Jewish attention. *Par., Guyse.* Indicates great grief. *Est.* Prophet's contention with the Jews on this subject. *Per.* Great earnestness and affection. *Doddr.* Solemn testimony openly borne. *D. Brown.* Allusion to the loud authoritative tone the prophets were authorised to assume. *Bloomf.* The word of Hosea a prophecy; that of Isaiah teaches the right understanding of it. *Von Hofm.*—Ὑπερ, concerning. *Or., Chrys., Eras., Vat., Beza.* Like περι, 1 Cor. x. 30; 2 Cor. vii. 4; ix. 2; xii. 5. So Heb. עַל. *Grot.*—Το καταλειμμα (κατα and λειπω, to leave; the part left; remains, as from a table. *Tol.*) Codd. Alex. and Sin. have ὑπολειμμα. Only a remnant. *Pisc., Flatt, Doddr., Con. & Hows.* Only a small remnant. *Mart.* The remnant. *Ellicot.* The remnant only. *Diod.* Elect remnant only. *D. Brown.* But a remnant only are the called and people of God. *Ferme.* But a remnant according to the election of grace. *Guyse.* The remnant or small portion reserved by God for the purposes of His will. *Middleton.* Only few out of the Ten Tribes returned to Judæa; few left by Sennacherib; few brought to Christ. *Tol., Tir.* Only those possessed of faith. *Theod.* Only a remnant shall be saved from the great destruction or reckoning in judgment. *Luther.* Only such as returned to Jehovah and joined the kingdom of Judah. *Brown.* Metaphor from bread-making, small portion of dough reserved for leaven; the residue only; implying that but a small number compared with those who had perished will return to the Lord. *Bloomf.* Only a small number, a chosen remnant, to be saved by faith. *Lange, Barth.* The LXX. limits the salvation to the surviving remnant of the formerly numerous people: the apostle makes the saved remnant the same with the people who then were as the sand; however great the number, they are the people that remain after tribulation. *Von Hofm.* If God saved only a remnant from captivity, He may do the same under the Gospel. *Cobbin.*—Σωθησεται, after the LXX. Heb. שׁוּב, shall return. LXX. probably read יִוָּשֵׁעַ, shall be saved. The same truth in either case.

28. *For He will finish the work, and cut it short in righteousness: because a short work will the Lord make upon the earth.*

For. Introduces another quotation from Isaiah, chap. xxviii. 22.
A work of judgment to be accomplished on the Jewish people.
Finish. What God purposes He will perform, Ps. xxxiii. 11; Isa. xlvi. 10.
Promises and threatenings receive their accomplishment.
When God begins He will also finish, whether in grace or judgment.
The Lord not slack as some men count slackness, 2 Pet. iii. 9.
Creation but a reservoir of means made ready for His use. *Cowper.*
Work. Work of judgment in reference to the Jewish nation.
Jerusalem completely destroyed by the Romans under Titus.
Levelled to the ground as if it had never been inhabited.
Only three towers and part of the wall left standing.
The temple furniture carried among the spoils to Rome.
The land of Judæa seemed converted into a desert.
Cut it short. Bring it to a speedy termination.
Heb., "The consumption decreed shall overflow."
Vengeance executed by sudden and overwhelming invasion.
Judgment comes in due time as a sweeping flood.
The war under Titus brought to a speedy and decisive close.
The Jews overtaken by the judgment in the time of the Passover.
In righteousness. Holy justice. Judgment laid to the line, Isa. xxviii. 17.
Mercy trifled with and abused gives place to justice.
God's severest judgments are still in righteousness.
Israel to be brought to acknowledge this, Lev. xxvi. 41; Dan. ix. 7.
Josephus ascribes his country's sufferings to its sins.
Short work. A speedy and decisive work of judgment.
A short work made at the siege of Jerusalem by Titus.
The city at the time full of people for the celebration of the Passover.
Type of judgment-work at Christ's appearing, Matt. xxiv. 37–41; 2 Thess. i. 7–9.
Work of judgment shortened for the elect's sake, Matt. xxiv. 22.
Shall the Lord make. The Lord's work whoever the instruments.
Titus acknowledged it was only through God he took the city.
Wished to spare the temple, and so gave orders, but in vain.
Josephus says the Jews fought not against the Romans but God.
God never in want of means to accomplish His purposes.
Upon the earth. *Heb.*, The whole land, *i.e.*, of Israel.
Destruction not completed by the Assyrian but by the Roman armies.

Josephus says the whole land was destroyed with the city. The country around Jerusalem entirely changed. One event of Scripture made to typify and foreshadow another. Judgment-work of Christ's coming universal, 2 Thess. i. 8; 2 Pet. iii. 7, 10–12.

"Wherever the carcase is there shall the eagles be gathered together."

Λογον, the law. *Or., Tertullian, Chrys., Ambr.* This interpretation from ignorance of the Hebrew. Speech (sermonem). *Eras., Tir.* Account (rationem). *Pag.* A certain terrible thing not mentioned. *Vor.* Matter. *Ferme.* But ῥῆμα, not λογος, is thing or matter. *Est.* Prophetic threatening. *Par.* Number of faithful Israelites which God will make small. *Men., Tir.* Work. *Calv.* Denied by *Alford.* Counsel accomplished in God's mind, decree determined. *Dickson.* The thing heard, and therefore spoken. *Beng.* Account laid in His eternal purpose, balanced between the elect and others. *Guyse, Doddr.* Word, counsel, matter; summary termination. *Meyer.* Determination. *Glöckner, Beck.* Fact, saying. *Lange.* Divine promise, counsel. *Thol., De Wette.* Divine threatening. *Reiche, Rück.* Λογος, without the article — only *something*. *Von Hofm.* Word. *Tischendorf.* Reckoning. *Con. & Hows., D. Brown.* Account, affair. *Bloomf.* —Συντελων (συν and τελος, end), perfecting (perficiens). *Eras., Tir., Vat.* Accomplishing (conficiens). *Pisc.* Will finish. *Ferme, Guyse.* Is finishing. *Pyle, Doddr., Locke, D. Brown, Ellicot.* Consummates. *Mart.*—Συντεμνων, will cut short (concidet). *Beza, Pisc., Pag.* Bring into small compass (in compendium rediget). *Pag.* Is cutting short. *Locke, Pyle, Doddr., D. Brown.* Decides. *Diod.* Abridges. *Mart.* Determines. *Flatt.* Deciding, bringing to an end, executing. *Stuart.* Will soon cut short the affair. *Bloomf.*—Συντετμημενον. This, with the preceding words from συντελων, omitted in some copies. A concise word. *Mor.* A concise affair. *Beza, Pisc.* Compendious account. *Pag.* Determined purpose. *Vat.* Severe affair. *Cast.* Speedily accomplished work. *Ferme, Alford.* Decision. *Diod., Glöck.* An abridged matter. *Mart.* Short work. *D. Brown.*—Γης, land of Israel. *Stuart.* The world. *Von Hofm.* The whole almost verbatim from the LXX. Heb., 'the consumption (כִּלָּיוֹן, destruction, Deut. xxviii. 65) decided (חָרוּץ, decree, surely determined) overfloweth with righteousness (צְדָקָה שׁוֹטֵף).' A destruction is strictly determined, bringing in righteousness as with a flood. *Delitzsch.* The destruction is determined; it bringeth destroying righteousness. *Gesenius.* Bringing overflowing righteousness, *i.e.*, righteous punishment. *De Wette.* Hostile bands inflicting punishment. *Frit.* Nothing of this in the Greek translation. *Rück.* Passed over as not adapted to his purpose. *Von Hofm.* This verse apparently adduced as confirming the certainty of the salvation of the remnant. *Alford.* While the present world remains, Israel's final salvation continues still in the balance: the Lord, therefore, makes an end and reckons with the world; and what the people of Israel shall then be, this remnant turns to Him and obtains salvation. *Von Hofm.* While a remnant is graciously spared to return from captivity, 'the decreed consumption' of the impenitent majority shall be 'replete with righteousness,' or illustriously display God's righteous vengeance against sin; the 'short reckoning' being the speedy completing of His Word both in cutting off the one portion and saving the other. *D. Brown.*

---

29. *And as Esaias said before, Except the Lord of Sabaoth had left us a seed, we had been as Sodoma, and been made like unto Gomorrha.*

Said before. 1. Foretold; 2. Said in a previous prophecy, Isa. i. 9.

Lord of Sabaoth—*i.e.*, Lord of Hosts. Title first found in 1 Sam. i. 3.
The Hebrew word retained in the Greek version in Samuel and Isaiah.
Elsewhere rendered by a word signifying "the Almighty," as Rev. i. 8.
Sabaoth = hosts, applied—1. To the heavenly bodies.
Hence the worship of these bodies called Sabæism. See on chap. i. 25.
2. Applied also to angels, the armies of heaven, Ps. ciii. 21; Dan. iv. 35.
Jehovah called the Lord of Hosts or of Sabaoth—
1. As the supreme Ruler of heaven and earth;
2. In opposition to the prevailing worship of the heavenly bodies.
Left us. The remnant according to free unmerited mercy.
The difference existing among men is not of man but of God.
Sovereign mercy alone the ground of a sinner's salvation.
Seed. The remnant spared at the destruction of Jerusalem.
From them were to spring the multitude of the saved, chap. xi. 26.
Seed small in itself but to be greatly mulitiplied.
Small but useful, the seed of future generations, Isa. vi. 13.
Had been as Sodoma—*i.e.*, Entirely given to sin and destruction.
A godly elect remnant the preserving salt to the mass.
Miserable state of the kingdom of Judah under Ahaz, Isa. i. 5-9.
Wasted by Pekah king of Israel, Syrians, Idumæans, Philistines.
120,000 slain in one day by Pekah, 2 Chron. xxviii. 5-7; xxix. 8.
Sodoma or Sodom one of the most ancient cities of Canaan.
Mentioned with Gomorrha and three others as "cities of the plain."
All destroyed except Zoar, spared at Lot's prayer, Gen. xix. 21; Hosea xi. 8.
Sodom the chief town in the settlement.
The plain one great oasis, "as a garden of the Lord," Gen. xiii. 10.
Situated west of the Jordan in the south of Canaan.
The site of the cities near if not under the Dead Sea.
Their inhabitants notorious for profligacy and vice.
Cities and people destroyed by fire and brimstone from heaven.
Not a vestige of the cities remaining. No elect seed left.
Monuments of the anger of a holy, sin-avenging God, 2 Pet. ii. 6.
Josephus makes his countrymen worse than the men of Sodom.

Gomorrha. A climax. Like Sodom from which only Lot's family escaped.

Yea like Gomorrha, from which escaped not even one individual.

Προείρηκεν, has before said. *Ferme.* In a former part of his prophecy. *Guyse, D. Brown.* Predicted; Israel's unbelief and rejection in the time of the prophet a true type of the future. *Nielson.*—Σαβαωθ, Heb. צבאות, hosts. All creatures who obey and war for God. *Pisc., Vor.*—Σπερμα. In Isa. i. 9, שָׂרִיד, a remnant, LXX. σπερμα, a seed; so in Deut. iii. 3, 'none left remaining.' A remnant, small at first, but in due time to be a seed of plenty. *D. Brown.* Reference to some invasions of Judæa by Resen and Pekah at the latter end of Jotham's reign. *Lowth, Koppe.* A spiritual seed, made the objects of His special love. *Guyse.*—Ὡμοιώθημεν, resembled in character and in doom. *D. Brown.*—Σοδομα, Sodom and Gomorrha with Admah and Zeboim generally believed to have stood at the south end of the Dead Sea, and to have been submerged by the lake. Their remains, walls, columns, and capitals said to have been long after discerned below the water. Both views unsupported by Scripture. *Dr Smith.* Their situation at the south end of the lake believed by Josephus, Jerome, and others after them. This view supported by Dr Robinson, as—1. Sodom was near Zoar, and Zoar stood at the south end of the present lake; 2. Similar names exist in that direction; 3. A salt mountain is found at the south of the lake, with a tendency to split off in columnar masses, presenting a rude resemblance to the human form. The destruction of the cities thought by some (Michaelis, Chateaubriand) to have been occasioned by the lightning igniting the combustible mass of bitumen over which they stood. Others (Captains Irby and Mangles) think that the lightnings swept the neighbouring cliffs containing nitre and sulphur, and that their flaming masses poured in a deluge of fire upon the plain.

---

30. *What shall we say then? That the Gentiles, which followed not after righteousness, have attained to righteousness, even the righteousness which is of faith.*

What shall we say then? What is the conclusion of all this? The object indicated at which the apostle has been aiming.

Gentiles. Their case the great stumbling-block of the Jews. Their salvation thought attainable only by adopting Judaism. Regarded with supercilous contempt by the Jews as dogs, &c.

Followed not after—*i.e.*, Earnestly as men in a chase. Reference to the life and aims of the Gentile world. All men pursue some object, few a worthy one.

Righteousness. Justification, with holiness as its fruit. With Paul, righteousness is generally acceptance with God. About this the Gentiles in general entirely unconcerned. Their object in the worship of their deities was either—

1. To obtain temporal benefits; or, 2. Be delivered from temporal ills.

Personal acceptance with a holy and righteous God unthought of.

Cornelius the centurion an exception through grace.
Acceptance with God the one object worthy a sinner's pursuit.
Have attained. Gained the prize of acceptance.
Not themselves seeking it, God presented it to them.
Presented as a gift, they were drawn to accept of it.
Righteousness of faith. Acceptance through faith in Christ.
The righteousness of Christ the only ground of acceptance.
That righteousness offered and bestowed on all who believe, chap. iii. 22.
Held out in the Gospel, chap. i. 17. Accepted by the Gentiles, Acts xi. 18.

Διωκοντα, pursuing, *i.e.*, earnestly. *Chrys.* As in a race. *Ham., Guyse, Alford.* As not having it. *Phil.* In order to *do* it, not *possess* it, Heb. xii. 14 ; Rom. xiv. 19. *Von Hofm.* Rabbins : Be thou running after the commandments. *Pirke Aboth.* Heb. רדף, Isa. li. 1, ' Ye that follow after righteousness' (רֹדְפֵי צֶדֶק).—Κατελαβε, laid hold of as a prize. *Guyse.*

---

31. *But Israel, which followed after the law of righteousness, hath not attained to the law of righteousness.*

Israel. Here the great body of the Jewish people.
The more religious portion especially regarded.
Followed after. By a religious life and legal observances.
Had a zeal of God but not according to knowledge, chap. x. 2.
Good to strive, better to strive lawfully, 2 Tim. ii. 5.
Good to run, better to run well, Gal. v. 7. *So* run that, &c., 1 Cor. ix. 24.
Law of righteousness. *Gr.*, A law of righteousness.
Law used in an indefinite sense, as in chap. iii. 27
A method or way of justification and holiness.
Israel pursued a way of righteousness but a wrong one.
Law of righteousness put for righteousness itself, as in ver. 30.
" Law " indicates the kind of righteousness sought.
All Israel's efforts were after a legal righteousness.
More anxious about the law than the righteousness of it.
Have not attained. Ran but so as not to obtain, 1 Cor. ix. 24.
Fell short even of the law they pursued after.
A right *way* necessary as well as a right *end*.
To obtain the prize the runner must keep to the course.
Acceptance with God only to be obtained in God's way.
Misguided zeal, however earnest, misses its aim.

Νομον δικαιοσυνης. Codd. Sin., Vat., and Alex. omit δικ. Righteousness of the law. *Chrys., Calv., Beza, Beng., Cobbin.* Legal righteousness. *Melv.* Fulfilment of the law; righteousness which the law demands. *Ferme.* Righteousness to justification by their own obedience to the law of Moses. *Guyse.* Expecting to obtain it by legal observances. *Doddr.* Way of righteousness. Νομος = תּוֹרָה, from יָרָה, to guide. *Grot.* A rule through which to obtain righteousness. *Flatt.* An ideal law of righteousness; a justifying law. *Meyer, Thol., Frit.* Νομ. = method, established order, way, as chap. viii. 2; a practicable method of justification. *Brown.* Following after the law and aiming at justification by it. *Bloomf.* A prescribed rule of apparent righteousness. *Alford.* Law of external righteousness. *Wells.* 'Law' here, as in chap. vii. 23, a principle of action; 'law of righteousness,' acceptance with God. *D. Brown.*—'Εφθασε (φθανω, in later Greek, 'to attain,' with the idea of overcoming difficulties. *Thol.*) Reached (pervenit). *Eras., Pag., Mor.* Reached the goal. *Par.* Obtained. *Syr.* Attained. *Flatt, Doddr., Bloomf.* Arrived at, came up to, apprehended. *Guyse.* Οὐκ ἐφθασε, fell far short. *Alford.* Missed. *D. Brown.*—Νομ. δικαιοσυνης, law of righteousness; law of the Spirit. *Or.* The righteousness of the law. *Chrys.* Rule according to which God justifies. *Calv.* Way or method of communicating righteousness through the doctrine of the Gospel. *Melv.* True rule of righteousness. *Flatt.* A righteousness which answers the demands of the law. *Guyse.* A law or *the* law which gives justification, viz., that of Christ. *Bloomf.* That which is most properly to be called the law of righteousness, *i.e.*, the blessings of that dispensation by which alone righteousness and life can be secured. *Doddr.* The law which was given them. *Alford.* Acceptance with God. *D. Brown.* New Testament law giving righteousness. *Rück.* In both places, the idea of a justifying law. *Thol., Meyer.* An ideal of righteousness presented for realisation. *Phil.* Law of Moses. *Nielson.* Νομ. δικ., and not δικ. νομου, because Israel and not the Gentiles had in the economy of mercy a law which taught what was right; law not making righteous, but declaring what is right. *Von Hofm.*

---

32. *Wherefore? Because they sought it not by faith, but as it were by the works of the law: for they stumbled at that stumbling-stone.*

Wherefore? Important to know the cause of miscarriage.
Sought it not by faith. The only way by which it could be found.
There is a way that seems right to a man, but the end of it is death, Prov. xiv. 12.
The reason of miscarriage is not God's purpose but man's pride.
Those who perish either do not seek or seek in a wrong way.
The treasure of salvation hid in a field, Matt. xiii. 44.
If sought elsewhere, sought in vain. The field Christ, Acts iv. 12.
The treasure becomes ours with the field. Ours by faith.
Everything to be sold in order to purchase the field.
All our own works to be given up to possess Christ, Phil. iii. 7, 8.
Christ the end of the law for righteousness to the believer, chap. x. 4.
As it were. Or, As if it were to be obtained by, &c.
Fatal mistake to seek heaven where it cannot be found.

By the works of the law. Rather, By works of law, as chap. iii. 20.
Thought to obtain acceptance, not by believing, but working.
To seek justification by our own works is to seek fire in ice.
To look for acceptance through these is to forget we are sinners.
Christ's works, not ours, the ladder that reaches to heaven.
The righteousness that justifies is God's gift, not our wages.
Righteousness through works, but works without a flaw.
Works out of Christ are works not *of* law but *against* law.
Christ's works alone justify. The Lord our Righteousness, Jer. xxiii. 6.
To seek acceptance out of Christ is to seek for the sun at midnight.
Israel missed the works by their very attempts at them.
Works trusted in are not salvation but damnation.
A man's righteousness trusted in keeps him from righteousness.
Men kept out of heaven by good works as well as bad ones.
A legal religion is man's bane instead of blessing.
A double curse in substituting our own works for Christ's.
The proud guest's clothing lost to him the feast, Matt. xxii. 11-13.
Men prefer their own rags to Christ's robe.
To trust in our own works is to make a saviour of our sins.
To cross the gulf by our own righteousness is to plunge into it.
Only the God-man's works bridge the chasm between God and man.
He doubly deserves hell who refuses God's way to heaven.
Man's own way to heaven is only another way to hell.
More guilt in resisting mercy's offers than law's commands.
Despising Christ's blood and righteousness man's crowning sin.
Stumbled. As persons running in a race.
A man who runs and stumbles loses the prize.
Christ either lifts to heaven or casts into hell.
The former realised by all who humbly trust in *Him;*
The latter by all who proudly trust in themselves.
Stumbling-stone—viz., That predicted by the prophet.
Christ a stone of stumbling as well as rock of salvation.
Set for the fall and rising again of many in Israel, Luke ii. 34.
The thoughts and disposition of men's heart to be thus revealed.
Christ only a Saviour to the humble and sincere.
Revealed to babes, hidden from the wise and prudent, Matt. xi. 25.
The proud stumble at Christ, the humble embrace Him.
The full soul loatheth the honey-comb, Prov. xxvii. 7.
The whole refuse the Physician, sick men welcome Him.

Israel would have embraced a Christ who would either—
1. Have suffered them to live in their sins; or,
2. Have allowed them to save themselves.
Christ crucified opposed both to Pharisaic and philosophic pride.

'Ωs ἐξ ἔργων νόμου. Codd. Sin., Vat., and Alex. omit νόμου. As if from the works of the law, their works being not really works of the law, but the fruits of their own hypocrisy. *Ferme.* Supply φθησόμενοι εἰς ν. δικ., as if they were to attain to it. *Phil., Thol.* As being thus attainable. *D. Brown.* 'Ωs indicates the supposition that their works were good works. *Frit.* Rather that they should fulfil the law by their righteous conduct. *Von Hofm.* Rabbins: 'Whoever keeps the law, behold paradise awaits him; but to those who keep it not, there is hell.' *Beresh. Rabba.* On Isa. xlvi. 12, it is said: 'The world in general is to be justified by the righteousness of God, but the Rabbies by their own merit.' *Talm. Ber.*—Προσέκοψαν (πρὸς, against, and κόπτω, to strike), struck against. *Syr., Eras., Cas.* Stumbled (offenderunt). *Vulg.* Stumbled against. *Ferme, D. Brown.* Allusion to a man's striking his foot against a stone or other obstacle, and so falling and losing the race. *Guyse.* Cases mentioned of chariots striking against the pillar round which they were to turn in the race. *Soph. Electra*, 730. Heb. בָּשַׁל, נָגַף.—Προσκόμματος, stumbling (offendiculi). *Per.* Striking and being hurt. *Vat.* Obstacle. *Eras.* Stone against which one strikes, Rom. xiv. 13. *Beza.* Christ. *Ferme, Melv., D. Brown.*—Γὰρ wanting in Cod. Sin. and some other MSS.

---

33. *As it is written, Behold, I lay in Zion a stumbling-stone, and rock of offence: and whosoever believeth on Him shall not be ashamed.*

Written. Isa. xxviii. 16; viii. 14. Both texts combined in one.
No new thing declared by Paul concerning God's Saviour.
No statement to be made without Scripture warrant.
The passages applied by the Jews themselves to the Messiah.
Behold. Attention called to the provided Saviour.
Implies—1. The excellence of the object; 2. The need of regarding it.
Christ's incarnation is God's crowning act and man's salvation.
When God says "Behold," man is bound to look.
Man's faith begins by attending to God's "Behold."
The Father says of Christ, Behold Him, Isa. xliii. 1; Zech. vi. 12.
Christ says of Himself, Behold me, behold me, Isa. lxv. 1.
I lay. Christ's incarnation and work from God himself, Ps. xl. 6.
Christ became God's servant for man's salvation, Isa. liii. 11.
It was God's—1. To say whether there should be a Saviour; 2. To say who the Saviour should be; 3. To provide Him.
The foundation-stone of man's salvation laid by God—
1. In His eternal purpose and decree, 2 Tim. i. 9;
2. In Christ's incarnation in the fulness of time;

3. In the effectual calling of each believer.
Terrible guilt to refuse to build on God's foundation.
In Zion. In the Church represented by Mount Zion.
Zion in *Heb.* = a dry place : original condition of the Church.
The Church at first Gentile, then Jewish, now mixed.
Salvation was to be of the Jews, John iv. 22. Christ a Jew, Rom. ix. 5.
The Gospel to be preached first at Jerusalem, Luke xxiv. 47.
The law to go forth out of Zion to the Gentiles, Isa. ii. 3.
In the Church Christ is revealed and made known, 1 Tim. iii. 15.
Zion a rocky eminence forming part of Jerusalem.
Originally a stronghold of the Jebusites, Josh. xv. 63.
At last taken by David and called the city of David, 2 Sam. v. 6–8.
The place to which David brought the ark, 2 Sam. vi. 12; Ps. cxxxii. 8.
The place of public worship and sacrifice before the Temple, 2 Sam. vi. 17.
House of Caiaphas, where Jesus was condemned, placed there.
The foundation thus laid literally in Mount Zion.
Stumbling-stone. Here the second quotation begins, Isa. viii. 14.
Pride and unbelief make God's foundation a stone of stumbling.
Unbelief makes the balm of Gilead a deadly poison.
The Gospel a savour of death unto death as well as life unto life.
God's counsel rejected by men against themselves, Luke vii. 30.
Men either build on Christ and are saved, or stumble and perish.
Rock of offence. A rock against which men stumble.
The rock intended for salvation made a rock of offence.
" Blessed is he whosoever is not offended in me," Matt. xi. 6.
Much in Jesus at which the Jews stumbled and were offended—
1. Birth and parentage, descended from poor parents, Matt. xiii. 54–58;
2. Education and place of bringing up, Nazareth, John i. 46; vii. 41, 52;
3. Mean appearance of Himself and followers, John vi. 42; vii. 48;
4. Obscurity of His kingdom, coming not with observation, Luke xvii. 20; xix. 11;
5. Company He kept and audience that attended on Him, Luke xv. 2;
6. Doctrines He taught, John v. 18; vi. 41, 60, 66; viii. 48, 52, 59;
7. Miracles He performed, John v. 16; ix. 16; Matt. xii. 10–14;

8. His death and the manner of it, Matt. xxvi. 31; Luke xxiv. 20, 21; 1 Cor. i. 23.
To fall on this rock in unbelief is to be broken, Matt. xxi. 44;
To have it falling on us in judgment is to be ground to powder.
Whosoever. Again, Isa. xxviii. 16. Christ a Saviour for mankind.
Jew and Gentile equally welcome to build upon Him.
None excluded who do not exclude themselves, Rev. xxii. 17.
Believeth on Him. Rests all his hopes of salvation on Him.
The right use to make of Christ is to trust in Him.
Faith or trust is that which gives saving interest in Him.
Faith builds on Christ, and so unites us to Him.
Preached by prophets and apostles as the only way of salvation.
Not merely to hear or to speculate about Him, but—
1. To believe God's testimony concerning Him; and, 2. To trust in Him.
To believe in Christ is an act not only of the head but the heart.
With the heart man believeth unto righteousness, chap. x. 9, 10; Acts viii. 37.
Fruits and evidences of such faith—1. Christ is precious, 1 Pet. ii. 7;
2. Peace and joy in believing, Rom. v. 1; xv. 13; 1 Pet. i. 8;
3. Love and obedience, Gal. v. 6; vi. 14, 15; 1 Pet. i. 8.
Ashamed. Disappointed. *Heb.*, Make haste, as needing more.
Christ as a foundation is solid rock; all else shifting sand.
Trusting in Him for salvation we shall not be ashamed—
1. Of our hope before God; 2. Our profession before man.

Γέγραπται, both passages applied by the Jews to the Messiah. Isa. viii. 14, the Targum applies it to the Word of the Lord, the essential Word. Talmud says: 'The son of David does not come till, &c., as it is said, He shall be for a sanctuary and a stone of stumbling,' San. xxxviii. 1. On Isa. xxviii. 16, the Targum has, 'Behold, I appoint in Zion King Messiah, a king powerful, strong, and brave.' Jarchi has, 'I have appointed King Messiah in Zion for a precious corner-stone,' &c. The author of Zohar says: 'The shekinah, which is called the tried stone, the stone of strength.'—Σιων (from 'צ, a dry region; or, 'a *sunny* mountain,' from ה;צ. *Gesenius*). Zion, or the city of David, that part of Jerusalem so called,—the higher city. Anciently and up to the taking of Jerusalem by Titus, the eastern hill on which the temple stood, 2 Sam. v. 7; 1 Chron. xi. 5-8. The northern hill. *Lightfoot*. The southern, including the more ancient part of the city, with the citadel and temple. *Gesenius*. Since the time of Constantine, the name applied to the western hill as at present. Surrounded by a deep ravine on south, east, and west. Rises abruptly on the west and south from the valley of Hinnom. On the east, slopes steeply down towards the Tyropœon, or valley of the cheesemakers, which also separated it from the lower city, or Acra, on the north. The summit along the western brow, a level tract of considerable extent, now partly ploughed

CHAP. X.] ST. PAUL'S EPISTLE TO THE ROMANS. 63

like a field (Micah iii. 12), the rest occupied by the Christian cemeteries and a few straggling buildings. On the north side, near the Zion gate, the house of Caiaphas is said to have stood, the site being now covered by an Armenian convent. About the middle of Mount Zion is the tomb of David, over which stands a Turkish mosque, formerly a Christian church of high antiquity, said to contain the room in which the Lord's Supper was instituted, and hence called the Church of the Cœnaculum. Only the north part of Mount Zion is enclosed within the modern walls, chiefly containing the Jewish quarter, the great Armenian convent, and the Protestant Church with the connected buildings.—Καταισχυνθησεται. LXX. καταισχυνθῇ. Heb. יָחִישׁ, shall not make haste; 'not betake himself to flight;' translated freely by the LXX. *Frit.* Grasp at any illegitimate means of safety. *Ferme.* Shall not be afraid. *Syr.* For יָחִישׁ, the LXX. probably read יֵבוֹשׁ. *Grot., Capell.* יחישׁ, itself susceptible of that sense. *Pocock, Rosenm., Gesen.*—Πας, wanting in Codd. Sin. and Alex.

CHAPTER X.

1. *Brethren, my heart's desire and prayer to God for Israel is, that they might be saved.*

Brethren. An affectionate and soothing appellation.
Addressed to Jewish believers. Paul's remarks might seem severe.
God's judgments only to be declared in the spirit of love.
Desire. *Gr.,* Good will; notwithstanding contrary appearances.
Christ's coming was "good will to men," Luke ii. 14.
His servants must have all good will to all men.
Heart's desire. No mere words of compliment.
While the lips denounce wrath, the heart must desire mercy.
Good desires must be heart desires, Prov. xxvi. 23.
Heart desires are the soul of acceptable prayer.
Cold desires only beg denials, James v. 16, 17.
Prayer. All desires should be turned into prayer.
Paul not only desired Israel's salvation but prayed for it.
Israel therefore not absolutely and entirely rejected.
Prayer *to* God must be based upon a promise *from* God.
Prayer must be according to God's will, not against it.
Hence the gift of the intercession of the Spirit, Rom. viii. 26, 27.
Supplications, prayers, intercessions, to be made for all men.
The reason given is, because God will have all men to be saved,
  1 Tim. ii. 1, 4.
God's predestination secures, not supersedes, man's prayer.
Prayer practicable when all other means are excluded.

Though apparently vain to labour, yet not vain to pray, Jer. xxxiii. 3.
Prayer to be made even for the most violent opposers of the truth. Among Christ's last words was prayer for His murderers.
Saved. The highest and best wishes for men are "that they may be saved."
Contrast—1. Between this and Paul's earlier zeal, Acts ix. 1, 2;
2. Between this and his treatment from the Jews, Acts ix. 23, 29; xiii. 50.
Views of God's sovereignty connected with love to men's souls. Salvation the one thing needful. Embraces time and eternity.
Saved—1. From sin, Matt. i. 21; Titus ii. 14; 2. From its consequences, 1 Thess. i. 10.
The salvation of *one* soul incalculably precious.

"Know'st thou the value of a soul immortal?
Behold that midnight glory; worlds on worlds.
Amazing pomp! Redouble the amaze,
Ten thousand add; add twice ten thousand more;
Then weigh the whole. One soul outweighs them all."
Young.

Μεν not followed by δε, the opposition lying in the blame which limits the praise. *De Wette.*—Ευδοκια (ευ, well, and δοκεω, to seem). Vehement desire. *Chrys., Theod.* Will (voluntas). *Trem.* Strong inclination (propensio). *Cas.* Good will. *Mor.* Earnest will (propensa voluntas). *Eras., Pag., Pisc.* Kindly wish (benevolentia). *Eras., Tol.* Ardent desire. *Ferme.* Most benevolent and affectionate desire. *Guyse.* Anxious wish. *Bloomf.* Benevolent kind desire, sincere and hearty wish. *Stuart.* Inclination. *Alf.* Great desire, what would afford pleasure. *Rück.* That wherein my heart would entirely acquiesce and be fully pleased. *Ellicot.* Entire complacency, that in which the heart would experience full satisfaction. *D. Brown.* Ευδοκια, 'good will,' Luke ii. 14; Phil. i. 15; 2 Thess. i. 11; 'good pleasure,' Matt. xi. 26; Eph. i. 5, 9; Phil. ii. 13. Heb. רצן.—Δεησις (δεομαι, to want, beseech). Supplication. *D. Brown.* Deprecation. *Ferme.*—Του Ισραηλ. Codd. Sin., Vat., and Alex. have αυτων, 'them.' The true reading. *D. Brown.*

---

2. *For I bear them record, that they have a zeal of God, but not according to knowledge.*

For. Gives the reason for his great concern.
Misguided religious zeal—1. Makes men the more to be pitied.
2. Makes their salvation all the more to be desired.
Bear them record. Wishes to say all the good he could.
Often something commendable even in unbelievers.

CHAP. X.]   ST. PAUL'S EPISTLE TO THE ROMANS.   65

Not to be ignored in preaching the Gospel. Paul at Athens, Acts xvii. 22, 23.
Hinders not damnation, but makes salvation more desirable.
The best construction to be put on men's words and actions, 1 Cor. xiii. 5, 7.
Zeal of God. Zeal in regard to God, His worship, truth, cause.
Shown in strict observance of the law, the Sabbath, &c.
Jewish opposition to the Gospel from zeal for the law.
Jews as a rule characterised for religious zeal.
No excuse for unbelief, but ground of greater pity.
Paul formerly an example of the character described, Phil. iii. 5, 6.
Zeal about religion no guarantee for the possession of it.
" Zeal of God " must be zeal *from* God as well as *for* God.
Godly zeal in appearance may be ungodly in reality.
Religious zeal, in order to be holy and acceptable, must be—
1. According to God's *character*, which is *love;*
2. According to God's *word*, which is *truth.*
Misguided zeal makes the devil's best servants.
Paul's zeal of God led him to persecute God's Son, Acts ix. 4.
Sincerity in error no plea or excuse before God, John xvi. 2, 3.
According to knowledge. Guided by and accompanied with knowledge.
Jews crucified Christ not knowing what they did, Luke xxiii. 34; Acts iii. 17.
Paul persecuted Christ ignorantly and in unbelief, 1 Tim. i. 13.
Jews knew not Christ nor the voices of their own prophets, Acts xiii. 27.
Ignorant of the hidden wisdom of God, 1 Cor. ii. 7–10.
Had a certain religious knowledge, but not a correct one. So 1 Cor. iii. 20.
No right apprehension of the truth revealed to them.
No right knowledge—1. Of the law; nor, 2. Of the Gospel.
Satan blinds the minds of them that believe not, 2 Cor. iv. 4.
True knowledge comes from the Holy Ghost and centres in Christ.
The Jews' guilt that they had not better knowledge.
Continued blind because they said, We see, John ix. 41.
Those who will do God's will shall know of the doctrine, John vii. 17.
Men loving darkness are often allowed to remain in it, John iii. 19.
Zeal not according to knowledge is often cruel and superstitious.
True zeal is—1. Enlightened; 2. Pure; 3. Full of love.
Contrast between Paul's earlier and later zeal, 1 Tim. i. 13; 2 Tim. ii. 10.

VOL. II.   E

Two evils—1. Zeal without knowledge; 2. Knowledge without zeal.

Μαρτυρω αὐτοις, I bear witness in their favour. *Bloomf.*—Ζῆλον (ζεω, to be hot, and λιαν, very), glow or fervency of soul, used in a good as well as a bad sense. *Nielson.* Zeal, a human affection compounded of love and anger. *Ferme.* Ζελ. Θεου, zeal for God; genitive of the object. *Bloomf., D. Brown.* For God and His law. *Guyse.* For God's honour. *Barth.* For God and His service. *Bloomf.* For religion. *Schött.* Much feeling and zeal in respect to religion. *Stuart.* Loved God and His glory so intensely as to be transported with vehement hatred against anything which threatened to deprive them of God, or to prove injurious to His worship. *Ferme.* Heb. הִנְאָה.—Κατ' ἐπιγνωσιν, according to knowledge. *Eras., Mor., Pisc., Beza.* Οὐ κ. ε. τ. = Ignorantly. *Cas.* Without knowledge. *Mart.* Ἐπιγνωσις = γνωσις. *Grot.* A living principle of the understanding, going beyond mere historical knowledge or γνωσις. *Lange.* True correct knowledge. *Meyer, Phil., Ferme.* Accurate apprehension of the way of righteousness revealed to them. *Alford.* That knowledge which supposes a disposition of the will towards the object of it. *Von Hofm.* Knowledge of God's word and will therein revealed. *Ferme.* Ζηλ. οὐ κ. ἐπιγ. = imprudent zeal. *Schött.* Misguided zeal. *Guyse.* Zeal not in conformity with, or regulated by, sound knowledge or true religion. *Bloomf.* Heb. דֵעָה, used for the true knowledge of God as a gracious affection, Prov. ii. 5; Hosea iv. 1, 6; vi. 6.

3. *For they, being ignorant of God's righteousness, and going about to establish their own righteousness, have not submitted themselves unto the righteousness of God.*

Ignorant. Not recognising it though revealed to them.
Ignorance in the midst of light is generally criminal.
Something wilful in Jewish ignorance, John iii. 19; 1 Thess. ii. 15, 16.
The effect of judicial blinding, John xii. 37–40; Acts xxviii. 24–27.
Jews did not know because not wishing to know, John v. 40.
Notable exceptions: Nicodemus, John iii. 1; the Bercans, Acts xvii. 11, 12.
Ignorance the mother of self-righteousness.
God's righteousness. 1. His administrative and retributive justice; 2. The justifying righteousness provided by Him. For both see chap. iii. 21–26.
The only righteousness that avails before Him.
That to be brought in by Messiah's doing and dying, Dan. ix. 24.
Indicated in the name, The Lord our Righteousness, Jer. xxiii. 6.
Foretold by Isaiah, Isa. xlv. 24, 25; li. 5, 6, 8; liii. 11.
Trusted in and declared by David, Ps. lxxi. 15, 16.
Prepared by God the Son in our nature, Matt. iii. 15; John xix. 30.
The God-provided garment for a sinner's nakedness, Gen. iii. 21; Isa. lxi. 10.

Freely held out to all in the Gospel, Rom. iii. 22 ; Matt. xxii. 9–13.
Its necessity grounded on two undeniable facts—
1. Man is a sinner ; 2. God is righteous.
Going about. *Gr.*, Seeking. The zeal of God referred to in ver. 2.
Sought to accomplish an impossibility, Rom. viii. 3.
The bootless labour of millions still.
Establish. *Gr.*, Set up, or make to stand as valid.
Our own righteousness is—1. Fallen ; 2. Unable to stand.
Man must have some ground of justification before God.
To attempt what God has forbidden is rebellion.
Much of man's morality and religion a Babel-building, Gen. xi. 3, 4.
Our most splendid works often mere splendid sins.
Men's good works often set up in opposition to Christ's.
Their own righteousness. A righteousness of their own—
1. Wrought by themselves ; 2. Approved by themselves.
Righteousness of the law ; legal duties and observances, Phil. iii. 9.
The Pharisee in the Temple an example, Luke xviii. 9–14.
What is highly esteemed by men often abomination with God, Luke xvi. 15.
Man's own righteousness but filthy rags, Isa. lxiv. 6.
A bed too short for a man to stretch himself on it.
A garment too narrow to wrap himself in, Isa. xxviii. 20.
Job abhorred himself and repented in dust and ashes, Job xlii. 6.
Isaiah's confession suited to every sinner, Isa. vi. 5.
Ignorance of God's righteousness leads men to set up their own.
Submitted themselves. Pride the parent of unbelief.
The Gospel made known for the obedience of faith, chap. i. 5.
Acceptance of Christ is submission to God, Ps. ii. 12 ; John vi. 29 ; 1 John iii. 23.
Humility required in order to accept God's righteousness.
The first lesson in Christ's school is to deny one's self.
Righteous self often harder to deny than sinful self.
God's way of justification requires only submission to it.
Its greatest antagonist the pride of the human heart.
Man's first attempt is to sew fig-leaves for an apron.
Unbelief refuses an amnesty proclaimed in the Gospel.
Ignorance of God's righteousness the cause of not submitting to it.
"They that know Thy name will put their trust in Thee," Ps. ix. 10.

'Αγνοουντες, having opportunity of knowing it, but remaining ignorant. *Stuart.* Not recognising; had it before them, but overlooked it. *Alford.* Not knowing; as

better expressing their misapprehending the nature of the righteousness. *Ellicot, Mart.*
—Τὴν τ. Θεου δικαιοσυνην, the righteousness by faith. *Chrys.* God's justice as demanding a perfect righteousness; or, the righteousness provided by God in Christ, like τῃ δικ. τ. Θεου. *Guyse.* God's method of justification. *Stuart, Bloomf.* Retributive justice against sinners. *De Wette.* The only righteousness that avails before God, that of Jesus Christ. *Alford.* Perfect fulfilment of the law by Christ. *Haldane.* His doings and sufferings. *Brown.* The righteousness approved and appointed by God for the justification of the guilty. *D. Brown.*—Τὴν ἰδιαν δικ., a justification of their own, *i.e.*, from the works of the law, making every one's salvation to depend on his own merits. *Bloomf.* Δικ. omitted in Codd. Vat. and Alex.—Ζητουντες, earnestly aiming (studentes); seeking with all earnestness. *Beza, Par.*—Στησαι, to set up (statuere). *Vulg.* Constitute. *Beza, Pisc.* Give it authority and strength. *Vat.* Set up and hold on its feet as weak and infirm. *Par.* Extirpate the Gospel that the law might stand. *Tol.* = יִצְדָּק, to approve, give right and authority to a thing. *Grot.* Prop up. *Doddr.* Metaphor from propping and buttressing a weak structure unable to stand by itself. *Bloomf.*—Ὑπεταγησαν, the subjection intimated in 2 Cor. x. 4. *Ferme.* The righteousness of God viewed as a dispensation, ordinance, law, chap. i. 5; iii. 27. *De Wette.* Have not obediently accepted. *Bloomf.*

---

4. *For Christ is the end of the law for righteousness to every one that believeth.*

For. Explains what he means by the righteousness of God. Christ is God's appointed way for making men righteous.
End of the law. Final end, object, and aim—
1. Of the moral; 2. Of the ceremonial law.
The moral law discloses the wounds sin has made;
The ceremonial law shadows forth the remedy.
The law given as a tutor to conduct us to Christ, Gal. iii. 24.
Its authority as a covenant terminates in Christ.
All its demands in precept and penalty satisfied in Him.
In Christ we have the law's object, viz., righteousness and holiness.
What the law cannot accomplish Christ has done, chap. viii. 3.
Christ fulfilled all righteousness, and that in our name, Matt. iii. 15.
Is made to us both righteousness and sanctification, 1 Cor. i. 30.
The object of the law was to give life by obedience to it, chap. vii. 10.
That life we have in Christ through His obedience, chap. v. 21; 1 John v. 11.
Christ gives righteousness and life, which the law shows but gives not.
The law in its Old Testament form ceased with Christ's death.
The Temple veil then rent in twain, Matt. xxvii. 51; Eph. ii. 13–18; Heb. vi. 19; x. 19–22.
The ministration of death succeeded by that of life, 2 Cor. iii. 6–11.
The law remains as a *rule*, but ceases as a *way*, of life.

Pursues with its curses till refuge is taken in Christ.
The manslayer pursued by the blood-avenger to the city gates, Josh. xx. 2-5.
Christ the kernel, the Alpha and Omega, of the Old Testament.
The law and the Gospel evidenced in man's moral nature ;
The law the ideal of its life ; the Gospel the life of its ideal.
For righteousness. That men may be justified before God.
A justifying, and as its effect, a sanctifying righteousness.
Both aimed at in the law ; both found in Christ, 1 Cor. i. 30.
Christ's never-to-be-forgotten name, The Lord our Righteousness.
Every one. Jew or Gentile, bond or free. No difference, chap. iii. 22.
The very chief of sinners not excluded, 1 Tim. i. 13-15.
Believeth. Faith the bond that unites to Christ.
Makes Christ and the merits of His life and death our own.
Accepts Him as the end of the law for righteousness to us.
When a man believes, the end of the law is attained in Him.
Faith signs the covenant that makes life our own, Ps. l. 5.

Χριστος, the promised Messiah. *Von Hofm.*—Τελος νομου, fulfilment of the law, *i.e.*, for us. *Eras., Vat., Par., Tol., Calv., Ferme.* What the law could not do Christ has done. *Schött.* Whoever believes has obtained everything, and has fulfilled the law. *Chrys.* The object or scope of the law, namely, to give a justifying righteousness. *Syr., Carpzov., Par., Est., Elsner, Doddr., Fell., Beng., Thol., Alf., Stuart, Bloomf., D. Brown.* Final end, viz., perfect obedience and justification. *Beza, Dick., Gom.* Its object, viz., to lead to Christ. *Theod., Calv., Ferme, Melv., Pisc., Grot., Chal., Colbin.* Its terminus, where it ends. *Vulg., Par.* Its termination, not as a rule of life, but as a covenant of works and as including the ceremonial law. *Flatt.* Its dominion terminated by Christ (chap. vii. 1, &c. ; Luke xvi. 16). *Aug., Luth., Ols., Meyer, De Wette.* Its fulfilment, and therefore removal in the Old Testament form. *Lange.* Its perfection, accomplishment, consummation. *Haldane.* Christ has so put an end to the law that it has received its true fulfilment in Him. *Nielson.* Refers to what Christ has done to terminate the law. *Phil.* In so far as the promised Saviour is present, no law (νομος, without the article) has any longer a place. *Von Hofm.* Refers more especially to Christ's active obedience,—' The man that doeth them shall live by them,' ver. 5. *Guyse.* —Εις δικαιοσυνην, as righteousness. *Mart., Diod.* For righteousness. *Beng., Knapp, Van Ess.* The obtaining of righteousness. *De Wette.* That He may impart to us the righteousness He has procured by obeying the law. *Ferme.* Whoever believes in Him is righteous. *Luther.*

---

5. *For Moses describeth the righteousness which is of the law, that the man that doeth these things shall live by them.*

For. Proves his position from the law itself. Shows—
1. That justification by our own obedience to the law is impossible ;

2. That Moses himself declares and commends the way of faith.
Moses. He in whom they trusted, John v. 45. See on *Moses*, chap. ix. 15.
Describeth. *Gr.*, Writes—viz., in Lev. xviii. 5. The expression hints—
1. That the law was a killing letter; 2. That it passes away. Important to understand what the righteousness of the law is.
Righteousness which is of the law. Justification through it.
That which the Jews laboured so much to establish.
What multitudes still labour in vain to accomplish.
The mode of acceptance with God to which the flesh clings.
We are only driven from it by the knowledge—1. Of God's character; 2. The law's demands; 3. Our own guilt and weakness; 4. Christ's better and freely offered righteousness.
Doeth these things. The law requires perfect obedience.
Doeth; not heareth, readeth, or approveth of them.
Not who desires or attempts to do them, but who actually does them.
The law's voice is, Obedience or death, Deut. xxx. 15.
Acknowledges no mere attempts, allows no failure, Deut. xxvii. 26.
Such the economy under which man was first placed, Gen. ii. 17.
Adam might at first have obeyed, but failed.
His posterity failed in him, and consequently in themselves.
The power to obey the law lost by the fall.
The law is spiritual, but man is now carnal, chap. vii. 14.
The law which is love (Matt. xxii. 37, 38) is only fulfilled—
1. By Christ; 2. By His members in and through Him.
Live by them. Have eternal life by obeying them.
Life the great prize of obedience, chap. vii. 10; Gen. ii. 17.
The comprehensive term for all true blessedness.
Not only existence but what makes existence happy.
Life to man's threefold nature, spirit, soul, and body.
To Israel, continuance in Canaan included, Deut. xxx. 16, 20.
Life is still by doing, but the doing of Jesus Christ the Righteous.
Failure acknowledged by the constant sacrifices under the law.

Μωϋσῆς. Accent on Μωϋσῆς, as on τέλος, in ver. 4. *Von Hofm.* Moses introduced as a witness for the statement in ver. 4. *Meyer, De Wette, Baumg.-Cr.*—Γράφει, writes; present tense, as indicating a continuous act in the Scripture. *Von Hofm.* Delineates and explains in his writings. *Guyse.* A popular ellipsis, — Moses, treating of the justification to be had from the law, thus writes or speaks of it. *Bloomf.* Κατα, understood before γράφει. *Knapp.*—Ὅτι after γράφει in Codd Sin. and Alex., but after νομου in Cod. Vat.—Ὁ ποιησας, who shall have done. *Ferme.* Hath done. *D. Brown.*—Ζησεται, shall have eternal life. *Targums.* Chief and primary sense, life and prosperity in this world, with an obscure promise of everlasting life. *Bloomf.* Shall have eternal life and happiness. *Guyse.*

---

6. *But the righteousness which is of faith speaketh on this wise, Say not in thine heart, Who shall ascend into heaven ? (that is, to bring Christ down from above).*

But. The way of faith contrasted with that of works.
Of faith. By faith or trust as the instrument.
Faith the hand that takes Christ and makes Him our own.
Does not work itself, but trusts in another's work, for life.
Allows Him to obey who alone can and has obeyed.
Rests on Him who came to do what man could not.
Speaketh. The righteousness of faith personified as speaking.
The righteousness of the law is described by another.
The righteousness of faith speaketh for itself.
Weakness, decay, and death in the one ;
Life, vigour, and permanency in the other.
The former described as a pattern for compliance ;
The latter speaks as an announcement for belief.
Describing applicable to that which passes away.
Speaking, to that which lives and proclaims to the end, Matt. xxviii. 20.
In the Gospel a living and life-giving voice, John v. 25 ; vi. 63.
The power of God, chap. i. 16.
On this wise. After this manner—viz., in Deut. xxx. 11–14.
The Gospel represented as speaking in this passage.
The Law-giver becomes for the time the Gospel-preacher.
Moses wrote of Christ, John v. 46. The Gospel imbedded in the law.
Even under the law men only saved by faith in Christ.
The dim dawn, with the Spirit, sufficed to show the way.
Where the moral law wounded, Christ in the ceremonial healed.
Typical atoning blood ever streaming before Israel's eyes.
The moral law told that better blood was required, Heb. x. 4.
Two covenants made with Israel—1. That at Sinai ;
2. That, after forty years' wandering, on the borders of Canaan.
With the former stands the quotation in ver. 5 ;
With the latter that now about to be given.
The law given at the beginning of the journeying ;
The Gospel revealed, though still obscurely, at the end.

The one a forerunner and preparation for the other, Gal. iii. 24.
Israel's experience in the wilderness (Acts vii. 39–43) proved—
1. The utter depravity of the human heart;
2. The inability of the law to make men holy;
3. The absolute necessity of another's righteousness.
Say not in thine heart. As if salvation were unattainable.
The inward struggles of an earnest and sincere inquirer.
Great difficulties seen in the way of salvation.
Nature and law show no way out of such difficulties.
Met and removed in the Gospel. Christ the true light, John i. 9; viii. 12.
The Jew especially addressed. Christ already come and risen.
All done that required to be done for light and salvation.
Who shall ascend into heaven? The wish but not the power.
Indicates unbelief. Anxiety. Embarrassment. Despair.
Refers—1. To salvation itself; 2. To the knowledge of it.
Christ already come—1. To save; 2. To reveal salvation.
Knowledge of God's will not far off or unattainable.
Not as if to be attained only by going up to heaven for it.
That is. Apostles explain what prophets darkly hinted.
The full meaning given to the supposed inquiry.
The Spirit in the New Testament interprets the dark sayings of the Old.
Salvation by faith obscurely preached by Moses.
To bring down Christ from above. 1. As if not already come;
2. As if His bodily presence were necessary to salvation.
The opposite of faith in and confession of Him as Lord, ver. 9.
Christ already come to put away sin by the sacrifice of Himself, Heb. ix. 26.
Has revealed the will of God for our salvation, John xvii. 23, 26.
Now lives at God's right hand to save all who trust in Him, Heb. vii. 25.
Christ the Saviour not brought down by men but sent by God, John iii. 16.
Men saved not by seeing but believing, John xx. 29; 1 Pet. i. 8.

Λεγει. Moses not mentioned because only the words borrowed from him. *Vat.* May be considered as expressing itself thus *Doddr.* Its language or import is to this effect. *D. Brown.* Righteousness of faith personified, in contrast with Moses. *Rückert.* Paul personifies the righteousness of faith and makes it say of its doctrines and precepts what Moses said of his commandments, though in a somewhat different sense. *Mackn.* Paul acts the interpreter and paraphrast. *Par.* Two sides of the law—1. As a covenant of works; 2. As a type of the Gospel; the former given in the quotation from Leviticus, pointing to *ordinances* to be performed; the latter from Deuteronomy, as a prophecy to be fulfilled. *Lange.* The righteousness of the law occurs only in a description of it by Moses (γραφει); that by faith *speaks* (λεγει) as a thing actually present. *Von Hofm.* Οὑτω, thus: an accommodation of the passage. *Ham., Doddr., Bloomf.* Not simply law of Moses spoken of, but his whole doctrine, comprehending the Gospel also. *Calv., Par., Dick.* Literally spoken by Moses of the law, but especially meant of and verified in the revelation of Christ and the Gospel, and the spirit in our hearts enabling us to obey the word. *Fell.* Spoken originally of the law as already near and accessible. *Theod.* The passage in Deuteronomy undeniably Messianic. *Ols.* So *Cap., Calv., Ch. Smidt, Reiche, De Wette, Meyer.* The passage very freely treated, but applied to the Messiah in the way of illustration. *Thol., Glück., Rück.* What Moses says of the law applies in a still higher sense to the Gospel; the main thought,—It is God's to communicate the truth in revelation, man's to receive it. *Nielson.* The passage in Deut. xxx. 13, 14, quoted in substance. *D. Brown.* Spoken with an ultimate view to Gospel days. *Guyse, Ainsworth.* Moses when about to die preaches the Gospel and delivers its covenant plainly to the Jews. *Goodwin.* Mosaic description of the righteousness of faith. *Ferme.* Described in the words of Moses, but from their meaning correctly applied to Christ. *Melv.*—Μη ειπῃς ἐν τ. καρδιᾳ σου, expressing the *self-confidence* with which unbelief usually originates. *Bloomf.*—Τις ἀναβησεται; who shall ascend? indicating unbelief in the Saviour who has already appeared. *Chrys., Calv., Melv., De Wette, Meyer.* Doing or attempting to do some hard impossible thing. *Ham., Ferme, Turner.* Wish, but want of power. *Beng.* A longing after such a word as might bring salvation. *Rückert.* Embarrassment. *Stuart, Rosenm.* Anxiety. *Thol.* Despair. *Guyse, D. Brown.* One struggling with anxious doubts about salvation, not having yet known of faith in Christ. *Knapp.* As a Jew might say, Who will fetch the law from heaven if once lost? so of Christ. *Lange.* Expresses despair of the wish being accomplished; the case not one of unreachable distance. *Von Hofm., Melv.* Ye have not to sigh over the impossibility of obtaining salvation. *D. Brown.* Adverts to those points on which the faith of the unbelievers chiefly staggered. *Bloomf.*—Εἰς τον οὐρανον. Ascending into heaven and descending into hell, used by the Hebrews of one wishing to hide himself in secret places or to investigate secret and attempt arduous things, which can by no means be known or done. *Knapp.* Proverbial expressions for what was impossible or very difficult; used by Moses to show that it is not impracticable to attain a knowledge of God's law. *Bloomf.* So, 'In coelum ire.' *Juvenal.* 'Coelum petere.' *Horace.*—Χριστον καταγαγειν, to bring the Messiah. *Eras.* As if He had not already come. *Vat., Ferme, De Wette, Lange.* To assure us of God's promised mercy. *Per., Melv.* To teach us, or atone for our sins. *Doddr.* Implies unbelief in Christ's session at God's right hand. *Calv.* As if the word concerning the Lord of heaven were not near enough to confess Him. *Beng.* Χριστον, the promised Messiah, not Ἰησουν; actually to bring the Messiah down from heaven; not the merely wishing to do so. *Von Hofm.* The Messiah according to the Jews' expectation has already come from heaven with the new word of salvation. *Rückert.*

---

7. *Or, Who shall descend into the deep? (that is, to bring up Christ again from the dead).*

Descend. Points prophetically to the death of Christ.
Heb., "Who shall go over the sea for us and bring it to us?"
The spirit-world viewed by the Jews as beyond the sea.
Salvation and the knowledge of it not to be thought far off.

Deep. The grave; spirit-world; place of the dead, *Heb.*, The sea. Proverbially, unknown and remote parts; prophetically, the grave. *Gr.*, The abyss. Spirits prayed not to be sent into it, Luke viii. 31. Christ's body entered the grave, His spirit the unseen world.
Bring up Christ from the dead. As if He had not risen. Opposite of believing that God raised Him from the dead, ver. 9. Unbelief doubts both Christ's incarnation and resurrection. His death and resurrection as needful as His incarnation. His resurrection God's great testimony to His Messiahship, chap. i. 4. Christ risen and become the first-fruits of them that slept, 1 Cor. xv. 20.
If not risen, our faith is vain; we are yet in our sins, 1 Cor. xv. 17. We have not to bring Him from the dead but believe on Him risen. What unbelief desiderated, God has done, Luke xvi. 30, 31. One has risen from the dead and brought immortality to light, 2 Tim. i. 10.
Appeared alive for forty days, teaching the things of the kingdom, Acts i. 3.
I can no more save myself than bring up Christ from the dead.
"Nor need you," replies the Gospel; God does both, Eph. i. 19, 20.

Τις καταβησεται; who shall descend?—to bring the Gospel from the remotest parts. *Vat., Gom., Dick., Melv.* To be assured that victory has been gained over hell. *Pisc.* As if Christ had not risen. *Ferme.* As if the word concerning the risen Christ were not at hand to believe in Him. *Beng.* Another case of impossibility, suggested by Prov. xxx. 4, and perhaps Amos ix. 2. *D. Brown.*—Την άβυσσον (from ά, not, and βυθος, a bottom), into the abyss. *Beza, Pisc., Ferme.* — Gehenna or hell. *Pisc., Par.* Deut. xxx. 13, 'Who shall go over the sea,' &c.; in the Jerusalem Targum, 'Oh that we had one like Jonah the prophet, to go down to the bottom of the great sea!' Hence applied to Christ's resurrection from the dead. *Whitby.* Jonah a figure of Christ in the heart of the earth (Matt. xii. 40), to be brought up again from the depths of the earth (Ps. lxviii. 20); the 'sea' called the 'deep' and 'depth' (Ps. civ. 6; cvii. 24, 26). *Guyse.* 'Αβυσσος, the place of departed spirits, supposed by the Jews to be far below the surface of the earth. *Bloomf., Mackn.* A supposed cavity in the globe, under the earth and sea, Job xxviii. 14, 22; — Hades, placed by the Jews beyond the sea. *Koppe, Bolton.* Used instead of hell; lower world (Amos ix. 2), or the grave. The doctrine not incomprehensible or afar off, to be fetched down from heaven or from beyond the sea. *De Wette, Melv.* The deep; Heb., 'beyond the sea,' thought to be impassable; hence what is difficult: the doctrine of the Gospel plain, intelligible, and easy of access. *Stuart.* Language of doubt and unbelief; who will die and go down into the lower world to redeem men by his death, as if Christ had not yet done so. *Turr., Glück., Rück.* Εις τ. άβυσσον, substituted by Paul for םיּ רבֵע, 'beyond the sea,' to direct the thoughts to Christ's resurrection. *Beng.* Classics: 'I would ascend to the stars or descend into the earth beneath.' *Eurip., Phœn.* Χρ. ἐκ νεκρων,—ἀναγαγειν, to bring Christ up or again from the dead: indicates unbelief in Christ's resurrection, the completion of salvation, and the possibility of it, Matt. xix. 25. *De Wette.* All one whether the sinner in his desire for salvation wished Christ out of heaven or out of the grave. *Thol.* The promised Saviour is come into the world, and has not remained among the dead, but is translated to that life where He can be a Saviour to us; and it were foolish to think so as if salvation lay at an unreachable distance. *Von Hofm.* The righteousness by faith does not require impossible things, our bringing Christ from heaven or raising Him from the dead, but simply to believe. *Cobbin.* Ἐκ νεκρων = ἐκ της ἀβυσσου. From some allusions in Scripture, several early Fathers, in the second and third centuries, inferred that Christ descended into the abode of the dead to announce to the souls of the patriarchs, and Old Testament saints kept there, the accomplishment of His work, and to conduct them into His kingdom. Thus Irenæus, Tertullian, Origen, and Clement of Alexandria. Clement inclined to extend the preaching of the Gospel to the souls of the deceased Gentiles. The idea of Hades (= שְׁאוֹל) was transferred to Christianity as an intermediate state for the soul after separation from the body. So Justin. According to Tertullian, martyrs go direct to paradise. Cyprian appears to acknowledge no intermediate state. A purifying fire maintained by Clement and Origen, not, however, as acting in connection with the intermediate state, but on earth with the conflagration of the last day. Augustine also connects this fire (ignis purgatorius) with the last day, but suggests whether there is not also such a fire after death in Hades, where the souls of the departed were supposed to remain till the general resurrection. This, with further additions by others, especially Cæsarius of Arles, and Gregory the Great, prepared the way for the doctrine of purgatory, afterwards brought forward in connection with the Mass. Gregory the Great rightly called the inventor of the doctrine. Set forth very distinctly by Gregory of Nazianzum, but made an article of faith by Gregory the Great, who propounds clearly the doctrine of deliverance from it by intercessory prayers, masses for the dead (sacra oblatio hostiæ salutaris), &c. Opposed by the Cathari, Waldenses, and Wycliffe. Never fully approved by the Greek Church. All Souls' Festival (November 2) founded on this doctrine at Clugny in 993. Different departments (receptacula) were ascribed to hell—1. Hell proper, the abode of devils and of lost souls; 2. Intermediate states (subterranean regions), between heaven and hell, subdivided into (1.) Purgatory, nearest to hell; (2.) Limbus infantium, for unbaptized children; (3.) Limbus patrum ('Abraham's bosom'), the abode of Old Testament saints, where Christ was said to go after His death, to preach redemption to the spirits in prison. An intermediate state admitted by the Greek Church, which, however, rejected the doctrine of indulgences and masses for the deliverance of souls. *Hagenbach.*

---

8. *But what saith it? The word is nigh thee, in thy mouth, and in thy heart: that is, the word of faith which we preach.*

Word. Deut. xxx. 14. Doctrine of salvation; revelation of God's will.

That word contained in the Old Testament, more clearly in the New.

The word of the truth of the Gospel, Col. i. 5; Eph. i. 13.

Words of this life, Acts v. 20; words whereby to be saved, Acts xi. 14.

Moses not only a mediator of the Old Testament, but a prophet of the New.

Paul by the Spirit sees the Gospel where appeared only the law.

What was said of the law the Spirit by him applies to the Gospel.
Nigh. 1. In types; 2. In prophecies; 3. In the preached Gospel.
Nigh in the Old Testament, much nearer in the New.
Nigh, as—1. Accessible; 2. Plain; 3. Ready for use.
If true of the law, much more so of the Gospel.
God brings His salvation within our reach, Isa. xlvi. 13.
Unable to cross your threshold, you can have it at home.
Christ stands at the door and knocks for admission, Rev. iii. 20.
The Gospel preached to the poor and illiterate, Matt. xi. 5.
Repentance and forgiveness in Christ's name preached to all, Luke xxiv. 47.
Faith requires no learned investigations. Believe and live.
A child can know the Scriptures and have life in them, 2 Tim. iii. 15.
The vision made plain that he that reads may run, Hab. ii. 2.
The way of faith a highway where a fool may not err, Isa. xxxv. 8.
In thy mouth. Capable of immediate and ready confession.
The subject of familiar conversation and private teaching, Deut. vi. 7.
God puts His words into our mouth as well as our heart, Isa. lix. 21.
Out of the abundance of the heart the mouth speaketh, Matt. xii. 34.
Christ's word to dwell in us richly, teaching one another, Col. iii. 16.
The Gospel in the mouth—1. In confession; 2. Preaching; 3. Praising.
Out of the mouths of babes and sucklings God thus perfects praise, Ps. viii. 2.
In thy heart. The subject of faith, meditation, and thought.
The word given to be not only in the mouth but in the heart.
Believed with the heart, then uttered by the mouth, 2 Cor. iv. 13.
Revealed to and impressed on the heart by the Holy Ghost.
Only in the mouth marks a hypocrite and formalist;
In the mouth and in the heart marks a true believer.
In the heart for our personal salvation;
In the mouth for God's glory and the salvation of others.
In the heart and not in the mouth is cowardice;
In the mouth and not in the heart is hypocrisy.
In the mouth in daily reading, in the heart in daily meditation.
Salvation made as near to us as we are to ourselves.
The Gospel believed is a fountain in the heart;
The Gospel confessed is the streams through the mouth.

That is. The meaning of Old Testament Scripture given in the New.
The preacher's part truly to expound the written word.
Word of faith. 1. As teaching faith ; 2. As producing it, ver. 17.
The whole doctrine of the Gospel a doctrine of faith.
Commandments given in the law to be obeyed ;
Declarations and promises in the Gospel to be believed.
The word not given for speculation but for faith.
The Gospel is God's testimony concerning His son, 1 John v. 9–11.
Redemption-work completed, men have but to believe it.
The foundation laid, it is ours to build upon it.
Moses declared the word of faith, for he spoke of Christ, John v. 46.
The righteousness of faith found in the Pentateuch ;
How much more in the apostolical epistles.
The Gospel in Leviticus; much more in the Evangelists.
We preach. Moses predicted, the apostles preached it.
To preach = to proclaim as a herald, openly, clearly, boldly.
A herald was a public officer ; so preachers of the Gospel.
Employed by Zion's King to announce His mercy to mankind.
In their commission we are the servants of Christ and not of men ;
In the discharge of it, men's servants for Jesus' sake, 2 Cor. iv. 5.

Τι λεγει; what saith it? viz., the righteousness of faith, or doctrine concerning it. *Guyse.* The quotation from Deut. xxx. 14 continued. *D. Brown.* Some MSS. (DEFG). add ἡ γραφη, the Scripture : so several ancient versions (Copt., Eth., Arm., Sclav., Vulg., and It.), and Church Fathers (Or., Chrys., Theod., Hil., Ambr., Ruf.)—To ῥημα, the word ; as well as of the Gospel as of the law. *Par.* Not only the Word itself, but Christ and His salvation, which it presents. *Spener.* The Gospel. *Melv., Stuart.* Revelation. *Thol.* Doctrine of justification by faith, or 'the word of faith.' *Bloomf.* Two covenants in Deut., the legal (from chap. i. to xxvi.) and the evangelical (chap. xxix.) *Junius.* The Gospel and word of faith ; to be revealed and written on the heart in the last days (Jer. xxxi. 31). *Ferme.* A spiritually enlightened interpretation of the passage. *Calv* A sweet and deeply significant parody on the words of Moses. *Beng.* A holy and sweet play of the Spirit on His own inspired Word. *Phil.* An allegorical exposition according to a true though Jewish mode, like Gal. iv. 24, &c. *Meyer.* Precept of active righteousness (לעשׂתו, 'that thou shouldst do it'). *Bp. Bull.* The word which indicates the righteousness of faith is not the word of a precept to be done, like that of which Moses speaks ; but the word published by the witnesses of Jesus, to be believed. *Von Hofm.* Though it is of the law that Moses more immediately speaks, yet the law as Israel shall look on it when the Lord shall circumcise their heart, ver. 6. *D. Brown.* The apostle not merely appropriates the language of Moses, but keeps in the line of his deeper thought. *Ols.* See also on ver. 6.—Ἐγγυς σου, nigh thee ; *i.e.*, easy. *Chrys.* While faith begins to believe, Christ already dwells in the heart. *Or.* Easy and ready at hand. *Tir., Gom.* Near to, and freely obtained by, those that believe. *Ferme.* Christ not to be sought afar off, but within us. *Beng.* Within the reach of an ordinary understanding to conceive, and of an ordinary Christian to perform. *Ham.* Easy to be confessed and believed. *Flatt.* Plain, intelligible, accessible, like the law given to Moses; brought before the mind and heart of each. *Stuart.* Accessible, apprehensible, and certain. *Alford.* Easily accessible. *D. Brown.*—Στοματι, in thy mouth; as ready at hand. *Melv.* As the subject of conversation and teaching. *Stuart.* To be talked about. *Cobbin.* To be read and spoken of in your prayers and praises to God, and your confessions before men. *Guyse.* 'In order to be in thy mouth.' *Brown.* To confess. *Alford.* When thou confessest Him. *D. Brown.* Whoever perceives it gets it into his mouth and heart; the will of God revealed in it becomes the contents of his speech and thought. *Von Hofm.* 'In your schools.' *Targum.*—Καρδιᾳ, in thy heart; as near. *Melv.* As the subject of meditation and thought. *Stuart.* In order to be in thy mouth. *Brown.* To believe. *Alford.* When thou believest on Him. *D. Brown.* When you cordially embrace it. *Guyse.*—Τουτ' ἐστι, that is; Paul gives the sense which the Old Testament passage has in the mouth of the righteousness of faith. *Von Hofm.*—'Ρημα τ. πιστεως, word of faith; faith in Christ being its subject and its effect. *Ferme.* The word which men have to believe for salvation (1 Tim. iv. 6). *D. Brown.* The Gospel the power of God to salvation by giving both righteousness and faith. *Melv.* The Gospel and way of faith foretold under the veil of the law. *Alford.* The word of which Moses speaks stands in the same relation to that which indicates the righteousness of faith, that the Old Testament does to the New. *Von Hofm.*—Κηρυσσομεν, we preach, viz., the apostles. *Ferme.* Κηρυσσω, from κηρυξ, a herald or public crier. In Greek writers—1. To be a herald (*Homer, Lucian*); 2. To make proclamation through a herald (*Diod. Sic.*) In the New Testament, to proclaim, announce publicly, publish. Among the Romans, a herald went round the city when public religious rites were to be performed, calling the people to rest from their labour, and inviting their attendance.

---

9. *That if thou shalt confess with thy mouth the Lord Jesus, and believe in thine heart that God hath raised Him from the dead, thou shalt be saved.*

Confess. Openly acknowledge by word and life.
Profess faith in, dependence on, and discipleship to, Jesus.
Confess Him before men to be Lord and Christ, Matt. x. 32, 33; Acts ii. 36.
Confession the complement and offspring of genuine faith.
Here placed before faith according to the order of Moses.
True and hearty confession of Christ the fruit of the Spirit, 1 Cor. xii. 3.
Faith first known and visible through confession.
Only reckoned as faith when confession follows it.
In man's view faith is non-existing without confession.
The more confession costs the more precious its evidence.
The dying thief, Luke xxiii. 41, 42. Joseph and Nicodemus, John xix. 38, &c.
With thy mouth. Allusion to the words, " In thy mouth," ver. 8.
Confession with the mouth originally made in baptism, Acts viii. 37.
Baptism the answer of a good conscience towards God, 1 Pet. iii. 21.

CHAP. X.] ST. PAUL'S EPISTLE TO THE ROMANS. 79

Hence so often connected in the New Testament with salvation.
The Lord Jesus. Or, Jesus as the Lord; or, that Jesus is the Lord.
Involves His Messiahship and divine Sonship.
Confession that He is Lord, Phil. ii. 11. Calling Him Lord, 1 Cor. xii. 3.
Implies—1. That He was crucified for our sins; 2. That He was raised again from the dead; 3. That He is exalted at God's right hand, Acts ii. 36; 4. That He is King and Head over all; 5. That He is the Son of God.
This confession the sum of faith and salvation.
A declaration of—1. Faith in Jesus; 2. Acceptance of Him; 3. Submission to Him as Lord and Saviour.
Believe. Confession only of value as connected with faith.
Valued only as the expression of a faith really existing.
To believe is to credit and appropriate Christ's death as an atonement for sin verified by His resurrection.
In thine heart. Only heart-faith recognised as true faith.
The faith required of the Eunuch before baptism, Acts viii. 37.
Confession without such faith only hypocritical.
The "heart" in contrast with—1. The head; 2. The mouth.
The seat—1. Of the affections; 2. Of all mental operations.
True faith—1. Flows from the understanding; 2. Moves the affections.
To believe with the heart is to believe—1. Sincerely; 2. Earnestly.
That God hath raised Him from the dead. Proof of His being Lord.
A God-given and God-raised Christ the object of faith.
His resurrection the completion and seal of redemption.
God's certificate of His finished and accepted work.
The virtual justification of all who believe in Him.
A risen Christ believed and confessed brings salvation.
"God raised Jesus from the dead" the genuine apostles' creed.
That at which both Jew and Gentile stumbled, Acts iv. 2; xvii. 18.
The great subject of the apostles' preaching, Acts ii. 32; iii. 15; iv. 33.
Saved. Delivered from sin and all its consequences.
Blessed with all a sinner needs for time and eternity.
Be restored to God's favour, friendship, and image.
Two requisites to salvation,—faith in Christ and confession of Him.
Faith and confession of Christ the complements of each other.

Faith leads to confession ; confession seals faith.
He who believes and boldly confesses his faith is saved.
The righteousness of faith therefore nigh and easily attainable.
The heart believing and the mouth confessing bring salvation.

Ὅτι, that; the language of the true method of salvation. *Calv., Beza, Ferme, D. Brown.* Because. *Vulg., Luth., De Wette, Stuart, Alford, Ellicot.* Gives the reason why it is that we have the word so nigh us. *Von Hofm.*—Ὁμολογήσῃς. Cod. Vat. adds τὸ ῥῆμα, shall confess or profess. *Beza, Pisc.* Acknowledge, believe, invoke, and follow. *Par., Beza, Tol.* Make a free, bold, and open confession. *Guyse.* A hysterosis ; the last in order first explained. *Ferme.* Put first to correspond with foregoing quotation : Similar inversion, 2 Pet. i. 10. *D. Brown.* Confessing with the mouth of greater consequence as regards *men* ; believing with the heart, as respects God. *Bloomf.* —Ἐν τῷ στόματί σου, with thy mouth ; — to have the word of the Gospel in the mouth. *Ferme.* With the mouth, life, and conduct. *Melv.* With sincere and open confession. *Beng.*—Κύριον Ἰησοῦν. Cod. Alex. adds Χριστόν. Cod. Vat. has ὅτι Κύριος Ἰησοῦς, 'that Jesus is Lord.' Acknowledge Jesus as thy Lord and only Saviour. *Par., Beza, Tol.* Confess that Jesus is Lord. *Luth., Ferme, Melv., Thol., Stuart, D. Brown.* Confess Jesus for thy Lord. *Con. & Hows.* Confess Jesus as the Christ who has appeared, and by His resurrection has been perfected as such. *Von Hofm.*—Ἐν τῇ καρδίᾳ, with the heart ; with a sincere faith, engaging the affections and influencing the actions. *Mackn.*

---

10. *For with the heart man believeth unto righteousness; and with the mouth confession is made unto salvation.*

With the heart. The heart is that with which we savingly believe.
Saving faith a thing of the heart ; inward, serious, sincere.
The heart more than the head. Devils believe and tremble, James ii. 19.
True faith in the heart embracing and resting on Christ for salvation.
Unto righteousness. So as to obtain acceptance with God.
To the receiving of that righteousness which makes us accepted.
Faith receives a justifying righteousness in and by Christ, chap. iii. 21.
God's appointed medium of union with Christ, and so of justification.
With the mouth. The mouth follows the heart, 2 Cor. iv. 13.
The order of Moses now changed by the apostle. Believe and confess.
Heart and mouth go together in the matter of saving faith.
Confession. 1. Before men in an open acknowledgment ;
2. Before God in thanksgiving, praise, and prayer.
Includes calling on the name of Christ, ver. 12, 13.

Seals us to Christ before the world. God's name in the forehead, Rev. vii. 3.
Confession of Christ the proper evidence and manifestation of faith.
In times of persecution a sufficient pledge of its sincerity.
The "fearful" or cowardly classed with the unbelievers, Rev. xxi. 8.
Universal confession of Christ as Lord part of His reward, Phil. ii. 6–11.
Faith lays the foundation, confession builds on it.
Faith and confession are to each other as existence and manifestation.
Unto salvation. Including sanctification and glorification.
Justification the beginning, not the whole, of salvation.
Righteousness followed by salvation, as faith is by confession.
Confession the flower of faith, as salvation is of justification.
The same distinction between justification and salvation, chap. v. 9, 10.
Salvation includes the happy consciousness of it.
Such consciousness in proportion to faith in and confession of Christ.
Faith obtains the gift, confession brings its enjoyment.
Faith gives the title, confession the realisation of it.
Justification is the foundation, salvation the superstructure.
Justification the planting of the tree, salvation the fruit.
Salvation the goal, justification the starting-place.
Salvation the end of faith, received at Christ's coming, 1 Pet. i. 5, 9.
Justification is one thing and completed at once;
Salvation is manifold and only completed when Christ comes.
Righteousness or justification is salvation in the bud;
Salvation is righteousness developed in the fruit.

Καρδιᾳ, with a man's whole heart, including the consent, approbation, and acceptance of his will and affections. *Guyse.*—Εἰς δικαιοσυνην, so as to attain justification. *Cobbin.* Justifying righteousness. *D. Brown.*—Ὁμολογειται, public profession is made. *Doddr.* Profession along with faith urged in the case of all who are to be saved. *Ferme.*—Εἰς σωτηριαν, final salvation; confession God's appointed means and method of bringing us to it. *Guyse.*

---

11. *For the Scripture saith, Whosoever believeth on Him shall not be ashamed.*

Scripture. Isa. xxviii. 16. Constant appeal to Old Testament Scripture.
Testimony borne by the prophets to justification by faith, chap. iii. 21.

Whosoever. Jew or Gentile, circumcised or uncircumcised.
Paul's aim to obliterate this distinction in the matter of faith.
No barrier to salvation but what we make ourselves.
Believeth on Him. Cordially trusts in the foundation laid.
Blessedness connected with trusting in the Lord, Ps. xl. 4; Jer. xvii. 7.
Trust in Christ the only way to trust in God, Ps. ii. 12; 1 Pet. i. 21.
Ashamed. 1. Disappointed of our hope; 2. Ashamed to confess.
Indicates—1. The future verification of our faith;
2. Its present victory over the world, 1 John v. 4, 5.
Faith in the heart emboldens to confess with the mouth.
Heb., Make haste; be thrown into perturbation and alarm.
Shall patiently wait for the fulfilment of the promise.
Shall not haste to lay any other foundation than that is laid.
Hope in Christ a hope that maketh not ashamed, chap. v. 5.
Not ashamed of Christ *now*, nor put to shame *hereafter*.

Καταισχυνθησεται (see on chap. ix. 33), ashamed to confess Christ. *Chrys* Be confounded. *Vulg.* Disappointed of their hope. *Vat.* Indicates—1. The duty of him who believes; 2. The grace or blessing of him who perseveres in the duty. *Ferme.* Heb. שׁיחִי, 'shall not make haste;' the ideas cognate. *Par., Beza, Dick.* Translated according to the LXX., shall not fly for escape as from conscious danger. *D. Brown.* 'Shall not be moved when trouble comes.' *Targum.*

---

12. *For there is no difference between the Jew and the Greek: for the same Lord over all is rich unto all that call upon Him.*

For. Reason and confirmation of the preceding.
No difference. The same great truth repeated from chap. iii. 22.
No distinction on the ground of nationality or privilege.
God no respecter of persons. The Gospel good news for all, Luke ii. 10.
Same Lord. *Gr.*, "The same (viz., Jesus) is Lord over all, rich," &c.
Jesus said to be Lord, ver. 9; Lord of all, Acts, x. 36.
Made Lord by God, Ps. cx. 1; Acts ii. 36; Head over all, Eph. i. 22; Phil. ii. 9–11.
Invoked by the Church as Lord of all, 1 Cor. i. 2; Acts i. 24; ix. 13; xxii. 16.
Of all. Jews and Gentiles; all creatures; men and angels.
Rich. *Gr.*, Being rich—1. In Himself; 2. In His gifts.

Christ is rich in Himself—1. As God ; 2. As Mediator.
As God, all is His ; as Mediator, all is put into His hand, John iii. 35.
Rich from eternity, for our sakes He became poor, 2 Cor. viii. 9.
As Mediator, all power is given Him in heaven and earth, Matt. xxviii. 18.
Made Head over all things to His body the Church, Eph. i. 22.
All fulness made to dwell in Him by the Father, Col. i. 19.
That fulness for believers to receive from, John i. 16.
Unsearchable riches of Christ, Eph. iii. 8 ; riches in glory, Phil. iv. 19.
Unto all. All distinction abolished in the Gospel.
All, without respect to nation, condition, character, sex, or age.
Call upon Him. As Lord and Saviour. Therefore God.
Included in the confession of Him. Implies—
1. A rendering divine homage to Him ;
2. An acknowledgment of His being Lord and Saviour ;
3. Believing prayer addressed to Him for salvation.
Calling on Jesus the first martyr's dying act, Acts vii. 59.
Prayer to Christ taught in Scripture. The dying thief, Luke xxiii. 42.
Men to honour the Son even as they honour the Father, John v. 23.
Prayer *to* Christ the means of obtaining the riches *in* Christ.
Christ the well, prayer the bucket in the hand of faith.

Διαστολη (δια, apart, and στελλω, to place), distinction. *Ferme, D. Brown.* Reference to Jews and Gentiles. *Melv.*—Ὁ γαρ αὐτος Κυριος παντων, there is one and the same Lord of all. *Mart.* One and the same is Lord of all. *Diod.* The same person is Lord of all. *Bloomf.* Κυρ. παντων, the primary predicate ; πλουτων, &c., the secondary. *Ellicot.* Ὁ γαρ αὐτος = God. *Calv., Grot., Ferme, Ols., Hodge.* — Christ. *Chrys., Melv., Guyse, Beng., Stuart, D. Brown.*—Πλουτων, rich in mercy. *Ferme.* Munificent. *Melv.* Benevolent and loving. *Schött.* Abundant. *Bloomf.* Being rich. *Ellicot.* A favourite Pauline term expressing the exuberant grace in Christ. *D. Brown.*—Παντας, all the elect. *Ferme.*—Ἐπικαλουμενους, religiously invoke and worship Him as a divine Saviour with faith in His name. *Guyse.* To be understood of every kind of precatory address to God. *Bloomf.* To call on the name of the Lord Jesus a customary expression. *D. Brown.* Invocation as the effect of faith, embracing the whole worship of God. *Melv.*

---

13. *For whosoever shall call upon the name of the Lord shall be saved.*

For. Confirmation from Old Testament Scripture.
Whosoever, &c. Quoted from Joel ii. 32. Also by Peter, Acts ii. 21.

The passage understood by the Jews of the times of Messiah.
Gr., Every one whosoever. Emphatic universality.
Such language characteristic of the Gospel, Isa. lv. 1; John iii. 16.
The well of salvation open to every comer, John vii. 37; Rev. xxii. 17.
Shall call. Implying faith in Him as able to save.
To call on the Lord is—1. An act of prayer; 2. An expression of faith.
Prayer originates—1. In sense of need; 2. In belief of power to help.
Calling on the Lord a mark of spiritual life. A living child cries.
Name. Put for the Lord himself. The Lord as revealed. First used, Gen. iv. 26.
The Lord. In the prophecy, Jehovah. Here applied to Christ. See on chap. i. 3.
Hence Christ is plainly regarded as Jehovah, the Eternal God.
To save a soul is the prerogative of Deity, Isa. xlv. 21, 22.
Christ was worshipped by patriarchs before His incarnation. *Origen.*
Calling on Jesus—1. Makes a Christian; 2. Proves him such.
The life-long practice of a believer, 1 Cor. i. 2; 2 Tim. ii. 22.
Characteristic of early Christians, Acts ix. 14. *Pliny to Trajan.*
God's will that men call on Jesus for salvation, Isa. xlv. 24, 25; Ps. ii. 12.
Shall be saved. Pregnant expression. Saved for time and eternity.

Κυριου. In Joel, יְהוָֹה. Double argument for Christ's divinity; called Jehovah, and invoked. *Bp. Horne, Whitby.* Christ here called Jehovah, or the apostle's argument inconclusive. *Bp. Pearson.* One of the many passages in the Old Testament where Jehovah is spoken of, applied to Christ in the New, *e.g.*, Matt. iii. 3. *D. Brown.* In the prophecy, the invoking is directed to Jehovah, the God of Israel; applied to Christ as God's sent Saviour, in whom God reveals Himself as the God of salvation. *Von Hofm.* Jehovah and Christ identified by the apostle. *Phil.* The Messianic contents of the passage justify the application to Christ. *Meyer.* This application certain from the words that follow. *Bloomf.* The prophecy of Joel understood by the Jews of the times of Messiah: 'At that very time (of Messiah), a more copious spirit shall be raised up and given to Israel; as it is said, I will pour out in those days of my Spirit, and they shall prophecy,' &c. *Zohar.* 'The Blessed and Holy One said, In this world (or age), single prophets prophesied; but in the world to come, all Israel shall be prophets; as it is said, I will pour out,' &c. *Bammidbar Rabba.* 'The Holy Blessed One said, In this world, the gift of prophecy was with individuals only; but in the world to come, it shall be with all men; as it is said, It shall come to pass in these days,' &c. *Tanchuma.*

14. *How then shall they call on Him in whom they have not believed? and how shall they believe in Him of whom they have not heard? and how shall they hear without a preacher?*

How, &c. Gospel to be preached to all that all may call on Him.
Joel's prophecy supposes a universal evangelisation.
The end implies and requires the use of necessary means.
The Jew again reasoned with out of his own Bible.
On Him—viz., Jehovah, in the prophecy; Christ, in the view of Paul.
Not believed. No calling on Christ without faith in Him.
Help only asked where it is believed to be found.
Faith in Christ the foundation of prayer to Him.
Necessity and faith unite in urging us to Christ's door.
Faith in His power to save is the condition of obtaining, Mark ix. 23.
Not heard. Application only made to a known Benefactor.
Faith in an unknown Saviour impossible, Ps. ix. 10.
For men to be saved they must believe, to believe they must hear.
The principle of missions and of preaching in general.
Hence Christ's commission to His disciples, Matt. xxviii. 19; Mark xvi. 15.
Without a preacher. To hear supposes a speaker.
Gr., One who publishes or proclaims, *i.e.*, about Christ.
A preacher is Christ's herald proclaiming forgiveness.
The bearer of God's good news to a dying world.
"Ye shall be witnesses to me to the end of the earth," Acts i. 8.
Preaching a necessity if men are to believe and be saved.
Christ and salvation to be published by men, not angels, Acts viii. 26, &c.; xi. 13, 14.
Yet the good tidings first announced by an angel, Luke ii. 10, 11.
Angels study the Gospel; men are employed to preach it, 1 Pet. i. 12.
The treasure in earthen vessels that the excellency may be of God.
To preach the Gospel is to be the Holy Ghost's fellow-worker, John xv. 26, 27; Acts v. 32.
The most blessed and honourable employment on earth.
Men may preach—1. With their presence; 2. With their pen.

Πως, &c. Objection by a Jew, as if opportunity for believing had not been afforded. *Chrys., Grot., Ham., Mackn., Stuart, Cobbin.* Rather, a question asked by the apostle himself, to vindicate the divine commission of preaching from the necessity of the case. *Young, Guyse, Bloomf., Haldane, D. Brown.* Shows the necessity of the apostleship, to convince the Jews of unbelief and disobedience. *Meyer.* Necessity and dignity of the preachers of the Word, and the universality of their preaching. *Alford.* Ordinarily no faith apart from the Word: God's ordinary administration treated of, His extraordinary operation not being bound or confined to ordinary means. *Ferme.*—Οὖν here indicates not *conclusion*, but *deduction*, or simple relation; 'now.' *Crellius.*—Κηρυσσοντος (κηρυξ, a herald), a person preaching or publishing, *i.e.*, the Lord as the God of salvation. *Von Hofm.* The reasoning in the text a sorites or prosyllogism of successive stages. *Ferme.* Ancient heralds among the Greeks and Romans employed as public criers to make proclamation—1. In the assemblies of the people; 2. In the courts of justice; 3. At the public sacrifices; 4. At public sales or auctions, &c. A Roman herald went round the city at the time of the public religious solemnities, inviting the attendance of the people, and calling them to rest from their labours. *Plutarch.* Preaching the Gospel at first rather outside than inside the church; rather designed for Jews and heathens than those already believers. Public addresses in the church at first by apostles, prophets, or teachers. Presbyters, or elders, as pastors, to be apt to teach. The address by the latter an exhortation founded on the portion of Scripture read. Short, not extending over eight or ten minutes. Generally several of them at one diet. The speakers called upon by the presiding presbyter, himself giving the concluding address. These addresses afterwards considerably extended, and usually delivered by the bishop or presiding minister. *Jamieson.*

---

15. *And how shall they preach except they be sent? as it is written, How beautiful are the feet of them that preach the gospel of peace, and bring glad tidings of good things!*

Sent. The first step after Christ's death to man's salvation.
God first sent His Son, then heralds to proclaim Him.
The sending is—1. Primarily by Christ; 2. Subordinately by man.
Christ sent the preachers in His great commission, Matt. xxviii. 19.
As the Father sent Christ, so Christ sent the preachers, John xx. 21.
A prince's ambassadors to be sent by the prince himself.
As Christ's agent the Holy Ghost also sends the preachers, Acts xiii. 2.
The Holy Ghost sends through the Church as His organ, Acts ii. 3.
The Church's duty to send qualified preachers to all the world.
The Church sends by giving—1. Preparation; 2. Commission; 3. Support.
" The Spirit and the Bride say, Come. And let him that heareth say, Come," Rev. xxii. 17.
The Lord of the harvest to be entreated to send forth labourers, Matt. ix. 37, 38.
Christ by His Spirit—1. Prepares; 2. Moves, the labourers.
Three things ordinarily necessary in a mission to preach—
1. The Spirit's inward motion; 2. The leadings of Providence; 3. The call of the Church.
Want of an evangelistic spirit in a Church to be deplored.
The true missionary impulse is—1. Love to Christ; 2. Love to souls.
In the sending of the Gospel Christ has His joy, men have salvation.

Many go abroad for gain, few for the Gospel.
Much spent on carnal lusts, little on saving souls.
Written. Isa. lii. 7. Preachers sent according to divine promise.
Nothing advanced without appeal to the Scriptures.
Beautiful. From the joyful message they carry.
The sweetness of the tidings transferred to the bearers of them.
Those who love the message love those who carry it.
Gospel-work makes the Church's feet beautiful, Cant. vii. 1.
Three things make the preacher's feet beautiful—
1. The preciousness of his message ;
2. The ardour of his zeal and love ;
3. The holy consistency of his life.
Christ washed His disciples' feet before sending them.
Isaiah's lips touched with a live coal before he was sent to preach.
Feet. 1. Of those who announced Israel's release from Babylon.
2. Especially of those who announce the salvation of Christ.
A nearer and more remote fulfilment of prophecy.
The more remote the principal one intended.
Israel's release by Cyrus a type of sinners' release by Christ.
Isaiah in spirit sees the ready steps of Gospel preachers.
Feet of Israel's messengers appeared on the hills of Palestine ;
Feet of Gospel-preachers in every part of the world.
Preachers to take care that their feet be beautiful.
Feet are for active motion. Preachers to be diligent, 2 Tim. iv. 2.
Gospel of peace. Good tidings of peace and happiness. See on chap. i. 1, 7.
A title sufficient to win the attention of mankind.
No news comparable to those of the Gospel of peace.
Announces—1. Peace with God through the blood of Christ ;
2. Free bestowment of all blessings as the result of it ;
3. Experience of these on the belief and acceptance of the message.
Its language—" All things are ready ; come to the marriage," Matt. xxii. 4.
Offers the richest blessings on the easiest terms.
Believing and accepting, the only conditions, John i. 12 ; iii. 14–18.
Gospel-preachers Christ's ambassadors of peace to men, 2 Cor. v. 20.
Glad tidings. Meaning of " Gospel." Evangel. Glad tidings, as—
1. Fitted to make men glad ; 2. Constantly doing so.
Christ's Gospel the foundation of all true joy in the world.
Good things. 1. Pardon ; 2. Peace ; 3. Holiness ; 4. Heaven.
Things that seem to one awakened too good to be true—

1. God as our reconciled Father and Friend;
2. Christ as our loving Redeemer and Saviour;
3. The Holy Ghost as our Teacher and Sanctifier;
4. Angels as our ministering attendants;
5. Heaven as our prepared everlasting home.

Ὡραῖοι (from ὁράω, to see; ὥρα, properly applied to physical beauty, that of which the sight affords pleasure, — speciosi : or perhaps from ὥρα, season ; 'formosissimus annus.' *Virgil*), beautiful ; for the sake of their message. *D. Brown.* To the elect. *Ferme.* To sensible sinners. *Gill.* Grateful, acceptable. *Bloomf.* Quoted according to the Heb. (אוֵֹי), but not after the LXX., as at present, which has ὥρα.—Πόδες, feet ; put instead of the persons themselves, as the instruments of motion in bringing the good tidings. *Gill.* Footsteps. *Doddr.* Arrival. *L'Enfant.* Approach ; exciting the idea of progress. *Jebb, Bloomf.*—Εὐαγγελιζομένων (εὖ, well, and ἀγγέλλω, to tell ; hence εὐαγγέλιον, evangelium, good tidings, the 'Gospel'), who publish good tidings ; not merely of Israel's deliverance from the Babylonish captivity, but the still much happier tidings of salvation by Christ. *Guyse.* Primarily and literally the return of the Jews, but with a secondary and mystical application to the times of the Messiah. *Bloomf.* Not of the messenger that brought the news of Cyrus's proclamation of liberty to the Jews ; but rather of John the Baptist : best, of Christ himself, the Messenger of the Covenant, and of His apostles, and preachers of the Gospel in general. *Gill.* Gospel-preachers. *Beng.* Deliverance from Babylon the pledge and foreshadowing of the redemption by Christ. *Barth, Alford.* The righteousness and salvation of God, mentioned Isa. li. 6 ; lii. 10. *Brown.* Rabbins : 'When King Messiah cometh, He openeth not His mouth except in proclaiming peace ; as it is said, How beautiful upon the mountains,' &c. *Vayikra Rabba.* 'From whence does He (the Messiah) come? By the way of the mountains ; as it is said, How beautiful,' &c. *Tanchuma.* 'Three days before the coming of Messiah will Elijah the prophet come on the mountains of Israel · as it is said, How beautiful,' &c. *Pesikta Rabbathi.* ' The Holy Blessed One announces nothing to Jerusalem which is to be redeemed but peace ; as it is said, Publishing peace.' *Debarim Rabba.*—Εἰρηνην των εὐαγγ., omitted in Codd. Sin., Vat., and Alex. The *importance* of the heralds of salvation implied in the high *commendation* of them. *Stuart.*

---

16. *But they have not all obeyed the Gospel : for Esaias saith, Lord, who hath believed our report ?*

But. Enjoyment of the blessing hindered by unbelief.
Not all. An unpleasant truth stated in the gentlest way.
Few Jews believed, though with the best evidence before their eyes.
No objection to the message that it is not believed by all.
Partial success no disparagement to a divine commission.
Obeyed—*i.e.*, The Gospel call. Submitted to God's way of saving.
Gospel not only to be known and believed, but obeyed.
God's command is to receive Christ as the only Saviour, Ps. ii. 12.
Esaias. Chap. liii. 1. Jews' unbelief foretold by their own prophet.

CHAP. X.] ST. PAUL'S EPISTLE TO THE ROMANS. 89

A confirmation of the divine character of the message.
The prophecy applied by the ancient Jews to the Messiah.
Wonderfully verified in the life, sufferings, and death of Jesus.
Applied to Him, Matt. viii. 17; Mark xv. 28; John xii. 38.
The text from which Philip preached Jesus to the Eunuch, Acts viii. 35.
Who hath believed? Believers in the Gospel message to be few.
Jews' rejection of Jesus therefore a confirmation of His Messiahship.
Unbelief is—1. Intellectual; 2. Practical. The result of depravity.
The Gospel announces a holy Saviour and a holy salvation.
Requires immediate and complete submission to God.
Reveals truths beyond the power of carnal reason to comprehend.
Comes in a way contrary to what the flesh desires.
The Jews expected and desired a Saviour, but a carnal one.
Man by nature too self-righteous to accept the Gospel.
Would rather live in sin than be saved out of it.
Acceptance of the Gospel is acceptance of the cross.
The Gospel is believed and received—1. By the humble-minded; 2. By the candid and sincere; 3. By the consciously guilty and lost; 4. By those who desire to be saved from sin.
No ambassador more clearly accredited than Jesus Christ.
No message so well authenticated as the Gospel.
The intellect often convinced while the heart is closed.
A cordial faith in the Gospel the work of God's Spirit, Eph. i. 19; ii. 8.
Report. That which is published and therefore heard.
The report concerning God's righteous Servant and Saviour.
Called also God's record or witness concerning His Son, 1 John v. 11.
The Gospel a report—1. Of God's amazing love to sinners;
2. Of the most wonderful events the world ever saw;
3. Of what concerns man's highest interests for eternity.
Makes known the way devised by God for man's salvation.
The incarnation, life, death, and resurrection of God's Son.
Claims therefore—1. The most earnest attention; 2. The most ready acceptance; 3. The most lively gratitude.

Ἀλλ' οὐ πάντες, but they have not all, &c. *Ferme.* Howbeit they did not all.
Ellicot. Spoken of the Jews. *Melv., Thol., Meyer, Phil., D. Brown.* Of the Gentiles.
Guyse, Frit. Of both. *Von Hofm.* An objection started by the Jews. *Crell., Locke, Taylor, Bloomf.* A statement by the apostle himself. *Ferme, Guyse, D. Brown.*
—Ὑπήκουσαν (ὑπο and ἀκούω, to hear), obeyed. *Ferme.* Hearkened. *Melv., Guyse,*

Bloomf. To obey supposes a command, and consists in doing it. *Von Hofm.* Shows the guilt of the heathen who perish. *Frit.*—'Ακοῃ (ἀκουω, to hear). Heb. לִשְׁמֻעָתֵנוּ. LXX. ἀκοῃ, hearing (audition). *Gill, Rück., De Wette, Phil., Est.* Preaching. *Pisc., Luth., Mar., Diod.* Discourse. *Beza, Grot., Eras.* Doctrine. *Vat.* That which others have heard from us. *Vor.* Our teaching. *Con. & Hows.* Our message. *Niel.* Refers to the act of hearing. *Beza.* To the Gospel heard. *Tir.* Spoken in the person of the prophets. *Jerome, Est.* Of the apostles. *Tol.* Of Christ and the apostles. *Melv.* The prophet includes with himself all the heralds of the Messiah. *Henry.* The prophet himself and Christ and His apostles whom he personated. *Gill.* The servants of Messiah. *Guyse.* Isaiah and the other prophets. *Fausset.* The speaker personates the repentant Jews in the latter ages. *Horsley.* The passage quoted to justify the preaching of the Gospel to the heathen. *Calv.* To show that the want of success was predicted and can be no objection to the divine commission of the apostles, or reason why the Gospel should not be preached. *Chrys., Theod.* To show the agreement with the prophet's experience. *Flatt, Ewald.* To confirm the fact that all have not believed. *Glöck., Meyer.* To show the agreement with the prophecy which has thus received its fulfilment. *Thol., Baumg.-Cr.* To meet the infidel's objection from the Jews' rejection of the Gospel. *Fausset.* Expresses the certainty of such a result after the prediction. *Rück., Phil.* The prophecy of which it forms a part (Isa. lii. 13–15 ; liii. 1, &c.) in many respects the most important of the Old Testament Scriptures. *Hengstenberg.* Anciently applied by the Jews to the Messiah. The Targum on chap. lii. 13, says : ' My servant the Messiah shall prosper.' The book of Zohar : ' Of thee, O Messiah, this scripture treats, My servant shall deal prudently,' &c. Tanchuma in Yalkut Shimeoni : ' Behold my servant shall prosper, &c. ; King Messiah is understood.' Abenezra says, ' Many have expounded these things of Messiah ; because our ancestors said that on the day in which the temple was destroyed Messiah was born, and was afterwards bound with fetters.' Abarbinel also says, ' Jonathan ben Uzziel (in the Targum) expounds this of Messiah, and his interpretation is also that of the Fathers of blessed memory ; I have also seen an interpretation of this prophecy by Moses, the son of Nachmon, who also explains it of King Messiah.' For the application of single verses, see on chap. iii. 25 ; iv. 25. The Messianic interpretation of the prophecy prevailed among the Jews up to the twelfth century. Sometimes, but rarely, it was referred to others ; *e.g.*, the Jewish people collectively, Abraham, Moses, Ezra, Zerobabel, and to any righteous man. Since the twelfth century it has generally been referred by Rabbies to the Jewish people ; *e.g.*, by Jarchi, Abenezra, Kimchi ; but by Abarbinel to King Josiah, and by Saadias Gaon to Jeremiah. Its application to Messiah is acknowledged in the prayers of the synagogue. In those for the Feast of the Passover it is said : ' Haste thee, let the shadows flee away ! Let Him that was despised be exalted, extolled, and be very high ! Let Him prosper, and rebuke, and sprinkle many nations.'

---

17. So then faith cometh by hearing, and hearing by the word of God.

So then. The conclusion,—the Gospel to be everywhere preached.
Faith. Belief in and acceptance of the provided Saviour. That which gives an interest in Him and in His salvation.
Cometh—*i.e.*, Into a man's experience and possession. Faith to be produced in man's heart. The question is, How ?
By hearing. Hearing a testimony, or a testimony heard. Same word rendered "report" in ver. 16, here alluded to.

Faith produced by hearing the Gospel record or report.
The report concerning Christ. Given to be heard.
The Holy Spirit's instrument in producing faith.
The Gospel to be published and heard with that object.
A twofold necessity—1. Of preaching ; 2. Of hearing, the Gospel.
God gives faith but gives it through the Gospel read or heard.
The simplicity of the way of salvation on man's part.
Hearing brings faith and faith brings salvation.
Word of God. 1. The warrant ; 2. Matter ; 3. Rule of preaching.
The Gospel message is from God and about God.
Preachers to declare not their own views but God's Word.
The Gospel not the word of man but of God, 1 Thess. ii. 13.
Perfect harmony between the Old and New Testaments.
Preachers to speak according to the law and the testimony, Isa. viii. 20.
God the author of the Gospel. Divine warrant for preaching it.

'Αρα, therefore; conclusive. *Bloomf.* Appears to avoid direct reference to his opponents the Jews, and to argue against the Church of God which has embraced the truth. *Ferme.* Shows the necessity of preaching the Gospel, and vindicates the divine authority of the Christian religion against the Jews. *Koppe.* Confirmation of the truth that faith supposes hearing the Word, and this a commission to preach it. *D. Brown.* Hearing is necessary to faith, which justifies our preaching. *Newcome.* So then ; the objector still speaks. *Cobbin.*—'Ρηματος Θεου. Codd. Sin. and Vat. have Χριστου. Word of God, *i.e.*, announced by the apostles or those heralds whom God sends. *Ferme.* The Gospel. *Melv.* Word which supplies what is to be preached. *Dickson.* Command of God who sends the preachers. *Pisc., Beza.* The preaching, as from God and about Him. *Tol.* God's word, not man's, to produce faith. *Vat.* God's express command. *Doddr., Flatt.* The Gospel, of which God is the author, and which He has given commission to publish. *Guyse.* The preached Word. *De Wette, Frit., Glöck., Meyer, Baumg.-Cr., Nielson.* The message of the prophets, but viewed as from God himself. *Von Hofm.*

---

18. *But I say, Have they not heard? Yes, verily: their sound went forth to all the earth, and their word to the ends of the world.*

But. They have not believed : but have they not heard ?
The Gospel to be preached whether men will believe or not.
They. The Jews ; but so as to include the Gentiles also.
Heard—*i.e.*, The Gospel or the preachers of it.
Yes, verily. The Gospel already preached to Jews and Gentiles.
Preached throughout most of the civilised world, chap. i. 5, 8 ; Col. i. 6.
Jews either heard or had the opportunity of hearing.

According to the Scriptures, the Gospel to be universally preached.
Their sound. Quoted from Ps. xix. 4, for confirmation.
The passage applied by the Jews to the times of the Messiah.
Testimony of the Gospel as wide as that of the heavens.
The Sun of righteousness to shine as wide as that in the sky.
In the psalm, the heavens a figure of the Word of God.
The comparison applied by the apostle to the Gospel.
The psalm prophetical. The Gospel to be universal.
Its light to be as free and far-spread as the light of the sun.
The Gospel and creation both the voices of God.
The heavens and Gospel-preachers have a common ministry.
The one proclaims a Creator, the other a Redeemer.

Ἀλλὰ λέγω. An anticipated objection that the Jews had heard, answered by admitting the fact. *Ferme.* Objection that the Jews had not heard answered by denying it. *Melv.* Cavil against preaching the Gospel to the Gentiles answered by referring to the matter of fact. *Guyse.*—Μὴ οὐκ ἤκουσαν; Have they not heard? viz., the Jews. *Chrys., Theod., Ferme, Melv., Beza, Stuart, De Wette, Meyer, Phil., Rück.* The Gentiles. *Theoph., Guyse.* Both. *Vat., Von Hofm.* Heard the Gospel. *Chrys.* The voice of the teachers. *Con. & Hows.*—Φθόγγος (φθέγγομαι). Heb. קַו, rendered by the LXX. ὁ φθόγγος αὐτῶν, 'their voice;' by Aquila, ὁ κανών αὐτ., 'their line,' as 2 Cor. x. 13. קַו, 'a line,' used in Isa. xxviii. 9, 10, 13, of the first elements of instruction, and so may be rendered by φθόγγος, a letter or sound of one. Perhaps the LXX. read קוֹלָם. *Grotius, Randolph.* קַו, line or delineation of the mundane fabric which proclaims without sound, and so transferred to 'sound.' *Melv.* קַו = a musical chord or string, and so may be rendered 'a sound.' *Rosenm., Koppe, Thol., De Wette, Meyer, Rück.* Signifies also a loud voice or cry. *Pococke, Guyse.* Universal teaching of the heavens by the heavens applied to the preaching of the apostles. *Hyperius, Bloomf.* Words of the Psalmist by the inspired apostle to a different subject. *Gom.* Gentiles taught by the created heavens; or by the Gospel to which they are compared. *Ferme.* Used not in the way of testimony but accommodation; yet so as to hint that, according to the prophet, the Gospel was to sound far and wide. *Melv.* God had already preached to the Gentiles by the material heavens; He follows it up by preaching to them through the Gospel. *Calv.* Paul perceives a spiritual meaning and prophecy in the psalm. *Par.* Uses the words as the vehicle of his own thoughts. *Stuart.* For illustration. *Hodge.* By way of accommodation, and hyperbolically, to enliven the address and animate hope. *Rück.* The publication of the heathen generally set forth in the psalm. *De Wette.* The comparison between the heavens and the Word of God followed up by the apostle. *Alford.*—Εἰς πᾶσαν τ. γῆν, to all the earth : all the Gentiles had now heard the Gospel. *Chrys., Theoph.* Paul's answer to the objector : all the ends of the earth have heard ; well might the Jews. *Chrys., Theod.* Rabbins : 'By the words "unto all the earth" the servants of Messiah are understood.' *Zohar.*

---

19. *But I say, Did not Israel know? First, Moses saith, I will provoke you to jealousy by them that are no people, and by a foolish nation will I anger you.*

Israel. Name applied—1. To Jacob, Gen. xxxii. 28. See on chap. ix. 4 ;

CHAP. X.] ST. PAUL'S EPISTLE TO THE ROMANS. 93

2. To the twelve tribes collectively as sprung from him, Exod. iii. 16.
3. To the ten tribes which separated from Judah and Benjamin;
4. To the returned exiles from Babylon as representing the nation;
5. To the people as distinguished from the priests and Levites, Ezra vi. 16.

Here the collective body of the Jewish nation.

Know. 1. That the Gospel should be preached in all lands; 2. That the Gentiles should enjoy Israel's privileges.

First. From the very beginning of their national existence.

Moses. The instrument of Israel's formation into a people.

Their very founder the first to foretell the Gentiles' faith.

Saith—viz., In Deut. xxxii. 21; a solemn prediction—
1. Of Israel's unbelief; 2. Of the calling of the Gentiles.

Provoke. By calling the Gentiles to be His people.

Jews to be finally excited to faith through that of the Gentiles, chap. xi. 13.

The object of the apostle in his Gentile ministry, chap. xi. 14.

Jealousy. Zeal, emulation. Same word employed, chap. xi. 14.

Men often made more sensible of their mercies—
1. By the loss of them; 2. By their passing to others.

No people. The Gentiles who were—1. Not the people of God; 2. Not a people at all,—so degraded, rejected, and disunited.

The light in which God regarded Egypt, Greece, and Rome.

A godless people not worthy to be called a people.

Separated from God, men cannot be united to each other.

The heathen brutified like the gods they worshipped.

In casting away God men cast away themselves, chap. i. 23-28.

Foolish. Idolaters like the senseless objects of their worship.

Their makers like them, Ps. cxv. 8. Led by a deceived heart, Isa. xliv. 20.

The foolishness of idolatry graphically described, Isa. xliv. 9-23.

Applicable to the most polished nations of antiquity.

The wisdom of the world foolishness with God, 1 Cor. iii. 19.

Israel a wise and understanding people through God's Word, Deut. iv. 6.

Void of counsel and understanding by their neglect of it, Deut. xxxii. 28.

Anger. The effect indicated rather than the intention.

The intention not to make them sin but to make them suffer.

Israel's sinful anger caused by God's righteous dealings.

Angry at the evangelisation of the Gentiles, Acts xiii. 45; xvii. 5, 13; 1 Thess. ii. 16.
The elder brother angry at the prodigal's reception, Luke xv. 28.
Neither accepted the call nor suffered those that would, Matt. xxiii. 13.
The greatest punishment is to be abandoned to evil passions.

'Αλλα λεγω. Introduces a supposed objection by a Jew. *Beza, Grot., Ferme.* Meets an objection raised on behalf of the Jews. *Melv.*—Μη ουκ εγνω 'Ισρ.; In some ancient MSS., versions, and Fathers, Μη 'Ισρ. ουκ εγνω; Has not Israel known it? *Luth., Mart.* Had some knowledge. *Diod.* Has not Israel known God? *Ferme.* The Gospel. *Melv., Vat., Est., Gom., Ham., Rück.* The truth of God. *Calv., Beza, Chal.* The righteousness of God; Israel could and ought to have known it, but would not. *Beng.* 'Εγνω has the same object as ηκουσαν, viz., the Gospel. *Von Hofm.* 'Εγνω = consider, recognise, viz., the different conduct of God towards the heathen and the Jews. *Thol.* Know that the Gentiles should be called. *Pisc., Par., Tol., Guyse, D. Brown.* That the Gospel should be preached in all lands, and so to the heathen. *Henry, Doddr., Flatt., Stuart, Bloomf., De Wette, Meyer, Alford.* That these were preachers sent from God. *Chrys.* Did not God know Israel only? *Reiche, Bretschneider.* —Πρωτος, first, in opposition to Isaiah. *Ols., Baumg.-Cr.* First in the line of prophets. *De Wette.* Connect with εγνω. Has not Israel first heard [the Gospel]? *Wetstein, Storr, Flatt, Von Hofm.*—Παραζηλωσω (ζηλος, zeal, emulation), provoke to emulation. *Par.* Excite your jealousy. *Bloomf.*—Ουκ εθνει, = a contemptible nation. *Grot.* Classics: 'Αργειον ουκ 'Αργειον. *Eurip. Orest.* Not a people of God by any peculiar covenant. *Bloomf.* A no-people; as they had provoked God by their no-gods. *D. Brown.*—'Ασυνετω (α not, συν together, and ιημι to put; not putting things together so as to reason from them), destitute of intelligence. *Mart.* Affected with the folly of idolatry, destitute of the knowledge of the only true God. *Grot.* Refers to their religious blindness. *De Wette.*—Παροργιω (Attic future for παροργισω; from παρα and οργη, anger), I will excite you (commovebo). *Eras., Vat.* Provoke you to anger. *Beza, Pisc., Pag.*

20. *But Esaias is very bold, and saith, I was found of them that sought me not; I was made manifest unto them that asked not after me.*

Very bold. 1. Speaks very plainly; uses still stronger terms. Moses hinted it; Isaiah boldly and openly declares it.
2. Speaks courageously and without fear of results.
Unwelcome truths require courage to utter them, Acts iv. 13, 29, 31.
Those who would be faithful to God must not fear offending man.
Saith. Isa. lxv. 1. Compare with the prophecy, Eph. ii. 11; iii. 6.
Found. As in the case of the woman of Samaria, John iv. 29; of the Eunuch, Acts viii. 26, &c.; of the jailer at Philippi, Acts xvi. 27, &c.
Christ a treasure to be found, Matt. xiii. 44. So Andrew, John i. 41.

The pearl of great price, Matt. xiii. 45. Whoso findeth me findeth life, Prov. viii. 35.

Sought me not. So chap. ix. 30, "followed not after righteousness."

Christ beforehand with His grace. Seeks us before we seek Him.

The shepherd seeks the sheep, not the sheep the shepherd, Luke xv. 3.

We love Him because He first loved us, 1 John iv. 19.

Christ found when not sought, much more when He is.

Counsels the careless and self-satisfied to take His grace, Rev. iii. 17, 18.

Seeking required by those who wish to find, Prov. ii. 2–5 ; Isa. lv. 6.

Gentiles sought not Christ but the things of the world, Matt. vi. 32.

The Greeks sought after wisdom, but not the wisdom of God, 1 Cor. i. 22.

The context applied by Rabbies to the Gentile nations.

Made manifest. Salvation in the knowledge of God and of Christ, John xvii. 3.

An inward revelation of Christ the work of God, Matt. xvi. 17 ; Gal. i. 16.

His manifestation to Israel the object of John's ministry, John i. 31.

Heb., I am sought ; *i.e.*, preached in order to their seeking me.

How shall they call on Him of whom they have not heard, ver. 14.

Asked not after me. So the Greeks inquired for Jesus, John xii. 20, 21.

Gentiles were neither asking *for* Christ nor *after* Him.

The wise men only asked for Christ when His star appeared to them.

Δε = imo vero. *Bloomf.* And still further. *Guyse.*—'Αποτολμᾷ κ. λεγει, speaks very plainly and openly. *Chrys.* Says boldly. *Diod.* Becomes quite bold and says. *Mart.* Useth boldness (audacia). *Beza, Pisc., Pag., Ferme.* With great confidence (fiducia). *Melv.* Is courageous, confident. *Est.* Open, plain. *Tir.* Τολμαω and ἀποτολμαω, often pleonastic, but generally implying difficulty, and the need of courage and boldness in the act. *Schött.* 'Αποτολ. κ. λεγ., a hendiadys for ἀποτολμως λεγει, pronounces confidently ; ἀπο, intensive. *Bloomf.* 'Απο gives more precision. Speaks with great freedom, openness, and undaunted courage. *Guyse.* Comes out boldly. *Stuart, Nielson.* Uses still stronger and more explicit terms. *Brown.* Is still plainer, and goes the length of saying. *D. Brown.*—Εὑρέθην, I was found ; used of God when exciting men by His benefits to seek and worship Him. *Koppe, Rosenm., Bloomf.* —Τοις. Cod. Vat. has ἐν τοις, among them.—'Εμφανης (from ἐν and φαινω, to appear) ἐγενομην (LXX. ἐγενηθην). Heb. נִדְרַשְׁתִּי, properly, 'I am explained,' revealed, made known, according to the rabbinical use of the word ; the Jews using the word דרש, not only for searching into the meaning of Scripture, but also for explaining it, on the supposition of previous search ; hence their expositions and schools called הָדְרָשִׁים,

midrashim, and their preachers דֹּרְשֵׁי. So נִדְרָשְׁתִּי, I was preached to them. *Gill.* LXX. perhaps read הדרשׁתי, I am consulted, as Hosea iv. 5. *Grot.* I am sought or inquired of, *i.e.*, was present at hand ; the parallel to נִמְצֵאתִי, I am found. *Beng.* Made known in a distinguishing and effectual manner by the preaching of the Word and the illumination of the Spirit. *Guyse.*—'Ἐπερωτῶσι (ἐπι and ἐρωταω, to ask), who asked (interrogabant). *Vulg.* Consulted. *Grot.* Used of a person inquired of, not a thing inquired about, as Matt. xii. 10 ; xvi. 1 ; Mark xi. 29. *Ham.* Rabbins : 'Even to the Gentiles that are not called by my name, I am preached.' *R. Moses the Priest*, on the passage. The apostle quoting from memory seems to transpose the words נִדְרָשְׁתִּי and נִמְצֵאתִי, the LXX. also having ἐμφανὴς ἐγεν. first. I am sought or inquired of as by true worshippers, and therefore found, as Ezek. xiv. 3 ; xx. 3. *Alford.*

---

21. *But to Israel he saith, All day long I have stretched forth my hands to a disobedient and gainsaying people.*

To Israel. Rather, of or in regard to Israel, as Heb. i. 7 ; Luke xx. 19.

All day long. *Gr.*, The whole day. With unwearied patience.
So far from any want of means being used to win them.
How often would I have gathered thy children, &c., Matt. xxiii. 37.
Continual means used for Israel's salvation, Hosea vi. 5.
God speaks of rising early and sending His prophets, Jer. vii. 13 ; xi. 7.
The day of divine patience and persuasion followed by a dark and silent night.

Stretched forth my hands. Calling for repentance and faith.
Attitude of suppliants ; "as though God did beseech you," 2 Cor. v. 20.
Metaphor from mothers fondly calling to wayward children.
Christ compares Himself to the hen calling her brood, Matt. xxiii. 37.
If so under the law, how much more under the Gospel !
Where the Gospel is preached, Christ holds out inviting arms.
God appears as a friend offering reconciliation and love.
The Creator stretches forth beseeching hands to the creature.
Offended God persuades and entreats offending man.
The hands now stretched forth are the pierced hands of Jesus.
Their wounds the most powerful plea with sinners to repent.

Disobedient. Not believing and obeying the divine call.
Their rejection therefore their own fault.
The Spirit's calls and ordinary operations resisted, Gen. vi. 3 ; Acts vii. 51.
The Gospel seeks the obedience of faith. Rendered by Gentiles, chap. i. 5, 6.

Gainsaying. The sin of the mouth added to that of the heart.
Disobedient instead of believing; gainsaying instead of confessing.
Gainsaying an aggravation of the sin of not believing.
Characterised the Jews in relation to the prophets, Jer. xv. 10, 15, 20; Ezek. ii. 6.
The same in relation to the apostles, Acts xiii. 45; xiv. 2, 19; xvii. 5–7, 13.
Two marvels—1. God's goodness not overcome by man's badness; 2. Man's badness not overcome by God's goodness.

Πρὸς Ἰσ., to Israel. *Vulg.* Against. *Beza, Pisc.* Of, as Heb. i. 7. *Est., De Wette.* In reference to. *Niel.* In regard of. *Ellicot.*—Ἐξεπέτασα (ἐξ, out, and πέταω, to spread), called with open and outstretched arms. *Gom.* Calling to faith and repentance; metaphor from mothers. *Par.* Or from the lively action of an orator. *Guyse.* Targum: 'I sent my prophets every day,' &c.—Ἀπειθοῦντα κ. ἀντιλέγοντα. So the LXX.; but in the Hebrew only סוֹרֵר, 'rebellious.' Two words used more accurately to represent the force of the *single* Hebrew term; ἀντιλέγ., the stronger of the two. *Bloomf.*

CHAPTER XI.

1. *I say then, Hath God cast away His people? God forbid. For I also am an Israelite, of the seed of Abraham, of the tribe of Benjamin.*

I say then. Anticipates an objection by a Jewish reader.
Unwarranted conclusions often drawn from Scripture truths.
Cast away. Rejected from being any longer His people.
Either—1. Externally and nationally; or, 2. Spiritually and personally.
Either—1. Universally and totally; or, 2. Partially and temporarily.
His people. Those whom He had chosen for His people.
The high position occupied by Israel as a nation.
Still more enjoyed by those who accept God's offers in Christ.
The promised blessing in the new covenant, Jer. xxxi. 33; Heb. viii. 8–12.
Men may be God's people—1. Nationally and collectively; or, 2. Personally.
1. By an outward visible bond; 2. By an inward spiritual relation.
God forbid. The Lord will not cast away His people, Ps. xciv. 14.
Will not forsake His people for His name's sake, 1 Sam. xii. 22.
Israel even as a nation not absolutely and finally cast away.

At present a remnant saved, ver. 5 ; hereafter the whole, ver. 26.
In Israel's case God had a people within a people.
The same in regard to the visible Church of Christ.
For. Proofs that God had not cast away His people.
I also. Paul himself an evidence of this non-rejection.
Absolute rejection must have included himself.
Preachers do well to support their statements by their own case.
Reference to Paul's own case here peculiarly emphatic.
Individually none had done more to be cast away, 1 Tim. i. 13–16.
An Israelite. Member of the Jewish nation and family. See chap. x. 19.
In the same sense, chap. ix. 4 ; 2 Cor. xi. 22. Of the stock of Israel, Phil. iii. 5.
The term used in a higher sense, chap. ix. 6 ; John i. 47 ; Gal. vi. 16.
A national and a spiritual Israel, chap. ii. 28, 29 ; ix. 6.
Paul belonged to both. Never lost sight of his nationality.
Not likely therefore to maintain an absolute rejection.
Of the seed of Abraham. A high honour and privilege.
One of Paul's gains, but counted loss for Christ, Phil. iii. 5–7.
External advantages, though not saving, yet to be valued.
Redoubled force given to his statement by this addition.
Tribe. Collective families from one of Jacob's twelve sons.
Name in Hebrew from the rod or sceptre borne by the head of each tribe, Num. xvii. 2.
Hence the sceptre still used as an ensign of regal power.
The tribes of Israel usually called " the Twelve Tribes."
In point of fact, thirteen, Joseph's being divided into two.
Geographically twelve, as Levi had no land-inheritance.
The tribe of Levi not included in the census, Num. i. 47–49.
The tribes divided into two kingdoms under Rehoboam.
Judah and Benjamin formed that of Judah ; the rest that of Israel.
The ten tribes or kingdom of Israel first taken captive to Assyria.
Judah and Benjamin taken captive to Babylon.
Only the latter, with a sprinkling of the former, returned.
The rest still greatly unknown. Traced in various countries.
Benjamin. The youngest of the sons of Jacob, Gen. xxxv. 18.
Rachel's second son, born seven years after Joseph.
The only son of Jacob born within the borders of Canaan.
His birth the occasion of his mother's death.
Hence called by his mother *Benoni*, " Son of my affliction."
Called by his father *Benjamin*, " Son of my right hand."

CHAP. XI.] ST. PAUL'S EPISTLE TO THE ROMANS. 99

Type of the Church; at first, sorrow and martyrdom, then exaltation.
Saul, the first king of Israel, chosen from that tribe.
Saul, the chief of the apostles, taken from the same.
Jacob's prophecy regarding Benjamin fulfilled in Paul, Gen. xlix. 27.
First made havoc in the Church, then in Satan's kingdom.
Benjamin's blessing fulfilled in the Church, Deut. xxxiii. 12.
The Temple said to have stood partly in Benjamin's lot.
Jerusalem numbered among the cities of Benjamin, Josh. xviii. 28.
Benjamin and Judah closely connected in Jewish history.
These, with Levi, were the tribes that remained faithful to God.
Formed together the kernel of the Jewish nation.
Paul's lineage deduced through a faithful tribe.
He establishes the purity of his descent—Hebrew of the Hebrews.
Magnifies his Jewish privileges for the sake of the Jews.
Particularity in the description strengthens the impression.
The genealogy perfects the idea of a genuine Israelite.
Paul a Christian and a patriot, and both with his whole heart.

Λέγω οὖν. Supposed to be asked by an objector, as following from Paul's statements. *Ferme, Melv., Mackn., Stuart.* The supposition groundless and unnecessary. *Haldane, Guyse.*—Ἀπώσατο (ἀπό and ὠθω, to thrust). Rejected (rejecit). *Beza, Pag. Repulit. Pisc.* Degraded, thrust down. *Syriac.* Literally, to push anything aside with abhorrence, as a nauseous potion; with the adjunct, to *push away,* cast off; implies here perpetual rejection and total abandonment. *Bloomf.* Same word rendered 'rejected,' Judges vi. 13; 'cast off,' Ps. xciv. 14. Heb. סָאַב, נָעַל, זָנַח, יָאַשׁ, נָטַשׁ. Cod. Alex. adds ὃν προέγνω.—Φυλῆς (φύω, to spring, be born; φύλον, a people, race), a tribe. Heb. מַטֶּה, שֵׁבֶט, originally a rod or staff, anciently borne by chiefs or heads of tribes. Various opinions regarding the Ten Tribes supposed to be lost. Found among the Affghans. *Sir. W. Jones.* In Bombay. *C. Buchanan.* In America and the West Indies. *Aaron Levi,* who travelled in 1644 under the name of Montesinos. In Daghestan, on the Caspian Sea. *Jacob Samuel.* Among the Nestorian Christians of Chaldæa. *Grant.*

---

2. *God hath not cast away His people which He foreknew. Wot ye not what the Scripture saith of Elias? how he maketh intercession to God against Israel.*

His people. Especially in the higher and spiritual sense.
The remnant according to the election of grace, ver. 5.
The proof that He has not cast away Israel absolutely.
Individuals still saved, and at last the whole nation.
Israel chosen as His people, not finally and absolutely cast off.
Foreknew. Loved and chose beforehand. So chap. viii. 29.
The reason why His people are not finally cast away.

Such foreknowing and casting off incompatible.
The gifts and calling of God without repentance, ver. 29.
Israel as a nation still beloved for the fathers' sake, ver. 28.
Individuals among them chosen to faith and salvation.
God's foreknowledge implies and involves His decree.
Sometimes mentioned along with the decree, Acts ii. 23.
Sometimes put instead of it, as 1 Pet. i. 20.
Wot. An old Saxon word signifying to "know." So Acts iii. 17.
Of Elias. *Gr.*, In Elias, *i.e.*, in the section about Elias.
Sections in the Old Testament named from their leading subject.
So Luke xx. 37.
Elias, *Heb.*, Elijah ; meaning "Jehovah is my God."
Next to Moses the most renowned prophet of the Old Testament.
Surnamed the Tishbite from Thisbe, where he was born.
A strenuous vindicator of the worship of the true God.
Opposed the idolatrous kings of Israel under whom he lived.
His life threatened by Jezebel, the wife of King Ahab.
Seeks safety in flight. Halts at Beersheba.
Wanders into the wilderness dejected and desponding.
Falls asleep under a juniper tree. Is awoke by an angel.
Partakes of food miraculously provided for him.
Travels to Horeb for forty days without more support.
Found by God in a cave, who asks, What dost thou here, Elijah?
In reply to the question he opens his grief, 1 Kings xix. 10-18.
In doing so, he "maketh intercession against Israel."
Elijah one of the two translated to heaven without dying.
Appears with Moses on the Mount of Transfiguration.
Foretold by Malachi as the forerunner of the Messiah, Mal. iv. 5.
Verified in John the Baptist, who came in his power and spirit,
    Luke i. 17 ; Matt. xvii. 12, 13.
Maketh intercession. Complains of their apostate state.
Excuses his flight by a charge against them of total apostasy.
Same word rendered "dealt," Acts xxv. 24. Elijah also sought help.
Prayer a dealing with God for the obtaining of an end.
To make intercession a believer's priestly office, 1 Pet. ii. 5.
To plead with God one of the privileges of His children.
Against Israel. As having abandoned Jehovah's worship.
Sad when faithful ministers have to complain against a people to God.
Abraham made intercession for Sodom, Elias against Israel.

Τον λαον αυτου, His elect people. *Tol.*, *Ferme*, *Melv.*, *Guyse.* The portion chosen to eternal life. *Or.*, *Aug.*, *Chrys.*, *Theod.*, *Theoph.*, *Calv.*, *Luth.*, *Hald.*, *Lange.* The whole people. *Ham.*, *Doddr.*, *De Wette*, *Meyer*, *Thol.*, *Phil.*, *Alf.*, *Niel.* To the apostle the election are the true people of God. *Lange.* Those whose acceptance of the Gospel he foreknew. *Mackn.* Israel chosen as God's people to be the foundation of Messiah's kingdom; therefore cannot as a people be cast away. *Thol.*—Προεγνω, knew before as receiving the faith. *Chrys.* Loved, favoured, approved, chose before. *Vat.*, *Vor.* Foreknew and chose in Christ. *Melv.* Indicates God's good pleasure and decree. *Calv.* Foreknew as His own people; to foreknow.— to decree, 1 Pet. i. 20. *Beng.* In His eternal counsels of love and grace distinguished from the rest and chose them to saving benefits. *Guyse.* Determined and decided who should be His people. *Stuart.* Who He foreknew would be His people. *Bloomf.* Loved and chose. *Hald.* Formerly acknowledged, Num. xvi. 5; Amos iii. 2. *Brown.* Probably indicates His peculiar gracious complacency. *D. Brown.* Determined beforehand, as in chap. viii. 29, viz., to be His people, *i.e.*, the family of Abraham: the reason given for their non-rejection. *Rück.*—Ἐν Ἐλια, in Elias. *Mor.*, *Est.* Concerning Elias. *Eras.*, *Pag.*, *Beza*, *Pisc.*, *Cas.*, *Vor.* In the history of Elias. *Arab.*, *Syr.*, *Vor.*, *Cam.*, *Est.*, *Diod.*, *Doddr.*, *De Wette.* In that section treating of Elias, and called by his name, *Stuart*, *D. Brown.* —Ἐντυγχανει τῳ Θ. κατα τ. Ἰσρ., addresses, appeals to (appellat). *Cas.* Talks with (colloquitur). *Pag.* Beseeches (postulat). *Amb.* Pleads with God for help. *Tol.* Complains of their apostate state and seeks help. *Est.* Pleads. *Guyse*, *D. Brown.* Ἐντυγχανω, with κατα, to accuse another of a crime, as 1 Macc. viii. 32. *Whitby.* = προσερχεται. *Hesych.*—Λεγων, omitted by Codd. Vat. and Alex., though found in Cod. Sin.

---

3. *Lord, they have killed Thy prophets, and digged down Thine altars; and I am left alone, and they seek my life.*

Killed Thy prophets. At the orders of Jezebel, 1 Kings xviii. 4, 13.
People guilty of the sins of their rulers when either—
1. They lend themselves as instruments; or, 2. Consent to the deed.
Herod killed James and sought to kill Peter, because it pleased the Jews, Acts xii. 1.
Killing the prophets charged also on Jerusalem, Matt. xxiii. 37.
Digged down. Altars usually made of stone, earth, or turf.
People not only neglected God's altars, but destroyed them.
When Baal's altars are set up, God's must be pulled down.
No man can serve two opposite masters, Matt. vi. 24.
The heart opposed to God is opposed to His worship also.
Altars. Erections on which to offer sacrifices.
Sometimes also erected as memorials, Josh. xxii. 26, 27.
Most probably originally made of earth.
That built by Noah after the flood the first mentioned, Gen. viii. 20.
Yet used long before in Adam's family, Gen. iv. 3, 4.

In early times usually built on certain hallowed spots.
Patriarchs built altars where God appeared to them, Gen. xii. 7; xiii. 18, &c.
By the law of Moses, to be made of earth or unhewn stone, Exod. xx. 24, 25.
Frequently built on high places, especially by idolaters, Deut. xii. 4.
The altars in the Tabernacle, and then in the Temple, were—
1. The altar of burnt-offering, standing in the outer court.
That in the Tabernacle, made of Shittim wood overlaid with brass;
That in the Temple entirely of brass, Exod. xxvii. 1; 1 Kings viii. 64.
Both square, but that in the Temple much larger.
2. The altar of incense, standing in the Holy Place.
That in the Tabernacle also of acacia wood overlaid with gold;
That in the Temple of cedar wood, also overlaid with gold.
Size of both, two cubits in height and one in length and breadth.
Both altars had projections or "horns" at the corners.
Altars of brick used in idolatrous worship, Isa. lxv. 3.
Altars used for sacrifice before the erection of temples.
Generally built beside a tree or in a grove for shade.
Such groves sometimes planted for the purpose, Gen. xxi. 33.
Trees forbidden to be planted near the altar of the Lord, Deut. xvi. 21.
Altars privileged places or places of refuge, Exod. xxi. 14; 1 Kings i. 50; ii. 28.
Erected by patriarchs and prophets, or at God's express command.
Probably also by the Ten Tribes when cut off from the Temple-service.
These silent witnesses for Jehovah not to be endured in the land.
Alone. The only one of Jehovah's prophets or even worshippers.
Elijah saw but himself, God saw seven thousand, faithful in the land.

Θυσιαστηρια (θυσια, a victim), altars; found in high places where patriarchs had sacrificed. *Est., Par.* Built by those of the Ten Tribes not allowed to go to Jerusalem to worship. *Grot., Est.* Altars put for worship. *Par.* Altars erected by pious persons from among the Ten Tribes, as Samuel and Elijah had done. *Doddr., Guyse.* Θυσ., also used by the LXX. for הבמה, a high place, 2 Chron. xiv. 4; and for נוה, a habitation, Ps. lxxxiii. 13 —Κατεσκαψαν (κατα, down, and σκαπτω, to dig), digged up (suffoderunt). *Beza, Pisc.* Overthrown (subruerunt). *Eras.* Subverted. *Vat.* Digged up the very foundation. *Doddr., Guyse.* Dug down; overthrown by digging under them as being solid edifices. *Bloomf.* Destroyed. *Diod.* Demolished. *Mart.* Heb. רֹגְזָם. LXX. καθειλαν. The apostle uses κατεσκαψαν, from the altars being made of earth. Και before τα θυσ., not found in the oldest and best MSS. (Sin., Vat., and Alex.)—Μονος, refers to worshippers and servants. *Melv., Guyse.* To prophets. *Bloomf.*

---

4. *But what saith the answer of God unto him? I have reserved to myself seven thousand men, who have not bowed the knee to the image of Baal.*

Answer. The divine voice or audible enunciation.
He who came to Elijah is called the "Word of the Lord," 1 Kings xix. 9.
The Word of God, who afterwards became flesh, John i. 1, 14; Rev. xix. 13.
The servant intercedes *against* Israel, the Master *for* them.
Divine condescension in the answer to the prophet.
Believers' privilege to have free access to God, Eph. ii. 18; Heb. x. 19-22.

I have reserved. God's purpose and grace alone make the difference.
"Who maketh thee to differ?" admits of an easy answer, 1 Cor. iv. 7.
Men act freely, but God inclines and strengthens the will.
A faithful remnant preserved in times of greatest apostasy.
God reserves to Himself a seed—1. By preserving their life; 2. By keeping them from apostasy; 3. By raising up others in their place.

To myself. 1. As His faithful servants and true worshippers;
2. As His own children, people, and property;
3. As His instruments for His own honour and glory.
God's interest to reserve to Himself a godly remnant.
Their highest honour to be reserved to God as His own.

Seven thousand. The preserving salt at that period.
Perhaps a definite put for an indefinite number: yet—
The number of the godly is—1. Known to God; 2. Determined by Him.
Seven a symbolical number; denotes sufficiency and completeness.
A goodly number to be left in idolatrous Israel.
Women and children not generally numbered, Matt. xiv. 21.
More true believers than the godly often imagine.
The faithful often hidden to man when not to God.
Much good seed in the ground waiting time to germinate.

A comfort to faithful ministers and preachers, Isa. xlix. 4–6.
God's mercy alone makes the number what it is.
Bowed the knee. The outward sign of idolatrous worship.
Connected with another,—kissing the image, 1 Kings xix. 18 ; Hosea xiii. 2.
The one denoted subjection, the other affection.
Such willing acts forfeited the title of God's servants, Job xxxi. 26–28 ; 2 Kings v. 18.
Compliance with the forms of a false religion sinful.
Worship expressed by bodily actions and postures.
God's people distinguished not only by profession but practice.
Character and conduct the criterion of election, 2 Pet. i. 10.
Believers preserved from following an idolatrous multitude.
A separate people, 2 Cor. vi. 17. Not conformed to this world, Rom. xii. 2.
A lily among thorns, Cant. ii. 2. A people wondered at, Zech. iii. 8.
Best evidence of sincerity to swim against the stream.
Image of Baal. *Gr.*, " To Baal," viewed as female. Baal = lord.
The name by which the sun was anciently worshipped.
Sun adored by Phœnicians and others as lord of the universe.
His worship introduced into Israel by Jezebel, Ahab's queen.
Occasionally put down, 2 Kings iii. 2 ; x. 27, 28. Never entirely abolished.
Formerly practised in the British islands.
Baal also a name given to idols in general in the Old Testament.
In Israel, God himself called Baali or " my Lord," Hosea ii. 16.
To be exchanged for a more endearing one, Ishi, " my Husband."
Baal contrasted with Jehovah, 1 Kings xviii. 21.
His worship celebrated with much pomp and ceremony.
Temples erected to him, 1 Kings xvi. 32 ; 2 Kings xi. 18. His image set up, chap. x. 26.
His altars numerous, Jer. xi. 13 ; especially on lofty eminences, 1 Kings xviii. 20.
Numerous priests of Baal, 1 Kings xviii. 19, &c. ; of various classes, 2 Kings x. 19.
His worship performed with appropriate robes and postures, 2 Kings x. 22 ; Ezek. viii. 16.
Accompanied with incense, Jer. vii. 9 ; sometimes with human sacrifices, Jer. xix. 5.
The priests danced frantically round the altar, 1 Kings xviii. 26.

Wounded themselves to excite the idol's attention and compassion, ver. 28.

Χρηματισμος (χρηματίζω, used of a divine supernatural intimation, Matt. ii. 12; Acts x. 22; also of a divine revelation and admonition, Heb. xii. 25), oracle. *Eras., Cas., Pisc., Melv.* Divine answer or response. *Eras., Fag., Beza, Mor., Stuart.* The Bath Kol (בַּת קוֹל, 'daughter of the voice'); the *still small voice*, 1 Kings xix. 12. *Grot., Bloomf., Thol.* This fiction of the Rabbins, which in later Judaism was substituted for the immediate voice of God, cannot be shown to be the apostle's idea here. *Rück.* = Ὀπτασια. *Hesych.* Heb. מַשָּׂא, burden or prophecy, Prov. xxxi. 1. Answers or oracles of heathen deities usually conveyed in dark and ambiguous terms. Supposed to have been given by demons, either by the mouth of the idol or of the priest. Called by Seneca, 'communications of the will of the gods by the mouths of men;' and by Cicero, 'the speech of the gods' (Deorum oratio). Consulted by the heathen on a variety of occasions both of public and private interest. Of all the heathen oracles, that of Pythian Apollo at Delphi the most celebrated. The responses interpreted and put into verse as the priestess uttered them in the time of her *furor*. The damsel with the spirit of divination (πνευμα Πυθωνος, 'spirit of Python'), Acts xvi. 16, akin to this; Python, the name of the serpent said to have been slain by Apollo, then transferred to Apollo himself, Pythian Apollo, and applied to soothsayers held to be inspired by him. At Dodona the answer given from the hollow of an oak. At the cave of Trophonius, mentioned by Herodotus, the oracle was known from what the applicant uttered before recovering his senses. Persons consulting the oracles not allowed to enter the sanctuaries where they were given. Neither Epicureans nor Christians allowed to come near them. Oracles of very remote date among the Egyptians. The Greeks as well as some other nations indebted to them for their institution. The question and the answer sometimes written and sealed up in a secret and ceremonious manner. Consultation attended with many prescribed sacrifices, omens, auguries, and lustrations. Answers usually delusive, and capable of quite opposite interpretations. So in the reply of the pretended prophets of Ahab, 1 Kings xxii. 5, 6. Heathen oracles spoke what rulers dictated, or tended to the interests of the priests. In later times, held by the wiser heathen in contempt. According to an ancient tradition, ceased altogether at the Saviour's birth. Lucan, in the time of Nero, laments the cessation of the Delphian oracle as one of the greatest misfortunes of the age. Porphyry, an enemy of Christianity, says that since Jesus began to be worshipped, no man had received any public help or benefit from the gods.—Κατελιπον (κατα, behind, and λειπω, to leave). I have reserved or kept remaining. *Schött.* Have made to remain. *Ferme.* Heb. וְהִשְׁאַרְתִּי. LXX. reading וְהִשְׁאַרְתָּ, have καταλειψεις, 'thou shalt reserve,'—evidently not the true reading.—Ἄνδρας, men and women. *Pisc.* Men, besides women and children. *Est.*—Ἔκαμψαν, have bent. Heb. כָּרְעוּ. LXX. ὤκλασαν. Here the apostle translates for himself.—Τῇ Βααλ, before Baal. *Luth., Mart.* To the image of Baal. *Ferme, Diod.* Heb. לַבַּעַל, to Baal. LXX. τῷ Βααλ, Baal = lord, from בַּעַל, to rule or possess. Spoken of here as female. So Tobit i. 5; Hosea ii. 10; Jer. ii. 8. All the tribes sacrificed to Baal the heifer (τῇ Βααλ τῇ δαμαλει), the golden calves being identified with Baal. *Alford.* The calves appear distinct from Baal, 1 Kings xvi. 31. *Grot.* Baal, like many others, a female as well as a male deity. Selden calls the idol ἀρρηνοθηλυς, male and female. Spoken of as a female by way of contempt. So Rabbies called heathen deities אלהות, 'female gods.' *Thol.* The feminine noun εἰκονι, 'image,' understood. *Eras., Beza, Schött.* In the quoted text the Septuagint reads τῷ B., as a male deity, but elsewhere τῇ B., as female So the apostle probably read it here also. *Alf.* Baal a general name of idols; here probably Hercules or the Sun, the most ancient god of the Tyrians. *Fuller.* Same with Moloch or King, the name given by the Phœnicians to the sun whom they worshipped as a male deity, called by Plautus *Baalsamon*, 'lord of heaven.' The name probably indicated also the moon, called the 'queen of heaven,' Jer. vii. 18. This, as worshipped by Jezebel, a female deity. So Dido's favourite deity was Juno. Baal the principal deity of the Canaanites, Carthaginians, Assyrians, and Babylonians. Also called by the Phœnicians *Adoni* or lord, and by the Greeks *Adonis*. According to Josephus, Ithobal, Jezebel's father, was a priest of Astarte, the Phœnician Juno. Baalberith (Judges viii. 33) also the name of a female deity among the Phœnicians. *Bra.* The worship of Baal and Astarte, the sun and moon, as symbolical of the active and passive powers of nature, seems to have been the earliest form of idolatry, as well as the most widely diffused. Baal, Bel, or Beal, the name of the principal deity of the ancient Irish,—adduced as a proof of their Phœnician origin. Heaps of stones found on the tops of many hills in Scotland, called by the common people Bel's cairns, where it is supposed sacrifices were offered by our Pagan ancestors. Baal the deity from whom the Greeks derived their Hercules, one of his Phœnician names being Harokel (הָרֹכֵל), 'the merchant,' corrupted into Hercules (Ἡρακλῆς). Much celebrated under the name of the Tyrian Hercules. Two specimens of coins representing this deity now in the British Museum. *Bib. Cycl.* Baal the domestic and principal deity of the Phœnicians, especially of the Tyrians; also worshipped with great devotion together with Astarte by the Hebrews, especially in Samaria. Among the Babylonians the same deity called in the Aramæan manner בֵּל, Bel, for בַּעַל. Among the Tyrians his full name appears to have been מַלְקֶרֶת בַּעַל צֹר, *Malkereth* (*i.e.*, 'king of the city,' for קִרְיַת), *lord of Tyre*. The planet Jupiter, as the ruler and giver of good fortune, rather to be understood by this name. Yet בַּעַל, with certain attributes, as בַּעַל חַמָּן (the sun Baal or sun lord), to be referred to the sun. *Gesenius, Frit., Rosenm.*

---

5. *Even so then at this present time also there is a remnant according to the election of grace.*

Even so. What God did under the Old Testament He still does under the New.
The same general principles of divine procedure in both.
This present time—viz., While Israel as a nation are—
1. Rejecting the Messiah; 2. Rejected by God on that account.
The Jews now filling up the measure of their sins, 1 Thess. ii. 16.
Remnant. A portion, though small, of the Jewish people.
A saved and believing remnant. A godly seed, chap. ix. 29.
Reserved by the Lord amid the general apostasy and unbelief.
To that remnant belonged Paul and all Jewish believers.
Comparatively small, yet embracing many thousands, Acts xxi. 20.
A seed of godly men and women which never dies out.
The Christian Church the continuation of the kingdom of God.
According to. In virtue or in consequence of.
Indicates the ground on which this remnant exists.

Election. A choosing or choice made out of many.
A godly remnant exists in virtue of a divine choice.
The faithful in Israel an elect or chosen remnant.
But for such election no such remnant should exist.
Reserved by God to Himself out of the ungodly mass.
True of believers in general, Eph. i. 4; 1 Pet. i. 2; 2 Pet. i. 10.
God's saved people are brands plucked out of the fire, Zech. iii. 2.
The question in the text not of nations but individuals.
Not an election to Church privileges but personal salvation.
Grace. The character and ground of the election or choice.
Not elected on the ground of man's merit but God's grace.
God's free, sovereign, and unmerited favour.
His pure good pleasure without regard to works or worthiness.
Grace strongly contrasted with works in the following verse.
Choice of a remnant not from foreseen merit but free mercy.
None faithful but through God's free gracious election.
Not chosen because faithful, but faithful because chosen.
Chosen to salvation *through*, not *for*, sanctification, 2 Thess. ii. 13.
Elected *unto* obedience and faith, not *because* of it, 1 Pet. i. 2.
The means appointed along with the end.
Election necessarily of grace. All equally undeserving.
Election is of grace, but in wisdom and prudence, Eph. i. 8.
Resulting in the greatest glory to God himself as its end, ver. 6.
Unconditional election thus again broadly and explicitly stated.

Λειμμα (λειπω, to leave). Remains (reliquias); in comparison with the great number of the ungodly, and to show that all were in themselves alive. *Calv.* The Jews converted to Christianity, the Christian Church being the continuation of the true theocracy. *De Wette.* While even a remnant is saved, Israel is not wholly cast away. *Rück.* Heb. שְׁאָרִית, 2 Kings xix. 4.—'Εκλογην χαριτος, gratuitous election. *Ferme.* Merciful choosing. *Cobbin.* Election to Christian privileges. *Bloomf.* Sovereign choice of some among Israel to believe and be saved. *D. Brown.*

---

6. *And if by grace, then is it no more of works: otherwise grace is no more grace. But if it be of works, then is it no more grace: otherwise work is no more work.*

If by grace. If the election be according to mere favour.
No more of works. Can no more be the result of our own works.
Election through grace and as the result of works incompatible.
The same thing stated of a sinner's justification, chap. iv. 4, 5.
Not of works, neither as past nor to come, actual or foreseen.
What is given on the ground of works is not favour but reward.

Salvation must be entirely either of works or of grace.
The mixture of the two in the matter of election impossible.
Good works only the effect of election and grace, 1 Pet. i. 2 ; Eph. ii. 10.
If of works. If the election be the result of our works.
The opposite case supposed for greater confirmation.
No more of grace. The same incompatibility from the converse.
Important truths often thus insisted on, John iii. 36 ; 1 John v. 11.
Grace and works must be clearly seen to exclude each other.
Their incompatibility as grounds of election placed in a strong light.
Each must be all in the matter of salvation or nothing.
Such commingling typically forbidden under the law, Lev. xix. 19.
Otherwise. Since in such a case. The conclusion obvious.
Work is no more work—*i.e.*, By any mixture of grace in the matter.
Work mixed with grace loses its nature of work or merit.
If any merit in the matter of salvation, it can be no more of grace.
Work implies merit ; but merit and grace are contrary to each other.
The reservation of the remnant acknowledged to be of grace.
The salvation of men proceeds on the same principle in all ages.

Ἐπεί, for [then]. *D. Brown.* For otherwise: 'otherwise' only a necessary insertion. *Ellicot.*—Εἰ δὲ ἐξ ἔργων, &c. This clause not found in Codd. Sin., Alex., and several others, though extant in Cod. Vat., which, however, has χαρις, instead of ἔργον, at the end. The clause is also wanting in the Vulgate, and some other ancient versions, but found in the most ancient Peschito Syriac, and in the Arabic. It is also absent in some Greek, and most of the Latin Fathers. Rejected, therefore, by many critics. Not sufficient grounds for its exclusion. *Bloomf., D. Brown.* Some copies omit the first clause and retain the second.

---

7. What then? Israel hath not obtained that which he seeketh for ; but the election hath obtained it, and the rest were blinded.

What then ? Comes to the point he wishes to establish.
Israel. The great body of the Jews. Israel as a nation.
A prominent subject before Paul in this Epistle.
The question was—1. As to Israel's real standing and state ;
2. The consistency of that standing with God's promises.
Hath not obtained. The conclusion is against Israel's state.
They have failed in obtaining a justifying righteousness.
Little matter what a man obtains if he misses salvation.
The world a small gain set over against the soul's loss, Matt. xvi. 26.

Israel did not obtain because not seeking aright, chap. ix. 32.
Did not strive lawfully, 2 Tim. ii. 5. *So run that ye may obtain,* 1 Cor. ix. 24.
That which he seeketh for, viz., Justification before God.
Sought righteousness, and not willing to receive it. *Chrysostom.*
Cain sought acceptance with God, but not in God's way.
Good ends must be sought through lawful and appointed means.
Israel's sin that they obtained not what they sought for.
Sought it by their own works instead of by faith, chap. ix. 32.
Rejected God's counsel and followed their own, Luke vii. 30.
Preferred their own righteousness to God's.
A proud, self-righteous heart rejected God's Saviour, chap. ix. 33.
Pride clung to its rags and rejected offered robes, Matt. xxii. 11-13.
Salvation is from God, condemnation from ourselves.
The election. Put for the elect. The remnant referred to, ver. 4, 5.
The ground of difference also indicated, God's electing grace.
The doctrine rejected as unjust and unreasonable by the world.
Only its truth can account for its being in the Bible.
Yet most agreeable to the dictates of sound reason.
Punishment of sinners not an arbitrary but a righteous act.
Election of any to salvation alone from God's sovereign will.
Salvation freely offered to all, but accepted only by the elect.
Election to salvation includes its acceptance and application.
Israel as a people rejected salvation; the election accepted of it.
Their acceptance of it the *result*, not the *ground*, of their election.
Sin and unbelief are man's own; saving faith is God's gift.
Faith not refused to any who earnestly ask it from God.
Indifference and pride the great causes of men's ruin.
Blinded. Or, hardened. Given over to judicial blindness.
Left in such a condition in righteous retribution.
The state declared without indicating the agent.
The blinding not God's act but Satan's; the blame men's own.
The god of this world blinds the minds of the unbelieving, 2 Cor. iv. 4.
Blinding a natural as well as righteous effect of unbelief.
Rejection of God's Saviour brings abandonment by God's Spirit.
Blinding or hardening *from* God, yet not *by* God.
Terrible judgment on obstinate unbelief.
Insensibility to the light and love revealed in the Gospel.
The light refused and hated is righteously removed.

Solemn responsibility connected with a preached Gospel.
All God's sayings true, and meekly to be received.
The text a hard saying to the natural mind, John vi. 60.
The mark and privilege of God's children humbly to receive it.
Smites down the proud, but opens a door of hope to the humble.
Makes salvation not an uncertain but a certain thing.

Τί οὖν ; what then? Supply ἐροῦμεν ; What shall we say then? *Hyperius, Bloomf.* What then do you reply to the objection? Still the words of an objecting Jew. *Ferme.* What then, on the whole, is the true state of the case? *Guyse.* How stands the fact? *D. Brown.*—Ἐπιζητεῖ (ἐπί, intensive, and ζητέω, to seek), earnestly desire and endeavour to acquire. *Guyse.* Is in search of. *D. Brown.*—Τούτου, the accusative τοῦτο found in all the early editions, and many of the best MSS., rightly adopted by critics. *Bloomf.*—Ἐκλογή, the election ; for 'the elect'—the abstract for the concrete, as 'the circumcision' for 'the circumcised.' *Grot., Vor., Guyse.* Chosen purposely, to indicate the source and ground of the difference. *Pisc., Ferme, Beng.* So כִּבְחִירֵי עָם, 'His chosen people ; literally, 'people of His choice,' Dan. xi. 15.—Ἐπωρώθησαν (were blinded, from πῶρος, blind ; or were hardened, from πῶρος, callosity in the joints or skin). Were blinded. *Vulg., Eras.* Were hardened. *Pisc., Melv.* Πωροῦν = ὀκληρύνειν, to harden, John xii. 40 ; 2 Cor. iii. 14 ; = הכב, to make dim ; to blind. *Grot.* Have become callous ; πῶρος, a white, hard, dry substance, by which broken bones are united, which grows upon the body, contrary to nature, like hard skin, and is so hurtful to the joints or lungs, that they become unfit for their natural motion ; here indicates a hardening, which renders unfit for every motion of the life of God, and for every good work. *Ferme.* Became hardened, or hardened themselves ; passive for the reciprocal, as John xii. 40. *Bloomf.* Became blind and stupid, hardened and obstinate, with regard to Christ, and the way of salvation by Him. *Guyse.* Were hardened. *D. Brown.* Πώρωσις = ἐξ ὀστέων συμφύσις κ. σύνδεσμος ; also, ἐπὶ σαρκῶν πῶρος ἡ ἀναισθησία. *Hesych.*

---

8. (*According as it is written, God hath given them the spirit of slumber, eyes that they should not see, and ears that they should not hear*) *unto this day.*

According, &c. Their state making good the prophet's words.
Written. Two passages combined, Deut. xxix. 4, and Isa. xxix. 10. Both passages prophetic as well as declarative.
Jews' unbelief a remarkable fulfilment of their own Scriptures.
A confirmation of the truth and divinity of the Gospel.
Given. The word used by Moses ; "poured" used by Isaiah.
Put negatively by Moses, "the Lord hath not given you eyes," &c.
Positively by Isaiah, " hath poured upon you the spirit," &c.
The good Spirit righteously withheld, and the evil one let loose.
God said to give what He purposely suffers to exist, Gen. xxxi. 7.
Gives good, but righteously appoints evil also.
When God withholds good, evil takes its place.

Light and heat being withheld, darkness and cold supervene.
From him that hath not shall be taken what he hath, Matt. xxv. 29.
Gifts and privileges misimproved are righteously withdrawn.
Spirit of slumber. Deep sleep or stupefaction.
A state of mental delusion. A reprobate mind.
Want of disposition either to duty or interest.
Confirmed indifference to eternal things.
The effect—1. Of natural depravity when grace is withheld;
2. Of the operation of circumstances on the depraved heart;
3. Of the co-operating influence of wicked spirits.
The punishment of abused or rejected light.
Strong delusion sent so that men believe a lie, 2 Thess. ii. 11.
The effect of not receiving the love of the truth, ver. 10.
God may righteously choose men's delusions, Isa. lxvi. 4.
Give them up to confirmed indifference, unbelief, and sin.
Deep unconcern one of the most solemn judgments.
Eyes that they should not see. Organs and no power to use them.
Jews saw Christ's miracles, but not their meaning.
Men may see God's works, but not receive their lessons.
Intellectual vigour often combined with spiritual blindness.
Light misimproved becomes confirmed darkness.
Men close their eyes, and God righteously makes them blind.
The text illustrated by the Jews' continued unbelief.
Terrible judgment, a mind unable to discern the truth.
Unto this day. Quoted from the passage in Deut. xxix. 4.
The judgment continued to the apostle's time and our own.
The veil still on the heart of Israel, 2 Cor. iii. 14.
Jews, with few exceptions, still reject their own Messiah.
All the marks given by the prophets found in that Messiah.
His humiliation, suffering, and death the great stumbling-block.
Yet declared beforehand as necessary to a sinner's salvation.
Foreshadowed by the sacrifices of their own law.
Their cessation itself a demonstration, Ps. xl. 6-8; Jer. xxxi. 31; Dan. ix. 27.
Some rejecting Jews yet forced to believe Messiah is come.
Others driven to the figment of two Messiahs, a suffering and a reigning one.
Rejecting the true Messiah, they have followed many false ones.
Always to their own confusion and destruction.

Καθως γεγραπται. Introduces a prediction of the present blinding. *Frit.*, *Rückert.* Messianic fulfilment of what had been said by Moses and Esaias. *Meyer.* Expresses the agreement of present fact with what is written. *Von Hofm.*—Ἔδωκεν, hath given. Indicates the effectual execution of the will of God, their own abuse of the ministry of the Word intervening. *Ferme.* For their obstinacy, He has permitted them to have, &c. *Wells.* Correspondent Hebrew and Greek terms, signifying 'to give,' often used in the sense of permission. *Whitby.* Brought them into a situation in which they were incapable of perceiving. *Von Hofm.*—Πνευμα κατανυξεως (from κατανυω, Gr. *Schol.*; νυω, νευω (Latin, nuto), to nod or sleep. *Pisc.*; the word only in the LXX. In this sense; elsewhere, = pain, compunction, from κατανυσσω, 'to prick,' as Acts ii. 37. Compare Dan. x. 9. Κατανενυγμενοις, 'in a deep sleep.' *Theodotion's Translation*). Spirit of compunction. *Vulg.*, *Eras.*, *Mor.* Spiritum transpunctionis. *Cyp.* As penetrating the whole man. *Vor.* As exasperating them, *i.e.*, against the Gospel. *Vat.* Spirit of hallucination or infatuation. *Dick.*, *Syr.* Of insensibility (torpentem). *Cast.*, *Arab.* Such a disturbance of mind as makes a man mad or stupid. *Mint.* Spirit of sleep or slumber (soporis). *Pisc.*, *Beza*, *Pag.*, *Cap.*, *Ham.* Of deep sleep, as of night. (νυξ) ; profound lethargy, through evil spirits. *Ferme.* Of obstinacy; fixed as by a nail. *Chrys.*, *Theod.* A spirit that pricks or incites to evil as a goad. *Anselm.* Blindness, from the eyes being picked out as with a needle. *Men.* A sleepy spirit. *Beng.* Κατανυξις, with Greek authors, = violent pain: the meaning of sleep perhaps from νυω, νυξω, to nod with the head, or because violent pain causes stupefaction. *Flatt.* A stupid and obdurate temper, with carnal security. *Guyse.* A state of mind stupid and destitute of all sense of good and evil. *Bloomf.* Spirit of intoxication or torpor. *De Wette.* Of insensibility. *Gossner.* Of deep sleep or stupefaction; a state of delusion. *Brown.* Of stupor. *Ellicot*, *D. Brown.* Exact idea uncertain. *Rück.* Κατανν. = λυπη, ησυχια. *Hesych.* Here, not from κατανυσσω, 'to prick,' but from κατανυω, or, as with the LXX., κατανυσσω, 'to nod or slumber,' = κατανυσταξω; as in Sir. xxi. 21, 'on his bed he will not slumber,' κατανυγησεται. The LXX. renders such Hebrew words as הַרְדֵּמָה, דּוּם, הֵרָדֵם, signifying slumber, by κατανυσσω and κατανυξις, as in Ps. lx. 3. Οἶνον κατανυξεως, rendered by Jerome 'vinum consopiens,' but by the Vulg. 'vinum compunctionis,' as in the text. *Grot.* Heb. רוּחַ תַּרְדֵּמָה.—Ἑως τ. σημερον ημερας, 'unto this day.' Separated from the quotation, and connected with επωρωθησαν, 'were blinded.' *Beza*, *Grot.*, *Ferme*, *Wolf.*, *Griesb.*, *Knapp*, *Diod.*, *Mart.* Form part of the quotation. *Carpzov.*, *Rück.* To show that the Jews had always the same vicious disposition. *Mackn.* The apostle intimates that their obduracy had continued to the present time. *Bloomf.* This present day. *D. Brown.*

---

9. *And David saith, Let their table be made a snare, and a trap, and a stumbling-block, and a recompense unto them.*

David. Speaking both as a prophet and a type of Messiah.
Saith, in Ps. lxix. 22, 23. The psalm prophetical of Christ, as to—
1. His sufferings from the Jews, His enemies and persecutors;
2. The judgments that should overtake them as such;
3. His exaltation and the success of His Gospel.
Also quoted and applied to Jesus, chap. xv. 3; John ii. 17; xix. 28, 29.
Applied to Judas, who betrayed Him, Acts i. 20.

CHAP. XI.] ST. PAUL'S EPISTLE TO THE ROMANS. 113

Similar denunciations to be similarly interpreted.
Not the utterances of personal or vindictive feeling ; but—
The denunciations and predictions of God's Spirit.
Table. What would otherwise have been for their good.
1. Daily and common mercies ; 2. Spiritual privileges.
That at which people sit at ease and enjoy God's gifts.
Sin brings a curse which converts food into poison, Mal. ii. 2.
Their table. A believer's table is prepared for him by *God*, Ps. xxiii. 5 ;
The table of the unbeliever is regarded by him as his own.
Snare. Cause of unexpected destruction.
Metaphor from birds falling into a snare or wild beasts into a trap.
Their very mercies an occasion—1. Of sin ; 2. Of misery.
To the godly, a token and means of blessing ; to the impenitent, a snare.
Sin multiplied and aggravated by the abuse of daily mercies.
To faith, the means of grace are salvation ; to unbelief, a snare.
Table a snare when the Gospel proves a savour of death to death.
The Gospel-table spread first for the Jews, "their table," Matt. xxii. 2, &c.
The preaching of forgiveness to begin at Jerusalem, Luke xxiv. 47.
Christ sent first to the lost sheep of the house of Israel, Matt. xv. 24-27.
Rejection of the Saviour the cause of all their miseries.
The Gospel a richly furnished table ; unbelief makes it a deadly snare.
Trap. *Gr.*, A capture. Animals caught in it and destroyed.
The sinner caught in Satan's trap when he rejects the Saviour.
Gradation,—a snare for the foot, a trap for the whole body.
The Old Testament falsely interpreted, confirms the Jews in unbelief ;
The New Testament disbelieved, becomes the occasion of deeper sin.
In opposing the Gospel, the Jews filled up their sins, 1 Thess. ii. 16.
In this sin, the wrath of God came on them to the uttermost.
Their passover-table made providentially their trap.
Multitudes thus unexpectedly caught in the siege and perished.
Stumbling-block. That which trips up and causes to fall.
Especially that which causes to fall into a pit or snare.
The Gospel, when believed, raises men to heaven ;
Rejected, it trips them into the bottomless pit.
Christ for the fall and rising again of many in Israel, Luke ii. 34.

A foundation to some; a stone of stumbling to others, chap. ix. 32, 33.

Recompense. Terrible consequences of a rejected Christ. The Jews judged out of their own mouth, Matt. xxi. 41. The rejected stone grinds its opposers to powder, ver. 44. "His blood be on us and on our children" awfully verified, Matt. xxvii. 25. Has been on them for 1800 years in terrible retribution. Crucifying their Messiah, they were crucified themselves. 500 crucified daily during the siege of Jerusalem. No more room found for crosses or crosses for the bodies.

Δαβιδ λεγει. Another passage referring to the blinding and hardening of Israel. *Baumg.-Cr.*, *Meyer*, *Phil.* Applicable first to David's own enemies, then by accommodation, as here, to the Jews as the persecutors of Christ. *Bloomf.* In such a Messianic psalm, the passage meant of the rejectors of Christ. *D. Brown.*—Τραπεζα, table,— that which serves for nourishment; here, the sacrifices and all the service of the law; the ministry of the Word. *Ferme.* The law which was Israel's food. *Phil.* Their own table, or food. *Bloomf.* Enjoyment of secure life. *Barth.* All they enjoy. *De Wette*, *Rück.* Privileges and advantages. *Brown.* Their very blessings. *D. Brown.*—Εἰς παγιδα (from πηγνυμι, to fix, a snare being fixed in the ground). For a snare; the law made a snare and death as leading them to reject the Gospel. *Ferme.* For destruction unexpectedly. *Schött.* Caught while securely at their food. *Beng.* Cause of their destruction. *Barth.* Occasion of their delusion and punishment. *Brown.*—Εἰς θηραν (θηρ, a wild beast, θηραω, to hunt). Capture (captionem). *Eras.*, *Mor.* Cause of tripping (offendiculum). *Beza.* Trap (decipulum). *Cast.* That which men hunt, *Pisc.* Prey taken by hunting (venationem). *Drus.* Taken by Satan and devoured by him. *Vat.* Let their food be hurtful to them. *Schött.* Θηρα, a net or snare to catch animals. *Flatt.* Εἰς θηρ., neither found in the Septuagint nor in the Hebrew; exegetical of εἰς παγιδα. *Bloomf.* The Septuagint rendering of רֶשֶׁת, 'a net,' in Ps. xxxv. 8.— —Εἰς σκανδαλον (σκαζω, to halt; σκανδαλον, what is placed in the way of another causing him to stumble; that part of a trap which, when struck, causes the animal to fall). Stumbling-block. = ἐμποδισμος. *Hesych.* Heb. לְמוֹקֵשׁ. Used elsewhere by the LXX. for כָּשׁוֹל. Παγ., θηρ., σκαν., snare, net, pitfall; kindred ideas. *Rück.* All signify here the cause or occasion of calamity and destruction. *Flatt.*—Εἰς ἀνταποδομα (ἀντι, ἀπο, and διδωμι). Retribution. *Pisc.*, *Drus.* And that for their recompense. *Mart.* And for a punishment. *Van Ess.* The just recompense of their sin in perverting the sacrifices and services of the law to another end than that intended by God. *Ferme.* The LXX. has εἰς ἀνταποδοσιν κ. εἰς σκανδαλον; the apostle, the more suitable form ἀνταποδομα, and suitably places it at the end. *Von Hofm.* In the Heb. 'a snare *to the secure*' (from שָׁלוֹם, peace); the LXX. and Paul appear to have read לְשִׁלּוּמִים (from שָׁלֵם, to recompense). *Thol.*, *Rück.*

---

10. *Let their eyes be darkened, that they may not see, and bow down their back alway.*

Darkened. The penalty and effect of rejecting the light, John iii. 19, 20.

Satan the agent in blinding the minds of unbelievers, 2 Cor. iv. 4.
Not see. 1. The glory of redemption in the cross of Christ;
2. The evident proofs of Jesus being the Messiah;
3. The means of advancing their own best interests;
4. Their duty both to God and to themselves.
Jewish blindness only to be explained as a divine judgment.
Infatuation marked their conduct in the war. So Josephus.
Absurdities of the Talmud accepted and believed in.
Synagogue-worship little else than a childish formalism.
Starvation preferred to eating food not Rabbinically prepared.
Bow down their back. Indicates bondage, feebleness, misery.
A humbled, weakened, and servile condition, Deut. xxviii. 65–67.
Contrasted with a state of liberty and enlargement, Lev. xxvi. 13.
As if doomed to be ridden and trampled on by the nations.
   Lisco.
Sordid, grovelling disposition. Affections bound to the earth.
Especially bent on the acquisition of worldly gain.
Bowed down as with anguish of spirit and bodily pain.
Pressed under the yoke of the law and human traditions.
Sinking beneath the burden of the wrath of God, 1 Thess. ii. 16.
Hebrew, " Make their loins to shake " as in great distress.
Active, as indicating God's righteous hand in their misery.
The effect of apprehension and alarm, Nahum ii. 10; Dan. v. 6;
Or of carrying heavy burdens under the yoke of oppression.
True picture of the state of Israel for eighteen centuries.
Visible in almost every land, especially in their own.
Have appeared everywhere a people doomed to contempt.
" Tribes of the wandering foot and weary breast."
Foretold by Moses as the penalty of disobedience, Deut. xxviii.
   20, &c.
Yet Israel free from image-worship for more than 2000 years.
Their sin the rejection of the Messiah, God's incarnate Son.
Rejecting grace and its blessings, they have clung to the law and its
   curses.
To fall from God is to fall into bondage and misery.
A rejected Saviour followed only by ruin here or hereafter.
Alway. Till God in mercy take the veil from their heart.
Divine curses long in coming and long in departing.
The present acknowledged to be Israel's great captivity.
Israel to be abandoned for " many days," Hosea iii. 4.
Afterwards to return and seek the Lord, and David their king.

The veil to be taken away, 2 Cor. iii. 16. All Israel to be saved, ver. 26.
Their final conversion treated in the following verses.

Σκοτισθητωσαν (σκοτος, darkness), be darkened ; so as to fall like blind persons into the evils prepared for them. *Bloomf.* Not to see the way of escape from deserved wrath and ruin. *Guyse.*—Νωτον, back ; symbol of strength. *Par.* Heb. חֲלָצַיִם, 'loins:' three parts in the back,—shoulders, spine, and loins. *Aristotle.*—Συγκαμψον (συν, together, καμπτω, to bend), bow down or together ; break their strength, that they may no more hurt. *Par.* Render their state miserable. *Schött.* Under the weight of God's anger. *Ferme.* Under a weight of sorrows. *Doddr.* As with anguish of spirit and bodily pain. *Stuart.* A picture of bondage, infirmity, and ruin. *Phil.* Bending misery. *De Wette.* Terror and bondage under the law. *Thol.* Lameness of loins preventing them from walking. *Von Hofm.* Decrepitude or a servile condition. *D. Brown.* A mind poring on earthly things. *Guyse.* 'O curvæ in terras animæ, celestium inanes.' Heb. הַמְעַד, 'cause to shake.'

---

11. *I say then, Have they stumbled that they should fall? God forbid: but rather through their fall salvation is come unto the Gentiles, for to provoke them to jealousy.*

I say then. Speaks in his own person or that of an objector.
Stumbled. At the Messiah in rejecting Him.
What the prophet predicted and the apostle declared, chap. ix. 32, 33.
That. 1. The object of their being thus left to stumble.
The object viewed in relation to God, not themselves.
2. The actual issue and result of their stumbling.
Is their final fall to be the result of their unbelief?
Fall. 1. Perish and be miserable here and hereafter.
Have they stumbled so as to be left in their fall?
Fall entirely and irrevocably as a people.
2. Fall into their present state of unbelief and apostasy.
God has wise reasons for leaving men to reject His Son.
Will overrule even their unbelief for His own glory.
God forbid. God has had other views in permitting this.
Israel's fall not the final end of their stumbling.
Their rejection of Christ to be followed with other results.
For themselves, their fall neither total nor irrevocable.
Others shall be graciously affected and themselves finally saved.
But rather. The object and result of this still mournful fact.
Through their fall. 1. Their sin ; 2. Their state in consequence.
Unbelief the great sin. Its consequence, misery and ruin.
Israel's fall their ceasing for a time to be God's people.

Salvation. Deliverance from a state of sin and condemnation.
Is come. 1. In the offer; 2. In the actual experience.
Gentiles. The nations of the world hitherto in darkness.
The salvation of the Gentiles the first object in view.
The refusal of some brought others to the feast, Matt. xxii. 4–10.
Exemplified in the apostle's own ministry, Acts xiii. 46.
Gentiles thus received the Gospel—1. Earlier; 2. More readily.
Antipathy between Jews and Gentiles no longer a hindrance.
Christianity not to wear a Jewish dress or Jewish bonds.
The Gospel rejected by one people to be carried to another.
The fall of some overruled for the salvation of others.
The glory of God to convert an evil into a blessing.
Nothing so bad but God overrules it for good.
To provoke. To awaken, stir up. The second object in view.
Jealousy. Emulation; sense of loss with concern to recover it.
Israel's feeling on seeing the Gentiles occupy their place.
Commendable emulation in the matter of salvation.
Gospel blessings not diminished by the number of partakers.
Christianity to be made the object of Jewish desire.
Christian inconsistency a barrier to Jewish conversion.
Gentiles' conversion designed to bring about Israel's restoration.
Condition of believing Gentiles to be contrasted with their own.

'Επταισαν (from πετω or πιπτω, to fall), stumbled (offenderunt). *Vulg.* Fallen (lapsi sunt). *Eras., Vat.* Πταιω = נגף, to stumble, fall down; πιπτω = נפל, to fall so as to lie in the fall, Rev. xviii. 2. *Grot.* Πταιω, properly to be tripped or totter with the feet. *Beng.* Rendered 'offend,' James ii. 10; iii. 2; 'fall,' 2 Pet. i. 10. Stumbled against Christ. *Ferme.* At Christ. *Guyse.* In rejecting the Messiah. *Brown.*—Πεσωσι, might fall (laberentur). *Pisc.* Fall off (exciderent). *Beza.* Fall entirely (conciderent). *Eras., Vat., Est.* Remain in their fall. *Grot., Ham.* Fall away from God. *Ferme.* Fall from their ancient privileges totally and irrecoverably. *Guyse, Beng., Doddr., Wells.* Remain fallen. *Stuart.* Perish or become miserable; their rejection neither total nor final. *Hodge.* Is their fall the object and end of their stumbling, viewed on God's side? *De Wette.* Only that they should fall; as if only to their punishment. *Thol.*—Παραπτωματι (παρα and πιπτω), through their offence (delicto). *Vulg.* Offensam. *Pag., Beza.* Fall (lapsum). *Est., Tol.* Stumbling against Christ. *Ferme.* Trespass, sin. *Flatt, Ellicot.* Ruin, decay. *Bengel.* Error, false step. *De Wette.* Misery. *Rück.*—Σωτηρια, knowledge and means of salvation. *Mackn.*—Παραζηλωσαι, provoke to emulate the faith and obedience of the Gentiles. *Wells.* Provoke to jealousy and emulation, and so to a desire of regaining their ancient state of favour with God. *Young, Bloomf.*

---

12. *Now if the fall of them be the riches of the world, and the diminishing of them be the riches of the Gentiles, how much more their fulness?*

Fall. Sin in rejecting Christ, with its consequences.

Their offence which brought temporary loss of God's favour.
Riches of the world. Occasion of rich and numerous blessings to it.
The happiness and salvation of the Gentile nations.
The Gospel alone the source of true riches.
Brings the unsearchable riches of Christ, Eph. iii. 8.
Makes men rich in faith and heirs of a kingdom, James ii. 5.
Rich even amid tribulation and poverty, Rev. ii. 9.
With Christ, all things are ours, 1 Cor. iii. 21–23 ; Rev. xxi. 7.
Grace and salvation the only true riches, Rev. iii. 18 ; Luke xvi. 11.
The world rich through the Gospel and believers in it.
Diminishing. Degraded, fallen condition as a people.
Israel's name *Lo-ammi*, "no longer my people," Hosea i. 9.
Nations and individuals are as they receive or reject Christ.
A small number of poor Jews brought the world its riches.
Riches of the Gentiles. The enriching of the nations.
The Gentiles enriched through Israel's impoverishment.
Kingdom of heaven taken from them and given to us, Matt. xxi. 43.
Persecuted disciples went everywhere preaching the Word.
Esau despised his birthright, and the blessing became Jacob's.
How much more. Greater riches in reserve for the world—
1. A more extensive ingathering of the Gentiles ;
2. Greater enlargement of spiritual knowledge, Isa. xxx. 26 ;
3. Large increase of joy and spiritual blessing, Acts iii. 19.
Converted Israel the world's best missionaries, Isa. lxvi. 18–20 ; Ps. lxvii. 1, &c.
Christ's coming connected with Israel's conversion, Matt. xxiii. 39.
Nations called to rejoice in Israel's restoration, Deut. xxxii. 43.
Fulness. 1. Restoration, with possession of promised blessings.
2. Conversion of the whole nation to the faith of Christ.
The more abundant the seed, the greater the increase.
So great blessing through the few, what through the many ?

Παραπτωμα, trespass, false step. *De Wette, D. Brown.* Rejection of the Gospel *Ferme.* Apostasy and ceasing to be God's peculiar people. *Guyse.*—Ηττημα (ἧττον, less), diminution. *Vulg., Eras., Pag., Mor., Beza, Diod., Mart.* Poverty (inopia). *Cast.* Want. *Syr.* Condemnation. *Arab.* Small number. *Tir.* Fewness of believing Jews. *Chrys., Beza, Par., Grot., Vor., Tol., Beng., Ols., De Wette, D. Brown.* Loss, damage. *Or., Ambr., Luth., Glöck., Meyer.* Rejection of the Gospel. *Ferme.* Ruin, decay. *Flatt.* Diminution by scattering the preachers. *Doddr.* Fault in losing their privileges and defect of believers among them. *Guyse.* Degradation and punishment. *Stuart.* Impoverishment, loss of advantages. *Calv., Hodge.* Temporary fall. *Hald.* Disadvantage, decay, loss *Rück.* Loss to the kingdom of God. *Phil.* Lessened and degraded condition. *Brown, Thol.* Lessening of their gain. *Con & Hows.* Worsening, worse condition. *Wetst., Carpzov., Koppe, Schleusner, Bloomf., De Wette* Disgrace. *Alford.* Diminution, defeat, discomfiture; from ἡττάομαι, used by LXX. for חתת, 'be broken in pieces,' Isa. viii. 9: here, the conversion of the few. *Schött.* Fault, as 1 Cor. vi. 7, the only other place in the New Testament where it occurs: the verb rendered 'be inferior,' 2 Cor. xii. 13; 'be overcome,' 2 Pet. ii. 19, 20: εἰς ἥττημα, used by LXX. for לְמַס, 'for tribute,' E. V., 'be discomfited,' Isa. xxxi. 8, *marg*, 'for melting:' the idea, defeat with loss of numbers and broken strength. *Lange.* State in which they come behind what they were to be. *Von Hofm.*—Πόσῳ μᾶλλον, how much more; arguing from the less to the greater, common with Jewish doctors, and called the 'light and heavy.' So chap. v. 10, 15 : 2 Cor. iii. 7–11.—Πλήρωμα, full number (plena copia). *Cast.* Full restoration or recovery. *Par.* Good estate, perfection. *Vat.* Multitude. *Grot.* The mass. *Theod., Beza.* Abundance. *Mart.* Conversion of the whole nation. *Chrys., Schött., Guyse.* Admission into the Church to fill up the vacancy caused by the unbelief of so many. *Ham., Henry.* Whole body of the nation, both as preachers and living witnesses of the truth of revelation. *Doddr.* The remaining part that shall fill up the number of the whole people. *Storr.* Large numbers. *Beng.* Whole number. *Ols., Glöck., De Wette.* State of completion. *Meyer.* Restoration to favour. *Hald., De Wette.* Full reception. *Stuart.* Restoration to the state in which they can again fulfil their destiny. *Rück., Köllner.* Restored and justified state. *Thol.* Fulness of blessing. *Brown.* State in which they are full and complete. *Von Hofm.* Full recovery. *D. Brown.* Heb. כִּלְאָה, כִּלְאת.

---

13. *For I speak to you Gentiles (inasmuch as I am the apostle of the Gentiles, I magnify mine office).*

You Gentiles. Church at Rome composed of Jews and Gentiles.
The bearing of the subject upon the Gentiles exhibited.
Apostle of the Gentiles. Designed especially for them, Acts ix. 15.
Gospel of the uncircumcision committed to Paul, Gal. ii. 7.
God's love to the Gentiles in giving them such a labourer.
Special qualifications given with special work.
Each to attend especially to the work assigned to him.
His own work assigned to every one by the Master, Mark xiii. 34.
Magnify. Glory in ; exalt by word and deed.
Nothing omitted which might ennoble his office.
The glory of that office to bring as many as possible to Christ.
Especially to preach Christ far and wide among the Gentiles.
The office of the ministry is one to be magnified.
Contemptible in the eyes of the world, glorious in God's.
Assumed and discharged by the Lord of glory Himself.
Office. To preach Christ's unsearchable riches to the Gentiles, Eph. iii. 8.
To convert the heathen to Christ, and through them the Jews.

Paul in love not with the dignity, but the duty of the office.
The office itself, not the status or emoluments of it.
Discharged the office and wrought as a tentmaker.
Treated on account of it as the offscouring of all things, 1 Cor. iv. 9, &c.
Saving souls the noblest office a creature can be invested with.

Γαρ. Codd. Sin., Vat., and Alex. have δε, 'now.'—'Εφ' όσον, begins a parenthesis ending with δοξαζω. So Peschito Syriac version.—Μεν. Codd. Sin., Vat., and Alex. add οὖν, 'therefore.'—'Υμιν—ἔθνεσι. The epistle addressed to Gentile believers. *D. Brown.*—Δοξαζω (δοξα), I will honour my office. *Vulg.* Will praise. *Luth.* Render honourable. *Mart.* I honour. *Diod.* Render illustrious (illustro). *Beza, Pisc.* By words and miracles. *Est.* Glorify. *Eras., Vat., Ellicot.* By spreading the Gospel far and wide. *Gom.* By bringing as many as possible of the Gentiles to Christ. *Or., Theod., Beza, Pisc., Calv., Par., Koppe, Thol., Rück., De Wette, Meyer.* By saying that many are converted by it to Christ, in order to stir up the Jews to emulation. *Grot.* In asserting that the Jews have stumbled for the salvation of the Gentiles, in order that they may be moved to emulation and return to God. *Ferme.* I omit nothing that may ennoble it. *Beng.* Exalt it, hold it in high estimation. *Benecke, Glöckler, Reiche, Baumg.-Cr.* Glory in the fruits of my office among the Gentiles; labour to make it fruitful; think highly of it. *Flatt.* Bestow all my labour on this my office. *Koppe.* Assert its dignity. *D. Brown.* By making his countrymen jealous of the salvation enjoyed by the Gentiles whom he had converted, and so saving some of them. *Von Hofm.*

---

14. *If by any means I may provoke to emulation them which are my flesh, and may save some of them.*

By any means. All lawful means to be used for saving souls.
Provoke to emulation. Awaken to a just and jealous concern.
Emulation in the matter of salvation desirable.
Many ways in stirring up sinners to seek Christ.
Wisdom required in winning souls, Prov. xi. 30.
Fervent love and earnest desire is fertile in expedients.
Holy ingenuity to be exercised in saving souls.
Conversion of the Gentiles a means to that of the Jews.
The former prosecuted by Paul with a view to the latter.
The Gentile Church never to forget the salvation of Israel.
Flesh. Kindred; countrymen; the Jewish people.
Salvation of kin and country to be earnestly sought after.
Save some. The election or remnant to be gathered in.
The body of the people blinded but a remnant to be saved.
Not to be saved without the use of appropriate means.
Preachers well rewarded if only some hearers are saved.

CHAP. XI.]   ST. PAUL'S EPISTLE TO THE ROMANS.   121

Εἰ πως, to try if. *Ferme, Diod, Koppe.* To see if. *Mart.* Equivalent to ἵνα εἰ δυνατον, that if possible. *Koppe, Bloomf.*—Παραζηλωσω, may be able to provoke to emulation. *Ferme.* May possibly excite to emulation. *Koppe.* Awaken zeal to obtain the like blessings. *Cobbin.*—Σαρκα, countrymen. *Bloomf.* Kinsmen. *Ferme.*—Σωσω, may put into the way of salvation. *Pisc., Vor.* Recover from impenitence and unbelief. *Guyse.*

---

15. *For if the casting away of them be the reconciling of the world, what shall the receiving of them be, but life from the dead?*

Casting away. Rejection, loss; suffered from unbelief.
Terrible word for a Jew. Rejection from being God's people.
The fearful consequence of impenitence and unbelief, Luke ix. 25.
Reconciling. Actual reconciliation; occasion of it.
Men reconciled to God only through the Gospel.
Reconciled through Christ whom the Gospel reveals.
Christ our peace. Peace made through the blood of His cross.
Nations without Christ still without God, Eph. ii. 12.
The world reconciled through the Gospel rejected by the Jews.
Receiving. Restoration to former state of favour.
Equivalent to the "fulness" mentioned in ver. 12.
Their casting away not final and irrecoverable.
God's gracious purposes in regard to Israel thus indicated.
Their recovery and restoration predicted, Isa. xi. 11-16.
Their reception more blessed to the world than their rejection.
A soul saved is a lost one received back to God, Luke xv. 27.
Life from the dead. Spiritual quickening to the world.
Life of grace to the unsaved, and of glory to the saved.
Israel's repentance followed by times of refreshing, Acts iii. 19.
Joy in Pharaoh's house when Joseph's brethren came to him, Gen. xlv. 16.
Israel's conversion bound up with Christ's appearing, Acts iii. 19-21.
The beginning of the last act in the world's great drama.
The termination of the groans of creation, chap. viii. 19-22.
The following events apparently connected with each other:—
1. Outpouring of the Spirit on the Jewish people, Zech. xii. 10;
2. Their repentance, faith, and restoration, ver. 26; Zech. xii. 10; xiii. 1;
3. Christ's glorious return from heaven, Acts i. 11; iii. 20;
4. Resurrection of the just, or first resurrection, 1 Cor. xv. 23;
5. Deliverance of a suffering creation, chap. viii. 19-22;
6. Destruction of Antichrist and his followers, 2 Thess. ii. 8;

7. Universal establishment of Christ's kingdom, Rev. xi. 15;
8. Judging of the quick and dead by Christ, 2 Tim. iv. 1;
9. Binding of Satan for a thousand years, Rev. xx. 1;
10. General conflagration of the earth, 2 Pet. iii. 12;
11. Renovation of the heavens and the earth, 2 Pet. iii. 13.
Israel's evangelisation the first object of Christian policy.

'Αποβολη (άπο and βαλλω, to cast; άποβαλλομαι, to suffer loss through one's own fault. *Beng.*), abjection or rejection. *Beza, Pisc.* Loss. *Vat.* Loss suffered through unbelief. *Beng.*—Καταλλαγη, reconciliation. *Beza, Pisc.* Occasion of the Gospel being preached to them. *Guyse.* Occasion and means of their being reconciled. *Bloomf.*—Προσληψις (προς and λαμβανω, to receive), full assumption. *Vor.* Restoration into the divine family. *Vat.* Final acceptance. *De Wette.* Recall. *Hald.*—Ζωη εκ νεκρων, a life from among the dead. *Mart.* To receive life from the dead. *Luth.* Spiritual quickening to the rest of the world. *Aug., Ans., Pisc., Beng., Guyse.* Justification of the world. *Est.* New life in a higher fulness of spiritual gifts. *Flatt, Rosenm.* An entirely new, mighty quickening or revival of God's kingdom on earth. *Barth.* General conversion of the Gentiles. *Wells.* Revival among the Gentile churches from a dead and almost lifeless state. *Hald.* An illustrious change in the face of the whole Church. *Guyse.* Change in the dominant mode of thinking and feeling on all spiritual subjects. *D. Brown.* An event in the highest degree beneficial to the Gentile world. *Hodge.* A spiritual revival resembling a resurrection, as Ezek. xxxvii. 1-14. *Brown.* Rich fructifying of the Gentile Church. *Thol.* The dead the Jewish people, the life that which shall be communicated to them from the Gentile world. *Calv.* Restoration of the Jews from unbelief and Satan's power; compared to a resurrection, like their return from Babylon, Ezek. xxxvii. 1. *Ferme.* General conversion of them to Christianity. Something great, wonderful, surprising; as it were a general resurrection. *Stuart.* Resurrection-life experienced by Israel. *Krehl.* Matter of the greatest joy. *Ambr., Grot., Vat., Koppe, Bloomf.* Especially as attended with the general conversion of the Gentiles. *Wells.* Resurrection of the body. *Or., Chrys., Theod., Tol.* Final perfection of believers; resurrection in the proper sense. *De Wette, Nielson.* A further blessed state of the reconciled world, possibly implying the glories of the final resurrection. *Alford.* Deliverance of the body from death in the resurrection of a reconciled world; such a gradation to its reconciliation as corresponds to the contrast in άποβολη (casting away), and προσληψις (receiving). *Von Hofm.* A spiritual resurrection which connects itself with the physical one. *Olshausen.* Israel's restoration thought of in connection with the end and the Lord's appearing; the time of transition to a higher and glorious state bound up with the final resurrection. *Rückert.* With the apostle, the ideas of a spiritual and corporeal resurrection not far apart. *Lange.*

---

16. *For if the first-fruit be holy, the lump is also holy: and if the root be holy, so are the branches.*

For. Further shows that Israel is not finally and for ever cast away.

First-fruit. First of the dough to be offered to the Lord, Num. xv. 19, &c.

Here, the patriarchs, and especially Abraham himself.
Holy. Consecrated to God, as 1 Cor. vii. 14; Jer. ii. 3; Isa. xxiii. 18; Zech. xiv. 20, 21.
Also, taken and employed by God for special purposes, Isa. xiii. 3.
The patriarchs and their seed taken by God to be His people.
A certain holiness in such adoption and consecration.
Requiring and furthering, but not necessitating, personal holiness.
Lump. Dough or mass from which the first-fruit is taken.
So the first-fruits offered to the Lord sanctified the whole harvest.
Here, the whole Jewish nation or seed of the patriarchs.
Also holy. Sanctified, and therefore fit for use, 1 Tim. iv. 5.
Jews share in the consecration and adoption of Abraham.
Israel thus considered a people holy to the Lord.
Set apart by solemn covenant for His service, Deut. vii. 6.
Holiness of consecration the point of comparison.
Jewish nation sanctified in Abraham the first-fruit.
Thus the children of believing parents holy, 1 Cor. vii. 14.
Also, an unbelieving wife sanctified in a believing husband.
Israel's restoration thus made reasonable and probable.
Root. The patriarchs, especially Abraham, like " first-fruits."
The root—1. Naturally; 2. Federally, in the covenant.
Patriarchs the root of Israel as a people holy to the Lord.
Israel compared to a green olive tree, Jer. xi. 16.
Branches. Descendants of the patriarchs; individual Israelites.
The nation physically and federally from a holy root.
Branches consecrated to God when the root was so.
The tree receives its character from the root.
The derived partakes of the nature of the original.
Israel's physical union with Abraham inalienable.
Out of a noble root may again come forth noble branches.
Blessing of pious ancestors not entirely lost on their seed.
Rank and privileges propagated, if not personal qualities.
A free and wise father has a free, if not a wise, son.
Abraham a holy root to Israel externally and typically;
Christ a holy root to believers spiritually and really.
Believers justified, adopted, sanctified, and glorified in Him, 1 Cor. i. 30.

Δε, furthermore. *Bloomf.* But. *D. Brown.*—Ἀπαρχη, from ἀπο and ἀρχη, the beginning. Bread of the first-fruits. *Luth* Corn for the two loaves of the new meat-offering. *Eras., Koppe, Küllner, Ols.* Either the sheaf of new corn waved before the Lord as the first-fruits of harvest, or the first-fruits after the seven weeks of harvest,

Lev. xxiii. 9-22. *Ferme.* First-fruit of the dough. *Beza, Grot., Guyse, Thol., De Wette, Meyer, Con. & Hows., D. Brown.* Cake of the first dough. *Hald., Bloomf.* First of the dough of the first-fruits. *Rück.* First-fruit of harvest, sheaf of first-fruits (Lev. xxiii. 10), which, when wrought, gives the dough. *Von Hofm.* Here, Abraham. *Chrys., Melv., Guyse, Meyer, Alf., Niel., Von Hofm.* Patriarchs or first-fathers. *Ferme, Beng., Whitby, Stuart.* Christ as to His human nature. *Or., Theod., Glöck.* First Christians sanctified to God out of the mass of Judaism. *Ambr., Ans., Carpzov., Schött, Flatt, De Wette, Chalm., Bloomf.*—Ἅγια, separated from the nations and consecrated to God as His people. *Ferme, Stuart.* Relatively holy as appropriated to God. *Locke.* Consecrated and acceptable to God. *Beng.* Holy, not morally but in destination. *Heubner.* The election morally holy also, and afterwards the whole. *Haldane.* Applied to the Jews in anticipation and hope, as Christian children in baptism, 1 Cor. vii. 14. *De Wette.* Hallowed. *Con. & Hows.*—Φυραμα (from φυραω, to knead or mix), the mass. *Pisc., Beza, Melv., Ferme.* Whole congeries. *Zeg.* Mass of dough. *Guyse.* Dough. *Bloomf.* The LXX. renders עֲרִיסֹתֵיכֶם רֵאשִׁית, 'the first-fruit of your dough' (Num. xv. 20, 21) by ἀπαρχη φυραματος; here, the Jews. *Melv.* Whole body of Abraham's descendants. *Guyse.* Majority of that people. *Ferme.* Whole nation. *Rück., Alford.* The rest of the Jews who, like the first-fruits, embrace Christianity. *Flatt.* The remaining mass who may also be received into the Church of Christ. *Carpzov., Schött.*—Ῥίζα, Abraham. *Melv., Mackn.* The first-fathers. *Ferme, Doddr., Stuart, Niel., Von Hofm.* Same with the first-fruits. *Grot., Gom., Vor., Flatt, Alf.* Root—1. Naturally; 2. In relation to circumcision and the promises. *Beng.* Christ. *Or., Glöck.* Mother Church of believing Jews. *Corn. a Lap., Schött., Carpz., Reiche, Rück.* The ideal theocracy founded in, and represented by, the patriarchs, but not identical with them. Cf. Isa. xi. 1-10; Rev. v. 5; xxii. 16. *De Wette, Lange.* Metaphor transferred from Isa. xi. 1; Jesse, the 'root,' Christ, the 'branch,' 'scion,' or 'sprout' (Zech. iii. 8). *Ferme.*—Κλάδος, the Jews. *Melv.* The Jewish nation. *Vor., Gom., Grot., Alf.* Descendants of the patriarchs to the latest posterity. *Ferme, Stuart.* Of Abraham. *Guyse.* The patriarchs themselves. *Or.*

---

17. *And if some of the branches be broken off, and thou, being a wild olive-tree, wert graffed in among them, and with them partakest of the root and fatness of the olive-tree.*

Some of the branches. Individuals of the Jewish nation. "Some," not as in chap. iii. 3; but with the view of checking Gentile pride.

Broken off. As unfruitful and useless branches.
Removed from their place in God's visible Church.
Cut off through unbelief from the blessing of Abraham.
God's sovereign justice shown in unbelieving Israel.
So sinning angels cut off, though without hope of recovery.

Wild olive-tree. A tree said to have various species.
Its branches graffed into the olive said to promote its fruitfulness.
Jews the olive-tree (Jer. xi. 16); Gentiles a wild olive.
Mighty difference made by the adoption of Abraham's seed.
Jews enjoyed—1. A covenant relation to God;
2. A revelation of His will and other means of grace.
An olive-tree supposed to be under cultivation.

Men's natural condition since the fall that of a wild olive.
Graffed in. A contrary process to what is usual.
Ordinarily a good branch is grafted into a worse tree.
Men graft to improve the tree, God to improve the branch.
In baptism men are grafted into the Church;
In regeneration they are grafted into Christ.
Among them. The remaining branches; the elect remnant.
The New Testament Church composed originally of believing Jews.
That Church only the continuation of the Old.
The same good olive-tree receiving Gentile grafts.
With them. Sharing with them, but not to their exclusion.
Fellow-citizens with the saints of the Old and New Testaments, Eph. ii. 19.
Members of the household of God with patriarchs and prophets.
Fellow-heirs and partakers of the same promise, Eph. iii. 6.
A favourite theme and object of the apostle, chap. xv. 10.
Partakest. Obtainest a share in the blessings.
Root. The covenant as made with Abraham.
Abraham the father and head of the visible family of faith.
Christ the root of all spiritual communication;
Abraham the root of visible Church organisation.
The covenant orginating a visible Church first made with him.
The Jews connected with the root by natural birth;
The Gentiles by faith in Christ and by baptism.
Fatness. Blessing connected with the visible covenant.
Church privileges and benefits in the right use of them.
In the New Testament Church the same grace as in the Old.
The difference, a larger measure in the former, John vii. 37.
Spiritual blessings only in connection with Christ and His Church.
Olive-tree. A tree most frequently mentioned in Scripture.
Very abundant in countries round the Mediterranean.
Among the most characteristic vegetation of Judæa.
Of moderate height; often two or three stems from the root.
A knotty gnarled trunk with smooth, gray bark.
Its appearance indicative of tenacious vigour.
Leaves oblong, green above and whitish below.
Not deciduous; the tree therefore ever fresh and green.
Grows slowly, but lives to an immense age.
Flourishes 200 years before it begins to decay.
Young trees spring up around it to take its place.
Thrives best in warm and sunny situations.

Almost every village in Palestine has its olive-grove.
Its cultivation closely connected with Jewish domestic life.
Its foliage mentioned in connection with the flood.
Selected therefore as the representative of peace.
Emblem of prosperity and the divine blessing, Ps. lii. 8; cxxviii. 3.
Symbol of beauty, luxuriance, and strength, Hosea xiv. 6.
Its oil used in consecrating priests, prophets, and kings.
Mixed with the offerings in sacrifice, Lev. ii. 1, 2, 6, 15.
Used on the hair and skin, indicative of cheerfulness, Ps. xxiii. 5; civ. 15.
Employed medicinally and in surgical cases, Luke x. 34.
Used in connection with prayer for the sick, James v. 14.
Olive-tree a symbol of God's faithful witnesses, Zech. iv. 3; Rev. xi. 3.
Symbol of the Church as the channel of grace to men.
Chosen—1. From the holy anointing oil produced by it, Exod. xxv. 6; 2. From its beauty, Hosea xiv. 6; 3. From its constant greenness, Ps. lii. 8; 4. From its fruitfulness; 5. Its usefulness; 6. Its long duration.
The Church of God the reservoir of divine influences.
Christ's kingdom in which He dispenses purchased gifts.
Not appointed by the Mosaic but the Abrahamic covenant.

Εἰ δέ, but if. *Ferme, D. Brown.*—Τινες, some; softening the apostasy of the Jews as a check to the triumphing of the Gentiles over them. *Ferme.* Main body of the natural seed. *Guyse.*—Ἐξεκλάσθησαν (ἐκ and κλάω, to break), were broken off or cut. *Beza, Pisc.* 'Summas defringi ex arbore plantas.' *Virg.*—Ἀγριέλαιος (ἄγριος, wild, from ἄγρος, a field or open country; and ἐλαία, an olive-tree). Supply κλάδος; a wild olive-branch. *Bloomf.* Wild olives unfruitful; hence the proverb, 'More fruitless than a wild olive.' *Schött.* Columella states that the ancients grafted not on the wild, but the cultivated olive, the graft causing the decaying tree to revive and flourish, a fact substantiated by modern travellers. *Stuart.* The wild olive (oleaster, = עֵץ שֶׁמֶן), used for grafting into barren olive-trees to promote their fruitfulness; two species in Palestine: one (Elæagnus Orientalis) chiefly distinguished for its straight, sharp thorns scattered over its branches. *Jahn.*—Ἐνεκεντρίσθης (ἐν and κέντρον, a prick, used for piercing the tree in grafting; *lit.*, to prick in), was inserted or grafted (insertus). *Vulg., Mor.* Wast grafted (insitus). *Eras.* Grafted with its buds,—believers with their children. *Guyse.*—Ἐν αὐτοῖς, among them (in illis). *Vulg., Mor., Bloomf.* Into them (in eos). *Cast.* Instead of them (pro illis). *Fag., Beza, Pisc.* Along with them. *Beza.* Along with the branches left, the believing remnant. *D. Brown.*—Συγκοινωνὸς (σύν, and κοινός, common; a partaker in common with others), partner (socius). *Vulg.* Partaker (particeps). *Pisc.* Heb. חָבֵר. *Grot.*—Ῥίζης, of the same dignity, excellence, and nature. *Chrys.*—Πιότητος (πίων, fat), fatness; faith and evangelical grace of the patriarchs. *Vat., Tol.* Promises made to Abraham. *Grot.* Advantages of those Jews who belong to the people of God. *Flatt.* Ῥίζης, = fellowship with the Church; πιοτ.;

CHAP. XI.]   ST. PAUL'S EPISTLE TO THE ROMANS.   127

blessings bound up with it. *De Wette.* Rich grace secured by covenant to the true seed of Abraham. *D. Brown.* 'Ρίζης κ. πιοτ., a hendiadys for 'fatness of the root;' promises to Abraham and the privileges of God's Church. *Bloomf.*—'Ελαιας, olive-tree ; the Church of God appointed by the Abrahamic covenant, promising salvation by a Redeemer, and justification by faith. *Grot., Whitby.* Visible Church. *Guyse.* True theocracy, which began with the believing Jews. *De Wette.*

---

18. *Boast not against the branches : but if thou boast, thou bearest not the root, but the root thee.*

Boast not. Glory not with supercilious contempt.
Gentile Christians probably already began to show—
1. An overbearing disposition towards the Jews ;
2. A feeling of complacency in themselves.
Such a spirit soon and long manifested by Gentile churches.
In Rome the Jews still obliged to live by themselves, A.D. 1870.
Faith excludes boasting—1. Of ourselves ; 2. Over others.
Charity vaunteth not itself ; is not puffed up, 1 Cor. xiii. 4.
Bearest not the root. The Church not sprung from Gentiles.
Jews owe nothing to the Gentiles ; Gentiles owe all to the Jews.
Salvation is of the Jews, John iv. 22. Christ himself a Jew.
Jewish Church the foundation ; Gentiles built upon it, Eph. ii. 20.
The root thee. Gentiles grafted in upon the Jewish Church.
Jews the first people of God and first Christians.
Gentiles have received all through and from the Jews.
Salvation experienced in fellowship with Jewish patriarchs.
Church only revived and extended by admission of Gentiles.
The true Christian and Jewish Church but one.
Abraham originally bore the Jews and now the Gentiles too.
The root belongs not to the Gentiles but to the Jews.
Hope of salvation transferred from the Jews to the Gentiles, not *vice versâ*.

Κατακαυχω (κατα, against, and καυχαομαι, to boast or glory ; from καυχην, the neck, to toss the neck like a spirited horse,—the gesture of persons insulting over others). *Vor., Pisc.* Glory. *Beza, Pisc.* Despise. *Grot.* Boast against and despise. *Bloomf.* In the clause εἰ δε κατακ., supply γνωθι or ἰσθι ὁτι, 'know that.' *Koppe.* Remember that. *D. Brown.*

19, 20. *Thou wilt say then, The branches were broken off, that I might be graffed in. Well : because of unbelief they were broken off, and thou standest by faith. Be not highminded, but fear.*

Thou. The Gentile Christian or Church still addressed.
Wilt say then. In objection to this, and as a plea for boasting.

Broken off. In the wise ordination and righteous judgment of God.
The thing spoken of as already an accomplished fact.
That I, &c. Indicating not only the result but the intention.
As if the Gentiles stood higher in God's esteem than the Jews.
Graffed in. And so occupy the place of the natural branches.
The unfaithful sometimes removed to make way for others.
Well. An apparent admission of the objection stated.
The fact admitted without implying Gentile merit.
God in sovereignty puts down one and sets up another, Ps. lxxv. 7.
Unbelief. The bane of churches, nations, and individuals.
Believers only kept through faith unto salvation, 1 Pet. i. 5.
Standest. As a branch in a tree; in union with the Church.
Hast obtained and still retainest thy present place.
A fact stated, but involving a principle.
By faith. Uniting us to Christ and so to His Church.
Faith possessed unites us to Christ; faith professed, to the Church.
Profession often made and retained without possession.
The result is a name to live while really dead, Rev. iii. 1.
Be not high-minded. A standing caution to the Church.
High-mindedness the fall both of angels and men.
Inconsistent with genuine faith, Hab. ii. 4.
Danger of its entrance among the disciples, Matt. xx. 20-28.
Early appearance of it in the Church. Diotrephes, 3 John 9.
Characteristic of the Church and Bishops of Rome.
Rome calls herself the mother and mistress of all churches.
Its bishops began to usurp authority over other churches in 203.
Lay claim to infallibility. The dogma proclaimed, July 1870.
Supremacy claimed over princes. Title, "Our Lord God the Pope."
Grace given not to make men proud but thankful.
Man's real dignity consists in humility, faith, and love, Matt. xx. 28.
Fear. 1. God's displeasure; 2. A fall from your estate.
Before honour goeth humility, a haughty spirit before a fall.
Fear not opposed to humble confidence but to proud security.
The evils that befall others should be warnings to ourselves.
God's dealings fitted not to excite pride but induce caution.
Fear a means towards believers' preservation, Phil. ii. 12; 1 Cor. ix. 27.

Careful fear to be cherished, slavish fear to be cast out, 1 John iv. 18.
Confidence in Christ consistent with fear over ourselves.

Οἱ κλάδοι, the branches; but Codd. Sin., Vat., and Alex. read κλάδοι, without the article.—Καλῶς, well; be it so. *D. Brown.* Granting it to be so; as Mark xii. 32; Luke xx. 39; John iv. 17. *Bloomf.* A *concessio rhetorica*; seeming to grant something, but carrying with it the assertion of something *farther*, here introduced by δέ. *Hyperius.*—Πίστει, faith in Christ credibly professed. *Guyse.* Faith alone. *Bloomf.* Not as a Gentile, but solely by faith. *D. Brown.* Faith by which Christ and the blessing of Abraham in Him are apprehended. *Ferme.*—Ἕστηκας, have been brought into the privileges of the Jews and have hitherto stood in the possession of them. *Guyse.* Continuest in the divine favour into which thou hast been admitted. *Bloomf.*—Ὑψηλοφρονει (ὑψηλός, high, and φρήν, the mind), be [not] high-minded; implies presumptuous glorying of the Gentiles against the Jews. *Ferme.* Conceit of your own worthiness, contempt of others, and self-confidence of your ability to persevere. *Guyse.* At μή ὑψηλοφ., the force of the admonition much increased by the *Asyndeton. Bloomf.*—Φοβοῦ, fear; the fear of children; lest by sinful glorying they should be deprived of God's presence and favour. *Ferme.* Fear of sinning and falling also by unbelief. *Guyse.* Of being rejected for a similar cause. *Bloomf.*

---

21. *For if God spared not the natural branches, take heed lest He also spare not thee.*

Spared not. Cutting them off and shutting them up in unbelief.
The greatest punishment to be bereft of God's Spirit, Ps. li. 11.
Israel made like the barren fig-tree, cursed, Matt. xxi. 19.
Kingdom of heaven taken from them and given to others, Matt. xxi. 43.
Similar threatening to Gentile churches, Rev. ii. 5, 23.
Natural branches. The Jews descended from Abraham's loins.
Jews as such interested in the Abrahamic covenant.
Children of the covenant, Acts iii. 25; of the kingdom, Matt. viii. 12.
Take heed. Watchfulness to be joined with humility, 2 Pet. iii. 17.
Heedfulness necessary in every condition on earth.
Spare not thee. God the same in the Old and New Testaments.
The Seven Churches of Asia impressive examples.
The apostasy and mystery of iniquity indicated, 2 Thess. ii. 3.
Rome the Church that has fallen farthest from the truth.
Yet "boasts" of her preservation and unchangeableness.
Gentiles not more likely to be spared than the Jews.

Κατα φυσιν [branches], 'according to nature;' naturally descended from Abraham. *Bloomf.*—Οὐκ ἐφείσατο, spared not; indicates righteous severity. *Melv.*—Μη πως, lest by any means: supply 'you have reason to fear.' *Guyse.* Ὁρα, 'see,' or the like. *Bloomf.*—Φεισηται. Codd. Sin. and Alex. read φεισεται. The indicative instead of subjunctive, as sounding more positively and perhaps prophetically. *Beng.*

---

22. *Behold therefore the goodness and severity of God: on them which fell, severity; but towards thee, goodness, if thou continue in His goodness; otherwise thou also shalt be cut off.*

Goodness. Kindness, showing itself in bestowing benefits.
The attribute which constitutes God's chief glory, Exod. xxxiii. 18, 19.
Exercised according to His own wise and sovereign will, chap. ix. 15.
Shown peculiarly in the first instance to Israel, Ps. cxlvii. 19, 20.
Abused by them through impenitence and hardness of heart, chap. ii. 4, 5.
Designed to lead to repentance, love, and obedience, chap. ii. 4.
Severity. Treatment of sinners according to justice.
Either no favour shown or shown no longer.
Sometimes shown in words, Titus i. 13; here in acts. So 2 Cor. xiii. 10.
Gr., " A cutting off;" the severity threatened, Matt. xxi. 43.
Metaphor from the amputation of a diseased limb.
Severity as well as goodness in a holy God.
Viewed as the opposite side of the divine government.
Severity necessary as a guard to goodness.
Goodness abused will be followed by righteous severity.
Long usage and faithful ancestry give no immunity.
God's goodness and severity both to be remembered;
The latter to keep from presumption, the former from despair.
Fell. Through unbelief and rejection of God's Messiah.
Severity after much goodness exercised on the Jews.
Threatened by God through Moses, Deut. xxviii. 15–68.
First exercised in the withdrawment of the Spirit.
Afterwards in the calamities which overtook them.
Those calamities recorded by Josephus, one of themselves.
Jews cruelly oppressed by Gessius Florus, the Roman governor.
Impelled to take up arms in the twelfth year of Nero.
Jerusalem besieged by the Romans under Titus, A.D. 70.
Fearful sufferings during the siege from famine.

Mary, a woman of position, killed her son for food, Deut. xxviii. 52–57.
Five hundred crucified daily during the siege.
The crucified mocked by the Roman soldiers, Matt. xxvii. 25, 39.
Temple set on fire by a soldier against the orders of Titus.
The very day that of its former destruction by Nebuchadnezzar.
The whole city overthrown except three towers and part of west wall.
The rest levelled with the ground, leaving no trace of a city.
Its conquest ascribed by Titus to God's special co-operation.
The whole land destroyed. Country completely changed.
Eleven hundred thousand perished during the siege.
Ninety-seven thousand were made captives.
Captives sold for a trifle from want of purchasers, Deut. xxviii. 68.
God's righteous retribution acknowledged by the historian.
Jews' blindness in the war viewed as inflicted for their sins.

On thee goodness. In transferring to them the kingdom of God.

God's greatest goodness to a people seen in giving them the Gospel.
The Gentiles made possessors of Israel's privileges.
Nations thus exalted and millions made happy.
No room for pride, but much for gratitude and humility.

If thou continue—*i.e.*, By faith, humility, and obedience.
We continue in God's goodness as we continue in faith.
Being in Christ's love we are to abide in it, John xv. 5-7.
Abiding in Christ the evidence of belonging to Him, Heb. iii. 6.
Churches and nations not guaranteed their privileges.

Thou also shalt be cut off. As unfruitful branches, John xv. 6.
Jews "broken off," as with the hand, at once, ver. 20;
Gentiles "cut off," as with the knife, more deliberately.
Most of the Eastern Churches already cut off.
Have long presented a mass of spiritual death.
In some places almost rooted out by Mohammedans.
Their churches overthrown or converted into mosques.
The cities themselves often a heap of ruins.
Ephesus sunk in the overthrow of the Greek Empire.
Its candlestick removed from its place, Rev. ii. 5.
Hardly a Christian left in its representative, Aiasaluk.
Corn everywhere growing among its forsaken ruins.
Sardis (now Sart) chiefly peopled by Turkish shepherds.
The city now represented by about fifty mud huts.
Laodicea mostly tenanted by wolves and jackals.

A solitude affording an occasional encampment for Turcomans.
Justification by faith formally renounced by the Church of Rome.

Χρηστοτητα, benignity. *Pag., Mor., Beza, Cas., Pisc.* Indulgence. *Jer., Eras.* Effects of His gratuitous favour which He bestows on His people. *Ferme.*—Ἀποτομιαν (ἀπο and τεμνω, to cut ; met. from amputating a limb or pruning a tree), severity. *Eras., Pisc., Pag., Mor., Cas.* Strict severity (præcisam severitatem). *Beza.* Resectionem. *Eras.* Strictness (præcisionem). *Pag., Vor.* Just judgment against the unyielding. *Ferme.* In rejecting the chosen seed. *D. Brown.* 'In God's right arm is life and goodness ; in His left, death and severity.' *Zohar.*—Χρηστοτητα. Codd. Sin., Vat., and Alex. have χρηστοτης Θεου. In admitting thee to a covenant standing. *D. Brown.*—Ἐπιμεινῃς τῃ χρηστ., remain in that state in which thou wast placed by God's goodness, viz., through faith in Christ ; retain the goodness by continuing to endeavour to be worthy of it. *Bloomf.* Stand fast in Christ by keeping the faith. *Ferme.* In believing dependence on that goodness which made thee what thou art. *D. Brown.*

---

23. *And they also, if they abide not still in unbelief, shall be graffed in: for God is able to graff them in again.*

Unbelief. The sin that caused their excision, ver. 20.
Israel as a nation still in unbelief after eighteen centuries.
Given up to unbelief in order to a restoration by faith.
Graffed in. Like branches from the wild olive-tree.
Israel to be re-introduced into the kingdom of God.
The children of the kingdom for a time cast out, Matt. viii. 12.
God is able. The engrafting of Jew or Gentile the work of God.
Faith, the means of the engrafting, is God's gift, Eph. ii. 8.
God's omnipotence required in any sinner's conversion.
No room for despair since the Almighty is the agent.
No abyss out of which Omnipotence cannot raise us.
Resurrection-power to be put forth in Israel's behalf, Ezek. xxxvii. 1, &c.
The same power put forth in believers generally, Eph. i. 19.
Appeal to the *power* of God implies the difficulty of the case.
Realised by all who labour for Israel's conversion.
Individuals always graffed in, the *nation* yet to be so.
The *supposition* turned into an explicit prediction, Ver. 26.
God's power to restore exercised only in connection with faith.
No restoration to a covenant state while still in unbelief.
God's ability to restore Israel implies His willingness.
As easy to restore them as to adopt them at the first.

Δυνατος, able ; refers not to individual conversions, but to national restoration. *Ferme, Guyse, D. Brown.* The Jews' reception into the communion of saints. *Melv.* Has the adjunct of *willing. Ferme, Rosenm., Koppe.* The will included. *Calv., Ham., Whitby.*

---

24. *For if thou wert cut out of the olive-tree, which is wild by nature, and wert graffed contrary to nature into a good olive-tree; how much more shall these, which be the natural branches, be graffed into their own olive-tree?*

Wild by nature. Nations before Christ without spiritual culture.
A revelation and divine ordinances with the Spirit confined to Israel.
All nations suffered to walk in their own way, Acts xiv. 16.
The times of that ignorance winked at by God, Acts xvii. 30.
Gentiles lived without hope and without God in the world, Eph. ii. 12.
Spiritual culture now confined to the Gospel, John xv. 1.
Contrary to nature. As in the case of a graft.
Grafting from a different kind of tree not natural.
Gentiles Christianised against their national nature.
Their whole national life pervaded with idolatry.
Notions and practices all opposed to the divine life.
Contrary to every man's natural bent to be a Christian.
This contrariety increased by continuance in sin.
Good olive-tree. Visible Church with all its blessings.
Place in Christ's Church an inestimable privilege.
Yet not sufficient of itself to secure salvation.
Outward union with the Church brings privilege, not pardon.
The only tree in which salvation is certain is the true Vine, John xv. 1.
How much more. More easy, natural, and probable.
Much more to be overcome among heathens in order to faith.
Jews acknowledge one God and the authority of the Scriptures.
Have a divine code of morals, though overlaid with traditions.
Accustomed also to the notion and hope of a Messiah.
The natural perversity of the heart alone to be overcome.
Natural branches. Seed of Abraham after the flesh.
Children of the prophets and of the covenant, Acts iii. 25.
Their continuance among the nations a phenomenon.
Kept in God's providence for the fulfilment of His purposes.
Own olive-tree. Church originally set up in Abraham's family.
Church of the Old and New Testament, one and the same.
In conversion Jews are graffed into their own tree.

Gentiles only foreign branches graffed in among them.
Dogs permitted to partake of the children's bread, Matt. xv. 26.

Παρα φυσιν, contrary to the nature of thy origin. *Estius, and the Fathers*. Contrary to the nature of a graft to bear a different kind of fruit from its own. *Beng*. As in the case of a graft, contrary to thy national nature. *De Wette*. Engrafting itself, as an artificial process, opposed to nature. *Nielson*.—Καλλιελαιον (καλος, good, and ἐλαια, an olive-tree), corresponds to ἀγριελαιος. The word found also in Aristotle. *Schleusner*. —Ποσῳ μαλλον, more probable. *Mackn*. More easy and natural. *Barth*. God much more able to engraft the Jews themselves into their own root. *Ferme*.

---

25. *For I would not, brethren, that ye should be ignorant of this mystery (lest ye should be wise in your own conceits), that blindness in part is happened to Israel, until the fulness of the Gentiles be come in.*

Brethren. Addressed to the Gentile portion of the Church.
Ignorant. Christians to be an enlightened people, Col. i. 9.
Ignorance the mother, not of devotion, but of superstition.
Mystery. 1. What has before been but very partially revealed;
2. What but for revelation could not have been known.
God's Word full of mysteries, though now well known—
1. Incarnation of the Word, "the mystery of godliness," 1 Tim. iii. 16 ;
2. Calling of the Gentiles to fellowship with the Jews, Eph. iii. 3 ; Col. i. 26 ;
3. Spiritual union between Christ and His Church, Eph. v. 32 ;
4. Resurrection of the body and rapture of the saints, 1 Cor. xv. 51 ;
5. Doctrines and truths of Christianity in general, chap. xvi. 25 ; 1 Cor. ii. 7 ; iv. 1.

Some mysteries essential to salvation, others only useful.
First the calling of the Gentiles a mystery, now the restoring of the Jews.
Truths taught by progressive development, John xvi. 4, 12, 25 ; Heb. v. 11–14.
"Brethren" bespeaks affection ; "mystery" awakens attention.
Israel's restoration possible, ver. 23 ; probable, ver. 24 ; certain, ver. 25, 26.

Wise in your own conceits. Think too highly of yourselves.
Form an undue estimate of your own importance.
Gentile Churches in danger of being puffed up with pride.
This mystery revealed to check high-mindedness.

Some kinds of knowledge may puff up, 1 Cor. viii. 1 ; others keep humble.
The need of this caution verified in the Church of Rome.
Ignorance the mother of pride and presumption.
Blindness. Incapacity to perceive the truth. Also hardness.
The state into which Israel has been judicially delivered, ver. 7.
Terrible consequence of obstinate unbelief.
In part. 1. Only a part of the nation blinded, though a great one ; 2. The blindness only for a limited period.
A softening expression in regard to Jewish unbelief.
Same expression in chap. xv. 15, "in some sort" or measure.
Is happened. Has come upon, or become the state of, Israel, ver. 7.
Until. Indicates the period of Israel's blindness.
The period of Gentile conversion that of Jewish unbelief.
Gentile evangelisation necessary to Israel's conversion.
Fulness of the Gentiles. 1. Abundance of the Gentile nations : 2. Totality of the elect from among the Gentiles ; 3. The fulness of the times of the Gentiles, Luke xxi. 24.
Nations apparently spoken of rather than individuals.
Gospel to be preached to all nations before the end, Matt. xxiv. 14.
A multitude to be gathered out of every nation, Rev. vii. 9.
The children of God scattered abroad to be collected, John xi. 52.
A people to be taken out from the Gentiles for His name, Acts xv. 14.
The other sheep not of the Jewish fold to be brought in, John x. 16.
A Gentile election to be gathered before the Jews' restoration.
Gap in the Church made by Israel's unbelief to be filled up.
Come in. To the kingdom of God, or fellowship of the Church.
The effect of the preaching of the Gospel to the world, chap. x. 17.
Coming in of the Gentiles not necessarily the world's conversion.
Gospel to be preached to all nations *for a witness;* then the end.
Israel's conversion bound up with the Lord's appearing, Acts iii. 19.

Μυστηριον (from μυω, to imitate), something not hitherto, or only very partially, revealed. *Bloomf.*, *D. Brown.* What before its revelation could not be arrived at by human calculation. *Thol.* With Paul a truth unknown, hitherto concealed from men, and undiscoverable without higher help, but made known, through the divine Spirit, in those whom God employs as prophets or apostles. *Rück.* Here, the conversion of the Jews. *Beng.* That hardening has happened to Israel in part and for a time. *Ferme.*— Παρ' ἑαυτοις φρονιμοι, from Prov. iii. 7. Puffed up, as if alone chosen. *Bloomf.* On account of your knowledge of Christ. *Fer.*—Πωρωσις (either from πωρος, blind, or πωρος, a hard substance), hardening. *Ferme.* Hardness. *Ellicot, D. Brown.* Blindness and obdurate unbelief. *Bloomf.* Excision. *Melv.*—'Ἀπο μερους, a softening expression. *Flatt.* Not in the whole, but only in part. *Chrys., Ferme, Guyse, D. Brown.* In some degree. *Calv., Frit.* Only for a definite time and in a part. *Barth.* Total and complete where it existed, but only in a part, though the greatest. *Flatt, Rück., Hald.* —Πληρωμα τ. ἐθνων, fulness of the nations. *Vulg.* The whole number of the Gentiles who should be converted. *Aug., Theoph., Ferme, Ernesti, Chal.* A great multitude, spreading themselves beyond their own territories. *Schött.* The full number. *Stolz, Van Ess, Knapp.* The appointed harvest of the many converted in the latter age of the world. *Whitby, Doddr.* General conversion of the Gentiles through all the nations of the world. *Guyse.* A definite number. *Flatt.* Great multitude. *Stuart, De Wette.* Totality, filling up of their number. *Meyer, De Wette.* The mass. *Thol.* Great bulk. *Bloomf.* Organic virtual totality of the heathen world. *Lange.* The completing of the Israel of God by believing Gentiles. *Ols , Wolf.* Supplement of, or equivalent for, the unbelieving Jews. *Olearius, Phil.* Multitude appointed by God out of all nations. *Barth.* Fulness of Gentile nations. *Brown.* Times of the Gentiles. *Chal.* Till the Gentiles have had their *full* time of the visible Church all to themselves. *D. Brown.* = Πληθος. *Hesych.* Heb., קְהַל לֹא, Gen. xlviii. 19, applied to Ephraim.—Εἰσελθῃ, be, or have, come in ; have drawn near. *Ferme.* Be converted. *Wells.* Have possession of the true religion. *Locke.* Be called and put into a state of salvation. *Whitby.* Shall have the means of salvation bestowed on them. *Mackn.*

---

26. *And so all Israel shall be saved : as it is written, There shall come out of Sion the Deliverer, and shall turn away ungodliness from Jacob.*

And so. In this way ; when this takes place with the Gentiles.
All Israel. The whole body of the Jewish people.
Only a remnant *now* saved, hereafter the whole.
Saved. Veil of unbelief to be taken from their heart, 2 Cor. iii. 16.
Spirit of grace and supplication to be poured on them, Zech. xii. 10.
Shall mourn on account of Him whom they have pierced, ver. 10–14.
Shall acknowledge the Crucified as their Messiah, Matt. xxiii. 39.
Be washed in the fountain opened for sin and uncleanness, Zech. xiii. 1.
Have the stony heart taken away and a heart of flesh given them, Ezek. xxxvi. 26.
Be cleansed from all their idols and from all their filthiness, ver. 25.
Shall experience a spiritual resurrection, Ezek. xxxvii. 1, &c.
Be placed again in their own land under Christ, ver. 21, 24, 25.
Only, however, after multitudes of them have perished, Zech. xiii. 9 ; xiv. 1, &c.
Written. Two passages combined in one, Ps. xiv. 7 ; Isa. lix. 20.

Israel's restoration distinctly foretold in the Scriptures.
Their predicted dispersion fulfilled; so their predicted restoration.
Come. In person, Matt. xxiii. 39; Acts iii. 19, 21; 2 Tim. iv. 1; Rev. i. 7.
In the power and grace of His Spirit, Zech. xii. 10; Ezek. xxxvi. 25-27; xxxvii. 9, 10.
In flaming fire, executing vengeance, 2 Thess. ii. 8; Isa. lxvi. 15, 16; lix. 17, 18.
Out of Sion. So Ps. xiv. 7. Sion the Redeemer's special abode. See chap. ix. 33.
Symbol of the Church, Ps. cxxxii. 13; and of heaven, Heb. xii. 22; Rev. xiv. 1.
From Zion and Jerusalem went forth the Gospel, Isa. ii. 3; Luke xxiv. 47-49.
From Zion the Lord will set up His kingdom on earth, Isa. lx. 2.
Heb., "To Zion," Isa. lix. 21. Comes to Zion and then goes forth out of it.
Zion the head-quarters of Israel's Redeemer and King.
To Zion and from it, different but contiguous parts of one process.
Zion first partakes of the blessing; other places afterwards.
Deliverer. *Heb.*, "Redeemer;" kinsman to the redeemed.
The same name given to Job's Redeemer, Job xix. 25.
Came first to redeem by price with His own blood, Rev. v. 9;
Comes afterwards to redeem by power with His Spirit, Isa. lix. 19.
His first coming in meekness, His second in majesty.
A Deliverer from sin and from all sin's consequences.
The Deliverer equally needed by Jews and Gentiles.
Shall turn away ungodliness, &c. *Heb.*, "To them that turn," &c.
Their turning from ungodliness the effect of His turning them, Jer. xxxi. 18.
Christ blesses Israel by turning them from their iniquities, Acts iii. 26.
Comes to Zion to them that turn, then goes forth to turn others.
To turn from ungodliness His errand into the world, Matt. i. 21.
Ungodliness the enemy of all true happiness.
No true deliverance till delivered from ungodliness.
Ungodliness deeply rooted in the nature of Jew and Gentile.
No deliverance from it but by an Almighty Deliverer.
None but the God-man able to deliver Israel and the world.
The penitent alone made partakers of Christ's kingdom.

Impenitent rejectors of the Gospel destroyed by His coming, 2 Thess. i. 8.

Jacob. The people of Israel. A national conversion promised.

Οὕτω, so; when this shall take place; = τότε. *Bloomf.* After the same manner, or by a similar general conversion. *Guyse.*—Πᾶς Ἰσραηλ, all Israel, in opposition to the 'part;' or the remnant; Israel as a nation. *Thol., Meyer, De Wette, Phil., Alf., Hodge, D. Brown.* The bulk of the nation, not each individual. *Aug., Greg. Naz., Beza, Par., Melv., Ferme, Henry, Guyse, Spener, Thol.* The whole without exception. *Or., Chrys., Hil., Ambr., Phil., Meyer, Reiche.* No warrant to make any limitation. *Haldane.* Without mathematical strictness, yet without contemplating any exception. *De Wette.* All, though only a remnant in respect to those who shall have perished. *Beng.* The spiritual Israel, embracing Jews and Gentiles. *Melanch., Bugenhagius, Oliander. Calv.*—Σωθήσεται, shall be saved eternally. *Commentators in general.* Shall be converted and received into the kingdom of God. *Theoph., Œcum.* Converted and saved from their dispersion and misery. *Doddr.* An election of Israel in the millennium as the most distinguished citizens of the New Jerusalem. *Beng.* Be put in the way of salvation, have the means of salvation bestowed upon them. *Bloomf.* Saved at the time of Christ's second advent. *Chrys.* When Elijah comes and brings to them the doctrine of faith before the second advent. *Theod.* Paul viewed the conversion of the heathen and of Israel as taking place shortly before the Lord's second coming. *De Wette.* The Reformers (Luth., Melv., Calv.), and the older Lutheran expositors, opposed to the idea of a future conversion of Israel as a body, as well as that of an earthly kingdom of Christ; Melanchthon, however, inclined to recognise it. *De Wette.*—Καθὼς γέγραπται, Ps. xiv. and Isa. lix. formerly quoted (chap. iii.) to show Israel's sinfulness, now quoted to show his salvation. *Beng.*—Ἥξει ἐκ Σιὼν ὁ ῥυόμενος. Instead of ἐκ, the LXX. reads ἕνεκα; ἐκ having perhaps crept in as an abbreviation from ἕνεκα. *Beza, Est., Koppe.* Probably taken from Ps. xiv. which the apostle now had in mind. *Vitringa, Bloomf.* The alterations in the passage intentional. *Reiche.* Denied by *Meyer and Rückert.* Paul gives the general sense while the particular costume of the passage is disregarded. *Stuart.* May have given the sense of prophecy rather than the wording of any particular passage; and may have in ἐκ Σιὼν summed up the prophecies which declare that the Redeemer should spring out of Israel. *Alford.* The apostle usually embraces in thought the Messianic prophecies, and treats single cited passages more as a substratum or point of union for the free presentation of the idea. *Phil.* Paul by inspiration supplements the sense from Ps. xiv. 7; Christ was and is to come *to Zion,* first with redemption, being sprung as man out of Zion. *Fausset.* All the glorious manifestations of Israel's God regarded as issuing out of Zion (Ps. xx. 2; cx. 2; Isa. xxxi. 9); the turn given to the words by the apostle merely adds the familiar idea. *D. Brown.* Heb. לְצִיּוֹן, to or for Zion; for Zion's welfare. *Beng.* Ὁ ῥυόμ., that Deliverer (Liberator). *Pag., Pisc., Vat., Eras., Mor.* Redeemer (Redemptor). *Drus.* Avenger (Vindex). *Beza.* Redeemer or Avenger as near kinsman. *Schött.*—Καὶ ἀποστρέψει. Codd. Sin., Vat., and Alex. omit καὶ. Shall turn away (avertet). *Beza, Pisc.* Heb. לְשָׁבֵי, 'to those who turn;' but LXX., the Chaldee Paraphrase, and the Syriac translate as if reading וְשָׁב, 'and shall turn,' or לְהָשִׁיב, 'to turn away.' So the Apostle Paul gives the full sense under inspiration: *they* turn from transgression because He first turns them from it and it from them. *Fausset.* The difference merely from a free translation. *Vitringa.* Seems to indicate a different reading. *D. Brown.* The Redeemer was to come for the behoof of God's own chosen people. *Alford.*—Ἀπὸ Ἰακώβ, from Jacob; so LXX., Chaldee, and Syriac. Heb. בְּיַעֲקֹב, in Jacob. The prophecy applied to the

Messiah in the Talmud and other Jewish writers, by Aben Ezra, and Kimchi, who by the 'enemy' understands Gog and Magog. *Gill.* Targum: 'And the Redeemer shall come to Zion, and to turn the transgressors of the house of Jacob to the law.' 'In the time to come God has purposed to remove the reproach of Israel from the rest of the nations, and to gladden them with the joy of Zion; as it is said, They shall come and sing in the heights of Zion; and again, The Redeemer shall come out of Zion.' *Zohar.* R. Acha said: 'As Israel was taken captive only by a powerful persecutor, so neither shall he be redeemed but by a powerful Redeemer; as it is said, The Redeemer shall come out of Zion.' *Echa Rabbathi.*

---

27. *For this is my covenant unto them, when I shall take away their sins.*

For. *Gr.*, "And." Gives the reason and meaning of this gracious procedure.

This is, &c. This is what I have engaged to do for them.
Then shall be fulfilled the covenant I made with them.
God ever mindful of His covenant and fulfils it.
The vision for an appointed time: at the end it shall speak, Hab. ii. 3.
The fulfilment of divine promises, if slow, yet sure.

My covenant. God's special covenant with Israel.
The same covenant solemnly declared, Jer. xxxi. 31–34.
The Redeemer comes at last to Israel in virtue of it.
Made originally with Abraham and with his seed in him.
Gentile believers made partakers with them in it, Eph. iii. 6.

Unto them. "With them," Isa. lix. 21; with the house of Israel, Jer. xxxi. 33.
The covenant made first with Christ and with them as in Him.

When I shall take away their sin. Reference to Isa. xxvii. 9, and Jer. xxxi. 34.
Their sins their greatest misery and the cause of all the rest.
Sin the cause of all suffering both here and hereafter.
Pardon of sin the foundation of all new covenant blessings.
When God blesses He begins at the beginning.
"Thy sins are forgiven thee;" then "Rise, take up thy bed and walk."
"The inhabitant shall not say, I am sick," because "forgiven their iniquity," Isa. xxxiii. 24.
Penitent Israel to wash in the opened fountain, Zech. xiii. 1.
Israel taken again into covenant when their sin is forgiven.
The veil taken from their heart when they turn to the Lord, 2 Cor. iii. 16.

Καί, and, moreover; still further to raise their faith and hope. *Guyse.*—Ἡ παρ' ἐμοῦ διαθήκη, the covenant from me. Heb. בְּרִיתִי, 'my covenant.' This is what I promise them. *Grot.* In this shall my covenant be fulfilled. *Est.* Made with the nation and Church of Israel. *Guyse.* Made first with Christ and with them as in Christ. *Fausset.* The covenant the same with each believer in all times and places. *Chalmers.*—Ἀφέλωμαι (ἀπό and αἱρέω), I take away; pardon their sins and turn them from them. *Guyse.* The passage rather a brief summary of Jer. xxxi. 31–34, than the express words of any prediction. *D. Brown.* The words και αὐτή, &c., taken from the same passage in Isaiah, left incomplete and to be supplied by the reader. *Koppe.* Ὅταν ἀφέλωμαι, &c., supposed to be taken from Isa. xxvii. 9, but possibly from Jer. xxxi. 31. *Bloomf.* His only mentioning the covenant supposed to be sufficient to lead to his design in referring to it, the promise being easily supplied by turning to the well-known passage in Jer. xxxi. 31. *Guyse.*

---

28. *As concerning the Gospel, they are enemies for your sakes: but as touching the election, they are beloved for the fathers' sakes.*

As concerning the Gospel. As to the case of the Gospel.
Here the ministration of the Gospel rather than its matter.
The Gospel was to be communicated to the Gentiles.
The Jews hardened themselves against it and rejected it.
This very rejection made the occasion of the Gentiles hearing it.
Enemies. In relation to God both actively and passively.
The nation viewed as a whole rather than individuals.
Israel, through unbelief, treated by God as enemies.
Enemies against God who gave the Gentiles the Gospel.
Opposed the Gospel and so opposed God himself.
Rejecting the Gospel, they showed themselves His enemies.
They pleased not God and were contrary to all men, 1 Thess. ii. 15.
They rebelled and vexed His Holy Spirit by unbelief;
So He turned to be their enemy and fought against them, Isa. lxiii. 10.
Terrible condition induced by sin and unbelief, Isa. xxvii. 4.
The Almighty the best friend but the worst enemy.
For your sakes. 1. Allowed to become enemies for your benefit.
The Jews' loss the unspeakable gain of the Gentiles.
The Gospel taken to the Gentiles when rejected by the Jews.
Gentiles to attain salvation through the Jews' unbelief.
2. Provoked to enmity on your account, 1 Thess. ii. 14–16.
Jews' enmity to the Gospel increased by the Gentiles' faith.
As touching the election. In respect to God's choice of them.
According to their original election and destination as His people.
Israel as a nation made God's people through election, Deut. vii. 6, 7.

Chosen—1. To peculiar privileges ; 2. To peculiar purposes.
That election made in Abraham and the fathers.
Israel's election typical of that of all believers.
The one external and national ; the other spiritual and personal.
The former made in Abraham, the latter in Christ, Eph. i. 3.
Beloved. Regarded with paternal favour and affection.
Love in God's heart even when obliged to take the rod in His hand.
Israel beloved by God, and should therefore be loved by us.
For the fathers' sakes. God's own reason for His love, Deut vii. 7, 8.
Nothing in Israel themselves to attract God's love.
Obstinate transgressors from the womb, Isa. xlviii. 4, 8.
A disobedient and gainsaying people, chap. x. 21.
So God loves sinners in Christ for His Son's sake.
God's love to the fathers remembered in behalf of the children, Lev. xxvi. 42.
Blessing of godly ancestors. Children loved for their fathers' sake.
Especial regard claimed for the offspring of godly parents.

Κατ' εὐαγγελιον, in respect to the Gospel (quod ad evangelium attinet). *Beza, Pisc., Est.* By occasion of the Gospel. *Grot.* According to the Gospel. *Luth.* In relation to the Gospel. *Mart., Diod., Lange.* That it might be borne to the Gentiles. *Con. & Hows.* In so far as they are hardened against it. *De Wette.* In the present ministration of it. *Henry.* Gospel of Christ and the way of salvation through Him. *Guyse.*—Ἐχθροι (ἐχθω, to hate), enemies ; actively to us and the Church. *Grot.* To the Gospel. *Par., Mor., Guyse, Ols.* To God. *Ferme, Wells, Beng., Henry.* To the apostle. *Theod., Luth., Flatt.* Of believers and unbelievers. *Lange.* Of the Gentiles. *Theod.* Passively, as to God ; hated by God. *Or., Pisc., Par., Thol., Meyer, De Wette, Rück.* Opposers of Christianity, and so treated as enemies by God. *Flatt, Brown.* Rejected by God and viewed no longer by Him as friends. *Doddr., Phil.* Regarded and treated as enemies ; in a state of exclusion through unbelief from the family of God. *D. Brown.*—Δι' ὑμας, on your account ; through the Gospel being preached to you. *Est.* Through your admission while uncircumcised into the Church of God. *Grot.* On account of your salvation brought about by the Gospel. *Vor., Tol., Pisc.* For your sakes against whom they have such antipathy. *Henry.* In favour of you. *Doddr.* For the benefit of you Gentiles. *D. Brown.* For your advantage, that the Gospel may come to you. *Bloomf.* That you through their unbelief might attain salvation. *De Wette.*— Κατα δε τ. ἐκλογην, in respect to the election (quod ad electionem attinet). *Beza, Pisc.* On the ground of the election (ratione electionis). *Grot., Tol.* His choice of that people, and the blessings bestowed on them. *Est., Par.* In relation to the election of Israel as the people of God. *De Wette.* According to their original destination and election as a covenant people. *Haldane.* Their election as a people. *Brown.* The election of Abraham and his seed. *D. Brown.*—Ἀγαπητοι, beloved ; by God. *Ferme, Melv., and most.* By the apostle. *Theod., Luth.* The objects of God's kind and merciful regards. *Guyse.* The same persons spoken of. *Chrys., Theod., Ambr., and most.* Different persons. *Or., Aug., Tol.* Beloved even in their state of exclusion. *D. Brown.*

—Διὰ τοὺς πατέρας, for the fathers' sakes; on account of the special favour He had for their fathers after the flesh, Abraham, Isaac, and Jacob, and the choice He made of them and their posterity to be a peculiar people to Himself. *Guyse.* His benevolence to the fathers on Christ's account. *Melv.* Because of their election in the fathers. *Ferme.* On account of their connection with the fathers. *Lange.* On account of the patriarchs, who were beloved and chosen. *De Wette.* From regard to the covenant made with their fathers. *Brown.* Their lineal descent from, and oneness in covenant with, the fathers, with whom God originally established it; the nation sprung from Abraham still an elect people and as such beloved. *D. Brown.*

---

29. *For the gifts and calling of God are without repentance.*

For. Gives the ground of the fact just stated.
Gifts. Special reference to the gifts bestowed on Israel—
1. Their relation as a covenant people; 2. The land of Canaan.
The special gifts promised to Abraham and his natural seed.
True of all His gifts. All from an unchanging God, James i. 17.
Here all hoped for from God's *goodness;* in ver. 23, from His *power.*
Calling. The instating of any in a distinguished position.
Here the calling of the Jews to be a covenant people.
In the New Testament sense, the calling into a saved condition.
Israel's calling as a nation typical of believers' calling.
Both effectual in reference to the end in view.
What God calls nations and individuals to, He makes them to be.
"Gifts" in general; "calling," the most excellent of the gifts.
Reference in the "gifts" to chap. iv. 13; in the "calling," to chap. iv. 17.
Without repentance. Without change of mind on God's part.
His gifts and calling unchangeable and irrevocable.
Subject to no regret or change of purpose, 2 Cor. vii. 10; Heb xii. 17.
God gives without variableness or shadow of turning, James i. 17.
His gifts to Israel only suspended or withdrawn for a season.
Has not repented of calling Abraham and his seed as His people.
Has not regretted the promises made to the fathers.
Man's conduct may change God's *manner* but not His *mind.*
God's dealings may vary but not His determinings.
His providences may alter but not His purposes.
The Strength of Israel will not lie nor repent, 1 Sam. xv. 29.
God's unchangeableness the ground of Israel's safety, Mal. iii. 6.
God will not cast away His people, Deut. iv. 31; 1 Sam. xii. 22.
Israel not to be deprived of what God has promised them.
The proposition is general in its form and force.

ἈμεταμέλητA (a, not, μετα, denoting change, and μέλομαι, to care for; μεταμέλομαι, to change one's care, or purpose; often including the idea of regret), not to be repented of. *Aug., Elsner, Doddr.* Immutable. *Tir., Men., Par.* Irrevocable. *Cast.* Such as He cannot repent of. *Eras., Pag., Beza, Pisc.* Not capable of recall; subject to no change of mind. *De Wette.* Cannot be repented of. *Ellicot.* Not to be repented of; the same love which rested on the fathers still rests on their descendants at large, and will yet recover them from unbelief and reinstate them in the family of God. *D. Brown.* The hardened and apostate majority not reckoned the Israelitish nation. *Ferme.*—Χαρίσματα (χαρις, free favour), gifts (dona). *Mor.* With κλῆσις, a hendiadys; gift of vocation or calling. *Par., Calv.* The gifts which through His Spirit He specially confers on His own. *Ferme.* Promises made to the fathers and spiritual blessings bestowed on their offspring. *Stuart.* Articles of the covenant God made with Abraham. *D. Brown.*—Κλῆσις (καλεω), calling (vocatio). *Mor.* Election. *Par.* To salvation by His Spirit. *Pisc., Est., J. Cap.* Effectual calling through which the gifts become known to the recipients themselves. *Ferme.* Gratuitous decree of election. *Melv.* Calling of the posterity of Abraham into God's covenant. *Calv.* To the external condition of a covenant people. *Thol.* Calling through the Gospel. *De Wette.* Gracious effectual calling. *Chalmers.* The sovereign act by which God in the exercise of His free choice called Abraham to be the father of a peculiar people. *D. Brown, Guyse.*

---

30. *For as ye in times past have not believed God, yet have now obtained mercy through their unbelief.*

In times past. Previous to the general preaching of the Gospel. Profitable to believers to remember their previous condition.
In time past Gentiles in the flesh, without God, Eph. ii. 11, 12.
Afar off, without Christ and having no hope, Eph. ii. 12, 13.
Children of disobedience, dead in trespasses and in sins, Eph. ii. 1–3.
Foolish, disobedient, deceived, serving lusts and pleasures, Titus iii. 3.
Remembrance of our former condition fitted—
1. To promote humility ; 2. To awaken gratitude ; 3. To soften our censures ; and 4. To strengthen our hopes of others.
Not believed God. Did not believe and obey the light they had. Heathen in unbelief even without the Gospel.
An unbelief including in it disobedience.
God speaks—1. In nature ; 2. In conscience ; 3. In revelation.
An evil heart of unbelief natural to fallen men.
Now. Blessed contrast between their present and former state.
God free and sovereign in the exercise of His mercy—
1. In regard to the subjects of it ; 2. The time of its exercise.
Obtained mercy. Believers made the subjects of God's mercy.
The previous state of the Gentiles—1. One of sin ; 2. Of misery.

Heathen justly condemned for the sin they lived in.
Might have been righteously allowed to remain in it.
Two great acts of divine mercy towards man—
1. To give Christ; 2. To open the heart to receive Him, Acts xvi. 14.
Through their unbelief. As the effect of the Jews' unbelief.
Gr., Disobedience; a proud, rebellious unbelief.
Resistance to the counsel and command of God, Luke vii. 30; 1 John iii. 23.
Unbelief viewed as disobedience and gainsaying, chap. x. 21.
Jewish unbelief designed to be the means of Gentile conversion.

Ποτέ, formerly; from the building of the tower of Babel till the incarnation of Christ. *Ferme.*—'Ηπειθήσατε, did not obey. *Pisc., Beza, Ham.* Were unbelieving. *Est.* Were unyielding and disobedient. *Ferme.* Disobedience and unbelief included. *Ols.* Were disobedient. *Con. & Hows., Ellicot.* By idolatry. *Hyperius, Bloomf.* Did not yield the obedience of faith. *D. Brown.* To the Gospel. *Ferme.*—'Ηλεηθῆτε (ἔλεος, mercy), have obtained mercy; in being brought into God's visible covenant, and made partakers of its saving benefits. *Guyse.* —Τῇ τουτων ἀπειθεία, on account of their unbelief. *Vulg.* By their unbelief. *Dick.* Contumacy. *Beza, Pisc.* Whilst they are disobedient. *Cam.* Because they were disobedient. *Par.* By occasion of their unbelief. *Grot., Pisc., Eras., Beza, Van Ess, Bloomf., D. Brown.* Upon their disobedience. *Con. & Hows.* By the disobedience of these. *Ellicot.* Unbelief considered as disobedience or resistance to the divine will. *Alford.* A proud rebellious unbelief. *Thol.* Rebellion. *Mart.*

---

31. *Even so have these also now not believed, that through your mercy they also may obtain mercy.*

Now. While the Gospel is preached to them. The Jew *first*.
Not believed. Not obeyed the call of the Gospel.
The Gospel is—1. A testimony; 2. An invitation.
Is therefore—1. To be believed; 2. To be obeyed.
Unbelief and disobedience united in rejecting the Gospel.
That. Indicates—1. The result; 2. The design.
Jews' unbelief designed as means to the Gentiles' faith.
Judas' sin designed to lead to the world's salvation.
Yet both the Jews and Judas acted according to their own will.
Man's wrath made to praise God and to further His designs.
Your mercy. Mercy experienced by you. So Isa. lv. 3.
The Gentiles' mercy in their hearing and accepting the Gospel.
No mercy experienced except in connection with Christ.
Gentiles' mercy was to be—1. The means; 2. The pattern, of the Jews' mercy.

Jews to be visited with the same mercy as the Gentiles.
Mercy shown to the Gentiles is—1. The occasion of Jewish unbelief;
2. Ultimately made the means of Jewish conversion.
Mercy experienced by Gentiles to be exercised by them to Jews.
May obtain mercy. Being brought to accept the Gospel.
Jews moved to seek mercy by the grace shown to Gentiles.
Jews and Gentiles to be the occasion of blessing to each other;
The Jews by their unbelief; the Gentiles by their faith.
Extinction of the Jews' light the kindling of the Gentiles'.
The continuance of the latter the rekindling of the former.
Japhet persuaded to occupy the tents of Shem;
Shem persuaded by Japhet to return to his own.
God's love and true grace opposed to monopolies.
Those who receive mercy are to seek its extension to others.
Jews' unbelief permitted with a view to ultimate faith.
Christ for the falling and rising again of many in Israel, Luke ii. 34.
In Jew and Gentile, mercy seen rejoicing against judgment, James ii. 13.

Τῷ ὑμετέρῳ ἐλέει, In or by your mercy—1. Connected with ἠπείθησαν; have not believed through the mercy shown to you. *Syr., Caiv., Brown.* Have not believed in the mercy shown to you (in vestram misericordiam). *Vulg., Luth., Lange.* 2. Connected with ἐλεηθῶσι; may obtain mercy through the mercy shown to you; ἵνα being placed after the emphatic noun in the sentence, as in 1 Cor. ix. 15; 2 Cor. ii. 4; Gal. ii. 10. So *Beza, Pisc., Pag., Glass, Beng., Stuart, De Wette, Alford.* Through your mercy, provoking them to emulation. *Ferme.* And preserving the Gospel in the world. *Guyse.* Jews apparently to be converted through the instrumentality of believing Gentiles. *D. Brown.* With the like mercy to yours. *Thol.* Because God has had mercy on you. *Ols.* On your obtaining mercy. *Con. & Hows.* Through your compassion, which will again bring back the Jews. *Cobbin.*—Ἵνα, indicates the design. *Ferme.* The result rather than the design. *Hodge, Flatt.*—Ἐλεηθῶσι, might obtain mercy on their believing in Christ. *Beng.* Being stirred up to seek restoration to divine favour. *Stuart, Ols.* Salvation of Jew and Gentile to appear to be of mercy and not of merit. *Haldane, Bloomf.* Codd. Sin. and Vat. have νῦν before ἐλεηθῶσι.

32. *For God hath concluded them all in unbelief, that He might have mercy upon all.*

For. The reason and explanation of this divine procedure.
Concluded. Shut up; given over; convicted, Gal. iii. 22.
As in a prison, where the guilty are shut up together.
Prominence given to God's own act in the matter.
A righteous thing with God to give men up to their own sin.

Softening and subduing grace has only to be withheld.
The righteous result of resisting light already given.
Obstinately choosing evil, God gives men up to their own choice.
When men *will* not believe, God may say, you *shall* not.
God's Spirit resisted both by Jew and Gentile, Gen. vi. 3; Isa. lxiii. 10.
Ultimate designs of mercy in this act of judgment.
Shows—1. The enormity of sin; 2. The riches of grace.
The fever allowed to reach its height before using a remedy.
The germ of sin in all races allowed to develop itself.
Heathen made ripe for mercy in the Old Testament dispensation;
The Jews in like manner made ripe for it in the New.
All. Both Jews and Gentiles; the reference to races.
Applicable also to individuals among both.
Men shut up in unbelief either—1. Judicially; or, 2. Graciously.
A conscious shutting up often the forerunner of enlargement.
A helpless state of conscious unbelief prepares the way for faith.
All might be judicially shut up in unbelief; some are graciously so.
In unbelief. *Gr.*, Unto unbelief or disobedience.
Jew and Gentile both allowed to sink into such a state.
Door of faith only opened to Gentiles when Cornelius believed, Acts xi. 18.
Faith God's gift, bestowed where and when He pleases, Eph. ii. 8; Phil. i. 29.
Felt power of unbelief makes the gift the more precious.
Have mercy. In opening to them the door of faith, Acts xiv. 27.
Mercy experienced only in a cordial acceptance of Jesus.
A sinner's greatest mercy is the removal of his unbelief.
Upon all. Jews and Gentiles. Jews still to be visited with mercy.
All equally dependent on God's sovereign mercy in Christ.
All nations to experience it, Num. xiv. 21; Isa. xi. 9; Ps. lxxii. 19.

Συνεκλεισε (συν and κλειω, to shut), has shut up, as in a prison. *Men.* As if with their hands tied. *Pisc.* Left them under the power of unbelief. *Vat., Cam.* Proved, convicted, demonstrated them to be unbelieving and disobedient. *Chrys., Schött., Vor., Wetst., Carpzov.* Delivered over. *Stuart, Hodge.* Involved in, made subject to. *Alford.* Given them into the power of. *Meyer.* Shut them up under their unbelief as their jailer. *Clarke.* Heb. הִסְגִּיר, 'gave over, delivered up,' Ps. lxxviii. 50, 62.—Τους ταυτας. Jews and Gentiles; each of these divisions of men. *D. Brown, Stuart.* Not strictly each individual. *Lange, Barth.* Men without limitation. *Hald.*—Εἰς ἀπειθειαν, into rebellion or disobedience (in contumaciam). *Pag., Pisc.* In rebellion. *Beza.* Under disobedience; in unbelief. *Ferme.* Under sin. *Melv.* To unbelief; the experience of an unhumbled, condemned state without Christ. *D. Brown.*—T. παντας, Gentiles first, and then Israelites. *Ols., Phil., Stuart, Hodge, D. Brown.* On their accepting God's mercy in Christ. *Ferme.* The elect. *Melv.* Mercy provided for, but not accepted by, all. *Alford.* The idea of a final general mercy. *De Wette.*

---

33. *O the depth of the riches both of the wisdom and knowledge of God ! how unsearchable are His judgments, and His ways past finding out !*

O the depth. The deep, inexhaustible fulness.
A burst of adoring admiration after contemplating—
1. The whole mystery of the Gospel in general, 1 Pet. i. 12;
2. Dispensations in regard to Jew and Gentile in particular.
God's works and ways fitted to excite wonder and intense delight.
Their contemplation the employment of the redeemed, Rev. xv. 2–4.
The desire of angels to look into and study Gospel truths, 1 Pet. i. 12.
The joy of renewed and sanctified minds on earth, Ps. xxvii. 4.
The more we know of God's works and ways, the more we admire.
God's thoughts and judgments a great deep, Ps. xcii. 5; cxxxix. 6.
Praise is silent in deep and adoring admiration, Ps. lxv. 1, *marg.*
Riches. 1. Treasures; "He treasures up His bright designs."
2. Goodness and mercy; "Earth is full of Thy riches," Ps. civ. 24.
In God is an unfathomable depth—1. Of riches, ver. 35; 2. Of
  wisdom, ver. 34; 3. Of knowledge, ver. 33.
"Depth of the riches" = either "rich depth," or "deep riches."
Deep riches in God's wisdom and knowledge.
Too deep to be fathomed, too rich to be exhausted.
His riches, wisdom, and knowledge to be admired for their depth.
Man's deepest thoughts compared with God's are shallow.
Those of profoundest thinkers the thoughts of a child, 1 Cor. xiii.
  9–12.
Sir Isaac Newton a child gathering pebbles on the sea-shore;
The ocean of knowledge lying unexplored before him.
Wisdom. That which seeks the best ends by the best means.
God's wisdom framed the purpose which His love prompted;
His knowledge prepared the means for accomplishing it.
God aims at His own glory and the best interests of creation.
The means infinitely well chosen for their promotion.
His wisdom fitted to awaken admiration and confidence.
Displayed especially in Christ and the plan of redemption by Him,
  1 Cor. i. 24; Eph. iii. 10.
Knowledge. Intimate acquaintance with persons and things.

Extends not only to things actual but possible.
Things in all their possible relations and combinations.
To His wisdom nothing difficult, to His knowledge nothing dark.
In God perfect knowledge accompanies perfect wisdom.
His knowledge keeps the object and issue ever before it.
Penetrates the most secret workings of men's hearts.
Foresees their actions and their most distant tendencies.
Scans the nature, properties, and connections of all beings and events.
Perceives what is best fitted to promote the end in view.
Provides the materials for wisdom to act upon.
Sees the end from the beginning; past, present, and future, Acts xv. 18;
All changes, motions, and operations, both in mind and matter.
Beholds all things in one clear, full, infallible view.
Counts the hairs of our head and the birds on the branches.
The universe a sea of glass before Him, clear as crystal.
Things exist according to His plan, and are known before they exist.
Unsearchable. Not to be comprehended by finite intelligence.
" Deep in unfathomable mines of never-failing skill."
Wise and gracious ends in His most terrible judgments.
The variety and extent of His designs beyond our knowledge.
Man's duty not to criticise and cavil but to acquiesce.
A wise restraint to be put upon inquiries and speculations.
Revealed truth to be firmly held fast, Deut. xxix. 29.
Perfect knowledge to be waited for, John xiii. 7; 1 Cor. xiii. 9-12; Ps. xxxvi. 9.
God's ways and judgments unsearchable; therefore be—1. Modest in your judgment; 2. Humble in your disposition; 3. Faithful in your work.
Judgments. Counsels; plans; purposes.
Extend to the universe, to nations, and to individuals.
Those of His mouth plain; those of His hand, dark and mysterious.
Things conducted to a glorious end, yet man left to his free-will.
Evil overruled for good, yet righteously punished.
God's acts are judgments, the results of wisdom and justice.
The reasons often hidden; but always wise, holy, and good.
Ways. Dealings; providences; procedure.
His ways the execution of His purposes.
His ways on the surface, His judgments beneath it.
Seen—1. In creation; 2. In providence; 3. In grace.

The manifestations of Himself; therefore holy, just, and good.
Past finding out. Not to be traced and followed to their origin.
Metaphor from the footprints left by animals.
His way is in the sea, His footsteps untraceable, Ps. lxxvii. 19.
His providence not to be judged by our feeble sense.
God to be trusted when we cannot trace Him.
Examples :—Abraham ; Joseph ; Moses ; David ; Christ.
The track soon lost in the pursuit of God's ways.
True in individuals, still more in the universe at large.

> " Lives there the man whose universal eye
> Has swept at once the boundless scheme of things ;
> Mark'd their dependence so and firm accord,
> As with unfaltering accent to conclude
> That *this* availeth nought ? Has any seen
> The mighty chain of beings lessening down
> From Infinite Perfection to the brink
> Of dreary nothing, desolate abyss ?" *Thomson.*

’Ω, &c. Yields himself to admiring contemplation. *D. Brown.* Magnificent epiphonema. *Ferme, Bloomf.*—Βαθος πλουτου, depth of the riches, *i.e.*, of the grace and mercy of God *Or., Chrys., Theod., Grot., Tol., Beng., Mart., Diod., Guyse, Meyer, Ellicot.* Depth of the riches of the wisdom, &c. *Beza, Pisc., Dick., D. Brown.* — Profound riches. *Beza, Pisc., Ferme.* Deep inexhaustible fulness. *De Wette.* Rich depth. *Bloomf., Brown.* Βαθος = αβυσσος, as 1 Cor. ii. 10; Rev. ii. 24. *Grot.* Και omitted by Beza.—Σοφιας, wisdom ; = γνωσις. *Pisc.* A species of knowledge, the highest judgment as to the best manner and order of doing things. *Per.* Γνωσις = perfect acquaintance with all things ; σοφια, that which orders all for the best ends. *Tol.* Points to the fitness to accomplish the ends intended. *D. Brown.*—Γνωσεως, of the knowledge ; points to the vast sweep of divine comprehension displayed in the purposes and methods exhibited in the chapter. *D. Brown.*—’Ανεξερευνητα (ἀ, not, ἐξ, out, and ἐρευναω, to search), inscrutable. *Fag., Melv.* Thoroughly concealed. *Cast.* Incomprehensible. *Vulg., Mor.* Metaphor from mining. *Melv.*—Κριματα (κρινω), judgments; counsels and purposes. *Ferme, Flatt, D. Brown.* In respect to unbelievers. *Beng.* In respect to the unbelief in the world. *Barth.* Governance of God's providence. *Bloomf.*—’Ανεξιχνιαστοι (ἀ, not, ἐξ, out, and ἰχνος, a trace or footprint), untraceable. *Eras., Fag., Melv.* Abstruse. *Cast.* Metaphor from hunting. *Melv.* Heb. אֵין־דַּרְכֵּי, Job v. 9 ; ix. 10.— 'Οδοι, ways ; works. *Est.* Secret counsels as to saving men. *Per.* Way of executing His decrees. *Grot., Tol., Ferme, Bloomf., D. Brown.* In regard to unbelievers. *Beng.* Dealings, especially in the way in which salvation is bestowed. *Barth.* Providential dispensations. *Brown.*

---

34. *For who hath known the mind of the Lord ? or who hath been His counsellor ?*

Known. Isa. xl. 13. Fully penetrated and comprehended.

Known by his own unaided faculties.
Much known of God's mind through revelation.
All saving knowledge thus communicated.
Believers also taught by the unction of the Holy One, 1 John ii. 20.
Still all our knowledge but that of a child, 1 Cor. xiii. 9-12.
God's plans and purposes unknown till revealed, Deut. xxix. 29.
Mind. His purposes in regard to His creatures.
The ends He has in view and His means of accomplishing them.
God's mind is directed to and embraces all He has made.
Seraphim and animalculæ alike its objects.
Nothing too great or too small for an Infinite mind.
God's plan embraced the universe before its existence.
Counsellor. Such as earthly monarchs have around them.
Giving counsel as to plans and means of executing them.
Sharing in the formation of His various designs.
Only God himself existing when the plans were made.
None able to comprehend, much less guide His counsels.
Infinite Wisdom requires no counsellor.
Finite creatures directing the Infinite Creator!

'Εγνω, hath known; rendering of the LXX. in Isa. xl. 13. Heb. תִכֵּן, 'has weighed or examined.' *Gesenius.*—Νουν, mind; so LXX.; Heb. רוּחַ, 'the Spirit.'—Συμβουλος (συν and βουλη, counsel), one with whom He might consult. *Tol., Pisc.* His counsellor in the conduct of His affairs. *Ferme.* Heb. אִישׁ עֲצָתוֹ, 'man of His counsel,' Isa. xl. 13. Divine self-sufficiency, αὐταρκεια. *Melv.*

---

35. *Or who hath first given to Him, and it shall be recompensed unto Him again?*

Given. Nothing received by God but what He has first given.
Impossible for man to be profitable to His Maker, Job xxii. 2.
The universe and all it contains owes its existence to God.
The Maker, Preserver, and Benefactor of all, Acts xiv. 17; xvii. 28.
No creature in a condition to make God his debtor.
Free therefore to dispose of Jew and Gentile as He pleases.
Recompensed. Paid back as a debt incurred or favour bestowed.
Impossible for God to be under obligation to man.
God absolutely independent of all His creatures.
Gives only out of self-moved sovereign goodness.
No claim on His favours either with Jew or Gentile.
God a most free agent, and debtor to none of His creatures.
His justice in His sovereign disposals fully vindicated.

As the potter, He has power over His own clay, chap. ix. 20, 21.
Has right to do what He will with His own, Matt. xx. 15.
No creature can put in a claim upon God, much less a sinner.
Yet nothing truly done in His service unrequited, Matt. x. 42.

Προεδωκεν, has given first (prior dedit). *Beza, Pisc.* Τις προεδ., refers to His goodness; τις εγνω, to His wisdom and knowledge. *Tol.*—Ανταποδοθησεται (αντι, απο, and διδωμι, to give), it shall be repaid in return. 'Is God in their debt? Let them say for what, and it shall be repaid.' *Locke.* Bears on all claims on God's favour preferred on the ground of merit or service. *Stuart, Bloomf.*

---

36. *For of Him, and through Him, and to Him, are all things: to whom be glory for ever. Amen.*

Of Him. 1. As the only source of existence in the universe;
2. The inexhaustible fountain of all good.
All things owe their origin to His simple will.
The beginning, origin, and efficient cause of all.

> "Happy the man who sees a God employ'd
> In all the good and ill that chequer life!
> Resolving all events with their effects
> And manifold results unto the will
> And arbitration wise of the Supreme." *Cowper.*

Through Him. As preserving, directing, and controlling all.
His sustaining power needed every moment.
Not only purposes the end but conducts to it.
God the author of providence as well as creation.
Seraph and insect alike dependent on His hand.
Conducts the created universe to its eternal destiny.

> "The Lord of all, Himself through all diffused,
> Sustains and is the life of all that lives.
> Nature is but a name for an effect
> Whose cause is God. He feeds the secret fire
> By which the mighty process is maintain'd."

To Him. As the end for which all exists and takes place.
God himself the true and worthy end of all He has made.
All things made for Himself, Prov. xvi. 4; for His pleasure, Rev. iv. 11.
Sustained and directed as well as created for His own glory.
God the beginning, middle, and end of all things.

"What is His creation less
Than a capacious reservoir of means,
Form'd for His use and ready at His will?"

The doctrine of the Trinity perhaps faintly indicated.
Paul ever conscious of the doctrine as a living reality.
The Father's love and purpose the origin of all things ;
The Son's mediation and rule their continuance and direction ;
The Spirit's agency in conducting all to the end designed.
All things *of* the Father, *through* the Son, *by* the Spirit.
To Him be glory. The feeling of every renewed heart.
Whatever the premises, God's glory is the conclusion.
God's glory the end in all His doings and dealings.
All thoughts about God and His ways to end in adoration.
Glory to God the song of the Church on earth and in heaven.
The Church the mouthpiece and priest of creation.
For ever. Begun on earth to be continued through eternity.
Earth now full of God's glory, hereafter full of His praise.
His procedure in time worthy of the praises of eternity.
Amen. Expresses—1. Satisfaction ; 2. Desire ; 3. Assurance
The whole soul poured out in a hearty Amen, Be it so !
Fitting conclusion to so glorious a chapter.
Here ends the doctrinal and dispensational part of the Epistle.

Ἐξ αὐτοῦ, from Him as the Creator. *Ferme.* Origin. *Beng.* Fountain. *Barth.* His will the source of all.—Δι' αὐτοῦ, through Him as the Preserver. *Ferme.* Their preserving and directing, governing and disposing cause. *Guyse.* Intermediate cause. *Stuart.* Conducting all to the best end. *Barth.*—Εἰς αὐτόν, in Him. *Vulg.*, reading ἐν αὐτῷ, towards Him (in ipsum) ; to His glory. *Beza.* On account of Him. *Cas.* As the last end of all. *Beng.* All for His glory and praise. *Theod.* Doctrine of Trinity alluded to. *Barth.* Though not formally. *Thol., Alf.* All of the Father, through the Son, in and by the Spirit. *Tol., Theod.*

CHAPTER XII.

1. *I beseech you therefore, brethren, by the mercies of God, that ye present your bodies a living sacrifice, holy, acceptable unto God, which is your reasonable service.*

Beseech. The doctrinal and dispensational succeeded by the practical.
Teaching lays the foundation ; exhortation builds upon it.

Paul "beseeches" as a friend earnestly desiring their best interests.
Ministers and preachers to *beseech* as well as teach, 2 Cor. v. 20.
Moses commands and threatens; the apostle beseeches.
A kindly and affectionate address the key to the heart.
Therefore. Reference both to the doctrinal and dispensational.
The use of these—1. General, ver. 1, 2; 2. Special, ver. 3 to the end.
Christian doctrine the foundation of Christian duty.
Brethren. Believers are children of God and brethren to each other.
Possess a common nature, experience, and hopes.
Roman Church composed of Jews and Gentiles, yet all brethren.
"Brethren," to remove all suspicion of guile or dislike.
Mercies of God. The exhibition of His love already treated.
Not common but covenant mercies. Sure mercies of David, Isa. lv. 3.
Mercies as seen—1. In their source, God's heart; 2. In the streams, God's hand.
Include—1. The gift of Christ; 2. Gift of the Spirit; 3. All real good.
Endless glory, and grace as the preparation for it.
Paul exhorts not by the power or authority of God, but His mercies.
Experience of mercies the best plea for obedience.
Covenant of works begins with service and ends with reward;
Covenant of grace begins with mercies and ends with service.
Perception of God's mercies moves to performance of God's will.
Large receivings to be answered by large returnings.
God's mercies as experienced by a believer are—
1. Everlasting both in their origin and continuance;
2. Sovereign, spontaneous, free, and undeserved;
3. Rich, precious, and meeting all requirements;
4. Dearly purchased by the blood of God's own Son.
Present. Offer; yield; surrender. Reference to chap. vi. 13, 16, 19.
To present as a sacrifice to God the act only of living men.
Surrender to God the spring of all duty and obedience.
Essence and fruit of love; the fulfilling of the law, chap. xiii. 10.
The presenting of a sacrifice which is no more to be withdrawn.
Implies—1. Readiness of the surrender; 2. Its entireness.
Every believer a daily ministering priest—
1. In the spirit by which he is moved and anointed;
2. In the service which he is continually presenting.

Bodies. The instruments of service, whether for good or evil.
Withdrawn from sin's service to be employed in God's.
Bodies fearfully and wonderfully made, Ps. cxxxix. 14–16.
Made to be employed in their Creator's service, Rev. iv. 11.
Believers' bodies redeemed, Eph. i. 14. Temples of the Holy Ghost, 1 Cor. vi. 19, 20.
Self-surrender to be so thorough as to include the whole body.
Extends to every member, organ, and separate part.
"Holiness to the Lord" from the crown of the head to the sole of the foot.
The body the instrument through which the soul acts.
The organ of all practical activity, holy or unholy.
Symbol of the present life in all its relations and actions.
The lowest part of man's threefold nature, 1 Thess. v. 23.
Often hindering the soul and seducing it into sin.
Subjugated by the fall to the bondage of iniquity, chap. vi. 19.
Redeemed and sanctified in Christ with soul and spirit.
The body presented to God by the sanctified spirit.
A holy God requires not men's beasts but their bodies.
God to be glorified with our body as well as our spirit, 1 Cor. vi. 20.
Worshipped with the body accompanied by the spirit, Isa. xxix. 13; John iv. 24.
God honoured by our bodies when employed—
1. In acts of immediate worship;
2. In works of benevolence and mercy;
3. In patient suffering for His sake.
Rome now presents to God not her body but her *bread*.
Living sacrifice. A sacrifice that which is offered to God.
Slain animals among the first recorded offerings, Gen. iv. 4.
Cain's fruits and Abel's lambs both called an offering.
In both cases the sign of worship and thanksgiving.
In Abel's the consciousness of guilt and faith in the seed, Gen. iii. 15.
The offering of slain animals apparently taught by God, Gen. iii. 21.
Intended to point forward to the Lamb of God, John i. 29.
Fallen man unable to approach God without a sacrifice.
The practice universal. An instinct of fallen humanity.
The distinction between clean and unclean founded on it.
Noah's first act after the flood to offer the former to God, Gen. viii. 20.

CHAP. XII.]   ST. PAUL'S EPISTLE TO THE ROMANS.   155

Practised in covenants, Gen. viii. 21, 22; ix. 9; xv. 7–18; xxxi. 44, &c.; Exod. xxiv. 4, &c.
Covenant made with God only by sacrifice, Ps. l. 5.
The idea of expiation especially prominent, Job i. 5; xlii. 8.
Three kinds of bloody sacrifices among the Jews—
1. Sin-offering, type of Christ as substitute and sin-bearer;
2. Burnt-offering, type of Christ in His active and passive obedience;
3. Peace-offering, sign of peace established between God and men.
In the sin-offering, Christ stood necessarily alone;
In the burnt-offering, His members made to resemble Him;
In the peace-offering, they as reconciled present their bodies, &c.
After Christ's death bloody sacrifices no longer needed.
Ceased during the siege of Jerusalem from want of lambs.
After the destruction of the Temple could no longer be offered.
Israel has now been without a sacrifice for eighteen centuries.
That of a cock at the Passover a mere human invention.
Besides bloody sacrifices, there were under the law—
1. Meat-offerings accompanying the daily burnt-offering;
2. The shewbread, renewed every Sabbath, Lev. xxiv. 5, 9;
3. Special meat-offering on Sabbaths and festivals, Num. xxviii.; xxix;
4. First-fruits at the Passover and Pentecost, Lev. xxiii. 10–14, 17–20;
5. Incense burnt on the altar morning and evening, Exod. xxx. 7, 8;
6. Scapegoat and incense on the day of Atonement, Lev. xvi. 10, 12.
Christ's one offering on the cross the only propitiation for sin.
The unbloody sacrifice of the Mass a human invention.
Believers' bodies called a living sacrifice—
1. In opposition to slain animals under the law;
2. As expressing the spiritual life of a believer's service.
Living, active powers to be dedicated to God.
A living soul makes the body a living sacrifice.
Dead sacrifices an abomination to God.
A living God to be worshipped with living sacrifices.
Holy love puts life into every religious service.
Living sacrifices only offered in union with Christ, the Life.
The religion of unrenewed men a religion of death.
Believers are priests who offer up *themselves*—
1. In the obedience of their lives, 1 Sam. xv. 22;
2. In the praises and thanksgivings of their lips, Heb. xiii. 15;

3. In their works of mercy and benevolence to others, Phil. iv. 18;
4. In their exercise of true penitence and contrition, Ps. li. 17;
5. In a life of self-denial and cross-bearing, Matt. xvi. 24, 25;
6. In their prayers and intercessions for others, Job xlii. 8; Ps. cxli. 2; 1 Tim. ii. 1.

Holy. Morally, as distinguished from ceremonial holiness.
Holy, what is—1. Set apart for the Lord; 2. Separate from sin.
Body to be holy as well as the spirit, 1 Cor. vii. 34; 1 Thess. v. 23.
A sanctified soul makes a sanctified body.
The believer's body a holy temple for a holy God.
Sacrifices under the law to be without blemish, Lev. i. 3.
The body a holy sacrifice when employed in God's service.
"Let the hands do good, the tongue bless, the ear listen to divine truth." *Chrysostom.*

Acceptable. Well pleasing. Sacrifices such as are—1. Holy;
2. Presented in union with, and through the hands of, Christ.
Jesus Christ the altar that sanctifies the gift.
All services acceptable only through Him, 1 Pet. ii. 5.
Living and holy sacrifices alone acceptable to a holy God.
True worshippers are those who worship in spirit and in truth.
Burnt-offerings only a sweet savour till Christ's death.

Reasonable. As opposed—1. To irrational animals;
2. To services in themselves not reasonable.
God's service to be reasonable, not blind and superstitious.
The exercise of an enlightened mind and understanding.
Nothing in scriptural Christianity but what is reasonable.
Some doctrines of men neither reasonable nor scriptural.
Examples :—Baptismal regeneration and transubstantiation;
Prayer to departed saints; worship of images, or of God by images.
Much in some Christian churches that is unreasonable service.
Acceptable service must be scriptural service.
Will-worship unacceptable, Col. ii. 23. "In vain do they worship me," &c., Matt. xv. 9.
God's service in itself most reasonable—
1. We are His creatures, made and sustained by Him;
2. We are endowed with faculties fitting us for it;
3. God has required such service at our hands;
4. He is in Himself infinitely worthy of our service;

5. Conscience dictates and approves such service;
6. Our own present and eternal peace connected with it;
7. Our nature elevated and improved by it.
Service. Reference to believers' priesthood, 1 Pet. ii. 8; Rev. i. 6.
Service not confined to acts of religious worship.
The whole of a believer's life to be one priestly service.
May be either active or passive, doing or suffering.
"They also serve who only stand and wait." *Milton.*

Οἰκτιρμων, mercies; operations and effects of God's mercy towards us. *Pisc.*, *Par.*, *Beza*, *Tol* , *Est.* = רַחֲמִים, Neh. i. 11. *Grot.* Plural, indicating the frequency and excellency of the gift. *Glass.* Different instances of divine compassion before enumerated. *Hald.* Doctrine in general treated in the whole Epistle. *De Wette.* Mercies whose unmerited nature, glorious channel, and saving fruits have been opened up at such length. *D. Brown.*—Παραστησαι, same word in chap. vi. 13, 16, 19. Exhibeatis. *Vulg.*, *Cam.* Afford (præbeatis). *Eras.*, *Vat.* Offer. *Tol.*, *Vor.* Place (sistatis); = προσφερω, Heb. הִקְרִיב, Lev. i. 2. *Grot.*, *Beza.* Present, as a sacrifice before the altar. *Elsner*, *Doddr.* Indicates readiness and entireness of surrender. *Lange*, *Alford.*
—Σωματα, bodies; as organ and symbol of our earthly life. *Lange.* Organ of practical activity. *Thol.*, *Alf.* Body most under the bondage of sin. *Ols.*, *De Wette.* Jews taught by their Rabbies to substitute their bodies for sacrifices by diminishing their fat and blood through fasting. *Zohar.*—Θυσιαν (θυω, to kill), sacrifice. Arguments in favour of their divine origin—1. Appropriateness as a means of keeping before the mind the desert of sin, and the Saviour, whose death was to take it away; 2. Animal food not granted to man till after the flood; hence the beasts slain (Gen. iii. 21) intended for sacrifice; 3. Adam could not have invented the rite, there appearing no natural congruity between such sacrifices and God's satisfaction; 4. Abel's bloody sacrifice offered in faith, therefore in obedience to God's will, and thus visibly accepted; 5. Universality of such sacrifices from the earliest period; 6. Early distinction of animals as clean or unclean made before the flood, and therefore not with reference to food. *Magee.* Gregory of Nazianzum, Basil the Great, and others, generally speak of a sacrifice in the Lord's Supper. Gregory the Great speaks more distinctly of a daily repeated sacrifice, 'quotidianum immolationis sacrificium.' Transubstantiation and the sacrifice of the Mass made an article of faith by the Lateran Council under Pope Innocent III., and expressed in a liturgical form, by the institution of Corpus Christi Day, by Pope Urban IV. (1264), and by Clement V. (1311).—Ζωσαν, living; in opposition to slain animals, and in the sense of the higher moral life. *De Wette.* Living active powers of the body to be continually devoted to God. *Stuart.* Philo and Josephus speak of the Essenes as not sacrificing animals, but desiring to prepare their minds as a suitable offering to God. *Alf.* Θυσιας οὐκ ἐπιτελουσι,—ἀφ' ἑαυτων τας θυσιας ἐπιτελουσι. *Jos. Antiq.*— Λογικην, rational; in opposition to the offering of irrational creatures. *Theod.* To what is superstitious. *Calv.* To the fleshly service of the Jews. *Stuart.* Rational, in respect to the understanding and will (rationalem cultum). *Eras.*, *Pisc.*, *Beza*, *Cast.*, *Pag.* Intelligent; — of the reason. *Ellicot.* The doctrine of the Gospel is λογικον ἀδολον γαλα, 1 Pet. ii. 2. Pythagoras required divine worship to be intelligent (ἐπιστημονικη). *Jamblichus.*—Λατρειαν, religious service, not sacrifice; the more general idea. *De Wette.*

2. *And be not conformed to this world ; but be ye transformed by the renewing of your mind, that ye may prove what is that good, and acceptable, and perfect will of God.*

Conformed. Assimilated ; made like in character and conduct. Reference to the spirit and practices prevailing in the world.
This world. 1. Present time or age, while Satan rules as prince ;
2. World which lies in wickedness or in the wicked one, 1 John v. 19 ;
3. Outward, visible, transitory state of things, 1 Cor. vii. 31.
The present the time in which Satan acts as prince of this world. Hence the character of the present age or period.
" This world" as contrasted with the age to come, 2 Pet. iii. 13 ; Rev. xxi. 1–4.
Believers formerly walked according to the course of it, Eph. ii. 2.
Its contents, lust of the flesh, lust of the eye, and pride of life, 1 John ii. 16.
Its character, fulfilling the desires of the flesh and mind, Eph. ii. 3.
Serving lusts and pleasures, and living in malice and envy, Titus iii. 3.
Minding earthly things, Phil. iii. 19. Earthly, sensual, devilish, James iii. 15.
Believers not to fashion themselves according to former lusts, 1 Pet. i. 14.
Past time sufficient to have wrought the will of the Gentiles, 1 Pet. iv. 3.
Believers to come out and be separate from the world, 2 Cor. vi. 17.
To have no fellowship with the works of darkness, Eph. v. 11.
Henceforth not to walk as other Gentiles walk, Eph. iv. 17.
To be faithful to God we must often be singular among men.

> " Among the faithless, faithful only he ;
> Among innumerable false, unmoved ;
> Unshaken, unseduced, unterrified ;
> His loyalty he kept, his love, his zeal ;
> Nor numbers nor example with him wrought,
> To swerve from truth nor change his constant mind,
> Though single." *Milton.*

Amidst outward changes, the spirit of the world unchanged.
Gr., " Be not of the same form and fashion with this world."
Believers' outward fashion to agree with their inward form. *Beng.*
Fashion of this world grovelling, mean, transitory, 1 Cor. vii. 31.
Things of time a *show,* those of eternity *realities.*

> "All, all on earth is shadow; all beyond
> Is substance; the reverse is folly's creed." *Young.*

Believers to be separate from the world—
1. As sacrifices presented at the Lord's altar;
2. As members of the Lord's regenerated family;
3. As soldiers in the Lord's consecrated army.

Transformed. Changed in form. So Christ, Matt. xvii. 2.
A moral transfiguration corresponding with His spiritual one.
Personal Christianity an entire moral change, 2 Cor. v. 17.
The world's show given up for the reality of holiness.
The life and character of the world to be exchanged for Christ's.
Not to be conformed to this world, we must be *transformed.*
Implies effort, Ezek. xviii. 31; Phil. ii. 12; 2 Pet. i. 5–9; Hosea v. 4.
Sin to be resisted, holiness cultivated, means employed.
The character of Christ to be contemplated in the Word, 2 Cor. iii. 18.
Promise corresponding to the precept, Ezek. xxxvi. 26, 27;
Its fulfilment to be pleaded for in prayer, ver. 37.
Always increasing transformation to be sought, 2 Cor. iii. 18.

Renewing. Transformation not by amendment but renewal.
Indicates both the means and magnitude of the change.
More than mere change; a new creation, Eph. ii. 10; 2 Cor. v. 17.
Not merely *another* man, but a *new* man, 1 Sam. x. 9: Eph. iv. 24.
A radical change, the effect of union with Christ, 2 Cor. v. 17.

Of your mind. Renewal of inner, not outward man.
Includes views, disposition, taste, affection, desire, will.
The central part of man's moral nature to be renewed.
Renewed in quality not substance,—"spirit of your mind," Eph. iv. 23.
Change not in mere outward walk but inward character.
Change of *heart* necessary to thorough change of *life.*
Understanding as well as will and affections renewed, Eph. iv. 17.

Prove. Discern so as to approve, experience, and practise.
Only a renewed mind successful in inquiring after truth.
Moral discrimination a Christian grace.
Certainty as to the will of God to be endeavoured after.
To be atttained to—1. After renewing of the mind;
2. After honest examination in connection with it.
To try the things that differ a Christian duty, Phil. i. 10, *margin.*
Believers' knowledge of God's will connected with experience.

Grace enables to *perceive*, and disposes to *receive*, the will of God.
A clever wit can *dispute* about duty;
An honest heart *sees* and *practises* it.
Good. *Gr.*, " That which is good ;" abstractly, " the good."
1. The good morally, as agreeing with God's commands ;
2. The good experimentally, as tending to life and happiness.
What is excellent in itself and profitable for us.
Good in itself, and good for the time and person, 2 Chron. xxvi. 18.
What is pleasing to God is profitable to man.
That is good which is according to God's will.
The good alone to be offered in sacrifice to God, Lev. ix. 10 ; xxii. 21.
Acceptable. *Gr.*, " The acceptable ;" what is pleasing to God, Heb. xiii. 21.
What is pleasing to God is excellent in itself.
First the good, then the acceptable. Only the good is acceptable.
What is acceptable to God is so to all wise and holy beings.
Further allusion to sacrifice ; sweet savour ; accepted, Lev. i. 4, 9.
The crown of a man's work is its acceptance with God.
The great question, Does God accept thy works? Eccles. ix. 7.
Perfect. Without blemish or defect, wanting nothing, James i. 4.
The sacrifice to be perfect in order to its acceptance, Lev. xxii. 21.
Gr., " The perfect ;" that which completes the moral character.
God's will is our perfection and sanctification, 1 Thess. iv. 3 ; v. 23 ; Matt. v. 48.
Believers to be perfect and complete in all the will of God, Col. iv. 12.
The law of the Lord is perfect, allowing no sin, Ps. xix. 7.
God's will can neither be more nor less holy than it is.
His requirements perfect like His own nature.
Nothing but what is perfectly holy satisfies a holy God.
Believers complete in Christ and accepted in the Beloved, Col. ii. 10 ; Eph. i. 6.
Will of God. *Gr.*, " The will of God ;" what God requires of man.
His will in reference to our disposition and conduct.
God's will is the good, the acceptable, and the perfect.
Only what is according to God's will is such.
God requires all that is good, acceptable, and perfect.
Romish doctrine of supererogation unscriptural.
Human doctrines and traditions not acceptable to God, Matt. xv. 9.

Συσχηματιζεσθε (συν, with, and σχημα, form or fashion, as 1 Cor. vii. 31), be not conformed (configuremini). *Pisc.* Configurate vos. *Beza.* Do not show yourselves like. *Cast.* Do not accommodate yourselves to the form or fashion. *Eras.* Do not take the form of the world. *Barth.* Do not adopt its sinful customs and practices. *Stuart.* Do not be assimilated. *Haldane.* Same word, 1 Pet. i. 14. Σχημα, show or appearance, used in reference to this world, as 1 Cor. vii. 31 ; μορφη, form, in reference to the new man or new life, as having form or beauty with a substratum of reality. *Origen.* The fashion of this world mean and transitory ; a mask, with no abiding substance. *Chrys.* The things of time a mere show. *Theod.* Σχημα, less inward and perfect than μορφη. *Beng.*—Τῳ αἰωνι τουτῳ, this world ; its corrupt, sinful practices *Jortin.* As of the Jews (chap. ii.) and of the Gentiles (chap. i.). *Boothroyd.* Heathen world. *Whitby.* Inhabitants of the world in every age. *Haldane, Barth.* This age or generation ; the customs, &c., of a corrupt age. *Cobbin.* Present age, in opposition to that of the Messiah yet to come. *De Wette.* Whole world of the ungodly, as contrasted with the spiritual kingdom of Christ. *Alford.* Whole external frame of things seen and temporal, including principles and maxims, characterising the great mass of mankind. *Brown.* Men outside the kingdom of Christ. *Nielson.*—Μεταμορφουσθε (μετα, denoting change, and μορφη, form), be transformed (transfiguremini). *Cast., Grot.* Transformate vos. *Beza.* Transformemini. *Pisc.* Transfigured, as Matt. xvii. 2 ; 2 Cor. iii. 18. *Ellicot, D. Brown.* Exchange the form of the world for that of Christianity. *Stuart.* Be changed in spirit. *Cobbin.* Not μετασχηματιζεσθε, but μεταμορφ. ; for holiness has real form and natural beauty, and has no need of paint. *Chrys.* Turn from the world which is a show to holiness which is a reality. *Theod.* Μορφη, form, more inward and perfect than σχημα, dress, fashion, or habit ; Christ in the 'form' of God (μορφῃ), but found in 'fashion' (σχηματι) as a man, Phil. ii. 6, 8 : our vile body changed in 'fashion' (μετασχηματισει), that it may be like Christ's in 'form' (συμμορφον), Phil. iii. 21. *Beng.* 'Intellige, Lucili, non emendari me tantum, sed transfigurari.' *Seneca.* Heb. בְּעֻזִּי הִשְׁתַּנָּה, 'when he changed his manner,' μεταμορφωσε, Ps. xxxiv. *title. Symmachus.*—Ἀνακαινωσει (ἀνα, again, and καινος, new), through the renewing. *Eras., Pag., Pisc.* In newness. *Vulg.* In the new form or pattern. *Beng.* A new and different spirit to be cultivated. *Stuart.* Indicates not the instrument but the manner of the change. *Alford.*—Νοος ὑμων, of your mind (mentis). *Eras., Pag., Pisc.* Spirit or disposition (animi) ; = רוּחַ. *Grot.* Mind itself corrupt. *Par.* Not its essence or faculties, but its operations ; disposition, higher consciousness. *De Wette.* Ἀνακαιν. τ. νοος, such an inward spiritual transformation as makes the whole life new,—new in its motives and ends, even when the actions differ in nothing from those of the world,—new, considered as a whole. *D. Brown.*—Εἰς το δοκιμαζειν, that you may prove by trial and experience. *Boothroyd.* Try, experience, so as to know. *Stuart.* Acquire the faculty of proving. *Ols.* Discern by an unerring test. *Con. & Hows.* Obtain practical proof by experience. *Alford.* Not to know it speculatively, but to realise it. *Brown.* So that you may *prove*,—not may be *able*; not ability or letter-knowledge indicated, but disposition, as Eph. v. 10 ; Phil. i. 10 ; higher consciousness to which the Christian is to be daily more renewed. *Nielson.* Ascertain, as metals are tried. *Cobbin.* Prove experimentally ; sentiment the same as in chap. v. 4, and Phil. i. 10.—Τι το θελημα τ. Θ., what is the will of God, even that which is good, &c. *Con. & Hows., Stuart, De Wette, Barth.* Christian truth in its whole extent. *Stuart.* What dispositions and actions are acceptable to God. *De Wette.* Will of God revealed in the Gospel. *Boothroyd.* His doctrines and commands. *Cobbin.*—Το ἀγαθον, that good, &c., will of God ; ἀγαθον, &c., qualifying θελημα. *Calv., Beng., Boothr., D. Brown.* Even what is good, &c. ; the thing in which the will of God consists. *De Wette, Thol., Phil., Con. & Hows.* God's will good as requiring a living holy sacrifice. *Beng.*

As demanding only what is essentially and unchangeably good. *D. Brown.* 'Αγαθον, εὐαρ., and τελ., contrasted with the Jewish ritual. *Grot., L'Enfant.*—Εὐαρεστον (εὐ, well, and ἀρεσκω, to please), well-pleasing; in contrast with all that is arbitrary, as demanding only what God has eternal complacency in. *D. Brown.* The acceptable. *De Wette.* What is excellent. *Roos.* What is pleasing to God. *Barth.*—Τελειον (τελος, end), perfect, according to the powers given. *Roos.* As the Christian advances. *Beng.* Blameless, holy, consistent with His wisdom and goodness. *Est.* Having no defect. *Stuart.* Requiring nothing else than the perfection of God's reasonable creature, who, as he attains it, reflects God's own. *D. Brown.* This and other requirements in the typical sacrifices transferred to better things, Lev. xxii. 21. *Grot.* The new life; that under the law was also the will of God, not preferred as being best, but only permitted from human infirmity. *Chrys.* Including all that is necessary to complete the character. *Brown.* The perfect, as without defect or error; the perfect love of God. *De Wette.*

---

3. *For I say, through the grace given unto me, to every man that is among you, not to think of himself more highly than he ought to think ; but to think soberly, according as God hath dealt to every man the measure of faith.*

For. 1. Reason for seeking the renewing of the mind.
2. Example of the need of ascertaining the will of God.
Renewing of the mind necessary—1. For right self-knowledge ;
2. For the right exercise of gifts and discharge of duties.
Comes now to particulars as to God's will and believers' duty.
Conformity to the spirit of the world to be guarded against—
1. In the Church ; 2. In connection with spiritual gifts.
Say. Command on the authority of an apostle.
The force of a command given to the exhortation that follows.
Grace given me. 1. As the apostle of Jesus Christ.
Apostolic office a gift of grace, chap. i. 5 ; xv. 15 ; Eph. iii. 2, 8.
Gives the reason for using the language he does.
2. Speaks not the words of carnal wisdom but by God's grace.
Believers' speech to be with grace, seasoned with salt, Col. iv. 6.
Grace given for the discharge of every duty and office.
Grace given to be duly exercised and employed.
Every man. 1. All the members of the Church in general.
2. Those endowed with spiritual gifts in particular.
Special reference to Jews and Gentiles in the Church at Rome.
These prone to boast against each other, chap. ii. 17, 23 ; xi. 18.
Is among you. 1. Is of your society as a professed believer ;
2. Is endowed with gifts or invested with office in the Church.
The exhortation that follows equally suitable to all.
Each to apply to himself the word intended for him.
Think more highly. Overestimate himself for his gifts.

Believers to judge of themselves—1. Modestly ; 2. Truthfully.
Modesty and humility required with the highest gifts.
Believers only receivers. "Who maketh thee to differ ?" 1 Cor. iv. 7.
Gifts bestowed not according to man's merit but God's will.
Difference of gifts implies no difference of merit.
Gifts, small or great, well employed, bring equal praise, Matt. xxv. 20–23.
Gifts increased as the reward of faithful use, Matt. xxv. 28, 29.
Believers to think highly of God's grace, lowly of themselves.
Men prone to overvalue themselves, even in the Church, 1 Cor. xii. ; xiv.
The sin into which the Church at Rome might readily fall.
History shows how much need it had to be thus cautioned.
One gift not to be overestimated against another, 1 Cor. iv. 6 ; xii. 1, &c.
Paul begins where his Master did,—with humility. *Chrysostom.*
Than he ought. 1. Than becomes a humble recipient ;
2. Than he is warranted to do by the facts of the case.
Possession of gifts no security against spiritual pride.
Think soberly. *Gr.*, Think so as to be sober-minded.
Modest and sober judgment to be formed of ourselves and our gifts.
A wise and sober use to be made of the gifts we possess.
Neither boast of your own nor envy those of others.
To think soberly of our gifts necessary to a right use of them.
Gifts in general to be soberly estimated.
Gifts are not grace, nor always accompanied with it.
Gifts various, yet all useful and necessary.
The most splendid not always the most profitable.
Each has only a share, and that according to God's will.
Dealt. Shared. Gifts and grace distributed by God—
1. Graciously ; 2. Sovereignly ; 3. Wisely.
Diversity of gifts to be recognised in the Church.
A liberal judgment to be formed of the gifts of others.
Measure of faith. Faith God's gift in every measure of it.
Exists in various degrees and under various forms.
Differs in respect—1. To its nature ; 2. To its object.
Chiefly of two kinds—1. That which *saves;* 2. That which *serves.*
Saving faith different from the faith that works miracles.
One faith saves our own soul, another heals a brother's body.
Faith classed with various gifts for the benefit of others, 1 Cor. xii. 9.

Faith that removes mountains possible without charity, 1 Cor.
xiii. 2.
Faith receives gifts as well as righteousness.
Faith necessary for, and appropriate to, each gift.
Qualifies for the reception of gifts as well as salvation.
The fountain of all gifts both for holiness and ministry.
The subjective principle of the gifts and services referred to.
Distinguished the gifted—1. From other believers ; 2. From each
other.
Receptivity for gifts itself dealt out by God.
Faith itself a gift ; therefore no room for pride.
Dealt out by measure after God's good pleasure.
Bestowed not according to man's merit but God's mercy.
In Christ's kingdom faith counts more than natural gifts.

Λεγω, I say, and give in charge. *Doddr.* Authoritatively. *D. Brown.*—Χαριν, grace, to be an apostle. *Cobbin.* Apostolical authority. *Ham.* Given to me as an apostle. *D. Brown.*—Μη υπερφρονειν παρ' ὁ δει φρονειν, not to think or savour (sapiat) above what he ought. *Beza, Pisc., Pag.* Not to arrogate to himself more than he ought. *Cas.* Not to think arrogantly of himself. *Eras.* Aim beyond his capacity and calling. *Par.* Levites not to affect the things of the priesthood. *Grot.* Not to arrogate to himself above what he ought to think. *Raph., Doddr.* Pretend to be wiser than he ought. *Mart.* Have any sentiment above what he ought. *Diod.* Have a higher judgment or esteem of himself than is just. *Schött.* Not to be high-minded above what he ought to be minded. *Ellicot, Alford, Calv.* Emphatic play of the words on each other ; a strong way of characterising all undue self-elevation. *D. Brown.* Not to over-estimate himself. *Stuart.* Teaches humility in respect to spiritual gifts. *Alf.* Not to aspire to such offices as they were unfit for. *Chal.* Irregularities in the exercise of gifts had either appeared at Rome or were likely to do so, as at Corinth, &c. *Macknight.* Φρονεω = to judge, as 1 Cor. iv. 6. *De Wette.* Ὑπερφρονα = ὑπερηφανον, ἀγνωμονα, ὑψηλοφρονα. *Hesychius.* Caution against excesses and extremes in matters of religion, as 1 Tim. iv. 1-3. *Origen.* Begins with humility, the chief virtue. *Chrys.*— Εἰς το σωφρονειν (σως, sound, and φρονεω, to think), unto sobriety. *Beza, Pisc., Pag.* So as may render him modest. *Calv.* That he may be modest and sober. *Eras.* Think with modesty or moderation. *Syriac.* Soberly. *Schött.* Modestly. *Flatt, Mart.* With sobriety. *Diod.* With modesty, sobriety, and humility. *Doddr.* Be modest and temperate in his estimate of himself. *Hodge, Alford.* Seek a sober mind. *Con. & Hows.* Think judiciously and modestly. *Brown.* With modesty ; not as better than others because having more faith. *De Wette.* Modestly, prudently ; not puffed up with his gifts. *Stuart.* A sound and moderate estimate to be made of one's gifts. *Haldane.* So as to be sober-minded. *Ellicot, D. Brown.* Σωφρονειν = φρονειν σωφρονως. *Flatt.* Σωφρονουντα, of a sound mind, Luke viii. 35. Applied to speech, 2 Cor. v. 13 ; to spirit and behaviour, Titus ii. 6 ; 1 Pet. iv. 7.—Ἐμερισε (μερος, a part), has shared or divided (partitus). *Beza, Pisc.* Heb. חלק, Paul wishes the recognition of the diversity of gifts, and a liberal judgment of those of others. *De Wette.* One not to make himself the measure of others. *Beng.*—Μετρον πιστεως, measure of faith ; the rule by which each is to judge of himself. *Rückert.* In correspondent proportion to the gifts. *Doddr.*

Πιστις, the faith to perform miracles. *Theoph.* Gifts given in faith or with faith. *Pisc.* Christian knowledge. *Beza.* Trust committed. *Tol.* Faith as the directress of other gifts. *Est.* Put for all spiritual gifts. *Macknight.* Gifts intrusted. *Flatt, Thol., Hodge.* Christian belief or knowledge which God has imparted. *Stuart.* Faith in Christ. *Haldane.* Receptivity of gifts. *Alford.* The subjective principle of the gifts and services. *De Wette.* Faith corresponding to the gifts received. *Brown.* The gift of faith as the source of miraculous powers; a firm persuasion that the power was given and would be successful. *Con. & Hows.* Faith as laying hold of the lost ideal life in confidence on God as reconciled through Christ to sinful man, the mother of all Christian virtue and perfection. *Rückert.* Faith viewed as the inlet to all the other graces and receptive faculty of the renewed soul. *D. Brown.*

4, 5. *For as we have many members in one body, and all members have not the same office; so we, being many, are one body in Christ, and every one members one of another.*

One body. Church compared to a body with its members.
Same comparison, 1 Cor. xii. 12, 14–27; Eph. i. 23; iv. 16; Col. i. 18, 24; ii. 19.
Christ the Head, each believer an individual member.
The Church one body with one Head and many members.
Paul's object to show that each member has its own office.
And all members. *Gr.*, But all the members, &c.
It belongs to the members of a body to have different offices.
Each member serves a different but a useful purpose.
Has its own function for the benefit of the whole.
So members of Christ's body have different gifts and functions.
Romans applied the figure to the state, Paul to the Church.
Office. Function; part to perform; duty to fulfil.
In the body a variety of functions necessary.
Some with special relation to the external world:
Various senses; means of voluntary motion and action.
Others having relation to the well-being of the body itself:
Natural functions; as, digestion, secretion, excretion.
Vital functions; as, nervous action, circulation, respiration.
The various functions performed by different parts and organs.
So, many functions necessary for the well-being of the Church.
These wisely distributed among the several members.
Each member has his or her own gift and office, chap. xvi. 1-3.
All the members *have* office, though all do not *bear* office.
Office used in two senses, a wider and a more restricted one.
All *have* office in the former, some *bear* it in the latter.
Each to know and fulfil his and her own function.
All to discharge their various offices harmoniously and well.

In Christ. The one Head to whom all are united, Ps. cxxxiii.
The members to live and act in fellowship with the Head.
Christ the source of life and spiritual energy to the whole.
The union not merely visible and economical, but—
Vital, personal, real, and effectual, John xv. 5 ; xvii. 21.
Union with Christ effects union with each other, Ps. cxxxiii.
All receive from Christ, and that for others as well as themselves.
Church membership gives visible union with Christ ;
Only regeneration and faith effect a real and vital one.
Saving union alone by the purpose and operation of God, 1 Cor. i. 30.
Visible union may bring gifts ; vital union secures grace.
The former only temporary, the latter eternal, John xv. 5, 6.
Members one of another. All believers joint-members.
Opposed—1. To sectarian partiality and exclusiveness ;
2. To latitudinarian laxity and false liberality.
All believers are members of each other, but *only* such.
Only the former considered as being in the Church.
Those only to be Church-members who credibly profess faith.
Christ's members only proper Church-members.
Baptismal water makes the latter, only the Holy Ghost the former.
Each believer virtually united with every other.
Each the receiver of grace and gifts to serve the rest.
Believers to love and serve each other—
1. As parts of Christ ; 2. As parts of themselves.

Πραξιν (πρασσω, to do or perform), action. *Beza, Pisc.* Function. *Grot.* Heb. הָיָה, 2 Chron. xiii. 22 ; xxvii. 7 ; xxviii. 25. LXX. use, office. *Stuart.*—Ἐν Χριστῷ, in the fellowship of Christ. *De Wette.* In Christ as the Head in the organic life. *Lange.* —Ὁ δὲ καθ' εἰς ἀλλήλων μέλη, for ὁ εἰς καθ' ἕνα, Rev. iv. 8. None to consider His gift without respect to others, as if having it only for himself. *Nielson.* Properly a solecism ; see also John viii. 9 ; Mark xiv. 19 ; 3 Macc. v. 34, ἀνὰ εἰς, Rev. xxi. 21. *Stuart.*

---

6. *Having then gifts differing according to the grace that is given to us, whether prophecy, let us prophesy according to the proportion of faith.*

Having then gifts. *Gr.*, And (or but) having gifts, *i.e.*, as members.
All members understood to possess gifts of some kind.
Office, strictly taken, belongs to few ; serving gifts to all.
Gifts may either be natural, acquired, or supernatural ;

Ordinary or extraordinary; temporary or permanent;
Either internal or external; with grace or without it.
Believers often endowed with various supernatural gifts.
Such gifts bestowed on the Church at Pentecost, Acts ii. 4.
Afterwards with imposition of hands by the apostles, Acts viii. 14–18; xix. 6.
Bestowed on Cornelius and his friends without this, Acts x. 44–46.
The outward sign then dispensed with for an obvious reason.
Gifts bestowed for Christian efficiency and service.
Extraordinary gifts confined to apostolic ministry, 1 Cor. ix. 1, 2; 2 Cor. xii. 12.
Given in connection with the establishment of the Church.
Apostles, as such, without successors; gifts of grace continued.
Gifts here specified divided into two classes—
1. Prophets or instructors, including teachers and exhorters;
2. Ministers or administrators; discharging the duties of—
1. Distribution; 2. Government; 3. Attendance on the sick.
Differing. As in the body, members having different uses.
Various gifts but modifications of one divine operation.
Diversities of gifts, but the same spirit, 1 Cor. xii. 4, &c.
Variety seen in every department of God's works.
Various gifts necessary both for the Church and the world.
Hence varieties of human individual talent.
Gifts differ; saving and sanctifying grace always the same.
Grace. Gifts bestowed as a matter of free favour, 1 Cor. iv. 7.
The Spirit divides to every man severally as He will, 1 Cor. xii. 11.
Gifts are not grace, yet all proceed from grace, 1 Cor. iv. 7.
Ministering gifts not according to sanctifying grace, 1 Cor. xiii. 1.
All believers stewards of the manifold grace of God, 1 Pet. iv. 10, 11.
Grace needed for the right employment of every gift.
Whether. Proceeds—1. To particularise some of the gifts and offices.
2. To give directions and exhortations in regard to them.
These to be exercised in a way suitable to their nature.
All to be employed humbly, diligently, faithfully.
Each to exercise his gift in peace and harmony with others.
Instruction intended for all Christians, especially ministers.
Each to keep within his own sphere and attend to his own duties.
Each doing his own work makes an efficient Church.
Manifold departments in the work of Christian ministry.

Pattern in David's allotment of services, 1 Chron. xxiii. 4, 5.
Division of employment a divine institution.
Exemplified in the most prosperous period of the Church's history.
Becoming more recognised by the Church in the present day.
Still a hurtful tendency to abridge and economise.
One man often required to discharge many offices.
Hence most done imperfectly and much not done at all.
Prophecy. Gift for—1. Communicating divine truth ;
2. Interpreting the divine will ; 3. Foretelling future events.
Implied occasional inspiration by the Spirit.
A prophet one who was in intimate relation with God.
In the New Testament an inspired teacher, ranking after apostles, Eph. iv. 11.
Gift of prophecy to distinguish New Testament times, Acts ii. 17.
To be bestowed on both sexes, Acts ii. 17, 18 ; xxi. 9 ; 1 Cor. xi. 5.
Given for edification, exhortation, and comfort, 1 Cor. xiv. 3.
Chief of the gifts, Acts ii. 17, 18 ; xi. 27 ; xiii. 1 ; 1 Cor. xi. 4 ; xiv. 3–6, 12, 13, 18, 19, 24.
A branch of usefulness not confined to the pulpit. *Chalmers.*
Proportion of faith. 1. Analogy or general teaching of Scripture ;
2. Measure of faith actually imparted and possessed ;
3. The special gift which has been bestowed ;
4. The revelation which has been received, Jer. xxiii. 28.
Every gift to be exercised within its proper limits.
The measure of faith and knowledge the limit of this gift.
True prophets speak according to the law and the testimony, Isa. viii. 20.
See the truth, and neither conceal nor go beyond it.

Ἔχοντες δέ, but having, &c. *Est., Beng., Brown, Young.* And possessing, &c. ; ἔχοντες agrees with ἡμεῖς, understood, and continues the sentence ; an anacoluthon. *Stuart.* Speaks of those possessing certain gifts and offices in the church. *Brown.* —Χαρίσματα (χάρις, free favour, χαρίζω, to give as a favour), gifts ; functions or offices according to gifts or talents. *Tol.* Ordinary and perpetual. *Par.* Necessary for that time. *Barth.* Two species of gifts,—προφητεία and διακονία ; two varieties under the first, and three under the second. *Beza, Par., Ham., Koppe.* Four gifts,— προφ., διακ., διδασκ., and παρακλ., the three last mentioned (μεταδ., προϊστ., and ἐλ.) being special exercises of the gift of ministry (διακονία). *Meyer.* Of the χαρίσματα (gifts), the power of working miracles the most striking. Gift of healing a peculiar branch of this power. Gift of faith the source of these miraculous powers. This faith distinct from saving or sanctifying faith. A firm persuasion that the power was given and would be successful. Such powers referred to by the apostle as matters of ordinary occurrence. Mentioned in letters to persons supposed to be constant eyewitnesses of them. Another remarkable gift, that of *tongues*. Exercised where no need existed for the knowledge of a foreign language. Not generally employed for the conversion of foreigners. The result of a sudden impulse of supernatural inspiration. Often received after baptism, and at uncertain intervals afterwards. The exercise of the understanding suspended, and the spirit in an ecstasy. The believer constrained to pour out his soul in thanksgivings. Often ignorant himself of the meaning of the words he uttered. Another gift, the interpretation of tongues. The former not to be exercised in public without this. A fourth gift, that of discerning spirits, for distinguishing the real possessors of gifts. Another prominent gift, that of prophecy. Widely diffused. The prophet spoke with the authority of inspiration. Uttered divine strains of warning, exhortation, encouragement, and rebuke. Marvellous effect of such inspired addresses on the audience, 1 Cor. xiv. 25. Regarded by Paul as the first instrument for the benefit of believers, 1 Cor. xiv. 1, 3, 5, 22. Gift of teaching less extraordinary. Exercised more frequently than that of prophecy. Teacher made a prophet by a larger measure of inspiration. Gift of government enabled its possessor to preside over the church and regulate its external order; that of ministry, to attend to the temporal benefit of the brethren. *Con. & Hows.* Gifts divided by Paul in 1 Cor. xii. into,—I. Those referring to the power of intellect,—1. Word of wisdom ($\lambda o\gamma os\ \sigma o\phi\iota as$); 2. Word of knowledge ($\lambda.\ \gamma\nu\omega\sigma\epsilon\omega s$): II. Those conditioned by a peculiar faith,—1. The faith itself ($\pi\iota\sigma\tau\iota s$); 2. Its active operations, *e.g.*, healing of the sick ($\iota a\mu a\tau a$), miracles ($\delta\upsilon\nu a\mu\epsilon\iota s$); 3. Its oral operation in prophecy ($\pi\rho o\phi\eta\tau\epsilon\iota a$); 4. Its discerning operation, the discerning of spirits ($\delta\iota a\kappa\rho\iota\sigma\iota s\ \pi\nu\epsilon\upsilon\mu a\tau\omega\nu$): III. Those relating to tongues ($\gamma\lambda\omega\sigma\sigma a\iota$),—1. The speaking with tongues; 2. Their interpretation. The faith not merely a 'miraculous faith,' but a higher degree of faith in Christ produced by the Spirit,—a heroism of faith; its effect seen in acts of healing, performance of miracles, prophecy, discerning of spirits. This last effect decided whether the spirit which operated was divine, human, or demoniacal. *Meyer.*—$\Delta\iota a\phi o\rho a$, which are diverse. *Stuart.* Modifications of the one divine grace in the varieties of human individual talent. *Lange.* After $\delta\iota a\phi o\rho a$, supply—'Let him keep himself within the limits of his gift.' *Grot., Par.* 'Let him attend to that.' *Will.* 'Let him have or use that.' *Cam.* 'As God gives a man, so let Him minister.' *Beng.* 'Let us employ the gifts.' *De Wette.* —$E\iota\tau\epsilon$, whether; serves to enumerate particular species of the genus $\chi a\rho\iota\sigma\mu a\tau a$. *Stuart.*—$\Pi\rho o\phi\eta\tau\epsilon\iota a\nu$, prophecy. See chap. i. 2. Whether [we have] prophecy. *D. Brown.* Not merely foreknowledge of the future, but the knowledge of things hidden. *Theod.* Gift of understanding and explaining Scripture. *Calv.* Implies either foretelling future events, or explaining Old Testament prophecies. *Boothr.* Office or gift of prophecy; referring, in a more general sense, to those who publicly uttered anything by special aid or inspiration on the subject of religion; $\pi\rho o\phi\eta\tau a\iota$, in the Christian Church, those endowed with a supernatural gift in regard to addressing the people, whether for instruction or devotion. *Stuart.* Occasional inspiration. *Hodge.* Preaching by inspiration. *Cobbin.* A prophet, in the New Testament sense, an inspired teacher. *Brown.* Prophecy, an unpremeditated utterance from the revelation and impulse of the Holy Spirit, revealing the depths of the human heart and the divine counsel, but not connected with any definite office. *Meyer.* In the Old Testament sense, the gift of speaking under the impulse of the Spirit, whether in exhortation or revelation of the future. *Nielson.* Inspired teaching; a prophet, any one speaking with divine authority, whether with reference to the past, the present, or the future, Acts xv. 32; Exod. vii. 1, &c.—Κατα τ. ἀναλογιαν τ. πιστ, according to the proportion of faith. *Eras, Diod.* By (per) the proportion of faith. *Pag., Beza, Pisc.* According to the rule, method, or proportion (rationem) of faith. *Vulg.* According to the agreement of the faith. the canon or interpretation of Scripture. *Est., Par., Beza.* Likeness of the faith, *i.e.*, like the faith. *Luther.* Analogy of faith, common universally acknowledged doctrine of Scripture. *Calv., Mart.* Confession or summary of faith. *Rhem. Tist.* Tertullian calls the apostles' creed, 'regula fidei,' the rule of faith, the doctrine being thus known and familiar. Accurate knowledge of divine truth. *Tol.* Like method; agreement or analogy. *Mintert.* Let his interpretation be agreeable to the faith; so Josephus uses the verb ἀναλογέω, Antiq. iv. 8, 4 *Schött.* According to the objective rule of faith. *Phil.* This rule in the interpretation of Scripture not explanation, but application. *Lange.* Standard or rule of faith. *Hodge.* Let him give all revealed truth its proper place. *Cobbin.* Let him prophesy in proportion to his knowledge and persuasion. *Morus.* According to the proportion of faith which has been intrusted to him. *Storr, Flatt, S. Clarke.* Proportion of his faith. *Ellicot.* The revelation received by him. *Brown, Boothr.* The extent of his information or measure of faith. *Hald.* Depth, energy, and illumination of faith naturally the measure to this gift. *De Wette.* According to the proportion of [our] faith; all the gifts of believers according to their respective capacity for them. *D. Brown.* Measure of faith or confidence; = μέτρον πίστεως. *Alford.* According to the gift received. *Thol.* Πίστις, the talent from which proceeds prophecy, the χάρισμα, or function. *Tol., Vor., Pisc.* The gift according to the capacity of the vessel which receives it. *Chrys.* Conferred according to the faith of him who received it. *Whitby, Doddr., Macknight.* So far as he has the gift of inspiration. *Pyle.* In proportion to his subjective faith, as Jer. xxiii. 28; none to speak, but as it is given him of God. *Nielson.* Ἀναλογια, from ἀνα, denoting comparison, and λογος, reason; ἀναλογισασθε, consider, in the way of comparison or for imitation, Heb. xii. 3.

---

7. *Or ministry, let us wait on our ministering; or he that teacheth on teaching.*

Ministry. 1. Church ministry in general, 1 Cor. xii. 5;
2. Special service in any particular Church;
3. Office of deacon as distinguished from that of elder, Phil. i. 1.
Denotes management rather than teaching.
Outer business of the house of God, Neh. xi. 16; Acts vi. 1, &c.
Mark thus profitable to Paul for ministry, 2 Tim. iv. 11.
Some endowed with special gifts for outward service.
Business tact; administrative talent.
" Deacon " used in an official sense in the apostolic age.
First occurs in the Epistle to the Philippians; = minister, servant.
The office itself discharged from the beginning, Acts v. 6, 10; vi. 1–7.
Those who discharged it at first called " young men," Acts v. 6.
The " seven " appointed in Acts vi., for a time without the title.
These called not " deacons," but the " seven," Acts xxi. 8.
The title probably given when the duties multiplied.
The office one of considerable importance, 1 Tim. iii. 8.
Those appointed to it who had received the gift of " ministry."
Required heads and hands. Discharged also by females, chap. xvi. 1.

CHAP. XII.]   ST. PAUL'S EPISTLE TO THE ROMANS.   171

Subordinate assistants afterwards appointed.
The office, in course of time, greatly changed in character.
Let us wait. Words not in the original. Reference to ver. 3.
Paul not now exhorting, but defining the sphere of the gift.
Let him attend to that, and be content with it. *Theophylact.*
Brethren to give themselves entirely to their proper work.
If any has an office, let him wait on his office. *Luther.*
Teacheth. Has the gift of communicating instruction.
Teachers distinguished from prophets, Acts xiii. 1 ; 1 Cor. xii. 28, 29 ; Eph. iv. 11.
Prophets spoke under the Spirit's immediate inspiration ;
Teachers not necessarily inspired but well instructed, 2 Tim. ii. 2.
Paul's own ordinary form of ministration, 1 Cor. iv. 17.
Natural gifts and acquired knowledge available for the office.
Reading and study enjoined with a view to it, 1 Tim. iv. 13, 15, 16 ; 2 Tim. ii. 15.
Even heathen poets made available, Acts xvii. 28 ; 1 Cor. xv. 33 ; Titus i. 12.
Gift of prophecy exercised for the conversion of sinners ;
Gift of teaching for the building up of believers.

Διακονιαν (διa, and κονις, dust), ministry. *Cam.* Church function. *Chrys.* Especial'y outward service, and more particularly care of the poor. *Theod., Theoph.* Office in general. *Luth.* Distributing the church's funds to the poor. *Tat.* Office of deacon. *Beza.* Care of the poor; distribution of church-alms. *Schött.* Deaconship. *Flatt, Hodge.* Office of ministry, as deacons. *Doddr., Boothr.* Service in preaching the Gospel, &c. *Parkhurst.* Work of an evangelist. *Whitby.* Official duty of the διακονοι, —care of the poor, sick, conveniences for public worship, &c., and generally, the external matters of the Church, like the חזן (chazan) or minister of the synagogue, Luke iv. 20. *Stuart.* Gift of ministration. *Con. & Hows.* Management rather than teaching. *Brown.* All that pertained to outward service. *Nicl.* Care of the poor and suffering. *Rück.* Church ministry in general ; special service in any church ; the diaconate as distinguished from the presbyterate or episcopate. *Lange.* Service of administering the temporal affairs of the church. *D. Brown.* The Greek term διακονος, out of thirty times in the New Testament, only used three or four times officially. *Con. & Hows.* Office described by deacon (διακονος) appears in the New Testament as the co-relative of bishop. The two mentioned together, Phil. i. 1 ; 1 Tim. iii. 2, 8. First used in its generic sense, implying subordinate activity (1 Cor. iii. 5 ; 2 Cor. vi. 4); afterwards more definitely, as applied to a distinct body of men in the Christian society. Questionable whether the 'seven' (Acts vi.) were not appointed to higher functions than those of the deacons in the New Testament. Indications of another body existing in the church at Jerusalem who may be compared with the deacons in Phil. i. 1. The 'young men' (Acts v. 6, 10) probably not merely young men, but persons occupying a distinct position and exercising distinct functions. Moral qualifications for the office of deacon substantially the same as those of the bishop, except not required to be 'given to hospitality,' or 'apt to teach.' Analogy of the synagogues and the scanty notices in the New

Testament point to the deacons, or 'young men' in the Church at Jerusalem, as preparing the places of assembly, taking part in the distribution of the church's alms, at first with no direct supervision, then under that of the seven, and afterwards under the elders, maintaining order at the daily meetings to break bread, baptizing new converts, and distributing the sacramental elements. Apparently not a part of the deacon's office to teach publicly in the church. *Smith's Dictionary of the Bible.*—Ἐν τῇ διακονίᾳ, let each be diligent in his office; let him abide in his ministry. *Cam.* In ministration. *Pag., Eras., Vat.* In ministering. *Pisc., Beza, Tol.* Let him exercise his ministry. *Pag., Beza, Pisc.* Think soberly of it. *Par.* Be wholly devoted to his ministration or service. *Stuart.* Wait on or be occupied with it. *D. Brown.*—Ὁ διδάσκων, he who teaches, or has the gift of teaching. *Tol.* Office next to that of prophet. *Grot.* The teacher. *Diod.* If any be called to teach. *Mart.* An instructor of catechumens. *Doddr., Boothr.* Preaches the gospel where already planted. *Ham.* For the conversion of others. *Whitby.* Ordinary stated teacher who was so by official station and taught according to degree of knowledge possessed, thus distinguished from προφήτης, who taught by inspiration. *Stuart.* Teacher not necessarily inspired. *Hodge.* Under inspiration, but working by secondary instruments, will, reason, rhetorical powers. *Alford.* Office probably consisted mainly in opening up the evangelical hearings of Old Testament Scripture, *e.g.*, Apollos, Acts xviii. 24. *D. Brown.*—Ἐν τῇ διδασκαλίᾳ, in doctrine. *Vulg., Tol.* To teaching. *Vat.* Let him employ himself in teaching. *Pisc, Beza, Pag.* Right to teach in the public assemblies at first universal. In consequence of improprieties very early occasioned by this (James iii. 1), the right apparently limited in the second century to those officers who publicly spoke in the congregation, though not formally abolished. Duty of teaching, as an office, not incumbent on the elders (πρεσβύτεροι), although these were to be διδακτικοί, 'apt to teach.' The distinction into presbyteri docentes and presbyteri regentes (teaching and ruling elders) first made by Calvin, 'verbi ministros sive episcopos,' and 'gubernatores sive seniores ex plebe delectos.' This distinction afterwards made a part of the constitution of the Presbyterian Church. The capacity of instructing and edifying in the assemblies at first considered rather as a free gift of the Spirit (χάρισμα πνευματικόν), which manifested itself in many Christians, although in different modes (προφήτης, διδάσκαλος, γλωσσηλαλών). Still less was a distinct priestly order known in the time of the apostles, the whole society of Christians forming a royal priesthood. Tertullian says, The authority of the church made the difference between clergy and laity. Hilary the deacon says, At first all taught and baptized whenever there was occasion for doing so. *Gieseler.*

---

8. *Or he that exhorteth, on exhortation: he that giveth, let him do it with simplicity; he that ruleth, with diligence; he that showeth mercy, with cheerfulness.*

Exhorteth. Has the gift of exhorting; a species of teaching, Acts xiii. 15.
One of the uses of the gift of prophecy, Acts xv. 32; 1 Cor. xiv. 3.
Included both warning and consolation, Acts xiv. 22.
Had special reference to practice and experience, Acts xv. 32.
Followed up the work of the teacher in the Church.
The teacher required the clearer head;
The exhorter the warmer heart. Both needful.
In New England these offices originally in two separate ministers.
Giveth. *Gr.*, Distributes, viz., 1. The Church's funds;

Or, 2. His own private liberality, as ver. 13 ; 1 Tim. vi. 18.
Special office of the deacons, Acts vi. 1-7 ; Phil. i. 1 ; 1 Tim. iii. 8.
Teachers and elders supported by the Church, 1 Cor. ix. 11, 14 ; 1 Tim. v. 17, 18.
Widows and poor also thus supported, 1 Tim. v. 9, 16 ; Gal. ii. 10.
Paul declined this right of support, yet asserted it, 1 Cor. ix. 7-14.
Exhorts the elders at Ephesus to imitate his example, Acts xx. 34, 35.
Believers to contribute to the support of ministers and the poor, Gal. vi. 6 ; ii. 10.
Simplicity. Purity of motives; uprightness; liberality, 2 Cor. viii. 2.
Single devotedness to Christ's glory and the Church's good.
In Scripture, the Christian quality of the benevolent, 2 Cor. ix. 11.
A single eye ; opposed to covetousness and selfishness, Matt. vi. 22.
Indicates, not the *sphere*, but the *character* of the service.
The disposition with which the gift or office is to be exercised.
Judas had the office but not the grace of it, John xii. 6.
First Christians liberal contributors to the poor, Acts ii. 44, 45 ; iv. 34, 35.
Ruleth. Exercises rule or presidency in the Church.
Has the care of the brethren committed to him.
Governments named among the gifts, 1 Cor. xii. 28.
A charge indicated without denoting its special character.
Same word used for ruling one's own house, 1 Tim. iii. 5.
Seems rather to have pertained to external matters.
Probably care of the outward affairs of the Church.
"Taking care of the Church of God," 1 Tim. iii. 5.
Ranked among the inferior gifts here, and in 1 Cor. xii. 28.
Those who ruled well entitled to double honour or pay, 1 Tim. v. 17.
Especially when also labouring in the word and doctrine.
To be esteemed very highly in love for their work's sake, 1 Thess. v. 12, 13.
The office exercised by elders or presbyters, 1 Tim. v. 17.
Same persons also called bishops or overseers, Acts xx. 17, 28 ; Titus i. 5, 7.
Elder denotes the rank, *bishop* the duties of the office.
"Elders" and "bishops" used in the N. T. as equivalent terms.
All of equal rank and authority in the time of the apostles.

Several in each church, Acts xi. 30; xiv. 23; xv. 2, 4, 6; Phil. i. 1; Titus. i. 5.

Their duty to watch over the Church—1. As to external order; 2. Internal purity, Acts xx. 28.

To exercise ministerial rule and promote the spiritual welfare of the Church's various members.

All required by Paul to be apt to teach, 1 Tim. iii. 2.

Yet some ruled without labouring as teachers, 1 Tim. v. 17.

Ruling in the Church afterwards confined to one of the elders.

This elder distinguished from the rest by the title of "bishop."

Diligence. Earnestness, zeal. Same word rendered "business," ver. 11.

Requisite in taking care of the Church of God, 1 Tim. iii. 5.

Elders or bishops exhorted by Paul, Acts xx. 28-35; by Peter, 1 Pet. v. 2-4.

Showeth mercy. Attends to the suffering and distressed.

Believers often in such circumstances by persecution.

Persons appointed to such a charge in the Church.

Sometimes women, 1 Tim. v. 10; Phœbe probably such, Rom. xvi. 1.

Not so much an office indicated as a service.

Early Christians distinguished for their care of the suffering.

Members to have the same care one of another, 1 Cor. xii. 25, 26.

An enemy's testimony,—"See how the Christians love one another."

Cheerfulness. Good-will and liking for the task.

Manner and spirit of the service. Kind looks, cheerful smiles.

The Lord loveth a cheerful giver, 2 Cor. ix. 7.

Not only good-doing, but cheerfulness in it.

Often more consolatory than the act itself.

Gives double value and efficacy to relief afforded.

Implies the gain experienced in good-doing, Acts xx. 35.

Mercy blesses both him that gives and him that receives.

Ὁ παρακαλων, he who exhorts, or has received the gift of exhortation. *Tol.* The pastor or presbyter who labours in the word and doctrine; special gift of comforting the afflicted. *Beza, Pisc., Par.* By exhortation souls are comforted from the Scripture. *Origen.* Who persuaded to virtue. *Theod.* Same as ποιμην, pastor. *Schött.* Who preached the practical use of the Gospel where already planted. *Ham.* Who urged Christians to duty and encouraged them in the discharge of it. *Dodlr.* Urged to practical duties, dwelt upon the threatenings and promises of the Gospel, and so aided and completed the work of the teacher. *Stuart.* The office of the bishop or pastor; implies not only enforcing Christian duties, but applying the doctrines of Christianity for the comfort, hope, and joy of the faithful. *Boothroyd.* Seems to have been a distinct office. *Cobbin.* One who delivered hortatory discourse, probably the interpretation of an Old

Testament passage; also as a prophet. *De Wette, Reiche, Meyer.* Teaching and exhortation subdivisions of prophecy. *Koppe.* Distinction probably not to be pressed. *Rück.* Gift of impressively preaching practical Christianity and divine comfort, and of exercising cure of souls by house and sick visitation. *Barth.* Not necessarily distinct from prophecy. *Alford.* Indicates inspired instruction, the character of the two classes of gifts. *Brown.* Reference perhaps to persons permitted to exercise themselves occasionally in exhorting either the brethren generally, or small parties of the less instructed. *D. Brown.* Heb. נָחַם, to comfort; קָרָא, to call, Prov. viii. 4; Isa. xl. 2; אָמֵץ, to strengthen; בָּשַׂר, to publish good tidings, Isa. xli. 27; הִסִּית, to persuade, Deut. xiii. 6. The addresses delivered in the early but post-apostolic church were exhortations founded on the portions of scriptures read, with a view to their practice. *Justin Martyr.* Of these, which lasted only eight or ten minutes, there were usually several by different persons at each diet. *Jamieson.*—Ὁ μεταδιδούς, he who distributes, *i.e.*, alms. *Tol., Beza.* His own property. *Church Fathers in general, Boothr., Doddr., D. Brown.* Alms of the Church. *Tol., Est., Beza, Mackn., Cobbin.* His own goods or those of others. *Ham.* Distributor of the church's alms, like the פַּרְנָס (parnas), of the Synagogue. *Schött.* Distributes the charities of the church or of individuals in it; διάκονος, the general overseer, collector, and provider of alms; ὁ μεταδιδούς, the actual distributor of them. *Stuart.* Chiefly deacon's office. *Hodge.* Either the deacon, or some distributor subordinate to him. *Alford.* Collecting and distributing the voluntary offerings of the church as a deacon. *Brown.* Attending to the distribution of alms. *Nielson.* The exercise of private benevolence rather than of diaconal duty. *D. Brown.* Μεταδίδ., to distribute what is our own, 1 Tim. vi. 18; διαδίδ., what is another's, Acts iv. 35. *Vitringa.* Εἶτα, here omitted, so that the strain becomes purely hortatory. *Stuart.* Omission of εἶτα seems to indicate a transition from public to private gifts. *Alford.*—Ἐν ἁπλότητι (ἁπλοῦς, simple), with simplicity. *Pisc., Beza, Pag.* Simplicity of heart. *Vat.* Kindness. *Drus.* Good faith. *Tir.* Without partiality. *Beza, Tol., Est.* Without self-interest. *Est.* Without fraud. *Tol.* With liberality. *Chrys.* Uprightness, fidelity; without avarice, favour, or prejudice. *Schött.* With liberality and disinterestedness. *Doddr., D. Brown.* Impartiality, liberality, or purity of motive. *Parkhurst, Mackn.* Single regard to the good of those on whom the charity was bestowed. *Stuart.* Integrity of aim. *Cobbin.* Uprightness. *De Wette.* Sincerity. *Brown.* Indicates rather the outward than the inward frame. *Alford.* Heb. בְּיֹשֶׁר לְבָב, in the uprightness of my heart, 1 Chron. xxix. 17; בְּתָם = ἁπλῶς, uprightly, Prov. x. 9; נֶפֶשׁ בְּרָכָה = ψυχὴ ἁπλῆ, the liberal soul, Prov. xi. 25 —Ὁ προϊστάμενος (πρό, before, and ἵστημι, to stand; middle, προΐσταμαι, to preside; προεστώς, a president or ruler, 1 Tim. v. 17). Cod. Sin. has προϊστανόμενος. He who presides (præest). *E(i)as., Pisc., Tol., Mart., Diod., Stuart.* Has charge over others. *Est., Beng.* Presides over the church. *Tir., Tol., Ham.* The presbyter or elder who rules the church. *Vor.* Joined with the pastor for church discipline. *Gom., Beza, Par.* Presbyter or elder, like the ruler of the Synagogue; so προεστῶτες, 1 Thess. v. 12. *Grot., Schött.* Who is over the brethren or the church. *Origen.* Aids the needy as well by words as bodily service. *Theoph.* Who presides in the distribution of charities. *Doddr.* Presides over the church's stock. *Whitby, Wells.* Has a charge. *Flatt.* Like 'governments' (κυβερνήσεις), 1 Cor. xii. 28; an office apparently among the lowest in the church; like προστάτις (chap. xvi. 2), or, one who receives and entertains strangers. *Stuart.* That of managing the external affairs of the church and attending to the poor. *De Wette.* One exercising a presidency or charge in general. *Rückert.* Who presides over distributions to the poor, and has the care of those imprisoned for the faith. *Boothr.* Exercises rule in the church. *Hodge.* Has the rule of a congregation, or even merely of a house. *Barth.* Presides in the assemblies and superintends the affairs of the church. *Brown.*

A higher activity than the διακονια (diaconate), proceeding from the gift of κυβερνησις, 1 Cor. xii. 28. *Nielson.* He who had care of the outward affairs of the church; a presbyter, but not exclusively. *Meyer.* Who acts as president of the congregation; might devote himself to distribution or care of the poor, to ruling or government in the restricted sense, or to healing the sick. *Lange* Who rules, whether in the church or in his own household, as 1 Tim. iii. 4, 5. *D. Brown.* Heb. קְהָתִין, his minister; LXX. τον προεστηκοτα του οἰκου, 'who was over his house.' 2 Sam. xiii. 17. Name applied to those who in Greek cities had the care of strangers committed to them, and who were responsible for their behaviour. *Meyer.* Justin Martyr speaks of one, probably an elder, as προεστως των ἀδελφων, presiding over the brethren. *Apol.* i. 67. Tertullian says: 'president probati quique seniores.' Church distinctions less developed at the time of this epistle than in that of the first Epistle to Timothy, but somewhat more than in the first Epistle to the Corinthians. *Lange.* A regularly constituted society arose by degrees among the brethren. For this the Jewish Synagogue presented itself as the most natural model. At first the apostles themselves performed the duties of the society, but by degrees special officers were appointed. First seven distributors of alms appointed to be chosen. Soon after this, elders chosen, not so much for the purpose of teaching, as for the management of common concerns, and maintaining the ordinances of the church. These appointments allowed to be determined by the church itself. The 'seven' regarded by most as the first deacons. So Cyprian. Distinguished from them by Chrysostom and the Council of Trulla. Appointment of deacons from the enlargement of the circle of duties required (Mosheim, Neander). New churches out of Palestine formed after the pattern of the mother-church at Jerusalem. Their presidents were the elders or bishops (πρεσβυτεροι, ἐπισκοποι); officially of equal rank, though in many churches individuals among them had a personal authority over the others, under the title of the 'bishop.' Both appellations originally the same, Acts xx. 17, 28; Titus i. 5, 7; Phil. i 1; 1 Tim. iii. 1, 8. Jerome says, With the ancients the same persons were called bishops and presbyters or elders. Long admitted even in the Romish Church. Pope Urban II., in the Council of Bonaventura (1091), says: 'We say that the sacred orders are the diaconate and presbyterate, since the primitive church is said to have had these alone.' Nicolaus Tedeschus (1428): 'Formerly presbyters governed the church in common and ordained priests.' Council of Trent declared that 'bishops, who succeeded to the place of the apostles, govern the church and are superior to presbyters,' without maintaining the superiority and distinction as a divine institution. This, however, afterwards became the general doctrine of the Roman Catholic Church. English Episcopalians adopted this view, while the other Protestant churches returned to the most ancient doctrine and regulation on the subject. *Gieseler.* Clement, Bishop of Rome, mentioned Phil. iv. 3, says: 'The apostles constituted bishops and deacons,' and elsewhere uses the terms 'presbyter' and 'bishop,' as denoting the same office. Polycarp: 'Ye must be subject to the presbyters and deacons.' Irenæus: 'It behoves us to hearken to those who are presbyters in the church, who have their succession from the apostles with the succession of the episcopate.' Ignatius (Epistle to the Church at Magnesia) speaks of their 'bishops' in the plural number. Tertullian says: 'Certain approved elders (seniores) preside.' Firmilian of Cæsarea: 'In elders or presbyters is vested the power of baptizing, imposition of hands, and ordination.' Jerome: 'The bishops are greater than the presbyters rather by custom than the appointment of the Lord.' Hilary: 'Presbyters were at first called bishops.' Theodoret: 'Of old they called the same persons both bishops and presbyters.' Mosheim: 'The rulers of the church were called either presbyters or bishops.' Dr Holland, Div. Prof. at Oxford: 'To affirm the office of bishop to be different from that of presbyter and superior to it, is contrary to Scripture, the Fathers, the doctrines of the Church of England,

and to the very schoolmen themselves.' Hooker: 'Sundry forms of discipline may be equally consistent with the general maxims of Scripture.' Milner: 'At first indeed, or for some time, church governors were only of two ranks, presbyters and deacons: the term "bishop" was confounded with that of "presbyter."' Waddington (History of the Church): 'It is even *certain* that the terms "bishop" and "elder" were in the first instance, and for a short period, sometimes used synonymously, and indiscriminately applied to the same order in the ministry.' 'Till the date of Clement's epistle, its government (that of the Church of Corinth) had been clearly presbyterial.' Dr Hinds (Early Progress of Christianity): 'At the period on which we are now dwelling, it is obvious that the terms "bishop" and "presbyter" were not only applied to the same order, but that no order of ministers (setting aside the apostles) was generally established superior to the presbytery.' Neander: 'It is certain that every church was governed by a union of elders or overseers chosen from among themselves.' The two titles (bishop and elder) originally equivalent; as—1. Nowhere named together as orders distinct from each other; 2. Bishops and deacons named as apparently an exhaustive division of the officers of the church (Phil. i. 1; 1 Tim. iii. 1, 8!; 3. Same persons described by both names (Titus i. 5, 7; Acts xx. 17, 18); 4. Elders discharge functions essentially episcopal, *i.e.*, involving pastoral superintendence (1 Tim. v. 17; 1 Pet. v. 1, 2). Elders had priority of time. Mentioned in Acts xi. 30, and Acts xv. 2. Earliest use of 'bishops' in the address to the elders at Miletus, and there rather descriptive of functions than given as a title. Duties of the bishop-elders:—1. General superintendence over the spiritual well-being of the flock (1 Pet. v. 2); 2. Work of teaching both publicly and privately (1 Thess. v. 12; Titus i. 9; 1 Tim. v. 17); 3. Work of visiting the sick (James v. 14); 4. Receiving strangers (1 Tim. iii. 2; Titus i. 8). Took part in deliberations (Acts xv. 6-22; xxi. 18); addressed other churches (xv. 23); were joined with the apostles in the work of ordaining and laying on of hands (1 Tim. iv. 14). Episcopal functions in the modern sense of the words, as implying special superintendence over the ministers of the church, belonged only to the apostles and those whom they invested with their authority. *Smith's Dictionary of the Bible,* voc. BISHOP. Baur infers from Titus i. 5 that every church had but one elder, and that where several elders are represented as being in one city, each governed independently a particular church. Analogy of the synagogue, however, is in favour of the plurality of elders in a church. Passages in which the collected elders of one city appear and act as a united whole (Acts xv. 4; xx. 17; Phil. i. 1; James v. 14), speak for the connection of the elders of one city into a college, and consequently of the churches in houses into one church, even if every house-church, as every synagogue, had its particular elder. *Gieseler.* In the Fathers, the term 'presbyter' always exclusively applied to ordained spiritual advisers, distinguished from the laity; in Latin, rendered by sacerdos, pastor, and the like. According to Mosheim, some presbyters governed and instructed the church at home, and were thus the presiding or governing presbyters ($\pi\rho o\epsilon\sigma\tau\omega\tau\epsilon s\ \pi\rho\epsilon\sigma\beta\upsilon\tau\epsilon\rho o\iota$); others occupied themselves in converting the Jews and heathen, labouring in the word and doctrine ($\kappa o\pi\iota\omega\nu\tau\epsilon s$). According to Neander, the existence of ruling elders as a distinct class of officers in the modern sense of the term, to be traced only to the North African churches in the fourth century, certain leaders in them being called 'seniores plebis,' but not presbyters or elders; being expressly distinguished from the clerical body, and constituting, as the representatives of the congregation, a middle class between the clergy and laity, for whose interests they consulted, being the remains of a similar arrangement in the previous ages. Officers, similar to 'ruling elders,' called by the ancients 'seniores,' and probably the 'helps, governments,' mentioned 1 Cor. xii. 28, and the 'brethren' who sat in the councils with the apostles; 'seniores' never being applied by the Fathers to ministers, but only to these laymen. *Smith on Presbytery, Note.* Where the apostles were themselves able to superintend the churches they had founded, the church-officers consisted of—(1.) Apostles; (2.) Bishops or priests; (3.) Deacons and evangelists. Where the apostles were unable to give personal superintendence, they delegated that power to one of themselves, as in Jerusalem; or to one in whom they had confidence, as at Ephesus and in Crete. As the apostles died off, these apostolic delegates necessarily multiplied. By the end of the first century, they would have been established in every country, as Crete, and in every large town where there were several bishops or priests. These superintendents apparently the angels addressed by John, Rev. ii., iii. Left to fill the places of the apostles in the government of the church, but with authority only to be exercised in limited districts. In the next century, these officers bore the name of bishops, those who in the first century had been called indifferently presbyters or bishops having now only the title of presbyters; the title 'bishop' being thus gradually dropped by the presbyters, and applied specifically to those who represented what James, Timothy, and Titus had been in the apostolic ages. *Smith's Dictionary*, voc. CHURCH.—'Εν σπουδῇ (σπευδω, to haste). With zeal (studio). *Eras., Pisc., Tol.* Diligence. *Pag., Beza, Vor.* Solicitude. *Mor.* Attention and zeal. *Hodge.* Earnest purpose. *D. Brown.* Solicitude for the welfare of his charge. *Origen.* —'Ο ἐλεων, who shows mercy or pity (misereretur); taken generally. *Mort.* In particular, who takes care of the afflicted, poor, exiles, strangers. *Est., Tol., Par., Vor.* The *parabolani* of a later age. An ancient church office committed to widows and others. *Calv.* Not who is only merciful, but has charge of the sick, &c. *Schött., Whitby, Wells.* Refers to personal cares and services bestowed on the sick and unfortunate. *Stuart.* The idea of gift, *i.e.,* the gift of church activity, extended by the apostle to Christian activity in general,—private benevolence, and especially of Christian women. *De Wette.* Perhaps attention to the sick and prisoners. *Nielson.* This and the two foregoing taken as subdivisions of ministry or administration of the church's affairs. *Koppe, Brown.* No church office intended. *Alf., Vitringa.*—'Εν ἱλαροτητι, with cheerfulness (hilaritate); with a cheerful mind and countenance. *Beza, Pisc.* Alacrity and kindness. *Hodge.* Giving in faith and hope, not sorrowing as if it were lost. *Origen.* Appearing not with sadness, but with a cheerful and tranquil countenance. *Theoph.* Early Christians remarkable for their care of their poorer brethren. The duty not left to the gratuities of private individuals, but devolved on the whole community of believers, who regarded it not as a burden but a privilege. At the close of the Sabbath service, lists of the poor, aged, widows, and orphans were produced by each in turn as they knew of a brother's or sister's necessity, and a donation forthwith ordered out of the funds of the church, supplied by the voluntary contributions of the faithful. Individuals also, especially women, as having readier access, held it a sacred duty to countenance the poor with their presence and their purse in their own homes, inquiring into their wants, and tendering the highly-prized comforts of Christian sympathy and counsel. Ladies of highest rank performed for the afflicted the meanest and most servile offices; sat beside the bed-side of the sick, conversing with and comforting them, prepared their victuals and fed them, administered cordials and medicine, brought them changes of clothing, made their beds, dressed their putrefying ulcers, and swaddled their bodies when dead. In times of famine and pestilence, the Christians, in contrast with the heathen, were busy on the streets and in the houses, distributing money, food, or clothing to the sufferers. Delivered thousands, by their self-sacrificing benevolence, from captivity and exile. To their brethren in prison, they begged admission in crowds, carrying with them beds, food, clothing, and fuel, washed their feet, and rendered them the most tender and endearing services. Not only sent relief to those condemned like slaves to the mines, but undertook lengthened journeys for their comfort and support. Some dedicated themselves to the task of searching out desolate orphans, helpless widows, unfortunate tradesmen, and heathen foundlings. Some sat by the highways, or hired persons to perambulate the fields, in order to direct wanderers and benighted travellers into the way. Others delighted to lead the blind, succour the bruised, and carry home the lame and the maimed unable to walk. In cases of great or public calamity, fasts were appointed, the savings from which were given for the aid of the needy. Many were in the habit of observing in private quarterly, monthly, or weekly fasts, giving the savings for the same purpose. Some voluntarily bound themselves to set aside the tenths of their income for the church's treasury in aid of the poor. Many sold their estates for the same purpose, devoting themselves to manual labour or preaching the Word. Others gave up their patrimony to objects of Christian benevolence, but retaining the management in their own hands. *Jamieson's Manners and Trials of Primitive Christians.*

---

9. *Let love be without dissimulation. Abhor that which is evil; cleave to that which is good.*

Let, &c. Comes to duties of Christians in relation to each other.
Love. First, special directions in regard to love.
Benevolence, kind feeling; to be shown in words and deeds.
General love to all men, fervent love to the brethren, 1 Pet. i. 22; iv. 8.
Love leads the way to all the duties that follow. *Chrysostom.*
Without dissimulation. Only undissembled love is love.
Such love insisted on, 1 Cor. xiii. 1, &c.; 2 Cor. vi. 6; 1 John iii. 14, 18.
Great danger of love being only in appearance.
Burning lips and a wicked heart, Prov. xxvi. 23. Hatred under deceit, ver. 26.
Love to be real must have God and His will for its object. *Origen.*
Men only love unfeignedly when they first love God.
Such love grudges neither trouble nor expense for its object.
Consistent with faithful admonition and leads to it, Lev. xix. 17.
Abhor. Not only shun but vehemently hate it.
To abhor evil necessary to truly loving good.
Love consistent with a hatred of evil and requires it.
Rejoices not in iniquity but rejoices in the truth, 1 Cor. xiii. 6.
Love to the sinner accompanied by abhorrence of the sin.
Evil. 1. Moral evil or sin in general;
2. Especially, what is malignant or injurious, Matt. v. 29.
Every temper and action having an injurious tendency.
Immoral and injurious thoughts, feelings, words and actions.
Cleave. Not only follow but stick to it. Metaphor from glue.
Implies—1. deliberate choice; 2. Sincere affection; 3. Perseverance.
Eagerly seek good; readily embrace it; strenuously follow it.
Affection of the heart coupled with action of the hand.

Good. 1. What is morally good and excellent;
2. What is beneficial and tending to the good of others, Matt. vii. 11, 12.
To love and seek the good of others marks the Christian.
Good-loving and good-doing the nature of God, Acts xiv. 17; 1 John iv. 16.
The spirit and character of Jesus, Acts x. 38; xx. 35; 2 Cor. viii. 9.
Not enough to abhor evil; believers earnestly to follow good.
Lofty tone of morality characteristic of the Gospel.
Evil to be shunned and good done, and both *with the whole heart*.

'Ανυπόκριτος (ἀ, not, and ὑποκρίνομαι, to feign, act the hypocrite), unfeigned; forbids simulation or pretence. *Ellicot.*—'Αποστυγοῦντες (ἀπό, from, and στυγω; to turn away from a thing with loathing) [be] abhorring; ἔστε, understood. *Stuart.*— Τὸ πονηρόν, the evil; especially what is unkind or injurious to a brother. *Calv., D. Brown.* Malice. *Stuart.*—Κολλώμενοι (κολλα, glue), keeping yourselves glued to the good. *Hart.* Hold firmly to the good. *Diod.* Be cleaving; ἔστε, understood. *Stuart.* Heb. דָּבַק.

---

10. *Be kindly affectioned one to another with brotherly love; in honour preferring one another.*

Kindly affectioned. As those who are near relations.
Condemns apathy and requires holy affection to all believers.
Expresses a natural affection, as of parents to children, &c.
Love more tender, intense, and tenacious than mere good-will.
Believers connected with each other by the closest relation,
Hence to cherish towards each other the tenderest affection.
Not only love required but readiness and inclination to love.
With; or, "In." Indicates the special kind of love intended.
Brotherly love. Distinguished from charity or general love, 2 Pet. i. 7.
Still more intensifying the love enjoined.
Believers are children of God, therefore brethren of each other.
Their love to each other to be that of brothers and sisters.
The happiness as well as holiness of true Christianity.
The sweetest thing on earth to love and to be loved.
Brotherly love the family feature of true believers.
Heathens could say, Behold how these Christians love one another!
Believers linked together by closer than earthly ties.
Their love a divine and not a mere earthly affection.
Christ's love to them the pattern of theirs to each other, John xiii. 34.

In honour. Moral respect essential to Christian love.
Love necessitates respectful thoughts and carriage.
All men to be honoured, 1 Pet. ii. 17; especially the brethren.
Love honours them that fear the Lord, Ps. xv. 4.
Is forward to notice the gifts, graces, and works of others.
Preferring one another. Vie with each other in true respect.
Lead the way; set the example; anticipate each other.
Love willingly accords pre-eminence to others.
Vaunts not itself; is not puffed up; seeks not her own, 1 Cor. xiii. 4, 5.
Believers learn of their Master to be lowly in heart, Matt. xi. 29.
Jesus humbled Himself, made Himself of no reputation, Phil. ii. 7, 8.
Each believer to esteem another better than himself, Phil. ii. 3.
Lowly thoughts of ourselves, high and honourable ones of others.
Contrast to the reigning morality of the heathen world.
Christianity the foundation of true courtesy and politeness.
"Be courteous," a New Testament precept, 1 Pet. iii. 8.
True love is tender of another's feelings.
Church at Rome in danger of jealousies and contentions.
Love of pre-eminence the bane of the Church, 3 John 9.
Church of Rome claims to be mother and mistress of all churches.

Φιλαδελφίᾳ (φιλεω, to love, and ἀδελφος, a brother). Through brotherly love. *Diod.* Carried by brotherly love to love one another. *Mart.* In love of the brethren. *Ellicot, Young.* In respect to brotherly love; dative of relation. *Stuart.* In brotherly love. *D. Brown.*—Φιλοστοργοι (φιλεω and στοργη, natural affection). Ready, strongly inclined (propensi) to love one another. *Pag., Beza, Pisc., Tol.* Στοργη, not only natural affection, but a charity equally strong,—vehement affection, 2 Macc. ix. 10. *Grot.* Φιλοστ., a strong affection like that of parents to their offspring, with delight in it. *Balguy.* Delight in the tenderest fraternal affection to each other. *Doddr.* Such affection as the relation of Christian brethren and the bonds of consanguinity demand. *Whitby.* Be affectionate. *Ellicot.*—Τιμη, respect. *Eras.* Aid. *Vat.* In respect to honour. *Stuart.* In civility. *Cobbin.*—Προηγουμενοι (προ, before, and ἡγεομαι, to lead). Going before each other. *Beza, Pisc., Pag., Par., Schött., Young.* Preventing each other. *Eras., Mor., Cas., Mart., Diod.* Let one go before another in showing respect. *Luth.* Ἡγεισθαι, to lead the way; to prefer to one's self, Phil. ii. 3. *Grot.* Preventing each other in every office of respect, *Doddr.* Mutually preventing one another with honour. *L'Enfant.* Leading on each other with respect. *Leighton.* Ready to think better of others than yourselves. *Wells.* Strive to anticipate each other; ἡγεισθαι, = to take the lead, go before, set the example. *Stuart.* By showing respect, let each seek to lead another to the same disposition and behaviour; dative of instrument. *Rück.* Outdoing one another. *Ellicot, Cobbin, D. Brown.* Shows how brotherly love may be continued. *Theoph.* 'When a man knows his neighbour is accustomed to salute him, let him be the first to give the salutation.' *Talmud.* 'Vixerunt mira concordia per mutuam caritatem et invicem se anteponendo.' *Tacitus.* Exemplification of the text in the primitive Love-feast. After the close of public worship, believers of all classes sat down to this repast in familiar company. No seats of honour appropriated to those in office. No invidious line of distinction between those at the head and those at the foot of the table. A true and literal feast of charity in brethren meeting together as such, forgetting all distinctions in their common union in the faith and service of Christ. Provisions supplied by the rich, and voluntary offerings of all were laid on a table spread in the church. After invocation of the divine blessing, the viands were distributed, each eating and drinking at discretion, but all with the strictest temperance. Edifying and Christian conversation occupied the time, the richer and better educated kindly mingling with their poorer brethren. At a convenient part of the evening, some one gave a short exhortation to unity and brotherly love, while others entertained the company with the singing of a psalm, or some sacred piece of his own composition. The repast ended as it begun, with prayer. *Jamieson.*

11. *Not slothful in business ; fervent in spirit ; serving the Lord.*

Not slothful. Christianity opposed to indolence and sloth.
Diligence and industry required in temporals, Eph. iv. 28 ; 1 Thess. iv. 11, 12.
Still more in spirituals, Luke x. 41, 42 ; John vi. 27 ; Phil. ii. 12 ; Heb. vi. 12.
Jesus an example of diligence,—" I must work while it is day," John ix. 4.
Rose for prayer a great while before day, Mark i. 35.
What our hands find to do, to be done with our might, Eccles. ix. 10.
The slothful servant accounted a wicked servant, Matt. xxv. 26.
Christian's life a race, Heb. xii. 1 ; a warfare, Eph. vi. 13 ; a work, Mark xiii. 34.
Business. *Gr.*, Diligence, zeal. Taken generally.
Grace makes a man diligent in his calling whatever it is.
Duties of the Christian life in general referred to.
Zeal for all good enjoined, especially for the kingdom of God.
Diligence in secular things included as part of God's service.
Every action and employment to be for the glory of God, 1 Cor. x. 31.
The service of God to be made a business, Luke ii. 49.
The kingdom of God and His righteousness to be first sought, Matt. vi. 33.
Love shows itself in deeds of earnest zealous good-doing.
Fervent. Not mere diligence, but fervency required.
Lukewarmness Christ's greatest abhorrence. Laodicea, Rev. iii. 16.
Zeal to be hot and glowing. Apollos an example, Acts xviii. 25.
Leads to action. Apollos, fervent in spirit, " taught diligently."
Christ the pattern of holy fervency, Luke ii. 49 ; John ii. 17 ; iv. 34.

In spirit. The spirit the sphere of true holy fervency.
So Apollos, Acts xviii. 25. God to be served with our spirit, chap. i. 9.
To be worshipped in spirit and in truth, John iv. 23; Phil. iii. 3.
True zeal a zeal of the spirit, not of the flesh.
Fleshly zeal, the greater it is, often only the more dangerous.
Holy fervour not from mere nature but from the Holy Spirit.
Only that acceptable to God which has His Spirit and our own in it.
Christianity enjoins fervour and a holy enthusiasm.
Lays hold first of the internal, then of the external life.
Is at once contemplative, devotional, and active.
Brings a holy earnestness into every employment.
Presents the body a *living*, not a dead sacrifice to God, ver. 1.
Holy zeal the fire that consumes it and carries it up to heaven.
True religion a zeal of God, but according to knowledge, chap. x. ii.
Ground of Zeuxis' care in his profession,—" I paint for eternity."
Believers' privilege and duty to do everything for eternity.
" Fervent," *lit.*, glowing, boiling. God's Spirit a fire in ours producing heat.
Acts on our spirit as fire placed under water, Isa. lxiv. 2.
Believers fervent in spirit when filled with the Spirit.
To be so filled at once their privilege and duty, Eph. v. 18.
Christ's office to baptize with the Holy Ghost and fire, Matt. iii. 11.
Exemplified in the disciples on the day of Pentecost, Acts ii. 3, 4.
Serving the Lord. Doing all as the servants of Christ.
Believers' privilege and duty to do all as to the Lord, Eph. vi. 5-7; Col. iii. 17, 23.
The high dignity of the Christian life, a serving Christ.

Τῇ σπουδῇ, in zeal (studio). *Eras., Cas., Pisc.* Earnestness in promoting the good of others. *Chrys.* In what you ought to do. *Luth.* Diligence in the discharge of office. *Vat.* Σπουδή, = ardour, zeal, earnestness; also that which requires it, business. *Flatt.* As to diligence; dative of relation; the word taken in a general sense. *Stuart.* Diligence in every duty of our state. *Pyle.* In any affair. *Boothroyd.* Especially in the duties of our calling. *Barkit.* In employing yourselves for others *Marl.* Zeal in defending and propagating religion. *Koppe.* Relates to Christian duties as such. *Alford.* Energy of action. *D. Brown.* Heb. חָפַז, 'haste,' Exod. xii. 11; Deut. xvi. 3; יָהַג, κατὰ σπουδήν, 1 Sam. xxi. 9. Early Christians gave no symptoms of a change of habit in respect to outward avocations, except that, being furnished with higher motives, they attended with an activity, a diligence, and fidelity greater than ever to all the claims of society and the offices of life. Those who in times of persecution withdrew to places of solitude, as soon as the occasion ceased, returned, for the most part, to the circle of their families and friends, and mingled as before in the wonted scenes and activities of life. *Jamieson.*—Ὀκνηροί (ὄκνος, fear,—'a lion in the streets'). Slothful;

remiss. *Stuart.* Heb. בְעַל.—Τῷ πνευματι, in spirit; one's own spirit. *Most.* The Spirit of God. *Flatt.* Refers both to internal and external life. *Beng.* Not only have the Spirit, but a fervent spirit. *Chrys.*—Ζεοντες (ζεω, to glow, boil). Glowing, boiling (ferventes), as water by fire. *Grot., Tol.* Τῷ πν. ς., having a warm and ardent desire for divine things. *Theod.* Warm and active in spirit. *Doddr.* Show in your employments a living zeal. *Flatt.* Warmly engaged, fervid action in serious earnest. *Stuart.* Having your spirit glowing with zeal. *Con. & Hows.*—Τῷ Κυριω δουλευοντες. Some copies read καιρῳ, 'the time or occasion,' instead of Κυριῳ. So *Or., Jer., Ambr., Luth., Frit., Ols.* Adapting yourselves to the present season *Meyer.* Testimony of MSS. Codd. Sin., Vat., and Alex.), Versions, and Fathers decidedly in favour of Κυριῳ. So. *Beza, Pag., Pisc., Beng., Lachm., Rück., De Wette.* Doing all for Christ. *Chrys., Theod., Theoph.* The object of all zeal to be the Lord's interest. *Thol.* Being true bondmen of your Lord. *Con. & Hows.* As servants of the Lord. *Alf.* The Lord Christ. *Stuart, D. Brown.* The Christian may, and should make use of the time, but not serve it. *De Wette.* Dative of relation; as to the Lord, obedient, or engaged in His service. *Stuart.* Primitive believers, animated by the sublime motive of consecrating their time, talents, and the whole powers of their nature to the service of Christ, were ready, above all classes of their contemporaries, to occupy themselves with the ordinary business of life. Their grand rule to make every pursuit subservient to religion, and to infuse its spirit into all the habits of every-day life. Hence accustomed to choose such employments only as were favourable to retirement and reflection. Carefully avoided all professions whose duties required religion to be banished, or allowed it to be attended to but rarely, and as a secondary concern; *e.g.,* the manufacture and sale of idols, at that time a most lucrative, and by far the most extensive employment; the stage; astrology, magic, and such like impostures; teaching the histrionic art; gladiatorship. Fishermen, shoemakers, masons, tentmakers, smiths, carpenters, mechanics of every name and degree, found among the early followers of Jesus. *Jamieson.*

---

12. *Rejoicing in hope; patient in tribulation; continuing instant in prayer.*

Rejoicing, &c. Passes to duties arising—1. From external circumstances;
2. From the believer's relations to those without.
Serving the Lord to be accompanied with rejoicing.
The contrary displeasing to God, Deut. xxviii. 47, 48.
If so in the Old Testament, how much more in the New!
Joy in the Lord a Christian's duty, Phil. iii. 1; his strength, Neh. viii. 10.
Serving the Lord naturally suggested rejoicing. So Ps. ii. 11.
Cheerfulness belongs to right zeal, joy to right service.
Paul often sorrowful, yet always rejoicing, 2 Cor. vi. 10.
Believers' full joy the Saviour's desire, John xv. 11.
Their rejoicing consistent with temporary heaviness, 1 Pet. i. 6.
Their joy at times unspeakable and full of glory, chap. i. 8.
In hope. In prospect of the glory before them, chap. v. 2; viii. 18.
Earthly hope the source of joy, much more the heavenly.

The world rejoices in hope, much more the Christian.
His present often painful, his future only glorious.
A cross now, a crown and kingdom hereafter, 2 Tim. iv. 7, 8.
Sighs and tears on earth, songs and triumph in heaven.
Night of weeping followed by a morning of endless rejoicing.
Hope paints a rainbow on a believer's tears;
Digs wells of consolation in the Valley of Baca.
Songs in the night, in the house of our pilgrimage, Job xxxv. 10; Ps. cxix. 54.
Believers now have sorrow, John xvi. 33; groan within themselves, chap. viii. 23.
At Rome and elsewhere exposed to persecution, 2 Tim. iii. 12.
Their joyful hope never brighter than in times of trouble.
Hope strengthens the soul both for duty and conflict.
Joyful hope makes patient endurance natural and easy.

Patient. Patience closely connected with hope, chap. viii. 25.
Needed by believers, Heb. x. 36. The reason why, Acts xiv. 22.
Believers not to faint or murmur under trials, Heb. xii. 5, 12.
Endurance to the end necessary to salvation, Matt. x. 22.
A terrible storm was soon to burst over the Church of Rome.
The persecution under Nero only about four years after.

Tribulation. Trouble of any kind; specially, for Christ's sake.
Tribulation the beaten path to the kingdom, Acts xiv. 22.
Part of Christ's legacy to His Church, John xvi. 33.
Tribulation for Christ's sake a precious privilege, Phil. i. 29.

Continuing instant. Persevering and importunate, Col. iv. 2.
Not cold *in* the duty, nor soon weary *of* it.
Men *always* to pray and not to faint, Luke xviii. 1, &c.
Examples:—Jacob at Penuel, Gen. xxxii. 23-29; Hosea xii. 3, 4;
Moses on the hill at Rephidim, Exod. xvii. 8-13;
Elijah on Mount Carmel, 1 Kings xviii. 42-45; James v. 17, 18;
The disciples in the upper room at Jerusalem, Acts i. 14.
Perseverance in prayer connected with patience in trial.

Prayer. Patience in tribulation supported by prayer.
The effectual help both for duty and conflict.
All-prayer a necessary part of the Christian's armour, Eph. vi. 18.
The best support in adversity and preservative in prosperity.
Prayer to be continued in—1. At regular set times, Ps. lv. 17; Dan. vi. 10;
2. By frequent and brief ejaculations, Neh. ii. 4;
3. By a prayerful spirit and heavenward tendency of soul.

Τῇ ἐλπίδι, as to hope; dative of relation, as in the other cases. *Stuart.*—Τῇ προσευχῇ προσκαρτερουντες (πρός, to, and κρατος, strength,—always applying strength, enduring). As to prayer, be persevering. *Stuart.* Continuing on (perdurantes . *Pag., Beza, Pisc., Tol.* Instant, urgent (instantes). *Eras., Mor.* Assiduous. *Cas.* Heb. הַתְמִיד, Num. xiii. 20. Among the primitive Christians, the family assembled at an early hour in the morning for prayer, praise, and reading the Word. During the day, they had, like the Jews, stated seasons, at the third, sixth, and ninth hours (nine, twelve, and three o'clock), when those who were able retired for a little for prayer. In the evening, the family again assembled as in the morning, but for a longer period. Dinner was prefaced by a prayer of considerable length, and concluded in like manner. Special and extraordinary seasons were, from time to time, set apart from worldly business for earnest and protracted prayer, accompanied with fasting. *Jamieson.*

---

13. *Distributing to the necessity of saints; given to hospitality.*

Distributing. *Gr.*, Communicating. Believers one family.
The necessities of the saints to be regarded as our own.
First Christians had all things common, Acts ii. 44, 45; iv. 34, 35.
All believers to make common cause with each other.
Each to share with others what God has given, 1 Pet. iv. 10, 11.
As co-members to suffer and rejoice with each other, 1 Cor. xii. 26.
Each has something to give and something to receive, 2 Cor. viii. 14.
Teachers communicate their gifts, the taught their goods, Gal. vi. 6.
The rich their substance, the poor their prayers, 2 Cor. ix. 14.
The soul to be drawn out to the poor, and the purse to follow, Isa. lviii. 10.

Necessities. Wants, not wishes; necessities, not niceties.
Believers to be content with food and raiment, 1 Tim. vi. 8.
Supply of wants guaranteed in the covenant, Ps. xxiii. 1; Phil. iv. 19.
Early believers often in necessities, Heb. x. 34; xi. 37, 38.
Paul now charged with a supply for the poor at Jerusalem.
Constant occasion for the exercise of this grace, Matt. xxvi. 11.
Kindness to Christ's poor viewed as done to Himself, Matt. xxv. 35–40.

Saints. Holy persons; usually applied to believers in the New Testament.
All professed Christians are saints by profession.
True Christians, saints in reality, 1 Cor. i. 2; 2 Cor. v. 17.
Saints may be in necessities like their Master, Matt. viii. 20; 2 Cor. viii. 9.
A saint chooses rather to suffer want than to sin, Heb. x. 34.
Poor saints, the peculiar care of the Church of Christ.

Given to hospitality. *Gr.*, pursuing kindness to strangers.

Not merely to wait for opportunities, but to seek them.
So Abraham, Gen. xviii. 2; Lot, Gen. xix. 2; Job, Job xxxi. 17, 32.
Poor not only to be received but brought to our house, Isa. lviii. 7.
Early Christians often driven from home and livelihood.
Preachers often without purse or scrip, Matt. x. 9, 10; 3 John 5, 8.
Entertaining strangers especially urged on believers, Heb. xiii. 2.
Christian hospitality to be practised without grudging, 1 Pet. iv. 9.
Entertaining Christ's poor viewed as done to Himself, Matt. xxv. 35.
A special blessing connected with it, Heb. xiii. 2.
A common love due to fellow-creatures;
A special love due to fellow-believers.
"Saints" and "hospitality," terms often misapplied.

Ταις χρειαις, in respect to the wants. *Stuart.* Necessary uses (usibus). *Beza, Pisc., Par.* Indigence. *Syr., Dick.* Some MSS., Fathers, and Versions read μνειαις, monuments or tombs. So *Vulg., Hil., Ambr., Sed., Opt.* Rejected by critics as both wanting authority and congruity.—Κοινωνουντες (κοινος, common). Be sympathetic; feel their wants as if your own; κοινωνεω, in classic Greek always with an *intransitive* sense; so here,—to be a partaker, to share in. *Stuart.* Distributing. *Boothroyd.* Communicating. *Young.* Partaking of your good things with the needy. *Cobbin.* You give money, they give faith in God. *Chrys.* A mutual benefit,—you give your money and receive their prayers. *Theoph.*—Φιλοξενιαν (φιλεω, to love; and ξενος, a stranger). Entertainment of strangers. *D. Brown.* Hospitality; the construction here changed,—the accusative after διωκοντες. *Stuart.*—Διωκοντες, pursuing. *Young.* Practising. *Boothroyd.* Readily practising. *Stuart.* Not only receive but search out the strangers. *Origen, Beng.* Not waiting for the needy coming to you, but running to them like Abraham. *Chrys.* Practise hospitality not only to the saints, but to strangers needing your help. *Theod.* Hospitality essential in those times to the spread of Christianity and connection among the churches. *Barth.* In the east, where houses of entertainment are still rare, hospitality is regarded as of the most sacred character. *Hodge.* Enjoined in the Talmud, especially in regard to those who went from city to city in order to teach the law. *Berachath.* Early Christians going abroad either on their own private affairs, or on missions connected with the state and progress of religion, were received with open arms by the Christians of the place as brethren. The traveller, on arriving at any town, sought out the church, in or about which liberal accommodation was always provided both for the temporal and spiritual comfort of the wayfaring man. No sooner, however, was the news of his arrival spread than the members vied with each other which should have the privilege of entertaining the Christian stranger at their homes. A minister was entertained by one of his own order; and a mechanic by one of the same craft or station. In consequence of abuses, each on setting out on a journey was furnished by the minister of the church to which he belonged with a letter of credence to the spiritual rulers of the place where he meant to sojourn. These were called *literæ formatæ*, from the particular form in which, to prevent forgeries, they were folded. Christians were thus admitted to the fellowship of their brethren in all parts of the world, treated by the family that received them as one of themselves, had their feet washed by the wife on their first arrival, and at their departure were tenderly committed to the Divine care in a prayer offered by the master of the house. *Jamieson.*

14. *Bless them which persecute you; bless, and curse not.*

Bless. Do good by word and deed. Enjoined by Christ, Matt. v. 44. Sermon on the Mount well known, 1 Cor. vii. 10; James iv. 9; v. 12; 1 Pet. iii. 9, 14; iv. 14.

Believers to imitate God their Father in blessing, Matt. v. 45, 48.

Christ prayed for His murderers, Luke xxiii. 34. So Stephen, Acts vii. 60.

Believers to bless as called to inherit a blessing, 1 Pet. iii. 9.

Contrast between the spirit of Christianity and that of the world.

Counted right by the heathen to remember injuries and avenge them.

Believers to invoke blessings in return for them.

Persecute. Christians a sect everywhere spoken against, Acts xxviii. 22.

Persecution the promised lot of Christ's disciples, John xv. 19; xvi. 2.

Servants not to expect better treatment than their Lord, John xv. 20.

The prophets persecuted in like manner, Matt. v. 12; Heb. xi. 36, 37.

Persecution of various forms and degrees, Heb. x. 32-34; xi. 35-38; xii. 4.

The truth necessarily persecuted by a world that hates it.

Bless. The exhortation repeated, to indicate—
1. Its importance; 2. The difficulty attending the duty; 3. The constant perseverance required in it.

Curse not. Believers to bless uniformly. Do nothing but bless.

Not utter a single imprecation against the persecutor.

Not to be surprised into an angry or bitter expression.

Not to curse even in the name of the Lord as Elisha, 2 Kings ii. 24.

Early Christians in danger of sometimes cursing, James iii. 10.

Official authoritative anathema expressed by a different word.

Such pronounced by the apostle under inspiration—
1. On those who preached a false gospel, Gal. i. 8, 9.
2. On those who love not the Lord Jesus Christ, 1 Cor. xvi. 22.

Εὐλογεῖτε (εὖ, well, and λέγω, to speak), speak well. *Pag., Beza, Pisc., Cast.* Pray well. *Vat., Tol., Est., Schött.* Instruct with kind words. *Eras.* Pray that blessings may descend on them. *Stuart.* Call down by prayer a blessing on them. *D. Brown.* Heb. בָּרַךְ, the repetition adds force to the precept. *Macknight.*—Καταρᾶσθε (ἀρά, a curse), imprecate. *Beza, Pag., Pisc., Cast.* Pray ill (male precemini). *Eras., Trem.* With desire of revenge. *Est.* Do not wish evil with dire imprecations. *Vat.* Heb. אָרַר, קָלַל. Early Christians suffering death for the truth, were heard praying for the judge who condemned them, for the emperor who authorised the persecution, for the executioner who was to be the agent of their punishment, and for the infuriated rabble who were driving them with execrations from the world; and beseeching the Almighty that their own death might not be remembered among the sins laid to their enemies' charge. *Jamieson.*

---

15. *Rejoice with them that do rejoice, and weep with them that weep.*

Rejoice. To rejoice a Christian duty. Required—
1. On our own account; 2. On account of others.
Here, an unselfish sympathy with another's joy.
Not merely not to envy it, but to rejoice in it.
The joy of others, especially of believers, to be made our own.
All united by a bond of brotherhood, especially Christians.
Hence reciprocation of each other's joys and sorrows, 1 Cor. xii. 26.
With them that do rejoice. As sharing in their joy.
To rejoice with them that rejoice is the means—
1. Of increasing their joy; 2. Of demonstrating your love; 3. Of engaging and confirming their love to you.
Less selfish and more difficult than to weep with the weeping.
Sympathy with other's joy to be real and manifested.
Exemplified in Jesus at the marriage in Cana, John ii. 2–10.
Weep with, &c. Sympathise with sorrow as well as joy.
Exemplified in Jesus at Bethany, John xi. 35.
We lighten another's affliction by sharing his tears.
A powerful charm in the fellow-feeling of others.
Sympathy relieves if it cannot remove the affliction.
Paul himself no stranger to its power, Acts xxviii. 15; Heb. x. 34.
To be extended to all, especially the members of Christ's body.
Sympathy in a church the sign of spiritual life.
Jesus sought it in His distress but found it not, Matt. xxvi. 36–45.

Χαιρειν, rejoice. The infinitive, as frequently in Greek classics instead of the imperative; δει properly understood,—'You must rejoice.' *Stuart.*—Και κλαιειν, and weep. Και omitted in Codd. Sin. and Vat. Possible allusion to the two gates said to have been in the temple, the one for the sorrowful the other for the joyful, who, as they passed through, were addressed by others in terms of condolence or congratulation accordingly.

---

16. *Be of the same mind one toward another. Mind not high things, but condescend to men of low estate. Be not wise in your own conceits.*

Same mind. Have the same affection one for another.
Connected with " having the same love," Phil. ii. 2.

With "having compassion one of another," 1 Pet. iii. 8.
Each to think and feel towards another as towards himself.
Believers to have a mutual care and regard for each other.
Includes unity of sentiment and affection, Phil. iii. 15, 16.
Unanimity, cordiality, and harmony the Church's beauty.
Good and pleasant for brethren to dwell together in unity, Ps. cxxxiii. 1.
Paul's earnest desire in regard to the Church, 2 Cor. xiii. 11; Eph. iv. 3.
True Christian unity based on mutual esteem, Phil. ii. 3.
Mind not high things. 1. Do not cherish high thoughts, Phil. ii. 3–8.
2. Do not aim at high positions, 3 John 9; Jer. xlv. 5.
Self-exaltation the greatest enemy to Christian unity.
Roman Christians especially exposed to this temptation.
Natural to corrupt fallen nature to mind high things.
Its early appearance in the Church, James ii. 1–7; 3 John 9.
Showed itself among the disciples in Christ's presence, Luke xxii. 24.
Inconsistent—1. With love to others; 2. With life in ourselves.
Condescend. The opposite of minding high things.
Has relation—1. To persons; 2. To things.
Believers to come down to the lowly, especially lowly brethren.
Humility the first lesson in the school of Christ, Matt. xi. 29.
Lowly condition to be no hindrance to fellowship or esteem.
David a king, yet companion to all who feared God, Ps. cxix. 63.
Christ received publicans and sinners, and ate with them, Luke xv. 1, 2.
Christian condescension does not regard itself such, Phil. ii. 3.
The spirit of Christianity one of community and sympathy.
Christ's mind carries us rather to the lowly than the high.
Readily performs the lowest services, John xiii. 4–16; 1 Tim. v. 10.
Goes down to another's poverty and makes the case its own.
Angels go down to Lazarus at the rich man's gate.
Nothing to be thought beneath a Christian but sin.
Wise in your own conceits. From Prov. iii. 7. *Gr.*, With or by yourselves.
Self-conceit the enemy of Christian love.
The evidence of ignorance and a weak mind.
Destroyer of Church harmony and individual progress.
Conceit in our own wisdom the bar to Christian unity.
Good to be wise, but evil to think ourselves so.

CHAP. XII.]   ST. PAUL'S EPISTLE TO THE ROMANS.   191

When Moses' face shone "he wist not of it," Exod. xxxiv. 29.
Men made to need each other's counsel and help.
Believers to be ready both to ask and give advice.
Rejection of our plans not to hinder co-operation with others.

To αὐτο εἰς ἀλλήλ. φρονοῦντες, mutually mind the same thing. *Boothr.* Mutually think the same thing, *i.e.*, be agreed in your opinions and views. *Stuart.* Think of another as you do of yourself. *Chrys.*, *Theoph.* Refers to the understanding,—unity of sentiment. *Ans.* Refers to the affections,—love others as yourselves. *Tol.* None to think more of himself because of station, &c. *Est.*, *Eras.* Be in peace and concord. *Grot.*, *Beza.* Unanimous in your views and counsels. *Par.*, *Cam.* Be entirely united in your regards for each other. *Doddr.* Desire the same things for others that you do for yourselves, and would have them to desire for you. *Whitby.* Enjoins consent in life, and mutual offices of Christian love. *Parkhurst.* Be united in your sentiments and affections. *Brown.* Have one mind among yourselves, as a little company in the presence of a hostile world. *Barth.* Live in concord. *Cobbin.*—Μὴ τὰ ὑψηλὰ φρονοῦντες, not thinking or savouring high things (sentientes, seu. sapientes, seu. cogitantes). *Eras.*, *Beza, Pag.* Not affecting the high things of this world. *Par.*, *Doddr.* Aim not after high things. *Barth.* Cherish not ambitious or aspiring purposes and desires. *D. Brown.* —Τοῖς ταπεινοῖς συναπαγόμενοι, consenting with the lowly (humilibus consentientes). *Vulg.*, *Mor.* Adhering to the lowly. *Syr.*, *Arab.* Abiding with the humble. *Ulfilas.* Accommodating yourselves. *Eras.*, *Cast.* Embracing lowly circumstances. *Beza, Est., Tol., Vor.* Go down to another's poverty, and give him your personal aid. *Chrys.* Condescend to those who appear to be low; reckon yourself among them. *Theod.* Go down to the lowly. *Luth.* Lowering yourselves to lowly things. *Pisc.* Complying (obsecundantes). *Beza, Pag., Par.* Be faithful in littles. *Calv.* Follow the example of the humble. *Grot.*, *Schött.* Adapt yourselves to what is lowly; attend to lowly things. *Beng.* Accommodate yourselves to men of low rank. *Doddr.* To lowly things. *Mart., Diod.* Walking with, or accompanying the lowly. *Dick.* Condescend to the humble; be not ashamed of connection with them. *Flatt.* Do not withdraw from fellowship with your afflicted brethren, as willing to suffer with them. *Kopfe.* Let yourselves be carried away with or by the lowly. *Rückert.* Associating with them. *Macknight.* Suffer yourselves to be borne along with them. *Con. & Hows.* Do not isolate yourselves from your brethren when in tribulation. *Thol.* Give yourselves up to the lowly. *Lange.* Let not pride separate you from the lowly. *Cobbin.* Be carried along with things that are lowly, not withdrawing yourselves from them. *De Wette.* Be led away by humble things. *Stuart.* Undertake lowly employments in life. *Meyer.* Consent to be evened with lowly things. *Chal.* Inclining to the things that be lowly. *Ellicot.* The difference of interpretation turns on the gender of ταπεινοῖς, regarded by many as the antithesis of ὑψηλά, and consequently neuter. Συναπάγομαι = συμπορεύομαι, συνέρχεται. *Iles.* = Συγκαταβαίνειν. *Cam.* Commonly used in a *bad* sense, viz., to suffer one's self to be led away by temptation, &c. (Gal. ii. 13; 2 Pet. iii. 17); here, to be taken in a *generic* sense. *Stuart.*—Φρόνιμοι παρ' ἑαυτοῖς, prudent with or by yourselves. *Beza.* Arrogant. *Eras.* Neglecting to seek divine counsel or the advice of others. *Est., Tir.* Do not depend on your own wisdom. *Chrys., Theod.* Romans proud of their wisdom and prudence in the management of affairs. *Tol.* Do not fancy yourselves wise. *De Wette, Barth.* Do not refuse to confer with others and to hearken to their suggestions. *Stuart.* Have no undue estimate of your own powers and acquirements. *Brown.* Be not puffed up with a high opinion of your wisdom and privileges. *Cobbin.* Refers to estimate of our own mental character. *D. Brown.* Heb. אַל תְּהִי חָכָם בְּעֵינֶיךָ, Prov. iii. 7.

---

17. *Recompense to no man evil for evil. Provide things honest in the sight of all men.*

Recompense. Retaliation of injuries. Forbidden, Matt. v. 39; 1 Pet. iii. 9.
The Spirit of Christ the opposite of a spirit of revenge.
Its characteristic to return good for evil, Matt. v. 44, 45.
Opposite tendency of our nature. Only produced by grace.
No man. Not even the worst, nor your greatest enemy.
Believers not to return evil for evil—
1. Under no pretence; 2. Under no circumstances; 3. To no individual.
Christians persecuted by all ranks and classes of the people.
Christ's followers to be hated by all men for His sake, Matt. x. 22.
Evil. Injury; injurious treatment. Under various forms.
Mockery; insult; calumny; violence to person or property.
Provide. Look well to; take care to have.
Believers to look well to their walk and conduct—
1. On their own account; 2. On that of others; 3. On their Master's.
No place for thoughtless indifference in the Christian life.
Things honest. Honourable, becoming, of good report.
Quoted from Prov. iii. 4. Same duty enforced, Phil. iv. 8; 1 Pet. ii. 12.
Exemplified in the apostle, 2 Cor. viii. 21. In Christ himself, Matt. xvii. 27.
Everything mean and suspicious to be carefully avoided.
Believers in their conduct to be sincere and without offence, Phil. i. 10.
A precious stone should have a proper setting.
In the sight of all men. Of the world as well as the Church.
Believers to walk in wisdom toward those without, Col. iv. 5.
To be epistles of Christ known and read of all men, 2 Cor. ii. 3.
God's glory and men's salvation bound up with a Christian's walk.
No cause of stumbling to be given to Jew, Gentile, or Christian, 1 Cor. x. 32.
The world's eyes on the followers of Christ, Zech. iii. 8; 1 Cor. iv. 9; Heb. x. 33.
Men often suspicious and watch for a fault, Jer. xx. 10; Luke xi. 53, 54.
Believers to live as in a house of glass, Matt. v. 14-16.

Ἀποδιδόντες (ἀπο, from, and δίδωμι, to give), giving back; participle, expressing habit.—Προνοούμενοι (Mid. of προνοέω; from προ, before, and νοῦς, the mind), caring beforehand; providing (procurantes). *Pisc.*, *Beza*, *Pag.* (parnutes). *Eras.* Diligently caring for. *Grot.* Seeking. *Mart.* Procuring. *Diod.* Seek after; be studiously attentive to. *Stuart.* Be provident of. *Con. & Hows.*—Καλά, honest things. *Pisc.*, *Beza*, *Pag.*, *Eras.*, *Mar.*, *Diod.* Honourable conduct. *Luth.* Right thing. *Young.* That which is good. *Stuart.* Honourable. *Ellicot.* Of good report. *Con. & Hows.* Προν. καλά, preconsider the tendency of your conduct so as to act aright; so ἀρετῆς προνοεῖ (Jos. Antiq.) *Krebs.*, *Wetstein.* Have such a walk as to avoid the appearance of evil. *Barth.* Give others no occasion of stumbling through your conduct. *Theod.* Give no occasion of others speaking evil of you. *Theoph.*—Ἐνώπιον παντ. ἀνθρ. Cod. Alex. has ἐν. τοῦ Θεοῦ καὶ π. ἀνθρ. The words from Prov. iii. 4, where for Heb. וְאָדָם אֱלֹהִים בְּעֵינֵי, the LXX. have ἐνώπιον Κυρίου κ. ἀνθρώπων; and for וְשֵׂכֶל טוֹב, 'and good understanding,' they have προνοοῦ καλά, reading בְּשֵׂכֶל, as the imperative of שָׂכַל, to understand or attend to. The idea is the care Christians should take so to demean themselves as to command the respect of all men. *D. Brown.* Pliny's letter to the Emperor Trajan (A.D. 99) sufficient testimony to the blameless morals of the early Christians:—'To satisfy myself still farther, I apprehended two female slaves, who had been deaconesses in the Church; and having examined them by torture, all I could discover by their evidence respecting the conduct of the Christians is, that on a stated day they are wont to assemble before sunrise to sing a hymn to Christ as the God whom they worship; and bind themselves by an oath not to commit any wickedness, but to abstain from theft, robbery, adultery; to keep faith, and, when requested, to restore any pledge committed to them.' The Emperor Severus observing the excellent conduct of the Christians, and their fidelity in every department of public and private life, and finding, on inquiry into their principles, that one grand rule of theirs was, 'Not to do to others what they would not have done to themselves,' was so charmed with it, that at all public executions he ordered it to be proclaimed aloud by a herald, and had it inscribed on the walls of his palace, and on all public buildings. *Jamieson.*

---

18. *If it be possible, as much as lieth in you, live peaceably with all men.*

If it be possible. Implying its difficulty. Not always possible—
1. From the conduct of others; 2. From the claims of the truth.
Every effort to be made for peace consistent with duty.
Enmity to the truth often makes peace impossible, Matt. x. 35.
As much as lieth in you. *Gr.*, So far as depends on you.
The limitation not to be on the Christian's side.
"I am for peace; but when I speak, they are for war," Ps. cxx. 7.
No breach of peace to be made on our account.
No just subject of complaint to be given to others.
All to be done for peace consistent with the interests of truth.
Avoid inflicting injury or offering affront.
The truth to be spoken, but spoken in love, Eph. iv. 15.
Jeremiah a man of strife, but not through his fault, Jer. xv. 10.
Believers' duty to contend earnestly for the faith, Jude 3.

To love the truth and peace, Zech. viii. 19 ; truth first, peace next.
The wisdom from above is first pure then peaceable, James iii. 17.
"Fightings without;" the apostle's frequent experience, 2 Cor. vii. 5.
Peace without purity the peace of Satan's kingdom, Luke xi. 21.
Live peaceably. Believers to be peacemakers and peace-livers.
To lead quiet and peaceable lives in all godliness, 1 Tim. ii. 2.
To sow the fruit of righteousness in peace, making peace, James iii. 18.
The Christian's most precious jewel a meek and quiet spirit, 1 Pet. iii. 4.
To live peaceably with men, it is necessary—
1. To avoid injuring and wounding others by word or deed ;
2. Patiently to bear injuries and overlook affronts from others ;
3. To bridle the tongue, James iii. 2–5;
4. To mind our own business, 1 Thess. iv. 11 ; 1 Tim. v. 13.
To live at peace without sacrificing truth both our duty and happiness.
The apostle specially earnest in enjoining peace, chap. xiv. 17, 19 ; 2 Cor. xiii. 11.
A believer's holy and peaceable life a powerful sermon, 1 Pet. iii. 1–4.
All men. Not only in the Church, but out of it. Even with the perverse.
The world can be at peace with *some;* Christians to be so with *all.*

Εἰ δυνατόν, if possible ; *i.e.*, if others will let you. *D. Brown.* Limitation, showing that it is not possible in all cases. *Stuart.*—Τὸ ἐξ ὑμῶν, as much as is in you. *Diod.* As much as depends upon you. *Mart., Ellicot.* On your side peaceableness is to be unlimited. *De Wette.* No breach of peace to be on our own account. *Barth.* Κατα το ἐξ ὑμ. ; ἐξ, in the sense of *belonging to ;* 'in proportion to that which belongs to you,' *i.e.,* according to your ability. *Stuart.*—Εἰρηνεύοντες (εἰρήνη, peace), be at peace ; part. for imper. *D. Brown.* Heb. שָׁלֵו, 1 Kings xxii. 45 ; Job v. 23, 24 ; שָׁקַט, שָׁלָה.

---

19. *Dearly beloved, avenge not yourselves, but rather give place unto wrath : for it is written, Vengeance is mine, I will repay, saith the Lord.*

Dearly beloved. Affectionate address introduced to show—
1. The importance of the exhortation ;
2. The apostle's earnest desire and concern on the subject ;
3. The difficulty of compliance under great provocation ;

4. That the counsel was from no indifference to their wrongs.
The tendency of our nature to love and seek revenge.
"Revenge is sweet,"—the language of corrupt nature ;
"Father, forgive them,"—the language of grace, Acts vii. 60.
Avenge not yourselves. Believers not to be their own avengers.
Personal revenge opposed to the spirit of the Gospel.
Not forbidden to appeal to magistrates in case of injury.
Christians to expect to suffer at the hands of men, Matt. x. 16.
To be in the world as lambs in the midst of wolves.
To be wise as serpents and harmless as doves.
Give place unto wrath. Leave it to God to avenge you.
Let the punishment come from God, not from yourselves.
Believers to indulge no resentful feelings, Matt. v. 39.
All bitterness, wrath, and anger to be put away, Eph. iv. 31.
Believers to be angry and sin not, Eph. iv. 26.
The sun not to go down upon our wrath, *ibid.*
"Wrath" often used for "punishment," as chap. iv. 15 ; xiii. 4, 5.
Written. Deut. xxxii. 35, 41. Appeal to Old Testament Scripture.
Duties to be enforced on the ground of God's Word.
Vengeance is mine. 1. As the righteous Judge of all ;
2. As the special Defender of His people, Deut. xxxii. 36, 43.
Vengeance belongs to God as well as mercy, Ps. xciv. 1.
A righteous thing with God to recompense persecutors, 2 Thess. i. 6.
Vengeance only safe in the hands of a holy God, Rev. xv. 4.
All recompensing of injuries to be left to Him, Acts iv. 29.
"I heard not"—"for *Thou* wilt hear," Ps. xxxviii. 14, 15.
I will repay. The "*I*" emphatic ; "leave it to *Me.*"
1. We *may* not take God's place ; 2. We *need* not.
God repays evil done *against*, and good done *to* His people.
Good done *by*, and injury done *to* His servants both remembered.

Ἐκδικοῦντες (ἐκ, from, and δίκη, justice, right), avenging ; redressing wrong, as Luke xviii. 3 ; for injury received. *Cobbin.* Heb. םָקָנ, בֵקָע, שָׁרַד, טַפָשׁ.—Δότε τόπον τῇ ὀργῇ, give place to wrath. Some copies add Θεοῦ ; doubtless a gloss. Ὀργῇ, referred—1. To God : leave the time and matter to Him. *Or., Chrys., Theod., Aug., Eras., Vor., Beza, Pisc., Grot., Cam., Calv., Dick., L'Enfant, Whitby, Beng., Rück., Meyer, Ellicot.* Commit it to God's judgment. *Van Ess, Flatt, Nielson.* Leave the injury to God, or the magistrate as His minister. *Wells.* To the wrath of God. *Boothr.* God's sin-avenging wrath. *D. Brown.* The punishment of God, as Rom. ii. 5, 8. *Schött.* Leave God to avenge the injury. *Brown.* 2. To the injured party : restrain your anger. *Vat., Semler, Cramer, Koppe, Paulus, Reiche.* Give time to it. *De Wette.* Time to settle. *Cram.* Interpose delay to anger ; make not the wrath your own, but leave it to God. *Alford.* Defer its execution. *Stuart.* 3. To the injurer or enemy : go out of the way of His anger. *Ambr.*, *Ans.*, *Ammon*, *Drus.*, *Gom.*, *Tol.* Keep out of its way; leave the place, and let wrath occupy it. *Henry.* Yield and give place to the wrath of the enemy. *Doddr.* Δοτε τοπον, give or make room, Luke xiv. 9 ; μη διδοτε τοπον, do not give place or yield, Eph. iv. 27. Heb. נֹתֵן מָקוֹם, gave place or yielded, Judges xx. 36.

---

20. *Therefore if thine enemy hunger, feed him ; if he thirst, give him drink : for in so doing thou shalt heap coals of fire on his head.*

Therefore if, &c. From Prov. xxv. 21, 22. A still higher Christian duty.
Believers not only not to retaliate, but to repay evil with good.
The highest morality taught in the Old as well as in the New Testament.
Enemy. One who hates you in his heart, and shows it in his acts.
A Christian may have enemies without making them.
Many may be *his* enemies, himself an enemy to none.
"Marvel not if the world hate you," 1 John iii. 13; John xv. 18, 19.
God's enemies not likely the friends of His children.
Hatred against the Head likely to be shared by the members.
Purity and love no guarantee against the world's hatred.
Virtue became incarnate and the world crucified it.
Hunger. Not unlikely to befal such enemies, Isa. lxv. 13.
The thought perhaps suggested by—" I will repay."
" My servants shall eat, but ye shall be hungry."
Feed. *Gr.*, tenderly with your own hand as an invalid.
Not only give him food, but in the kindest manner.
Contrive so to do it as to show him your love.
Christ gave His flesh for the world that killed Him ·
Believers may well give their meat and drink.
Heap coals of fire. 1. Melt him down ; 2. Make him ashamed.
Kindness shown to an enemy will either—
1. Remove his enmity ; or 2. Display its unreasonableness.
So David with Saul, 1 Sam. xxiv. 17, &c. ; xxvi. 21 ; Ps. cxli. 6.
To show kindness to an enemy is the noblest revenge.
" Heap ; " not only one or two, but repeated kindnesses.

Ἐαν οὖν, if then. Codd., Sin., Vat., and Alex. have ἀλλα ἐαν, but if.—Ψωμιζε (ψωμος, a mouthful, bit of bread), feed. *Eras.*, &c. Feed with the hand, as 2 Sam. xiii. 5 LXX. *Grot.* Heb. הַאֲכִלֵהוּ לֶחֶם, ' cause him to eat bread,' Prov. xxv. 21.—Ποτιζε (ποτος, drink, from πιω, to drink), give to drink. Heb. הַשְׁקֵהוּ מָיִם, Prov. xxv. 21.

—'Ανθρακας πυρος, coals of fire. Ignited coals. *Pisc.* Glowing coals. *Cas.* Burning coals. *Eras.* Heb. גַחֲלֵי־אֵשׁ, burning coals — vengeance of God, Prov. xxv. 22; Ps. cxl. 9, 10; Isa. xlvii. 14; Ezek. x. 2. *Whitby.* Pain denoted, but rather that of shame and contrition than punishment. *Stuart.* An oriental figure for constantly burning pain: 'Coals of fire shall burn on the head of him who denies he has sinned,' 3 Esdras xvi. 54. —Σωρεύσεις (σωρος, a heap), thou shalt heap. Heb. חָתָה. 'Ανθρακας—αὐτοῦ, = make him feel compunction for his sin and suffer in his conscience. *Origen.* Make him liable to greater punishment from God unless he repent. *Chrys., Theod., Cam., Est., Beza, Grot., Wetst., Koppe.* He will be ashamed and repent. *Aug., Tol., Vat., Par., Eras., Vor., Pisc.* Shalt either by kindness bring him to a better mind or increase his punishment. *Schött., Chal.* He will repent and give himself up to you, the end of all revenge. *Beng.* Thou wilt touch him so sensibly that he will submit to seek thy friendship. *Doddr.* Wilt mollify and bring him to a good temper. *Macknight.* He will be grieved to have injured thee. *Flatt.* Wilt produce pain enough from shame and remorse. *Cobbin.* Wilt take the most effectual vengeance, under which he will be fain to bend. *D. Brown, Alford, Hodge.* The feeling of shame will not allow him to rest till he has repaired the injury. *Barth.* The object of these expressions of love must be the same as those of Christ on the Cross. *Lange.* Met., taken from the melting of metals by covering the ore with burning coals. *Macknight, Con. & Hows.* Words of the wise compared by Rabbies to coals of fire, as capable both of benefiting and burning: 'Warm thyself at their fire; but take care of the coals lest thou be burned. *Pirke Aboth.*

---

21. *Be not overcome of evil, but overcome evil with good.*

Overcome of evil. By allowing yourselves to resent it.
The worst defeat is to be overcome—1. By our own passions; 2. By the evil done us by the passions of others.
Believers neither to be overcome by evil—1. As existing in themselves; nor 2. As done to them by others.
The greatest conqueror is he who—1. Conquers himself; 2. Conquers his enemy by kindness.
He is the bravest man who can *bear* most.
Overcome evil with good. Disarm enemies by kindness.
Evil only to be overcome by its opposite.
For evil done to you, do as much or more good in return.
The noblest heroes those who conquer evil—
1. In themselves; 2. In those who injure them.
Grace makes men heroes in the degree they possess it.
The noblest victories those recorded in heaven.
The world's heroes often gain their victories by evil;
God's heroes gain theirs only by good.
Names of the former emblazoned on the page of earthly history
Those of the latter enrolled in the annals of eternity.
At the head of these stands Jesus Christ, the Crucified.

"Father, forgive them"—the greatest victory ever won on earth.
Noble testimony to Cranmer, "To get a favour, do him a wrong."
To return good for good is merely human;
To return evil for evil is carnal;
To return evil for good is devilish;
To return good for evil is divine.
This last peculiar to Christianity. Bible morality.
Maxims of this chapter unequalled in any philosophy.
The brightest tablet of social moralities earth ever saw.

Μη νικω, be not overcome, *i.e.*, by wishing to avenge yourself or doing evil like the other. *Beza, Pisc.*—Νικα ἐν τῳ ἀγαθῳ το κακον, overcome evil with the good; an evil thing with a good thing (bono malum). *Pisc., Beza.* Malice with kindness (bonitate malitiam). *Pag.* 'Vincit malos pertinax bonitas.' *Seneca.* Early Christians especially in circumstances to require the exhortation. Maliciously charged by Nero, four years later, with setting fire to Rome. Endured the most shocking cruelties as the consequence. 'Nero proceeded with his usual artifice. He found a set of profligate and abandoned wretches who were induced to confess themselves guilty; and on the evidence of such men, a number of Christians were convicted, not indeed upon clear evidence, of their having set the city on fire, but rather on account of their sullen hatred of the whole Roman race. They were put to death with exquisite cruelty; and to their sufferings, Nero added mockery and derision. Some were covered with the skins of wild beasts, and left to be devoured by dogs. Others were nailed to a cross. Numbers were burnt alive. Many, covered with inflammable matter, were lighted up when the day declined, to serve as torches during the night.' *Tacitus.* Pliny, reputed a just and humane governor, says that of the Christians in his jurisdiction (Bithynia), some he degraded, others he tortured, and all who, after being thrice interrogated if they were Christians, persevered in the avowal, he put to instant death. *Letter to Trajan.* Christians in the provinces treated in the same manner even under the reign of Marcus Aurelius, a philosopher extolled for his humane and amiable disposition. 'The evidence of slaves, and the prejudiced testimony of the lower rabble was readily entertained by numbers of the governors and judges, whom fear or bribes had gained over; and the property of the condemned was given as a reward to the accusers.' Thus 'every Christian whose money or lands excited the cupidity of his envious neighbours, or whose virtuous presence overawed their fraudulent transactions in business, or whose removal might promise an accuser advancement to a lucrative office or a more extended trade, was forthwith dragged before the public tribunals. If the usual question "Art thou a Christian?" was answered in the affirmative, from that moment his fate was sealed.' *Jamieson.* 'That we who have in faith given our names to Jesus, do not draw back from our profession while we are beheaded, crucified, exposed to wild beasts, and tortured by hooks, fire, and all kinds of torture, is sufficiently manifest; and the more that such tortures are exercised upon us, so much the more do others become believers and worshippers of the true religion through the name of Jesus.' *Justin Martyr.* 'To the Christians alone it is not permitted to speak anything which may clear their cause or defend the truth, or not allow the judge to be unjust. That alone is expected which is demanded by the public odium,—confession of the *name*, and not examination of the charge.' *Tertullian.* Quarters from which early Christians suffered were :—1. Heathen governors; 2. Heathen philosophers, who held them up to public ridicule and contempt; 3. Priests and others interested in the prevalent idolatry; 4. The multitude, especially when instigated by these ; 5. Their own relations, and those under whose roof they lived. Grounds on which they were made to suffer:—1. The alleged novelty or newness of their religion ; 2. Their exclusiveness in maintaining it to be the only true one, and refusing to participate in the idolatrous rites or customs of their neighbours ; 3. The charge of disloyalty, illegal assemblies, and conspiracy against the State ; 4. That of being useless members of society ; 5. That of atheism, and therefore of being the cause of all the public calamities of the empire ; 6. That of practising the most horrible enormities at their nocturnal meetings. *Jamieson.*

CHAPTER XIII.

1. *Let every soul be subject unto the higher powers. For there is no power but of God : the powers that be are ordained of God.*

Let, &c. Duties in relation to magistrates and civil powers.
Rome the seat of empire. Special reason for what follows.
Importance of such a testimony for Christianity at Rome.
Jews charged with resisting the government, Acts xviii. 2.
Probably the occasion of these instructions to believers.
Christians often confounded by the Romans with the Jews.
Sometimes also held mistaken views of Christ's kingdom.
That kingdom not mentioned as such in this Epistle.
Every soul. The nobler part of man put for the whole.
Man's nobility not opposed to subjection, but to servility.
Subjection to magistrates to be matter of conscience.
In chap. xii. 1, the *body* prominent—here the *soul.*
In things of God the soul has to bring the body to duty ;
In things of the world the body has to bring the soul, 1 Cor. x. 23.
" Every soul" marks more strongly the universality of the duty.
Hebraism for "each." Includes apostles, prophets, and evangelists. *Chrys.*
The clergy not exempt from subjection to civil tribunals.
Bishops of Rome have exalted themselves above all earthly rulers.
Be subject. *Gr.*, Subject yourselves, 1 Cor. xvi. 16 ; Eph. v. 22.
Willing subjection to authority the spirit of Christianity, ver. 5.
The obedience enjoined both active and passive—
1. Do what is commanded ; 2. Submit to what is appointed.
Obedience to be rendered in all lawful matters.
Only clearly unlawful commands to be disobeyed, Acts iv. 19 ; v. 29.
No reference here to duty in seasons of revolution.

The precept respects obedience to any established power.
No exception as to the nature or constitution of the government.
The Roman government at that time an absolute monarchy.
The only limits—conscience, faith, and God's command.
Property and life to be given by the subject, but not conscience.
Subjection to the civil magistrate requires—
1. The cherishing of an inward honour ;
2. The manifestation of outward respect ;
3. Ready obedience to all lawful commands ;
4. Rendering all due personal and pecuniary support

Higher powers. Persons invested with civil power, Luke xii. 11
Rulers of whatever name—emperors, kings, consuls, presidents, &c.
All orders of magistrates, supreme or subordinate, 1 Pet. ii. 13, 14.
" Higher "—those who are over you ; ground of the subjection.
Rulers here viewed as " powers," not as individuals.
Powers to be revered though the persons be contemned, Ps. xv. 4.

For. The reason given for the subjection enjoined.
God's commands reasonable, and require reasonable obedience.

Of God. Of divine origin and appointment.
Applicable even to persecuting powers. Power abused. *Origen.*
The "power," without reference to the person exercising it. *Chrys.*
" Power" of divine origin ; exercise of it by divine arrangement.
Civil power includes, but does not rest on social compact.
Christian obedience placed on the footing of conscience.

That be. That actually exist, of whatever kind they are.
No question as to either—1. What is their character ;
Or 2. How they came into actual possession.
Jeroboam established idolatry ; Augustus subverted the laws.

Ordained. Arranged, ordered, arrayed ; a military term.
Subordination *in* the magistracy as well as *under* it.
Civil rule originates in circumstances divinely ordered.
Established not only with God's permission, but by His providence.
Not merely the office, but the holding it of God, Dan. iv. 17 ;
    Jer. xxvii. 5.
God is judge : He puts down one and sets up another, Ps. lxxv. 7.
The shields of the earth belong to the Lord, Ps. xlvii. 9 ; Prov.
    viii. 15.
Rules in the kingdom of men, and gives it to whom He will, Dan.
    iv. 25, 26.
Subjection required even under usurped power.
The worst government in any country still of God.

CHAP. XIII.]   ST. PAUL'S EPISTLE TO THE ROMANS.   201

Rulers appointed by God for his own purpose and glory, Exod. ix. 16.
Either for the happiness or chastening of a land, Job xxxiv. 29, 30.
Wicked rulers God's scourge for guilty nations.

Πασα ψυχη, every soul; every office-bearer as well as member of the Church. *Or.,
Chrys.* Jewish as well as Gentile converts. *Pyle.* A Hebraism = כָּל־נֶפֶשׁ, = every
one, each one. *Stuart.* Every person. *Cobbin.* Every man of you. *D. Brown.*—
'Εξουσιαις, authorities. *Ellicot.* Office and person. *Beza, J. Cap., Ham.*—Ὑπερ-
εχουσαις, superior (præcellentibus). *Eras., Vat., Tol.* Supreme. *Cap., Ham., Hald.*
All powers or orders of magistrates. *Par., Brown.* Pre-eminent or supreme; in this
case the civil magistracy or power of civil rulers. *Stuart.* That are above him. *Ellicot,
D. Brown.* Heb. יָרַד, אֶצְיָן, אַדִּיר. 'Sublimes potestates.' *Anim. Marc.* 'Supreme,'
applied to the king as above other magistrates as well as subjects, 1 Pet. ii. 13. The
'power' to be distinguished from the means of obtaining it and the manner of employing
it. *Est., Thom.* Hosea viii. 4. Compare 1 Kings xi. 31, &c. *Par.*—Ὑποτασσεσθω,
submit himself (middle). *Ellicot, D. Brown.* Connection with the preceding exhortations: a hostile magistracy likely to be softened by a submissive Christian spirit and
conduct. *Nielson.*—Ἀπο Θεου. Codd. Sin. and Alex. have ὑπο Θ. Of or from God;
mediately through men. *Est.* By divine permission. *Stuart.* Divine appointment.
Haldane. Divine origin. *De Wette.* Even persecuting powers of God. *Origen.*—
Αἱ δε οὐσαι ἐξουσιαι. Codd. Sin., Vat., and Alex., omit ἐξουσιαι. Those which are,
i.e., true and legitimate rulers, not robbers. *Beza.* Existing [magistracies]. *Stuart.*
That actually exist. *Alford, Nielson.* Form of government left to human discretion.
Sanctioned by God so long as exercised for its proper ends. No encouragement here
given to passive obedience. Opposed to factious resistance. *Locke.* Resistance to
heathen rulers made by the Jews on the ground they had no king but God, and so
inculcated by the Pharisees. *Jos. Antiq.* This, and the suspicion likely thereby to fall
on the Christians, the occasion of these exhortations. *De Wette.*—Τεταγμεναι (τασσω,
to put in order), arranged, ordained (ordinatæ). *Beza, Pisc.* Instituted. *Est.* Distributed in order. *Pag., Tir.* Ranged, disposed, and established. *Doddr.* Are of God's
appointment. *Stuart.* Arranged, set in order. *Brown.* Have been ordained. *D. Brown.*
—Ὑπο Θεου, by God. *Doddr., &c.* Under God. *Brown.* At the commencement of the
Christian era, the Roman Empire had now for its boundaries the Atlantic on the west, the
Euphrates on the east, the deserts of Africa and Arabia on the south, and the British
Channel, the Rhine, the Danube, and the Black Sea on the north. Subsequently, Britain
was added by Claudius, and Dacia by Trajan. Population of the Empire under Augustus
calculated at eighty-five millions. Countries conquered by Rome became subject provinces,
governed directly from Rome by officers sent out for that purpose. Petty sovereigns sometimes left in possession of a nominal independence on the borders or within the natural
limits of the province. Provinces divided by Augustus into two classes—1. Imperial, or
those retained in his own hands and requiring the presence of a large military force; such
as Syria, Phœnicia, Cilicia, Cyprus, and Egypt; 2. Senatorial, or those more peaceful and
unarmed, and therefore committed to the Senate. The governor of an Imperial province
(Legatus Cæsaris) styled by New Testament writers ἡγεμων, or 'governor:' those of
Senatorial provinces, by the correct title ἀνθυπατοι, 'pro-consuls' or 'deputies,' Acts
xiii. 7; xviii. 12; xix. 38. Provinces heavily taxed for the benefit of Rome and her
citizens. Better governed under the Empire than under the Republic, and those of the
Emperor better than those of the Senate. Augustus, on becoming sole ruler of the
Roman world, was in theory simply the first citizen of the Republic, intrusted with
temporary powers to settle the disorders of the state. Old magistracies retained, but

the various powers and prerogatives of each conferred on Augustus. 'Emperor' (Imperator) originally designated one intrusted with the full command of an army; but acquired a new significance when adopted as a permanent title by Julius Cæsar, who thus asserted a paramount military authority over the state. The Empire nominally elective, but practically passed by adoption; a sort of hereditary right seemingly recognised up to the time of Nero. *Dr Smith*. After the fall of the Republic and the establishment of a Monarchy, the dignity of *consul* as chief magistrate, after existing about five hundred years, was allowed to continue for a time to deceive the people with the show of a Republic, the power and respect of the office gradually sinking to a shadow and a mockery till it disappeared entirely under Justinian. Belisarius the last consul, A.D. 543. *Prætors* next to consuls; their province to administer justice; at first one, and afterwards two: one chosen from the patricians as city prætor, the other from the plebeians as foreign prætor. Their number increased by Julius Cæsar and afterwards by Augustus to sixteen, but reduced by Valentinus and Martian to three. Each bound to declare, supply, and improve the law; and at his entrance into office, issued an edict or manifesto declaring the mode of his administration, and consisting of formulas of justice collected from the laws of the Twelve Tables and the edicts of his predecessors. *Censors* originally appointed to take the value of each person's estate, and to register his name in the class to which he belonged. Their duty afterwards to let out the public tributes, customs, and taxes, take charge of the public roads, buildings, and marriages, and exercise a moral police over the manners and conduct of the people. Two held office at once; the election for five years. With the fall of the Republic the office came into disuse, the Emperor himself assuming its duties. *Quæstors* at first charged with criminal processes and the pecuniary affairs of the state. Subsequently only state treasurers. Two in number and chosen annually; during their office in Rome, called city or treasury quæstors; afterwards, sent into the provinces to draw the revenues, and called provincial quæstors. In the time of Julius Cæsar, the state treasurership was committed to two ædiles, the quæstors being appointed to other offices as cabinet secretaries. Delivered over by Augustus to the prætors, but restored by Claudius to the quæstors till Nero, his successor, again finally transferred it to the prætors. *Proconsuls* usually those who had been consuls and afterwards sent into the provinces, generally with the command of an army, having under them two lieutenants (legati) and two quartermasters or provincial quæstors (proquæstors). *Proprætors* usually those who had been prætors, and then sent into a province where no army was kept, for the administration of justice, having also under him proquæstors.

---

2. *Whosoever therefore resisteth the power, resisteth the ordinance of God; and they that resist shall receive to themselves damnation.*

Resisteth. 1. By disobeying; 2. Refusing to support; 3. Attempting to overthrow.
Opposition to the state not only civil crime, but moral delinquency.
No Christian warranted to disturb a settled civil government.
Rulers to be obeyed while not enjoining what is sinful, Acts iv. 19.
Power. 1. Government abstractly; 2. The persons exercising it.
Believers not to resist the persons, much less the power. *Chalmers*.
Ordinance of God. Not a mere human appointment.
Hence rulers called " Gods," as in God's place, Ps. lxxxii. 6.

Called also an ordinance or creation of man, 1 Pet. ii. 13.
The form human, the institution itself divine.
Originally of God, mediately of man.
To rule, a divine right, but not to rule wrong.
The power itself of God, but not the abuse of it.
No reference here to any special form of government.
Civil government the result of God's moral government.
Damnation. 1. Condemnation ; 2. Punishment.
Condemnation from God ; punishment from the power itself.
God's authority resisted in that of the magistrate.
Civil punishment one form of God's chastisement.
Obedience to magistrates urged by the apostles—
1. On the ground of conscience ; 2. On that of consequences.
The Gospel favourable to magistracy and civil order.
Yet Christ and His apostles charged with sedition, Luke xxiii. 2, 5.
   Acts xvii. 7 ; xxiv. 5.
Exhortations to obedience in this epistle necessary—
1. From the tendency of the Jews to rebellion ;
2. From the heathen character of the civil powers ;
3. From their probable hostility to Christianity.

'O ἀντιτασσομενος, whoever resists (obsistit) ; a military term. *Beza.* Opposes. *Pag., Pisc., Grot.* With violence. *Ham.* Rises up against ; refuses to obey a just law or edict. *Grot.*—Διαταγη (δια and τασσω). Ordination. *Eras., Pag., Mor.* Institution. *Cast., Schött.* Commandment. *Syr., Stuart.* Equivalent to what was called by the Roman emperors διαταγμα and διαταξις. *Grot.* Disposition of God for the public peace and order. *Doddr.* Same word applied to angels in connection with the giving of the law,—εἰς διαταγας ἀγγελων, Acts vii. 53.—Κριμα, judgment ; from the magistrate, or, escaping that, from God himself. *Whitby.* Punishment from God, but through the organ of the magistrate. *Thol.* Civil punishment. *Stuart.* Condemnation, not from the magistrate, but from God, whose authority in the magistrate's is resisted. *D. Brown.*

---

3. *For rulers are not a terror to good works, but to the evil. Wilt thou then not be afraid of the power ? Do that which is good, and thou shalt have praise of the same.*

For. 1. Proof that rulers are an ordinance of God ;
2. Reason for obedience and subjection.
Terror. Object of fear ; terrible. A general fact declared.
None need to fear who practise only good, 1 Pet. iii. 13.
Good works. Conduct morally and socially good.
Works fitted to promote the good of society.
Works really good, as conformable to God's law.

Such not only good in their nature but their tendency.
Not the works which disturb society, but uphold it.
Such works the opposite of those usually punished by rulers.
The text true in general of the worst government.
Works enjoined by the Roman law in general good.
Roman code one of the best the world has ever seen.
Administration of Roman law in general good.
Christianity not yet persecuted by the Roman government.
Laws of all civilised states favour peaceable subjects.
Protection of the good the design and general effect of all rule.
Evil. 1. What is criminal in its own nature;
2. What is contrary to the law of God and man;
3. What is injurious in its tendency to society.
Be afraid. Two kinds of fear in regard to evil works—
1. A fear that precedes, to deter from them;
2. A fear that follows, as their punishment.
Praise. Commendation with reward, 1 Cor. iv. 5; 1 Pet. ii. 14.
Praise within certain limits a lawful motive to well-doing.
Only becomes sinful when predominant or supreme.
Praise of man vain without the praise of God, John xii. 43.
Truly good works will generally obtain both, Luke ii. 52.
Good works entitled praise, as well as entitled to it, Phil. iv. 8.
Christians commended by the heathen, except for their religion.

Φοβος, fear, terror; i.e., φοβεροι, terrible; abstract for concrete. *Stuart.*—Των ἀγαθων ἐργων ἀ. τ. κακων. Codd. Sin., Vat., and Alex. have τῳ ἀγαθῳ ἐργῳ ἀ,—τῳ κακῳ, to the good work but to the evil.—'Επαινον, praise of obedience. *Par.* Reward; so 1 Cor. iv. 5; ἐπαινειν, used in this sense in connection with Grecian judicature. *Schött.* Commendation of being a peaceful and obedient citizen. *Stuart.* 'Leges improbos supplicio afficiunt, et defendunt ac tuentur bonos.' *Cicero.* 'Bonus vir Caius Seius, tantum quod Christianus.' *Tertullian.*

---

4. *For he is the minister of God to thee for good. But if thou do that which is evil, be afraid; for he beareth not the sword in vain: for he is the minister of God, a revenger to execute wrath upon him that doeth evil.*

Minister. A servant, or one who works for another.
Magistrates and ministers of the Word called by the same name, Eph. iii. 7.
Rulers, though lords to their subjects, are servants to God.
They do His work, and shall render to Him their account.
To thee. 1. As an individual citizen; 2. As a Christian.

Civil government especially a benefit to believers.
Rulers often their shield from the people, Acts xxi. 30–32 ; xxv. 11.
Nero a wicked ruler, yet for a time Paul's protector.
"To the lions with him," a common cry of the Pagan multitude.
For good. The enjoyment of a quiet and peaceable life, 1 Tim. ii. 2.
Tendency and design of civil government good and salutary.
Promotes the good of society. True of the worst government.
The worst civil government better than a state of anarchy.
Persecution for Christ's sake not here in the apostle's view.
Indicates what governments were to be and generally are.
Beareth. Weareth ; is invested with it, *i.e.*, by God himself.
Sword. Token of power over the subject's life, Acts xii. 2.
Often carried before rulers as the insignia of their office.
An axe carried before Roman consuls with the same view.
Expresses all sorts of punishments, especially that of death.
Text in favour of capital punishment for certain crimes.
The foundation of it the law given after the flood, Gen. ix. 5, 6.
Power over human life given to rulers by God, John xix. 11.
In vain. 1. For no purpose ; 2. By mere chance.
The Roman government strong, active, and jealous.
Not backward in visiting crime with punishment.
Governments generally made successful against evil-doers.
Best-planned crimes and conspiracies generally detected and punished.
The sword given by God, and that for a definite purpose.
Christians desired to be punished if found evil-doers.
Revenger. One who exacts the claims of justice.
Punishment to be viewed as righteous retribution.
Crime is wrong done—1. Against God ; 2. Against man.
Its punishment demanded by the claims of society.
Pain inflicted to be atoned for by pain endured.
Wrath. Punishment, viewed as an expression of anger.
Anger justly excited by wilful evil-doing.
All wilful crime to be viewed with indignation and abhorrence.
Punishment the expression of displeasure on the part—
1. Of God ; 2. Of the magistrate ; 3. Of society in general.
The judge's wrath here viewed as a righteous infliction.
Executed not to gratify a feeling, but to fulfil a duty.

Διακονος, minister or servant who attends to any business for another. Applied to Christ, Rom. xv. 8 ; to apostles and preachers of the Word, 1 Cor. iii. 5 ; to those in the Church who had charge of temporal matters, 1 Tim. iii. 8, 12; Rom. xvi. 1. Here applied to the magistrate. The ruler is a minister of God. *Boothroyd.* It (the civil government) is an instrument in the hands of God,—is of divine appointment. *Stuart.* —Εἴκη (εἴκω, to yield); yielding to impulse or passion, and so acting rashly and inconsiderately, and hence often without effect. *Pisc.* By chance. *Con. & Hows.* As a mere show. *Cobbin.*—Μάχαιραν (μάχομαι, to fight), sword; emblem of punishment. *Stuart.* Symbol of magistrate's authority to punish. *D. Brown.* Sulpicius carried a dagger (pugio) as the symbol of the power of the magistrates over the life of the subject, and gave one as such to officers of state.—Φορεῖ (φέρω, to carry; φορέω, to carry habitually, as a garment, Matt. xi. 8), wears; more than. φέρω, to indicate the divine institution and give weight to the injunction.—Ἔκδικος εἰς ὀργήν, exercising judgment unto punishment; judging, condemning to punishment. *Stuart.*

---

5. *Wherefore ye must needs be subject, not only for wrath, but also for conscience' sake.*

Must needs. Strong expression. It is matter of necessity.
Some duties require to be particularly enforced.
Christians to attend carefully to every department of duty.
Hence to be instructed—1. As to what is duty; 2. The reasons and grounds of it; 3. The importance of attending to it.
For wrath. On account of the punishment incurred.
Fear of punishment the lowest motive to obedience.
For conscience' sake. In obedience to conscience.
As a matter of duty, and a question of right and wrong.
Conscience the vicegerent of God within us.
Believers to act in all things from sense of duty.
Conscience views matters in relation to God, 1 Pet. ii. 19; Acts iv. 19.
Regard to God's authority the best security to loyalty.
A Christian obedience is to be free, pure, and conscientious;
From sense of what is right, without regard to consequences.
Subjection to magistrates to be made matter of conscience—
1. As subjection to God's institution and His own command;
2. As enjoined and exemplified by Christ himself, Matt. xxii. 21; xxvi. 63, 64.
3. As a due return for benefits received;
4. As an example to others, and for the benefit of society;
5. As a testimony in favour of Christianity.

Ἀνάγκη, moral necessity, as 1 Cor. ix. 16. *De Wette.* We ought. *Stuart.*—Ὀργήν, the wrath or punishment mentioned in preceding verse. *Ellicot.* Indignation; not merely to shun the evils of a different course. *Stuart.*—Διὰ τὴν συνείδησιν, for conscience' sake,—because of God's institution and command. *Tol.* Christ's command. *Grot.* Taught by natural instinct. *Est.* Example to others and testimony to Christianity. *Eras., Vat.* From a principle of duty to God. *Stanhope.* Conscientious regard to our obligations. *Stuart.* Return for benefits. *Chrys., Theod.*

6. *For, for this cause pay ye tribute also : for they are God's ministers, attending coninually upon this very thing.*

For. Passes to details of duty in relation to the state.
For this cause. That thing being a matter of conscience.
Pay ye. Contributions to the state a debt of the subject.
Public debts to be paid as punctually as private ones.
No reference here to contributions unconstitutionally levied.
Tribute. *Gr.*, Tributes; public dues of every kind.
Taxes imposed for the support of civil government.
The power being of God, tribute to be paid for its support.
Jewish believers especially tempted to withhold the tribute.
Principles of Judas Gaulonitis still in operation, Matt. xxii. 17.
Early Christians known as conscientiously paying taxes.
God's ministers. Public officers under God himself.
God's agents in upholding and protecting society.
His servants as employed in accomplishing His purposes.
So Nebuchadnezzar, Jer. xxv. 9 ; and Cyrus, Isa. xliv. 28.
A higher title given here than in ver. 4; appropriated by Paul xv. 16.
Gives to magistrates a kind of sacred character.
Both Zerubbabel and Joshua God's anointed ones, Zech. iv. 2–14.
Subordinate officers employed about the taxes included here.
Attending continually. Employing all their time.
Magistrates and other officers reminded of their duty.
Reason for the faithful payment of taxes.
A diligent ruler should have a faithful people.
Rulers to be duly furnished with means for doing their work.
On this very thing. Business connected with the public good.
Their duty as ministers of God in civil matters.
The lowest official in the state needful as well as the highest.
Each to be supported as God's minister in his work.

Διὰ τοῦτο, for this cause ; for the sake of conscience, as we . as to avoid civil penalties. *Stuart.* This is the reason why. *D. Brown.*—Γὰρ, added for the sake of further illustrating and confirming the subject ; διὰ τοῦτο γάρ, perhaps an intensive causal formula, like ἐπειδήπερ, &c.,—on this very account. *Stuart.*—Φόρους (from φέρω, to bear), tributes ; applied to tribute paid to Roman emperors, Luke xx. 22 ; a tribute imposed on the provinces : first imposed on the Jews by Pompey. *Schött.* Contributions requisite for maintaining civil government. *D. Brown.* The question of paying tribute to heathen princes agitated by the Jews not only in Judæa but elsewhere. *Macknight.* Principles of Judas Gaulonitis widely spread, and might have infected the Christians. *De Wette.* Revenues of the Roman Empire consisted chiefly—1. Of the rents of public lands, farmed by *publicani*, and collected by tax-gatherers employed by them, the 'publicans' in our version; 2. Customs or taxes on goods; 3. Tithes; 4. Pasturage, &c.; 5. Poll or personal tax; 6. Property-tax; 7. Army-tax, imposed on all free Roman citizens, but especially on the inhabitants of the provinces. *Keil.*—Τελεῖτε, ye pay; indicative. *Beza, Pag., Mor., Eras., Pisc., Cast., Calv., D. Brown.* Pay; imperative. *Stuart.*—Λειτουργοί (λαος, people, and ἔργον, work; a public officer, whether in Church or State), ministers; more frequently used of church officers; applied to the Levites by LXX. for מְשָׁרֵת. *Grot.* Διάκονος, a general term for service; λειτουργός used of service of a public, and more especially of a sacred character. God's ministers or instruments, in the same sense as the magistracy above-mentioned. *Stuart.*—Εἰς αὐτὸ τοῦτο, to this very matter; magisterial office. *Calv.* To this one affair, the execution of their high office. *Doddr.* Executing judgment between man and man. *Whitby.* Administering justice. *Mart.* The whole extent of their magisterial duty. *De Wette.* Affairs of the public. *Haldane.* Collecting the taxes. *Brown.* —Προσκαρτεροῦντες, labouring. *Beza.* Applying themselves. *Calv., Eras., Pag., Pisc., Doddr.* Vigorously. *Mor.* Assiduous. *Cast.* Persevering, watching, toiling. *Par.* Employing themselves in. *Mart.* Who attend to; indicates habitual persevering attention. *Stuart.*

---

7. *Render therefore to all their dues: tribute to whom tribute is due; custom to whom custom; fear to whom fear; honour to whom honour.*

Render. Not "give;" the case is one of debt, not of favour. For protection by the magistrate, support is due from the subject.
Therefore. On account of the place of rulers as God's ministers.
To all. State officers of every description, and men in general.
"To every one his own," the Christian's motto. Applied—
1. To the civil magistrate, Matt. xxii. 21; 2. To all men.
Their dues. Whether as superiors, inferiors, or equals.
Each has a debt against us, whatever his station or relation.
To all their dues—1. In the state; 2. In the market; 3. In the church.
Taxes and customs not favours, but public debts.
Debts to the state to be paid as well as debts at the store.
Tribute. Tax laid on persons and land; property-tax.
To be paid according to the valuation of a man's estate.
Custom. Tax levied on goods and merchandise.
Paid on goods both imported and exported.
Fear. Duty owed to superiors—magistrates, parents, &c., Mal. i. 6.
Reverence, or a higher degree of honour and respect.
Civil authorities to be feared as an institution of God.
Honour. An inferior degree of reverence, 1 Pet. ii. 17.
All customary civil honour and respect to be paid to men.
Difference of rank in society God's appointment, Ps. cxiii. 7, 8.
Civil rule to be honoured in all its forms and departments.
Reverence the sovereign invested with supreme authority.

Venerate the legislature and administrators of law.
Honour municipal and local authorities.
Respect the police and each government officer.
Fear God. Honour the king. Honour all men, 1 Pet. ii. 17.
Honour to be—1. Inwardly cherished; 2. Outwardly expressed in words and actions.

Ἀπόδοτε οὖν. Codd. Sin., Vat., and Alex. omit οὖν.—Ὀφειλάς, dues; what is due on the ground and spirit of such precepts. *Stuart.* Comprehends the various duties owed to magistrates, viz., rendering due honour, obeying their edicts, and paying the revenues. *Calv.* Applied to pecuniary debt, Matt. xviii. 32. = χρέος, δάνειον, ἀνάγκη. *Hes.*—Φόρον, a fixed tax. *Boothroyd.* Direct taxes. *Cobbin.* Land-tax. *D. Brown.* A tax either on persons or land, or rather here on both. *Stuart.*—Τέλος (from τελέω, to pay), a tax on goods, &c., customs, especially harbour-dues, Matt. xvii. 25; whence in New Testament, τελῶναι, tax-gatherers, improperly rendered 'publicans.' The tenth of the produce of public lands paid by the occupier; rent for the privilege of pasture on public lands. *Adam's Antiq.* Φόρος, paid as capitation money according to census; τέλος, paid on any other account. Φόρος, paid on things immoveable, as farms; τέλος, on things which may be conveyed. *Beza.* τέλος answers to our present term *customs*, i.e., a tax on goods, wares, merchandise, &c. *Stuart.*—Φόβον, reverence, obedience, fear of offending. *Par.* Fear in such a sense as to deter from sedition and civil disobedience. *Stuart.* A greater degree of honour. *Bengel.*—Τιμή, all kinds of reverence; outward respect, love, obedience, gratitude, forbearance. *Par.* Respect paid to equals in rank; but here that paid to magistrates. *Stuart.* Φόβος, inward disposition; τιμή, external behaviour proceeding from it. *Doddr.* Φόβ. used especially of judges; τιμή, more general. *De Wette.* Enrolment in the censor's books, and payment of taxes according to fortune, regarded among the *rights* of Roman citizenship. Census taken every five years. Citizens appeared in the Forum in martial order, under pain of losing property and liberty. Name, age, fortune, race, family, and condition declared. Censors also charged with the general inspection of manners. Could punish the guilty with degradation of rank and loss of citizen-rights. Other public rights of citizens were:—*Personal liberty*, as against power of tyrants, severity of magistrates, cruelty of creditors, and insolence of the great; *Suffrage*, or right to vote in the assemblies of the people; *Public employments*, or right of holding offices in the State, civil or sacerdotal,—at first only held by patricians; *Military service*, or right to be enrolled among the legions, at first confined to Roman citizens; *Religious worship*, or right to celebrate the religious rites belonging to the family or gens. Private rights were:—Those of *family*, more especially in transmitting the religious rites above mentioned; *Marriage*, union between slaves being only cohabitation; *Paternal rights*, or power over the liberty and life of the children to the third generation, sons only being free and able to acquire property at the death of father and grandfather; *Property*, which might either be *sacred*, as altars, temples, tombs, &c., or *human*, which again might either be public or private; *Inheritance*; *Guardianship.*

---

8. *Owe no man anything, but to love one another: for he that loveth another hath fulfilled the law.*

Owe no man. Withhold from no man what is his due.
Passes from duties to magistrates to general and mutual ones.

No man to be in debt against his creditor's will.
Private as well as public debts to be punctually paid.
A duty especially incumbent on the followers of Christ.
The breach of it either from inability or unwillingness to pay.
The former may be either a misfortune or a sin.
The latter the mark of a wicked person, Ps. xxxvii. 21.
Some think little of the *trouble* of being in debt;
More think little of the *sin*. *M. Henry.*
But to love one another. Love, a debt due to all men.
Especially due by believers to one another.
Love the only debt for a Christian to owe.
A *great* debt—1. As due to so many—all men;
2. Requiring so much to pay it—sometimes our life, 1 John iii. 16, &c.
A *lasting* debt; though always paid, yet never discharged.
The more that is paid the more is felt to be due.
The principle of love deeper and more active by the practice of it.
A *pleasant* debt; comfort in love, Phil. ii. 1.
Every payment of it gladdens and enlarges the heart.
An *honourable* debt; necessary to our moral nature.
Love makes us God-like and Christ-like, Eph. iv. 32; v. 1, 2; 1 John iv. 8.
Men viewed in the context under a threefold regimen—
1. Of fear, ver. 4; 2. Of conscience, ver. 5–7; 3. Of love, ver. 8–10.
In Christ an ascent from a lower to a higher discipline.
Supremacy of law makes place for the supremacy of love.
Fulfilled the law. 1. Love secures performance of every duty;
2. Is itself in principle that performance.
All duties the development of one principle, *viz.*, love.
Love, the higher duty, includes all the lower ones.
All duties but different ways of performing this one.
Love the mother of all goodness. The nature of God, 1 John iv. 16.
The law itself is but love in manifold dutiful action.

'Οφείλετε, owe, or ye owe. Cod. Sin. has ὀφείλοντες, 'owing.' An injunction. *Stuart, Hald., D. Brown.* An assertion,—'ye owe.' *Brown.* Special reference to the duties enjoined in relation to magistracy. *Calv.*—Εἰ μὴ τὸ ἀγαπᾶν ἀλλήλους, except mutual love; a debt that is ever due. *Hodge.* A debt which is multiplied by paying. *Augustine.*—Τὸν ἕτερον, the other; his neighbour. *Ellicot.*—Νόμον, the law; that part of it which relates to our neighbour. *Bp. Hall, Wells.* True love to our neighbour can only spring from love to God, of which it is both the evidence and the effect. *Calvin.*

9. *For this, Thou shalt not commit adultery, Thou shalt not kill, Thou shalt not steal, Thou shalt not bear false witness, Thou shalt not covet ; and if there be any other commandment, it is briefly comprehended in this saying, namely, Thou shalt love thy neighbour as thyself.*

Commit adultery. Put first, perhaps, from its prevalence, chap. ii. 22.
Order of commandments not everywhere the same.
Love makes each careful of another's comfort and chastity.
Preserves a wife from impurity, a husband from pain.
So-called "love affairs" often diametrically opposite to love.
The foulest things often called by the fairest names.
Any other. For example, the fourth, relating to the Sabbath.
The fifth, in relation to parents, quoted Eph. vi. 2.
Commandments. The law contained in commandments.
Those written on the two tables of stone especially in view.
Law the general term ; commandment the special duty.
The nature and fulfilment of each commandment is love.
Briefly comprehended. Summed up under one head.
Summarily contained and concisely expressed.
United in the one principle of love, from which all flow.
The law summed up by Christ under two heads, Matt. xxii. 38–40.
Both comprehended under one principle, love.
Love. The one word that includes all man's duty.
The nature of God and the perfection of man, 1 John iv. 16, 18.
The bond of perfection, and essential in religion, Col. iii. 14 ; 1 Cor. xiii. 1, &c.
Beginning, middle, and end of true holiness and obedience.
The root, stem, and branches of the law. *Chrys.*
Love is—1. Desire for; 2. Delight in ; 3. Endeavour after, another's good.
Is—1. Cherished in the heart ; 2. Exhibited in the life, 1 John iv. 18.
Its pattern and example in God and the Lord Jesus Christ, Eph. v. 1.
Neighbour. Term applicable to and including all men, ·Luke x. 29–37.
Sharers of our common humanity. All of one blood, Acts xvii. 26.
All men the offspring of God by creation, Acts xvii. 28, 29 ; Luke iii. 38.
As thyself. 1. As truly as thyself; each loves himself, Eph. v. 28, 29.
2. With the same love in kind and degree.
His happiness and well-being to be as dear to us as our own.

Μοιχευσεις, the commandments in the order in which they are read by the LXX. in Exodus. *Grot.*—Οὐ ψευδομαρτυρησεις, omitted in Codd. Vat. and Alex.—Ἀνακεφαλαιουται (ἀνα and κεφαλη, a head, κεφαλαιον, a sum or summary), are gathered into one head or sum (recapitulantur). *Aug., Pisc., Mor.* Comprehended. *Calv.* Summarily comprehended. *Eras., Pag., Cas., Par., Est., Mar., Diod.* Summed up. *Booth royd.* Term borrowed from rhetoric, to recapitulate; or from military tactics, to gather into one band, Eph. i. 10. *Rückert.* = ἐπαναλαμβανω. *Hes.* Love to God and love to man said by the Jews to be the great sums or heads of the law, כללים גדולים. *Grot.*—Ἑαυτον. Codd. Sin. and Alex. have σεαυτον.

---

10. *Love worketh no ill to his neighbour ; therefore love is the fulfilling of the law.*

Worketh no ill. So 1 Cor. xiii. 5. To project evil is in effect to do it. Love's delight, desire, and aim is another's good.
The negative side expressed, the positive implied.
Love not only works no evil, but works all good.
To work no evil to another the lowest form of love.
Not only restrains from doing evil, but constrains to do good.
All evil done to others the effect of want of love.
We cannot even willingly displease the person we love.
Fulfilling of the law. Love to God the fulfilling of the first table ;
Love to man the fulfilling of the second table of the law.
The latter at present especially in the apostle's view.
Yet never found except in connection with the former.
Love to God the only true foundation of love to man.
The whole law in both its tables fulfilled in love.
Love is what the law demands, and all that it demands.
Hence called the "royal law" and the "law of liberty," James ii. 8, 12.
No part of the Decalogue, therefore, ever to be repealed.
The unchangeable rule of Christian life, chap. vii. 12 ; Eph. vi. 2, 3 ; James ii. 8-12.
Never spoken of in the New Testament except as being still in force.
Its prohibitions no unreasonable restraints of liberty.
All its commands the just requirements of love.
To love is liberty ; and to love is the requirement of the law.
The commandments kept without effort where love prevails.
Law of God wonderful in its simplicity and comprehensiveness.
The Bible the only book that promulgates such a law.
Thus carries in its bosom the evidence of its divine origin.

CHAP. XIII.] ST. PAUL'S EPISTLE TO THE ROMANS. 213

'Αγαπη—ἐργαζεται, omitted in Cod. Alex.—Πληρωμα, completion. *Beza, Pisc.* Consummation. *Eras., Pag., Vat.* Filling up (complementum). *Tol., Est.* Perfection. *Arab.* Πληρωμα = πληρωσις ; the completing of what the law demands, the filling up of the measure of its requirements. *Stuart.* Indicates the genuine disposition of love as the sum of all the single manifestations of love required by the law. *Nielson.*

---

11. *And that, knowing the time, that now it is high time to awake out of sleep: for now is our salvation nearer than when we believed.*

And that. And this do especially; or, And this I say. The following verses give the Christian's daily directory :—
1. When to awake, ver. 11 ; 2. How to dress, ver. 12, 14 ; 3. How to walk ; ver. 13 ; 4. What to provide, ver. 14.

Knowing. Considering ; taking cognizance of ; understanding. Believers to be like Issachar, understanding the time, 1 Chron. xii. 32. Men required to discern the signs of the times, Matt. xvi. 3. Watchmen to be able to answer, "What of the night?" Isa. xxi. 11.

Time. Present season, with its circumstances and duties. The time then present, as well as that in which we are, was—
1. A time of gracious visitation, chap. iii. 26; v. 6 ; 2 Cor. vi. 2 ;
2. A time of tribulation and conflict, chap. viii. 23; Eph. vi. 10, &c. ; 2 Thess. iv. i. 4-7.
3. A time of approaching glory, chap. viii. 18; 1 Cor. xv. 51-58 ; 1 Thess. iv. 15-17.
4. A time of coming danger and apostasy, Acts xx. 29, 30 ; 2 Thess. ii. 3-12 ; 1 Tim. iv. 1.
5. A time of transition, night still, but far advanced, ver. 12.
6. A time of restlessness, dissatisfaction, and activity.

Indefinite expectation of the Lord's speedy return.
Light had broken in upon the darkness of the Pagan world,
Already betokening the approach of a glorious day.
Gospel everywhere preached and everywhere believed, Col. i. 6.
Time advanced as compared with that of Pentecost.
More than eighteen centuries since Paul wrote these words.
The present a time of renewed evangelization of the world. ·
Great and general restlessness and activity among men.
Old systems of Paganism shaking and losing their hold.
Awakened expectancy as to the Lord's appearing.
Anticipated approaching apostasy, conflict, and suffering.
Infidelity and Romanism putting forth their utmost strength.
General belief of some important crisis at hand.
Preparations rapidly making for some great event.
Ends of the earth brought together by railroads and telegraphs.

Everything done with rapidity, haste, and dispatch.
Steam almost everywhere superseding manual labour.
Extraordinary diffusion of knowledge and information.
One of the first nations of Europe now in a state of prostration.
One of the greatest European wars now raging, and another still greater anticipated, Nov. 1870.
The Pope's temporal power, after existing little more than 1260 years, now brought to an end.
Rome belongs no longer to the Pope, but to the King of Italy.
Yet the revival of the defunct Holy Roman Empire spoken of.
Now. Already; no more time to be lost.
High time. *Gr.*, Hour; a certain portion of the day.
Here the hour shortly preceding daybreak.
The time for awakening out of sleep. Applicable—
1. To the Church in general; 2. To individual believers.
Allusion here and in what follows to military life.
Roman soldiers awakened early by sound of trumpet.
Awake. Rouse ourselves to watchfulness and activity.
No time for sloth or slumber, Eph. v. 14; 1 Cor. xv. 34; 1 Thess. v. 6.
Refers to the past as a time of sleep and inactivity.
Sleep. Fallen man's natural condition, Eph. v. 14. A state of—
1. Unconsciousness as to one's real circumstances;
2. Unconcern as to one's present and eternal state;
3. Inactivity in regard to the interests of eternity;
4. Indulgence of fleshly appetites and desires;
5. Delusive dreams as to one's real condition;
6. Helplessness and exposure to danger.
An awakening at the time of conviction and regeneration.
Tendency to fall asleep again even after conversion.
Both wise and foolish virgins slumbered and slept.
Exhortations needed to wake up and keep awake, Eph. v. 14; 1 Thess. v. 6.
Imagery borrowed from Christ's discourses, Matt. xxiv. 22; Luke, xxi. 28–36.
The present a time of partial awakening and comparative drowsiness in the churches.
From 1858, great awakenings over Europe and America.
Our. Applies to Paul himself, and every believer.
Salvation. Full salvation at the Lord's appearing, Heb. ix. 28.
Day of perfect redemption, chap. viii. 23; Eph. i. 14; Luke xxi. 28.
Manifestations of the sons of God, chap. viii. 19; Col. iii. 4; 1 John iii. 2.

Glorious liberty of the children of God, chap. viii. 21.
Salvation has various stages of development—
1. Time of union with Christ, and justification through faith;
2. Progressive sanctification extending through life;
3. Deliverance from sin and suffering at death;
4. Glorification in soul and body at Christ's appearing.
Nearer. A believer's full salvation ever approaching.
Christ's second appearing at that time constantly in view.
Salvation possessed, yet always progressing to perfection.
Not now a being, but a becoming. Not a leap, but a walk.
Greater nearness of salvation a motive to diligence.
Sloth to be shaken off as the glory approaches.
The nearer the King's approach the more need to prepare.
The nearer the goal the more earnest the race.
Foolish to relax when the prize is so near.
The nearer Canaan, the less care about the wilderness.
Fewer sands in your glass to-day than there were yesterday.
Believed. Believed with the heart to justification.
Began to believe; entered on the path of faith.
Faith a race, Heb. xii. 1; 1 Cor. ix. 24–26; Acts xx. 24; 2 Tim. iv. 7, 8.
Faith begins by laying hold of Christ, and ends with beholding Him.
"Believing" the commencement of the Christian's life.
Characterizes its whole course. A life of faith, Gal. ii. 20.

Καὶ τοῦτο, and this; this especially. *Theod.* And because we know this, viz, the time. *Luth.* Therefore. *Dickson.* Besides. *Par., Calv.* And this we ought the more to do. *Diod.* Also this I command. *Macknight.* And this do. *Est., Flatt, Stuart, Con. & Hows., D. Brown.* Farther, because we know, &c. *Stier.* Added for amplification. *Beza, Eras., Tol.*—Εἰδότες, considering. *Grot.* Understanding. *l'isc.* Seeing. *Mart., Diod.* Taking cognizance of; participle used causally,—because or since ye know. *Stuart.* Duly estimating. *Cobbin.* Being acquainted with. *Brown.*—Καιρόν, the time. *Mor., Eras.* Occasion or opportunity. *Tol., Eras., Pag., Beza, Calv.* Season. *Mart.* Circumstances of the present season. *Doddr.* Time you live in, and what it demands of you. *Flatt.* Gospel time, the beginning of a glorious day. *Stuart.* Time then present, contrasted with that when they believed. *Haldane.* Real state of present circumstances and the duty rising out of them. *Brown.* Time on earth. *Boothroyd.* Season wherein we stand. *Con. & Hows.*—Ὥρα, hour. *Vulg., Mor.* Time. *Beza.* Due time (tempestivum). *Eras.* Καιρός, season; ὥρα, an hour, a more limited space of time; certain time of day. *Beng.* Allusion to military life. *Grot.* 'Nec excitutur classico miles truci.' *Hor.* Time; the commencement of the dispensation and the beginning of light in your own souls. *Stuart, Calv.* The hour has already come. *D. Brown.* We have been in the dark, but let us awake with the light. *Cobbin.*—Ἡμᾶς, Codd. Sin. and Alex. read ὑμᾶς, you.—Ὕπνου, deep sleep; dreams of the present life; physical death. *Chrys.* Spiritual stupor; the image of death. *Calv.* Life of sensuality and sin; a state of blindness, inactivity, and danger. *Stanhope.* Sleep of sin. *Schött.* Of heathenism and vice; Roman converts only progressively awaking. *Mackn.* State of comparative inaction. *Stuart.* Christian's condition on earth as one of anticipation and hope. *Reiche.* As having more or less of the sinful element. *Meyer.* Indicates worldly carelessness and indifference to sin, allowing works of darkness. *De Wette, Alford.* State of darkness and enslavement of the judgment and conscience, by the blinding influence of sin. *Lange.*, As applicable to men in general, a state of spiritual ignorance, delusion, and inactivity; as applicable to believers, a state of spiritual languor. *Brown.* State of stupid, fatal indifference to eternal things. *D. Brown.* Consciousness of the nearness of the Lord's appearing should move to greater earnestness than ever in seeking to fulfil all his commandments in love. *Rückert.*—'Εγερθῆναι, to awake; to gird ourselves and prepare to perform the duties incumbent on us. *Calv, Flatt.* Rouse up to a state of strenuous effort. *Stuart.* To the full consciousness of salvation. *Reiche.* Includes reference to the resurrection of the body. *Chrys.*—Νῦν, now; ἤδη, now already, no time to lose; νῦν, at this present time as distinguished from the past. *Beng.*—'Εγγύτερον, nearer, in point of time; refers to time before believing. *Calv.* Doctrine of the Gospel now better understood. *Mackn.* Spoken in the view of Christ's speedy return. *Meyer, Alford.*—'Ημῶν, our [salvation]; or salvation nearer *to us.* connecting ἡμῶν with ἐγγύτερον. *Beng., Ellicot, D. Brown.*—Σωτηρια, salvation; the resurrection a salvation to those prepared for it. *Chrys.* Spiritual salvation and future glory. *Est., Par.* Deliverance as from a besieged city. *Grot.* Wider and more complete publication of the Gospel. *Wolf, Carpzov.* Deliverance from Jewish persecutions. *Hammond.* From ceremonial law. *Schött.* Knowledge of the doctrine of the Gospel. *Mackn.* Knowledge and experience of the benefits of Christianity now greater. *Flatt.* Great expected salvation. *Doddr., Bp. Hall, Stanhope.* The salvation to be brought at Christ's appearing. *Beng., Meyer, De Wette, Thol.* Greater inner perfection of believers. *Mor., Glöckler.* Redemption from all evil. *Rückert.* Spiritual salvation in the world of glory. *Stuart.* Blessedness of heaven at death. *Haldane, Cobbin.* Full spiritual salvation and day of perfect redemption viewed as connected with the universal spread of Christianity. *Lange.* Overthrow of Paganism. *Brown.* Day of Christ's second appearing always represented as at hand, to keep believers in a state of wakeful expectancy, though without reference to the *chronological* nearness or distance of that event. *D. Brown.*—'Ὅτε ἐπιστεύσαμεν, when we believed; while trusting in the Mosaic law. *Eros.* When we thought salvation lay in external things, and had no certainty of it. *Melanch.* Before Christ's coming. *Corn. a Lap, Baldwin.* When we became believers. *Beza, Grot., Rück., Ellicot.* Began to believe; referring to the time before faith. *Calvin.* Time when we first believed. *D. Brown.*

---

12. *The night is far spent, the day is at hand: let us therefore cast off the works of darkness, and let us put on the armour of light.*

Night. 1. The time previous to the full light of the Gospel;
2. The period of a believer's sojourn in this world;
More especially, the time till Christ's second appearing.
Night a time of darkness and sleep; indicating—
1. Ignorance; 2. Sin; 3. Discomfort; 4. Dangers; 5. Dreams.
Believers not *of* the night, yet still *in* it, 1 Thess. v. 5; 2 Pet. i. 19.
No daylight till the Sun of Righteousness arise.
All the days of sinful nature are the darkness of night.
No right discerning of spiritual things, 1 Cor. ii. 11, 14.

All is night here, in respect of ignorance and daily ensuing troubles. *S. Rutherford.*
Eighteen centuries have passed, and still night continues.
Christ the true Light, but men shut out His beams.
Men's heads full of dreams that keep them sleeping.
Creation still groaning and travailing together in pain, chap. viii. 22.
Believers still groaning within themselves, waiting for the adoption, viz., the redemption of their body, chap. viii. 23.
Darkness still in great part covering the earth, Isa. lx. 2.
Far spent. Probably two-thirds at least then gone, A.D. 58, A.M. 4062.
After eighteen centuries the night much nearer its end.
The world's seventh millennium may bring the day.
Time between Christ's first and second coming the dawn. *Beng.*
Gross darkness already past, and some daylight appears. *Leighton.*
The bright day believers look for is posting forward. *Ibid.*
Day. Termination of night to—1. The Church; 2. Believers; 3. The world.
Day breaks and shadows flee away at Christ's return, Cant. iv. 6.
The Sun of Righteousness yet to arise on the earth, Mal. iv. 2.
Christ the bright and morning star, Rev. xxii. 16.
His twofold appearing, Heb. ix. 26, 28 ; Luke i. 78 ; 2 Pet. i. 19.
Day a time of light—1. Knowledge; 2. Holiness; 3. Happiness.
New earth promised, wherein dwells righteousness, 2 Pet. iii. 13.
At hand. Christ's coming so represented, Phil. iv. 5 ; Jas. v. 8 ; 1 Pet. iv. 5, 7.
His own last promise that He would come quickly, Rev. xxii. 20.
The Lord is not slack concerning His promise, 2 Pet. iii. 9.
The Bridegroom was to tarry, Matt. xxv. 5.
The nobleman to go into a far country, and to return, Luke xix. 12.
One day with the Lord as a thousand years, 2 Pet. iii. 8.
A watchful and enlightened eye required to discern the time.
When ye see these things begin to come to pass, look up, Luke xxi. 28.
Believers to lift up their heads, their redemption drawing nigh. *Ib.*
Yet a little while, and He that shall come will come, Heb. x. 37.
Cast off. As we do our night-clothes in the morning.
The process of an ever on-going repentance.
In sanctification some things always to be put off, Eph. iv. 22 ; Col. iii. 8, 9.
The old man and his works viewed as a clothing, Ps. cix. 18.
All our righteousness as filthy rags, Isa. lxiv. 6.
Every weight and besetting sin to be laid aside, Heb. xii. 1.

All malice, guile, hypocrisy, envy, evil-speaking, 1 Pet. ii. 1.
Works. Those both of the outward and the inward man.
Include thoughts, feelings, tempers, dispositions, words.
Works of the flesh—hatred, wrath, strife, variance, Gal. v. 20.
Some works visible to man, others only to God, 1 Tim. v. 24, 25.
Darkness. Sin, moral darkness, 1 John i. 5, 6 ; ii. 9, 11 ; Eph. v. 8.
The opposite of God's nature, who is Light, 1 John i. 5.
Works of darkness all kinds of sin, Eph. v. 11 ; as—
1. Proceeding only from a sinful heart, Matt. xv. 19 ;
2. Suitable only to a sinful state, John iii. 19, 20.
Works done in the dark, and fit only for the dark, Eph. v. 12, 13.
Works of darkness belong only to those who are of the night.
Believers children of the light and of the day, 1 Thess. v. 5.
Works of darkness hang on them as Lazarus',grave clothes.
Put on. The Christian's life a constant putting on, 2 Pet. i. 5-7.
Always something to be put on as well as off, Eph. iv. 24.
Believers to be constantly adorning themselves, 1 Pet. iii. 3-5.
Zion to be putting on her beautiful garments, Isa. lii. 1.
Adorning herself for her royal Husband, Rev. xxi. 2 ; xix. 7, 8.
Armour: The believer a warrior, 1 Tim. i. 18 ; vi. 12 ; 2 Tim. ii. 3, 4 ; iv. 7.
The armour offensive and defensive described, Eph. vi. 13, &c. ; 1 Thess. v. 8.
The enemy—sin, Satan, and the world, Heb. xii. 4 ; Eph. vi. 11, 12 ; 1 John v. 4.
The Leader, Christ, 2 Tim. ii. 3, 4 ; Heb. ii. 10 ; Rev. xix. 11-14.
The Christian life one of vigilance, activity, endurance, conflict.
The believer dressed and armed at once. His dress his armour.
Light. Holiness ; the divine nature and character, 1 John i. 5.
The opposite of darkness and sin—divine truth, Eph. v. 13.
Armour of light is—1. Such as becomes a soldier of light ;
2. Provided in and by the Gospel which is light ;
3. Consisting only of what is according to His nature who is Light.
This armour bright and glorious. Intended for the light.
Reflects the glory of Christ the Sun of Righteousness.
Used only in the conflict against darkness and sin.
The Christian's banner displayed for the truth, Ps. lx. 4.
His armour is Light, and can bear the light, John iii. 21.
Armour of Righteousness on the right hand and the left, 2 Cor. vi. 7.
Armour of light or of the day, which calls to battle.
Armour needed in the day, scarcely even garments in the night.

Light the symbol of joy. Christians fight and feast at once.
Power to fight allied with perception of divine truth.
Christian's armour moral, intellectual, and divine.
Armour of light contrasted with works of darkness.

Νύξ, night; time of Mosaic law, previous to Christ's first coming. *Cyp.*, *Aug.*, *Tol.*, *Beza.* Time of ignorance of God, in which we both err and sleep. *Calv.*, *Schött.* Time before conversion. *Par.* Present state of darkness, error, and sin. *Tol.*, *Pisc.*, *De Wette, Hald.* Time of persecution from the Jews. *Ham.* Dark state of the present life. *Doddr.* Life of sin and error. *Stanhope.* Of Pagan ignorance. *Macknight, Brown.* Of darkness in which believers had once been. *Stuart.* Time preceding Christ's second advent. *Thol., Meyer, Rück.* The whole of life in this present world, in comparison with the kingdom of glory. *Nielson.* Time of evil. *D. Brown.*—Προέκοψεν (πρό, forward, and κόπτω, to cut; to cut off in the way of advance; to advance further and further, as Luke ii. 52; 2 Tim. ii. 16; iii. 9, 13; also, to be far advanced, as Gal. i. 14; so *Jos. War*, ix. 4, 17, νυκτὸς προκοπτούσης), has advanced (præcessit, gone before). *Vulg.* Is past (præteriit). *Pag., Pisc.* Has passed (transivit). *Cyp., Mart.* So *Syriac.* Is gone (discessit). *Cast.* So *Arab.* Has advanced, gone forward (processit). *Pag., Beza, Vat.* Has progressed. *Eras., Calv., Pisc.* Is mostly gone. *Grot., Vat., Est.* Has reached its highest point. *Beng.* Is far advanced. *Doddr.* The last part of the night indicated; the time of twilight, that between Christ's first and second appearing. *Rückert.* The night is advanced; now nearly gone. *Stuart.* Believers not now overwhelmed in that deep darkness in which unbelievers still are, and have before their eyes the hope of resurrection. *Calv.*—Ἡμέρα, day; gospel light and knowledge. *Mor., Vor., Pisc., Vat., Cas., Grot., Schött.* Full brightness of celestial glory. *Calv.* Conversion. *Par.* Day of Christ, the last day. *Est.* Destruction of Jerusalem and consequent deliverance from Jewish persecution. *Ham.* Full salvation. *Beng.* Eternal day, or more perfect knowledge of divine things. *Stuart.* Salvation, the time of light, purity, perfection, and blessedness. *De Wette.* The endless period of glory and blessedness commencing with Christ's appearing. *Rückert.* Fulness and perfection of salvation at Christ's coming, viewed as near. *Nielson.* Second advent. *Meyer.* Deliverance from this present evil world and admission into heaven. *Haldane, Hodge.* Period of Christian knowledge, purity, and happiness. *Brown.* Night the heathen condition of Rome; day, the coming of Christian Rome; day, a gradual and constantly renewing daybreak; breaks a hundred times, and with ever increasing potency, between Christ's first and second advents. *Lange.* Consummated triumph over the night of evil. *D. Brown.* The Hebrews, like the Athenians, reckoned the day from sunset to sunset; the Babylonians from sunrise to sunrise. The Egyptians, like the Roman priests, reckoned from midnight to midnight. *Pliny.* The natural day from sunrise to sunset was in the oldest times, from want of clocks, loosely divided, as still in Arabia, into six parts:—
1. Dawn or morning twilight (נֶשֶׁף, שַׁחַר), having among the Persians as also among the Hebrews, at least after the exile, two parts (עַרְפַּיִם, dual), 1 Chron. viii. 8, and in the Jerusalem Talmud four parts; 2. Morning, sunrise (בֹּקֶר); 3. The time when it becomes hot, heat of the day (חֹם הַיּוֹם), Gen. xviii. 1; 1 Sam. xi. 11,—about nine o'clock; 4. Mid-day (צָהֳרַיִם); 5. The cool of the day or time of the breeze (רוּחַ הַיּוֹם, breath of the day), Gen. iii. 8,—some hours before sunset; 6. Evening (עֶרֶב), consisting of two parts (עַרְבַּיִם, dual), the first, according to the Karaites and Samaritans, at sunset, and the second at the commencement of the night; but according to the Rabbins, the first at the decline of the day and the second at sunset. The Arabs make their division of the evening more like the former, the second part being the first watch of the night.

So the ancient Hebrews, Deut. xvi. 6, compared with Exod. xxix. 39. Water-clocks invented at a very early period by the Egyptians. Dials first mentioned, 2 Kings xx. 11. In very early use among the Babylonians, from whom Ahaz probably brought or borrowed his. At first indicated only mid-day, and gradually the hours afterwards. Division of hours first mentioned, Dan. iii. 15. In the Saviour's time, the day divided into twelve hours counted from sunrise to sunset, of different lengths according to the season of the year and length of the day, as still in Egypt and the East. Among the Egyptians and Greeks, the hours were named from the planets; among the Jews, only numbered, the principal being those fixed for prayer,—the third, sixth, and ninth (Acts ii. 15; iii. 1; x. 9). In Persia and many other countries the day still divided into four such parts of three hours each. In the longest day in Palestine the sun rises a little before five, and sets a little after seven o'clock. In the shortest, it rises about seven, and sets about five. The Jews in early times had probably not only sun, but water-clocks, made as they are still found in the East,—a round dish of thin copper with a small hole in the bottom, placed on the surface of the water kept in a vessel for that purpose, the water passing through the hole into the dish and so filling it in the space of three hours, when it sinks. The night was anciently divided, among the Hebrews, into three parts or watches, probably according to the watches of the Levites in the temple. The first from the beginning of night to midnight (רֹאשׁ אַשְׁמֹרָה, Lam. ii. 19), fixed according to the course of the stars. The second, till cock-crowing,—the middle watch (אַשְׁמֹרֶת הַתִּיכוֹנָה, Judges vii. 19). The third, till sunrise, the morning watch (אַשְׁמֹרֶת הַבֹּקֶר, Exod. xiv. 24). At the time of Christ the Jews divided the night into four parts, received from the Romans after becoming subject to that power; the first, evening (ὀψέ), from the beginning of the night till nine o'clock; the second, from nine till midnight (μεσονύκτιον); the third, from midnight till three o'clock (ἀλεκτροφωνία, cock-crowing); the fourth and last, from three till dawn (πρωΐ), Mark xiii. 35. With the Jews the days had no name. Named by the Egyptians after the sun, moon, and five planets. The Egyptians followed by the Romans, and the Romans by ourselves. —'Ἤγγικεν, is near; they had come to the confines of eternal day. *Stuart.* Ere long it would be meridian day over the Roman world. *Brown.* Daylight is every moment growing, and the perfect morning light is near. *Leighton.* 'Though I have not skill enough to the exposition of hard prophecies to make a particular determination about the thousand years' reign of Christ on the earth before the final judgment, yet I may say that I cannot confute what such learned men as Mr Mede and Dr Twiss and others (after the old fathers) have hereof asserted.' *Richard Baxter.* 'The world therefore beginning thus, doth show how it will end, viz., by the reign of the second Adam, as it began with the reign of the first. These long-lived men therefore show us the glory that the Church shall have in the latter day, even in the seventh thousand years of the world, the Sabbath when Christ shall set up His kingdom upon earth, according to that which is written, They lived and reigned with Christ a thousand years.' *J. Bunyan* on the first chapters of Genesis. 'Christ will bring His kingdom not only by His Spirit and the effusions of His grace, but He will personally appear in His glory; hence His appearing and kingdom put together as contemporary, 2 Tim. iv. 1. This glorious and visible kingdom of Christ will not take place till after the resurrection of the just and the renovation of the world. This kingdom will be bounded by two resurrections; by the first resurrection, a resurrection of the just, at which it will begin, and by the second resurrection or the resurrection of the wicked, at which it will end. In the interval between these two resurrections will be the millennium, or the thousand years' reign of Christ and His people together.' *Gill.* 'I am more inclined to the literal interpretation of this psalm (the 50th) than that which would restrict it to the mere preaching of the Gospel in the days of the apostles. It looks far more like the descent of the Son of man on the Mount of Olives with all the accompaniments of a Jewish conversion, and a first resurrection, and a destruction of the assembled hosts of Antichrist.' *Dr Chalmers.* The belief of a world destroyed, renewed, and replaced by a better order of things, is reproduced under various forms among various religions. The basis of the Fourth Eclogue of Virgil and of the fictions of the Hindoos as to the return of the Golden Age. Found in the Third Book of the Natural Questions of Seneca. The Persians used the period of a thousand years for a day in the creation, saying that twelve thousand years are fixed for the duration of the world, the half of this period having passed before the introduction of evil by Ahriman under the form of a serpent. The millesimal period preserved by the ancient Tuscans, who say the Creator consecrated twelve thousand years to the works He produced, creating in the first the heaven and the earth; in the second, making the firmament or heaven; in the third, the sea and the waters which flow on the earth; in the fourth, the great lights of nature; in the fifth, the lower animals inhabiting air, earth, and waters; and in the sixth, man, who was thus to subsist six thousand years.—'Ἀποθώμεθα (ἀπο, off or away, τίθημι, to put), let us cast away; as night-clothes. *Par.*—'Ὅπλα τ. φωτος. Cod. Alex. reads ἔργα τ. φ. Garments suited to the light. *Pag., Pisc., Beza, Schött.* Graces of the Spirit produced by the light of faith. *For.* 'Ὅπλα = Heb. לְּבֻ, applied to dress as well as armour. *Drus.* Arms belonging to one who is of the light. *Alford.* Armour consisting in the power and disposition of light, truth and righteousness. *De Wette.* Roman armour kept bright. 'Curate ut splendor meo sit clypeo clarior quam solis radii.' *Plautus.* 'Ὅπλα, more especially denoted the defensive armour of the Greek soldier,—the shield and the breastplate. By wearing these the heavy-armed soldiers, hence called ὁπλίται, were distinguished from the light-armed (ψιλοί, ἄνοπλοι, γυμνοί, γυμνήται), who instead of being defended by the shield and breastplate, had a much slighter covering of skins, leather, or cloth; and instead of the sword or spear, commonly fought with darts, stones, bows and arrows, or slings. The Roman legions consisted, as the Greek infantry for the most part did, of heavy and light armed troops. All the essential parts of the Roman heavy armour, except the spear, mentioned together in Eph. vi. 17. *Smith's Dict. of the Bible.*

---

13. *Let us walk honestly as in the day; not in rioting and drunkenness, not in chambering and wantonness; not in strife and envying.*

Walk. Comes to duties in relation to ourselves.

We rise and dress to go abroad or work.

" Walk," the believer's daily life and conduct.

This verse and the following the means of Augustine's conversion.

Honestly. Decently, becoming, gracefully, 1 Pet. ii. 12; 2 Pet. iii. 11, 14.

Like persons who go abroad in decent apparel.

Believers not only to *be* good but to *appear* good.

Hypocrites care for appearance more than reality;

The followers of Christ to be careful of both.

Good works commend and adorn the doctrine of Christ.

Great stress laid by Paul on appearance as means to an end.

In the day. As becomes the children of the light.

Our whole conduct to be such as to bear exposure.

Christians to walk as before the eyes of God and men.

What we are inwardly we must appear outwardly.
Internal good to have also a good external form and colour.
Apples of gold to be presented in baskets of silver, Prov. xxv. 11.
Rioting. All meetings for intemperance and debauchery.
Amusements that minister to men's impure passions.
Revelling, more especially connected with feasting.
Rioting and drunkenness sins usually of the night.
The exception, to riot in the daytime, 2 Pet. ii. 13.
Drunkenness. *Gr.*, Drinking bouts; excess in wine and strong drink.
Noah the first recorded example of it, Gen. ix. 21.
Lot twice made drunk by his daughters, Gen. xix. 33, 35.
The case of a drunkard supposed in the law, Deut. xxi. 20.
Drunkenness not uncommon among the Jews.
Denounced by the prophets, Isa. v. 22; xix. 14; xxviii. 1; Jer. xxiii. 9; Hosea vii. 5.
Its effects described by Solomon, Prov. xxiii. 29–35; xx. 1.
One of the greatest destroyers of mankind.
Poverty, disgrace, crime, disease and death in its train.
Murders, drunkenness, and revellings named together, Gal. v. 21.
More than anything else the ruin of families and individuals.
The rock on which thousands make shipwreck of faith.
The plague-spot of Britain, and waster of the Church of Christ.
To be shunned as worse than the pestilence.
Every approach to it to be vigilantly guarded.
Formation of intemperate habits to be most carefully avoided.
Mistaken hospitality often the occasion of intemperance.
Christians to eat and drink only to the glory of God, 1 Cor. x. 31.
Chambering. Unholy intercourse between the sexes.
Frequent accompaniment of rioting and drunkenness.
Wantonness. *Gr.*, Wantonnesses. Various forms of the sin.
Lasciviousness; includes all that leads to uncleanness.
Lascivious thoughts, looks, words, books, songs, dances, &c.
Chambering and wantonness all kinds of licentiousness.
Strife and envying. Works of the flesh like the former, Gal. v. 20.
Usually their accompaniments and effects, Prov. xxiii. 29–35.
The opposite of the love enjoined in preceding verses.
The venom of the serpent infused into mankind.
Love makes earth a heaven, strife and envying a hell.
Strife and envying also named together, but in inverse order, Jas. iii. 14, 16.

"Envying" the inward feeling, "strife" its outward fruit. Wars and fightings the offspring of fleshly lusts, Jas. iv. 1.

Εὐσχημόνως (εὖ, well, and σχῆμα, fashion, form; εὐσχήμων, beautiful and symmetrical. *Phrynicus*). Honestly. *Cas.*, *Pisc.* Decently or becomingly. *Mor.*, *Beza*. Modestly. *Eras.*, *Vat.* As with garments well arranged (composite). *Eras.*, *Pag.* In decent apparel. *Beng.* Decently, honourably, and gracefully. *Doddr.*, *Whitby.* Becomingly. *Haldane*, *Stuart*. In seeming guise. *Con. & Hows.* Respectably. *Brown.* Seemly; appears to be parallel with 'orderly,' Acts xxi. 24. *Ellicot.* Seemingly. *D. Brown.*—Ὡς ἐν τ. ἡμέρᾳ, as in the day; as in full day. *Mart.* In the public and open view of others. *Bp. Hall.* As Christians. *Whitby.* As by day; as those who enjoy the light. *Stuart.* As children of the light and of the day, only doing what is fit to be exposed to the light of such a day. *D. Brown.*—Κώμοις (κῶμα, sleep; κῶμος, banqueting till overpowered by sleep. *Eustathius:* hence Comus, the god of revelry ; also, a company of immodest musicians at a banquet. *Suidas.* = Ἀσελγῆ ᾄσματα, πορνικὰ συμπόσια, ᾠδαί, lascivious songs, impure banquets. *Hes.*), revellings (comessationibus). *Pag.*, *Pisc.*, *Beza*. Banquets, drinking feasts. *Est.* Nocturnal amours. *Grot.*, *Ham.* Noisy crowds of drunken men often ran dancing and singing through the streets. *Flatt.* Lascivious banquets (Gal. v. 21; 1 Pet. iv. 3) often seen at Corinth where Paul now was; nocturnal processions of pleasure parties, usually leading to misconduct and revelling. *Rückert.*—Μέθαις (μέθυ, wine; μετὰ τὸ θύειν, after sacrificing. *Suidas*), drunken festivals such as were celebrated by the heathen in honour of their gods, when after they had sacrificed they drank to excess. *A. Clarke.* Heb. ןוֹרָכִּשׁ, drunkenness, Ezek. xxiii. 33 ; xxxix. 19; רָכֵשׁ, strong drink, Prov. xx. 1; xxxi. 6; סִיסָע, new wine, Joel i. 5. Three kinds of drinks besides water used by the ancient Jews and others—1. Simple wine; 2. Medicated wine; 3. Strong drink. The vine a principal branch of agriculture in Palestine and the adjacent countries. Mentioned in almost every prophetical promise and threatening as a figure of peace and prosperity, Amos ix. 14; Zech. ix. 17; Micah vi. 15. After being pressed from the grape, the juice was partly put in skins (Job xxxii. 19; Matt. ix. 17), and in large earthen pitchers to be left to ferment, and partly boiled to a syrup called שַׁבְדּ (debash), or honey, in modern Arabic *debs*. The latter, thinned with a little water, still used instead of sugar and butter, and given to patients instead of wine. Was also used by the Greeks and Romans mixed with milk or wine (*Virg. Georg.* i. 296 ; *Ovid. Fast.* iv. 780). Applied externally to wounds (Luke x. 34; *Mishnah*, *Shabb.* viii. 1). The vine-juice used also before fermentation as a refreshing drink (Judges ix. 13 ; Hosea iv. 11 ; Joel i. 5). In Egypt before the time of Psammiticus, the juice of the vine was drunk only in an unfermented state as pressed out of the grape (Gen. xl. 11). The fermented wine was allowed to remain for some time on the lees, and thus undergo a second fermentation by which it obtained a stronger taste (Isa. xxv. 6 ; Jer. xlviii. 11). Often used with bread (1 Sam. xvi. 20; xxv. 18; Neh. v. 15; Lam. ii. 12). Usually strained in a cloth before use (Isa. xxv. 6; Matt. xxiii. 24). Talmud speaks of mixing water with the wine. Wine often medicated with spices and aromatic herbs to make it stronger (Isa. v. 22; Ps. lxxv. 9; Prov. ix. 2, 5). Then called 'spiced wine' (חַקְרֶ ןִיֵי, Cant. viii. 2), the '*vinum aromatites*' of the Greeks and Romans. Strong drink coupled with wine in Lev. x. 9; Num. vi. 3; Deut. xxix. 6; Judges xiii. 4, 7, 14; Prov. xx. 1; xxxi. 4. According to Jerome, any intoxicating drink, whether made from grain, apples, dates, &c. These drinks called by the Romans 'vina factitia.' Among the Egyptians a drink called *zythos* made from barley. Date-wine at present a common drink in the East. The drunkards in Israel preferred the medicated wines to all others

(Prov. xxiii. 29, 30). Strong drink also their favourite indulgence (Isa. lvi. 12). Like Oriental debauchees still, they rose early in the morning to their revel (Isa. v. 11). Jews as a rule accustomed to drink to intoxication at the Feast of Purim (*Mishna*). Wine drunk during their meals as among the Romans, but especially after them, and often then only, as among the ancient Egyptians and Persians, and as among the Arabians and Persians at present. *Winer.* In the earliest period of their history the Romans had but one meal in the day, viz., at 3 P.M, called the supper (cœna), usually consisting of a very simple dish prepared from meal, water, and honey, or from beans, barley, and water. In later times, as wealth and luxury increased, breakfast (jentaculum, prandium) was added, as also an evening meal (comessatio). At the principal meal or cœna the most costly dishes were served in three courses,—the first consisting of honied wine (mulsum), salad, sausages, and eggs, to whet the appetite; the second, forming the substance of the meal and consisting of many various dishes; and the last, consisting of pastry, nuts, and fruit. After the meal wine was again brought on the table and freely drunk. Male and female singors and dancers as well as buffoons were often introduced to enliven the company during the meal, and dice formed the common employment after it. *Keil.* The abominable practices that followed in Paul's time and named by him above are indicated by Seneca: 'Alius [servus] vini minister in muliebrem modum ornatus, cum ætate luctatur: in tota nocte pervigilat, quam inter ebrietatem domini ac libidinem dividit, et in cubiculo vir et in convivio puer est.' 'Transeo puerorum infelicium greges quos post transacta convivia aliæ cubiculi contumeliæ expectant.' *Epist.* xlvii. and xcv.—Κοίταις (κεῖμαι, to lie), beds (cubilibus). *Pag., Eras., Mor., Pisc., Beza.* (Concubilibus). *Cast.* Indulgence in sleep. *Leighton.* Beds,—a euphemism for unchastity. *Rückert.* Debauchery. *Boothroyd.* Dalliance. *Con. & Hows.* Unholy intercourse of the sexes. *Alford.* Heb. מִשְׁכָּב, שָׁכַב.— Ἀσελγείαις (according to some, from Σελγη, a city in Pisidia, remarkable for the vice in question, or according to Suidas, for the absence of it), wantonnesses (proterviis). *Eras., Pag., Pisc.* Lasciviousnesses. *Mor., Beza, Men.* Lusts. *Par.* Unchastity; all offences in relation to the sexes. *Grot.* Effeminacy and lasciviousness. *Doddr.* Plural, —various kinds of wantonness. *Alford.* Κοιτ. and ἀσελγ. varied forms of impurity; the one pointing to definite acts, the other more general. *D. Brown.*—Ἔριδι κ. ζήλῳ. Cod. Vat. has ἔριδι κ. ζήλοις. Contention and emulation, the latter the source of the former, and ambition the cause of both. *Calvin.* Probably viewed by Paul as consequences of the preceding sins. *Nielson.* Here he begins to give up the allegory, in order to drop it entirely in the affirmative part of the exhortation. *Rückert.*

---

14. *But put ye on the Lord Jesus Christ; and make not provision for the flesh to fulfil the lusts thereof.*

But. Indicates—1. The contrast of the sins mentioned; 2. The means by which they are to be avoided. The change effected, not by excision, but by substitution. The heart not simply to be dispossessed and left empty. The expulsive power of a new affection. *Chalmers.* The Spirit's joy substituted for that of wine, Eph. v. 18, The love of the Father for the lusts of the flesh, 1 John ii. 15, 16; Psalms in the place of carnal songs, Jas. v. 13.

Put on. As your dress. Implies—1. Intimate union, Gal. iii. 27. 2. Personal appropriation of Christ;

3. Thoroughness of application and imitation of Him.
Christ to appear in us as our dress in the eyes of men.
To pervade our whole life and daily conduct.
As dress and armour, to surround and protect us on all sides.
To be put on—1. For justification ; 2. For sanctification.
To be not merely read in the Bible, but put on in our life.
The only dress that can make us comely before God and men.
Christ put on our humanity that we might put on His divinity.
Was made naked on the cross to clothe us before the throne.
Lord Jesus Christ. Christ not only our food but our dress.
Is given both for comfort, ornament, and defence.
Made to us in Him both righteousness and holiness, 1 Cor. i. 30.
Reference here especially to His Spirit and example.
Conformity *to* Christ the fruit of acceptance *in* Christ.
Receiving the Lord Jesus, we are so to walk in Him, Col. ii. 16.
Christ's image in us the true adornment of the soul.
Christ *in* us is our beauty, Christ *around* us our defence.
He who has Christ has all virtue. *Chrys.*
Believers by His Spirit to imitate His example, John xiii. 15.
To clothe themselves with all the graces of His character.
As mirrors to reflect His moral glory to the world, 2 Cor. iii. 18.
To walk in His steps of humble love and patient suffering, 1 Pet. ii. 21.
His image to be seen in our spirit and life, 1 John iv. 17.
Christ is put on—1. By faith ; 2. By imitation.
Christ put on man that man might in Him put on God.
Sinners accepted only in Christ the Elder Brother's garments.
Jacob obtained his father's blessing in His brother's clothes.
What he did by deceit we do by divine appointment, Isa. xlv. 24, 25.
Christ put on gives all we need for time and for eternity.
The wedding garment, Matt. xxii. 11, 12 ; robe of righteousness, Isa. lxi. 10.
Typified in the skins which He put on Adam and Eve, Gen. iii. 21.
The believer's dress casts every other into the shade. It is—
1. Costly,—cost the King of glory His life and death, Phil. ii. 6–8 ;
2. Comfortable,—fills the soul with peace and joy, Rom. xv. 13 ;
3. Complete,—leaves no part of body or soul exposed, Col. ii. 10 ;
4. Comely,—in the eyes of God, angels, and men, Ezek. xvi. 14 ;
5. Glorious,—the image of Christ, the Lord of glory, 2 Cor. iii. 18 ;
6. Durable,—never wears away or waxes old, Heb. xiii. 8 ;
7. Divine,—Jehovah our righteousness, Jer. xxiii. 6.

Clothes the believing beggar in more than royal splendour.
Make no provision. Take no forethought or care.
By a common figure of speech, more meant than expressed.
Fleshly lusts not only not to be cared for, but to be mortified.
The body to be provided for, but not the flesh.
Man's forethought to be exercised on higher and holier things.
Flesh. The sinful principle of our depraved nature.
The desires, appetites, and passions of fallen humanity.
Whatever tends to excite its lusts to be avoided.
Without Christ men only aim at serving the flesh.
To fulfil the lust thereof. To gratify its sinful desires.
Bodily wants to be attended to, but not fleshly lusts.
Bestow care on the body for health, not for lasciviousness. *Chrys.*
To feel lust implies the presence of sin *in* us;
To fulfil it, implies the power of sin *over* us.
To provide food for our body a duty;
To provide food for our lusts a sin, Ps. lxxviii. 18.
To fulfil lust worse than to feel it;
To provide for its fulfilment worse than both.
Fleshly lusts may be fed, but never filled.
To feed the lusts of the flesh is to fit it for hell fire.
To put on Christ the best way of putting off the flesh.
He who has Christ feels no need to beg elsewhere.
Christ's sweetness puts the sweetness of sin out of credit.
Clothed with Christ, and trampling on the flesh, the true picture of the spouse of Christ.

'Ενδύσασθε (ἐν, in, and δύω, to enter), be clothed (induimini). *Vulg., Pisc., Beza.* Put on (induite). *Vat.* Imbibe His Spirit. *Grot.* Imitate His charity. *Tol., Vat.* Exhibit Him both before men and God, both outwardly and inwardly. *Tol.* Appropriate Him ; be united to Him. *Est.* Put Him on—1. In His obedience and merit ; 2. In His divine presence. *Strig.* Put Him on—1. For justification by imputation ; 2. For sanctification by impartation : or—1. By profession ; 2. By participation : or—1. In conversion ; 2. In conversation. *Gataker.* Be fortified on all sides by the Spirit of Christ and so be made fit for all the parts of holiness. *Calv.* Christ all our salvation, light, holiness, and strength. *Beng.* Conform to his doctrine and life ; Greek phrase for imitating another. *Whitby.* Imitate him, according to the use of the Greek term ; or like the Heb. לָבַשׁ, 'be filled' with Him, *i.e.*, with a Christian spirit. *Stuart.* Imitate Him, His principles, example, spirit. *Cobbin.* Put Him on so that He only may be seen in you. *D. Brown.* Intimate union with Christ indicated, *Nielson.* The expression 'to put on a person' for becoming his follower and imitator, still common in Chrysostom's time. *Boothr.* So 'induere' used by Tacitus.—Τῆς σαρκός, the flesh ; our body. *Luth., Doddr., Calv.* Sinful principles of our nature. *Haldane.* Corrupt nature. *Hodge, D. Brown.* For the sake of the flesh ; a latitude in the use of the genitive in the New Testament. *Stuart.*—Προνοιαν (προ, forward, and νοεω, to think), provision. *Vat.* Providence. *Aug., Eras.* Care. *Calv., Mart., Diod.* Solicitous provision. *Doddr.* Thought. *Con. & Hows.* Forethought. *Ellicot, D. Brown.*—Ποιεισθε (ποιεω, to make; middle voice, make or exercise); προν. μη ποιεισθε, have no care. *Mart., Diod.* Do not attend to, &c. *Dutch Bible, Knapp.* Take no thought. *Con. & Hows.*—Εις επιθυμιας, to [fulfil] its desires or lusts. *Pag., Pisc., Beza.* So as to make it wanton. *Luth.* With respect to its lusts. *Dutch Bible.* So as to attend to the necessity of the flesh, but not indulge its lusts. *Calv.* Care of the flesh permitted, but not its lusts. *Chrys.* That not a true care of the body which inflames its lusts. *Theoph.* To fulfil its irregular desires or gratify the senses. *Doddr.* To the kindling of its lusts. *Thol., De Wette.* In order to gratify its lusts. *Stuart.* To fulfil its evil desires. *Boothr.* For the sake of its lusts. *Knapp.* To supply its lusts. *Stolz.* To please your fleshly lusts. *Con. & Hows.* In order to excite or gratify its desire. *Brown.* How you may provide for the gratification of the cravings of your corrupt nature. *D. Brown.*

CHAPTER XIV.

1. *Him that is weak in the faith receive ye, but not to doubtful disputations.*

Him. The believer. Mutual duties of the strong and the weak.
Weak. 1. Not firmly settled; 2. Not fully enlightened; 3. Not far advanced.
Refers both to doctrine and duty, to conviction and conscience.
Various stages of growth in the Christian life.
Various degrees of faith and knowledge in believers.
Great variety in the spiritual condition of God's family.
Some are babes and little children, some young men, some fathers.
Probably Jewish Christians here more especially in view.
Most of believing Jews still held to the ceremonial law, Acts xxi. 20.
Almost all Gentile Christians believed it to be abolished.
Difficulty with some early Christians as to meats, 1 Cor. viii. 1, &c.; x. 19, &c.
Faith. 1. The Christian religion; 2. Conviction as to doctrine and duty.
Faith is either subjective or objective. As subjective it is—
1. Belief, trust; 2. Conviction. As objective it is—
That in or upon which the trust or conviction is exercised.
Weak in *the faith* and weak in *faith* two different things.
Weak in the faith identical with a weak conscience, 1 Cor. viii. 7, 10.
Weakness in the faith leads to doubts and scruples in the life.
Defective knowledge in doctrine brings uncertainty in duty.

Faith not only saves the soul but directs the life.
To be weak in the faith no absolute blame;
To be strong in the faith no absolute praise.
Weakness in *faith* more blameable than weakness in *the faith*.
The latter may arise—1. From imperfect information;
2. From the prejudices of early education;
3. From peculiar natural temperament;
4. From a less abundant measure of the Holy Spirit.
Paul throws the shield of his protection over the weak.
Receive. 1. Admit to your fellowship; 2. Treat with kindness.
Probably more than church membership intended, Acts xviii. 27; xxviii. 2.
The weak require the more tender care and treatment.
The Church to receive the weak as well as the strong.
Want of faith, not weakness in the faith, a ground of exclusion.
Church members to be mutually kind, forbearing, and helpful.
Stones in an arch, differing in size, support each other.
Pharisaic consciousness and Sadducean laxity both evils.
To unite church parties in love one object of this epistle.
To **doubtful disputations.** 1. So as to dispute on doubtful matters;
2. So as first to settle the points on which he has doubts.
The question here not so much of doctrine as of duty.
Duties as to external matters and legal observances.
The directions relate to the class of things indifferent.
Strivings about the law unprofitable and vain, Tit. iii. 9.
Discussion to be—1. On proper subjects; 2. In a proper spirit.
Sincere though weak believers to be received, not disputed with.
Unanimity seldom the result of disputation.
Discussion may either resolve doubts or increase prejudice.
The Spirit's teaching more to be trusted than man's disputing.
Paul urges a discreet silence and respectful toleration.
A sound liberalism as well as a spurious one.
The former from the Spirit, the latter from the god of this world.
Room for abridgment of the church's controversies. *Chalmers.*
Inflexible *up to* what is written, be flexible *beyond* it.
A cedar in essentials, a willow in circumstantials.
Christians to look more to points of agreement than of difference.
Zeal best expended on matters in which the Church is agreed.
Truth to be contended for, not victory over brethren's scruples.

CHAP. XIV.]   ST. PAUL'S EPISTLE TO THE ROMANS.   289

'Ασθενοῦντα (ἀ, not, and σθένος, strength), weak (infirmus). *Pisc., Beza.*
'Ασθενής = לְשׁוּט, one ready to stumble or easily made to fall. Not fully instructed.
Grot., Tol. Milder term than the adjective ἀσθενῆ: Paul does not apply the epithet
to a brother, but describes the case. *Beng.* Not yet fully convinced or enlightened.
Stuart. 'Sum paullo infirmior,' a little too weak, *i.e.*, scrupulous. *Hor.*—Τῇ πίστει,
Christian doctrine, the truth believed. *Beza.* Persuasion as to things indifferent. *Est.*,
Pisc., Beza. Knowledge of Christian doctrine. *Calv., Grot., Semler.* Persuasion as to
his Christian liberty. *Wells.* The Christian faith. *Doddr.* His belief; τῇ, either equivalent to the pronoun *his*, or referring to the Christian belief or persuasion; πίστις,
here not *saving* faith, but *belief* or *persuasion* in a more general sense. *Stuart.* The
doctrine of the Gospel as a whole. *Haldane.* Persuasion as to duty and certain truths.
Hodge. As to faith. *Chal.* In *the* faith, not *his* faith; moral soundness conferred by
faith. *Alford.* In the standing of faith and its consequences. *Lange.* Moral conviction
and sentiment; conscience; faith in a practical view. *De Wette.* Christian disposition
of the entire spirit, resting on faith in Christ. *Rückert.* On the subject of Christian
liberty. *Cobbin.* In faith. *Boothr., D. Brown.* 'Ασθεν. τ. πίστ., defective in faith,
and so an anxious observer of external things. *Rück.* In bondage to things indifferent.
Theod. Applied to converted Jews. *Grot.* Who still wished to observe the law of
Moses. *Calv.* Who still retained the prejudices of a Jewish education. *Doddr.* Who
were doubtful about the lawfulness of certain things. *Boothr.* Not fully persuaded of
their Christian liberty. *Wells.* Not fully enlightened as to its extent. *Stuart.* One
who doubts and hesitates. *Brown.* Who wants broad and independent principles and
is in consequent bondage to prejudices. *Alford, De Wette.* Whose faith wants that
firmness and breadth which would raise him above small scruples. *D. Brown.*—
Προσλαμβάνεσθε, take to you (assumite). *Eras., Pag., Pisc., Mor., Beza.* Take under
your care, relieve (suscipite, sublevate). *Calv., Cam.* Assist. *Vat., Zeg.* (Opitulemini).
Cas. Tolerate. *Vat.* Cherish. *Men.* Associate to the church. *Grot.* Kindly correct,
teach him better. *Schött.* Support, assist, admit to intimate intercourse. *Beng.* Receive
and treat him kindly. *Flatt.* Receive with kindness, admit to your society and friendship. *Stuart.* Receive to yourselves as a Christian brother and treat him kindly.
Hodge. Receive kindly. *Boothr.* Receive into your fellowship. *Con. & Hows., Brown.*
Treat as a brother, tenderly and lovingly. *Barth.* Give him your hand, count him one
of you. *Alford.* Receive to cordial Christian friendship. *D. Brown.* Not proper
church communion intended. *Lange.* Heb. לָקַח. For 'The Lord was pleased to make
you His people' (אֶתְכֶם לוֹ לְעָם נַחֲלָה), 1 Sam. xii. 22, the LXX. have ' προσελάβετο
ὑμᾶς ἑαυτῷ εἰς λαόν.'—Μὴ εἰς διακρίσεις διαλογισμῶν, supply 'however.' *Pag.*,
Pisc., Beza. Do not challenge him. *Est.* Do not precipitate him. *Par., Cam.* To
discussions of thoughts. *Vulg.* To the discussions of questions; the language elliptical.
Calv. To altercations or contentions of disputes. *Pag., Eras., Beza.* Into discussions
of disputes. *Mor., Cam.* To questions of disputes. *Diod.* To the settlement of disputes.
Eras. To the judging of his thoughts. *Dickson.* Do not disturb them and yourselves
with various disputations, but attend to them as sick persons. *Theoph.* And do not be
divided in your opinions. *Syr.* Do not perplex their consciences. *Luth.* Have no
contests or disputes with him. *Mart.* Not so as to throw him into more difficult
thoughts. *Schött.* Not to run into debate and distinctions about matters in doubt.
Doddr. Not to reasonings about lawful or unlawful things. *Ham.* So as not to lead to
doubtful thoughts by seeking to make him do as you do. *Beng.* Not to discrimination
of persons according to their inward thoughts or reasonings. *Whitby.* Not so as to
make decisions in respect to his opinions. *Stuart.* Do not irritate him by perverse
disputes. *Boothroyd, Cobbin.* Do not contend with him about his opinions. *Burk.*
Not for the purpose of examining with him doubtful or disputed points. *Bluomfield.*

Not to sit in judgment on a brother in such matters as disputations or opinions. *Hodge.* Imposing no determinations of doubtful questions. *Con. & Hows.* Not to the discussion and determination of his peculiar opinions. *Brown.* Not to have disputes to settle the points on which he has scruples. *Alford.* Yet so that you do not sit in judgment on his thoughts (views, principles), 1 Cor. xii. 10; Heb. v. 14. *Meyer.* Not so as to decide upon his motives. *Lange.* Not to raise doubts and uncertainties of thoughts. *Ols.* Not so as to awaken doubt in his mind. *Phil.* Not to the stirring up of doubting thoughts ; εἰς indicates the possible consequence of admission into fellowship. *De Wette.* Not so that thoughts and feelings be divided. *Rück.* Without strife about opinions. *Van Ess.* Without being contentious. *Knapp.* Do not decide about his opinions. *Stolz.* Without embarrassing the conscience. *Stier.* Without regarding their opinions or severely judging their thoughts. *Flatt.* Not to altercation about disputed points. *Thol.* Not to the deciding of doubts. *Ellicot.* Not to the deciding of doubts or scruples, *i.e.*, not for the purpose of arguing him out of them. *D. Brown.* Διακρίνω = to distinguish; to examine ; to settle a controversy ; to separate clearly. Διακρίνομαι (middle) = 1. To contend with another ; 2. To contend with one's self, *i.e.*, to doubt. Hence διάκρισις, controversy, disputation. *Calv., Par., Beza, Glöck.* Doubt. *Cram., Beng.* Judgment. *Scholz.* Distinguishing, dividing, splitting. *Rückert.* Distinction, decision, discrimination. *Stuart.* — Heb. הִכְרִיעַ, a balancing, Job xxxvii. 16. Διαλογίζομαι = to reason, think. Hence διαλογισμοί, opinions, views, thoughts. *Scholz, Reiche, Ols., De Wette.* Rendered 'thoughts,' Matt. xv. 19 ; 'disputing,' Phil. ii. 14 ; 'doubting,' 1 Tim. ii. 8. — Heb. מַחֲשָׁבוֹת. Often much disputing among the Rabbies on receiving proselytes on account of some supposed disqualification. *Mishna.*

---

2. *For one believeth that he may eat all things ; another who is weak eateth herbs.*

Believeth. Is persuaded as the effect of his faith.
Reference to the faith or persuasion in preceding verse.
"Has confidence ; " this not mentioned of the weak brother.
That only to be done which we "believe" to be God's will.
Eat all things. All kinds of meat suitable for food, 1 Tim. iv. 3, 4.
1. Without respect to the Mosaic distinction of meats, Lev. xi. 2, &c.
2. Without regard to their having been in an idol's temple, 1 Cor. x. 25, 28.
The ceremonial law now virtually abolished, Acts x. 11, &c. ; xv. 19-21.
Especially in regard to the Gentile converts, Acts xv. 19, 23.
Yet these to abstain from idol-meats for the sake of the Jews, Acts xv. 20, 21.
Weak. Not fully persuaded ; having needless scruples, ver. 1.
One with a less instructed and enlightened conscience, 1 Cor. viii. 10, 12.
Converted Jews brought their scruples with them into the church.
Eateth herbs, *i.e.*, only ; to avoid the chance of pollution.
Careful lest in eating he violate a divine command.

CHAP. XIV.]   ST. PAUL'S EPISTLE TO THE ROMANS.   231

Similar examples of abstinence, Dan. i. 8, 12, 16 ; Est. iv. 16.
A common faith consistent with minor differences.
Diversity in opinion and practice gives occasion for charity.
The spirit to be harmonized more than views and practices.

'Ος μεν, he who indeed; followed by ὁ δε ἀσθενῶν, an anacoluthon. *Stuart.*—
Πιστεύει, has confidence. *Beng.* Ventures, as Acts xv. 11. *Alford.* The believing
Gentile. *Theod.*—Φαγειν (2d aor. of obsolete φαγω, to eat'.—Παντα, with βρωματα,
'meats' understood; anything eatable. *Stuart.* Things unlawful by the law of Moses.
Men., Tir., Tol. Things offered to idols. *Tol.* The sacrificial character of the flesh and
wine not here spoken of, as in 1 Cor. viii. 10. *Lange.* Abstinence and scruples of a legal
not an ascetic kind, in ver. 14; but the meats mentioned in ver. 21, 22, those offered to
idols. *De Wette.*—Λαχανα ἐσθίει, eateth herbs ; supply μονον after ἐσθίει. *Stuart.*
Thinking that by eating meats they were defiled, and as practising greater temperance
and self-denial. *Theod.* Thinking to be more tolerated by abstaining not only from
swine's flesh but all flesh. *Theoph.* Not Jewish but moral social motives in operation
on the part of the Jews, who feared mingling with heathen sacrificial practices. *Aug.*
Both motives operated. *Eras.* Jewish Christians intended, who wished still to observe
the law of Moses. *Calv.* Who could not find in a Gentile country such animal food as
they considered clean. *Boothr.* Who feared lest by eating what was in the shambles
they might eat what had been offered to idols. *Stuart.* And so be made unclean. *D.
Brown.* Not ascetic motives ; in Rome as elsewhere were Jewish Christians who
avoided meats sacrificed to idols and wine used for libations, some, from fear of possible
defilement, abstaining from flesh and wine entirely. *Thol., De Wette.* Paul speaks not
to dogmatic Judaizers, to whom he uses a different tone ; but to tender Jewish Christians, less enlightened as to practice. *Alford.* Josephus speaks of some Jewish priests
at Rome who, to avoid uncleanness, abstained from all prepared food. *Hodge.* Among
the Jews, flesh from an idol's temple held to be unclean, and that only lawful to be used
which is prepared in a particular and prescribed manner. *Mishna.* Pythagoreans
among the Heathens, and Essenes among the Jews, believed it improper to eat animal
food. Egyptian priests, Persian magi, and many among the Indians, ate only herbs.
James, the Lord's brother, abstained from flesh and wine, and many Christians from
flesh.

---

3. *Let not him that eateth despise him that eateth not ; and let not him which eateth not
judge him that eateth : for God hath received him.*

Despise. As weak, narrow, scrupulous, and unenlightened.
The more enlightened apt to despise those who are less so.
The pride of knowledge holds the ignorant in contempt.
Knowledge puffeth up, but charity edifieth, 1 Cor. viii. 1.
Conscientious scruples, though mistaken, to be respected.
Weak but conscientious brethren to be tenderly treated.
Kindly help to be given rather than contempt entertained.
The evil on the part of the weak here treated tenderly, as—
1. It was confined to mere individual practice ;
2. It proceeded from a tender though less informed conscience.

Same thing treated differently in the Galatians, Gal. iv. 9, 10.
The Galatians Gentile Christians seduced by Judaizing teachers.
Desired to give up Christian liberty for bondage, Gal. v. 1.
Weakness in the Romans was wilfulness in the Galatians.
Roman Jewish Christians followed the law, weeping, to its grave.
Galatian Gentile Christians sought to restore it to life.
Paul pre-eminently and characteristically a peacemaker.
Mild persuasives of Gospel charity better than stern decrees of ecclesiastical uniformity.

Judge. Condemn, as not believing him to act uprightly.
The less enlightened apt to judge those who are more so.
The weak prone to condemn those who are more free from scruples.
Too ready to ascribe evil motives to stronger brethren.
The weak as liable to *condemn* as the strong to *contemn*.
Believers differing in judgment to respect each other's character.
Mismanaged differences of opinion mar the church's peace.
Faults usually on both sides, and both have still to learn.

Him that eateth. The *thing* may be condemned, not the *person*.
Men bound to condemn what they believe unlawful.
Persons are condemned when motives are imputed.
The abstainer condemned the eater of meats as—
1. Seeking only to gratify his fleshly appetite;
2. Unwilling to practice a godly self-denial;
3. Wishing to conform to the world and its practices;
4. Afraid to incur the reproach of unbelievers;
5. Despising divinely-appointed institutions.

Received. 1. Accepted him as righteous in Christ;
2. Adopted him into his family as his own child;
3. Approved of that for which the weak brother condemns him.
This acceptance indicated by the gift of the Spirit, Acts x. 44–48.
Both parties, perhaps, partakers of His extraordinary gifts.
The strong said to be received, not the weak who doubted it.
Their conduct pleasing to God, because according to Gospel truth.
Not from laxity or flesh-pleasing, but from religious principle.
Man often condemns where God receives, and *vice versa*.
Believers to be temperate in judging as well as in enjoying.
God's views and conduct to guide us—
1. In our judgment of things; 2. In our treatment of persons.
The question in regard to a brother is, Does *God* receive him?
The great question for ourselves is, Does God receive *me*?

Ἐξουθενειτω (ἐξ and οὐδέν, to count as nothing), hold in contempt. *Or*. Look down superciliously upon. *D. Brown*. Heb. אַף, בָּזָה.—Και ὁ μη ἐσθιων. *Codd*. *Sin*. and *Alex*. have ὁ δε μη ἐσθ.—Κρινετω, judge or condemn; exercise an uncharitable and condemning spirit. *Stuart*. Condemn, as a conscious violator of the divine law. *Brown*. Sit in judgment censoriously upon him. *D. Brown*.—Προσελαβετο has received into His fellowship as His child. *De Wette*. Among His people. *Con. & Howes*. Accepted in respect to this particular conduct. *Haldane*. Received him into His church and to His favour, evident from the spiritual gifts conferred upon him. *Boothr*. Received him into His redeemed family, and admitted him to its privileges. *Stuart*. Received him as one of His dear children, who in this matter acts not from laxity but religious principle. *D. Brown*. Applies to both parties; evident from their being enlightened with the knowledge of God. *Calvin, Stuart*.

---

4. *Who art thou that judgest another man's servant? To his own master he standeth or falleth. Yea, he shall be holden up: for God is able to make him stand.*

Who art thou. The language of rebuke. Addressed to the weak.
Judgest. It is Christ's prerogative to judge His servants.
A grave offence to usurp Christ's judgment-seat.
Impertinent to condemn another man's servant.
Christians responsible to Christ, not to one another.
Servant. Every believer belongs to Christ as his Master.
A creature's highest honour to be Christ's servant.
Master. *Gr.*, Lord. Christ so calls Himself, John xiii. 13, 14; xv. 20.
Christ's authority absolute in and over His church.
His peculiar reward and office to be its Lord, Acts ii. 36.
All to be made to confess that He is Lord, Phil. ii. 11.
Christians accountable only to Him in matters of conscience.
His honour and interest involved in His people's conduct.
Standeth. Continues in faith and holiness, and so approved, Ps. i. 5.
A strong and standing Christian Christ's honour, 2 Cor. viii. 23.
None so interested in believers standing as Christ Himself.
The believer to be a palm in beauty, and a cedar in strength, Ps. xcii. 12.
Weak brethren fear or forbode the strong one's fall.
Falleth. 1. From his steadfastness, 2 Pet. iii. 17; 2. Into sin, 1 Cor. x. 12.
A Christian's fall brings loss to his Master Christ.
" Falls " in his Master's judgment; is disapproved and condemned.
Holden up. Made to stand fast in His Christian liberty, Gal. v. 1.
His feet on the rock, and His goings established, Ps. xl. 2.
The believer's security insured in Christ, Phil. i. 6; 1 Pet. i. 5.

Path of the just as the shining and ever-increasing light, Prov. iv. 18.
Consistent with occasional falls, Ps. xxxvii. 24; Prov. xxiv. 16; Micah vii. 8.
For. The ground indicated on which his security rests.
God is able. God's power the believer's security, chap. xvi. 25; 1 Pet. i. 5; Jude 24.
Lawful in things of grace to reason from the *can* to the *will*.
What God *can* do for His people in Christ He *will* do.
Because he *can*, he *does* perform all things for them, Ps. lvii. 2.
Because he *can*, He will perfect that which concerns them, Ps. cxxxviii. 8.
"I am the Almighty God," the believer's charter, Gen. xvii. 1.
Make him stand, *i.e.,* steadfast in His faith and Christian life.
He who gives life at first is able to preserve it.
He who sets a sinner's feet on the rock can keep them there.
Standing in Christ's grace, we stand in the Church's fellowship.
God able to acquit the servant whom his brother condemns.
Concerning a brother believer, charity hopes all things good.

Συ, thou ; nominative absolute, addressed to both parties. *Stuart.*—Ὁ κρινων, who condemnest. *Beza, Pisc., Stuart, Booth.* Judgest. *D. Brown.*—Τῷ ἰδίῳ κυρίῳ, to his own master, *i.e.,* Christ. *Theod., De Wette.* By his own master. *Mackn., Stuart.* It is his master's matter and his alone. *Alford.*—Στηκει (from στηκω, a non-classical verb formed from ἕστηκα, perfect of ἵστημι, to stand), stands ; is absolved, *i.e.,* if he do well. *Vor., Est., Grot., Clarke, Wolf, Koppe, Storr., Thol., Wells.* Is accepted. *Calv.* Acquitted. *Stuart, Brown.* Does well, or is of advantage. *Anon.* Abides firmly in what is good. *Flatt, Semler, De Wette, Glöck., Rück.* Remains in the true Christian life. *Meyer, Chr. Schmidt.* In the possession of his faith. *Haldane.* In the place and estimation of a Christian. *Alford.* In true fellowship of the church. *D. Brown.*—Πιπτει, yields to temptation and sins. *De Wette.* Is condemned. *Stuart, Brown.* Στηκ. ἢ πιπτ., it is with the Lord either to disapprove or accept. *Calv.* To his master he is for profit or loss ; it is his matter alone ; or, according to his decision alone he is confirmed or rejected. *Nielson.*—Σταθησεται, shall be supported. *Eras.* Established. *Pag., Beza, Pisc., Tol., Boothr.* Shall continue to stand in firm knowledge. *Beng.* In his liberty of faith. *Lange.* Shall be acquitted. *Ham., Stuart, Cobbin.* Be approved. *Brown.* Even this weak Christian shall be made firm. *Mar.*—Δυνατος γαρ ἐστιν ὁ Θεος. Codd. Sin., Vat., and Alex. have δυνατει γαρ ὁ Κυριος. Indicates God's merciful inclination. *Calv.* Power with will. *Par.* The *esse* concluded from the *posse. Beng.*—Στησαι, to save him. *Grot.* Keep him steadfast. *Vat.* Cause him to be absolved. *Est.* Acquit though you condemn. *Stuart.* Reconcile his conduct with a due regard to divine authority. *Brown.* Preserve him upright, give him light and strength. *De Wette.* Preserve him upright in faith and practice. *Alford.* Make good his standing in the true fellowship of the church. *D. Brown.* Heb. יְקִימֶנּוּ, יָקוּם, יַצִּיב.

CHAP. XIV.]   ST. PAUL'S EPISTLE TO THE ROMANS.   235

5. *One man esteemeth one day above another: another esteemeth every day alike. Let every man be fully persuaded in his own mind.*

One man, *i.e.,* one believer. All believers not of one opinion.
In essentials unity, in circumstantials variety and charity.
Saving faith consistent with imperfect views of duty.
Esteemeth. Judges; distinguishes; makes a difference.
Another instance of difference in opinion and practice.
One day above another. As in itself more sacred and holy.
Reference to Jewish festival days, Col. ii. 16; Gal. iv. 10.
Such days called Sabbaths, or days of rest, Lev. xxiii. 32, 38, 39.
All manual labour suspended on such days, Lev. xxiii. 31.
Such Sabbaths and festivals simply Jewish and ceremonial.
Characterized by Paul as beggarly elements, Gal. iv. 9.
Intended only for temporary observance.
Freedom left in the New Testament to observe them or otherwise.
Their observance continued by many Jewish converts.
The weekly Sabbath probably not here in view.
The Decalogue, enjoining its observance, of perpetual obligation.
Part of the law which is spiritual, holy, just and good, chap. vii. 12.
Its commandments quoted by Paul as still in force, Eph. vi. 2.
The Sabbath command very prominent in the Decalogue.
The institution of the Sabbath not Jewish, but universal.
Coeval with man's creation and the institution of marriage.
Its object the glory of God and the benefit of mankind.
Its observance before Moses indicated, Exod. xvi. 22-30; Gen. ii. 3; viii. 8-12.
A type of the heavenly rest, therefore in force till the antitype comes, Heb. iv. 9.
Great antiquity of a weekly division of time, Gen. xxix. 27, 28.
Day changed by Christ Himself as Lord of the Sabbath, Mark ii. 8.
First day of the week early known as the Lord's day, Rev. i. 10.
The day of holy convocation in the early Church, Acts xx. 7; 1 Cor. xvi. 2.
Old Testament Sabbath commemorative of God's work of creation;
New Testament Sabbath commemorative of His work of redemption.
Christ's resurrection the completion of the latter.
Took place at the end of one week and beginning of another.
His resurrection day "the day which the Lord made," Ps. cxviii. 24.
The new creation to be remembered before the old, Isa. lxv. 17.
The Sabbath law unaffected by the change of the day.

The seventh day also kept at first by Christians as well as Jews.
Observed as a day for sacred services, but not cessation from work.
Same religious services on both days till the fifth century.
The first day of the week gradually took the place of the seventh.
Work first publicly forbidden on that day in the fourth century.
The day kept joyfully in memory of Christ's resurrection.
Regarded by early Christians as the "queen of days."
No fasting on that day, nor kneeling in public prayer.
Every day alike. *Gr.*, " Every day," *i.e.*, judges every day holy.
This more likely to be the case with Gentile converts.
" Alike," to be omitted, as not in the text, and injuring the sense.
Jewish converts abstained from work on the seventh day.
Gentile Christians did not yet abstain entirely on any day.
Yet both days distinguished by special religious services.
The seventh day of the week only gradually superseded as sacred.
Jewish converts observed other days appointed in the law.
Gentile converts in general disregarded such days.
What God has made holy man may not make profane.
Where God has not spoken the conscience is free.
Persuaded. Fully convinced as to what is God's will.
To act conscientiously is man's highest duty.
His next duty is to have his conscience duly enlightened.
Nothing should satisfy as to duty short of full assurance.
Such assurance to be grounded on the Word of God, Isa. viii. 20.
Paul decides nothing, but urges firmness of conviction.
Wrong persuasion only an obliquity of the intellect ;
Conduct not according to persuasion an obliquity of heart.
To think one way and act another is to sin against God.
Firm Christian conviction valuable as—
1. Enabling us to act according to definite principles ;
2. Preserving us from vacillation and change ;
3. Keeping ourselves in inward peace ;
4. Fitting us for counselling and directing others.

Ὃς μέν, one person, the Jewish convert ; ὃς δέ, another, educated among Gentiles. *Doddr.* Cod. Sin. adds γάρ after μέν.—Κρίνει, thinks or estimates (æstimat). *Pag.*, *Beza, Pisc., Drus., Grot., Vat., Pur.* Judges (judicat). *Vulg., Mor., Eras.* Distinguishes (discernit). *Cas.* Pleads, disputes, or contends for. *Dick.* Prefers. *Raph.* Values or judges. *Flatt.* Holds to. *Knapp.* Approves, selects. *Thol., Lange.* Attends to, makes the object of religious observance. *De Wette.* Esteems, deems, makes a distinction between days. *Stuart.*—Ἡμέραν παρ' ἡμέραν, one day before another. *Pag., Beza, Pisc.* Various days (diem diemque). *Cas.* Between days (diem inter diem). *Vulg., Mor.* Thinks their Sabbaths and new moons and early fasts or feasts have something inviolably sacred in them. *Doddr.* Ἡμέραν, a day chosen for a fast day. *Chrys., Theod.* For abstaining from swine's flesh. *Theoph.* Days appointed in the Mosaic law. *Flatt, Wells, Burk.* Perhaps here taken for *time, festival,* and such like; reference to Jewish institutions, especially festivals as the Passover, Pentecost, Feast of Tabernacles, New Moon, Jubilee, &c., the weekly Sabbath not included. *A. Clarke.* Jews esteemed many days as holy. *Boothroyd.* Jewish festivals, as Sabbaths, &c. *De Wette, Thol.* Jewish festivals or Christian memorial days. *Rück.* Day for a festival. *Lange.* The Lord's day (ἡμέρα Κυρίου) not likely included here, as observed by all ✓ Christians. *Henry, Stuart.* The seventh-day Sabbath included, but not the first day or Christian Sabbath, which was of apostolic authority. *Brown.* No one day acknowledged by the apostle as of divine authority, but all days to the Christian strong in faith alike. *Alford.* Days here spoken of peculiar to the Jewish dispensation, as meats. *Haldane.* Respects only the ritual and instituted part of the observance. *T. Edwards.* The weekly Sabbath not included, as more ancient than Judaism. *D. Brown.* The Jewish Sabbath continued to be observed in the church till the fifth century. *Thol.* Justin Martyr (A.D. 130, says of the first day of the week : 'On the day called Sunday, there is a meeting of all who live either in town or country, when, as time permits, the narratives (commentaries) of the apostles and the writings of the prophets are read, prayers offered, and bread, wine, and water distributed to all present.' Work first publicly ✓ forbidden on the Lord's day (first day of the week) by Constantine the Great in the fourth century. The people still left free to labour in the field on that day, till an edict of the Emperor Leo, in the fifth century, made this also unlawful. The seventh day of the week kept by the early church as a *festival*, except that before Easter, which was made a *fast*. In most of the Western churches, the custom of fasting on that day was introduced in the third century, but abolished in the following one. The Council of Laodicea, in the fifth century, ordained that the same services should be held on the Sabbath (seventh day of the week) as on the Lord's day ; but forbade manual labour to be entirely suspended on that day. The observance of the seventh day, Sabbath, not held as a necessity, entire rest being confined to the Lord's day. *Baumgarten.* Athanasius says, 'Christians met on the Sabbath (seventh day), not because they were infected with Judaism, but in order to worship the Lord of the Sabbath.' Cassian says that in the churches of Egypt, the service of both days was always the same. *Bingham.* Assyrians, Egyptians, Indians, Arabians, in short, all Oriental nations, have been accustomed to reckon seven days as a definite fixed period. Also among the Romans, ancient inhabitants of France, Britain, Germany, Northern regions, and even in America, the same practice has been found to exist. First trace of weeks found in Gen. vii. 4. Week expressly named in Gen. xxix. 27, 28, as a well-known thing. Week reckoned from Sabbath to Sabbath ; hence in later times itself called σαββατα, or the Sabbath, and the rest of the days of the week the first, second, &c., day of the Sabbath. —Κρίνει πασαν ἡμέραν, equally esteems every day. *Pisc., Beza, Pay.* Judges every day. *Mor.* Holds every day in the same place. *Cas.* Judges the same, thinks equally of every day. *Eras.* Judges every day equal. *Par.* Approves every day. *Ham.* As fit for God's worship. *Grot., Pisc.* As equally holy. *Vat.* Makes no distinction of days in regard to eating. *Est.* Holds or judges every day, *i.e.*, alike suitable for doing good, or simply as a day and nothing more. *Beng.* No controversy here either about the first day of the week or the weekly Sabbath. *Brown.* No Sabbath obligation recognised in apostolic times ; the Lord's day an institution of the Christian church, analogous to the ancient Sabbath, binding on us from considerations of humanity, religious expediency, and the rules of that branch of the church in which Providence has placed us. *Alford.* Same incorrect views prevalent on the Continent. The apostolic church had no divinely-appointed weekly or annual festivals : the church, in virtue of the living Spirit ruling in her, has introduced the Christian festivals and the Sunday, not as law, but as a necessity of Christian fellowship, and as an excellent external discipline. *Barth (Calv. Bible).* The following, from the 'Kirchenfreunde' *(Riggenbach, &c.)*, much better : 'From all it appears that the Sunday can perfectly claim the right of divine institution and ordinance, which the rest in Paradise, after the finishing of creation, the holy ordinance of the Sabbath-command of the Decalogue, and the Lord of the Sabbath, the Mediator of salvation, secure to it as the weekly festival of the New Testament Church, ordained by God himself, in which all the ideal and lasting rights of the Old Testament Sabbath are realised, and are, therefore, contained ; while the temporary sheath, which protected the flower of the full Gospel-contents, was burst by the risen Saviour.' 'That thus the day of festive service is no longer for the Christian the Sabbath [of the Old Testament or seventh day of the week], but the Sunday, has by no means been made accidentally or arbitrarily by man, and thus the divine Sabbath-command altered and transgressed ; but God himself has made this day, and indicated it to His church. It is the natural fruit of the Old Testament development. As the fruit is distinguished from the bud and blossom, and yet from the beginning was contained in it, so the Sabbath is distinguished from the Sunday, and yet again is one with it.' Christian church early began to observe other days as festivals. At first the same with those of the Jews ; observed especially by Jewish Christians. These afterwards celebrated with a Christian instead of a Jewish reference. The earliest of these, the Passover or Easter, kept in commemoration of Christ's death and resurrection. *Con. & Hows.* The name 'Passover' ($\pi\alpha\sigma\chi\alpha$, pascha) was retained, taken either in a wider sense as extending over fourteen days, divided into two parts, viz., the Passover of the Cross ($\pi. \sigma\tau\alpha\nu\rho\omega\sigma\iota\mu\o\nu$, pascha crucis), called also the Great Week, known now as Passion Week, and the Passover of the Resurrection ($\pi. \alpha\nu\alpha\sigma\tau\alpha\sigma\iota\mu\o\nu$, pascha resurrectionis) ; or taken in a narrower sense, and called also $\pi\alpha\sigma\chi\alpha\lambda\iota\alpha$, or the paschal feast. The festival called Easter from the heathen goddess Astarte, called in Nineveh, as read on the Assyrian monuments, Ishtar, and by our Saxon ancestors Easter, Œster, or Oster, the same with the Latin Venus, whose festival was observed by the Pagans at the same time. The occurrence of the word Easter in Acts xii. 4, an example of the want of consistency in the English translators, who in the last revision substituted Passover for Easter as the translation of $\pi\alpha\sigma\chi\alpha$, in all passages where it had been used except this. *Dr Smith.* This festival, mentioned in church history in the third or fourth century, agreed originally with the time of the Jewish Passover, believed by Tertullian at the end of the second century to have been the 23d of March. Was preceded by no Lent. Cassian, of Marseilles, in the fifth century, says 'the observance of Lent had no existence so long as the perfection of the primitive church remained inviolate.' The forty days fasting borrowed from the worship of Astarte. Also observed by the ancient Egyptians, as still by the Yezidis or devil-worshippers of Koordistan. At first in the Roman church, when fasting before the Christian Pasch was held to be necessary, a fast was held of not more than seven days after the Jewish model of the days of unleavened bread. After the time of the Nicene Council, three weeks came to be the appointed period of fasting. About the end of the sixth century, the whole Chaldæan Lent, of six weeks or forty days, in conformity with the Pagan practice, was made imperative on all within the Western Roman Empire. Among the Pagans, this Lent seems to have been an indispensable preliminary to the festival in commemoration of the death and resurrection of Tammuz, which was celebrated by alternate weeping and rejoicing, and which in many countries was considerably later than the Christian festival, being observed in Palestine and Assyria in June, in Egypt about the middle of May, and in Britain some time in April. To conciliate the Pagans to nominal Christianity, measures were taken to amalgamate the Christian and Pagan festivals, by throwing the former later, and somewhat advancing the latter. The first

CHAP. XIV.]   ST. PAUL'S EPISTLE TO THE ROMANS.   239

attempt to enforce the new calendar made in Britain, where the observance of the Christian Pasch was a whole month earlier than that enforced by Rome, and was only exchanged for the latter after violence and bloodshed. *Hislop* (The Two Babylons). A lengthened contention existed also between the Eastern and Western churches as to whether this festival should be observed on the 14th day of the month, when the Jews kept their Passover, or on the Sunday after the full moon, the Eastern Church, with the pretended authority of John and Philip, adhering to the former, and the Western, after the alleged example of Peter and Paul, to the latter. The dispute settled by the Council of Nice deciding in favour of Sunday. *Baumgarten.* Christmas as a festival not heard of till the third century, and but little observed till the fourth was far advanced. *Gieseler.* Admitted by all that the day of Christ's birth is unknown. Certain not to have been on the 25th of December, when flocks were never kept out in the field at night. The 24th or 25th of December, or about the winter solstice, chosen as the time of a heathen festival at Rome, and among other nations, in honour of the birth of a god, supposed to be incarnate, and represented by the sun. 'Yule,' its name among our Saxon ancestors, derived from a Chaldee word for an 'infant' or 'little child;' and 'Yule-day' and 'Mother-night' given to the 25th of December and the night preceding it long before Christianity came in contact with Paganism. *Hislop.* The time of the celebration of this festival at first various. Observed by the Eastern church in Egypt, Jerusalem, Antioch, and Cyprus, on the 6th of January; by the Western on the 25th of December, the time of the Saturnalia at Rome. The latter date ultimately adopted also by the Eastern church. *Baumgarten.*—Πληροφορεισθω ($πληρης$, full, and $φερω$, to carry), let him abound. *Vulg., Mor.* Be certain. *Eras., Pisc., Beza.* Satisfy his own mind. *Vat.* Be fully certain. *Pag.* Have fulness of persuasion. *Est.* Be certain of his own opinion. *Calv.* Freely enjoy his own sentiment. *Doddr.* Have sufficient grounds for his conduct. *Flatt.* Go on comfortably in his own conviction. *Beng.* Act with full persuasion that what he does is lawful. *Whitby, Rückert.* Act conscientiously. *Stuart.* Satisfy himself in his conviction. *Knapp.* Hold by his own opinion. *Van Ess.* Have firm conviction. *De Wette.*

---

6. *He that regardeth the day, regardeth it unto the Lord ; and he that regardeth not the day, to the Lord he doth not regard it. He that eateth, eateth to the Lord, for he giveth God thanks ; and he that eateth not, to the Lord he eateth not, and giveth God thanks.*

He that, &c.   Only the believer still spoken of.
Regardeth.   Makes account of and pays attention to it.
Such regard is—1. In spirit ; 2. In practice.
Another word used in Gal. iv. 10 in much the same sense.
The Galatians condemned for it from the motive and principle.
To the Lord.   As a believer.   Shown from his general life.
He regards the day—1. Believing it of divine appointment.
2. Desiring thereby to honour and please his Master.
An erring act may be dictated by a pure motive.
The Lord marks not only the act but its motive and spirit.
The same thing may be blamed and praised in different persons.
To the Lord he doth not regard it.   As more according to his will.
The consistent believer acts or refrains from acting—

1. From the desire to honour the Lord; 2. The wish to obey Him.
Eateth to the Lord—1. In obedience to Him; 2. For His glory.
Believers only to eat and drink to the glory of God, 1 Cor. x. 31.
Christ here intended. His Godhead distinctly intimated.
For. Proof that he eats flesh in faithfulness to Christ.
Giveth God thanks. Believing the earth to be His, 1 Cor. x. 26, 28.
Thanksgiving to accompany our meals, 1 Tim. iv. 3.
Exemplified in Jesus, John vi. 11, 23; in Paul, Acts xxvii. 35.
Thanks at meals universal among early Christians.
Thanksgiving sanctifies actions that do not weaken it.
Hearty thanks from the good conscience of the eater.
Eateth not and giveth God thanks. Eats not flesh but herbs.
Same faith, love, and obedience shown in both cases.
Grace sanctifies and sweetens the humblest meal.
A gracious heart gives thanks in everything, 1 Thess. v. 18.

Ὁ φρονων, he who savours (sapit). *Vulg.* Honours. *Arab.* Makes account of. *Cast.* Observes. *Grot., Vat.*—Τῷ Κυριῳ, to the Lord; the Lord Christ. *D. Brown.* To his honour. *Grot., Pisc., Vor.* To please him. *Tol., Par., Est.* Not to you who are not interested in it. *Eras.* It is the Lord's to judge. *Beza.* To the Lord, who examines the spirit and motives. *Theod.* On account of his grace, and because he fears the Lord. *Theoph.* Regarding it, though erroneously, in obedience to the Lord. *Haldane.* Each doing what he believes to be the Lord's will. *D. Brown.* Και ὁ μη φρονων omitted in Codd. Sin, Vat., and Alex., and others, as well as in some ancient versions and Fathers; but retained by critics as authentic.—Ευχαριστει γαρ, for he gives thanks, *i.e.*, for the food. *Est.* And for liberty to eat anything. *Pisc.* Proof he eats flesh out of faithfulness to Christ. *De Wette.*—Και ευχαρ, and gives thanks; *i.e.*, for his sparing meal. *Flatt., Lange.* For his dinner of herbs. *Alford.* For other food enjoyed. *Henry, De Wette.* For the supposed light given him in making such a distinction. *Stuart.* Jews and early Christians universally gave thanks at meals. Jewish form of thanksgiving: 'Blessed art Thou, O Lord our God, King of the world, who createst the fruit of the earth [or, who producest bread out of the earth; or, who createst the fruit of the vine].' Early Christian form: 'Blessed art Thou, O Lord, who rememberest me from my youth up, who givest food to all flesh: Fill our hearts with joy and gladness, that always having all-sufficiency in all things, we may abound to every good work; through Jesus Christ our Lord, through whom to Thee be glory, honour, and might for ever. Amen.' *Apost. Constit.* See also under chap. xii. 12. Instead of thanksgiving, the ancient Greeks, before drinking, poured out a little wine as a libation to the good Spirit, and drank their first cup to Jupiter the Saviour. The libation at feasts often accompanied with the singing of the Pæan or hymn to Apollo. *Dr Smith.* The more ancient Romans regarded their table as holy as an altar, and sanctified it to the gods by setting salt on it, and sprinkling the salt with wine, with the wish that the gods might be favourably present at their meal, the image of their household tutelary deities being at the same time placed near the salt. *Keil.*

CHAP. XIV.]   ST. PAUL'S EPISTLE TO THE ROMANS.   241

7. *For none of us liveth to himself, and no man dieth to himself.*

None. No believer while acting in his proper character.
Marked contrast between believers and the world.
All others live and die to themselves, Ps. xii. 4 ; Job xxi. 15.
Believers to serve Christ in every action of their lives.
Stand pledged to be entirely devoted to His service and glory.
Our state and character tested by these two verses.
Liveth to himself—1. For his own benefit and pleasure ;
2. According to his own will and inclination.
Bought with a price, we are His who bought us.
A Christian living to himself a contradiction in terms.
The believer's true life one of self-renunciation and love.
Dieth to himself. Our death as well as life not for ourselves.
Our whole course on earth comprehended in these two terms.
Our life and death in our Master's hand, and to be for His glory.
The believer's life, therefore, one—1. Of highest dignity ; 2. Of noblest liberty ; 3. Of sweetest peace.
Believers are Christ's both in the present and future world.
Our spiritual life or death Christ's gain or loss as well as our own.

Ἑαυτῳ ζῇ, lives to himself; to live spiritually, Christ's gain as well as our own. *Chrys.* We are not our own masters. *Theod.* Act according to our own judgment and follow our own opinion. *A. Clarke.* Live for our own pleasure and obey our own inclinations. *Stuart.* Dispose of ourselves or shape our conduct after our own ideas and inclinations. *D. Brown.*—Ἑαυτῳ ἀποθνησκει, dies to himself; to die spiritually in the loss of faith. Christ's loss as well as our own. *Chrys.* In life and death, in the present and future world, we are the Lord's. *Stuart.* We are not to follow our own humour or seek our own objects in life or death. *Brown.*

8. *For whether we live, we live unto the Lord: and whether we die, we die unto the Lord: whether we live therefore, or die, we are the Lord's.*

Live unto the Lord. For Jesus our Lord and our God, John xx. 28.
The divine dignity, power, and majesty of Christ indicated.
The Proprietor, aim, and end of the believer's life.
Property, character, life, yielded up to His service.
We submit ourselves to His disposal, as not our own but His.
His will our rule ; His approval our aim ; His glory our end.
Die unto the Lord. The believer dies as he lives, for Christ.
Our death to be an act of consecration to His glory.
Christ to be magnified in our body, by life or by death, Phil. i. 20.

VOL. II.   Q

It is His to say by what death we shall glorify God, John xxi. 19.
Believers' death precious to Christ as well as their life, Ps. cxvi. 15.
Our fellowship with Christ both in life and in death, Phil. i. 21, 23.
"Lord Jesus, receive my spirit," the believer's dying prayer, Acts vii. 59.
We are the Lord's—1. We are His property, and so at His disposal;
2. We are His servants, and bound to seek His glory;
3. We are His members, and under His care and protection.
Christ's lordship over this world and the next, Rev. i. 18; iii. 5.
Believers recognise His property in them and authority over them.
Christ the centre in which the lines of our life and death meet.
The Christian's dignity, blessedness, and responsibility.
That is true Christianity which makes Christ all in all.
This verse the believer's motto for each day, week, and year
Expresses the common faith of all true Christians.

Τῷ Κυρίῳ, to the Lord, *i.e.*, Christ. *Vat., Grot., Beng.* Made certain by ver. 9. *Stuart.* Unendurable to a Christian ear were Christ a mere creature. *D. Brown.*—Ἐάν τε οὖν ζῶμεν, ἐάν τε ἀποθνῄσκωμεν, whether we live or die; from ver. 9, the state of the living and of the dead, not the act of living or dying. *Stuart.* Both act and state. *Haldane.* Under all circumstances. *Alford.* Living and dying the stronger form of 'eating' and 'not eating.' *Lange.*—Τοῦ Κυρίου ἐσμέν, we are the Lord's; the objects of His care. *Chrys.* His property; our spiritual life or death His gain or loss. *Theoph.* Christ's lordship over this world and the next. *Tol., Est.* Christ is our Lord both here and hereafter. *Stuart.* As His professed subjects and servants we seek His honour and glory both by our life and our death. *Boothr.* We are His property. *Alford.* It is His to decide our lot in both worlds. *De Wette.*

---

9. *For to this end Christ both died, and revived, and rose again, that He might be Lord both of the dead and living.*

To this end. One great design of Christ's death and resurrection.
His mediatorial dominion over mankind and His church.
Acquired by His death, and exercised afterwards in His life.
Exercised for God's glory and man's salvation, Ph. ii. 6-11; Isa. liii. 11, 12.
Died. As a substitute and sacrifice, the just for the unjust, 1 Pet. iii. 18.
All power given to Him as the result of it, Matt. xxviii. 18; John xvii. 2.
His kingly sceptre the reward of His priestly sacrifice.
The former swayed to secure the fruits of the latter, Ps. cx. 1-3.

Rose. As the first step to His kingly throne, Luke xxiv. 26, 46.
Rose to be the living Head of living members, who live in and to Him.
Revived. Lived again after His resurrection, Rom. vi. 8-10.
Lives to secure and carry out the objects of His death, chap. v. 10.
Resurrection-life common to the Head and members, John xiv. 19.
That He might be Lord. Possess universal lordship.
Be manifested as the righteous Head over the race of man.
Exercise sovereign rule in the visible and invisible worlds.
Man and man's world now the rightful property of Christ alone.
Indicates believers' safety and duty both as to their life and death.
Christ's lordship the end of His death, resurrection, and ascension.
Of the dead. Has dominion over the invisible world, Rev. i. 18.
Disembodied spirits, therefore, still living, Matt. xxii. 32.
As Lord of the dead, Christ shall also raise the body to life.
His universal lordship an evidence of His divinity, Isa. xlviii. 11.
Dying believers may well rejoice in a dying and risen Christ.
Of the living. Who live now and shall live again hereafter.
The living believer rejoices in a living Redeemer, Job xix. 25-27.
Christ Lord of the dead to raise them—of the living, to rule them.
The living responsible to Christ for their opinions and actions.
The dead raised by Him to receive their final award,

$_x$Καὶ ἀπέθανε κ. ἀνέστη κ. ἀνέζησεν. Codd. Sin., Vat., and Alex. omit the first καί, and also καὶ ἀνέστη. The clause 'κ. ἀνέστη' generally rejected by critics as spurious and unnecessary.—Κυριεύσῃ, may exercise lordship (dominetur). *Pisc.*, *Beza*. Obtain full lordship. *Men.* The full exercise of His lordship. *Tol.* Universal dominion a fruit or consequence of Christ's death, and one of the ends He had in view as necessary for the accomplishment of His benevolent purposes. *Stuart.* That He might show His saving rule. *Barth.* Not only His moral rule, but His future reign indicated. *De Wette.* Might be manifested the righteous Head of the race of man *Alford.* 'Having done all this to make us His property, will He not take care of His own?' *Chrys.*— Νεκρῶν κ. ζώντων, dead and living, as making up all the human race. *Stuart.* Separate as well as embodied spirits under His authority. *A. Clarke.*

---

10. *But why dost thou judge thy brother? or why dost thou set at nought thy brother? for we shall all stand before the judgment-seat of Christ.*

But why. *Gr.*, more emphatic—"but thou, why dost thou, &c.?"
This addressed to the weak brother according to ver. 3.
It is not thine to judge, but His who is Lord of dead and living.
Or why dost thou. *Gr.*, "Or thou again,"—turning to the strong.
Each class required reproof, though on different grounds.
The weak erred in judging, the strong in despising their brethren.

The superstitious prone to judge; those not superstitious, to despise.
Each has his own weaknesses and besetting sins.
Necessitates humility, forbearance, and self-examination.
Set at naught. Despise, as in ver. 3. Respects thoughts and conduct.
Seen in eating flesh notwithstanding offence to the weak.
For. The reason given for neither judging nor despising.
Appear. *Gr.*, Be made to stand, be sisted as parties.
"Appear," in 2 Cor. v. 10, = be manifested, stand revealed.
Here the *fact* indicated, there the *manner* of our standing.
Judgment-seat. The tribunal of the universe.
Great white throne, Rev. xx. 12; throne of His glory, Matt. xxv. 31.
Glorious contrast with the manger and the cross.
Angels as well as men sisted before the judgment-seat, 1 Cor. vi. 3.
All nations, civilised and savage, Jew and Gentile, Matt. xxv. 32.
All classes. Cæsars and sultans, emperors and kings, side by side with the humblest of their subjects.
Difference of place determined only by a difference of character.
Believers there to receive their gracious reward.
Unbelievers there to hear their righteous doom.
Each according to the measure of his faithfulness or sin.

> "I see the Judge enthroned! The flaming guard!
> The volume opened! Opened every heart,
> A sunbeam pointing out each secret thought." *Young.*

The secrets of six thousand years revealed, chap. ii. 16.
Wrongs redressed; errors corrected; mysteries solved.
The judgment-seat surrounded by myriads of angels, Dan. vii. 10.
Christ. The Son of God and man, the final Judge, chap. ii. 16; John v. 22, 23.
Judges the quick and dead at His appearing and kingdom, 2 Tim. iv. 1.
Comes to give every man according to his work, Rev. xxii. 12.
The best manuscripts read "the judgment-seat of God."
God himself the Judge, Ps. l. 6; Rom. ii. 16; Acts xvii. 31.
Christ therefore God. The judgment ascribed to Him, 2 Tim. iv. 1.
The judgment-seat said to be His, 2 Cor. v. 10; Matt. xxv. 31.
The apostle's argument requires Christ to be here understood.
Christ declared to be Lord of dead and living, therefore their Judge, ver. 9.
No clearer proof needed of Christ's divinity.

Συ δε, but thou. *Calv.* Συ, the nominative absolute, as in ver. 4; δε, but, the sentiment being adversative. *Stuart.* The original more lively than the English version: But thou (the weaker believer), why dost thou judge, &c. *D. Brown.* Κρινεις, condemnest. *Stuart.*—Και συ, and again thou. *Mart., Diod.* Important to keep apart the separate addresses. *Ellicot.*—Παραστησομεθα, we shall be placed (statuemur). *Vat.* (sistemur), *Pisc., Eras., Beza.* Be compelled to appear. *Grot.*—Βηματι, from βαω or βαινω, to go, the tribunal being ascended by steps). Heb. קְרָיַב, 'a pulpit,' LXX., Neh. viii. 4. Βημα, the elevated place among the Greeks from which the speaker addressed the public assembly. The 'tribunal' among the Romans. The chair from which judicial sentence was pronounced by the magistrate. Of two kinds—the one fixed in some open and public place; the other movable, and taken wherever the magistrates sat in their judicial character. The fixed tribunal was a raised platform at the end of the Basilica, or court of law on which the prætor and judges sat while administering justice. There was also a tribunal in the camp, generally formed of turf, but sometimes, in a stationary camp, of stone, from which the general addressed the troops, who stood in order around it with the standards in front, and where the consul and tribunes of the soldiers administered justice. *Dr Smith.*

---

11. *For it is written, As I live, saith the Lord, every knee shall bow to me, and every tongue shall confess to God.*

For. Proof adduced from Scripture that Christ is Judge of all.
Written. Isa. xlv. 23. Old and New Testaments given by one Spirit.
In harmony with each other in all their parts.
All religious teaching to be supported by Scripture, Isa. viii. 20.
The quotation teaches the universal acknowledgment of Jehovah.
Applied by Paul to prove that Christ is universal Judge.
The inference obvious that Christ is Jehovah.
Judgment of the world universally ascribed to God.
As I live. In the prophet, "I have sworn by Myself."
The meaning given by the apostle, but not the words.
Because He can swear by no greater, God swears by Himself.
Only the Self-existent, Independent, Eternal can say, "As I live."
Another unanswerable proof of Christ's divinity.
Saith the Lord. Added by the apostle speaking by the Spirit.
Paul quoted from memory, but under divine guidance.
Every knee shall bow. Applied directly to Christ, Phil. ii. 10.
Bowing the knee a common form of subjection.
The understanding to be subjected to Christ's truth;
The will and conduct to be subjected to His law;
The whole man to be subjected to His authority.
Men shall bow to the award passed on their conduct and actions.
Confess. Acknowledge, more especially with praise, chap. xv. 9.

Acknowledge His divinity and universal lordship, Phil. ii. 10.
Give account as to their supreme and final Judge.
In the prophet, "Every tongue shall swear." Same sense.
Shall swear, as subjects swear allegiance to their sovereign.
To swear by Christ is to acknowledge Him to be God.
Friends shall bow and confess freely, foes by force, Ps. ii. 8-12.
"Bow and confess" indicate subjection, adoration, and praise.
To God. Added by the apostle as implied in the passage.
Added as if expressly to indicate Christ's divinity.

Ἐξομολογήσεται (ἐξ, forth, ὁμοῦ, together, and λέγω, to speak). Cod. Vat. has 'shall swear,' according to the Hebrew text and the translation of the LXX. Shall confess, *i.e.*, that I am God. *Vat.*, *Schütt.* Worship and acknowledge as God. *Beza, Tol., Est.* Praise my mercy and justice. *Men.* The text applied by the ancient Jews to the Messiah. 'Can it be said that the Redeemer will accept persons? By no means; but rather He will save all who with mouth, works, and heart confess Him. As it is said, In His days Israel shall be saved, namely, those who confess Him. And again, Look unto me, and be ye saved, &c. (Isa. xlv. 22, 23).' *Bereshith Rabba*, in Raymond Martini, quoted by *Schöttgen*. Comp. Rom. x. 9. Heb. ידה.—Τῷ Θεῷ, to God; the apostle has translated *ad sensum*, not *ad verbum*. *Stuart.*

---

12. *So then every one of us shall give account of himself to God.*

Every one of us. Strong and weak; each believer; the apostle himself.
The highest office-bearer and humblest member of the Church.
Each has duties to perform and talents to improve for the Master.
Give account. As a steward or servant of the Master, Christ.
How we have spent our time and improved our opportunities.
What we have done, and how we have done it.
Believers only stewards of the manifold grace of God, 1 Pet. iv. 10.
Stewards to give account of their stewardship, Luke xvi. 2.
Required of stewards that a man be found faithful, 1 Cor. iv. 2.
The fact of a future judgment to influence our daily conduct.
Of himself. Emphatic; of *himself*, not of his brother.
Each to be judged himself, therefore not to judge another.
To God—*i.e.*, Christ who is Lord both of the dead and living.
The man Christ is judge, *only* because He is also God.
Talents committed to be accounted for to Christ, Matt. xxv. 19.
Christ alone Lord of the conscience.
Man responsible to God for his views and opinions.
The doctrine in the text consistent with—
1. The Church judging its members in the way of discipline, 1 Cor. v. 1-5.

2. Subjection to civil tribunals, Rom. xiii. 3–5;
3. Believers judging the life and doctrine of teachers, Matt. vii. 20; 1 John iv. 1, 2.

Λογος, account; so Matt. xii. 36; Acts xix. 40; 1 Pet. iv. 5; Heb. xiii. 17; iv. 13. *Stuart.* Τῳ Θεῳ, to God; omitted in Cod. Alex.

---

13. *Let us not therefore judge one another any more: but judge this rather, that no man put a stumbling block or an occasion to fall in his brother's way.*

Let us. Paul's humility; includes himself in the exhortation.
Aims at uniting strong and weak, Jew and Gentile believers.
Therefore. As having to give account of ourselves to God.
He who judges others forgets he is to be judged himself.
Judge one another. Addressed both to the strong and weak.
Both virtually judged and condemned each other.
Christians forbidden to indulge a censorious spirit, Luke vi. 37.
Charity believeth all things, hopeth all things, 1 Cor. xiii. 7.
The duty enjoined limited by the circumstances of the case.
Lawful to judge officially and collectively,—not as individuals.
Any more. The gentleness of the apostle, 1 Thess. ii. 7.
"Henceforth," a suitable motto for the believer, 2 Cor. v. 15, 16.
His life to be a forgetting the things that are behind, Phil. iii. 13.
Judge this rather. Allusion to the word just used, as in John vi. 28, 29.
"If you will judge, judge this,"—make this judgment.
Use your faculty of judging, but use it lawfully.
Sin leads to a perverted use of all our faculties.
These only exercised aright when directed by love.
Stumbling-block. Cause of sin to others by your conduct.
The danger especially of the strong believer, 1 Cor. viii. 9.
Christian liberty not to be used to the injury of others.
Occasion to fall. By acting contrary to his conscience.
The weak tempted and emboldened by the conduct of the strong.
What might be right in the strong might be sin in the weak.
The "stumbling-block" staggers, hinders, and hurts.
The "occasion to fall" overthrows and may ruin the soul.

Κρινωμεν, assume the office of judge over another. *D. Brown.*—Τουτο κρινατε, judge this; κρινω here used in a different sense from that in the former clause. *Calv.* Use discernment in this. *Mart.* Exercise your judgment in what relates to your duty, and you will come to this conclusion, not to put, &c. *Booth.* Make or come to this determination ; used in this sense by a kind of *paronomasia* frequent in Paul's writings, called by rhetoricians *autanaclasis*. *Stuart.* Let this be your judgment ; beautiful sort of play in the word 'judge.' *D. Brown.*—Προσκομμα, stumbling-block (offendiculum) ; anything against which one strikes or stumbles. *Beza.* Omitted in Cod. Vat.—Σκανδαλον, occasion of falling (scandalum). *Pisc*, *Eras.*, *Vat.* Προσκ., the occasion of his not embracing the Gospel ; σκανδ., the occasion of his forsaking it, a more serious injury. *Grot.*, *Beza.* Both used indiscriminately ; προσκ., where there is not a fall ; σκανδ., where there is. *Tol.* Jewish Christians guilty by imposing Judaism ; Gentile Christians by repelling scrupulous Jews. *Grot.* Προσκ., what you strike your foot against ; σκανδ., what trips you up. *Beng.* What may make remiss in duty, hinder from becoming Christians, or discourage in their new profession. *Parkhurst.* The two words not materially different—an occasion or cause of stumbling. *Stuart.* Rabbins : ' When I enter the school to expound the law, I pray that no occasion of stumbling may arise through me to any.' *Talm. Ber.* ' If a man cause his neighbour to stumble or fall through him, though without intending it, it is visited upon him.' *Zohar.*

---

14. *I know, and am persuaded by the Lord Jesus, that there is nothing unclean of itself : but to him that esteemeth anything to be unclean, to him it is unclean.*

Am persuaded. Gr., Have been persuaded, personal conviction.
A believer may think otherwise from want of knowledge.
Light both as to doctrine and duty given by degrees.
" Persuaded," a strong expression for the benefit of the weak.
Characteristic of the strong to " know and be persuaded."
By the Lord Jesus. Christ enlightens by His Spirit, John xvi. 14.
The Spirit promised by Christ to guide unto all truth, John xvi. 13.
Gr., " In the Lord Jesus,"—as vitally united to Him.
In Christ the curse entailed by the fall removed from the creatures.
The liberty given by the Gospel opposed to the bondage of the law.
Believers, and apostles especially, have the mind of Christ, 1 Cor. ii. 16.
Paul's persuasion not from mere human reasoning.
Divine authority had made a distinction of meats.
The same authority required to remove it, Acts x. 15.
Needful to state this on account of Jewish prejudices.
True light and conviction only obtained in union with Christ.
Nothing. No creature of God that is suitable for food, 1 Tim. iv. 3, 4.
Unclean. Morally impure, and bringing such impurity.
" Not that which entereth the mouth defileth the man," Matt. xv. 11.
Of itself. Its own nature, not being forbidden by God.
Many animals rendered unclean by divine prohibition.
The law that made such distinctions now abolished, Acts x. 15.
Two grounds of uncleanness according to the Jews—

CHAP. XIV.]   ST. PAUL'S EPISTLE TO THE ROMANS.   249

1. The prohibition of the law; 2. The contact with idolatry.
To him it is unclean. As if actually prohibited.
Partaking of what is forbidden defiles the conscience.
Same result in partaking of what we *believe* to be forbidden.
The lawful becomes unlawful when believed to be so.
Dangerous to trifle with conscience even when erroneous.

Πεπεισμαι (perfect passive of πειθω, to persuade), have been persuaded; Paul himself once thought otherwise.—'Εν Κυριῳ 'Ιησου, in Christ Jesus; by His appointment—connected with κοινον. *Calv.* Not a private opinion, but the revealed will of his Master. *Chrys.* Christ the ground of the persuasion, His death having removed the curse. *Calv., Henry.* By the faith of Christ. *Whitby.* By revelation from Him. *Macknight.* By His inspiration. *A. Clarke.* I, being in the Lord Jesus. *Stuart.* As having the mind of Christ. *Alford, D. Brown.* In virtue of my fellowship with Him. *Nielson.*—Κοινον, common. *Vulg., Eras., Mor.* Impure. *Beza, Pisc., Pag., Vat.* — βδελυκτον, ακαθαρτον. *Hes.* Heb. חנד, profane, unclean. *Grot.*—Δι εαυτῳ (Lachman reads αὑτου, him), by him (per ipsum, reading αὑτου). *Vulg.* By itself. *Beza, Pisc.* In its own nature; many Jews thought certain meats naturally and morally unclean. *Est.* By ordination of God. *Tol.* On its own account. *Stuart.*

---

15. *But if thy brother be grieved with thy meat, now walkest thou not charitably. Destroy not him with thy meat, for whom Christ died.*

But. Notwithstanding. Believers to have *love* as well as *light.*
Grieved. Made to experience—1. Grief; 2. Injury, 1 Cor. viii. 12.
Both the result of acting against conscience, 1 Cor. viii. 7.
To grieve a brother a sin, still more to injure him.
Joy a part of the kingdom of God (ver. 17); hence grief an evil.
With thy meat. Seeing thee eat what he believes unlawful.
Grieved at seeing thee, a brother, act inconsistently.
Emboldened by thy example to do the same.
Now. *Gr.,* No longer. Brotherly love to *continue,* Heb. xiii. 1.
Love to mark the *whole* of a believer's life, 1 Cor. xiii. 1, &c.
Charitably. *Gr.,* In, or according to love or charity.
Love to be the rule of a believer's life and conduct.
The connecting point between this and the preceding chapter.
Love worketh no ill to his neighbour, chap. xiii. 10.
Will not allow us to injure or even grieve another.
Regards the souls and consciences of others as well as our own.
Leads to self-denial for the benefit of others.
Makes us tender of another's peace and purity.
Want of love a greater evil than want of light.
Knowledge good, but charity the more excellent way, 1 Cor. xii. 31.

Destroy—1. As to his peace; 2. His purity; 3. His soul. 1 Cor. viii. 10–12.
The effect of all sin, if not prevented, is to destroy the soul.
Uncharitable use of liberty may cause another—
1. To do what his conscience feels to be wrong;
2. To fall into condemnation and lose his peace;
3. To commit sin, and if grace prevent not, lose his soul.
Souls may suffer from our want of charity and consistency.
To lead another into sin is to be guilty of destroying his soul.
Believers sometimes found doing Satan's work instead of Christ's.
Brethren to be cared for as if their perdition were possible.
Profession of Christ not necessarily possession of Christ.
With thy meat. Flesh eaten in the exercise of Christian liberty.
The meat which some thought no Christian could lawfully eat.
Sad to regard meat and drink more than a brother's soul.
For whom Christ died. Who cost Christ His life to save him.
If Christ gave up His life for him, we may well give up our meat.
A brother's soul precious in Christ's eyes, and should be so in ours.
Christ's love to men's souls contrasted with our indifference.
No sacrifice to be held too great for a soul's salvation.
Christian liberty to be coupled with self-denying love.
Christ died for the weakest as well as the strongest.
For all the children of God scattered abroad, John xi. 52.
For the sheep given him by the Father, John x. 11, 29.
For the church whom He loved as His bride, Eph. v. 25.
For all who by Him believe in God, 1 Pet. i. 20, 21.
In a more general sense, for all, 2 Cor. v. 14.
Gave His flesh for the life of the world, John vi. 51.
Gave Himself a ransom for all, 1 Tim. ii. 6.
A propitiation for the sins of the whole world, 1 John ii. 2.
Died generally for all, peculiarly for the elect.
His death sufficient for all, effectual for His own.
Made salvation certain to some, possible to all.

Εἰ δέ, but if. Codd. Sin., Vat., and Alex. have εἰ γάρ, for if.—Λυπεῖται, is saddened. *Eras., Pag., Pisc., Beza.* Grieves. *Vat.* Eating against his conscience by thy example. *Eras.* Sinning by a rash judgment against thee. *Est.* Grieved that he is blamed by thee as a Judaizer. *Par.* Grieved at thy conduct. *Vor., Pisc.* Is upbraided for his ignorance. *Grot.* Saddened to see thee eat. *Mar., Diod.* Injured in his conscience, and so impeded and driven from his Christian profession. *Ham.* Injured, being induced to do what his conscience forbids. *Schött.* Wounded, led into sin. *Doddr.* So as to be driven into a scandal. *Bp. Hall.* Grieved, of itself an evil. *Beng.* Distressed with anxieties and doubts. *Boothr.* Has his weak conscience hurt. *D. Brown.* Through the offence given, ver. 13. *De Wette.* Δυπεω, used for being hurt; λυπουντα τους ποδας. *Ten. Mem.* Heb. עָצַב, יָרֵע, חָרָה, קָצַף, רָגַן, 'fretted,' Ezek. xvi. 43.—Κατα ἀγαπην, according to what love and benevolence requires. *Stuart.*—Δια βρωμα, on account of some particular kind of meat on which neither thy life nor well-being depends *A. Clarke.* Because of *meat* ; purposely selected as something contemptible. *D. Brown.*—'Απολλυε, destroy (perdito). *Beza, Pisc.* Giving occasion to a rash judgment of you. *Or.* To an unhappy imitation of you. *Est.* Causing him to resile from Christianity and return to Judaism. *Men., Vor., Pisc.* Inchoately, by injuring his charity and faith. *Gom.* Give occasion of perishing, as 1 Kings xiv. 16; Acts i. 18. *Glass.* Give not pain. *Schleusner.* Eternal perdition not meant here. *Ham., Locke.* The soul's ruin implied. *A. Clarke.* 'Απολλυμι, sometimes with the Greeks = to *torment, vex;* here more probably to *destroy.* Compare ver. 20, and 1 Cor. viii. 11. *Stuart.* Destroy by causing him to act against his conscience, and so to commit sin. *De Wette, Thol.* The tendency is to lead him to apostatize. *A. Clarke, Boothr.* To bring him into condemnation. *Haldane.* To quench the Spirit within him. *Alford.* Whatever tends to make any one violate his conscience tends to the destruction of his soul. *D. Brown.* Heb. שָׁחֵר, הָאֲבִיד, הִשְׁמִיד, הֶחֱרִים, כָּשַׁל, 'to fall,' נָדַח and דָּחָה, 'to cast out.'—'Υπερ οὐ Χριστος ἀπεθανε, for whose benefit Christ died. In whose stead; hence some may perish for whom Christ died. *A. Clarke.* The worth of even the poorest and weakest brother most emphatically expressed by the words, 'For whom Christ died.' *Ols., D. Brown.* A general as well as a particular reference in Christ's death held by theologians till about half a century after the death of Calvin in 1564; *e.g.,* Irenæus, Clement of Alexandria, Tertullian, Origen, Cyprian, Eusebius of Cæsarea, Hilary, Athanasius, the two Gregories, Ambrose, Chrysostom, Jerome, Augustine, and the Fathers in general; Luther, Melancthon, Calvin, Peter Martyr, Bucer, Parcus, Bullinger, Zanchius, Pelican, Latimer, Becon, Jewel, Dr Twiss, &c. *Biblical Notes and Queries.*

---

16. *Let not then your good be evil spoken of.*

Then. Since some may receive injury from what you do.

Your good. The good—1. Received ; 2. Practised ; 3. Professed.

The liberty wherewith Christ makes us free, Gal. v. 1 ; 1 Cor. x. 29.

The kingdom of God, ver. 17. Christ's doctrine and cause. The Gospel.

The believer's life one of true excellence, Eccles. i. 14.

Such a life to be carefully guarded against just reproach.

Believers therefore to be tender in respect to weak brethren.

No fly to be in the apothecary's pot of ointment, Eccles. x. 1.

Others may sin in speaking evil, *we* in giving occasion to it.

Evil spoken of. *Gr.,* Blasphemed—1. By the world ; 2. By weak brethren, 1 Cor. x. 30.

Christian liberty abused appears as licentiousness.

Strife among Christians a stumbling-block to the world.

Contention in the Church a hindrance to the Gospel.

The honour of Christianity in the keeping of its professors.

David's sin gave occasion to the enemies of God to blaspheme, 2 Sam. xii. 14.
Believers so to live that the word of God be not blasphemed, Tit. ii. 5.
Their whole conduct, therefore, to be without reproach, Phil. ii. 15.
In all things to adorn the doctrine of God our Saviour, Tit. ii. 10.
So to do good as to give no occasion to evil-speaking.
Guilt of the Jews that through them God's name was blasphemed, Rom. ii. 24.

Βλασφημεισθω (βλαπτω, to hurt, and φημι, to speak), be evil spoken of ; because of your divisions. *Chrys.*, *Est.* When Christian liberty is abused by offence given to the weak. *Luth.* For the evil it does to others. *D. Brown.* By the heathen. *Chrys.* By the Jews, because of your defilement. *Anon.* By the weak brethren. *Nielson.*—Ύμων το ἀγαθον, your good, *i.e.*, your Christian liberty. *Or.*, *Calv.*, *Grot.*, *Tol.*, *Est.*, *Vor.*, *Pisc.*, *Ham.*, *Beng.*, *Doddr.*, *Wells*, *Stuart*, *Ols.*, *Hald.*, *D. Brown.* The Gospel. *Ambr.*, *Cast.*, *Luth.* The Christian religion. *Chrys.*, *Theoph.*, *De Wette*, *Phil.* Faith, knowledge, hatred of superstition. *Cam.* The advantage you enjoy. *Mart.* Freedom from Jewish rites. *Mackn.* The good you do. *A. Clarke* The truth as it is in Jesus. *Chal.* What you deem right. *Cobbin.* Your just views of Christian freedom. *Boothr.* The kingdom of God, including both the Gospel and faith. *Lange.* Your strength of faith. *Alford.* The Christian cause. *Brown.*

---

17. *For the kingdom of God is not meat and drink; but righteousness, and peace, and joy in the Holy Ghost.*

Kingdom of God. God's rule in the heart set up and exercised by Christ.
1. The kingdom in the believer ; 2. The kingdom he is now in.
A twofold kingdom of God—1. That of grace ; 2. That of glory.
The two never separated. One preparatory to the other.
" The Holy to the Holiest leads." Flower and fruit. Dawn and day.
Kingdom of God in the New Testament. Economy. Ministration of the Spirit.
Meat and drink—1. Liberty to use or abstain from these ;
2. The enjoyment of outward and carnal things ;
3. Attention to matters in themselves indifferent.
Men prone to cling to what is external in religion.
The law stood much in meats and drinks, Heb. ix. 10 ; Lev. xi. 2-24.
The Gospel otherwise. No rule given in such matters.
Undue attention to externals hostile to the inner life.
The kingdom of God consists in what is spiritual, not external.
But. Three elements given in which it really consists.

Righteousness. Here a holy and obedient life. Conformity to God's will.
Righteousness of life as the fruit of righteousness by faith.
Righteousness practised as the effect of righteousness imputed.
Righteousness before men as the evidence of righteousness before God.
Believers to be filled with the fruits of righteousness, Phil. i. 11.
Death to sin and life to righteousness fruits of Christ's death, 1 Pet. ii. 24.
Peace. Peace in ourselves and with others as the fruits of peace with God.
A peaceful and gentle demeanour flowing from inward peace.
Harmony with God, the brethren, and ourselves.
Peace a mark of God's children and Christ's followers, Matt. v. 9.
The wisdom from above is first pure, then peaceable, James iii. 17.
Peace numbered among the fruits of the Spirit, Gal. v. 22.
Joy in the Holy Ghost. Such joy as the Holy Spirit imparts.
Joy as well as peace a fruit of the Spirit, Gal. v. 22.
Joy in the Holy Ghost contrasted with meats and drinks.
Experience in the fellowship of the Holy Ghost, 2 Cor. xiii. 14.
Has its foundation in the Spirit, 1 Thess. i. 6; Phil. iv. 4.
True joy the feeling of His presence and the fruit of His power.
The Spirit's part to show us the causes for rejoicing.
Reveals and sheds abroad God's love in the gift of Christ, chap. v. 5.
The grounds of spiritual joy as revealed by the Spirit are—
1. Christ himself and His work on earth and in heaven, John xvi. 13–15.
2. Our interest in Christ and His redeeming work, Gal. iv. 5, 6.
3. The glory in reserve for believers in heaven, 1 Cor. ii. 9–12.
True joy only found in things spiritual and eternal.
Given by the Spirit in connection with righteousness and peace.
God to be served with joy as well as righteousness, Deut. xxviii. 47; Isa. lxiv. 5.
Compliance *with* God and complacency *in* God, the life of religion.
True religion the opposite of moroseness and gloom.
The Spirit gives a gladness within which radiates without.
The kingdom of God consists in—1. Righteousness in respect to God; 2. Peace in respect to others; 3. Joy in respect to yourself.
Beautiful and comprehensive division of living Christianity.

Βασιλεια τ. Θεου, the kingdom of God, *i.e.*, what commends us to God, as 1 Cor. viii. 8. *Tol.* Our salvation. *Par.* Christianity, saintliness. *Vat.* That in which He specially reigns in us. *Est.*, *Tir.* Christ's kingdom. *Calv.* When a man is under God's authority. *Beng.* The religion which God has sent from heaven. *A. Clarke.* Spiritual kingdom of God or Christ ; His moral dominion over the hearts of men ; true Christianity. *Stuart.* His reign in us. *Cobbin.* The earthly moral kingdom. *Thol.* Includes also the eternal and happy one. *De Wette.* Messiah's kingdom at His second advent. *Meyer.* The reign of a heavenly life in which God's word and Spirit rule, and whose organ is the church. *Lange.* Religion,—the proper business and blessedness for which Christians are formed into a community of renewed men in thorough subjection to God. *D. Brown.*—Βρωσις κ. ποσις, meat and drink. *Stuart.* Eating and drinking. *D. Brown.* Christ's kingdom not set up and preserved by these. *Calv.* Not greatly promoted by them. *Par.* Does not consist in such external matters. *Ham.* In liberty in regard to them. *Beng.* In things indifferent. *De Wette.* In using or abstaining from them. *A. Clarke*, *Haldane*, *Stuart.*—Δικαιοσυνη, righteousness of faith. *Vat.*, *Par.* Pursuit of righteousness as prescribed in God's law. *Vor.*, *Tir.*, *Pisc.*, *Est.*, *Tol.*, *Per.* Virtuous life. *Chrys.* Pardon of sin and holiness of heart and life. *A. Clarke.* Holy conformity to God. *Stuart.* Righteousness in the full sense of the term, including justification. *De Wette.* Righteousness of life springing from righteousness by faith. *Alford.* Rectitude in its widest sense, as Matt. vi. 33. *D. Brown.*—Ειρηνη, peace of conscience. *Par.* Concord and union with God. *Tol.* Pursuit of peace. *Grot.*, *Pisc.*, *Vor.* Peace with the brethren and one's neighbour. *Vat.*, *Est.* Inward cheerful peace springing from peace with God. *Calv.* Peace in the soul from a sense of God's mercy ; peace regulating, ruling, and harmonising the heart. *A. Clarke.* Peace, in opposition to discord and contention among brethren ; a peaceful and gentle demeanour. *Stuart.* Inward and outward peace. *De Wette.* Peace with God through Christ, and with it brotherly forbearance. *Lange.* Concord among brethren ; plain from ver. 19. *D. Brown.*—Χαρα εν Πνευματι αγιῳ, joy in the Holy Ghost, *i.e.*, effected by Him. *Pisc.* According to Him ; hence, spiritual. *Per.* Solid joy arising from true peace. *Calv.* Joy in others' welfare. *Ham.* A cheerful temper inspired by the Holy Ghost. *Doddr.* Solid spiritual happiness brought into the soul and maintained there by the Spirit. *A. Clarke.* Joy imparted by Him. *Stuart.* In fellowship with Him. *Barth.* Joyful sense of the love of God shed abroad in the heart by Him. *Burk.* Its foundation in Him. *De Wette.* Joy in communion with Him, and under His influence and indwelling. *Alford.* Christians represented as so thinking and feeling under the Spirit's operation, that their joy is viewed rather as His than their own. *D. Brown.* Only moral virtues here spoken of. *Lange.* Doctrinal and moral. *De Wette.*

---

18. *He that in these things serveth Christ is acceptable to God, and approved of men.*

For. Reason why peace and joy follow the practice of Christian principles.
In. Referring to the life-element, or state of mind and life.
These things. The marks of the Christian life just named. These Christian graces to be cultivated and blessings to be sought. Righteousness, peace, and holy joy, Christ's true service.
Serveth. Christ to be served in these things, therefore God. Christ to be served as our Master and our God, John xx. 28. Paul and all true believers servants of Christ, chap. i. 1.

Christ's service not in forms and in outward observances.
To serve Christ is to obey Him and further His interests.
His object to reconcile us to God and then to one another.
We may well serve Him who became a servant for us, Phil. ii. 6–9.
To serve Christ is man's most blessed freedom.
Acceptable to God. Well pleasing to Him. The true worshipper, Phil. iii. 3.
Those most pleasing to God who are best pleased with Christ.
To serve the Son faithfully is to be acceptable to the Father, Ps. ii. 10.
To be acceptable in duties we must serve Christ in them.
Approved of men. Men in general; good men in particular.
In these things men will find nothing to condemn.
A natural light and conscience in men to approve the good.
Consistent Christians gain even the testimony of the world.
The true service of Christ profitable to society.
Believers to seek—1. To please God; 2. To be approved of men.
Men's approbation desirable—1. For their own sakes;
2. For the sake of the Master whom we serve;
3. For our own personal comfort and influence.
To please God the surest way to be approved of men.
Persons and things acceptable to God should be approved by us.

Ἐν τούτοις. Codd. Sin., Vat., and Alex. have ἐν τούτῳ, in these things, *i.e.*, righteousness, &c. *Calv.* In this, *i.e.*, eating or not eating. *Beng.* In these marks of the Christian life. *De Wette.* In respect to these things. *Stuart.* Cultivating Christian graces and enjoying Christian blessings. *Brown.* In this threefold life. *D. Brown.*— Εὐάρεστος τ. Θεῷ, acceptable to God, the things being required by Him. *Theod.*— Δόκιμος τ. ἀνθρώποις, approved of men; is profitable to them. *Theod.* Affords them a good example. *Tol.* Commends himself to their sincere judgment. *Calv.* Approved of good men. *Henry.* Wise, charitable, and good men. *Burkitt.* Well spoken of by men for such a demeanour. *Stuart.* Men constrained to approve. *D. Brown.* Saying of the Rabbies: 'He who conscientiously observes the law, is acceptable to God and approved of men.' *Schöttgen.* Heb. פָּקִיד, 'refined,' applied to the precious metals, 1 Chron. xxviii. 18; xxix. 4; so מְצָרֵף, 2 Chron. ix. 17; 1 Kings x. 18; עֹבֵר כֶּסֶף, ἀργυρίου δοκίμου, 'current' money, Gen. xxiii. 16, LXX.

---

19. *Let us therefore follow after the things that make for peace, and things whereby one may edify another.*

Follow after. Not merely wish for it and talk about it.
Peace with, and edification of, others to be earnestly pursued.

Things that make for peace. *Gr.*, Things of peace, or belonging to it.

Not only peace itself, but the things that lead to it.
The end to be sought by a diligent attention to the means.
Dispositions and conduct tending to unite brethren in holy love.
Three things make for peace—1. Humility; 2. Meekness; 3. Self-denial.
If we cannot make peace we can follow what makes for it.
Things calculated to break peace to be carefully avoided.

Peace. Especially with and among the brethren, Mark ix. 50; 2 Cor. xiii. 11.
Peace also with men in general, Heb. xii. 14.
But not at the expense of truth or salvation, Gal. ii. 5.
Contendings for the truth should aim at peace and edifying.
The sword not to be separated from the trowel, Neh. iv. 17.
The Gospel often an occasion of dispeace, Matt. x. 34–36.
The cause in man's unrenewed nature which hates the truth.

Things wherewith one may edify another. *Gr.*, Things of mutual edification, or of building up in respect to each other, 1 Cor. xiv. 12.

Promote the advancement and perfection of the whole body.
The church and each individual believer a building, 1 Cor. iii. 9.
Others' growth and stability to be sought as well as our own.
"Am I my brother's keeper?" the language of the first murderer.
Believers to live not only peaceably but profitably.
Peace and mutual edification closely connected.
Want of peace one of the greatest hindrances to edification.
Peace opposed to contention; edification to offence.
Things often against peace because not for edification.
Believers may especially edify one another—
1. By their spirit; 2. By their converse; 3. By their life.
No brother so strong as not to need edification;
None so weak as not to be able to impart it.
The Spirit works in each to the edifying of the rest, 1 Cor. xii. 7.
In edifying another we are edifying ourselves.

Διωκωμεν, let us pursue. Codd. Sin., Vat., and Alex. have διωκομεν, we pursue.— Τα της ειρηνης, things of peace; a periphrasis for τα ειρηνικα, or for the simple ειρηνη. *Stuart.*—Τα τ. οικοδομης (οικος, a house, and δεμω, to build) της εις αλληλους, mutual edification. *Beza, Pisc., Stuart.* The things of it. *D. Brown.*

20. *For meat destroy not the work of God. All things indeed are pure ; but it is evil for that man who eateth with offence.*

Meat. This or that kind of food. Flesh-meat here intended.
A very insignificant object. Fleshly gratification.
Trifles in themselves often serious in their effects.
What was said of "meat" may now be applied to *drink*.
Destroy. Pull down as a building. Satan's aim and work.
Mournful effects often from what in itself is not sin.
Still more from the real inconsistencies of Christians.
Divisions in the church destructive to the cause of Christ.
Bitter and needless controversies the bane of religion.
Work of God—1. In a brother's soul ; 2. In the church at large.
The weakest brother's spiritual life the work of God.
Men's creation God's work ; not less so their salvation.
In creation God made man after His own image.
In salvation He renews that image after being lost.
God's work in a soul contrasted with perishable meat.
Sad to prefer the gratification of our appetite to God's work.
That work promoted in a soul by edification, in a church by peace.
Progress of the Gospel interrupted by early controversies.
Same effect from contentions after the Reformation.
A united church would soon lead to a converted world.
God's work not destroyed absolutely or finally ; but—
1. May suffer for a time ; 2. But for God's purpose, be destroyed.
The church, as God's building, united by the bond of peace, Eph. iv. 3.
Pure. In themselves as creatures of God ; lawfully eaten.
No distinction of meats under the Gospel dispensation.
The ends of those legal distinctions already served, Heb. ix. 10, 11.
Designed for the time to point symbolically to moral distinctions.
Connected with typical sacrifices to be abolished.
Evil—1. Morally ; 2. In its effects. *Gr.*, "Evil to the man."
Things lawful in themselves may be unlawful in their use.
Things harmless in themselves often baneful in their circumstances.
Eateth, *i.e.*, meat of any kind ; especially those in question.
The same principle applicable to drinking, dressing, &c.
With offence—1. As the effect of offence ; 2. So as to cause offence.
Sinful to do what we believe unlawful in imitation of others.
Equally sinful to do what we believe will have this effect.
The reproof chiefly directed against the authors of offence.

'Ενεκεν βρωματος, for the sake of meat. *D. Brown.*—Καταλυε (κατα, down, and λυω, to loose), pull down, Acts vi 14; Gal. ii. 18; 2 Cor. v. 1; contrasted with οἰκοδομη, building up; the verb accommodated to the figurative expression ἐργον Θεου. *Stuart.* Undo. *Ellicot.* Incipient destruction. *D. Brown.* Cod. Sin. has ἀπολλυε.—'Εργον τ. Θ., work of God; faith of a fellow Christian. *Theod.* The kingdom of God. *Calv.* A weak brother. *Wells.* Christian converts. *Whitby.* Progress of the Gospel; soul of a Christian brother. *A. Clarke.* A Christian. *Stuart.* The Christian life planted under God's co-operation. *De Wette, Alford.* Peace and edification. *Cobbin.* Work of grace in the soul. *Barth.* Christian personality, or status of the believer. *Meyer.* A converted man. *D. Brown.*—Καθαρα, clean; allusion to meats. *Wells.* A various reading in Cod. Sin. adds τοις καθαροις, 'to the pure.' —Κακον, evil, *i.e.*, hurtful, destructive. *Chrys., Theoph.* Morally wrong. *De Wette.* Evil is the meat; or, everything is evil; or, it is an evil thing. *Stuart.* There is criminality in the man. *D. Brown.*—Δια προσκομματος, through offence, *i.e.*, the weak scrupulous Jewish Christians. *Chrys., Theoph., Haldane. Barth.* While giving offence, *i.e.*, the strong. *Theod., Calv., Vat., Est., Grot., Beng., Mackn., De Wette, Alford, Brown.* So as to offend and endanger others. *Burkitt.* So as to stumble a weak brother. *D. Brown.* Δια with a genitive often — with, as in chap. ii. 27; iv. 11; 2 Cor. v. 10; 1 John v. 6. Often designates the *manner* in which a thing is done, as in Luke viii. 4; Acts xv. 27; 2 Cor. x. 11; Heb. xiii. 22. *Stuart.* Προσκομμα = ζημια, βλαβη. *Hes.*

---

21. *It is good neither to eat flesh nor drink wine, nor anything whereby thy brother stumbleth, or is offended, or is made weak.*

Good. Morally; according to charity or love, ver. 15.
Paul's own resolution and practice, 1 Cor. viii. 13.
Eat flesh. The thing which gave occasion to these remarks.
Not absolutely necessary. Other kinds of food to live upon.
Permission to eat flesh only expressly given after the Flood.
Fruits originally man's sustenance in Paradise.
To eat flesh a matter of liberty, not necessity.
Daniel and his brethren preferred pulse and a good conscience.
Their physical condition better than theirs who fed on royal dainties.
Drink wine. Wine a common beverage in the South and East.
Lawful in itself, but may be unlawful in its use.
Held unlawful by the Jews if brought from an idol's temple.
The case with much of the flesh and wine used in Pagan lands.
Water the ordinary beverage of the Jews, John iv. 6, 7.
The usual drink also of the Egyptians, Exod. vii. 17, 19.
Vinegar, a drink made from pure wine, also used, Num. vi. 3.
Used at meals with vegetables or bread, Ruth ii. 14.
Used also by Roman soldiers, and given to Christ, Matt. xxvii. 48.
Timothy for a time a constant water-drinker, 1 Tim. v. 23.

CHAP. XIV.]   ST. PAUL'S EPISTLE TO THE ROMANS.   259

Nazarites and Rechabites refrained from wine, Num. vi. 3; Jer. xxxv. 1, &c.
The sect of the Essenes abstained both from wine and flesh.
Nor anything. Christian charity to be unlimited, 1 Cor. viii. 13.
Christ's example to be followed by His members, 1 John iii. 16.
Life itself, if necessary, to be sacrificed for the brethren.
Stumbleth. Is staggered, or put in danger of falling.
Receives hurt, though not yet actually made to fall.
Offended. *Gr.*, Tripped up; made actually to fall into sin.
Is led to do what conscience forbids. Receives injurious prejudice.
Made weak. Or, is weak. Disturbed with doubts. Is weakened—
1. In his graces; 2. In his comforts; 3. In his convictions.
An aggravated sin to make the weak still weaker.
Different degrees and forms of spiritual damage.
Each influenced more or less by the conduct of another.
An insensible influence constantly exercised for good or evil.

Μηδὲ ἐν ᾧ, nor [to eat or drink] anything by which, &c. *Calv.*, *Haldane.* Nor [to do] anything. *Beng.*, *Mackn.*, *Stuart*, *Con. & Hows.*, *D. Brown.* Ἐν ᾧ, whereby. *Stuart.* Wherein. *D. Brown.*—Προσκόπτει (Cod. Sin. has λυπεῖται, is grieved or injured). *Lit.*, strikes against (impingit). *Beza*, *Pisc.*, *Pag.* Falls. *Calv.* Is offended (offenditur). *Vulg.*, *Tol.* Strikes against, and is wounded by imitating you. *Beng.* Stumbles without falling. *Haldane.* Is perplexed so as to be hindered from making due progress in the divine life. *A. Clarke.* Stumbles. *Stuart*, *D. Brown.*—Σκανδαλίζεται (this with ἢ ἀσθενεῖ, omitted in Codd. Sin. and Alex., as also in the Syr., Arab., Copt., and Æth. versions, and in *Or.*, *Ruf.*, and *Aug.*; regarded by some critics (Mill and Koppe) to be a gloss or repetition of προσκόπτει, and by Griesbach as dubious), is offended (offenditur). *Beza*, *Calv.*, *Pisc.*, *Pag.* His conscience shaken with serious perturbation. *Calv.* Is scandalised, so as to abandon Christianity. *Tol.* Made to stumble. *Schött.* Tripped up or impeded, shocked at your conduct. *Beng.* Is made totally to apostatize. *A. Clarke.* Has ground of offence. *Stuart.* Stumbles so as to fall. *Haldane.* Be obstructed in his Christian course. *D. Brown.*—Ἀσθενεῖ, is made weak (infirmatur). *Vulg.*, *Calv.*, *Stuart.* Is weak. *Est.*, *Beza*, *Pisc.*, *Pag.*, *D. Brown.* Whose conscience is thrown into some trepidation. *Calv.* Is disturbed with doubts and temptations. *Tol.* = בְּוּ, in LXX.; stumbles, doubts. *Grot.* Hesitates what to do. *Beng.* Is without power sufficiently to discriminate between what is lawful and unlawful; comes under the dominion of an erroneous conscience. *A. Clarke.* Ἀσθενεῖ = to render incompetent, *i.e.*, to walk safely or securely. *Stuart.* Whereby he is made to vacillate in his convictions. *De Wette.* Wherein he continues weak; unable wholly to disregard the example, and yet unprepared to follow it. *D. Brown.* Each term intentionally weaker than the preceding. *Calv.*, *D. Brown.* Three forms of spiritual damage, corresponding with the three blessings in ver. 17, which are prejudiced by them. *Beng.*, *Brown.*

22. *Hast thou faith? Have it to thyself before God. Happy is he that condemneth not himself in that thing which he alloweth.*

Thou. Emphatic. Addressed to the strong. The other lacks it.
Faith. Persuasion as to the lawfulness of a thing, as ver. 5. Here especially as to the distinction of meats, days, &c., ver. 6. Conviction grounded on the word of God a blessing. Faith that saves the soul informs and confirms the conscience. Faith gives—1. A foundation for hope; 2. A rule for daily life.
Have it. Hold it fast; enjoy and exercise it.
To thyself. For your own comfort and satisfaction; but—
1. Do not injure another by the use or display of it;
2. Do not attempt to impose it on your brother.
Before God. As between God and yourself, and as in His sight. Let your persuasion be grounded on the word of God. Act conscientiously in respect to your views of liberty. So use your liberty as not thereby to sin against God. " Whether ye eat or drink, do all to the glory of God," 1 Cor. x. 31.
Happy—1. In the approval of God and his own conscience;
2. In freedom from disquieting doubts as to what he does. The conscientious Christian happy both here and hereafter.
Condemneth not himself—1. Is free from doubts and scruples;
2. Acts in such a way that he cannot condemn himself. Happiness to have an enlightened and settled judgment; A still greater happiness to act according to that judgment; The greatest of all, to use our liberty so as to further others' good.
Alloweth. As a thing which he deems it right to do, 1 Cor. xvi. 3.
Gr., proves, or approves after examination, chap. ii. 18; Phil. i. 10.
Happy—1. To do a lawful thing in a lawful manner;
2. To act according to the dictate of an enlightened conscience. Doubts as to our actions indicate weakness or want of knowledge. The cause of frequent suffering to tender consciences. Miserable to approve one thing and practise another.

Συ πιστιν ἔχεις (Codd. Sin., Vat., and Alex. have συ πιστιν ἥν ἔχεις, thou, the faith which thou hast), hast thou faith? *Chrys., Pisc., Calv., Grot.* Thou hast faith. *Beza, Pag., Taylor.* Πιστιν, firm persuasion. *Beza, Par., Vor., Calv., Grot., Flatt.* Faith in a higher exercise, just persuasion as to the indifference of these things. *Doddr.* Persuasion as to the equality of meats. *Or., Beng., Whitby, Stuart, Haldane.* Right persuasion. *Taylor.* Belief as to the point in question. *Brown.* Faith on such matters. *D. Brown.* Thou knowest what thou shouldst believe. *Knapp.* Faith in Christ in whom the law is kept. *Or., Theod.*—Ἔχε, hold fast; forming, with ἔχεις, an *anadiplosis*, a word repeated with a different meaning. *Taylor.*—Κατα σεαυτον, with thyself. *Calv.* In respect to thyself. *Taylor.* As to thyself. *Boothr., Brown.* Within thy own breast. *D. Brown.* For thy own comfort. *Con. & Hows.* In thy own heart. *De Wette.* Let it be enough to regulate your conduct in private. *Stuart.* Make no display of it. *Barth.* Do not let your faith in Christ bring detriment to your neighbour. *Theod.*—'Ενώπιον τ. Θεοῦ (omitted in Cod. Sin.), before God; let your own consciousness of it suffice. *Chrys.* Be content with the tranquillity of conscience before God. *Calv.* Use it betwixt God and yourself, but not always before men, when in danger of hurting them. *Ham.* In the sight of God. *Taylor.* Not exercising it before men so as to give offence. *Boothr.* As seen only by the eye of God. *Stuart.* Without acting upon it. *De Wette.* Rejoice before God in the privilege, but do not hurt a brother by its exercise. *Hald.* As under God's eye. *Brown.* When your relation to God is considered, not your relation to others. *Nielson.* The conviction to be formed in the sight of God. *D. Brown.*—Μακάριος, blessed beatus'. *Pag., Pisc., Beza.* Has peace in his conscience. *Stuart.*—'Ο μὴ κρίνων ἑαυτὸν, who does not judge himself. *Vulg., Beng.* Doubt, or make distinctions. *Theod.* Does not condemn himself. *Pag., Pisc., Beza, Mart., Diod., Stolz, De Wette.* Does not judge himself,—is not conscious of evil. *Calv.* Does not make himself condemnable. *Par.* Judge himself erroneously, as if he did right. *Tol.* Whom his conscience does not condemn. *Eras., Vat.* Is free from the reproaches and even suspicions of his conscience. *Doddr.* Whose conscience does not upbraid and accuse him. *A. Clarke.* Who so uses his Christian liberty as not to bring on himself condemnation and blame by the abuse of it. *Stuart.* Has not to reproach himself. *Van Ess.* Who has no scruples about the lawfulness of what he does. *Alford, D. Brown.* Implies a firm, clear faith. *Ellicot.*—'Εν ᾧ δοκιμάζει, in what he proves (probat). *Vulg.* Approves. *Pag., Pisc., Beza, Mart.* Practically approves,—chooses to do and actually does. *Eras., Tir.* ' Examines. *Calv.* Prefers. *Grot., Flatt.* Has settled or decided. *Dick.* Discerns. *Diod.* Makes distinctions. *Syr., Trem.* Who does not eat in order not to give offence, though he knows it to be lawful. *Cas.* Spoken in reference to the strong. *Tol.* To the weak who acts against his conscience. *Est., Tir.* A non-accusing conscience only valuable after due examination of one's actions *Calv.* Κρίνω (to judge, question, doubt, condemn), and δοκιμάζω (to approve), finely express in their combination the doubting conscience. *Beng.* Δοκιμάζει, allows by his passions. *A. Clarke.* By his judgment. *Con. & Hows.* 'Εν ᾧ δοκ., in that which he chooses. *Barth.* Considers right. *De Wette.* Approves, justifies. *Rückert.* About things in which he allows himself. *Alford.* Which he allows himself to do. *D. Brown, Ellicot.*

---

23. *And he that doubteth is damned if he eat, because he eateth not of faith: for whatsoever is not of faith is sin.*

Doubteth—1. Regarding some meats as lawful and others not; 2. Doubting as to whether this or that is lawful to be eaten. Allusion to the weak. The opposite of having faith, see chap. ii. 22.
Damned. *Gr.*, Has been judged or condemned already in the act. Self-condemned as doing what he does not know to be right. No reference to eternal damnation, except as all sin deserves it.
Eat, viz., That about whose lawfulness he doubts.
Sinful to act in the face of *doubts*, much more of *conviction*.
Acts lawful in themselves become unlawful to the doubter.
Sinful to act *once* against doubts, much more *habitually*.

Faith. Conviction of its being right and pleasing to God. To act without such conviction is to make light of sin. **Whatsoever is not of faith.** Grounded on conviction. Believers only to think and act in the light of truth. Nothing to be done while its lawfulness is doubted. **Is sin.** To the individual, even though not so in itself. The thing may, so far as the doubter knows, be a sin. To act without conviction indicates indifference to sin. To be indifferent as to sin is sin itself. Every *appearance* of evil to be abstained from, 1 Thess. v. 22.

'Ο δε διακρινομενος, he who distinguishes (discernit). *Vulg.* Is divided in his judgment (dijudicat). *Eras., Calv.* Discusses with himself *Beza.* Is in two opinions (ambigit). *Pag., Pisc.* Doubts. *Luth., Grot.* Hesitates. *Vat., Eras.* Stands in doubt. *Diod.* Has scruples. *Mart., Alf.* Makes a difference between one sort of food and another. *Doddr.* Doubts as to whether it is right to eat. *Hald.* The opposite of faith. *Brown.* The sense of 'putting a difference' given to the active verb. *Est.* Expresses an uncertain and vacillating judgment. *Calv.*—Κατακεκριται, has been condemned; or, as Gal. ii. 11, is to be condemned. *Beng.* Is worthy of condemnation. *Stuart.* Self-condemned in the act itself. *Meyer.* Smitten and judged with the very act. *Lange.* Condemned by his conscience, his brethren, and God; but without reference to eternal damnation. *Brown.*—'Εκ πιστεως, from a persuasion of its lawfulness. *Chrys., Cas., Calv.* Approval of conscience. *Vat., Grot.* Moral conviction. *De Wette.* Conviction of its lawfulness. *Stuart.* Faith that he may eat. *Con. & Hows.* Conviction of its being right. *Barth, Brown.* Persuasion of rectitude grounded on and consistent with the life of faith. *Alford.* Christian believing disposition, in so far as it submits undoubtingly to the recognised will of God. *Nielson.* Christian saving faith. *Aug.* Faith in general; or faith in Christian doctrine in opposition to heresy. *Origen.*—'Αμαρτια εστιν, is sin : he eats sinfully because he eats doubtfully. *Bp. Hall.* Codex Bezæ adds at Luke vi. 4: 'As Jesus passed by, he saw a man ploughing in a field on the Sabbath day, and said, If thou knowest what thou doest, happy art thou ; if not, thou art accursed as a transgressor of the law.' *Ols.* Cod. Alex. and others, as well as some ancient versions (Arabic, later Syriac, and Sclavonic), and some Fathers (Cyril, Chrys., Theod., Œcum., Theoph., &c.), place the three last verses of the epistle at the end of this chapter. Their place here approved by Ham., Grot., Griesb., and others ; but opposed by Beza. who says, 'Marcion ends the epistle here, by whose fraud the difference occurs.' External grounds favour their place at the end of the epistle. *Thol., De Wette.*

CHAPTER XV.

1. *We then that are strong ought to bear the infirmities of the weak, and not to please ourselves.*

We. Probably the greater part of the Gentile Christians. Paul includes himself—1. As a believer; 2. As an apostle.

His principles on the subject in question those of the strong.
Then. *Gr.*, However. The weak in danger, but we ought to help.
Strong. Having an enlightened conviction as to meats, days, &c.
To know God's mind as revealed in the word is to be strong, 1 John ii. 14.
The really strong not always those of most vigorous intellect.
Most talented Christians may yet be weak in the things of God.
Bear. *Gr.*, Carry; so Gal. vi. 2. Bear each others' burdens.
The weak not to be depreciated, but borne with and helped.
Metaphor from travellers. The weak waited for and assisted.
Unencumbered pilgrims to help forward the weak and burdened.
Meekness and love the Christian's precious ornaments, 1 Pet. iii. 4.
Infirmities. Doubts and scruples of the less enlightened.
Mistaken views, and the conduct arising out of them.
Practical inconveniences from these to themselves and others.
The law of Moses a burden unable to be borne, Acts xv. 10.
Paul, here as elsewhere, an example of his own teaching, 1 Cor. ix. 22; x. 33.
Please ourselves—1. Consult our own pleasure and convenience; 2. Act according to our own views and inclinations.
Self-denial the first lesson in the school of Christ, Matt. xvi. 24.
Unchristian to act without regard to our neighbour's profit.
He who seeks to please himself cares little about profiting others.

'Οφείλομεν, we ought; emphatic,—we are bound as by a debt, viz., through the gracious revelation of salvation. *Nielson.* Allusion perhaps to xiii. 8, μηδενι μηδεν ὀφείλετε, ' owe no man anything, but to love,' &c.—Δε, adversative,—but. *Stuart.* —Οἱ δυνατοι, the more strong. *Pag*, *Pisc.*, *Beza*. Strong in faith and knowledge. *Tol.*, *Est.* = Οἱ πνευματικοι, the spiritual, Gal. vi. 1. *Beng.* Who have greater strength. *Schött.* Who have knowledge. *De Wette.* Knowing the mind of God as revealed in the Scriptures, that there is no longer any distinction as to meats. *Hald.* Who have no scruples about meats and drinks, &c. *Stuart*. Strong on such points as have been discussed. *D. Brown.*—Ἀσθενήματα, weaknesses (imbecillitates). *Pag*, *Pisc.*, *Beza.* Infirmities. *Grot*, *Vat.* Errors, ignorances in things indifferent. *Vor.* Things done in ignorance, though annoying to us. *Tol.* Scruples. *Beng.*, *Stuart.* Mistaken views and modes of conduct arising out of them. *Brown.*—Βασταζειν, to carry. *Pag.*, *Pisc.*, *Beza.* So Matt. iii. 11.—To bear with. *Grot.*, *Stuart.* So Rev. ii. 2, 3. Gently to instruct and strengthen. *Eras.*—Ἀρεσκειν, to please. *Pisc.* Indulge. *Pag.*, *Beza.* Do what is agreeable. *Grot.* Study to please. *Beng.* Act in a way merely to gratify our own views and inclinations. *Stuart.* Without considering how our conduct may affect others. *D. Brown.*

---

2. *Let every one of us please his neighbour for his good to edification.*

Every one of us. Takes both parties together and includes himself.

Please. Avoid whatever may give pain or offence.
Believers to aim at pleasing each other, not themselves.
The only way to benefit may be to please, 1 Cor. x. 33.
Christianity softens and meekens the spirit.
Renders us complaisant and obliging to others.
Selfishness and self-pleasing the antipodes of true religion.
For his good. *Gr.,* For good. The object and limit of the pleasing.
Please others not to obtain their praise, but promote their benefit.
Our duty to please subordinate to that of doing good.
Possible to please to the hurt both of others and ourselves.
To edification. To build him up in faith and holiness.
The person to be pleased already a brother in Christ.
The kind of good to be specially sought, spiritual improvement.
The strong to please the weak, not—1. By adopting his views;
Nor 2. By encouraging him in his prejudices; but—
3. By seeking to build him up in faith and knowledge.
Forbearance and love may lead to clearer views of truth.
No part of a servant of Christ merely to seek to please, Gal. i. 10.
To seek to please for good to edification is to follow the Master.
To please is Christ-like as a means, unlawful as an end.
A preacher to seek to please, but only that he may profit.
A pleasing preacher not always a profitable one.
To please may be to injure, to profit may be to offend.
Paul sought to please, 1 Cor. x. 33; yet no man-pleaser, Gal. i. 10.

'Αρεσκετω, let [each] please; act so as to please. *Stuart.* Lay himself out to please. *D. Brown.*—Εἰς τὸ ἀγαθόν (omitted in Cod. Sin.), unto good. In respect to that which is good. *Stuart.* Not for mere gratification, but for his good. *D. Brown.*—Πρὸς οἰκοδομήν, to edification. Εἰς, indicates internal end in respect to God, πρός, external in respect to our neighbour; εἰς, the ulterior end, πρός, the nearer or proximate. 'Αγαθόν, the genus, οἰκοδομή, the species; ἀγαθόν, the end, οἰκοδ., the means.

---

3. *For even Christ pleased not Himself; but, as it is written, The reproaches of them that reproached thee fell on me.*

Even Christ. His example ever exhibited, 2 Cor. viii. 9; Eph. v. 2, 25; Phil. ii. 5.
Imitation of Christ makes a trifle the highest virtue.
Christ the true and only strong one, Rom. v. 6; Luke xi. 22.
Pleased not Himself. Consulted not His own ease and comfort.
Humbled Himself and took the form of a servant, Phil. ii. 6.

Though rich, for our sakes became poor, 2 Cor. viii. 9; Matt. viii. 20.
Self-denyingly bore the infirmities of the weak, Matt. viii. 17; xvii. 17.
Condescended to the meanest capacities, Mark iv. 33; John xvi. 2.
Written. ‘Ps. lxix. 9. Psalms and Old Testament Scriptures full of Christ.
This psalm generally applied by the Jews to the Messiah.
Reproaches. The part of man's fallen nature to reproach God.
Adam in the garden, Gen. iii. 12; Israel in the desert, Exod. xvi. 3.
Sinners reproach God as if He were the author—
1. Of their sufferings; 2. Of their sins.
Fell on me—1. As partaking of them with the Father, John xv. 23, 24.
2. As enduring their punishment in the sinner's room.
The reproach of the Father in the Old Testament falls on the Son in the New.
Christ suffered the Father's reproach as—1. Revealing the Father; 2. Doing His will; 3. Coming as His servant.
Reproach no small part of the Saviour's suffering, Ps. lxix. 20.
Embittered His last hours on the cross, Matt. xxvii. 38–44.
Reproach against God was Christ's affliction, and should be ours.
Christ bore the Father's reproach, and we should bear His, Heb. xiii. 13.
Christ bore the reproaches of the wicked; we may well bear the infirmities of the weak.

Οὐχ ἑαυτῷ ἤρεσεν, pleased not Himself. Did not consider His own interests, but ours. *Chrys.* Bare others' burdens, which He did for the sake of God and men; the second member omitted for brevity. *Tol., Grot.* Had not respect merely to His own pleasure or pain, convenience or inconvenience. *Stuart.* Did not live to please Himself. *D. Brown.*—Οἱ ὀνειδισμοί, the reproaches (convitia). *Pag., Pisc., Beza* (opprobria), *Eras., Men.* Accursed deeds, *Tir.* Blasphemies. *Par.* All our sins. *Men., Par.* Outrages. *Mar., Diod.* Not only their insults, but the punishment due to them. *A. Clarke.*—Τῶν ὀνειδιζόντων σε, of them who reproach thee; the Father as well as Christ suffered reproach. *Chrys.*—Ἐπέπεσον ἐπ' ἐμέ, fell on me; affected me as if done against me. *Men., Tir.* I made satisfaction to thee for them that reproached thee. *Vat.* Bore the punishment of those reproaches in my flesh. *Tol.* Grieved as much as if I had endured them myself. *Calv.* The whole of the passage referred to. *Beng.* The general sentiment accommodated to a particular case; Christ suffered reproaches rather than desist from His beneficence towards others. *Stuart.* Suffered reproaches for others. *Cobbin.*

4. *For whatsoever things were written aforetime were written for our learning, that we through patience and comfort of the Scriptures might have hope.*

For. Shows the ground for the quotation just made.
Indicates the proper and legitimate use of Old Testament Scripture.
Old Testament Scriptures written for New Testament times.
Designed for the use of the Gentiles as well as the Jews.
Whatsoever things. Precepts, promises, threatenings, prayers.
Experience of Christ and Old Testament saints recorded for our benefit.
Written. Holy men of God not only spoke but wrote God's will.
Directed by the Holy Ghost what to write as well as what to speak.
Precious blessing to have a divine revelation in a written form.
Aforetime. Before the New Testament dispensation.
Old Testament Scripture written with a view to the future.
Pointed to Christ as the Head, and believers as the members.
Our learning. Instruction. Old Testament Scripture written for New Testament disciples.
The best learning that which is derived from the Scriptures.
Patience—1. Perseverance in faith and holiness;
2. Patient endurance of suffering and wrong;
3. Gentle forbearance with prejudice and ignorance.
Required both in regard to those without and those within.
Exemplified in the Saviour's life and suffering, Heb. xii. 2; Matt. xvii. 17.
Also in the Old Testament saints, *e.g.*, Job, Jas. v. 11; Moses, Num. xii. 3; David, 2 Sam. xvi. 5, &c.
Old Testament written to train New Testament saints to patience.
Blessed learning that has patience for its fruit.
Comfort—1. Consolation, 2 Cor. i. 4-7; 2. Exhortation, 1 Cor. xiv. 3.
Powerful, persuasive, and consolatory instruction.
The Bible the true and inexhaustible source of comfort.
The Old Testament such; still more with the New added.
Old Testament Scripture written for the comfort of New Testament believers.
Patience and comfort suppose trial and affliction.
Scriptures. Inspired writings; here especially the Old Testament.
God's word called scriptures or writings by excellence.
Lit., "The writings;" none to be compared to them, see chap. i. 2.
Prophetical writings called by Daniel "the books," Dan. ix. 2.

Same name applied by Alexandrian Jews to the Old Testament generally.
Hence the name still in use, the Bible or Book, *lit.*, " the books."
Given to both Old and New Testament since the fifth century.
Have. Or, hold fast, as xiv. 22 ; Heb. iii. 6 ; vi. 11 ; 1 Tim. iii. 9. 2 Tim. i. 13.
Hope. A leading part of a believer's experience, chap. v. 2, 4, 5 ; viii. 24.
Hope in Christ, 1 Cor. xv. 19 ; hope of the inheritance, 1 Pet. i. 3 ; Rom. viii. 25.
Strengthened and established by patience and perseverance, chap. v. 4.
Hope and patience mutually beget each other.
Christian hope is—1. To be held fast ; 2. To be increased.
Scriptures to be read in order to beget, strengthen, and increase it.
Christ and the promises held forth in them as the ground of hope.

Προεγραφη (προ and γραφω), were written beforehand. Cod. Vat. has ἐγραφη, ἐγραφη παντα.—Διδασκαλιαν, instruction. *D. Brown.*—Της ὑπομενης, patience. *Calv.* Perseverance. *Beng., Reiche, De Wette, Brown.* Examples of patience exhibited in the Old Testament Scriptures. *A. Clarke.* Patience under suffering, or tolerance of prejudice and ignorance. *Stuart.* 'The patience,'—this, as well as the comfort, being that to be found in the Old Testament Scriptures. *Ellicot.* Patience, needed for forbearance with the weak, taught from the Scriptures. *D. Brown.* Τ. παρακλησεως (Codd. Sin., Vat., and Alex. have δια τ. π.), consolation ; more appropriate here than 'exhortation.' *Calv., Beng.* Comfort received from God by Old Testament saints. *A. Clarke.* Admonition, exhortation to acts of self-denial. *Stuart, Hald.* Consolation, especially that which sustained Christ as exhibited in the Scriptures. *D. Brown.*—Των γραφων, the Scriptures or writings. Αἱ βιβλοι, or more frequently τα βιβλια, the books (lit., papyrus-books), applied by the Jews of Alexandria to the collected books of the Old Testament. The use of the phrase ἡ παλαια διαθηκη, the old covenant or Testament (2 Cor. iii. 14), for the Law as read in the Synagogue, led gradually to the extension of the word to include the other books of the Jewish Scriptures. The inspired Christian writings came in like manner to be called the New Testament or covenant (ἡ καινη διαθηκη). The Latin term 'Novum Testamentum' first used by Tertullian, about 200 A D. For reading in the Synagogue, the Law was divided into fifty-four sections or Parashioth, a lesson being thus provided for each Sabbath in the Jewish Intercalary year The sections of the prophets called Haphtaroth. Since the ninth century, the larger sections have been divided into verses (Pesukim). This verse-division adopted by Stephens in his edition of the Vulgate in 1555, and appeared for the first time in English in the Geneva Bible of 1560. Transferred from thence into the Bishops' Bible of 1568, and the Authorised Version of 1611. This division first adopted in the New Testament in the edition published by Henry Stevens in 1551, and used for the English Version published in Geneva in 1560.—Ἐχωμεν, may have. *Fag.* Hold. *Pisc., Beza.* Obtain. *Stuart.* Cod. Vat. adds της παρακλησεως, hope ' of comfort.'

5. *Now the God of patience and consolation grant you to be like-minded one toward another according to Christ Jesus.*

God of patience. God the source of patience; His word the means.
True patience a plant not of nature but of grace.
All virtues and graces produced in us by the Holy Spirit.
God not only gives patience, but gives it abundantly.
Name of God taken from the graces which He inspires.
His titles often given from the matter in hand.
Consolation. Comfort, as in ver. 3; in the same sense as in 2 Cor. i. 4–7.
God the giver—1. Of all matured patience in the New Testament; 2. Of all prepared consolation in the Old.
Like-minded. One in sentiment and affection.
Patience and comfort connected with unity, Col. ii. 3.
The more of patience and comfort the more of love.
Unity of sentiment among believers progressive, Phil. iii. 15, 16.
Knowledge partial and imperfect on earth, 1 Cor. xiii. 12.
Real harmony more in unity of heart than sentiment.
Its true principle, love to Christ's people for Christ's sake.
Unity of sentiment desirable, unity of heart essential.
Forbearance in cases of difference a test of grace.
Christian like-mindedness the gift of God.
According to Christ Jesus—1. According to His will and precept; 2. In accordance with His spirit and example; 3. In the belief and maintenance of His truth.
Christ's example exhibited—1. As an argument; 2. A pattern.
A like-mindedness *against* Christ as well as according to Him.
Truth, then peace, Zech. viii. 19; first pure then peaceable, James iii. 17.
Christ himself the centre of true unity.
Paul's wonderful delicacy and tact in uniting parties.

Δῴη, a later form of 2d aorist optative for δοίη, not acknowledged by older grammarians. *Stuart.*—Τὸ αὐτὸ φρονεῖν, think the same thing. *Calv.* Think, or savour that very thing (id ipsum sapere). *Vulg.* Be affected in the same manner. *Beza.* With the same mind. *Pag., Pisc., Tol.* May have like affection. *Tir.* Grant you all that makes for mutual concord. *Grot.* To have the same mutual affection. *Raph., Doddr.* In matters of belief; practical unity of sentiment. *Stuart.* In will and affection. *Hald.* Of the same mind; unanimity. *D. Brown.*—Κατὰ Χρ. Ἰησ. (Codd. Sin. and Alex. have Ἰησ. Χρ.), according to Christ Jesus; His command. *Tir.* His doctrine. *Tol., Est., Vat.* His example. *Doddr., Raph., D. Brown, Hald.* His Spirit and religion. *Stuart.* His will and precept. *De Wette.* In Christ as the bond of unity. *Cal.* Such concord as is not opposed to Christian piety. *Grot.* Christ not only the example, but the motive and spring of the Christian mind. *Nielson.*

6. *That ye may with one mind and one mouth glorify God, even the Father of our Lord Jesus Christ.*

One mind. One accord, like the disciples at Jerusalem, Acts i. 14.
So on the day of Pentecost, Acts ii. 1; and afterwards, ver. 46; iv. 24; v. 12.
Indicates unity of sentiment, feeling, and purpose.
Such unity sometimes in a bad sense, Acts vii. 57; xviii. 12; xix. 29.
The expression used also in an indifferent sense, Acts xii. 20.
Harmony of hearts the soul and strength of united worship.
Inner unity consistent with external variety.
One mouth. Unity of worship and confession, as chap. x. 9, 10.
Unity of mind first, unity of mouth next as its effect.
Praise and prayer to be as from one heart and by one mouth.
Believers' converse to be rather on points of agreement than of difference.
Reference to the two different parties in the church at Rome.
Jews and Gentiles, weak and strong, to be united in affection and praise.
Glorify God—1. Show forth His perfections; 2. Promote His glory.
God to be glorified in every action of our lives, 1 Cor. x. 31.
Especially glorified in acts of worship, Rev. xv. 4; Ps. xcvi. 8, 9.
Glorified also in and by the unity of believers.
The harmonious praise of God the highest fruit of unity.
Even. Or, "The God and Father," &c., as 2 Cor. xi. 31; Eph. i. 3; 1 Pet. i. 3.
Father of our Lord. The special object of Gospel worship.
To be praised for His love in the gift of His dear Son.
God both the God and Father of Jesus Christ, Eph. i. 17; John xx. 17.
His God as to His humanity, His father as to His divinity.
Christ's double relationship to the Father for our sakes.
Our double relationship to the Father through Him.
God to be worshipped not merely as God, but as Christ's Father.
Otherwise the object of fear, not of fellowship.
God as the Father of Jesus Christ the author of our salvation.

'Ομοθυμαδον (ὁμος, one, united, and θυμος, mind). Union of mind or sentiment. *Stuart.* Accordance in affection and heart. *Haldane.*—'Ενι στοματι, with one mouth; probable reference to acts of public worship. *A. Clarke.*—Τον Θεον κ. Πατερα τ. Κ. ἡμων 'Ι. Χ., God and Father of our Lord Jesus Christ. *Tol., Ham.* God of the man Christ Jesus, Father of the Divine Word. *Est., Whitby.*

---

7. *Wherefore receive ye one another, as Christ also received us, to the glory of God.*

Wherefore—1. This being your duty ; 2. To show your unity.
Receive—1. Into your fellowship ; 2. Into your affection.
Receiving Christ in faith, receive His members in love.
Mutual kindness and forbearance the duty of Christians.
One another. Christians addressed ; Jewish and Gentile.
Difference of opinion to be no barrier to affection.
The weak to overcome their prejudice, the strong their pride.
As. Indicates—1. The manner ; 2. The reason, of the duty, Acts x. 47 ; xi. 17.
Christ also received us. To pardon and save, Luke xv. 2 ; Acts xi. 18.
Received us into His fellowship, His family, and His fold.
Whom Christ has received we may not reject.
The weakest believer received by Christ, chap. v. 6.
Receives those who trust in Him though with much error.
Receives weak and strong ; these therefore to receive each other.
Receives cordially and rejoicingly, Luke xv. 5.
Christ receives sinners, we may well receive saints.
To the glory of God. God's glory the end of our salvation.
Christ received sinners to manifest God's glory.
We are to do the same with saints, John xv. 8, 12.
God's glory the end of all Christ did and we are to do, John xvii. 4 ; 1 Cor. x. 31.
God glorified in Christ's humiliation and love to sinners.
Also in our forbearance and love to one another.
Believers, differing in many things, to be one in glorifying God.
Participation in God's glory the happy lot of believers, chap. v. 2.

Προσλαμβανεσθε, take to you *Pag., Pisc., Beza.* Relieve, support (sublevate). *Vat.* Kindly receive and cherish. *Men.* Aid, support, and instruct. *Est., Tol.* Embrace and succour. *Ham.* Receive into mutual love. *Wells.* Treat with brotherly kindness and affection. *Stuart.* Receive into fellowship. *Con. & Hows., Brown.* Receive and compassionate. *D. Brown.* Both Jewish and Gentile Christians addressed. *De Wette.* —Προσελαβετο, received us to Him. *Mart.* Into fellowship with Himself. *Lange.* Showed kindness. *Stuart.* Received though with much error. *Hald.* Cordially.

CHAP. XV.] ST. PAUL'S EPISTLE TO THE ROMANS. 271

Brown. Codd. Sin., Vat., and Alex. have ὑμας, 'you,' instead of ἡμας, 'us.'—Εἰς δόξαν Θεοῦ, to the glory of God; that God may be glorified in the unity, harmony, and love of believers. *Chrys., Eras., A. Clarke, Stuart, D. Brown.* That we might be made sharers of the divine glory. *Grot.* Into the glory of God. *Diod.* Into the enjoyment of the divine glory with Christ awaiting believers. *Thol., Lange.* For the glory of God. *Mart.* To the praise and glorifying of God. *Nielson.* To the manifestation of His glory. *Hald.* His glory the end of all Christ did on earth or does in heaven. *Brown.* God glorified in Christ's humiliation and in taking men into fellowship with Himself. *Dickson, Lange.*

---

8. *Now I say that Jesus Christ was a minister of the circumcision for the truth of God, to confirm the promises made unto the fathers.*

Now, I say. Redoubles his efforts to accomplish his object.
His aim to soften Jewish prejudices and unite parties in love.
Speaks now—1. To the favour of the weak; 2. The guidance of both.
Explains how Christ has received men, both Jews and Gentiles.
Jesus Christ. Jesus the name, Christ the surname.
Jesus indicates the person, Christ the office and destination.
"Jesus" first in addressing Jews, "Christ" in addressing Gentiles.
Minister. Christ a servant—1. To God; 2. To men, Matt. xii. 18; xx. 28.
Allusion to His personal ministry. Points to His humiliation.
Circumcision. Used—1. For the law; 2. For the Jewish people.
Christ made under the law, Gal. iv. 4; Matt. iii. 15; v. 17.
A Jew of the seed of Abraham, Matt. i. 1: John iv. 9; Rev. v. 5.
Ministered when on earth almost exclusively to the Jews, Matt. xv. 24.
Minister of the circumcision for the salvation of Jews, John iv. 22.
So called here—1. To exalt the covenant people to their true dignity;
2. To humble the pride of the strong, viz., the Gentiles.
Truth of God. His faithfulness in performing His promises.
Not because the Jews were worthy, but because He is faithful.
Confirm. Fulfil, as Deut. xxvii. 26; make sure, as 2 Pet. i. 19.
The best confirmation of promises is their fulfilment.
Promises. Made to the patriarchs concerning their seed.
Christ the central point of all the promises, 2 Cor. i. 20; Rev. xix. 10.
Promises are either general or special; here the latter.
Made to the fathers. *Gr.*, Of or belonging to the fathers.
The fathers of the Jewish people, Abraham, Isaac, and Jacob.

The Saviour promised to be of their seed, Gen. xxii. 18; xxvi. 4; xxviii. 14.
Jews the children of the covenant, Acts iii. 25; salvation of them, John iv. 20.
Christ and His benefits the children's bread, Matt. xv. 26.
Israel beloved for the fathers' sakes, Rom. xi. 28.

Λεγω, I say; further argument to show that Jewish and Gentile believers should bear with each other, as all redeemed by grace,—the Jew in fulfilment of God's promise, the Gentile in the exercise of His mercy. *Nielson.*—Δε, now; 'accuratius definit,'—inserted for more full and entire explanation. Codd. Sin., Vat., and Alex. have γαρ, for. 'For' the true reading. *D. Brown.*—'Ιησ. Χριστ. Some copies omit 'Ιησους; others have Χριστ. 'Ιης.,—preferred by *Bengel* as more suitable to the passage, the *office* being the main idea.—Διακονον, attendant or laborious servant, = שָׁמָשׁ, from the same root as שֶׁמֶשׁ (shemesh), the sun, who doth ' his daily stage of duty run.'—Περιτομης, of the circumcision; Christ ministered to the circumcision. *Arab.* Fulfilled the law. *Chrys.* The peculiar minister of the Jews. *Par., Grot., Vor.* Preached, taught, laboured for their salvation. *Men.* Was sent to them. *Calv.* Discharged His office for them. *Vat.* Subjected himself to circumcision and the law for their sakes. *Par.* First preached the New Testament to them. *Eras.* Ministered the circumcision, fulfilled it, as a servant does his master's will. *Dickson.* Confined His ministry to them in the days of His flesh. *A. Clarke.* Served the cause of divine truth among them. *Stuart.* The Father's servant for their salvation. *D. Brown.* Christ, while fulfilling the law, was the ministering attendant on the Jews. *Lange.*—Ὑπερ ᾰληθειας Θεου, on account of the truth of God; to fulfil it. *Calv.* To promote the interests of divine truth. *Stuart.* To fulfil the truth contained in the promises. *A. Clarke.* For the faithfulness of God. *Con. & Hows.* For the sake of God's truth. *Ellicot.* To make good His veracity towards His ancient people. *D. Brown.*—Εἰς το βεβαιωσαι τ. ἐπαγγελιας τ. πατερων, to confirm the promises of the fathers. *Calv., Pag., Eras., Beza.* To keep the promises and prove them, thus gaining a title to them; βεβαιω = to obtain the title in a purchase. *Strip.* To make them good. *Schütt.* Carry them into execution. *Stuart.* The Messianic promises made to the Fathers. *D. Brown.* Heb. הֵקִים, to confirm, fulfil, establish; as Ps. cxix. 38, 'establish (הָקֵם) thy word,' &c. 'My daughter, thy promise has been fulfilled' (נִבְּיָה, confirmed). *Talm. Sota.*

---

9. *And that the Gentiles might glorify God for His mercy; as it is written, For this cause I will confess to thee among the Gentiles, and sing unto thy name.*

Glorify God. Exalt, adore, magnify Him; show forth His glory. God's glory the end of Christ's work and the sinner's salvation.
Mercy. Gentiles had no promise to claim like the Jews. What was faithfulness to the Jews was mercy to the Gentiles. Christ's ministry confined to the Jews, but not God's mercy. The salvation of any sinner is mercy, that of some especially so. Faithfulness as well as mercy in the salvation of some. Some children saved in faithfulness to their parents.
Written. Ps. xviii. 49. David in the psalm a type of Christ.

Christ therefore the subject of the prophecy.
Foretold to be a Saviour to Gentiles as well as Jews.
Jews regarded the Psalms as prophetic of Messiah, Luke xx. 41, &c.; xxiv. 45.
Paul's plentiful quotation of the Old Testament Scriptures to be noted.
The sword of the Spirit is the Word of God, Eph. vi. 17; Heb. iv. 12.
Confess. Praise, acknowledge, give thanks.
The Gentiles confess to God in the Psalms of David.
Thus David still confesses to Him among the Gentiles.
Christ confessed to God in the person of David, His type;
Still confesses to Him in the person of His members.
Among the Gentiles. These therefore to be His true worshippers.
Believing Jews therefore cordially to unite with them.
The calling of them part of the promise to Abraham, Gen. xi. 3.
That promise repeated down to the last of the prophets, Mal. i. 11.
Gentiles, as such,—without incorporation with the Jews.
Sing. David and David's Lord do this among the Gentiles—
1. Virtually in the church on earth through David's Psalms.
2. Personally in the church in heaven, Rev. vii. 9, 10; xiv. 1–4.
The church to consist greatly of Gentile converts.
Singing a leading part of Christian worship, 1 Cor. xiv. 5; Eph. v. 19; Col. iii. 16.
Jews and Gentiles to unite in praising God for His mercy in Christ.
Redeeming love gives songs of praise for wails of woe.

'Εξομολογησομαι, I will confess. *Calv.* Celebrate. *Diod.* Celebrate thy praise. *Mart.* Will praise thee; like Heb. ידה. *Stuart.* Will glorify thee. *D. Brown.* Cod. Sin. adds Κυριος after ἐθνεσιν. The psalm applied by the Jews to the Messiah: 'King Messiah, whether He be among the living or the dead, His name is David.' R. Tanchuma said, 'I thus prove it, He showeth mercy to David and to his seed' (Ps. xviii. ult), *Jerus. Tal. Ber.* R. Huna said, Messiah is called David,—' He sheweth mercy to David,' &c. *Midr. Mishle.*—Ψαλω (ψαω, to touch, ψαλλω, to touch the strings, to play, to sing praise), I will sing. For Heb. אזמר, will sing with an instrument. *Beng.* רני, to sing, properly in rhythmical divisions; to play on a stringed instrument (ψαλλω). *Nork.* From ψαλλω, the LXX entitled David's psalms or praise-hymns ψαλμοι, 'psalms,' Heb. תהלים, 'praises.' The Christian obviously received the Psalter from the Jews not only as a constituent portion of the sacred volume of Holy Scripture, but also as the liturgical hymn-book which the Jewish church had regularly used in the Temple. *Dr Smith.* Singing praise one of the principal parts of worship in the Christian church from the earliest period (Col. iii. 16). Pliny (A.D. 130) states that the Christians met before sunrise on a stated day and sang a hymn to Christ as God. At first only David's psalms and inspired portions of Scripture sung. Uninspired hymns afterwards gradually introduced. The Doxology, Gloria Patri, &c., 'Glory be to the Father, and to the Son, and to the Holy Ghost, world without end, Amen,' in early use. To this the Western churches added in the sixth century, ' As it was in the beginning, is now, and ever shall be.' The Angels' Song, 'Gloria in Excelsis,' &c., 'Glory to God in the highest,' &c., also early used. So the Trisagion, ' Holy, holy, holy, Lord God of Sabaoth, heaven and earth are full of His glory ;' Mary's Song or the Magnificat ; the Songs of Moses, Anna, Habakkuk, the Three Children, Simeon, and Zecharias. Human compositions not at first used in all places in public worship. The Creed sung in many places. Hymns for public worship were composed by Ambrose of Milan ; Nicetius, a century later, author of the Te Deum, wrongly ascribed to Ambrose; Hilary of Poitiers ; Claudianus Mamertus ; Ephraim the Syrian ; Nepos and Athenagoras. The hymns or poems of Gregory Nazianzum, Paulinus, Prudentius, and Sedulius, not probably used in public worship. Sometimes the precentor sung alone, but generally joined by the people, at first in the last line, and afterwards responsively. Responsive singing introduced into the West by Ambrose, and into the East by Flavian of Antioch, or perhaps by Ignatius. Instrumental music introduced in the West only in the thirteenth century by Marinus Sanutus, A.D. 1290. Organs in private use four centuries earlier. Singing, in all the public services, alternated with reading. On Sundays and Festivals, practised also at the beginning and end of the service. At other times alternated with prayer. The people stood while singing. At first the singing very simple, differing little from reading. Gradually more music introduced, at first at Antioch, Constantinople, Milan, and Rome. *Baumgarten.*

---

10. *And again he saith, Rejoice, ye Gentiles, with His people.*

Saith. In Moses' prophetic song before his death, Deut. xxxii. 43. Refers to Christ's victories over His and His people's enemies. Understood by the Jews as pointing to the days of Messiah.
Rejoice. Redeeming mercy the foundation of lasting joy. A duty to rejoice when God calls us to do so. Believers to rejoice in the Lord always, Phil. iii. 1 ; iv. 4 ; To rejoice evermore, 1 Thess. v. 16 ; Eccles. ix. 7, 8. The grounds—1. What the Lord is; 2. What He has done ; 3. What He will yet do.
Gentiles. Gentiles to share in the joy of Christ's victory. Fellow-heirs and partakers of the promise in Christ, Eph. iii. 6. To unite with God's people in their songs of praise. Especially bound to rejoice at having long been outcasts.
With His people. Gentiles therefore to be in fellowship with them. Made fellow-citizens with the saints, Eph. ii. 19. Form the innumerable multitude before the throne, Rev. vii. 9. Beheld by John after the sealing of the tribes of Israel, Rev. vii. 4. A universal burst of praise to come from Jews and Gentiles. The Gospel therefore to be preached to all nations, Matt. xxviii. 19. Done probably more than ever in the present day, A.D. 1870. The Bible already translated into 183 languages and dialects.

Εὐφράνθητε ἔθνη μετα τ. λαου αὐτου, rejoice, nations, with His people ; according to the LXX, who seem to have read עִמּוֹ עַם. Heb. עַמּוֹ גּוֹיִם הַרְנִינוּ, *lit.*, sing, ye nations, His people ; therefore to be in fellowship with them. *Dickson.* Sing, O Gentiles, as His people; therefore to become such. Sing, O Gentiles, with His people ; ו or עַם omitted. *Grot.* Both Jews and Gentiles to rejoice together in God's salvation. *Eras., Vat., Est.* Imperative used in apostrophes for the indicative.—Λαου αὐτ., His people, *i.e.*, Israel. *D. Brown.* On Deut. xxxii. 12, it is said in Zohar: ' This shall take place in the days of Messiah, when there shall be impurity in Israel.'

---

11. *And again, Praise the Lord, all ye Gentiles ; and laud Him, all ye people.*

Again. Ps. cxvii. 1. Paul multiplies quotations from the Old Testament.
Truth to be exhibited to gainsayers in all its strength.
The wise householder brings out of his treasure things new and old.
The word of Christ to dwell richly in us, Col. iii. 16 ; Matt. xiii. 52.
Praise. True praise implies—1. Knowledge and understanding, Ps. xlvii. 7 ; 1 Cor xiv. 15 ;
2. Faith, Ps. cxvi. 10 ; 3. Love, Ps. cxviii. 1 ; 4. Life, Ps. cxv. 17.
The Gentiles, therefore, to praise, must be preached to.
Praise implies experience of pardoning mercy, Ps. cxvi. 1–19 ; cxvii. 2.
Praise an exercise of public worship, Ps. cxxxiv. 1–3 ; cxxxv. 1–3.
Gentiles therefore to be incorporated with the church.
Laud. Another expression for praise. All sorts of praise due to God :
Public and private ; individual and collective ; internal and external ; vocal and instrumental, Ps. cl. 3–5.
God to be praised to the best and utmost of our ability, Ps. xxxiii. 3.
All ye people. Not only some, but all nations and peoples.
The Gospel to be preached to every creature, Mark xvi. 15.
Believers to be gathered from north, south, east, and west, Luke xiii. 29.
Christ a ransom for all to be testified in due time, 1 Tim. ii. 6.
God's will that all should be saved and come to the knowledge of the truth, ver. 4.
Christ, when lifted up, to draw all men unto Him, John xii. 32.

Αἰνεῖτε, praise ; ἐπαινέσατε, praise after (ἐπι, upon or after, and αἰνέω). Επαινεω, used more of responsive singing. *Beng.* Αἰνεῖτε = Heb. הַלְלוּ ; ἐπαινέσατε αὐτον = שַׁבְּחוּהוּ, Ps. cxvii. 1. הָלַל (Gen. xii. 15) and שָׁבַח, used for both αἰνέω and ἐπαινέω by the LXX. Αἰνέω used also for הוֹדָה, בָּרַךְ, רָנַן, שׁוּר.

12. *And again, Esaias saith, There shall be a root of Jesse, and He that shall rise to reign over the Gentiles ; in Him shall the Gentiles trust.*

Again. Quotations accumulated for greater confirmation.
Truths likely to be controverted to be well supported from Scripture.
Esaias saith. Isa. xi. 10. Esaias the evangelical prophet ; see under Rom. ix. 27.
The prophecy understood by the Jews to relate to Messiah.
A root. *Gr.*, The Root. A root out of a dry ground, Isa. liii. 2.
A Rod out of the stem of Jesse, and a Branch out of his roots, Isa. xi. 1.
As the Root He must flourish, bloom, and bear fruit, Ps. cxxxii. 17.
Christ, as the Root, the source of all spiritual life, Gal. ii. 20.
Indicates the oneness between Christ and His members.
Jesse. The son of Obed and father of David, Ruth iv. 17.
Christ the Root of Jesse, or Root in Jesse's family, Matt. i. 16.
The Root as well as offspring of David, Jesse's son, Rev. xxii. 16.
As man, David's offspring ; as the God-man Mediator, his Root.
On Him hangs all the offspring and issue of His Father's house, Isa. xxii. 24.
Christ the everlasting Father of the saved family, Isa. ix. 6 ; Heb. ii. 13.
Rise—1. Out of the depressed family of David and Jesse, Luke ii. 4-12.
2. Out of a state of humiliation ; 3. Out of the grave, Ps. xvi. 10 ; Phil. ii. 7-10.
Reign. *Heb.*, Be for an ensign. Christ a Prince and Leader, Isa. ix. 6 ; lv. 4.
The true King of the Jews, John i. 49 ; Matt. ii. 2-6 ; xxi. 5 ; ix. 15; xxvii. 37.
The Prince of the kings of the earth, Rev. i. 5 ; King of kings, xix. 16.
Head over all to His church and people, Eph. i. 20-22.
His kingdom not of this present world, John xviii. 36.
Now exercised through—1. His Word ; 2. His Spirit ; 3. His providence.
His true subjects all who receive and obey Him, John i. 11-13.
Over the Gentiles. Gentiles as well as Jews to be His subjects.
Christ as an ensign the bond of all nations.
Jews and Gentiles united to Him are united to each other.
Christ to be honoured by all peoples as their King and Lord.

CHAP. XV.]   ST. PAUL'S EPISTLE TO THE ROMANS.   277

Trust. *Gr.*, Hope. Men without Christ also without hope, Eph. ii. 12.
Christ the common hope and trust of Jews and Gentiles.
No other name whereby men must be saved, Acts iv. 12.
Christ our hope, 1 Tim. i. 1. The anchor of our soul, Heb. vi. 19.
Heb., "Shall seek," repair to Him as their hope and refuge, Heb. vi. 18.

Ἐσται, there shall be. *Grot.*, &c. It shall come to pass; not connecting with ἡ ῥίζα, as its nominative. *Dickson, Vat., Est.*—Ἡ ῥίζα (from ῥέω, to flow, and ζάω, to live; that from which the life flows) τοῦ Ἰεσσαί, the root of Jesse [shall have a shoot]. *Dickson, Vat., Est.* There shall be the root of Jesse, *i.e.*, of Jesse's root shall continue. *Tol.* There shall be a shoot from the root of Jesse. *Grot., Calv., Pisc., Est.* A root from the stock of Jesse. *Doddr.* A King shall spring from the root of Jesse. *Whitby.* By synecdoche, ῥίζα = the tree which springs up from the root; 'it will come to pass that the heathen shall betake themselves to the Root of Jesse.' *Hengstenberg.* The root of Jesse; not from which Jesse sprung, but 'He who is sprung from Jesse,' *i.e.*, Jesse's son, David. *D. Brown.* Ῥίζα, by meton. = a shoot from a root, as נֵצֶר = יֶלֶד, a stem (κλάδος), hence offspring, Rev. xxii. 16. *Schött.*—Ὁ ἀνιστάμενος, who rises; Heb. עֹמֵד, אֲשֶׁר for which the LXX., whom Paul follows, probably read עֹמֵד. *Stuart.*—Ἄρχειν, to reign; Heb. נֵס, for an ensign or standard,—the sign of authority and command. *Grot.* Power of calling to war belongs to the prince alone. *Ham.* Christ compared to a standard around which the nations, hitherto far from salvation, should assemble; Jacob's prediction as to the obedience of the nations to Messiah being thus fulfilled. *Hengstenberg.*—Ἐθνῶν, of the Gentiles or nations. The so-called Apostolical Constitutions (perhaps written in the third century) give the following list of bishops ordained by the apostles and their coadjutors: Zacchæus, the publican, Bishop of Cæsarea; Cornelius, his successor, and Theophilus, the third in the same place; Euodius, of Antioch, ordained by Peter; Ignatius, of the same place, ordained by Paul; Annianus, of Alexandria, by Mark the Evangelist; Avilius, of the same place, by Luke; Linus, of Rome, by Paul; Clement, his successor, by Peter; Timothy, of Ephesus, by Paul; John of the same place, Aristo of Smyrna, Strataeus his successor, Aristo who succeeded him, Gaius of Pergamos, Demetrius of Philadelphia, all ordained by John; Lucius, of Cenchreæ, by Paul; Titus, of Crete; Dionysius, of Athens; Marones, of Tripolis in Phœnicia; Archippus, of Laodicæa in Phrygia; Philemon, of Colosse; Onesimus, his slave, of Beræa in Macedonia; Crescens, of the churches in Galatia; Aquila and Nicetes of the parishes in Asia; Crispus, of Ægina.—Ἐλπιοῦσιν, shall hope or trust. Heb. יִדְרֹשׁוּ, 'shall seek.' Implies a religious seeking of the Messiah, and the ascription to Him of more than human dignity; דרש = to seek for counsel, help, protection; to manifest reverence; to consult as an oracle. *Hengst.* The passage belongs to the section read in the Synagogues on the eighth day of the Passover, probably about the time when this epistle was written. *Beng.* Quoted *ad sensum,* not *ad literam,* as the Hebrew vowels now are. *Stuart.* Applied by the Jews to the Messiah: 'When Messiah shall be revealed, all the nations of the world shall be collected to Him; as it is said, A root of Jesse,' &c. *Zohar.* ' R. Chanina said, Messiah shall only come to teach the Gentiles two precepts, those of the Tabernacles and the Palm branches; as it is said, A root of Jesse,' &c. *Midr. Tehill.* 'Israel shall not require to learn the doctrine of the Messiah in the age to come; as it is said, A root of Jesse, &c., implying that the Gentiles alone shall need to learn of Him.' *Ber. Rabba.*

13. *Now the God of hope fill you with all joy and peace in believing, that ye may abound in hope, through the power of the Holy Ghost.*

God of hope. God the author as well as object of Christian hope.
True hope grounded on His love in the gift of His Son, chap. v. 5; 1 Pet. i. 3.
All other hope a spider's web, Job viii. 14; house built on the sand, Matt. vii. 26.
God the object of our hope by raising Jesus from the dead, 1 Pet. i. 21.
The hope God gives is—1. A good hope, 2 Thess. ii. 16; 2. A lively or living hope, 1 Pet. i. 3; 3. A blessed hope, Tit. ii. 13; 4. Sure and steadfast, Heb. vi. 19; 5. Which never disappoints, Rom. v. 5.
"God of hope"—the title taken from the matter in hand.
God the giver of every good and perfect gift, Jas. i. 17.
God's titles become pleas in the mouth of faith.
The false goddess of Hope familiar to all the Romans.
The true God of hope known only to believers.
Fill. Joy and peace exist in various degrees.
The believer's privilege to be filled with them, Ps. lxxxi. 10.
Spiritual joy a thing to fill and satisfy, Ps. lxiii. 5; lxv. 4; iv. 6, 7; xxxvi. 8.
Carnal joy puffs up the soul, spiritual joy fills it.
Christ's desire that His people's joy may be full, John xv. 11.
All—1. All kinds; 2. All degrees, of joy and peace.
Joy and peace in the richest abundance and highest degree.
Paul's ordinary mode of expressing the superlative, Col. i. 9, 11; iii. 16.
Joy. Delightful sensation from the possession of good.
That possession either actual or anticipated; our own or another's.
Everything presented in the Gospel to fill with joy, Luke ii. 10, 14.
Christ, the pearl of great price, a believer's own, Matt. xiii. 45, 46.
Joy desired by all, desirable to a believer.
The joy of the Lord is his strength, Neh. viii. 10.
Makes him run in the way of God's commandments, Ps. cxix. 32.
Enables him cheerfully to carry his cross, Acts v. 41.
Prepares him to give a good report of the Lord's ways, Num. xiv. 7-9.
Fits him for persuading others both by his lips and his life, Num. x. 29.
Joy the first feeling on believing, Matt. xiii. 44; Acts xvi. 34.

Peace. Serenity and satisfaction of soul.
Peace with God the foundation of inward peace.
Christ our peace, Eph. ii. 14 ; peace by His blood, Col. i. 20 ;
His own peace made over to the believer, John xiv. 27.
The peace of God which passes all understanding, Phil. iv. 7.
A peace that preserves and guards both heart and mind, *Ib.*
The mind kept in perfect peace, because stayed on God, Isa. xxvi. 3.
A peace spoken and created by God himself, Ps. lxxxv. 8 ; Isa. lvii. 19.
God the God of peace through the resurrection of Christ, Heb. xiii. 20.
Peace to be spoken by Christ to the heathen, Zech. ix. 10.
Joy on believing followed by a calm and settled peace.
That joy and peace continued and ever increasing.
Joy and peace in a world of sorrow and unrest, John xvi. 33.
No real joy which flows not from true peace.
In believing. True joy and peace the fruit of faith, Rom. v. 1–3, 11.
Obtained, preserved, and increased through believing.
The glad tidings concerning Christ the source of both, Luke ii. 10, 11, 14.
Peace and joy stream from the fountain of Gospel truth.
A joyful proclamation of amnesty for faith to embrace.
The Gospel gives in Christ a trust-deed to a heavenly inheritance.
Joy and peace the necessary effect of believing God's record, 1 John v. 11.
Enjoyed in proportion to the clearness, simplicity, and extent of faith.
Abound. Believers not only to have hope but to abound in it.
Have ground for the highest hope. Their hope to abound—
1. In its strength and firmness ; 2. In its compass and extent.
Variety of experience. Believers to *increase* in hope.
Christ came to give life and give it more abundantly, John x. 10.
Hope. Of the glory of God, chap. v. 2 ; the heavenly inheritance, 1 Pet. i. 3 ; Christ's appearing and our likeness to Him, Tit. ii. 13 ; 1 John iii. 2, 3.
All joy and peace here a foretaste of that hereafter.
Hope the spring of action and stimulus to holiness, 1 John iii. 3.
Hope connected with joy and peace. Mutually feed each other.
Power of the Holy Ghost. The Spirit the author of Christian hope.

Hope is—1. From God's love; 2. Christ's work; 3. The Spirit's power.
Divine power needed to produce a living hope, 1 Pet. i. 3.
The believer's hope is often hope against hope, Rom. iv. 18.
Natural to have hope, but not a well-grounded one.
Same result ascribed to the Spirit and the Scriptures, compare ver. 4.
The Spirit the agent, the Scriptures the instrument.
God the Father the fountain of all blessing in the church;
Faith in Christ the means of its appropriation;
The Holy Ghost's power the agency in producing it;
Peace, joy, and abounding hope the blessed fruits.
The economy of the Godhead in the matter of redemption.
Each person in the Trinity occupies His distinctive place.
The prayer in the text worthy of the great apostle.
Suggested by the whole preceding subject-matter of the epistle.
More especially by the concluding word in the last quotation.
Peace, joy, and hope, the fruits of the faith so largely treated of.

Ὁ Θεος, τ. ἐλπιδος, the God of hope; contrasted with the pagan goddess of hope. Her temple at Rome first struck with lightning and afterwards burnt.—Πληρωσαι ὑμας, fill you. Cod. Alex. has πληροφορησαι ὑ. ἐν παση χ. κ. εἰρ.—Ἐν τῳ πιστευειν, in believing, *i.e.*, from faith already received. *Tol.* Through faith as the means of it. *Vat.* In maintaining faith. *Est., Grot.* In believing not only the promises given you, but in Christ in whom they are all yea and Amen. *A. Clarke.*—Εἰς τὸ περισσευειν (omitted in Cod. Vat.), that you may abound; be excited to take more enlarged views of the salvation of God, and have all your expectations fulfilled. *A. Clarke.*

---

14. *And I myself also am persuaded of you, my brethren, that ye also are full of goodness, filled with all knowledge, able also to admonish one another.*

I myself. Notwithstanding I have thus written to you.
Am persuaded of you. Paul's characteristic delicacy.
Corresponds with his statement at the outset, chap. i. 8.
No flattering compliment, but just commendation.
Exhortations to be accompanied with courtesy, 1 Pet. iii. 8.
Christian gifts and graces to be duly commended.
Love esteems a brother *above* rather than *below* his wrath.
Paul's rule exemplified—" In honour preferring one another," chap. xii. 10.
Full. Fulness of spiritual blessing our privilege in Christ.
Fulness and abundance characteristic of the Gospel, Isa. lv. 3; Luke i. 53.

Goodness—1. Moral excellence in general, Eph. v. 9
2. Kindness to one another in particular, 2 Thess. i. 11.
Mutual kindness and forbearance already largely treated of.
Filled. Not only having knowledge, but filled with it.
Paul's large-hearted love seen in the terms he employs.
Delights to point to the fulness believers enjoy in Christ.
Various degrees of knowledge and other spiritual gifts.
The light progressive to the perfect day, Prov. iv. 18.
All knowledge. Spiritual knowledge a believer's privilege.
The Spirit's office to impart it, John xvi. 13; 1 Cor. ii. 10, 12;
  1 John ii. 20, 27.
Such knowledge to be greatly desired, Phil. i. 9; Col. ii. 2.
All treasures of wisdom and knowledge hid in Christ, Col. ii. 3.
Christ made wisdom to those who are in Him, 1 Cor. i. 30.
"All knowledge;" all necessary to comfort, holiness, and usefulness.
Knowledge embracing all the subjects of revealed truth.
Comprises—1. Doctrines; 2. Duties; 3. Dispensations.
Knowledge of the Triune God, His will, and ourselves.
The deep things of God; things freely given us of God, 1 Cor.
  ii. 10, 12.
Goodness and knowledge rarely combined in the world.
Both given and enjoyed together in and with Christ.
Perfect in the Head, real though imperfect in the members.
Goodness and knowledge the heart and head of the new man, Eph.
  iii. 24.
Admonish one another. Put each other in mind of duty.
May be done either privately or publicly.
For the latter the gift of utterance bestowed, 1 Cor. i. 5.
Superadded to goodness and knowledge for the benefit of others.
Church members to be able to admonish one another, Heb. v. 12.
Mutual exhortation frequently enjoined, Heb. iii. 13; x. 25; Col.
  iii. 16.

Δε, serves for continuing the discourse, as in ver. 13. *Stuart.*—Και αυτος εγω, even I myself, though I have thus reminded you. *Beng.* Who have thus warned and cautioned you. *Stuart.* I myself also, as well as others. *Rückert.* I, in and of myself. *Thol.*—'Αγαθοσυνης, goodness. *Pag., Pisc., Beza.* Love (dilectione). *Vulg.*, reading αγαπην, found in some MSS. To be exercised in admonishing one another. *Eras.* Mutual kindness. *A. Clarke, Stuart.* General goodness. *Hald.* Inclination to all I have been enjoining. *D. Brown.*—Γνωσεως, knowledge, *i.e.*, of divine things. *Vat.* Of the nature of Christian liberty. *Grot.* Of all things pertaining to the doctrine of salvation. *Pisc.* Necessary to mutual instruction. *Eras., A. Clarke.* Of Christian truths and principles. *Stuart.* Of the truth expounded. *D. Brown.*—'Ἀλλήλους (some copies have ἄλλους) νουθετεῖν (νοῦς, the mind, and τίθημι, to put), to admonish (monere) one another. *Pag., Pisc., Beza.* Instruct, teach. *Eras.* Heb. יָכַח׃, Job iv. 3.

---

15. *Nevertheless, brethren, I have written the more boldly unto you in some sort, as putting you in mind, because of the gift that is given to me of God.*

Nevertheless. Although I know you to be thus able.
Boldly—1. In the manner of writing ; 2. In writing at all.
"I have taken the liberty to write thus freely to you."
Thus courteously apologises for the freedom of his exhortation.
In some sort. *Gr.*, In part—1. With some degree of boldness ;
2. In some parts of the epistle ; 3. Partially on these subjects.
Divine truth can only be stated in part, John xvi. 12 ; xxi. 25.
Tongues of men and angels fail to state it fully, 1 Cor. xiii. 1, 9 ;
1 Pet. i. 12.
Putting you in mind. Bringing to your remembrance ; stirring
you up.
Good to be reminded of known truths and duties, 2 Pet. i. 12 ; iii. 1 ;
Jude 5.
Truths often forgotten and dissipated by contact with the world.
Hence the value of regular Sabbath instruction.
Grace. His apostolic office, chap. i. v. The ground of his boldness.
Demanded by fidelity to God and the grace given to him.
Necessity laid upon him to preach the Gospel, 1 Cor. ix. 16.
Believers responsible for the use of their gifts and graces.
These to be faithfully employed for the benefit of others.

Τολμηρότερον (τολμάω, to dare), more freely (liberius). *Eras., Pisc., Mart.* More boldly. *Diod.* Confidently. *Tol., Calv.* Familiarly. *Eras.* Rather boldly (audaculè). *Beza, Par.* The more boldly. *Stuart.* In writing the epistle. *Beng.* In the manner of writing. *Rück.* Refers perhaps especially to the admonitory part of the epistle (chap. xiv. and xv. 1-13).—'Ἀπὸ μέρους, in part ; a little. *Syr., Grot.* Only part of what might be written. *Or.* In some little measure (aliquantulum). *Vat.* Somewhat (aliquatenus). *Beza, Diod.* In some part. *Pag., Pisc.* In part, or partially (ex parte). *Calv.* In some sort. *Mart.* A softening expression. *Eras., Est.* In this part of my epistle. *Doddr., Paulus.* To a part of you, viz., the Gentiles. *Taylor* In some parts of the epistle. *Stuart.* Here and there. *Nielson.* In some measure. *Ellicot, D. Brown.* Connected with 'written boldly.' *Par., Grot.* Only with written (ἔγραψα). *Reiche, Stuart, De Wette.* With ἐπαναμιμ., 'putting you in mind.' *Scholz, Benedek.*—'Ἐπαναμιμνήσκων (ἐπί, ἀνά, and μνεία, memory), bringing back to memory. *Vulg., Mor., Cas.* Putting in mind (commonefaciens). *Pag., Eras., Pisc, Beza, Calv.* Reminding (submonefaciens). *Tol.* = מַזְכִּיר, stirring up. *Grot.* Adding to or repeating admonition, or something in the way of reminiscence. *Stuart.*

16. *That I should be the minister of Jesus Christ to the Gentiles; ministering the Gospel of God, that the offering up of the Gentiles might be acceptable, being sanctified by the Holy Ghost.*

Minister. Indicates not only public but priestly service.
Not the same word as that in ver. 8, or in chap. xiii. 4, but in xiii. 6.
The faithful preacher the true evangelical priest.
Of Jesus Christ. The Apostle and High Priest of our profession, Heb. iii. 1.
Minister of the true tabernacle, Heb. viii. 2; chief shepherd, 1 Pet. v. 4.
Paul officiated in the Gospel under Christ the Chief Minister.
True ministers and preachers are ministers of Jesus Christ—
1. As receiving their appointment from Himself.
2. As serving Him in His own great work of ministry.
As High Priest, Christ—1. Walks among the churches;
2. Holds the ministers of them in His right hand;
3. Disposes of them according to His own pleasure, Rev. ii. 2.
To the Gentiles. Paul's especial calling, ver. 13; Gal. ii. 7, 8; Eph. iii. 8.
Ministering the Gospel. Discharging a priestly office in it.
The apostolic preaching of the Gospel the sphere of his priesthood.
Preaching the Gospel a priestly service—*to* God and *for* men.
To be attended to with priestly consecration and devotion.
The only priesthood connected with the Christian ministry.
Employment in the Gospel, not the sacrifice of the Mass.
Not offering again Christ's body, but ministering Christ's Gospel.
Bringing men to Christ, not offering Christ to God.
Presenting Christ to men in the Gospel, not to God at the altar.
Sacrificial style here adopted as familiar to Jews and Gentiles.
Language of temple service only figuratively employed.
Paul only a priest as the Gentiles were a sacrifice.
A priest in contrast with those both of Jewish and Pagan worship.
Offering up of the Gentiles—1. The Gentiles themselves;
2. The spiritual sacrifices which they presented.
Gr., That there might be made an offering up of the Gentiles.
Converted believing souls a true sacrifice to God.
Legal sacrifices typical—1. Of Christ the one Atoning Sacrifice;
2. Of His members as burnt-offerings in Him, Lev. i. 4; Rom. xii. 1.
Believers a meat-offering with oil and frankincense, Lev. vi. 15.
Sanctified souls offered to God in the fire of holy love.
Christ the Altar that sanctifies both the gift and the giver.

Great work of the Gospel preacher to present true converts to God.
Believers both spiritual priests and sacrifices, 1 Pet. ii. 5.
Acceptable. Well-pleasing ; a sweet savour, Lev. i. 9 ; Eph. v. 2.
Both believers' persons and praises an acceptable sacrifice.
Acceptable—1. Through Christ the only ground of acceptance, 1 Pet. ii. 5 ;
2. Through faith as that in which they are offered, Heb. xi. 6.
Sanctified. Consecrated and made clean as sacrifices.
Sacrifices under the law to be without blemish, Lev. i. 3.
Here a real, not a ceremonial or figurative holiness denoted.
Sanctified by a personal moral purification in Christ, 1 Cor. i. 2, 30.
By the Holy Ghost. The Great Agent in conversion and sanctification.
Sacrifices under the law sanctified by salt, Lev. ii. 13 ;
Those under the Gospel by the Holy Ghost, Tit. iii. 5 ; 1 Cor. vi. 11.
The Spirit the sacrificial fire accompanying the Gospel, Matt. iii. 11 ; 1 Pet. i. 12.

Λειτουργον 'Ιησ. Χρ. (Codd. Sin., Vat., and Alex. have Χρ. 'Ιησου), a minister; indicating ministerial priestly service. *Chrys.* Any public minister, civil or ecclesiastical, Acts xiii. 2; Rom. xiii. 6 ; Heb. viii. 2. *Vor.* A minister in sacred things, a priest. *Est., Tol.* Jesus the Priest, Paul the minister of the Priest. *Beng.* A ministering servant. *Doddr.* A public servant. *Berl. Bib.* A sacrificing priest. *Knapp.* Properly a state servant, a servant in a public office, as chap. xiii. 6 ; but used here, as often in the LXX. and the New Testament, of a priestly office. *Rück.* A ministering priest of Jesus Christ. *Alford.* The word commonly employed to express the office of the priesthood, from which accordingly the figurative language of the rest of the verse is taken. *D. Brown.*—'Ιερουργουντα (ιερος, sacred, and εργον, work ; ιερουργεω, to sacrifice, perform sacred rites. *Hes.*) το ευαγγελιον, ministering the gospel as a priest ; offering as a sacrifice the preaching of the Gospel. *Chrys.* Consecrating the Gospel ; makes himself a priest in the ministry of the Gospel, offering as a sacrifice to God the people whom he gains for Him, and so performing the sacred mysteries of the Gospel. *Calv.* Administering the Gospel. *Eras.*, who afterwards corrected this for 'sacrificing' (as *Luther*), which is worse ; the Gospel rather the sacrificial knife than the sacrifice itself. *Calv.* Performing (operans). *Pag., Pisc., Beza.* Teaching the sacred Gospel. *Vat.* Performing its sacred rites. *Dick.* Preparing the victim. *Strig.* Discharging the priesthood not of the Levitical but the Christian dispensation, according to Isa. lxvi. 11. *Grot.* Employing myself in the sacred service of the Gospel. *Diod.* In the sacrifice of the Gospel. *Mart.* Performing sacred rites according to the Gospel ; κατα understood. *Schött.* Ministering the Gospel as a priest. *Beng., Berl. Bib.* As a priest performing his sacred functions, preparing his sacrifice to be offered. *Whitby.* Acting as a priest. *A. Clarke.* Performing the office of a priest in regard to the Gospel. *Stuart.* Ministering as a priest in the Gospel. *Ellicot, D. Brown.* The sacrifice not the Gospel, but the people brought by it to Christ. *Alford.* Labouring as a priest in the Gospel. *Stier.* Discharging a sacred office in relation to it. *Rückert.* Executing the priestly office of the Gospel. *De Wette.* Acting as a priest of the divine Gospel. *Van Ess.* Sanctifying to God the evangelical sacrifice. *Knapp.* Carrying the Gospel round like a priest of the Lord, as if spiritual incense (2 Cor. ii. 14), that the sacrifice of the heathen may be consecrated thereby. *Niel.* So 'τους ἱερουργουντας τον νομον ἰδίῳ αἱματι,' performing the sacred rites of the law with their own blood, 4 Macc. vii. 8.—Προσφορα τ. ἐθνων, offering or oblation of the Gentiles. *Pisc., Pag.* Libation. *Cas.* Sacrifice which the Gentiles offer. *Strig.* The Gentiles themselves. *Vor., Par., Grot., Est, Pisc., Beza, Cal., Whitby, Stuart, Con. & Hows., D. Brown.* Believers offered as a burnt-offering in Christ. *Lange.* Heb. נקיה.—Εὐπροσδεκτος, acceptable, as the sacrifice of the Old Testament;—רצון. *Grot.*—Ἡγιασμενη ἐν Πν. ἁγ., sanctified by the Holy Ghost. *Pag., Pisc., Beza.* As the sacrifice by fire. *Chrys., Tir., Men.* By salt. *Grot.* The Holy Ghost is the *libamen* poured upon the sacrifice. *Whitby.*

---

17. *I have therefore whereof I may glory through Jesus Christ in those things which pertain to God.*

I have therefore. From this grace of apostleship given me.
Spoken not for his own aggrandizement but his reader's profit.
An apologetic tone here assumed, as in 2 Cor. x. 13.
Perhaps suggested by what he had experienced in Corinth.
More immediately occasioned by his intention of visiting Rome.
Whereof I may glory. *Gr.*, Glorying; ground for exultation, chap. xi. 13.
God's abundant and unmerited favour true ground of glorying, Ps. xxxiv. 2.
Not the *ground* of acceptance, but the *fruits* of it, here indicated.
High honour to be employed and made successful in Christ's work.
Our privilege to extend Christ's kingdom and win souls to Himself.
Man's highest glory to serve God faithfully in the Gospel.
Through Jesus Christ. *Gr.*, In Jesus Christ—1. Through His mediation;
2. In fellowship with Him and in His service, 1 Cor. xv. 31.
No glorifying in but through Christ our Righteousness.
Christ is—1. The only ground of our acceptance with God;
2. The only medium in the enjoyment of its fruits.
He—1. Calls to office; 2. Qualifies for it; 3. Gives success in it.
United to Christ we are made kings and priests to God, Rev. i. 6; v. 10.
Man's highest joy and dignity attained only through and in Christ.
In things pertaining to God. *Gr.*, Before, or in respect to God.
In the view of and in regard to the world, poor and despised, 1 Cor. iv. 9–13.
Preaching of the Gospel and conversion of souls God's own cause.

'Ἔχω οὖν, I have therefore, &c. ; apologetic, like 2 Cor. x. 13, &c. *De Wette.*— Καυχησιν (best MSS. add the article την). glory. *Vulg., Tol.* Glorying. *Est* Occasion of glorying. *Tir.* That I may glory. *Calv.* Or, whence I may glory. *Pag., Vat., Beza, Pisc., Eras.* That I may rejoice ; καυχωμαι = to lean on or rejoice in anything ; — Heb. יעל, הלל. *Grot.* Καυχωμαι = to speak great things of one's self,—in certain cases and from certain motives right, 2 Cor. x. 2, &c. ; xii. 1, &c. *Tol.* Cause for glorying or rejoicing. *Stuart.* True ground of glorying. *Hald.* I can glory. *De Wette.* Can glory in a Christian and legitimate manner ; have real ground of glorying. *Alford.* The power of boasting. *Con. & Hows.* I have my boasting. *Ellicot.* My glorying. *D. Brown.*—'Ἐν Ἰησου Χριστῳ, in Christ. *Vulg., Tol.* In the cause or things of Christ. *Cas., Per.* Through Christ. *Calv.* Things done through Him, not myself. *Grot., Tol.* On account of Christ, who works by me in the conversion of the Gentiles. *Vor.* Through His aid, or being in Him. *Stuart.* In my connection with Christ and in His service. *De Wette.*—Τα προς Θεον 'some copies add the article του), to God (ad Deum). *Vulg.* Before God. *Syr., Arab.* In those things which pertain to God. *Pag., Pisc., Eras., Tol., Vor., Est., Calv., Beza, Mart.* As to God (quoad Deum), the Author of my success. *Vor., Ham.* In things pertaining to the service of God. *Diod.* With respect to the things of God. *Doddr.* Offerings presented to God. *T. Edwards.* The things of the ministry committed to me of God. *D. Brown.*

---

18. *For I will not dare to speak of any of those things which Christ hath not wrought by me, to make the Gentiles obedient in word and deed.*

For. Explains what he means by his glorying in Christ.
Conciliates the Romans by his apostolic activity and success.
Dare. Will not claim praise from other persons' labours, 2 Cor. x. 13.
Allusion to the conduct of others in regard to his own work.
A faithful man will not dare to lie, however tempted.
A true labourer will only speak of what *Christ* has done by him.
Wrought by me. Has effected by me as His instrument.
Paul ascribes to himself no success which he really had not had.
Will only glory in what Christ has actually done by him.
Recognises other men's labours in the same blessed cause.
Paul's labours only ministerial. Christ the true worker.
Occasion everywhere taken to ascribe to Him the praise, 2 Cor. ii. 14.
Divine power the cause of His success, 1 Cor. xv. 10 ; 2 Cor. x. 4 ; Acts xiv. 27 ; xv. 12.
The Acts of the Apostles properly Christ's acts through them.
While on earth Jesus only *began* to do and teach, Acts i. 1.
Wrought with the apostles and confirmed their word, Mark xvi. 20.
Proofs of the contact of a strong divine hand with our fallen race.
To make the Gentiles obedient. The obedience of faith, chap. i. 5.

Gentile disciples the proofs of Paul's apostleship, 1 Cor. ix. 2;
2 Cor. ii. 3.
The object of the apostle to bring sinners to Christ's feet, 2 Cor. x. 5.
Christ's own power makes the sinner willing, Ps. cx. 3.
Repentance and faith the gifts of God, Acts xi. 18; Eph. ii. 8.
Ascribed also to Christ, Acts v. 31; Heb. xii. 2. Christ therefore
God.
Human instrumentality employed by Christ in His work.
Repentance and faith produced through the Gospel, chap. x. 17.
Word and deed. Includes preaching, labours, and miracles.
Describes both the means of his success and proofs of their obedience.
The symbols of his priesthood and signs of his ordination.
More awe-inspiring than vestments, mitre, and bells. *Chrys.*
Word and deed combined as the true means of conversion.
The most successful preachers those who add deeds to words.
Conversion here set forth—1. In its nature,—obedience to Christ;
2. In its Author,—Christ himself working by His Spirit;
3. In the means employed,—the Gospel preached and lived by men.

Οὐ τολμησω, I may not dare (ausim). *Calv.* Could not endure (sustinuerim), as Rom. v. 7. *Pag., Beza.* Will not arrogate praise. *Or., Eras., Men., Tol.* Could not. *Diod., Mart.* Will not presume. *Stuart.* Will not dare, as some do. *Con. & Hows.* As others may do. *De Wette.* Will only boast of what Christ has veritably done by me. *Alford.*—Λαλειν τι, to mention anything. *Stuart.* Speak aught. *D. Brown.*—Λογῳ κ. ἐργῳ, by word and work; preaching and miracles. *Chrys., Tol., Est., Beng.* Ἐργῳ, extending beyond miracles. *Calv.* The doctrines taught and the miracles wrought by him. *A. Clarke.* Preaching, and other personal effort. *Stuart.* Preaching and working; ἐργῳ explained by what follows. *D. Brown.* Profession and practice,—proofs of their obedience. *Brown.*

---

19. *Through mighty signs and wonders, by the power of the Spirit of God; so that from Jerusalem and round about unto Illyricum I have fully preached the gospel of Christ.*

Mighty signs and wonders. *Gr.*, By the power of signs and wonders.
The deeds through which the Gentiles were made obedient.
These proofs of his apostolic office also appealed to in 2 Cor. xii. 12.
Wrought all along his apostolical tour, Gal. iii. 1, 5.
Miracles in themselves no absolute proof of truth, Deut. xiii. 1–3.
Pharaoh's magicians, Exod. vii. 11, 22; viii. 7; Antichrist's prophets, 2 Thess. ii. 9; Rev. xiii. 13, 14.

Miracles, however, serve—1. To confirm the truth, Mark xvi. 20 ;
2. To draw attention to the doctrine, Acts viii. 6 ; xiii. 12 ;
3. To indicate its character and design, John x. 32 ;
4. As channels for its conveyance to the heart, Acts xxviii. 7–10.
Proofs of supernatural interposition in favour of the truth.
The character of the doctrine indicates the source of the miracle.
Benevolent miracles accredit a divine mission, John x. 25, 37, 38.
Sight of miracles not enough to secure faith, Luke xvi. 31 ; John xii. 37.
Satisfactory evidence of Paul's miracles having been wrought.
Strongest proof afforded by this and other epistles.
These letters preserved by the churches from the earliest times.
Copies of them speedily multiplied and everywhere diffused.
Miracles appealed to in them as evidences of his mission.
In some cases wrought in presence of those he addressed.
Appealed to while administering remonstrance and rebuke.
Apostolic miracles carried infallible marks of reality.
Performed before the eyes of many persons together.
Open to men's senses which could easily judge of them.
Specimens : Acts iii. 1–9 ; viii. 6–13 ; xiii. 11 ; xiv. 8–10 ; xix. 11, 12 ; xx. 10, 12 ; xxviii. 8, 9.
God's love makes miracles, in the circumstances, probable.
The world sunk in the licentious superstitions of idolatry.
These superstitions handed down through twenty centuries.
The Jews had received a religion confirmed by miracles.
Miracles required for that which was to supersede it.
Power of the Spirit—1. Internal influence ; 2. Gifts bestowed.
The Spirit the Agent through whom Christ wrought.
Promised and sent by Him for that purpose, Acts i. 8 ; ii. 1–18, 33.
Apostolic preaching and miracles through His operation.
The obedience of the Gentiles the fruit of His work.
Jerusalem. Mentioned as the starting-point of his work—
1. As presenting the greatest extent of space from S.E. to N.W.;
2. As being the metropolis of the Christian church ;
3. As conforming to the commission, Luke xxiv. 47. Jew first, chap. i. 16.
Paul passes from the character of his labours to their extent.
Jerusalem, called also the Holy City, the capital of Judea.
Believed by Jewish writers the same with Salem, Gen. xiv. 18 ; Ps. lxxvi. 2.
Earliest notice of the city, Josh. xv. 8 ; xviii. 16, 28.

Then called Ha-Jebusi, *i.e.*, The Jebusite, or City of the Jebusites.
Called also Jebus, Judges xix. 10, 11 ; and Jerusalem, Judges i. 7 ;
   Josh. x. 1.
Divided by a valley gradually rising from south to north, called the
   Tyropœon, or Valley of the Cheesemakers.
The city itself mainly on the west, and the temple on the east.
Zion first applied to the western, subsequently to the eastern hill.
The southern continuation of the latter called Ophel.
Its northern continuation called by Josephus, Bezetha.
Acra, northward of Zion, formed the lower city.
First siege by Judah and Simeon, after Joshua's death, B.C. 1400.
The citadel or fortress of Zion taken by David, B.C. 1046.
The city taken by the Philistines and Arabians under Jehoram, B.C.
   886.
Taken by the Israelites in the reign of Amaziah, B.C. 826.
Thrice taken by Nebuchadnezzar, in the years 607, 597, and 586 B.C.
In the last of these sieges utterly destroyed.
Its restoration begun under Cyrus, B.C. 538.
Completed under Artaxerxes I., King of Persia.
Commission to rebuild it given to Ezra, 457 ; to Nehemiah, 445, B.C.
Taken by Alexander the Great, B.C. 332.
Sacked by Antiochus Epiphanes, B.C. 170.
Free under the Maccabees till taken by the Romans, B.C. 63.
Besieged and destroyed by the Romans under Titus, A.D. 70.
Restored by the Emperor Adrian as a Roman colony, A.D. 135.
Temple of Jupiter Capitolinus erected on the site of the temple.
Name of Ælia Capitolina given to the city by Adrian.
A church erected by Constantine the Great on the supposed site of
   the Holy Sepulchre, A.D. 336.
Several churches and hospitals added by Justinian, about 532.
Taken by Chosroes II., King of Persia, 614. Recovered by Heraclius, 628.
Surrendered by the patriarch Sophronius to the Khalif Omar, 637.
Bestowed on Ortok, chief of a Turkoman horde, 1084.
Taken by the Crusaders, 1099, and held by them for eighty-eight years.
Retaken by Saladin after a siege of several weeks.
Nominally annexed to the kingdom of Sicily, 1277.
Came under the sway of the Ottoman Sultan, Selim I., 1517.
Present walls of the city built by his successor Suliman, 1542.
Taken possession of by Mahomet Ali, Pasha of Egypt, 1832.
Again restored to the Sultan of Turkey, who still holds it, 1840.

Population in its greatest prosperity, probably from 30,000 to 45,000.
Present population estimated at about 18,000.
Composed of 5000 Mohamedans, 9000 Jews, and 4000 Christians.
The Holy City annually resorted to by from 6000 to 8000 pilgrims.
Jerusalem to be trodden under foot of the Gentiles, Luke xxi. 24.
But only until the times of the Gentiles be fulfilled, Dan. xii. 7.
Present condition extremely wretched, but improved and improving.
Round about. *Gr.*, In a circle. Perhaps including Arabia and
    Damascus, Gal. i. 17.
The circuit embraced Asia Minor, Macedonia, and Greece.
Hence this epistle written after Paul's second visit to Greece.
The apostle's progress chiefly westward ; see Acts xx. 1, 2.
Illyricum. North-west of Macedonia, on the shores of the Adriatic.
Dalmatia, a part of Illyricum, touched by Macedonia, 1 Tim. iv. 10.
Apollonia, a city in that region, visited by Paul, Acts xvii. 1.
In his first missionary tour Paul had visited the southern parts of
    Asia Minor and the northern parts of Syria.
In his second, the cities of Macedonia near the Ægean Sea.
In his third, the interior of Macedonia to the shores of the Adriatic.
Greek Illyricum incorporated with Macedonia.
Roman Illyricum, towards the head of the gulf, under a separate
    governor.
Under the emperors more frequently called Dalmatia.
A vast extent of country lying south of the Danube.
Includes Bosnia, Dalmatia, and parts of Croatia and Albania.
These regions at that time most densely populated.
Distance marked out by the apostle 1400 miles in a straight line.
Fully preached. *Gr.*, Filled or fulfilled the Gospel.
Fulfilled his office as a preacher of the Gospel.
Declared the whole counsel of God for man's salvation.
Kept back nothing that was profitable, Acts xx. 27.
Not doing the work superficially or by halves.
The apostles had filled Jerusalem with their doctrine, Acts v. 28;
Paul sought to fill the cities of the Gentiles with it.
To fill a country with the Gospel better than to fill it with gold.

Ἐν δυναμει σημειων κ. τερατων, by its power (virtute) of signs and prodigies. *Pisc., Beza.* (Per virtutem). *Pag.* By the influence, &c. *Stuart.* By the power of signs and wonders. *De Wette.* In the power, &c. *Cal., D. Brown.* Σημ. κ. τερ., the deeds mentioned in ver. 18. *Beng.* Miracles are σημεια (signs), as conveying to us some signification from God ; τερατα, as exciting our wonder and admiration. *Est.*

Σημ. are miracles which may be produced by nature, though not so suddenly, nor in the same manner; τερ. are miracles which cannot be so produced, as giving sight to the blind: hence σημ., the lesser, τερ., the greater miracles. *Tol.* Σημ. κ. τερ., signs and wonders, or wonderful signs,—a Hendiadys, the latter noun qualifying the former according to Old and New Testament idiom; otherwise, σημ., = *miraculous proofs* adapted to convince, τερ., *wonderful occurrences*, adapted to strike with awe. *Stuart.* Σ. κ. τ., = glorious miracles. *D. Brown.* Σημ. κ. τερ. correspond in meaning to the Heb. אֹתוֹת וּמֹפְתִים, (*e.g.*, Exod. vii. 3). In the New Testament, τερατα, occurs always in this connection. Σημειον, = אוֹת (from אוה, to make an incision, to notch), is any thing, act, or occurrence, fitted to direct attention to and guarantee the truthfulness of a person or saying; τερατα, = מוֹפֵת (perhaps from יפע, to glisten), an absolutely supernatural (παρα φυσιν), astounding, and powerfully imposing fact or appearance, especially in the heavens (Acts ii. 19). *Delitzsch*, on Heb. ii. 4. 'Under the Law, miracles were wrought only in cases of necessity; but under the Gospel, many heathens have been healed by us from all manner of diseases; we possess such a fulness of miraculous power, that even the dead are raised; and often, when it must be so, we bring individuals to a sense of their wrong-doing by striking them with blindness through a mere threat, or inflict sudden death on the malevolent.' *Theodore of Mopsuestia.* Early Christians appealed to miracles in support of the truth of their religion. Hence important to define more precisely the idea of a miracle. According to Augustine, miracles are events which deviate not so much from the order of nature in general, as from that particular order of nature *known to us*. It was necessary to distinguish the miracles of Jesus and His apostles from those of Apollonius of Tyana, to which Hierocles and others appealed. Augustine therefore directed attention to their *benevolent design*, distinguishing them from those whose object was merely to gain the applause of men. Christians did not directly deny the existence of miracles in the heathen world, but ascribed them to the influence of demons. Origen preferred the evidence from prophecy as the evidence of *spirit*, that from miracles being the evidence of *power*. He also distinguishes between visible miracles and those which are spiritual and moral (as regeneration), of which the former are only the symbols, and which are the 'greater works' of which Christ spoke. Healing the sick and prophesying only an indifferent thing (μεσον). Justin appeals to visible miracles as even then wrought. From the time of Spinoza and Hume, Rationalists opposed the reality and credibility of miracles, while the adherents of modern Supernaturalism rested their belief in Revelation especially on that branch of evidence, differing in this from the Reformers, *e.g*, Luther. Bonnet's theory of preformation, viz., that God has *à priori* included miracles in the course of nature, did not meet with general approbation. Olshausen makes miracles a more advanced process of nature. According to Lavater, miracles are still taking place. Kant taught that it is neither possible absolutely to prove the reality of miracles, nor can their possibility be absolutely denied. The Rationalists endeavoured to comprehend the miraculous as something natural; while the Philosophers asserted that the natural made perfect by the spiritual, the perfection consisting in their close union, was the only true miracle. The adherents of modern speculative philosophy gave the preference to that hypothesis which makes the Scripture miracles myths, or disguised facts or fables embodying some moral idea. The adherents of modern orthodoxy in Germany use a more liberal, but also a considerate and cautious mode of reasoning, in order to defend the credibility of the Scripture narrative; some of them, however, as De Wette and Schleiermacher, admitting mythical elements. They distinguish between the objective and the subjective in miracles, and generally speaking adopt the principle of Augustine. *Hagenbach*.—'Εν δυναμει Πνευματος Θεου (in Cod. Alex. Πνευματος ἁγιου), the power of the Spirit of God; not by that of demons: or as indicating another means of success,—σημ. and τερ., being the external, the Holy Spirit's power the internal means.

Grot., Est. The Spirit the author of the miracles. *Chrys., Theod., Eras., Calv.* Gift of prophecy, tongues, &c. *Beza., Thol.* Allusion to λόγῳ, by word; converted souls being the signs of Paul's apostleship. *Beng.* Internal spiritual gifts of Christians. *Stuart.* Indicates the power of *word* as well as deed. *De Wette.* The Spirit-life, in which the Holy Ghost was one with his spirit. *Lange.* Explains the efficacy of the word preached. *D. Brown.*—Καὶ κύκλῳ, by a circuit. *Vulg., Cas.* On all sides, or in a circuit. *Eras.* In the circumjacent regions. *Pag., Pisc., Vat., Beza.* In a circuit,—not hastening on in a straight direction, but going through the intermediate regions. *Calv., Tol.* And around; indicating the region *around* Jerusalem, *i.e.*, Phœnicia, Syria, and part of Arabia. *Grot., Stuart.* Round about, as in Mark vi. 6, 36. Heb. מִסָּבִיב. = Μέχρι τοῦ Ἰλλ., even to Illyricum. *Stuart.* As far as Illyricum. *D. Brown.* From Jerusalem, Antioch, and Arabia in the East, round about through all Asia Minor and Greece, even to the western shores of Illyricum. *Doddr.* Illyricum the terminus ad quem. *Thol.* A Macedonian journey had brought him to Illyricum. *De Wette.* An excursion made to it. *Meyer.* His stay in Arabia and Damascus not here included. *Lange, Brown.* Nor what had been done later in Cilicia, Acts ix. 30. *De Wette.* The labours referred to extended over Asia Minor, Macedonia, and Greece. *Theod.* Brought him to the most north-western part of Greece. *Stuart, D. Brown.* It was on a second visit to Macedonia, almost immediately before writing this epistle, that he approached Illyricum. *Paley.* —Πεπληρωκέναι τ. εὐαγγ., accomplished, finished [the preaching of] the Gospel. *Arab.* Fulfilled (impleverim). *Vulg., Cas., Eras., Pag., Pisc., Calv., Beza.* Fully preached, omitting nothing that pertains to the faithful Evangelist. *Vat., Eras.* Completed what was lacking in the labours of others. *Calv.* Filled the Gospel net with the multitudes of the converted. *Tol.* Filled all places with the Gospel. *Cas., Pisc., Luth., Par., Mar.* With its report. *Vor.* Fulfilled the office of preaching the Gospel. *Pag., Pisc., Grot., Beza, Diod., De Wette, Alford.* Perfectly taught the Gospel as to both matter and manner. *Schött.* Preached it successfully. *A. Clarke.* Fully declared it, as Col. i. 25. *Stuart.* Fulfilled my task in making known the glad tidings of Christ. *Con. & Hows.* Perfectly spread the Gospel. *Lange.* Heb. מִלֵּא, but in LXX, מָלֵא, מָלָה.

---

20. *Yea, so have I strived to preach the Gospel, not where Christ was named, lest I should build upon another man's foundation.*

Yea, so have I strived. *Gr.*, And thus making it my endeavour. *Lit.*, Making it a point of honour—matter of holy ambition. Christian love always tender of the rights of others. True ambition, to serve God in the best and most devoted manner. Worldly ambition the perversion of a right principle. The Gospel brings into right play all the principles of our nature. The objects worthiest of men's effort and ambition are—
1. To bring the greatest glory to God and to Jesus Christ;
2. To impart the greatest amount of happiness to men;
3. To act with the greatest uprightness and courtesy to all.

Grace excites to the noblest and most arduous enterprises. Paul's ambition the principle in many a missionary:
E.g., Morrison and Carey, Martyn and Judson, Williams and Moffat.
Not where Christ was named. Sought new fields of labour.

Such fields are—1. More difficult and laborious to cultivate;
2. More rich and abundant in the return.
Speaks generally; Christ already known at Damascus and Rome.
The Gospel preached by the apostles in many lands.
Said to have been preached in Persia by Simon and Jude;
In Idumea, Syria, and Mesopotamia, by Jude;
In Egypt and other parts of Africa, by Mark, Simon, and Jude;
In Ethiopia, by Matthias; in Parthia, by Matthew;
In Pontus, Galatia, and adjacent parts of Asia, by Peter;
In Scythia, by Philip and Andrew;
In the northern and western parts of Asia, by Bartholomew;
In Media, Caramania, and other eastern parts, by Thomas.
Foundation. Work of preaching begun; church gathered, 1 Cor. iii. 10.
Paul called to plant and leave others to water, 1 Cor. iii. 6.
Experienced trouble from others building on his foundation, 1 Cor. iii. 10, 12; 2 Cor. x. 12-16.
Peculiarly skilled in introducing the Gospel into new parts.
Reasoned with idolaters from their own superstition, Acts xvii. 27.
With the learned out of their own literature, Acts xvii. 28.
With Pharisees from the tenets of their own sect, Acts xxiii. 6.
With Jews in general out of their own Scriptures, Acts xiii. 26-41.

Φιλοτιμουμενον (φιλεω, to love, and τιμη, honour), anxiously caring. *Syr.* Desiring. *Vulg.* Earnestly endeavouring. *Beza.* Fondly endeavouring. *Mor.* Striving (annitens). *Eras., Vat., Calv.* Going about like a candidate for office (ambiens). *Pisc.* Having still in some measure the ambition. *Diod.* Engaging myself with affection. *Mart.* Φιλοτιμωμαι, to aim ambitiously at a thing; 'from a kind of holy ambition, I have abstained,' &c. *Eras., Vor.* Φιλοτιμ. = 1. To do a thing from a desire of honour; 2. To attempt anything with great earnestness. *Grot.* To covet as an honour; hence, as here, to act with great earnestness, to labour or study, 2 Cor. v. 9; 1 Thess. iv. 11. *Schött.* It has been the object of my ambition. *Els., Doddr.* 'I was earnestly concerned,' with the additional idea of counting it as an honour. *Flatt.* Have considered it my honour. *A. Clarke.* Was strongly desirous; φιλ. construed with με in ver. 19. *Stuart.* The idea of honour in the word, but probably effaced from the apostle's usage. *De Wette.* Counting it a matter of honour. *Meyer, Alford.* My ambition was to preach according to this rule. *Con. & Hows.* Making it my ambition. *Ellicot.* My study. *D. Brown.*—Ουχ οπου ονομασθη Χρ., not where Christ was [already] named; avoiding places where He was already known. *Beng.*—Αλλοτριον θεμελιον, another's foundation; foundation laid by another. *Tol., Beza,* &c. Elsewhere, Christ the only foundation. *Calvin.*

21. *But as it is written, To whom He was not spoken of, they shall see, and they that have not heard shall understand.*

Written. Isa. lii. 15. Applied by the Jews to Messiah. See at x. 16.
A prophecy concerning the extent of Christ's kingdom.
Paul's holy ambition God's means for its fulfilment.
When God's purposes are ripe, suitable means are made ready.
When a work is to be done, God gives a heart to do it.
Not spoken of. Allusion to the Gentile world.
Christ, as minister of the circumcision, preached to the Jews.
Israel's distinguishing honour and privilege.
Christ a Saviour for all nations, Luke ii. 10, 11 ; John xi. 51, 52.
See. With the eye of the understanding and of faith, Rev. iii. 18.
Contrasted with bodily sight, John xx. 29 ; 1 Pet. i. 8.
Heard. The Jews had already heard of Christ—
1. Through the law and the prophets, John v. 39 ; Luke xxiv. 27 ; 1 Pet. i. 10, 11 ;
2. Through the preaching of Jesus and His apostles, Luke xxiv. 47 ; Acts i. 8.

Ἀλλα καθως γεγραπται, but [might act] as it is written. *D. Brown.*—Οἷς οὐκ ἀνηγγελη π. αὐτου, to whom no declaration was made respecting Him. *Stuart.* To whom no tidings of Him came. *D. Brown.* The words form part of the prophecy contained in Isa. lii. 13 ; liii. 1, &c., referring to Jehovah's servant. Heb. אֲשֶׁר לֹא־סֻפַּר לָהֶם, ' to whom He was not announced.'

---

22. *For which cause also I have been much hindered in coming to you.*

For which cause. The reason for not visiting them sooner.
Rome had already had the Gospel for some time.
Other places therefore first to be evangelised.
Hindered. Like "let," chap. i. 13. No want of inclination.
His only hindrance the work in which he had been engaged.
Paul's labours under the Spirit's direction, Acts xiii. 2.
Sometimes intended what the Spirit did not permit, Acts xvi. 6, 7.
Allowable to *intend*, indispensable to *obey*.
As many as are led by the Spirit of God are the sons of God, chap viii. 14.
Coming to you. Paul's object in wishing to visit Rome was—
1. To instruct believers further in the Gospel, chap. i. 11 ;

2. To preach to the mass of heathens in that city, chap. i. 13–15.
3. To spread the Gospel farther as from another centre, ver. 24, 28.
Paul, as an apostle, could act both as pastor and evangelist.
Preaching and teaching combined in the great commission, Matt. xxviii. 20.
Exemplified in Christ's personal ministry, Matt. iv. 23.
Paul's plan of operation wisely formed and clearly defined.
Three things necessary in order to much efficiency—
1. A *plan* ; 2. A *good* plan ; 3. *Adherence* to that plan.

Καί, intensive, augmenting the sense of what follows. *Stuart.*—Ἐνεκοπτομην (ἐν, in or against, and κοπτω, to cut or strike ; ἐγκοπτω, to stop by an incision or barrier; to cut off retreat ; to cut short), I was hindered. *Calv.*, &c. Inhibited. *Eras.*, *Grot.*, *Beza.*—Τα πολλα, very often (sæpius). *Calv.* Greatly; with και, = altogether. *Stuart.* For the most part ; in most instances. *Ellicot.*

---

23. *But now having no more place in these parts, and having a great desire these many years to come unto you.*

Place. Occasion for such apostolic and evangelistic work.
Gospel first preached and churches planted in large cities.
Cities made the central points of the apostle's labours.
Churches left to extend the Gospel to the villages around.
Paul always sedulously engaged in his Master's service.
Like Alexander, conquering and planning new conquests.
Time to be diligently employed to the greatest advantage.
"The night cometh when no man can work," John ix. 4.
Parts. Regions ; here, *Greece*, where he had now been preaching.
Great desire. Like chap. i. 11, "I long to see you." So Phil. i. 8.
Paul's fervent and affectionate spirit like his Master's.
Desire as to fields of labour, within certain limits, allowable.
Many years. So "oftentimes," chap. i. 13. No new feeling.
Personal feeling to be subordinated to public advantage.
Duty before desire. The Lord's will to be waited for.
The apostle's faithfulness and obedience to Christ.
His predilections and desires kept under holy restraint.
Indications as to the plan of labour given—
1. By direct intimation from without, Acts xvi. 6–10 ;
2. By strong, holy, and abiding desires kindled within ;
3. By the leadings of Providence prayerfully watched ;
4. By the pressure of hostility and persecution, Matt. x. 23.

Our purposes wisely overruled by God's providence.
The stars in Christ's hand to dispose of as He pleases.
Places visited with the Gospel not by chance, but God's purpose.
Love seeks not our own pleasure, but others' profit. ver. 1.
Evangelising at Rome more honourable and less laborious.

Μηκετι τοπον, no more place free for me to preach in. *Tol., Men.* Where the foundation is to be laid. *Grot.* No object to detain me. *Mart.* Occasion or opportunity for preaching. *Schött.* No more work of this kind to be done. *Doddr.* Opportunity of breaking up new ground. *A. Clarke.* Scope, room. *Meyer, Lange.* Room enough for my labours. *Con. & Hows.* No longer any considerable place where I have not preached the gospel. *Stuart.* Occasion for apostolic work. *Alford.* Paul thought it enough to preach and plant churches in the principal places. *De Wette.* The apostles planted churches in large cities, leaving them to extend the gospel to the villages around; hence the inhabitants of villages (pagani) came to be a term to designate the heathen or unchristianised in general (in English, 'pagans'). *Thol.*—Ἔχων, having. Codd. Sin., Vat., and Alex. read ἔχω, I have.—Κλιμασι (κλινω, to bend, incline; κλιμα, the space between two parallels, but used either in a wider or more restricted sense. *Grot.*), in these regions. *Pag., Pisc., Beza.* Greece. *Grot., Est., Tol.*—Ἐπιποθιαν (ἐπι, intensive, and ποθος, desire), a longing. *Ellicot, D. Brown.*—Πολλων ἐτων, for many years. *Stuart.* Many times. *Alford.* Jews reckoned their years from the creation, the flood, the exodus, the building of the temple, &c.; Greeks, by Olympiads beginning 776 B.C., fifty-five years before the captivity of the ten tribes; Romans, from the foundation of Rome, 753 B.C. At Argos the year was reckoned by the succession of the priestesses of Juno; at Sparta by that of the Ephori; at Athens by that of the Archons; but for the whole of Greece by the victor at the Olympic foot-race. Jews had two kinds of years: the civil, from which they reckoned the Jubilee, dated contracts, and noted the birth of their children and the reign of their kings; and the ecclesiastical, according to which they computed their annual festivals. The civil year began with the month Tisri, corresponding with part of September and October; the ecclesiastical, with Nisan or Abib, agreeing with part of our March and April. The year said by some to have originally consisted of only one month, divided afterwards into three, four, six, and twelve. Months already distinguished as now at the time of the flood. Before the exile, months among the Jews, as among the Egyptians, were only numbered, not named, except the first of the ecclesiastical year, which was called Abib, or month of green corn, Exod. xiii. 4. During the exile, Babylonian names were adopted for the months, viz., Nisan for Abib; Zif or Tyyar (1 Kings vi. 1, 36); Sivan (Est viii. 9); Tammuz (July); Ab; Elul (Neh. vi 75); Tisri or Ethanim (1 Kings viii. 2); Bul or Marchesvan (1 Kings vi. 38); Kislev (Zech. vii. 1; Neh. i 1); Tebeth (Est. ii. 16); Shebat (Zech. i. 7); Adar (Est. iii. 7). A year of 360 days the rudest known, formed of twelve spurious lunar months, and probably the parent of the lunar year of 354 days, and the vague year of 365. The Hebrew year from the time of the exodus evidently lunar, though in some way rendered virtually solar. *Dr Smith.* The intercalation or addition of a thirteenth month made whenever the twelfth ended too long before the equinox for the offering of the first-fruits to be made at the time appointed. The division of time into weeks or periods of seven days appears to have been universal, having prevailed among the Assyrians, Egyptians, Indians, Arabians, and all oriental nations; also among the Romans, the ancient inhabitants of France, Britain, Germany, and Northern Europe, and even of America. Its first trace, Gen vii. 4; mentioned as a thing well known, Gen. xxix. 27, 28.

CHAP. XV.]   ST. PAUL'S EPISTLE TO THE ROMANS.   297

24. *Whensoever I take my journey into Spain, I will come to you ; for I trust to see you in my journey, and to be brought on my way by you, if first I be somewhat filled with your company.*

My journey. Purposed, but uncertain if ever accomplished.
Man proposes, God disposes. Events in God's hands, not ours.
According to tradition, the journey made but not recorded.
Silence of Scripture no proof to the contrary.
Opportunity found between first and second imprisonment.
God's will made known in the way of His providence.
Spain. Originally including the present Portugal.
Hebrew name Tarshish, given also to a city in the south.
Colonised by descendants of Tarshish, son of Javan, Gen. x. 4.
Early traded with by Phœnicians, on account of its mines, &c.
The Gospel early preached and churches planted in Spain.
Favourable for the apostle's activity among the Gentiles—
1. Many Jews there ; 2. A place of Greek-Roman culture.
Trust. *Gr.*, Hope. Paul's plans subject to God's approval.
Common discourse to be according to godliness, James iv. 13-15.
The language of believers to be the language of Canaan, Isa. xix. 18.
Brought on my way. Escorted, conducted, sent forward.
Way through Gaul already well-known to the Romans.
Usual custom of churches with preachers, Acts xv. 3 ; xvii. 14, 15 ; xx. 38 ; xxi. 5.
Included the providing of external necessaries, 3 John 6.
God supplies His servants' wants by the hands of His people.
Believers expected to be ready to further every good work.
The privilege of all to be fellow-helpers to the truth, 3 John 8.
In my journey. *Gr.*, Passing through. Only a short stay in Rome.
Work to be so planned as not to involve waste of time.
Somewhat. *Gr.*, In part. Delicacy and affection of the expression.
The wish greater than could possibly be realised.
As if never able to have enough of their society.
Fellowship of believers enjoyed here only in part—
1. As to its degree ; 2. As to its duration.
Saints' society only "somewhat" fills ; that of God, altogether.
Filled. Anticipates rich enjoyment and refreshment.
Paul alive to the sweetness and benefit of holy society.
Highest social enjoyment in "the communion of saints."
Fellowship of believers on earth a foretaste of heaven.
With your company. *Gr.*, With you. Not their company but themselves.

His ardour and susceptibility. Not to see, but be *filled* with them.
His modesty and humility. They more likely to be filled with *him*.
His spirituality of mind. Filled with the *saints*, Ps. xvi. 2.
The saints were Rome's greatest attraction for Paul.
A seraph would have made the same choice.
Everything else in reality poor and contemptible, 1 John ii. 15-17.

Πορενωμαι. Subjunctive, as indicating *possible* or *probable* action; some MSS. have πορευομαι, which would have indicated certain expectation or resolution to go. *Stuart.* The journey never accomplished. *Meyer.* Whether made depends on the question of a second imprisonment at Rome. *Thol.* The journey affirmed by Clement of Rome, but not mentioned by Origen or Eusebius. Placed by some ecclesiastical historians between his first and second imprisonment. The presumption against the journey. *A. Clarke.* A second imprisonment, and consequently the journey most probable. *D. Brown.*— Εἰς τὴν Σπανιαν, into Spain. Called by the ancients Iberia and Hispania. The Tarshish which formed the celebrated emporium to which the Phœnicians and Hebrews traded; hence all large ships called 'ships of Tarshish,' Ps. xlviii. 7. A lake, city, and river in the south of Spain, near to Guadalquiver, called by the Greeks Tartessus, and the whole district Tartessis, doubtless identical with Tarshish. Richest country in the ancient world in the precious metals. Distinguished also for its vegetable productions. Phœnicians had built about twenty towns on the coast, including Gades (Cadiz) and Malaga. Had already gone to Spain in the time of Moses, Gen. xlix. 3; x. 4, &c. Several names of cities, and probably that of Spain itself, Phœnician. Carthaginians, or Phœnician colonists of Carthage, had obtained considerable parts of the country before their treaty with the Romans in 509 B.C., and had reduced the whole under subjection, except the mountainous districts of Biscay and Asturias. After the breaking out of the first Punic war, they were obliged to withdraw their army from Spain; but after its termination the country was again conquered by the Carthagenian general Hamilcar, the father of Hannibal. During the interval the Romans had formed an alliance with the cities of Saguntum and Ampurias. Hasdrubal, son-in-law of Hamilcar, on founding Carthagena, bound himself by a treaty not to attack Saguntum. Hannibal, who succeeded him in the command, attacked that city, and thus occasioned the second Punic war. During that war Spain was the battle-ground between the Romans and Carthagenians. After various defeats, in which the two Scipios were slain, Spain was completely wrested from the Carthagenians by the younger Publius Cornelius Scipio, and henceforward regarded as a province of Rome. The original language of Spain was a branch of the Celtic. The Phœnicians and Carthagenians introduced their tongue, which was cognate to the Syriac. Before the time of Paul, however, the Latin language, the basis of the modern Spanish, had obtained nearly general diffusion. Dionysius the Areopagite sent Eugenius, one of his disciples, from Gaul into Spain, who was so far successful that a church was founded in Toledo under his pastoral care. Irenæus, Bishop of Lyons, A.D. 184, alludes to the churches of Spain in his day. —'Ελευσομαι πρὸς ὑμᾶς. Not found in Codd. Sin. and Alex., nor in many ancient versions. Necessary to be supplied. *D. Brown.* Unnecessary, if the first clause of the verse be connected with the second. *A. Clarke.*—Προπεμφθῆναι (προ, forward, and πεμπω, to send), be conducted (deducar). *Pag., Pisc., Beza.* Hoped he should have companions of his journey. *Tol.* Respect and assistance. *Est.* Jewish custom to accompany strangers a part of their way; 'He did not come to us and was sent away without food; neither did we see him and send him away without a convoy.' *Mishna, Sotah.*—

Ἐμπλησθῶ (ἐν, in, and πληθῶ, to fill), be filled or satisfied (expletus). *Pag., Pisc., Beza.* Shall have enjoyed you (fruitus). *Vulg.* Be gratified. *A. Clarke.* Have my fill. *D. Brown.* Speaks as a parent to his children. *Chrys.* Writes familiarly, as to friends well known. *Beng.*

---

25. *But now I go to Jerusalem to minister to the saints.*

I go. Paul now at the end of his second journey to Greece.
When writing to Corinth, his Jerusalem journey uncertain, 1 Cor. xvi. 4.
This epistle therefore written after those to the Corinthians.
Paul probably now at Corinth, and ready to set out. See at chap. xvi. 1, 23.
To Jerusalem. Duty now called to Jerusalem, not to Rome.
Takes money to Jerusalem rather than the Gospel to Rome.
A time for every work. Everything beautiful in its season.
To be faithful in littles is to be faithful in all.
Obedience to every call of duty learned in the school of Christ.
To Jerusalem with its peril before Rome with its pleasure.
A visit fraught with danger, yet of deepest importance—
1. To overcome the prejudices of Jewish against Gentile believers;
2. To unite both parties more closely in Christian love.
Christian union even before evangelising new countries.
A necessary step to the success of future labours.
Minister. Convey supplies for their temporal wants.
Had carried out the council's recommendation, Gal. ii. 10.
Usually ministered to the souls, but now to the bodies, of men.
Ministering to poor saints not beneath an apostle.
So Christ ministered to men's bodies as well as their souls.
Often the best way to the heart is to help with the hand.
The cost of sympathy the best proof of its sincerity.
Tenderness to the poor one of a preacher's requisites.
What Paul could not give himself he moved others to give.
A double benefit conferred in exciting the liberality of others.
Giver and receiver both blessed, Acts xx. 35; 2 Cor. ix. 10–14.

Διακονῶν (Codd. Sin. has διακονήσων), ministering; supplying the wants of the saints. Διακονέω, often used in the New Testament for supplying with food and other comforts of life. *Stuart.*

26. *For it hath pleased them of Macedonia and Achaia to make a contribution for the poor saints which are at Jerusalem.*

Pleased. The contribution a matter of free-will
So he desired it to be, 2 Cor. viii. 1–5 ; ix. 5–7.
Yet recommended and enjoined it, 1 Cor. xvi. 1, 2 ; 2 Cor. viii. 6–11.
Our gifts to be free-will offerings of cheerful love, 2 Cor. ix. 7.
[Them of] Macedonia. The believers in that country, 2 Cor. viii. 1, &c.
Macedonia at that time a Roman province.
Lay to the north of Achaia, and east of Illyricum.
Included Thessaly and a large tract along the Adriatic.
Under the jurisdiction of a proconsul at Thessalonica.
Seat of the third or Grecian monarchy of the world, Dan. ii. 39 ; vii. 6.
Macedonian Christians placed in a favourable light, 2 Cor. viii. 1, &c.
Thessalonian believers objects of Paul's special affection, 1 Thess. ii. 8, 17, &c.
Philippians distinguished for liberality and self-denial, Phil. iv. 10, 14–19.
Bereans highly commended for their candour, Acts xvii. 11.
Contribution. *Gr.*, Fellowship. Rule in making it, 1 Cor. xvi. 1, 2.
Largely referred to in his Second Epistle to the Corinthians, chap. 8 and 9.
Probably made at the apostle's suggestion, Gal. ii. 9, 10.
Called a "fellowship," as being—1. A symbol of fellowship ; 2. Made up of the united contributions of believers.
No trace of community of goods in the apostle's letters.
Nor of such having been established at the beginning.
Believers freely to contribute to each other's wants—
1. As an expression of gratitude and love to Christ ;
2. As a token of their love to His members.
Contribution made—1. Deliberately ; 2. Cheerfully ; 3. Systematically.
Each step in the matter showed Paul's prudence and delicacy.
No constraint laid upon the churches, 2 Cor. viii. 12 ; ix. 7.
Spoken rather as by advice than by command, 2 Cor. viii. 10.
Wished to prove the reality of the converts' love, 2 Cor. viii. 24.
Stimulated one church by the example of another, 2 Cor. viii. 1–5 ; ix. 2.
Delicately contrasted the wealth of the Corinthians with the poverty of the Macedonians, 2 Cor. viii. 2, &c.

CHAP. XV.]   ST. PAUL'S EPISTLE TO THE ROMANS.   301

Presented as their motive Christ's self-denying love, 2 Cor. ix. 8.
Guarded against all suspicion in the conveying of it, 1 Cor. xvi. 3;
   2 Cor. viii. 20, 21.
The contribution is—1. A model for all Christian churches;
2. A beautiful display of the spirit of Christianity.
A delicate hint given to the Romans to imitate it.
Paul ingenious in pleading the cause of others.
Speaks more boldly to his own converts on the subject, 1 Cor.
   xvi. 1, 2.
An internal mark of the authenticity of these epistles.
Achaia.   Another Roman province, including—
1. The whole of the Peloponnesus, or the Morea;
2. The greater part of Hellas, or Greece proper;
3. The adjacent islands, Euboea or Negropont, &c.
With Macedonia, comprehended the whole of Greece.
Nearly coincided, except on the west, with modern Greece.
Its principal city, Corinth, here especially referred to.
Governed, in the reign of Claudius, by a proconsul, Acts xviii. 12.
Poor saints.   *Gr.*, Poor of the saints.   Only part of them poor.
Poverty of Jerusalem-believers appears from Acts. ii. 44; Heb.
   x. 34.
Comparison of Scriptures a pleasing and confirming exercise.
God's saints often poor in this world, James ii. 5; Heb. xi. 37, 38;
   Rev. ii. 9.
Such a dealing tends—1. To magnify God's kindness;
2. To show His sovereignty in disposing of His gifts;
3. To exalt the blessings of grace and salvation;
4. To hinder or keep down pride in His children;
5. To preserve them from many temptations;
6. To promote patience, faith, and heavenly-mindedness;
7. To lead to the exercise of mutual sympathy and love;
At Jerusalem.   Special interest attaching to that church.
The mother-church of Christendom.
The first object of persecution from the world.
Its effects experienced chiefly by the poorer classes.
Believers there cut off from ordinary Jewish relief.
Charity at home had nobly done its part, Acts ii. 44, 45; iv. 34–37

Εὐδόκησαν (εὖ, well, and δοκέω, to seem), were well pleased; thought good. It has pleased them (libuit). *Beza.* Placuit. *Calv.* Seemed good. *Eras., Vat., Stuart.* The contribution heartily approved of. *Eras.* Made cordially and cheerfully. *Beza.*—

Μακεδονια. Previously called Æmathia. Peopled by a number of tribes regarded by the Greeks as barbarians. Probably descended from Chittim the son of Javan, 1 Macc. i. 8; viii. 5. Its monarchy had continued about 400 years when King Philip added Thessaly, with great part of Epirus and Illyricum, to his territories. His son Alexander made himself master of Greece, the Persian empire, and part of India. This third great monarchy of the world quickly broken in pieces; and Macedonia, after having been a kingdom for 646 years, at length subjugated by the Romans, B.C. 168. Afterwards formed a portion of the eastern Roman empire, but in the fifteenth century fell into the hands of the Turks, its present occupants.—'Αχαια, Achaia, strictly so called, is the northern region of the Peloponnesus, bounded on the north by the Gulf of Corinth, on the south by Arcadia, on the east by Sicyonia, and on the west by the Ionian Sea. The name used by the apostle in the wider and Roman acceptation, including various regions, 2 Cor. xi. 10. What is called Achaia in Acts xix. 21, is called Hellas or Greece in Acts xx. 2. The title of proconsul or deputy given to its chief magistrate, Acts xviii. 12. Had not long been so when the Acts of the Apostles was written, nor continued long after—an internal evidence of the authenticity of the book.— Κοινωνιαν (κοινος, common), a communion or communication. *Eras., Vor., Pisc., Vat., Calv.* Collation. *Eras., Vor.* Contribution. *Stuart.* It was required among the Jews, in times of scarcity or dearness of provisions, that those who were able should contribute of their substance to the necessities of the poor. *Zohar.* Jews residing in Gentile lands sent the tithes for the poor every third year to Judea.

---

26. *It hath pleased them verily; and their debtors they are. For if the Gentiles have been made partakers of their spiritual things, their duty is also to minister unto them in carnal things.*

Verily. Special reason for their liberality in this case.
Some even of Christ's poor have claims on us above others.
Gentiles had good reason for contributing cheerfully.
Debtors. Not by a legal, but a moral obligation.
The gift not merely one of benevolence, but of repayment.
A double motive in it—1. Brotherly love; 2. Gratitude.
In Christ's kingdom, liberty and necessity, will and duty, are one.
Gentiles were debtors—1. To the Jews in general;
2. To the saints at Jerusalem in particular.
We are debtors to others to a greater extent than we suppose.
Spiritual things. Gentiles have received from the Jews—
1. The Gospel; Jews the first preachers of it;
2. The Scriptures; Jews their appointed guardians;
3. The Saviour; Himself a Jew and of Jewish parentage.
Jerusalem the channel of Gospel blessings to the world.
For spiritual blessings men are debtors—
1. To God; 2. To the instruments He employs.
Gentile obligations to Jews but little recognised.
Higher benevolence due to them than they have yet received.

A spurious Christianity long the persecutor of the Jews.
Their duty is. *Gr.*, They owe it as a debt, *i.e.*, to Jewish saints.
The debt one of fraternal equity, as in 1 Cor. ix. 11.
We owe love to all, gratitude to some, chap. xiii. 8.
Men's greatest debts ordinarily most forgotten.
Minister. *Gr.*, To minister as to God in holy things.
Term applied by Paul to himself as a minister of Christ, ver. 16.
To magistrates, as ministers of God, chap. xiii. 6.
To Epaphroditus, as ministering to Paul's wants, Phil. ii. 25.
This contribution called in like manner a service, 2 Cor. ix. 12.
The same Greek word applied to common prayer—Liturgy.
To do good and communicate a spiritual sacrifice, Heb. xiii. 16.
Carnal things. Things needful for the body and this life.
Claimed for preachers of the Gospel on similar grounds, 1 Cor. ix. 11.
Gratitude manifested by means of temporal gifts.
Carnal things are to spiritual as chaff to wheat.
Through Jewish believers Gentiles obtained eternal gain.
A small return, to contribute to their temporal wants.
Love embraces the whole man, body, soul, and spirit.
Ministering to the saints' wants a test at the last day, Matt. xxv. 25.

Εὐδοκησαν γαρ., it has pleased them I say; reading with the point at γαρ. *Calv.* It has seemed good; for they are truly their debtors; the point to stand after εὐδοκησαν. *Stuart.* They have thought it good; and their debtors verily they are. *D. Brown.*—Και ὀφειλεται αὐτ. εἰσι., and their debtors they are. *Calv.* Και, intensive, — truly, really. *Stuart.*—Λειτουργησαι, to minister; the verb properly indicating public service, and then transferred to sacred ones; gives a view of this contribution as a spiritual sacrifice. *Calv.*

---

28. *When, therefore, I have performed this, and have sealed to them this fruit, I will come by you into Spain.*

Performed. *Gr.*, Finished, completed. The wish realised, Acts xxi. 17.
The work finished when the saints received the contribution.
A good work to be persevered in till it is finished.
Paul's eager zeal did not break off an unfinished work.
Sealed. Made sure, Matt. xxvii. 26; delivered safely into their hands.
Paul had pledged himself to this to the churches, 1 Cor. xvi. 34.
His activity and fidelity worthy of all imitation.

Paul careful to avoid all ground of suspicion, 1 Cor. xvi. 3, 4 ; 2 Cor. viii. 19-21.
Ministers to be specially careful as to pecuniary trusts.
Fruit. 1. Fruit of faith on the part of the contributors ;
2. Fruit for enjoyment on the part of the Jerusalem saints ;
3. Fruit of the apostle's own labours among the Gentiles.
So he speaks of contributions to his own necessities, Phil. iv. 17.
Fruit is either—1. That which is produced ; or,
2. That by which another is benefited. Here both.
Much produced by the Gospel, and that for the good of others.

'Επιτελεσας, when I shall have finished or perfected (perfecero). *Calv.* Discharged this duty. *Stuart.* Heb. פָּרָה, עָצַר.—Σφραγισαμενος (σφραγις, a seal), when I shall have sealed (obsignavero). *Eras., Men., Calv.* Assigned. *Vulg., Mor.* Consigned. *Pag., Diod.* Have delivered sealed, as money was wont to be. *Vat.* Safely and faithfully deposited it. *Par., Beza.* Delivered up as a faithful guardian ; allusion to sealing deposits with a ring. *Calv.* As treasures, letters, or public documents. *Par.* Have answered for it as well and faithfully kept. *Luth.* Deposited it in the treasury as in a safe and secure place. *Chrys.* Delivered safely as under seal. *Hamm., Elsn., Doddr.* Faithfully delivered up. *Mart., A. Clarke.* Made sure, seen the distribution actually made. *Stuart.* Handed in safely. *De Wette.* Stamped as genuine ; exhibited to Jewish believers this seal or evidence of the Gentiles' faith. *Haldane.* Consigned, put the last hand to the work. *Brown.* Secured. *Cobbin, Ellicot.* Σφραγιζω, used by the LXX for חתם (E. V., 'that he might *sum* the money,' 2 Kings xxii. 4), but which they probably read חתם, 'that he might *seal.*' *Schött.*—Καρπον, fruit ; increase to the Jews from the sowing of the Gospel among the Gentiles. *Calv.* Benefit. *Schött.* Fruit of the success of his ministry and the conversion of the Gentiles. *A. Clarke.* Fruit of the contribution which the benevolence of the believers in Macedonia and Achaia had produced. *Stuart.* Fruit of their faith. *Hald.* Of the apostle's labours. *Brown.*—'Απελευσομαι, I shall set out on my journey (proficiscar). *Calv.* Pass through. *Stuart.* Return. *D. Brown.*

---

29. *And I am sure that, when I come unto you, I shall come in the fulness of the blessing of the gospel of Christ.*

Sure. Speaks of his *coming* with *hope*, of its *effects* with certainty.
Certainty from—1. Faith in the promise ; 2. Past experience.
Such belief in the preacher brings blessing to the hearer.
Indicates—1. His confidence in the Lord's power and love ;
2. In the preciousness of His message, chap. i. 16 ;
3. In the good-will and candour of his hearers ;
4. His affectionate desire for their welfare ;
5. His heartiness and cheerfulness in his work.
Hopefulness heartens both ourselves and others, Num. xiii. 30.

A preacher's success often according to his faith.
Fulness. Not only blessing, but fulness of blessing.
Expression of faith and love. Paul's large and affectionate heart.
Looks forward to an activity largely blessed by Christ.
To a prepared people rich blessing from such a preacher.
A fulness of blessing promised in the Gospel, Ps. lxxxi. 10.
Christ gives not only life, but life more abundantly, John x. 10.
Blessing—1. Conversion of sinners; 2. Confirmation of saints.
Blessing in the growth—1. Of knowledge; 2. Faith; 3. Holiness.
Christ's rich blessing to be sought and expected for others—
1. As the effect of our visits; 2. As the fruit of our labours.
Blessing the proper effect of the Gospel, Ps. lxxii. 17; Luke ii. 10, 11, 14.
Gospel of Christ. Christ's blessing to men comes through His Gospel.
The Gospel message to be preached in all its blessed fulness.
A rich blessing usually accompanies a full Gospel.
Sad to live under the Gospel without its blessing.
"The Gospel" may be dropped from the text, but necessary to the blessing.

Ἐν πληρώματι εὐλογίας τ. εὐαγγελίου τ. Χ. Codd. Sin., Vat., and Alex., as well as most Latin MSS., omit του εὐαγγελίου, though found in Chrysostom's copy, the Syriac Version, and in more recent Greek MSS., and restored by the Roman correctors. Generally rejected by critics. In or with the fulness of the blessing of the Gospel of Christ. *Eras., Mor., Calv.* With the full blessing. *Pag., Pisc., Tol., Beza.* With the richest gift of Christ. *Ambr., Grot.* Will fully make known to you the Gospel. *Vat., Est.* Shall find you replete with all spiritual gifts, and approved in all things. *Chrys.* Will find you abounding in the fruits of the Gospel; or, will have much fruit in preaching it. *Calv.* With full power of plentifully imparting to you the gifts of the Spirit. *Whitby, Wells.* With the full, abundant blessing; πληρ., according to Hebrew idiom, serving as an adjective. *Stuart.* Richest measure of success. *Hald.* In the fulness of the blessing of Christ. *Ellicot, D. Brown.* Endued with all the gifts and graces of Christ himself; the blessing of Christ *exceeds* even that of the Gospel. *A. Clarke.*— Εὐλογια = benefit, gift; Heb. בְּרָכָה; but used once by the LXX for פְּרִי, fruit, Isa. xxvii. 9. *Schött.*

---

30. *Now I beseech you, brethren, for the Lord's sake, and for the love of the Spirit, that ye strive together with me in your prayers to God for me.*

I beseech you. The journey was both hazardous and important.
Believers' prayers to be earnestly sought in times of need.
Request for prayer here made of persons not yet seen.

So Paul asks for the prayers of the Colossians, Ephesians, Thessalonians, and Hebrews, Col. iv. 3 ; Eph. vi. 19 ; 1 Thess. iv. 25 ; 2 Thess. iii. 1 ; Heb. xiii. 18.
Not of the Corinthians and Galatians, whom he had to rebuke.
The Lord's sake. The Jerusalem journey undertaken—
1. As a thing agreeable to the Lord's will ;
2. For the advancement of His honour and glory ;
3. From a principle of love and obedience to Him.
Those who are Christ's are to do all for Christ's sake.
Christ's cause and honour bound up with our life and labour.
" For Christ's sake," the strongest plea with a believer.
All our prayers and labours to be for His sake.
By the love, &c.—1. As you have tasted it ; 2. As you would show it.
Another argument. Shows Paul's earnestness in the matter.
Love looks not only on our own things, but those of others.
The undertaking commended to their prayers was one of love.
Prayer for others, to be effectual, must proceed from love.
Love a powerful argument with believers.
Christian love embraces all the brethren however distant.
Is concerned for the cause of Christ in all parts of the world.
Of the Spirit. Christian love a special fruit of the Spirit, 1 Pet. i. 22.
The Holy Ghost the Author of every Christian grace, Gal. v. 22.
Love, wrought by the Spirit, the only true, holy, and enduring love.
Strive. *Gr.*, Agonise, wrestle. Expresses the apostle's earnestness.
Not only help or pray, but strive, wrestle, agonise.
To prevail like Jacob, we must wrestle like him, Gen. xxxii. 24-30.
Prayer a stirring up of yourselves to take hold of God, Isa. lxiv. 7.
Earnest prayer a conflict or wrestling, Col. iv. 12.
Especially when made for the removal of evil, Matt. xvii. 21.
Evil spirits oppose us in prayer. *Origen.*
Great effort needed for right and successful prayer.
Prayer to be—1. In faith, nothing doubting, Jas. i. 6-8 ; Mark xi. 23 ;
2. With perseverance, without fainting, Luke xviii. 1-7 ;
3. With fervency and earnestness, Jas. v. 17 ; Luke xviii. 44 ;
4. With fixity of mind ; represented in Abraham, Gen. xv. 11 ;
5. With meekness and forgiveness of others, Mark xi. 24-26.
Prayer for others, to be effectual, must be fervent, Jas. v. 16.
Example of the power of intercessory prayer, Acts xii. 5-12.

All Abraham asked on behalf of Sodom granted, Gen. xviii. 23, &c.
Believers can strive in prayer when they can do nothing else.
Together—1. With himself; 2. With one another, as Matt. xviii. 19.
With me. Paul himself thus agonised in prayer.
Love as earnest in praying for others as for ourselves.
Those who truly ask the prayers of others will pray themselves.
Union both a help to prayer and the success of it, Matt. xviii. 19.
Those separated in person can be together in prayer.
In your prayers. Believers necessarily praying persons.
Their prayer for him to be not once nor twice, but often.
The cause of Christ greatly helped by believers' prayers.
Interest in those prayers a precious privilege.
Their value seen in Paul's earnest request for them.
The only favour he asked of the churches or his converts.
Interchange of prayers expressive of interchange of love.
Prayers of saints *on earth* desired, not of those in heaven.
To God. Not to the Virgin Mary, or the saints or angels.
The believer's privilege to pray directly to God his Father.
No Mediator or Intercessor but Christ the God-man, 1 Tim. ii. 5.
No scriptural example of departed saints invoked in prayer.
The practice in the Church of Rome a part of the apostasy.
For me. Prayer to be mutual. Paul had often prayed for *them*.
His humility. Sought aid even of the "weak" at Rome.
If the apostle needed the help of believers' prayers, well may we.
Especially needed by ministers and labourers in the Word.

Παρακαλω δε, moreover, I beseech; δε, continuative. *Stuart.*—'Αδελφοι, omitted in Codd. Vat.—Δια τ. κ. ἡμ. Ιησ. Χρ., by our Lord Jesus Christ. *Calv.* For the sake of our Lord Jesus Christ; out of love and regard for Him. *Stuart.*—'Αγαπης τ. Πν., the love of the Spirit; love which the Spirit has shown. *Chrys.* The uniting love which proceeds from the Spirit. *Calv.* Love which Christ requires and the Spirit works. *Ham.* Which the Spirit has shed abroad in our hearts. *A. Clarke.* The genuine fruit of the Spirit. *Doddr.* Love which the Spirit has given us. *Stuart.* Which the Spirit works. *De Wette.* Gives. *Con. & Hows.* 'Love of the Spirit,' a Hebraism for 'spiritual love.' *Hald.* The peculiar love which Christians have for each other. *Brown.* —Συναγωνισασθαι μοι, that ye strive together with me (concertetis mihi). *Calv.* Semel contendatis. *Mor.* Labour with me. *Syriac.* Aid me. *Cas.* Aid me in my labour. *Eras., Est.* With great earnestness and fervency join your prayers to mine. *Ham.* Join your utmost strength and fervency with mine. *Elsner, Doddr.* Strive together; unite with me in my Christian warfare by helping with your prayers. *Stuart.* Συναγωνιζομαι = to assist, as συναγωνισασθαι ἡμιν, 'he endeavoured to assist us.' *Luc. in Trag. Schött.* To pray is an ἀγωνη or conflict when *men* resist. *Beng.* Implies he had grounds for anxious fears in the matter. *D. Brown.*

31. *That I may be delivered from them that do not believe in Judea; and that my service which I have for Jerusalem may be accepted of the saints.*

That. The special want named. Particularity in prayer.
" What will ye that I shall do for you ?" Matt. xx. 32.
God knows our wishes, but will know them from ourselves.
Delivered. Paul knew that dangers awaited him, Acts xx. 22, 23.
Lawful to pray for deliverance from danger and death.
Prayer the means of relieving from carefulness, Phil. iv. 6, 7.
Paul glad to lay down his life, yet prays for its preservation, Phil. ii. 17.
His not being delivered a proof of the genuineness of the epistle.
Yet preserved from open violence and secret conspiracy, Acts xxi. 30 ; xxiii. 16.
Do not believe. Unbelief the ground of enmity to believers.
Describes the great majority in Judea and elsewhere.
Judea. The country of the Jews, in a wider or stricter sense.
Taken widely, embraced the whole of Canaan.
First mentioned as "Jewry," Dan. v. 13; province of Judea, Ezra v. 8.
More strictly, the south part of Canaan west of the Jordan.
South of Samaria, which again lay south of Galilee.
Paul especially obnoxious to the unbelieving Jews—
1. From his antecedents,—the hope of Judaism, Acts xxii. 3-5 ;
2. From his activity and zeal in spreading Christianity ;
3. From his doctrine of free justification, Gal. v. 11.
Jews his bitterest persecutors even among the Gentiles.
His life in greater danger in Judea than in heathen lands.
Not on that account deterred from duty, Acts xxi. 11-13.
Service. In the highest office he performs the humblest service.
Service humble, yet dignified ; important, but perilous.
The believer shrinks from no service his Master assigns him.
Accepted. What is kindly given should be gratefully received.
The acceptance of the contribution doubtful, from—
1. The unfavourable view entertained of Paul by Jewish believers, Acts xxi. 20, 21.
2. Their prejudice against Gentile Christians.
Paul's fears shared in by the Jerusalem elders, Acts xxi. 20.
The success of his service depended on its acceptance.
His aim the union of Jewish and Gentile believers.
The acceptance of his service to be also matter of prayer.
It is God's not only to restrain enmity, but generate good-will.

All that lies in our heart to be poured into God's ear.
Grounds to believe this prayer was largely answered.
Saints. Saints' as well as sinners' hearts in God's hand.
Even saints on earth liable to prejudice and passion.
Believers only partially sanctified in this life.

'Απειθουντων (ἀ, not, and πειθω, to persuade), the unbelieving (incredulis). *Calv.* Unbelievers. *Stuart.* Who do not obey, *i.e.*, the truth. *D. Brown.*—Ιουδαιᾳ, Judæa. This designation followed the overthrow of the ancient landmarks of the tribes of Judah and Israel in their respective captivities. Resulted from the division of the Persian empire under Darius, Est. viii. 9; Dan. vi. 1. In the Apocryphal books the word 'province,' found in Ezra v. 8, is dropped, and the terms used are 'Judæa' and the 'land of Judæa.' In the Greek period a noble and vigorous independence enjoyed under the Maccabees. Hyrcanus reigned over a prosperous and independent kingdom, 100 B.C. In 63 B.C. Pompey came to Jerusalem, and Judæa was made subject to Rome. In Antipater, an Idumæan, who was made procurator of Judæa by Julius Cæsar B.C. 47, a new native dynasty was raised to the throne. A foreign civilisation gradually introduced and extended. Herod the Great, who succeeded his father Antipater, reigned under the protectorate of Augustus. The period under Herod remarkable for great architectural works, promotion of commerce, influx of strangers, diffusion of the Latin and Greek tongues, and above all, for the birth of the promised Saviour. After the deposition of his son Archelaus as ethnarch of Judæa, A.D. 6, Judæa was placed under the jurisdiction of a procurator residing at Cæsarea, who was subject to the Governor of Syria at Antioch. In the time of this epistle it had been added by Claudius to the dominion of Herod Agrippa, who had received from Caligula the grant of an independent principality in the north of Palestine.—Διακονια (Codd. Vat. has δωροφορια, ministration of alms. *Tisch.*), ministry. *Calv.* Service. *Stuart.*—Ευπροσδεκτος, accepted. *Calv.* Acceptable. *Stuart, D. Brown.*

---

32. *That I may come unto you with joy by the will of God, and may with you be refreshed.*

May come. Third petition. Journeys and visits to be subjects of prayer.
Joy. Arising—1. From the success of his undertaking;
2. From the pleasure of enjoying their fellowship;
3. From the exercise of his ministry among them.
Desirable for ministers and preachers to meet their hearers with joy.
Not only visits but the joy of them to be matter of prayer.
Prayer answered. Came as a prisoner, but a joyful one, Acts xxviii. 15.
Our visits to believers and labours in the Lord to be with joy.
Will of God. Paul desired to visit Rome only by God's will, chap. i. 10.
Prayer to be made, not to change God's will, but to fulfil it.

God's unchangeableness no argument against prayer.
Prayer an appointed means for obtaining a purposed blessing.
Personal desire to be subordinated to the divine will.
Example of conditional as distinguished from absolute prayer.
A visit to be truly joyful must be according to God's will.
Abundant sources of joy to God's children even here.
Communion of saints on earth a foretaste of heaven.
Refreshed—1. In the fellowship of each other, Prov. xxvii. 17 ;
2. In the united contemplation of divine truth ;
3. In the seeing and hearing of the Lord's work.
Refreshment of spirit needed by the strongest believers.
Christian fellowship a means of spiritual refreshment.
Refreshment provided by the Lord for weary labourers, Mark vi. 31.

Ἵνα, so that; connected in sense with the preceding. *Stuart.*—Ἔλθω, I may come. Codd. Sin. and Alex. read ἐλθών, 'coming.'—Χαρᾷ, with joy ; desirable for the Romans themselves among whom he might labour. *Calv.*—Διὰ θελήματος Θεοῦ. Cod. Sin. reads διὰ Θ. Ἰησοῦ Χριστοῦ ; and Cod. Vat., δ. Θ. Κυρίου Ἰησ. Other MSS. read δ. Θ. Θεοῦ καὶ Ἰησ. Χρ.—Συναναπαύσωμαι ὑμῖν (omitted by Cod. Vat., while some copies read, συναναπαύσω ὑμᾶς ; others, ἀναψύξω μεθ' ὑμῶν); may with you be refreshed (refociller). *Calv., Pag., Pisc., Beza.* Recreer. *Cas., Mor.* With mutual intercourse. *Men.* Seeing your advancement. *Tol.* May be refreshed among you. *Stuart.* May rest. *Ellicot.* May with you refresh myself. *D. Brown.*

23. *Now the God of peace be with you all. Amen.*

God of peace. So xvi. 20 ; 1 Cor. xiv. 33 ; 2 Cor. xiii. 11 ; Phil. iv. 9 ; 1 Thess. v. 23 ; Heb. xiii. 20.
So called here with reference—1. To the apostle's own conflicts ;
2. To the differences about which he had written.
God not only at peace *with us*, but gives peace *to us*.
Gives peace—1. By giving us Christ and faith in Him, Rom. v. 1 ; Eph. ii. 8.
2. By inspiring confidence in His gracious providence, Phil. iv. 7.
3. By assuring us of victory in Christ over all enemies, xvi. 20.
God in the Old Testament the Lord of Hosts ; in the New, the God of Peace.
As the God of peace He bestows the peace of God, Phil. iv. 7.
The God of peace through Christ who makes peace, Col. i. 20.
"God of peace," an encouragement to take to Him every want.
As "God of peace," He takes pleasure in the prosperity of His servants, Ps. xxxv. 27.

With you. God reconciled dwells with His people, John xiv. 33.
Christ's name Emmanuel, "God with us," Matt. i. 23.
Believers not only have God *for* them, but *with* them.
Peace may well be among those who have the God of peace.
The *God* of peace with us will make us *men* of peace.
Peace is good,—the God of peace still better.
God a man of war to His foes ; a God of peace to His friends, Exod. xv. 3.
Amen. Expresses hearty desire and confidence of the writer.
The epistle properly ends here. The rest a postscript,

Θεος τ. εἰρηνης, God of peace ; the lover of peace. *Men.* Author of it. *Grot., Calv.* Procurer of it. *Tol.* Εἰρηνης, as uniting them all in harmony. *Calv.* As giving happiness and prosperity. *Stuart.* As reconciled with them, giving the peace of that reconciliation, and making them disseminators of peace. *D. Brown.*—Ἀμην, omitted by Cod. Alex

CHAPTER XVI.

1. *I commend unto you Phœbe our sister, which is a servant of the church which is at Cenchrea.*

Commend. To your Christian love and kind offices.
Believers travelling carried letters of recommendation.
Such letters referred to in 2 Cor. iii. 1 ; 3 John iii. 9, 10.
The member of one church admissible into any other.
Phebe. Probably a convert from heathenism.
Name denotes "the moon," an object of Pagan worship.
Like Diana, and adopted by females in her honour.
Heathen names usually retained by believers.
Sister. Term expressive of the new relationship in Christ.
A real relation involving responsibilities and duties.
Those so closely related should cherish corresponding affection.
Servant. Ministering female, probably in an official capacity.
Deaconesses an early institution in the church.
Female office-bearers corresponding to elders and deacons.
Such probably referred to in 1 Tim. iii. 8, 11 ; v. 10, 11 ; Titus ii. 3.
Their duty especially to attend to female members.
Needful from Oriental manners in regard to the sexes.
Women in the East not permitted to mix with male society.

Deaconesses attended to the baptism of female converts.
Took charge of poor and afflicted female church-members.
Also exercised an oversight over their morals.
Each member, male and female, may serve Christ in His church.
Women followed Christ and ministered to Him of their substance, Luke viii. 3.
Inspired authority for female agency in the church.
Example of apostolic times too little followed in our own.
The epistle authenticated by these personal references.
The facts again authenticated by its genuineness.
Character of living Christianity here illustrated.
Exhibited—1. In the writer; 2. In the parties referred to.
Church. Congregation of professed believers in Christ.
Term applied to the collective body of the elect, Eph. v. 25.
Name borrowed from the congregation of the synagogue, Matt. xviii. 17.
Applied also to the company of the redeemed in heaven, Heb. xii. 23.
Never given in the New Testament to the place of meeting.
"Church" an altered form of a word denoting "the Lord's house."
The church viewed either as visible or invisible.
The former may include hypocrites and formalists.
Tares among the wheat. A Judas among the twelve.
The latter includes only the renewed and justified.
Cenchrea. Eastern port of Corinth, four or five miles distant.
Corinth, standing on an isthmus, had two harbours.
Cenchrea likely to be visited by Paul when at Corinth.
The place where he assumed the Nazaritic vow, Acts xviii. 18.
Mention of Cenchrea, taken with ver. 23; 1 Cor. i. 14; Acts xix. 22, serves—
1. To confirm the genuineness of the epistle;
2. To indicate the quarter whence it was written.

Συνίστημι (σύν, together, and ἵστημι, to stand), I commend. Letters given by church rulers to members travelling to other places, called ἐπιστολαὶ συστατικαί (2 Cor. iii. 1), and συστάσεις, in the Apostolic Constitutions. Rules in regard to them laid down by the Councils of Antioch and Constantinople.—Δέ, continuative. *Stuart.* Omitted in some copies.—'Ἀδελφή (ἅμα, together, and δελφύς, the womb), sister. Instead of ἡμῶν, 'our,' Cod. Alex. has ὑμῶν, 'your.'—Οὖσαν, being, or who is. Cod. Vat. adds καί, also.—Διάκονον, a servant or female minister (ministra). *Calv., Pag., Pisc., Beza.* The *ministræ* in Pliny's Letter to Trajan. *A. Clarke.* Deaconesses. *Diod., Mar., Doddr., A. Clarke, Stuart, Alford, Brown, Ellicot, D. Brown.* A ministering servant. *Con. & Hows.* A pious noble and wealthy lady. *Par.* Who willingly contributed her substance to the church. *Vat.* Was wont to entertain and attend to God's servants. *Est.* Ministered to the sick members of the church. *Pisc.* Discharged an office in it. *Calv.* Was appointed to the office of deaconess. *Or., Chrys., Est., Men.* One of the deaconesses described in 1 Tim. v. 10, 11. *Tol., Flatt.* One of those who accompanied Paul on his journeys and ministered to him out of their own property. *Ham.* Pliny speaks of two female Christians 'quæ ministræ dicebantur.' Such deaconesses set apart by the laying on of hands and prayer. Their duty to instruct the female candidates for church-membership, attend at their baptism, visit Christian females and report concerning them to the bishop, take his commands to them or bring them to his presence, attend to martyrs, confessors, strangers, and sick, but especially those of their own sex, keep the women's door of the church, and see that good order was observed in the women's side during the public service. Generally widows at first, afterwards elderly unmarried females. Gradually the order fell into disuse, and was abolished in the Western Church in the sixth, and in the Eastern about the twelfth century.—Ἐκκλησιας (ἐκ, out of, and καλεω, to call), church or congregation of professed believers. ' A holy Catholic Church, which is the Communion of Saints,' the Christian confession of faith. No distinct definitions of the Church before Cyprian. According to early Christian writers, the church a mother, Noah's Ark, &c. No salvation out of it, but all the fulness of divine grace to be found in it. Clement of Alexandria, and still more Cyprian, maintained the *unity* of the church. Cyprian did not sufficiently distinguish between the visible and invisible church. The apostolic doctrine of a universal priesthood more and more superseded by the hierarchy of the bishops, and the internal converted into the external. Ἐκκλησια καθολικη, 'Catholic or universal church,' first met with in the inscription of the epistle of the church of Smyrna concerning the death of Polycarp, A.D. 169. Ignatius in his epistle to the same church says, 'Wherever Jesus Christ is, there is the Catholic Church.' Clement derives the term and the idea of ἐκκλησια (church, assembly) from the elect forming a society. Precedency accorded to the Roman church by Tertullian before his conversion to Montanism. He says, the words 'Tibi dabo claves' ('To thee will I give the keys') were addressed to Peter *alone* and not to the bishops, and views spiritual men as the successors of Peter. Distinguishes also between the church of the Spirit or spiritual men in whom the Holy Spirit dwells, and the church which is composed of the sum-total of the bishops. According to Cyprian, he who does not take part with the bishop no longer belongs to the church. Novatian maintained that the church is composed only of saints. Followed by the Donatists. Opposed by Optatus of Mileve, 368, and by Augustine. According to Augustine, the church consists of the sum-total of all who are baptized. These last advanced the idea of a universal Christian Church. Bishops of Rome applied this to the Papal system, and thus prepared the way for the hierarchy of the Middle Ages. Pelagius considered only the individual Christians as the church. The Manichæans, separating the elect from the rest who were only hearers, gave countenance to the principle of a church within a church (ecclesiola in ecclesia). Augustine advocated a rigorous exercise of church discipline, but not to the depopulating of the church. In subsequent centuries, the church, in the person of Peter and his successors, said to have the two swords united, ecclesiastical and secular. The contrary termed heresy. Bernard of Clairval (1146) the first to apply Luke xxii. 36–38 figuratively. John of Salisbury also gave both swords to the Popes. Others maintained that the power was divided. Papal power and infallibility claimed in opposition to the doctrine that councils were superior to the Pope. So the Bull of Boniface III. (1302). The contrary maintained by the Council of Basle, 1431. Mystical idea of the church and the universal priesthood of Chirstians propounded by Hugo of St Victor, Wycliffe, Huss, Wessel, and Savanarola. According to the Roman Catholic doctrine, the church is the visible society of all who by their baptism pledge themselves to the adoption of a certain external creed and the use of the same sacraments, and who acknowledge the Pope as their common head. According to the Protestant doctrine, the church is the invisible association of all who are united by the bond of a true faith, imperfectly represented by the visible church. The principle, 'extra ecclesiam nulla salus' ('no salvation out of the church'), also maintained by the Protestant Church, though in a somewhat different sense. According to Luther, every Christian man is a priest, and every Christian woman a priestess, whether they be young or old, master or servant, mistress or maid, scholar or illiterate. Protestants distinguish between sacerdotium (priesthood) and ministerium (ministry). According to the Roman Catholic doctrine, the church is a state, therefore independent of every other state. According to the Protestant view, the church is independent of all secular power. Cæsaro-papacy established by the church committing the government of the visible church into the hands of the state, the civil ruler taking the place of the Pope. Reformers proceeded on the idea of a Christian government analogous to the theocracy of the Old Testament. Hence some, as Zuingle, left ecclesiastical discipline to the magistrate, without making it necessary to have an ecclesiastical court. Others, as Œcolampadius and Calvin, retained the ecclesiastical institution of excommunication, but reduced it to the primitive apostolic form. A controversy on the subject was begun by Thomas Erastus (or Liebler, of Heidelberg, 1568), whose views were hence called Erastianism. According to him and Thomasius, the reigning prince possesses the right to regulate the ecclesiastical affairs of his country, banish disturbers of the church's peace, &c., but cannot himself be subject to church discipline,—the so-called territorial system. Opposed by Chancellor Pfaff of Würtemberg (1720), who advocated the system of ecclesiastical *collegia*, viewing the church as a collegium or society with laws and privileges of its own. *Hagenbach.*—Κεγχρεαις, in Cenchrea, now called Kikreis. Some remains of the ancient town still visible. The western port, called Lechæum, distant about a mile and a half from Corinth, and united to it by a long wall. A third smaller port was called Schœnus, now Kalamiki, at the narrowest part of the Isthmus. Corinth itself, where this epistle was written, situated on the Isthmus connecting the Morea and the continent, built on a steep rock two thousand feet above the sea. The common resort and universal mart of the Greeks. Noted for its wealth, luxury, and profligacy. To 'Corinthianise,' or play the Corinthian, was to act the wanton. Destroyed by the Roman Consul Mummius, B.C. 146, and rebuilt by Julius Cæsar. Rapidly increased in size and splendour, and at the time of this epistle had become the capital of the Roman province of Achaia. The Isthmus celebrated for the games held at the Posidonium or sanctuary of Neptune every two years. The road leading from Corinth to Cenchrea, through the avenue of pine trees which furnished the leaves for the victors' crowns, often traversed by the apostle. The games themselves alluded to in his epistle to the Corinthian Church, 1 Cor. vii. 25. Jews settled at Corinth in great numbers for the purpose of commerce.

---

2. *That ye receive her in the Lord as becometh saints, and that ye assist her in whatsoever business she hath need of you ; for she hath been a succourer of many, and of myself also.*

Receive—1. Into fellowship ; 2. Into hospitality.
In the Lord. As a Christian sister and member of the Lord's body.
In a Christian manner, worthy of the Lord, and for His sake.

All to be done as to the Lord, and in the Lord's name, Col. iii. 17, 23.
He who receives another in the Lord will do it heartily.
Those to be received by us who come as in the Lord.
Union with Christ the true ground of church fellowship.
As becometh saints. Saints the ordinary title of believers.
A professed Christian a professed saint, and should be a real one.
Believers to be received in a manner worthy of saints.
Saints, however poor, worthy of honourable reception by believers.
Certain kind of conduct due *to* saints and *from* saints.
Christ's members to be received as Christ himself—
1. With kindness ; 2. Esteem ; 3. Readiness to assist.
Assist. Believing strangers to be not only received but assisted—
1. With counsel ; 2. Protection ; 3. Temporal supplies.
Believers to help each other with their purses as well as their prayers.
The collective church to aid individual believers.
Whatever business. Whether of a public or private nature.
Whether her own or undertaken for another.
Whether of a sacred or a secular character.
Christianity does not abolish worldly transactions.
All business to be done in the Lord and for His sake.
Business thus sanctified and blessed to ourselves and others.
Need. One believer made to need another's aid.
The need may be—1. For ourselves ; 2. Another ; 3. Christ's cause.
Faithful servants of Christ have often need of aid.
Phebe a representative of all such applicants.
Christ himself comes to our door in the person of such.
No such application to be rejected,—missions, churches, schools, &c.
Help to be given—1. According to our ability ; 2. The actual need.
For. Additional claim presented on Phebe's behalf.
Applicants for the church's aid to be properly accredited.
Character and work entitled to confidence and regard.
Succourer. *Gr.*, Protectress, patroness ; more than mere helper.
Either—1. As a deaconess, caring for the sick and poor ;
Or 2. As employing her private means in doing good.
Wealth consecrated when used in helping Christ's cause.
Finds its proper place when laid at Christ's feet.
Love an active principle ; not in words, but deeds, 1 John iii. 18.
In the power of all in some way to succour others.
Help given to others gives a claim upon it in return.

Close and widely-extended relationship among believers.
Phebe commended to kindness at Rome for kindness elsewhere.
Of many. Probably while suffering persecution.
All Jews banished shortly before from Rome.
Believers scattered from Jerusalem after Stephen's death.
Thanks due from us not only for aiding ourselves but others.
Phebe's large-heartedness, wide and unwearied benevolence.
"The liberal soul deviseth liberal things," Isa. xxii. 28; Eccles. xi. 1, 2, 6.
Of myself also. Probably personally; the occasion unknown.
Paul often in circumstances requiring succour.
Remained long at Corinth amid dangers and difficulties, Acts xviii. 1-17.
Grateful acknowledgment of Phebe's kindness and service.
Grace teaches both to forget injuries and remember benefits.
Phebe had cast in her lot with Christ's despised and suffering saints;
Obtains an honourable and lasting place in the Book of God.

Προσδέξησθε, that ye receive her (suscipiatis). *Beza, Pisc., Calv.*—Ἐν κυρίῳ, in the Lord; for Christ's sake. *Chrys.* In Christ's name. *Beza, Par.* On Christ's account. *Grot., Vat., Tol.* Being in the Lord,—referring to Phebe as a true believer and member of Christ's spiritual body; or rather to the Romans as a Christian church,—ye, being in the Lord. *Stuart.* As a member of His body. *Hald.* As His genuine disciple. *D. Brown.* In a Christian manner, mindful of your common Lord. *Alford.* —Ἀξίως τ. ἁγίων, suitably for saints. *Beza.* As is worthy of saints. *Pag., Cas., Pisc., Calv.* As becomes saints. *Eras., Vat., Est.* As it becomes saints to receive saints. *Est., Tol., Brown, D. Brown.* As it becomes saints to be received. *Tol.* In a manner worthy of your Christian profession. *Stuart.* In a way worthy of you and her. *Haldane.*—Παραστῆτε, assist (adsitis). *Beza, Pisc., Eras., Pag., Cas., Calv.* (Assistatis). *Mor.* Be helpful (auxilio sitis). *Vat.* Julian ascribes the great increase in the number of Christians to their kindness to strangers.—Πράγματι (πράσσω, to do), business (negotio). *Eras., Pag., Beza, Mor., Calv.* In whatever way you may be able to help her. *Tol.* Legal terms used; probably some lawsuit or appeal to the Emperor. *Con. & Hows.*—Προστάτις (πρό, forward, before; and ἵστημι, to stand; προΐσταμαι, to preside, defend as a patron, Rom. xii. 8), has aided (adfuit). *Eras., Cas., Calv.* Afforded hospitality. *Pag., Pisc., Beza, Dickson, Mar., A. Clarke.* Been a protectress. *Diod.* A helper. *Mor.* A hostess, receiving those into her house who were the church's guests. *Locke.* Partly as a deaconess. *Alford.* Προστάτης, in the Grecian states, one who undertook the care of strangers and became responsible to the authorities for their behaviour. *Eustathius.* Προστάτις, a nobler word than παραστάτις, a mere helper. Προστάτης = Heb. ־ֹ֣ש, a ruler, one appointed over a charge, 1 Chron. xxvii. 31; xxix. 6; 2 Chr. viii. 10.

---

3. *Greet Priscilla and Aquila, my helpers in Christ Jesus.*

Greet. Salute. Express kindly feeling and good wishes. In Paul's case an indication of peculiar esteem and love.

Exhibits his courtesy and warmth of affection.
Love shows itself in a loving carriage and address.
Ordinary forms of courtesy to be used with sincerity.
Needless singularity not countenanced by the Word of God.
This and the following salutations valuable, as—
1. A source of gratification to the persons named;
2. A stimulus both to themselves and others;
3. A tribute to the Christian community at Rome;
4. A corroboration of the genuineness of the epistle.
Fitted also to unite Jews and Gentiles at Rome—
1. To each other; 2. To the apostle himself.
True Christianity characterised by—
1. Whatever is tender and amiable in human nature;
2. The graceful proprieties of an advanced civilisation;
3. The gentle charities and delicacy of refined friendship.
Grace sanctifies the courtesies of life and refines the manners.
Can clothe a peasant with the courtesy of a peer.
Friendly to the graces and amenities of social intercourse.
The truest courtesy proceeds from the love of the Spirit.
Forms of politeness most beautiful when animated by spiritual life.
Five classes in the salutations of this epistle—
1. Those to helpers and fellow labourers, as Aquila, Mary, &c.
2. Those to relatives and countrymen, as Andronicus, &c.;
3. To his own converts and well-known friends, as Epenetus, &c.;
4. To societies, as the church in Aquila's house, &c.;
5. To households, or parts of such, as that of Narcissus, &c.
Neither Peter nor any apostle at that time in Rome.
The number of the salutations accounted for from—
1. The knowledge Paul had of so many now in Rome;
2. His desire to promote harmony and love in the church;
3. The fact that he had never yet personally visited them;
In these salutations may be noted—
1. The kindness of Paul in naming so many;
2. Special regard to individuals combined with love to all;
3. Grateful remembrance of past kindnesses;
4. Those specially distinguished who had laboured most.
Care of the churches did not efface remembrance of persons.
Believers least likely to forget their friends.
Their mutual remembrance lively, because—
1. Founded in a spiritual, therefore deep affection;
2. Kept always fresh at a throne of grace.

Those well remembered who are remembered before God.
In the persons here saluted we have—
1. A group of star-pictures of the apostolic times;
2. A lovely representation of living Christians;
3. A splendid testimony to the riches of divine grace.

Roman, Greek, and Hebrew names promiscuously introduced.
Paul had already preached the Gospel for twenty-five years.
Priscilla. Called also Prisca by contraction, 2 Tim. iv. 19.
Or, Priscilla, a diminutive by way of endearment.
Mentioned also with her husband, Acts xviii. 2, 26; 1 Cor. xvi. 19.
Named here and in 2 Tim. *before*, elsewhere *after* her husband.
Perhaps more gifted, or of more energetic character.
Zealous in the Lord's service and in aiding the apostle.
Female devotedness marked in the history of the church.
Women last at the Saviour's cross, and first at His tomb.
Christ especially honoured by woman, Matt. xxvi. 7, 10; Luke vii. 37, &c.
Woman elevated and honoured by the Gospel.
Aquila. A Jew of Pontus, in Asia Minor, Acts xviii. 2.
Had learned and followed the trade of tentmaking, Acts xviii. 3.
Lived in Rome till banished with the Jews by Claudius, A.D. 52.
Well acquainted with Scripture and the way of salvation, Acts xviii. 26.
Useful with his wife in instructing young Apollos.
Their house used for meetings of the brethren, ver. 5; 1 Cor. xvi. 19.
Probably persons of considerable wealth and influence.
Both names Roman. Perhaps connected with a Roman family.
Met with Paul at Corinth after their banishment, Acts xviii. 1.
Received him as their guest, following the same trade, ver. 3.
Followed him to Ephesus, where he left them, Acts xviii. 19.
At Ephesus when he wrote his First Epistle to the Corinthians, 1 Cor. xvi. 19.
Had now returned to Rome when this epistle was sent.
At Ephesus again when he wrote his Second Epistle to Timothy, 2 Tim. iv. 19.
Example of high spirituality and zeal combined with diligence in a worldly calling.
A constant influx at Rome from all parts of the empire.
For some time Christians safer there than elsewhere.
As yet no regular church officers there known to Paul.
Christians had just returned from their banishment.

CHAP. XVI.]   ST. PAUL'S EPISTLE TO THE ROMANS.   319

Probably as yet no regular church organisation there.
No mention made by Paul of any bishop or presbyter.
My helpers. *Gr.*, Fellow-workers, *i.e.*, in spreading the truth.
Paul not ashamed to acknowledge these as his helpers.
Humility ever an accompaniment of true greatness.
Privilege of private Christians to help Christ's servants.
Ministers and preachers to avail themselves of such help.
Women as well as men fellow-labourers with the apostle.
Out of office as well as *in* it, we can labour for Christ.
Aquila and his wife a beautiful specimen of sanctified wedlock.
In Christ Jesus. In union with Christ and His cause.
All labour, to be of real value, must be in Christ Jesus.
Such testimonies the stars and ribands of true knighthood.
Resplendent when earthly orders and insignia have perished.

'Ασπασασθε (ἁμα or ἁ, together, and σπαω, to draw), salute. Heb. שָׁלוֹם לָךְ.
—Πρισκιλλα (Codd. Sin., Vat., and Alex. have Πρισκα, as Acts xviii. 2. 26; so Origen'.
Prisca, a contraction of Priscilla. *Beng., D. Brown.* Priscilla, an affectionate diminutive
of Prisca. *Stuart.* So Livia and Drusa called also Lavilla and Drusilla, by way of endearment. *Con. & Hows.* Better known and of pre-eminent zeal; therefore mentioned
before her husband. *Est.* Of a more energetic character. *Con. & Hows.* The persecution of Claudius not of long continuance. *Grot.* Aquila and Priscilla had returned
lately to Rome on the death of Claudius and the accession of Nero. *Est., Tir.* Banishment of Jews from Rome had made many acquainted with Paul, and had led to their
conversion. *Lightfoot.*—Συνεργους (συν, together, and εργον, work), fellow-workers.
Calv.—Ἐν Χριστῳ Ιησου, in the Christian cause. *Stuart.*

---

4. *Who have for my life laid down their necks; unto whom not only I give thanks,
but also all the churches of the Gentiles.*

For my life. Paul in great danger at Corinth, Acts xviii. 12-17.
Also at Ephesus, where Aquila and Priscilla were, Acts xix. 30-35.
"After the manner of men I fought with beasts at Ephesus," 1 Cor.
xv. 32.
Could testify in that city, I die daily, 1 Cor. xv. 31.
Writing to the Corinthians could say, In deaths oft, 2 Cor. xi. 23.
Laid down their neck. *Gr.*, placed their neck under, viz., the
sword.
The sword the ordinary mode of capital punishment.
Gave their neck as a pledge or deposit for Paul's life.
Acted on Paul's behalf so as to imperil their own lives.
Were willing to save his life by exposure of their own.

Love disposes us to lay down our lives for the brethren, 1 John iii. 16.

Give thanks—1. For their hospitality ; 2. Their devotedness ; 3. Their zeal in the cause of Christ and the Gospel.
Paul forward in expressing his obligations to others.
A generous nature not only renders services, but thanks.
An ungrateful heart an ungracious one, 1 Thess. v. 18.

Churches. Societies of believers. So Gal. i. 2 ; 1 Cor. xi. 16 ; xvi. 1, 19 ; 2 Cor. viii. 1, 18 ; xi. 28.

Of the Gentiles. 1. Gentile churches served in Paul's person ; 2. Personally assisted by their service and property.
Aquila and his wife fellow-workers with the apostle of the Gentiles.
Their service known to the Gentile churches in general.
Beautiful example of what a Christian couple can effect.
Enabled to lay all the Gentile churches under obligation.
Grace makes men princes on earth without the title.
Their true nobility displayed at the Lord's appearing.

T. ἑαυτῶν τράχηλον ὑπέθηκαν (ὑπο, under, and τίθημι, to put), exposed (supponuerunt) their own neck, *i.e.*, to the sword. *Beza.* To the danger of death. *Vat., Men., Est., Vor.* Laid down their neck (posuerunt). *Calv.* Gave up their neck as a kind of pledge or deposit. *Beng.* A proverbial expression ; derived from supporting a falling burden or suffering for another. *Est.* Risked their lives. *A. Clarke, D. Brown.*

---

5. *Likewise greet the church that is in their house. Salute my well-beloved Epenetus, who is the first-fruits of Achaia unto Christ.*

Church. Company of believers meeting statedly in Christ's name.
More or less fully organised with office-bearers.
The ordinances of Christ administered among them.
Not dependent on numbers. Christ's presence promised to two or three, Matt. xviii. 20.
Various such churches already at Rome, ver. 14, 15.

In their house. Either—1. The Christian members of their family ; Or rather, 2. The believers who met in their house for worship.
Their house, as commodious, given up for this purpose.
All the meetings of Christians first held in this manner.
" They brake bread from house to house," *i.e.*, in private houses, Acts ii. 46.
The private house the birthplace of Christian worship.
The upper room at Jerusalem so used, Acts i. 13.
Buildings erected for Christian worship in the third century.

CHAP. XVI.]   ST. PAUL'S EPISTLE TO THE ROMANS.   321

At Rome believers often met for worship in the catacombs.
Aquila's house a place for meeting wherever he went.
Zeal and love for Christ's cause to be carried about with us.
Mere professors often leave their religion behind them.
Grace in a family converts a house into a church.
Religion to be manifest in the family as a household thing.
Wherever Abraham had a tent Jehovah had an altar.
Well-beloved. Epenetus, probably one of Paul's own converts.
Strong affection between a minister and his spiritual children.
Epenetus remembered with peculiar pleasure.
No small commendation to be Paul's well-beloved.
The law of love in the heart puts the law of kindness on the tongue.
First-fruits. Among the earliest converts in that quarter.
First consecrated offering. Early believers first-fruits to God, James
    i. 18.
"First-fruits" often used for the best of the kind.
Favourite expression with Paul, viii. 23; xi. 16; Eph. i. 12; 1 Cor.
    xv. 20, 23; xvi. 15.
To be among the first who are brought to Christ a noble distinction.
Such the leaders of others—1. By their example; 2. By their efforts;
    3. By their prayers.
Paul forward in noticing any distinguishing excellence.
Achaia. The region of which Corinth was the capital, xv. 26.
Stephanas also mentioned as the first-fruits of Achaia, 1 Cor. xvi. 15.
Probably several converted about the same time.
Epenetus possibly one of the household of Stephanas.
Christ had much people in Corinth, Acts xviii. 10.
Very ancient manuscripts here read Asia for Achaia.
Unto Christ. Believers are offerings to Christ: Christ therefore God.
So those mentioned, Rev. xiv. 4, "first-fruits to God and *the Lamb.*"
Christ the Captain; all believers enlisted under Him.
The end of a preacher's labours is to bring men to Christ:
To Christ,—not to the preacher, nor a sect, nor even the Church.

T. κατ' οἶκον ἐκκλησίαν, the church which is in their house, *i.e.*, their Christian household. *Tol., Est., Men., Par., Whitby, Flatt, Thol.* A domestic church. *Calv.* Marriage no hindrance to piety. *Theod.* Used their house for the preaching of the Gospel and the entertaining of believing strangers. *Chrys.* The church who assembled there for worship. *Œcum., Par., Beza, Mede, Mackn., A. Clarke, Reiche, Stuart, Hald., De Wette, Ols., Meyer, Niel., Hodge, Con. & Hows., D. Brown.* Uncertain. *Rückert.* Name of 'church' given to the smallest company of believers. *Est.* ' Ubi tres, ecclesia est, licet laici.' *Tert.* Believers met where each one could and would. *Justin.* Build-

VOL. II.   X

ings erected or set apart for Christian worship at first called '*a house of the Lord*' (œdes dominica, Dominicum; Κυριακον, κυριακη, *i.e.*, οἰκια; hence kirche, kirk, church;); also the '*church-house*' (domus ecclesiastica, ἐκκλησιαστικον); *oratory*, or house of prayer (oratorium, domus precationum, προσευκτηριον); *synod* or *council* (synodus, concilium, conciliabulum); *conventicle*, or meeting-house (conventiculum); *assembly* (ecclesia, ἐκκλησια). At a later period called *basilicæ*; public buildings so called still retaining their name when converted into places for public worship; *temples* (templum, the name given to the places of Pagan worship). Called also *martyria*, from being built at the martyrs' graves, or containing their relics; or *cemeteria*, because often situated in cemeteries or burial-grounds. Consecration of churches not older than the fourth century. Services held in the catacombs or subterranean burying-grounds at Rome first in times of persecution, and afterwards in honour of the martyrs. The principal of these about three miles from Rome, on the Appian Way. Each catacomb three feet broad and eight or ten high, running in the form of an alley or gallery terminating in large open spaces, and communicating with others. The dead laid lengthwise, three or four rows over one another, in the sides of these alleys and parallel to them, the apertures being commonly closed with large thick tiles and sometimes pieces of marble, with the name of the deceased and some symbol or sentiment painted or carved on them. These symbols or sentiments, in the case of Christians, often expressive of the peace and hope in which they fell asleep under the care of the Good Shepherd,—an olive branch, an anchor, a shepherd with a lamb in his arms.—The order of service in the assembly was usually the reading of the Old Testament writings, of the apostles and evangelists, and occasionally other productions, by presbyters, deacons, or readers, with psalmody intervening; a discourse (sermo, oratio sacra, tractatus, exhortatio, disputatio, λογος), begun and ended with a short prayer by the president or other presbyter, and sometimes by a deacon, or, with permission, by an ordinary member,—in the apostolic times by those possessing the gift of prophecy; prayers; the Communion; the Agape or Love-feast, which also sometimes preceded the Communion. *Baumgarten.*—Ἀπαρχη, first converts. *Chrys., Men., Tir., Tol., Eras.* Distinguished among believers. *Or., Chrys., Eras.* Epenetus, a son of Stephanas, and first brought to Christ. *Schol.* Perhaps part of his household. *A. Clarke.* Several converted at the same time. *Par., De Wette.*—Ἀχαιας. Codd. Sin., Vat., and Alex. read Ἀσιας, as also various ancient versions and fathers. In 1 Cor. xvi. 15, ἀπαρχη connected with Ἀχαια, which may have led to the change from Ἀσια. *Beng.* Proconsular Asia. *Nied., Ellicot, D. Brown.*

---

6. *Greet Mary, who bestowed much labour on us.*

Mary. An honoured name in Scripture. The three, John xix. 25. This Mary the sixth in the New Testament. Same as Miriam in the Old Testament.
The honour of Christianity to produce such women.
Women dignified and honoured by the Gospel.
Mary an example to all, especially those of her own sex.
Richly rewarded for her labour in the place here given her.
Natural weakness mighty when strengthened by grace.
The least of Christ's true servants greater than the world's heroes.
Bestowed much labour. *Gr.*, Laboured much or in many ways.
Her activity probably not confined to one department.

Followed up the labours of apostles and evangelists.
Not only teaching privately, but ministering in other things. *Chrys.*
Women recipients of the gift of prophecy, Acts ii. 17, 18; xxi. 9.
And exercised that gift among believers, 1 Cor. xi. 5.
Forbidden to preside and teach in public, but not in private.
Our honour to labour for Christ, still more to labour *much.*
Not only in the work of the Lord, but *abounding*, and that *always*, 1 Cor. xv. 58.
Each believer has his and her work in the Lord's house, Mark xiii. 34.
On us. Himself and his fellow-labourers. So Luke viii. 23.
Aided the preachers of the word as Christ's ambassadors.
Those who help the workmen help the work, 3 John 8.
Mary, like others now at Rome, had met Paul elsewhere.
Probably a Jewess, and among those who had been expelled from Rome.
Or one who, as Epenetus, had resided in Asia and removed to Rome.

'Εκοπιασεν (κοπος, labour, toil), laboured. *Calv.* Her labours undertaken for the truth. *Theoph.* No doubt of a womanly kind. *D. Brown.*—Εἰς ἡμας (Codd. Sin., Vat., and Alex. read ὑμας; so Origen, Ambrose, and others), for us (erga nos). *Pag., Pisc, Beza, Calv.* Pro nobis. *Grot.* Among us (in nobis). *Vat.* On our account, to accommodate me and my companions. *Doddr.* Paul naturally mentions what she had done for himself. *De Wette.*

---

7. *Salute Andronicus and Junia, my kinsmen and my fellow-prisoners, who are of note among the apostles; who also were in Christ before me.*

Andronicus and Junia. The latter, as here read, that of a female.
Andronicus and Junia probably husband and wife, or brother and sister.
Grace adorns, sanctifies, and sweetens every relation in life.
Natural relationships not absorbed by union with Christ.
Kinsmen. Either in a wider or more restricted sense.
Paul's sister's son at Jerusalem warmly attached to his uncle.
Grace recognises the ties of natural kindred.
These ties drawn still closer by a common faith.
Fellow-prisoners. Where and when they were so, unknown.
Valuable undesigned coincidence with 2 Cor. vi. 5; xi. 23.
Paul had already been often in prison before being in Rome.
Yet the history only speaks of one imprisonment, Acts xvi. 23.

Others mentioned afterwards as his fellow-prisoners, Col. iv. 10; Phil. ii. 2, 3.
Chains for Christ greater honour than chains of office.
A threefold fellowship recognised in this verse—
1. Of faith; 2. Of family; 3. Of fiery trials.
Of note. Distinguished. Different ranks among believers.
Degrees among David's worthies according to bravery and zeal.
Not only *sincerity* but *eminence* in grace to be desired.
A man diligent in business stands before kings, Prov. xxii. 29.
All in Christ equally justified, but all not equally honoured.
Grace distinguishes more than gifts, and love than learning.
Best gifts to be coveted, but love the more excellent way, 1 Cor. xii. 31.
Apostles. 1. In the strictest sense, those appointed by the Lord, Matt. x. 2;
2. In a wider sense, those who laboured like them; "messengers," 2 Cor. viii. 23.
Paul's relations apparently lived in Jerusalem, Acts xxiii. 16.
Andronicus and Junia therefore in circumstances to be well known to apostles.
The Gospel possibly brought by them to Rome.
In Christ. The distinguishing characteristic of a true Christian.
The believer in three positions—1. In Adam by nature;
2. In Christ by faith; 3. In the Church by baptism.
"In Christ" is to be spiritually one with Him as a member of His body.
Before me. Paul's humility. Readily accords pre-eminence.
These kinsmen probably among the converts at Pentecost.
Priority of union with Christ to be regarded as an honour.
Age makes venerable, especially age in Christ.
Paul's delight to refer to his conversion and espousals.
The time of our union with Christ never to be forgotten.

'Ιουνιαν, Junia, or possibly 'Junias,' a contracted form of Junianus. *D. Brown.*— Συγγενεις (συν, together, and γινομαι, to be born), relations. *Eras., Pag., Pisc., Reza, Est., Calv., Meyer.* Countrymen. *Men., Reiche, De Wette, Ols.* Of the same tribe. *Tir., Est.* Andronicus may have married a relation who was ἐπικληρος, or an heiress. *Eras.* Of the same nation or tribe. *Beng., Bar., Brown.*—Συναιχμαλωτους (συν, together, and αἰχαλωτος, a captive; from αἰχμη, a spear, and ἁλισκω, to take), fellow-captives. *Eras., Pag., Pisc., Beza, Calv.* Formerly in the same prison. *Tir., Eras., Men.* Paul said to have been seven times in prison. *Grot.* In a more general sense, sharers with him in his hardships. *Chrys., Theod., Theoph.*—Ἐπισημοι (ἐπι, upon, and σημα, a mark), illustrious (insignes). *Eras., Pisc., Pag., Beza, Calv.*

CHAP. XVI.]   ST. PAUL'S EPISTLE TO THE ROMANS.   325

Known. *Cast.*, *Syriac.* Sometimes used in a bad sense, as Matt. xxvii. 16, 'notable.'—
'Ἐν τοῖς ἀποστόλοις, among the apostles, in a general sense; persons who spread
the Gospel and planted churches in various places. *Calv.* With or among the apostles.
Tol., *Beza.* In their judgment. *Vat.* Distinguished among the teachers and preachers
of the Gospel. *Men.* Early in great reputation among the apostles, strictly taken.
Doddr., *Bp. Hall*, *Flatt*, *Stuart*, *Meyer*, *Lange.* Apostles taken in a wider sense for
any minister of the Gospel, as Acts xiv. 4, 14; 1 Thess. ii. 6. *Chrys.*, *Theod.*, *Est.*, *Vor.*,
Par., *Wolf*, *Thol.*, *Ols.*, *De Wette*, *Nielson*, *Alford.* Evangelists. *D.od.* Clement of
Rome called an apostle by Clem. Alex.; Ignatius, by Chrys.; and Timothy, by Photius.
Ham. So the Fathers in general. So called, as having seen the Lord. *Beng.*—Οἵ κ.
πρὸ ἐμοῦ γεγόνασιν ἐν Χ., who also were in Christ before me; were grafted into Christ
by faith. *Beza*, *Par.* Were in the church, or were Christians. *Tir.*, *Men.*, *Est.* Pro-
bably among the seventy-two disciples, or converted under Peter's sermon at Pentecost.
Grot. Γ'εγον., began to be in Christ. *Beng.* Became Christians. *Stuart.*

---

8. *Greet Amplias, my beloved in the Lord.*

Amplias. Probably another of Paul's converts.
My beloved. 1. As his own son in the Gospel; or,
2. From special grace observed in him; or,
3. From his warm attachment shown to Paul; or,
4. From his eminent devotedness to the cause of Christ.
Degrees of attachment consistent with Christian love.
Of the twelve, Peter, James, and John most beloved, Matt.
   xvii. 1.
Of these, John especially the beloved disciple, John xiii. 23.
In the Lord. Beloved not after the flesh but in the Lord.
"Henceforth know we no man after the flesh," 2 Cor. v. 16.
Beloved—1. For Christ's sake; 2. With true Christian love; 3. As
   members of the same body of Christ.
Those truly beloved who are beloved in the Lord.

'Ἀμπλίαν, Amplias. Codd. Sin. and Alex. read 'Ἀμπλιᾶτον. So Origen and the
Vulg. Amplias contracted from Ampliatus. *D. Brown.*—'Ἐν Κυρίῳ, in the Lord, *i.e.*,
on the Lord's account, whom he zealously served. *Vat.* With Christian love. *Tol.*
Loved not for his talents or his wealth, but his faith and piety. *Par.* An expression of
dear Christian affection. *D. Brown.*

---

9. *Salute Urbane, our helper in Christ; and Stachys my beloved.*

Urbane. Or, Urbanus; a man's name, = Urban.
Our helper. Not Paul's only, but the helper of others also.
Urbane commended for his kind and devoted zeal.
Not in close relation to Paul as some, yet kindly named.

Gr., "Our fellow-helper." Might be at Rome or elsewhere.
Each has his work assigned him by the Master, Mark xiii. 34.
To labour in Christ's cause is to be helpers with apostles.
Paul delights to acknowledge the brethren's help.
The privilege of all believers to be helpers in Christ's work.
My beloved. Stachys probably another of his converts.
Rejoiced to think of his children walking in the truth, 3 John 4.
To be beloved of a faithful servant of Christ a high praise.
To be Paul's beloved greater honour than to be Cæsar's friend.
New, tender, and delightful relationships opened up by the Gospel.
Paul speaks the language of love as one who had been in paradise,
    2 Cor. xii. 4.
Truly loving language evinces love and engages it.

Συνεργον (συν and έργον), helper (adjutor). *Calv.* Fellow labourer. *D. Brown.*

---

10. *Salute Apelles, approved in Christ. Salute them which are of Aristobulus' household.*

Approved. Tried and found trustworthy. Irreproachable.
Of approved knowledge, judgment, courage, and sincerity.
A tried and approved Christian—1. By time; 2. Works; 3. Sufferings.
High praise. Paul's own care to approve himself, 2 Cor. vi. 4.
Diligence to that end urged upon Timothy, 2 Tim. ii. 15.
The Lord's people widely diversified. Some peculiarly tried.
Trials, meekly and patiently endured, the evidence of grace.
Well-tried Christians entitled to especial honour.
We are not only to be believers, but be approved as such.
Commendation to be given wherever it is due.
In Christ. 1. As a member of Christ's spiritual body;
2. In Christ's cause and work; 3. As evincing Christ's spirit.
Aristobulus. Probably a person of distinction.
May or may not be included in the salutation.
Not clear whether he himself belonged to Christ.
Not many mighty, not many noble called, 1 Cor. i. 26.
Household. Children, slaves, or other members; so 1 Cor. i. 11.
Some of the family or household brought to Christ.
Divine sovereignty. Son or daughter called, Matt. x. 35, 36.
Servant taken and master left. Sometimes both taken, Philem. 16.
Happy household when the whole become Christ's, Ps. cxxxiii.

Examples of converted families, Acts xvi. 15, 34; 1 Cor. i. 16.
Believers in godless families entitled to special regard.
Such saluted, though probably unknown to Paul.
Kindness and courtesy learned in the school of Christ.

Δοκιμον ἐν X., approved in Christ (probatum). *Pag., Beza, Pisc., Calv.* A sincere disciple. *Men., Tir., Vor.* Highly esteemed for his faith in Christ. *Vat.* A well tried and proved Christian. *Grot., Tol., Stuart, Brown.* Approved by sincerity of faith and integrity of life. *Whitby.* The approved. *Ellicot, D. Brown.* Tried and found trustworthy in Christ's work. *Con. & Hows.* Blameless in matters pertaining to Christ. *Chrys.*—Τους ἐκ των Ἀριστοβούλου, his house or family. *Drus., Par., Est.* Servants or domestics. *Cam., Pisc.* Master dead or absent at the time. *Grot.* Master not a believer. *Par.* Already dead or spiritually so. *Barth.* Probably dead. *A. Clarke.* Those of the domestics who were in Christ saluted. *Stuart.* Very possibly some of his slaves. *D. Brown.*

---

11. *Salute Herodion my kinsman. Greet them that be of the household of Narcissus which are in the Lord.*

Kinsmen. Relatives or countrymen, as in ver. 7.
Household. Family or establishment, as in ver. 10.
Roman villas often vast establishments of slaves.
Number of slaves belonging to rich citizens immense.
Narcissus. Some rich Roman citizen of that name.
Narcissus, the well-known favourite of Claudius, now dead.
His establishment possibly still called by his name.
Who are in the Lord. A limitation probably meant also in ver. 10.
Only some of the household the subjects of grace.
Good men often found in wicked families, 1 Kings xviii. 3, 12.
Courtesy to all; Christian greeting only to the brethren.

Ναρκισσου, of Narcissus; the favourite and freedman of the Emperor Claudius. *Grot., Par., Calv, Neander.* Had died in A.D. 58 before this epistle was written. *De Wette.* Overthrown and put to death by Nero's mother in the beginning of his reign; his immense estate probably confiscated and his body of slaves sold. *Rückert.* Indicative of the number and condition of slaves is the following from Petronius as taken from the Acta Diurna, a kind of newspaper or gazette published in Rome, containing an authorised statement of all transactions thought worthy of notice: 'On the 26th July, thirty boys and forty girls were born on Timalchi's estate at Cumæ. At the same time a slave was put to death for uttering disrespectful words against his master.'

---

12. *Salute Tryphena and Tryphosa, who labour in the Lord. Salute the beloved Persis, which laboured much in the Lord.*

Tryphena and Tryphosa. Two active females, probably sisters.

Beautiful pair of stars glowing in the Christian firmament.
Further examples of Christian women working for Christ.
Labour. *Gr.*, Laboured; had laboured, and were still doing so.
An evidence of grace not to be weary of well-doing.
Not only wrought, but "laboured," endured suffering.
Laboured in a way becoming their sex and Christian order.
Abundant occasion for self-denying female labour.
The glory of the Gospel still to produce many such examples.
In the Lord. 1. In union with Christ; 2. In His cause; 3. In His Spirit.
Labour in the Lord the only labour that shall not be in vain, 1 Cor. xv. 58.
Other labour spent for that which satisfieth not, Isa. lv. 2.
Beloved. Either for her amiable disposition or devoted zeal, ver. 8, 9.
Some distinguished by their amiability and lovely character.
Persis. Apparently a slave or freed woman of Persia.
Grace lifts the poor from the dunghill and sets them among princes, Ps. cxiii. 7.
Made this slave "beloved," and an honour to the Christian name.
Laboured much. So of Mary, ver. 6. Good to labour, better to labour much.
Different degrees of activity even among Christ's faithful servants.
Much love indicated by much labour for Christ, Luke vii. 44-47; 2 Cor. v. 14.
The disciple who labours much peculiarly noticed by Paul.
Appropriate praise encourages the praised and stimulates others.
Females often the most active labourers and patient sufferers for Christ.
Owing much to the Gospel, they acknowledge it by their labours of love.

Τρυφαιναν κ. Τρυφωσαν, probably sisters. *Bengel.*—Περσιδα, Persis. Slaves often named from the countries to which they belonged. So Mysa. Syrus, Davus. *Grot.*—Ἐκοπιασεν, laboured; promoting the Gospel among others. *Tir., Est., Men., Tol.* In the ministry of the word. *A. Clarke.* In such higher Christian labours as Priscilla bestowed on Apollos and others,—in a way competent to their sex. *D. Brown.* This last salutation omitted in Cod. Alex.

---

13. *Salute Rufus, chosen in the Lord, and his mother and mine.*

Rufus. Not unlikely the son of Simon the Cyrenian, Mark xv. 21.

Rufus mentioned by Mark as well known in the church.
Christ's cross, laid on Simon, brought blessing to his children.
Chosen. 1. Elected from eternity, as proved by his works, 1 Thess.
i. 4–6 ;
2. Distinguished, excellent, choice ; seen in his life and labours.
Applied to those whose faith verified itself by works, 2 John 1, 13.
Good to be a *chosen* Christian ; better still to be a *choice* one.
In the Lord. In union with Christ. Believers chosen in Him,
Eph. i. 4.
Union *with* Christ the evidence of election *in* Christ.
True excellence only attainable in union with Christ.
His mother. The godly mother of a godly son.
Double blessing when both parent and child are in the Lord.
If Simon's wife, the blessing of the cross still more conspicuous.
And mine. Beautiful mixture of delicacy and tenderness.
Simon's mother by nature, Paul's by her motherly attention.
Paul distinguished by grateful recognition of past kindness.
High honour given to Rufus's mother in being also Paul's.
So John honoured in being a son to the mother of Jesus, John xix. 26.
Services to Christ's members and servants well rewarded.

'Ρουφον, Rufus, the son of Simon. *Church Fathers*, *Grot.*, *Glöck.*, *Meyer.* Probably. *D. Brown.* The name a common one. *De Wette.*—'Εκλεκτον ἐν Χ., elect (electum). *Calv.* Select, or choice (selectum). *Pag.*, *Pisc.*, *Beza.* Distinguished. *Grot.* Of most choice faith. *Vat.* Chosen from eternity to salvation. *Schött.* One of great excellence. *Whitby.* Choice. *A. Clarke.* The sense of election not suitable here. *De Wette*, *D. Brown.* A choice Christian. *Brown.* The elect. *Ellicot.* Heb. בָּחִיר, בָּהִיר, כִּבְהָר, כַּר, נִבְהָר, 'choice,' Song vi. 9.—Και ἐμου, and mine. His mother literally, mine figuratively. *Stuart.* So Terence : '*Natura tu illi pater es, consiliis ego. Adelphi.*

---

14. *Salute Asyncritus, Phlegon, Hermas, Patrobas, Hermes, and the brethren which are with them.*

Asyncritus, &c. Pleasant even to be saluted only by name.
These perhaps some of the more gifted and ministering of the brethren.
Centres of influence among those in their own neighbourhood.
High distinction to be thus named in this epistle.
Believers to rejoice that their names are written in the Book of Life, Luke x. 20.
Brethren. Ordinary believers connected with the above.

To be saluted by Paul only as brethren no small honour.
Believers brethren of Christ, and so brethren of each other.
Glorious privilege to be so nearly related to Christ and His saints.
With them—1. As members of their various households;
2. Assembling with them as a church or congregation, as ver. 5.
More houses than Aquila's used as places of meeting.
Number of believers at Rome already considerable.
Various congregations, yet only one body in Christ.

Ἑρμᾶν, Hermas, author of 'The Shepherd.' *Or.*, *Euseb.* The author of that book really the brother of Pius, Bishop of Rome, and lived about the year 150. *Lange.* This book, pretending to give the revelations of an angel in a dream, once contested for authority with the Epistle to the Hebrews, and was held by some, especially of the Alexandrian School, in equal esteem with the Scriptures, and quoted as such. Never, however, admitted into the canon; and in the fourth century ranked among the spurious. It arose out of the controversy about those who in time of persecution had lapsed and again returned to the church. Hermas was one of the lapsed, and contended for their re-admission to communion.—Σὺν αὐτοῖς, with them; another house-congregation; perhaps united by a common trade. *Phil.* Another mission-society. *Reiche.* Each of those named probably a centre of some few Christians who met at his house for religious objects. *D. Brown.*

---

15. *Salute Philologus and Julia, Nereus and his sister, and Olympas, and all the saints which are with them.*

Philologus and Julia. Probably husband and wife, as in ver. 3, 7.
Their house also probably a meeting-place for the brethren.
Sanctified marriage a furtherance to the kingdom of God.
All. Implying a considerable number. Believers multiplied.
Saints. Holy persons. All church members such by profession.
Creation *made* men saints; redemption *remakes* them such.
Saintship or holiness the proper destination of rational creatures.
Allies men with God and all the heavenly intelligences.
The distinguished vocation of every believer.
Only to be realised in union with Christ the Head.
Commences in regeneration, ends in full glorification.
Its progress a growing conformity to Christ's image.
Exists in many degrees. Babes, young men, fathers. Strong and
  weak.
The church with its institutions a training-school for saints.
With them. As in ver. 14. Members of their families, or fellow
  church members.
Probably residing with them in the same neighbourhood.

Believers in a locality met for worship in some convenient house.
Times came when even this was not permitted in Rome.

Φιλολογον, &c. These with those in the preceding verse form two pairs of five each, each pair having 'brethren' or 'saints' connected with them; hardly, however, warranting the supposition that each of the five in both pairs had 'a church in his house.' *D. Brown.*

16. *Salute one another with a holy kiss. The churches of Christ salute you.*

Salute one another. So 1 Cor. xvi. 20; 2 Cor. xiii. 12; 1 Thess. v. 26; 1 Pet. v. 14.
Mutual salutation to be given in Paul's name.
What he could not do personally he does through themselves.
Implies an exhortation to mutual love and peace.
Brethren to live in the kind exchange of Christian salutations.
Kiss. Jewish form of salutation among friends.
Mutual love to be manifested and expressed as well as felt.
The mode to be according to the custom of the time and place.
The kiss still common in Oriental and Southern lands.
Became a practice in connection with the Lord's Supper.
Continued for a time—1. As a friendly salutation;
2. As an act symbolical of love and Christian brotherhood.
Betokened an equality among believers as God's children.
Holy kiss. Expression of true and holy love. Kiss of charity, 1 Pet. v. 14.
With Christians, the ordinary salutation must be holy and sincere.
The kiss holy as—1. Grave and becoming; 2. Guileless; 3. Chaste.
Contrasted with Joab's, 2 Sam. xx. 9; and Judas's, Matt. xxvi. 49.
The sign of a holy spiritual affection as members of Christ.
Churches of Christ. Christian congregations in various places.
Here, more especially those in the neighbourhood of Corinth.
Paul's intended journey and letter to Rome probably widely known.
Had on him daily the care of all the churches, 2 Cor. xi. 28.
These churches mostly house congregations like that in ver. 5.
Salute you. 1. Had evinced their affection and good-will to them;
2. Had given commission to Paul to express it for them.
Custom of early churches to send expressions of mutual affection.
Distant churches to be interested in each other's welfare.

'Ασπάσασθε ἀλλήλους, salute one another,—in my name. *Beng.* His affectionate greeting resolves itself into one general reciprocal salutation. *De Wette.* Supposes the epistle to be read in presence of the whole church. *Thol., De Wette, Nielson.*—Φιλή-ματι, with a kiss; the custom of the times both among Jews and Gentiles; among Christians after prayers. *Grot., Tol., Est., Par., Ham.* Among Orientals, equals kissed the lips of each other, inferiors the hand of their superiors. *Grot.* Eastern practice, especially on festive occasions. *Lange.* In early times, before communicating, the deacon said to the members of the church, Salute one another with a holy kiss. The presbyters then saluted the bishop, and the members those of their own sex. He added, Let none have any grudge against any: Let none act hypocritically. *Apost. Const.* Justin Martyr speaks of the kiss as the 'brotherly kiss after prayer,' and says, 'We mutually salute each other by a kiss, and then we bring forward the bread and the cup.' Tertullian calls it the 'kiss of peace' (osculum pacis), and the seal of prayer. Discontinued from the scandalous reports to which it gave rise. Still practised in the Greek and Oriental churches. In the Latin Church the kiss given only by the Pope. Rabbies ascribed much importance to the kiss: 'Every kiss causes that spirit cleaves to spirit.' *Zohar.*—Ἁγίῳ, holy; sincere and guileless. *Theod.* Not profane, lascivious, feigned, or treacherous. *Tir., Est.* Chaste, honest, modest, and fraternal. *Tol.* Such as becomes saints. *Est.* Proceeding from a mind full of holy love. *Beza.* Symbol of chaste and spiritual love. *Men.* Αἱ ἐκκλησίαι, the churches. Codd. Sin., Vat., and Alex. and others, with ancient versions and Fathers, add πᾶσαι, all. All those in the vicinity or recently visited. *Stuart.* Churches generally; all that knew he was writing to Rome. *D. Brown.*

---

17. *Now I beseech you, brethren, mark them which cause divisions and offences contrary to the doctrine which ye have learned, and avoid them.*

Beseech. As deeply sensible of the importance of the subject. Divisions and scandals eat out the life of religion.
Witnessed at Corinth, 1 Cor. i. 11; 2 Cor. xii. 20. In Galatia, Gal. i. 6-9; v. 15.
Mark. Believers to be watchful and observant, Exod. ii. 14.
Damage often sustained before danger is apprehended.
"Try the spirits," an apostolic injunction, 1 John iv. 1.
In time of war all approaches to a city guarded.
Suspected spies or other suspicious characters marked.
Cause—1. By false teaching; 2. Ambitious aims; 3. Unholy living.
Divisions—*i.e.*, among the brethren; factions; parties.
So Paul warned the elders at Ephesus, Acts xx. 29-31.
Judaising teachers already in the churches, Phil. iii. 2, 18; 2 Cor. xi. 20.
Probably not yet at Rome. Yet the danger to be feared.
Such teachers were increasing both in numbers and zeal.
Their aim to make the new converts Jewish proselytes.
Differed from the Jews only in acknowledging Jesus as the Christ.

As a party, were rather Jews than Christians.
Required the Gentiles to be incorporated into the body of Israel.
Made circumcision essential to full salvation.
Their success in the churches of Galatia proved—
1. Their unwearied activity and zeal;
2. Their skill in the acts of conciliation and persuasion.
Maintained a long and desperate struggle against Paul.
Converted Jews or proselytes the nucleus of all the churches.
The Judaisers flattered these in order to gain them over, ver. 18.
Invented many charges against Paul, 1 Cor. ix. 1; 2 Cor. x. 10; xii. 16.
Caused great divisions in the churches.
Some of the members held to Paul's views as to Christian liberty.
The strong. These much opposed to the Judaisers.
In danger of forming a party and becoming high-minded.
Tempted into bitterness of feeling against their opponents, Gal. v. 15.
Judaisers soon ceased as an influential party except in Palestine.
Others combined with the Gospel a Greek philosophising spirit.
Regarded it intellectually as a new system of philosophy.
Such found especially in Alexandria, the city of Apollos.
Hence probably a party formed at Corinth, under his name, 1 Cor. i. 12.
This spirit afterwards developed into Gnosticism.
Led to the idea that Christians were freed from the precepts of the law.
Also to the denial of the resurrection of the body, 1 Cor. v. 12; 2 Tim. ii. 18.
These views found at first chiefly in Rome and Corinth.
Increased gradually with the growth of the church.
Gnosticism a mixture of Grecian and Oriental speculation, with Jewish superstition.
Pretended a deeper insight into the mysteries of religion.
Oppositions of science (or knowledge) falsely so called, 1 Tim. vi. 21.
Attention to fables and endless genealogies, 1 Tim. i. 4.
Speculations on the origin and emanation of spiritual beings.
Christ viewed as an angelic emanation, and Jesus a mere man.
Connected with voluntary humility and angel-worship, Col. ii. 18.
Jewish fables and traditions of men, Col. ii. 8; Tit. i. 14.
Distinctions between different kinds of food, Col. ii. 16; 1 Tim. iv. 3.
Observance of Jewish festivals viewed as obligatory, Col. ii. 16.
Attention to outward rites and ceremonies, Col. ii. 8, 20.

Will-worship, or an arbitrary mode of worshipping God, Col. ii. 23.
Self-humiliation and mortification of the flesh.
Forbad marriage, 1 Tim. iv. 3. Held the essential evil of matter.
Pretended to a knowledge of magic and witchcraft, Rev. ii. 20;
    ix. 21; xxi. 18.
Indulged in the sensualities and idol-feasts of the heathen, Rev.
    ii. 20.
Jewish and Ascetic element prevailed in Colosse and Crete.
The Gentile and Antinomian in Corinth and Asia Minor.
These perverted views the foundation of the apostasy, 2 Thess. ii. 3.
Perpetuated in that corruption which led to the Reformation.
Still traced in the corrupt churches of the East and West.
Offences. Causes of stumbling by their teaching and practice.
Divisions in a church among the greatest offences.
Contrary. Different from; opposed to. Duty to examine.
Doctrines and practices to be compared with Scripture.
Doctrine ye have learned. Pattern given in this epistle.
More learned at that period from hearing than reading.
Many at Rome had heard from Paul's own lips.
Some of his epistles also already in the churches.
Apostolic teaching the only standard of comparison.
That teaching now found in the written word, Isa. viii. 20.
Divisions and offences themselves contrary to that doctrine.
Also occasioned through departure from it.
Truth unites believers; error separates them.
Believers capable of judging between truth and error.
Avoid them. *Gr.*, Turn away from them, 2 Tim. iii. 5; 2 John x. 11.
No fellowship to be held with such persons, 1 Cor. v. 11; 1 Tim.
    vi. 3–5.
Teachers of error not to be listened to, Prov. xix. 27.
Separation from such not a sin but a duty, 1 Cor. xi. 19.
To separate such as agree in the truth is sacrilege;
To uphold error on the plea of unity a stratagem of Satan.
False teachers and makers of division to be avoided—
1. In order to incur no responsibility for their procedure;
2. To give no countenance to them in it.

Σκοπειν (from σκεπτομαι, to see, look). Some copies read ἀσφαλῶς σκοπεῖτε.
Mark, observe (observetis). *Calv.* Carefully watch and observe, as enemies from a
watch tower. *Eras., Beza.* Look out (speculemini). *Pag., Mor.* Consider. *Eras., Grot.*
Beware of. *Syr., Arab.* Pay attention *Schött.* Look sharply after. *A. Clarke.* Con-

sider attentively; beware of. *Stuart.* Lest the evil should be done ere fully discovered. *D. Brown.* Heb. צָץ, דְּבָץ.—Διχοστασιας (διχα, implying division, and ἱστημι, to stand), divisions (dissidia). *Eras., Pisc., Pag., Beza, Calv.* Seditions. *Cas.* Judaisers especially referred to. *Par., Grot.* Uncertain what kind of persons are meant. *De Wette.* Probably similar to those mentioned Phil. iii. 2, 18; 1 Tim. vi. 3; 2 Cor. xi. 20. *Alford.* Either Judaising Ebionistic zealots of the law, or Gnosticising Antinomian spirits. *Lange.* Jewish zealots, not members of the church at Rome themselves, but who went about to cause disturbance. *Thol.* Judaisers known afterwards as Nazarenes and Ebionites. Nazarenes taught that the law, and in particular, circumcision, was obligatory on Jewish Christians only, and that Jesus was the son of the Virgin Mary, but only a mere man. The Ebionites sought to impose the yoke of the law upon Christians generally, and regarded Jesus as the son of Joseph and Mary from mere Jewish notions. Of the Gnostics (from γνωσις, *gnosis*, knowledge), some more opposed to Judaism than others. In some respects Docetic, holding the divinity of Christ, but merging His human nature into a mere phantom by denying the reality of His body; also Antinomian, opposing the spirit to the letter, the ideal to the real. Distinguished between those who only had faith, and those who had knowledge. Gnosticism established afterwards in the system of Manes (Manichæism), distinguished for the doctrine of two principles, and the inherent evil of matter. Cerinthus probably blended Judaism with Gnosticism, maintaining that the world was not created by the Supreme God, and that the Emanation Christ descended on the man Jesus at His baptism. *Hagenbach.* Basilides and Valentinus, the leaders of the Gnostics in the second century, distinguished mainly for their doctrine concerning the æons or emanations of spiritual beings, derived from the Sephiroth or ten divine emanations taught in the Jewish Cabbala, adopted by the Rabbies from Oriental sources and engrafted into Judaism. *Con. & Hows.* The views of Antinomian Gnostics in regard to morals indicated by Irenæus: 'As gold deposited in the mud does not lose its beauty, so they, whatever be their outward impurity or immorality, cannot lose their spiritual nature or be injured by it.' Also by Justin: 'They live sinful lives; yet if they know God, the Lord will not impute sin to them.' Early division and scandal in the church itself caused by the bishops of Rome in regard to the time of celebrating Easter (see at chap. xiv. 5). In 197, Victor, successor of Anicetus, assumed the right to impose the Roman mode on all the churches that followed the contrary practice. Polycrates, bishop of Ephesus, strenuously resisted the usurpation, and refused to relinquish the practice of his own church, introduced by St John and St Philip, and handed down to him by seven bishops of his own family. Victor threatened, in reply, to cut him off from his communion unless he submitted to conform to Rome. Polycrates, anxious to avoid any violation of the union which had subsisted among the bishops of the church, assembled a Council at Ephesus and laid the matter before them. The Council was unanimously of opinion that there was no necessity for changing their uniform practice. Victor then published an edict containing the most severe and bitter invectives against all the churches of Asia, declaring them cut off from his communion, sending letters of excommunication to their several bishops, and exhorting other bishops to follow his example. Some of these bishops, and especially Irenæus, bishop of Lyons, reproved and censured Victor for disturbing the peace of the church; others, however, as the bishops of Palestine, Pontus, Gaul, and Corinth, conceded to his views. Victor kept his word, and thus became, after Montanus, the author of the second schism in the church. *Fysh.* The Rabbies say: 'After backsliders in heart increased, divisions increased in Israel: after the disciples of Hillel and Shammai increased, who did not hearken as they ought to have done, divisions increased and the law was split in two. *Talm. Sotah.*—Σκανδαλα, offences; schisms. *Par.* Which cause men to forsake the faith. *Tol.* Which mar the church by the violation of ecclesiastical discipline. *Par.* Διχοστασιαι precede, σκανδαλα, follow as the result. *Est.* Errors and falls. *Flatt.* Scandals produced by the divisions. *A. Clarke.* Those who are the occasion of others stumbling and falling, by their uncharitableness or superstition. *Stuart.* Doctrinal, moral, or both. *De Wette.* Refers to those who haughtily disregarded the prejudices of the weak. *D. Brown.* 'Εμαθετε, ye learned; formerly by your teachers, and now by my epistle. *Par.* From the chief of the apostles, who formerly may have been there. *Theod.*—'Εκκλινατε (ἐκ, from, and κλινω, to turn), turn from them (declinetis). *Calv., Eras., Pag.* Stand off from them as from a pestilence. *Tol.* Shun their company. *Eras., Men.* Avoid them; give them no countenance or approbation. *Stuart.* And have no religious fellowship with them. *A. Clarke.* Nothing said here of excommunication, there being as yet no regular church or presbyters. *Grot.* 'People responsible for themselves, and not the bishop alone for them, because endowed with reason; pernicious pastors to be therefore avoided' (φευκτεον ἀπο των φθορεων ποιμενων). *Apost. Const.*

---

18. *For they that are such serve not the Lord Jesus Christ, but their own belly; and by good words and fair speeches deceive the hearts of the simple.*

Serve not the Lord Jesus Christ. Their motive and profession insincere.

Professed to serve Christ, but in reality sought themselves.

Our motive in religious matters to be carefully examined.

Satan often served under the Saviour's uniform.

The Lord Jesus Christ the object of service in the church.

God's King set by Him on His holy hill of Zion, Ps. ii. 6.

Entitled to our service—1. As God; 2. As Mediator.

To serve Christ is—1. An act of obedience to God;

2. An act of gratitude to Himself as our Redeemer.

Christ to be served with all our powers; therefore God.

To serve Christ is—1. To aim at His glory; 2. To promote His interest; 3. To do His will.

Their own belly. Gratification of the flesh; a mere living, 2 Cor. xi. 12, 20.

Character of false teachers in the church, Tit. i. 10, 11; Phil. iii. 18, 19; Gal. vi. 12.

Private interests served under the cloak of zeal for Christ.

Men can make gain of godliness instead of godliness a gain.

Their own belly their god, Phil. iii. 19; men become flesh, Gen. vi. 3.

Good words. Pretending great interest in your welfare.

"Words smoother than butter and softer than oil," Ps. lv. 21.

Speaking great swelling words of vanity, 2 Pet. ii. 18.

Wolves in sheep's clothing, Matt. vii. 15; Acts xx. 29.

Satan himself transformed into an angel of light, 2 Cor. xi. 14.

His ministers appear as ministers of righteousness, ver. 15.

Fair speeches, *Gr.*, Blessing; a stronger word than the former.
1. Speaking well of you; 2. Promising well to you.
Having men's persons in admiration for advantage, Jude 16.
Showing not only a bland spirit but an affected piety.
Foulest errors often introduced under fairest promises.
Satan a skilful fowler, knowing how to set his snare.
Soul-destroyers remarkable for seductive address.
Eve beguiled by Satan with promises of good, Gen. iii. 2, &c.; 2 Cor. xi. 3.
Flatterers and pretenders to be always suspected.
Fair speeches often false. Sweet tastes not always wholesome.
Deceiving. Deceived themselves, they seek to deceive others.
"Deceiver" Satan's most characteristic title, John viii. 44; Rev. xii. 9.
Practises his deception through his deceived followers.
Deceivers more to be feared than open persecutors.
Simple. Innocent; unsuspecting; inexperienced.
Not sufficiently guarded and grounded in the truth.
More distinguished for honesty than penetration.
Without malice in themselves, and suspecting none in others
The simple the natural prey of designing men.
Deceivers practise on tender consciences and superstitious fears;
Beguile unstable souls, 2 Pet. ii. 14; lead captive silly women, 2 Tim. iii. 6.

Τῳ Κ. ἡμ. 'I. X. Codd. Sin., Vat., and Alex. read τῳ Κ. X., the Lord Christ.—Κοιλιᾳ, belly; fleshly appetite. *Theod.* Their own gain. *Vat., Tol.* Luxurious living. *Est., Men.* Freedom for themselves and others from the cross. *Grot.* Secular support. *A. Clarke.* An idle and luxurious livelihood. *Chal.* Private interests; a maintenance. *Stuart.* Earthly gain; indicative of low, mean self-seeking. *Barth.* Their own low ends; κοιλια not to be taken in the grosser sense. *D. Brown.*—Χρηστολογιας (χρηστος, good, and λεγω, to speak), sweet discourse. *Vulg., Vat.* Bland speech. *Calv., Schött.* Sweet words. *Mar., Diod.* Χρηστολογος, one rather smooth than kind. *Grot.* One who makes fair promises. *Mint.* Pertinax so called as 'one who spoke well and acted ill.' Insinuating address, affecting elegance and good-breeding. *A. Clarke.* Flattery. *Theoph., Schött, Stuart.*—Εὐλογιας (εὐ, well, and λεγω), blessing (benedicentiam). *Vulg., Mor.* Flattery. *Eras., Men., Tir., Calv., Mar., Diod., Mint.* Praise. *Grot.* Eulogy. *Stuart.* Fine speaking. *De Wette, Van Ess, Rückert.* Flattery, praise. *Meyer.* Praising Christ and Christianity. *Flatt.* Χρηστολογια, speaking well of themselves in *promising;* εὐλογια, speaking well of you in *praising.* *Beng.*—Ἀκακον (ἀ, not, and κακος, evil), simple. *Eras., Vat., Drus., Calv., Men.* By no means bad. *Pag., Pisc., Beza, Schött.* Easily seduced. *Grot., Cam., Flatt.* Unsuspecting, incautious. *Eras., De Wette.* Little acquainted with the world. *Cam, Drus.* Honest, ignorant, and well-meaning persons. *Pyle.* Guileless, simple-hearted, *Stuart.* Unwary. *D. Brown.* Heb. בר, תם.

19. *For your obedience is come abroad unto all men. I am glad therefore on your behalf: but yet I would have you wise unto that which is good, and simple concerning evil.*

For—1. The reason for his giving the warning; 2. The ground on which he hopes it will be received.
Desirable that they should not tarnish their fair fame.
Their very obedience exposed them to designers' arts.
Instruction most likely to profit the obedient, Ps. ix. 9.
Obedience. Teachableness; forwardness to obey the Gospel, chap. i. 5.
Obedience not to human inventions, but to God's Word.
Faith in Christ is obedience, and leads to further obedience—
1. To a tractable temper; 2. To an obedient life.
Childlike submission to God's Word the highest praise.
Come abroad—1. In its report; 2. In its influence.
Believers' obedience should be influential on others.
Believers to be a guiding light and preserving salt, Matt. v. 13–15.
Unto all men. Widely; "throughout the whole world," chap. i. 8.
Am glad. Love rejoices not in iniquity, but in the truth, 1 Cor. xiii. 6.
Faith in Christ opens up countless sources of joy.
Paul "as sorrowful, yet always rejoicing," 2 Cor. vi. 10.
On your behalf. *Gr.*, As to what respects yourselves. Emphatic.
Obedient fruitful believers a joy to true ministers.
Deceivers and disturbers of the church their care and grief.
Self-seekers glad when things go well with themselves;
Faithful ministers, when they go well with their people.
But yet. Obedience good, but needs to be guarded.
Teachableness needs discretion for its companion.
Pliable tempers require a double guard.
The greater the grace received, the more need of caution.
Richest vessels require the strongest convoy.
Living churches and Christians Satan's most coveted prey.
Holy joy in others leads to holy jealousy over them, 2 Cor. xi. 2.
I would have you. Admirable sweetness and prudence.
Wise. Having good understanding and discrimination.
Wisdom is—1. To know what is good; 2. Embrace it; 3. Hold it fast.
Includes prudence and discretion. Wise as serpents, Matt. x. 16.
Necessary to avoid being ensnared by the crafty.

CHAP. XVI.]   ST. PAUL'S EPISTLE TO THE ROMANS.   339

The wisdom of the wise is to understand his way, Prov. xiv. 8.
False teachers usually pretend to superior wisdom, Col. ii. 2-4.
Believers to be not only harmless but intelligent.
Able to distinguish clearly between truth and error.
Roman believers perhaps already not sufficiently cautious.
Unto; *i.e.*, 1. In respect of; 2. To the practice of; 3. To the promotion of.
Good; viz., 1. In itself; 2. For yourselves and others.
Good—1. In doctrine; 2. In practice; 3. In experience.
The highest wisdom is to know the will of God and do it;
The most profitable that which makes us wise to salvation.
Wisdom becomes Christians, but only that which is unto good.
Simple. *Gr.*, Harmless; like an animal without horns.
Believers, in respect of malice and evil, to be as children, 1 Cor. xiv. 20.
Wise as serpents, harmless as doves, Matt. x. 16.
As contrasted with " wise,"—without cunning, dexterity, or skill.
Unknowing and unpractised in the ways of evil-doing.
Have not known the depths of Satan, as they speak, Rev. ii. 24.
Concerning. *Gr.*, Unto, *i.e.*, in respect to, or in the practice of.
Evil—1. Moral evil, sin; 2. Evil as done to others.
In malice be children, in understanding be men, 1 Cor. xiv. 20.
Believers to have skill to do good, but none to do evil.
Strangers to its wishes, unskilled in its methods and ways.

To ἐφ' ὑμῶν (Codd. Sin. and Alex. omit το), concerning you. *Calv.* In respect to you; for κατα το ἐφ' ὑμ. *Stuart.* Over you; omitting the article as the true reading. *D. Brown.*—Σοφους, wise, discriminating *Or.* Prudent. *Theoph., Tol.* Intelligent. *Beza.* Implies practical knowledge requiring prudence. *Est.* Sagacious. *Doddr.* Cautious. *Alf.* Susceptible, ingenious. *Lange.*—Εἰς το ἀγαθον, unto good (ad bonum). *Calv.* The truth. *Beza.* To the obtaining and retaining of what is good. *Pisc., Vor.* So as to persevere in what is good. *Grot.* To know how to do good. *Eras.* To pursue what ought to be pursued. *Tol.* With respect to every opportunity of doing good. *Doddr.* In respect to that which is good. *Stuart.* To understand and hold fast the good. *De Wette.* After good. *Lange.* To know what is to be obeyed and what resisted. *Or.* As to their own salvation and advantage. *Theoph.*—Ἀκεραιους (κερας, a horn, or κεραω, to mix), harmless, upright. *Theoph.* Simple. *Mor., Beza, Cas., Pisc., Calv.* Sincere. *Eras., Vat., Trem.* Free from committing evil. *Vor., Pisc., Vat.* Without skill in hurting. *Beza, Tol.* As if you knew not how to do evil. *Men., Est.* 'Wise' so as not to be deceived; harmless so as not to deceive others. *Grot.* Simple, inoffensive, hurting no one. *Schött.* Willing to be accounted simpletons. *Stuart.* Unsusceptible and slow, as if simple people. *Lange.* = ἀπλους, πραΰθυμος. *Eustath.*—Εἰς το κακον, in regard to doing evil. *Stuart.* In learning evil. *Lange.* In respect to false, impure wisdom. *De Wette.* So as to render evil for evil. *Or.*

20. *And the God of peace shall bruise Satan under your feet shortly. The grace of our Lord Jesus Christ be with you. Amen.*

God of peace. The author of peace and of all blessing, chap. xv. 33.
God who loves and approves, gives and continues peace.
God who—1. Is at peace with us, chap. v. 1 ; Eph. ii. 16 ; Col. i. 20–22 ;
2. Speaks peace to us, Ps. lxxxv. 8 ; Zech. ix. 10 ;
3. Ordains peace for us, Isa. xxvi. 12 ; 4. Bestows peace upon us, Num. viii. 26 ; Ps. xxix. 11.
Peace in opposition to the divisions and offences just named.
God's part and good-will to prevent or remove these.
Gives peace even in the midst of enemies, Job. v. 23 ; Prov. xvi. 7.
Rest and peace in the church God's gift, Acts ix. 31 ; Josh. xxii. 4 ; xxiii. 1 ; 2 Cor. xiv. 6.
Peace in the world enjoyed through His overruling providence.
God's presence in the church the only pledge of true peace.
Bruise. As Gen. iii. 15. Crush—1. His plans ; 2. His power ; 3. His person.
A prophetic assurance given for believers' encouragement.
Promises given to quicken, not to supersede watchfulness.
No true lasting peace in the church till Satan is bruised.
The serpent's head already bruised by Christ, the woman's seed.
Bruised effectually on the cross, finally at His coming.
Successive bruisings of Satan in the history of the church.
The enemy of the church's peace bruised by the God of peace.
Victory comes from God, not as the God of war, but of peace.
Satan. A Hebrew word signifying "adversary," 1 Pet. v. 8.
The enemy of God and Christ, of mankind and the church.
So called in the Old Testament, 1 Chron. xxi. 1 ; Job i. 6 ; Ps. cix. 6 ; Zech. iii. 1.
Still more in the New, Luke x. 18 ; xxii. 31 ; Acts v. 3 ; xvi. 18 ; 1 Cor. v. 5 ; vii. 5, &c.
Other names—Beelzebub, Matt. xii. 24 ; Belial, 2 Cor. vi. 15 ; the devil, or the slanderer, Rev. xii. 9 ; Matt. iv. 1, compared with Mark i. 14 ; the old serpent or dragon, Rev. xii. 9, compared with Gen. iii. 1 ; 2 Cor. xi. 3 ; the tempter, Matt. iv. 3 ; 1 Thess. iii. 5 ; accuser of the brethren, Rev. xii. 10.
A liar and murderer from the beginning, John viii. 44.
The deceiver of the nations, Rev. xii. 9 ; xx. 3, 8, 10.
The god and prince of this world, 2 Cor. iv. 4 ; John xii. 31 ; xiv. 30 ; xvi. 11.

Prince of devils and of the power of the air, Matt. xii. 24 ; Eph. ii. 2.
Originally an angel, who left his first estate, Jude 6 ; 2 Pet. ii. 4.
The enemy who sows tares in the field, Matt. xiii. 39.
False teachers and sowers of division his ministers, 2 Cor. xi. 15.
His attempts are—1. To defile ; 2. To disturb ; 3. To destroy.
Hates the church's purity, prosperity, and peace.
To be steadfastly resisted and overcome, 1 Pet. v. 9 ; Rev. xii. 11.
Bound at the first resurrection for a thousand years, Rev. xx. 1–3.
To be afterwards loosed again for a short season, ver. 3, 7.
After his last attempt against the saints, cast into a lake of fire, ver. 10.

Under your feet. As your conquered adversary, Josh. x. 24.
Token of subjection, humiliation, and destruction, Ps. cx. 2.
The believer's life a contest with Satan, Eph. vi. 11 ; 1 Pet. v. 9 ; Jas. iv. 7.
Conquered by Christ, he is to be bruised under His people's feet, Col. ii. 15.

Shortly. Mainly at Christ's coming, thought of as not far distant.
Partial and temporary bruisings in the meantime—
1. Deliverance from Pagan persecutions under Constantine ;
2. Deliverance from the darkness of Popery at the Reformation ;
3. Success in missionary operations in the present century.
Every victory of faith brings new grief to Satan. *Bengel.*

Grace, &c. The apostle's favourite benediction ; so 1 Cor. xvi. 23 ; Gal. vi. 18, &c.
Grace=1. Favour, love, kindness ; 2. Spiritual blessing as its effect.

Our Lord Jesus Christ—1. The source of spiritual blessing as God, John i. 16 ; Col. ii. 9 ;
2. The treasury of spiritual blessing as Mediator, John iii. 34 ; Col. i. 19.
Nothing but grace and love in Christ's heart to His church, 2 Cor. viii. 9.
The favour and blessing of Christ viewed as those of God.
The church continually in need of grace and blessing.
The care and keeping of it in the hands of Jehovah, Isa. xxvii. 3.
Christ's grace the good-will of Him who dwelleth in the bush, Deut. xxxiii. 16.
Mentioned here as the pledge of the church's final deliverance.
The best security against internal division.
His grace more than a match for all Satan's attacks.
The strongest armour and an impregnable wall. *Chrys.*

With you. Christ's love and blessing for ever with His people, John xiii. 1.
Naphtali's blessing theirs,—"Satisfied with favour," &c., Deut. xxxiii. 23.

Συντρίψει (σύν, together, and τρίβω, to bruise), future for optative. *Stuart.* Cod. Alex. has συντρίψετω, may he bruise (conterat). *Vulg., Tol.* Shall bruise (conteret). *Calv.* Take away his power from among you. *Barth.* At Christ's second coming. *Vat., Vor.*—Σατανάν. Heb. שָׂטָן = Rabbin., הַקַּדְמוֹנִי נָחָשׁ, the old serpent, ὄφις ἀρχαῖος, Rev. xii. 9. Personal existence of a spirit of evil clearly revealed in Scripture, but gradually, in accordance with the progressiveness of God's method. First temptation referred only to the serpent. Throughout the patriarchal and Jewish dispensation this vague and imperfect revelation of the source of evil alone given. In the Book of Job no power of spiritual influence, but only a power of outward circumstances attributed to him. The captivity brought the Israelites face to face with the great dualism of the Persian mythology, and the conflict of Ormuzd, the good Being, with Ahriman, the co-ordinate spirit of evil. But no resemblance between the Satan of Scripture and the Persian Ahriman. His subordination and inferiority as strongly marked after the captivity as before it. The apocryphal books, while dwelling on demons, have no notice of Satan. So with Josephus. The New Testament first brings Satan's existence and nature distinctly forward. There the whole description of his power implies a spiritual nature and spiritual influence. Probably a fallen angel, who once had a time of probation, but whose condemnation is now irrevocably fixed. *Dr Smith.*—Ἐν τάχει, shortly; as to the beginning of the bruising. *Beng.*—Χάρις, &c., found here and at ver. 24 in almost all the Greek and Latin MSS., and also in Chrys. and Ambrose. Beza, with the Syriac, retains it only at the end.—Ἀμήν, omitted in Codd. Sin. and Alex.

---

21. *Timotheus, my workfellow, and Lucius, and Jason, and Sosipater, my kinsman, salute you.*

Timotheus. A native of Lycaonia, born in Derbe or Lystra, Acts xvi. 1.
His father a Greek, and his mother a Jewess, Acts xvi. 1–3.
Mixed marriages not unfrequent among the dispersed Jews.
His father probably a proselyte of the gate, inclined to Judaism.
His mother Eunice, and his grandmother Lois, pious women, 2 Tim. i. 5.
His mind early imbued with scriptural knowledge, 2 Tim. iii. 15.
Probably converted during Paul's first tour in Asia Minor, Acts xiv.
At his second visit, found well reported of by the brethren, Acts xvi. 3.
Chosen by him to be the companion of his travels and labours.
Circumcised in order to remove Jewish prejudices.
Ordained by Paul and several elders with imposition of hands, 1 Tim. iv. 14; 2 Tim. i. 6.
Enjoyed the highest place in Paul's confidence and affection.

Was with him at Corinth when this epistle was written, Acts xx. 4. The latter part of his history involved in obscurity. Said to have gone to Rome after receiving Paul's second letter (2 Tim. iv. 9, 21), and to have attended him till his martyrdom, then returned to Ephesus, and at last to have also received the martyr's crown.
Not joined with Paul at the beginning of this epistle as elsewhere—1. From its nature and object; 2. From his not having yet been in Rome.

Workfellow. As in ver. 9, "helper." Paul's humility. Working together for Christ endears believers to each other.
Lucius. Either Luke the Evangelist, now with Paul, Acts xx. 5; Or, according to others, Lucius of Cyrene, Acts xiii. 1; or both. One name often appears under various forms.
Jason. A convert of Thessalonica, Acts xvii. 5, 7. Entertained Paul in his house there at much risk. Accompanied him to Corinth, as usual in those times, chap. xv. 24; Acts xx. 4.
Sosipater. Probably the same with Sopater of Berea, Acts xx. 4. A Jew with a Greek name. Now with Paul at Corinth.
Kinsmen. See at ver. 7, 11. Relations both by nature and grace. Holy and useful lives of relatives a joy to believers.
Timothy, a *workfellow*, named before Lucius, &c., who were *kinsmen*. Coincides with such passages as Phil. ii. 19-22; 1 Tim. i. 2; 2 Tim. i. 2.
Too recondite to be intended, and too exact to be accidental.
Other manifestly undesigned coincidences here with Acts xx. 4. The truth of the narrative and the genuineness of the epistle mutually prove each other.
Salute you. Jewish salutations to Gentile believers, Ps. cxxxiii. 1. Some Jews rose above the prejudices of their nation, Acts xv. 22. These salutations natural additions or postscripts.
Several apparent conclusions to the letter, xv. 33; xvi. 20, 24, 27. Shows Paul's intense interest. Occasion to add, as in 1 Cor. xvi. 23; Phil. iv. 20.

Λουκιος, Lucius; probably Luke the evangelist. *Or., Est, Lightfoot, A. Clarke, Stuart.* Lucius the Cyrenian. *Grot.* Not the evangelist, and uncertain whether the Cyrenian. *Lange.* Lucas not identical with Lucius; rather the Cyrenian. *De Wette.* The fuller form of Lucas is not Lucius, but Lucanus. *D. Brown.*—Ἰασων. Jason appears the same with Secundus, his Latin name. *Lightfoot.* Appears to have followed Paul from Thessalonica to Corinth, Acts xvii. 5. *D. Brown.*—Σωσιπατρος, probably Sopater of Berea. *De Wette.* Identity at least not improbable. *Lange.*

22. *I, Tertius, who wrote this epistle, salute you in the Lord.*

I. The change of person corroborative of the genuineness of the chapter.
Love seeks to express itself on all proper occasions.
Tertius expresses his affection for the church at Rome, and bespeaks it for himself.
Tertius. Probably an Italian, or Silas under a Latin name.
Apparently known to some believers at Rome.
Out of fervent brotherly affection sends his salutation.
Wrote this epistle. Acted as the apostle's amanuensis.
Such aid usually employed by Paul, 1 Cor. xvi. 21; Col. iv. 18; 2 Thess. iii. 17.
Concluded his epistle with his own hand for identification, Gal. vi. 11.
An amanuensis perhaps used from defective sight, Gal. iv. 13–15.
Appears to have written a large and not very legible hand, Gal. vi. 11.
Each his own gift. The greatest needs the aid of the least.
A humble service made the name of Tertius immortal.
In the Lord. As a Christian brother and member of Christ's body.
All our words and actions to be in the Lord,—
1. In union with Him; 2. In His strength; 3. In His sight.
His presence to be realised, and His glory sought in everything.

'Ἐγώ, marks the chapter as genuine. *Thol.*—Τέρτιος, Tertius, a Roman name, and probably known at Rome. *Beng.* Thought to be Silas, from the meaning of the name. *Doddr.* But without grounds, the Latinised name of Silas being Silvanus. *Lange.*—Ὁ γράψας, who wrote. From Paul's dictation. *Beza, Tol., Eras.* From Paul's copy, to be sent to Rome. *Beza, Tol.* Shows what sort of assistants Paul employed. *D. Brown.* No account in the Bible of the origin of writing. No allusion to its practice or existence in the Book of Genesis. Pliny believed the Assyrians had always known the use of letters. Every fragment of remote antiquity discovered at Nineveh bears characters perfectly expressed. The Egyptians in the time of Joseph acquainted with writing of a certain kind. First distinct mention of writing in Exod. xvii. 14. This apparently not used for the first time, but so familiar as to be employed for historic records. The tables of the Testimony written by the finger of God (Exod. xxxi. 18), and the names of the tribes engraven on Aaron's breast-plate, show the existence of alphabetic characters. Curses written in the book, Num. v. 23. The king to write out a copy of the law, Deut. xvii. 18. A writing of divorcement to be given to a wife put away, Deut. xxiv. 1, 3. Name Kirjathsepher or 'Book-town' (Josh. xv. 15) indicates a knowledge of writing among the Phœnicians. The characters used by the early Hebrews most probably Phœnician. Invention of letters ascribed to them. Cadmus, a Phœnician, said by Pliny to have brought with him into Greece sixteen letters. At the time of the Trojan war (1190 B.C.) Palamedes added other four, and Simonides of Melos four more. Writing most generally employed in the time of the Trojan war. Oldest documents containing the writing of a Semitic race probably the bricks of Nineveh and Babylon. Wood used on some occasions by the Hebrews, Num. xvii. 3. Lead probably poured into the cavities of the stone made by the letters of an inscription, Job xix. 24. The ancient and most common material used by the Hebrews probably dressed skins. Herodotus, after saying that the Ionians learned the art of writing from the Phœnicians, adds that they called their books 'skins,' because they made use of sheepskins and goatskins when short of paper. Parchment (2 Tim. iv. 13) used for the MSS. of the Pentateuch in the time of Josephus. The provisions of the Talmud require that the Law should be written on the skins of clean animals. The Egyptians imparted to the Greeks the use of papyrus, a kind of reed (hence our 'paper'), the most easy and convenient material known to the ancients for writing Originally called byblos; hence 'byblos,' a book (Bible). Tablets of wood covered with wax served for the ordinary purposes of life, Luke i. 63. Several of these fastened together formed a volume. Writing performed with a pointed style or pen (Job xix. 24), sometimes of iron (Jer. xvii. 1). For harder materials a graver employed (Exod. xxxii. 4; Isa. viii. 1). For parchments or skins a reed-pen used (3 John 13). The ink, lamp-black dissolved in gall-juice, carried in an ink-horn suspended, as still in the East, at the writer's girdle (Ezek. ix. 2, 3). In Assyria, writings on stone and metal passed from left to right; those in ink or colour on a smooth surface from right to left, or retrograde. The latter method at first employed by the Greeks, especially in inscriptions of a single line. The next variety in early inscriptions a double course given to the letters, the lines reading in alternate directions. This mode called Boustrophedon, from the resemblance to the ploughing of oxen, seen in the Sigean inscription now in the British Museum, one of the most ancient specimens of writing.—Ἐν τῷ Κυρίῳ, in the Lord; connect with γράψας, 'on the Lord's account.' Tol. For the Lord's glory. Eras. With ἀσπάζομαι, 'wish you the blessing which is from the Lord.' Beza, Pag., Pisc., Grot., Vor.

---

23. *Gaius mine host, and of the whole church, saluteth you. Erastus the chamberlain of the city saluteth you, and Quartus a brother.*

Gaius. Probably the Corinthian mentioned 1 Cor. i. 14.
Also possibly the Gaius of Derbe, Acts xx. 4; and of Macedonia, xix. 29.
Among the first whom Paul baptized at Corinth, 1 Cor. i. 14.
Apparently a person of wealth, and a leading member of the church.
Probably the same who is commended for his hospitality, 3 John 5-8.
Mine host. Paul lived with Gaius on his second visit to Corinth.
At his first visit, wrought with Aquila at his own trade, Acts xviii. 3.
Aquila now at Rome. Another undesigned coincidence.
Gaius naturally much attached to Paul as one of his converts.
Also as distinguished for hospitality. Additional coincidence.
Of the whole church. The brethren probably met in his house.
His large-hearted hospitality further commended.
His house much frequented on Paul's account.
Gaius's wealth consecrated to Christ and His cause.
Erastus. Perhaps the apostle's helper in Ephesus, Acts xix. 22.

Mentioned in connection with Corinth, his own city, 2 Tim. iv. 20.
Another confirmatory undesigned coincidence.
Probably, on receiving the truth, accompanied Paul for a time.
Chamberlain. Public steward or treasurer; town-clerk or recorder.
An office of high respectability, mentioned by Josephus.
The Gospel suits and gains all classes. Yet not many noble called, 1 Cor. i. 26.
Grace compatible with high position and manifold avocations.
Christians may hold office under heathen rulers, Neh. i. 1.
To serve Christ we need not abandon worldly business.
City. Corinth, where this epistle was written, see in ver. 1.
A place of great mental activity and commercial enterprise.
Proverbial for its wealth, vice, and profligacy of manners.
Worship of Venus attended there with shameful licentiousness.
Now a wretched village under the corrupted name of Gortho.
The church there planted by Paul himself, Acts xviii. 1; 1 Cor. iii. 6.
Paul in Corinth eighteen months, and then followed by Apollos, Acts xviii. 11; xix. 1.
Two parties then formed in the church, those of Paul and of Apollos, 1 Cor. i. 12.
Paul's First Epistle to the Corinthians written from Ephesus about 57 or 58.
Occasioned by information given respecting—1. The divisions existing among them, 1 Cor. i. 11; 2. A grievous case of incest, 1 Cor. v. 1; 3. Their defective habits (vi. 1, &c.), church-order (xi. 20, &c.), and doctrine, (xv. 1, &c.)
A former epistle, now lost, probably referred to, chap. v. 9.
The second written from Macedonia some months after the first.
Occasioned by cheering information from Titus and Timothy.
A visit to Corinth, while staying at Ephesus, probably not recorded, 2 Cor. xii. 14; xiii. 1.
A brother. Name common to all believers. All one in Christ.
Believers usually so called by the apostle, and ought to be so by us.
Quartus only mentioned by name and as a brother; a high honour.

Γαιος, Gaius, the Corinthian mentioned 1 Cor. i. 14. *Theod.*, *Flatt*. Probably. *De Wette*, *Lange*. Possibly also in Acts xix. 29; xx. 4. *De Wette*, *Lange*. Three Gaiuses mentioned. Perhaps originally of Derbe, and now residing at Corinth. *Est*. Church met in his house. *Grot*. John's epistle written to him. *Men.*, *Est*., *Par*. Probably had the charge of strangers committed to him. *Lightfoot*. Afterwards bishop of Thessalonica. *Or*. His Latin name Caius. *Grot*.—Ἔραστος, Erastus; same as mentioned 2 Tim. iv. 20. *Flatt*, *D. Brown*.—Οἰκονόμος (οἶκος, house, and νέμω, to tend or rule),

CHAP. XVI.]   ST. PAUL'S EPISTLE TO THE ROMANS.   347

steward. *Chrys., Theod.* Dispensator. *Eras., Vat.* Overseer (præfectus). *Zeg.* Procurator. *Beza, Pisc., Pag., Mar.* Anciently the name of a private office, now transferred to a public one, like Quæstor among the Romans. *Grot.* Dispenser of the public money alone or with others. *Eras., Tol., Est., Vat., Schött.* Only formerly one. *Pelagius.* Favoured by the fact that he was sent by Paul, Acts xix. 22. *Est.* Treasurer. *Stuart.* Heb. הבית על, 1 Kings iv. 6; בית רב, Est. i. 8.

---

24. *The grace of our Lord Jesus Christ be with you all. Amen.*

The grace, &c. As he began so he ends with prayer. *Theophylact.*
Preaching and teaching to be well seasoned with prayer.
Its repetition indicates—1. Its importance; 2. Paul's fervent affection.
Another of the various conclusions of the epistle.
The repeated farewells of a loving father to his children.
The same benediction as in ver. 20, but here invoked on "all."

Χαρις, &c. Omitted by Codd. Sin., Vat., and Alex. Repeated by Paul with his own hand. *Grot.*

---

25. *Now to him that is of power to stablish you according to my gospel and the preaching of Jesus Christ, according to the revelation of the mystery which was kept secret since the world began.*

To Him—1. To Him I commend you; 2. To Him be glory.
Of Him, to Him, and through Him are all things, chap. xi. 36.
That is. God described—1. As to His power; 2. His wisdom; so Jude 24.
Believers safe in the hands of such a God and Father.
Of power. Believers only kept by the power of God, 1 Pet. i. 5.
Christ the Author and Finisher of our faith; therefore God, Heb. xii. 2.
Of ourselves we can neither begin nor continue it.
God's power in the New Testament often implies disposition and will, iv. 21.
In the covenant of grace, what He can do He will do, xiv. 4.
His almightiness our greatest comfort and security, Gen. xvii. 1, 2.
Stablish. Make firm and steadfast—1. In faith; 2. In grace.
Establishment an unspeakable mercy, Heb. xiii. 9; Col. ii. 7; Eph. iii. 17.
Establishment in grace as necessary as conversion, Ps. xl. 2.
The apostle's great desire for the Roman Christians, i. 11.

According to, &c.—1. In relation to it ; 2. According to its teachings.
The Gospel the means, matter, and rule of our establishment.
Establishment in the Gospel is *salvation*,—in error, *ruin*.
The doctrine of the Gospel fitted to establish us in grace.
My Gospel. Gospel preached by me. So chap. ii. 16 ; 2 Tim. ii. 8 ; Gal. ii. 2, 7.
Paul's not as to its origination, but its publication.
Establishment by no other means than the true Gospel.
Other doctrines preached under that name, 2 Cor. xi. 4 ; Gal. i. 6.
Many gospels still preached that are not Paul's.
Paul's Gospel alone brings glory to God and salvation to men.
Exalts Christ and humbles the sinner.
Paul's only in common with the other apostles, Eph. ii. 20 ; 2 Pet. iii. 15.
Preaching of Jesus Christ—1. As made known to Paul by Christ, 1 Cor. xv. 1 ; Gal. i. 12.
2. As preached by Christ himself in the days of His flesh, Mark i. 14.
3. As preached by Him through His apostles, 1 Cor. vii. 10.
Christ both the authority and pattern for Gospel preaching.
Jesus Christ also the subject-matter of Paul's Gospel.
The Gospel is God's Gospel and record concerning His Son, chap. i. 1 ; 1 John v. 11.
According to, &c. Enlarges further on the nature of the Gospel.
Revelation of the mystery—1. The mystery now revealed ;
2. The actual revelation of the mystery now made.
The Gospel preached in virtue of that revelation.
Redemption and atonement through Christ a mystery, Eph. iii. 3.
Mystery of godliness, 1 Tim. iii. 16 ; mystery of Christ, Eph. iii. 4.
Not the product of human wisdom, but God's eternal counsel.
A mystery, because hitherto comparatively hidden, Eph. iii. 5.
Hid in dark figures under the Old Testament dispensation, Heb. ix. 8 ; 1 Pet. i. 11.
Now revealed to apostles and prophets by the Spirit, ver. 26 ; 1 Cor. ii. 10.
Made known to Paul by divine revelation, Eph. iii. 3 ; Gal. i. 12 ; 1 Cor. xv. 3.
Redemption a mystery—1. Of love that passes knowledge, Eph. iii. 19 ;
2. Of wisdom that angelic powers cannot fathom, 1 Pet. i. 12.
Reference also to the introduction of the Gentiles to an equality with the Jews, Eph. iii. 1-10.

Kept secret. *Gr.*, Kept back in silence ; not fully revealed. Little or nothing said of it in the earlier generations of men. The Old Testament a clock which only struck in the New. Life and immortality only now brought clearly to light, 2 Tim. i. 10. Concealment only comparative, Col. i. 26; Eph. iii. 5, 10; 1 Pet. i. 12. Concealed under various shadowy representations—
1. Historical types ; 2. Symbolical rites ; 3. Obscure prophecies. The mystery first indicated in the address to the serpent, Gen. iii. 15.
Next in the obscure promises to the patriarchs, as Gen. xii. 3. Salvation by God's crucified Son hidden till New Testament times.
Since the world began. *Gr.*, In eternal times. The ages before Christ—
1. Earliest ages of the world, touching on eternity ;
2. Eternity itself before the creation of the world.
The Gospel had its rise in the purposes of eternal love, Eph. i. 3, &c. God's grace given us in Christ before the world began, 2 Tim. i. 9.

Τῷ δὲ, &c. This and the following verses taken away by Marcion. *Est.* Wanting in most Greek MSS. *Eras.* But found in the oldest and best, *e.g.*, Sin., Vat., and Alex. Placed after chap. xiv. 23 in some copies, and in the Greek Fathers. In one MS. found in both places. Its proper place doubtless at the end of the epistle, as in various MSS. and versions, and in Origen and the Latin Fathers. *Alford.* The involved character of the passage indicative of the apostle's fervour on the general survey of the epistle. To Him [I commend you]. *Con. & Hows.* To Him [be glory, ver. 26]. *D. Brown.*—Στηρίξαι, to confirm. *Vulg., Est.* So as to persevere in the faith begun. *Tol.* This confirmation the object of the apostle's desired visit to Rome (i. 11). *Rückert.*
—Κατα το εὐαγγελιον μου, according to my Gospel. *Calv.*, &c. In relation to or in the faith of it. *De Wette.* In the Gospel, *i.e.*, in their adherence to it. *Rückert, Meyer.* So that you may live and act according to it. *Köllner.* In conformity with the truths of it. *D. Brown.* The ground of the certainty of His being able to stablish them. *Thol.*
—Κηρυγμα, preaching, heralding (præconium). *Pisc., Beza.* Predicationem. *Vulg. Tol.* Omitted in Cod. Sin.—'Ιησου Χριστου, of Jesus Christ, *i.e.*, which is in Him. *Vat., Tol., Pag.* That doctrine which I teach, nay, which Christ himself preached. *Grot.* Which Christ himself preached, and which is therefore His laws and not our opinions. *Chrys.* That which Christ published through us the apostles. *De Wette.* The preaching about Christ. *Calv., Luth., Doddr., Thol., Hald.* The preaching that was His own, or that was published by His messengers. *Rückert, Meyer.*—Κατα ἀ., according to (ex). *Pag., Beza, Pisc.* Secundum. *Vulg., Tol.*—'Αποκαλυψιν, revelation ; real historical revelation. *Most Interpreters.* Internal revelation. *Nielson.* The matter of the preaching such as is not discoverable by nature's powers, but is only revealed by God. *Tir., Tol.* The preaching takes place in virtue of the revelation of the mystery. *De Wette.* Μυστ. = arcanum. *Beza.* Divine secret. *Vat.* Refers to the calling of the Gentiles, as Eph. iii. 4. *Beza, Beng., Ham., Pyle, A. Clarke, D. Brown.* Redemption and salvation of all nations by Christ. *Tir., De Wette, Niel.* Whole doctrine of Christ. *Grot.* Refers to the entire plan of redemption, including the participation of the heathen in its blessings. *Calv.* More especially the latter. *Rückert.*—Χρονοις

αἰωνίοις, in eternal times. *Stier.* From the beginning of the world. *Luth.* For a very long time (longissimo tempore). *Grot., Flatt.* All the ages from the beginning of the world to the time of Christ. *Vor., Est., Beza.* From eternal times. *Vulg., Pag., Schött, Van Ess.* From the times of the ages (a temporibus secularibus). *Pisc.* A temp. seculorum. *Beza.* In past ages. *Vor., Mar.* Αἰών and Heb. עוֹלָם, not always eternity. *Beza.* Χρον. αἰωνίοις = πρὸ χρόνων αἰωνίων, before the times of the world, as 1 Tim. i. 9. *Schött.* Time when not only men but angels were created, the mystery being hid from both. *Beng.* For many ages back. *Diod.* In ancient times. *Doddr.* In the Jewish dispensation. *Whitby, Macknight.* From the earliest times; most ancient times before the law. *Stuart.* Earlier generations of our species. *Chal.* Ages before Christ. *De Wette, Hald.* From the ancient times before Christ; = ἕτερ. γενεαῖς, Eph. iii. 5. *Niel.* During eternal ages. *Ellicot, D. Brown.* Compare Col. i. 26.—Σεσιγημένον, kept silent (tacitum fuit). *Beza, Pisc., Pag.* Concealed. *Schött, Mar., Rück.* Only obscurely revealed. *Whitby.* Remained as it were concealed. *Stuart.* Kept in silence. *Ellicot, D. Brown.* Concealed, viz., in the Scriptures. *Nielson.* Something of it spoken by the prophets, but understood only by the event. *Grot.* Nothing heard of it in past ages. *Vat.* Never before so fully exhibited. *Doddr.*

---

26. *But now is made manifest, and by the scriptures of the prophets, according to the commandment of the everlasting God, made known to all nations for the obedience of faith.*

Now. Since the time of Christ's appearing, 2 Tim. i. 9.
In Him the dayspring from on high has visited us, Luke i. 78.
Made manifest. So chap iii. 21. Brought to light, 2 Tim. i. 9.
The veil of the temple rent at Christ's death, Matt. xxvii. 51.
The veil on Moses' face done away in Christ, 2 Cor. iii. 13-15.
Great plainness of speech in preaching the Gospel, 2 Cor. iii. 12.
Scriptures of the prophets. Christ testified of by the prophets, chap. iii. 21.
Salvation made known in the Old Testament Scriptures, John v. 37; 2 Tim. iii. 15.
Prophetic declarations only now understood, 1 Pet. i. 12; 2 Pet. i. 19.
Explained by Christ to His disciples in person, Luke xxiv. 27, 44-46.
Afterwards by the Spirit given to them, John xvi. 13-15.
They reveal the Gospel mystery by the light now cast on them—
1. In their fulfilment; 2. Through the illumination of the Spirit.
Old and New Testaments mutually throw light on each other.
Paul supports each doctrine in this epistle by Old Testament Scripture.
Writings of the prophets the armoury of New Testament preachers, Acts xviii. 23.
Commandment. Decree or appointment, as Ps. ii. 7, 8.

Christ's last words, Preach the Gospel to every creature, Mark xvi. 15.
A dispensation committed to the apostle so to preach it, 1 Cor. ix. 17.
Apostles ambassadors for God and Christ to the world, 2 Cor. v. 21.
Ministry of reconciliation committed to them and all preachers, ver. 18, 19.
A necessity laid on Paul to preach the Gospel, 1 Cor. ix. 16.
This command eternally sending forth its echo still.
Everlasting God. His dispensations change, but not Himself.
The same from everlasting to everlasting, Ps. xc. 1, 2; cii. 26, 27.
Same command and same character ascribed to Christ, Matt. xxviii. 20; Heb. i. 10-12.
"Everlasting" suggested by the different and distant ages referred to.
God himself from everlasting, though as to revelation *silent*.
Divine silence presupposes eternal knowledge, Acts xv. 18.
The everlasting God necessarily a hidden God, Isa. xlv. 15.
God's purposes formed in eternity, executed in time.
Each successive stage in man's history provided for.
Jewish economy only a temporary arrangement in the divine plan.
To all nations. Including the Jews, to whom it was first made known.
Preaching the Gospel to all nations the command of God.
Roman and all Christians thus reminded of their duty.
Obedience of faith. Object of the Gospel announcement, chap. i. 5.
That obedience furthered by inquiry into the Scriptures, Acts xvii. 11, 12.
Right faith is that which has obedience connected with it;
Right obedience is that which is produced by faith.
The epistle begins and ends with a description of the Gospel and its object.

Φανερωθεντος δε νυν δια τε, &c. (τε retained by Griesbach', but which is now manifested by, &c. *Mart.* And now manifested and made known by, &c. *Diod.* Expounded and understood. *Est.*—Γραφων προφητικων, prophetic scriptures; which predicted Christ and the Gospel. *Men.* Which prove the doctrine by their correspondence with the event. *Grot.* The mystery now laid open by the Gospel, but formerly by the prophetic scriptures. The calling of the Gentiles predicted by the prophets, but not understood by the Jews *Beng.* According to the tenor of the prophetic scriptures.

Doddr., *Koppe*. Next disclosed or comparatively brought to life by the prophetic scriptures. *Stuart*. Paul's teaching grounded on the Old Testament writings. *Rückert.*
—Κατ' ἐπιταγην, according to the command (preceptum'. *Vulg.* (Ex imperio'. *Pisc., Pag.* By the delegation given to the apostles. *Eras., Men.* Ordination of God from eternity. *Par., Tol.* Prophets commanded to reveal it to others. *Tol.* Four important points :—1. Δια γρ. προφ., for the sake of the Judaising teachers ; 2. Κατ' ἐπιτ. τ. αἰων. Θ., the authority for the Gospel's universal promulgation, with allusion to change of dispensation ; 3. Εἰς ὑπακ. πιστ., its object *faith* instead of *works ;* 4. Εἰς παντ. ἐθν., the extent of it. *Niel.*

---

27. *To God only wise, be glory through Jesus Christ for ever. Amen.*

Only wise. The Gospel scheme the product of divine wisdom, 1 Cor. ii. 7.
The object of redemption the exhibition of that manifold wisdom, Eph. iii. 10.
God alone wise—1. Originally ; 2. Essentially ; 3. Unchangeably. Creature wisdom only a drop from the ocean of the divine.
God only wise, as He is only holy and only good, Rev. xv. 4 ; Matt. xix. 17.
The wisdom of God exhibited in the contents of this epistle, chap. xi. 33.
Meet doxology at the close of such an exhibition of divine truth.
The declarations of such a Being to be meekly received.
His purposes deep, and only to be revealed by Himself.
Glory. The divine glory the end of all his doings, chap. xi. 36.
The highest and worthiest end the creature can seek.
Glory to be ascribed to God at the contemplation of His words and works.
The more He is known the more He is to be glorified.
God's wisdom entitles Him to endless glory and praise.
In thanksgiving we remember His benefits, in adoration His perfections.
Paul makes the end of his epistle what was the end of his life.
Through Jesus Christ. God's highest glory comes through Jesus Christ.
God revealed through Christ as the only wise God.
His purposes of wisdom executed through Him, Col. i. 16.
His mission into the world to declare the Father, John i. 18.
Glory and thanks to be presented to God through Him, chap. i. 8.
Christ the Mediator of our praises as well as of our prayers.

For ever. Boundless perfections worthy of endless praise.
The anthem begun in time to be carried into eternity.
Worthy and delightful employment for men and angels.
New discoveries of divine wisdom evoke new songs of praise.
The song of the redeemed ever a new song, Rev. v. 9; xiv. 3; Ps. xcvi. 1.
Immortal natures to be employed in immortal praise.
Amen. Expresses—1. Hearty consent; 2. Desire; 3. Affirmation; 4. Faith.
Added here—1. To the ascription; or, 2. To the whole epistle.
Glory to the only wise God the wish of each renewed heart.
In this "Amen" the Holy Ghost seals the truth of all that has been said.
Worthy peroration to so divine a composition.
Embodies the assurance that all will be realised.
The wish of the writer accompanies that assurance.
Each devout reader will add his own cordial Amen!

Thus ends the examination of this mine of spiritual wealth.
Perused a thousand times, yet ever found still new.
The oftener read the more delightful and valuable.
For the preciousness of its truths and the sublimity of its sentiments;
For the discoveries of divine grace and wisdom which it contains;
And for the influence which it has exercised on the human race;
Unrivalled by any composition in ancient or modern times.
A monument of divine love, and a treasury of blessing to man.

Μονῳ σοφῳ Θεῳ, to the only wise God [I say]. *Beza, Pisc., Pag.* To him [I commend you]. *Con. & Hows.* To Him I say. *D. Brown.* God the Author of all wisdom. *Grot.* Only wise in Himself and in His own essence. *Est.* Way of salvation discovered only by God himself. *Tol.*—Δια Ἰησου Χ., glory to be given only through Jesus Christ. *Est.* Through the Gospel and by men professing faith in Christ. *Men.* The wisely-contrived scheme of salvation executed by Him. *Doddr.* All that displays the wisdom of God made by Him. *Chrys.* All God's purposes of wisdom conceived and executed by Him. *Barth.* God has revealed Himself as the only wise God through Jesus Christ. *Orig., De Wette.*—Ω ἡ δοξα, *lit.* to whom be. *D. Brown.* An important alteration necessitated by the Greek. *Ellicot.* Ω wanting in some editions. Expunged by Beza. Found in almost all Greek and Latin MSS. Retained by critics. Apparently superfluous. *Niel.* Sentence imperfect; supply 'let us give thanks.' *Eras.* Redundant; assumed for the sake of repetition after the long hyperbaton. *Est.* Hebrew pleonasm. *Vor., Par., Beza.* For αὐτῳ or ἐκεινῳ, as Matt. xxvi. 50. So ὠν for αὐτων, Rom. iii. 14; Acts xxvi. 7. Relates grammatically and most naturally to Jesus Christ; if to Θεῳ, must be read for αὐτῳ, or rather in the demonstrative sense, as employed for οὑτος, or ὁδε. *Stuart.* An example of the apostle beginning a complex sentence with one construction and ending with a different one. Mark of genuineness. Peculiarities of style and composition not affected by inspiration.—Εἰς τ. αἰῶνας, unto ages never to be terminated. *Aug., Est.* The plan is to last for ever, and to have no issue but in eternal glory. *A. Clarke.* Codd. Sin. and Alex. add τῶν αἰώνων, for ever and ever. The subscription, πρὸς τοὺς Ῥωμαίους, found in Codd. Sin., Vat., and Alex. Some MSS. of less value add ἐγράφη and Κορίνθου; and others, διὰ Φοίβης διακόνου τῆς ἐν Κεγχρεαῖς ἐκκλησίας. The subscription adscititious, occasioned doubtless by chap. xvi. 1. The matter probably correct, but not written by Paul. *Stuart.*

INDEX.

A.

ABBA, Father, vol. i. 453, 454
Abelard, his view of Christ's death, i. 226; of original sin, i. 298
Abraham, i. 239, 251; his faith, i. 254, 261; his inheritance, i. 255; his seed, i. 255, 259, 261
Abraham's bosom, ii. 75
Abstinence from meats, ii. 230, 231
Abyss, ii. 74
Acacius of Cæsarea, ii. 14
Accursed, ii. 5, 7
Achaia, ii. 300, 302, 321, 322
Acra, part of Jerusalem, ii. 289
Acta Diurna, ii. 327
Acts of the Apostles, ii. 286
Adam, i. 294, 296; meaning of the name, ii. 39; a type of Christ, i. 301-303, 313
Adaptation in nature a proof of an intelligent Creator, i. 80, 82
Addresses in the early church, ii. 175
Admonition, mutual, ii. 281
Adonibezek, i. 113, 116
Adonis, i. 106, 178, ii. 106
Adoption, i. 452, 454, 479, 480; different kinds of, ii. 8
Adoption-interpretation of Christ's Sonship, ii. 14
Adultery, i. 176, 177
Ælia Capitolina, ii. 289
Æmathia, ii. 302
Æons, i. 95, ii. 335
Ætius, bishop of Antioch, ii. 13
Agape, or love-feast, ii. 322

Agonising in prayer, ii. 306, 307
Agrippa, Herod, ii. 309
Ahriman, i. 95, 476, ii. 221, 342
Aiasaluk, ii. 131
Albigenses, i. 510, 512
Alcibiades, i. 115
Alcuin, i. 500, ii. 14
Alexander the Great, i. 56
Alexander of Hales, i. 324
Alexandrian school of theology, ii. 14
All Souls' Festival, ii. 75
Altar, different kinds of, ii. 101, 102; Christ the true, ii. 283
Amanuensis used by Paul, ii. 344
Ambition, ii. 292, 293; that of the apostle, ii. 292-294
Ambrose, bishop of Milan, i. 298; first who recommended invocation of angels, i. 516; his views of Christ's death, ii. 251; a composer of hymns, ii. 274; introduced responsive singing into the Western Church, ib.
Amen, i. 110, ii. 13, 311, 353
Ammon, i. 178
Amosis, perhaps the Pharaoh of the Oppression, ii. 32
Amplias, ii. 325
Amyraldus, i. 501
Anabaptists, i. 325
Analogy of faith, ii. 168, 170
Anastatius of Alexandria, ii. 14
Anathema, ii. 7
Anaximander, his views of God, i. 99
Anaximenes, his views of God, i. 99.

Ancestors, worship of, i. 91
Andrew the Apostle, ii. 293
Andronicus, ii. 323, 325
Angels, i. 515, 516; invocation of them first recommended by Ambrose, i. 516; their worship prohibited, *ib.*
Anguish, i. 143, 145
Animals, bodies of, i. 82; worship of, i. 91, 96, 101
Animal soul, i. 410
Annianus, bishop of Alexandria, ii. 277
Anselm, archbishop of Canterbury, his views of Christ's death, i. 226; of original sin, i. 298; of election, i. 500
Answer of God, ii. 103
Antichrist, i. 465, ii. 121; his prophets, ii. 287
Antinomianism, ii. 333–335
Antiochus Epiphanes, i. 64, 189
Antipater, ii. 309
Antisthenes, his views of God, i. 99
Anubis, i. 104, 179
Apis, i. 91, 96, 179
Apocrypha, the, i. 15
Apollinaris, his views of the person of Christ, i. 23, ii. 14
Apollonia, ii. 290
Apollonius of Tyana, ii. 291
Apollos, ii. 346
Apophis, perhaps the Pharaoh of Joseph, ii. 32
Apostle, meaning and use of the term, i. 8, ii. 324, 325; how distinguished, i. 9, 11
Apostle of the Gentiles, ii. 119
Apostles, their traditional spheres of labour, ii. 293
Apostles' Creed, so called, ii. 170
Apostleship, i. 31
Apostolical Constitutions, i. 326, ii. 277
Appearance, external, of Paul, i. 6
Appian Way, ii. 322
Approved, ii. 326, 327
Aquila, ii. 277, 318, 321
Aquila, translator of the Old Testament into Greek, i. 151, 195
Aquinas, his views of Christ's death, i. 226; of faith, i. 274; of the fall, i. 298; of the sacraments, i. 324; of infant baptism, i. 325; of the cup in the Lord's Supper, i. 327; of election, i. 500

Arabia, i. 11
Arabs, their form of salutation, i. 41
Archelaus, ii. 309
Archippus, bishop of Laodicea, ii. 277
Areopagus, i. 56
Arianism, i. 23
Arians, ii. 13
Aristides, i. 118
Aristo, bishop of Smyrna, ii. 277
Aristobulus, ii. 326, 327
Aristotle, his views of God, i. 93
Arius, i. 23, ii. 13
Ark, the, i. 229, ii. 8
Arminians, their views of Christ's death, i. 226; of justification, i. 274; of the sacraments, i. 324; of baptism, i. 325; of election, i. 500, 501
Arminius, i. 500
Armour, Grecian and Roman, ii. 221; spiritual, ii. 218
Artemon, i. 23
Artemonites, ii. 13
Ashamed, ii. 62, 82
Ashtaroth, i. 106, 177
Asps, i. 208
Assyrians, their mode of writing, ii. 345
Astarte, i. 106, 177, 178, ii. 106, 238
Astronomy, its revelations a proof of creative power, i. 85
Asyncritus, ii. 329
Atergatis, i. 177
Athanasius, i. 23; his view of Christ's person, ii. 13, 14; of His death, i. 226, ii. 251; of the Holy Spirit, i. 283; his statement regarding the Sabbath, ii. 237
Athenagoras, a composer of hymns, ii. 274
Athens, i. 56, 57, 102, 105
Atonement, i. 249, 293, 394; view of Rabbies in regard to, i. 229; made by one man for another, ii. 7
Augustine, i. 283; theory of, i. 297, 298; his remark on the ministerial office, i. 31; his views of sin, i. 298; of the sacraments, i. 324; of baptism, *ib.*; of infant baptism, i. 325; of the millennium, i. 465; of predestination, i. 500; of angels, i. 516; of Christ's death, ii. 251; of an intermediate state and a purifying fire, ii. 75; of miracles, ii. 291; of the church, ii. 313; of church discipline, *ib.*

INDEX. 357

Augustus, ii. 200, 201, 309
Authenticity of Epistle to the Romans, i. 1
Avilius, bishop of Alexandria, ii. 277
Avitus of Vienne, i. 500
Awake, high time to, ii. 214
Awakening, ii. 214; the present a time of, *ib.*

B.

Baal, i. 96, 177, ii. 104, 105, 106
Baal-berith, ii. 106
Baal-peor, i. 177
Baal-zebub, i. 177
Baaltis, i. 178
Babes, i. 172, 174
Babylon, ancient bricks of, ii. 345
Banishment of Jews from Rome, ii. 318, 319
Banqueting, ii. 223
Baptism, i. 250, 321-326; of infants, i. 325; of proselytes, i. 322; views of the early church regarding it, i. 324; of the Latin church, *ib.*; mode of administering it, i. 324, 325; by whom administered, i. 326; high notions of it in the fourth century, i. 324
Barbarians, i. 54, 55
Barnabas, brings Paul to assist in the work at Antioch, i. 4; attends with him the Council at Jerusalem, *ib.*
Basil, St., i. 283, 298; his views of baptism, i. 326; of angels, i. 516, 517
Basil of Ancyra, ii. 13
Basilicæ, ii. 322
Basilides, i. 18, ii. 13, 335
Bassæ, temple of, i. 93
Bath-Kol, ii. 105
Baxter, Richard, his remark on the millennium, ii. 220
Beal, Bel, or Baal, ii. 106
Becon, his views of Christ's death, ii. 251
Bede, i. 500
Beelzebub, ii. 340
Bel, i. 94, 178, ii. 106
Bel's cairns, ii. 106
Belial, ii. 340
Believe, meaning of, in reference to Christ and the Gospel, i. 63, 245, ii. 62, 215

Believers, how called and addressed, i. 52; the three positions of, ii. 324
Belisarius, ii. 202
Benedictions, ii. 347
Benjamin, ii. 98
Berenger of Tours, i. 324; his views of the Lord's Supper, i. 327
Bernard of Clairvoix, his views of Christ's death, i. 226; of the two swords, ii. 313
Beza, i. 501
Bezetha, a part of Jerusalem, ii. 289
Bible, meaning and origin of the term, ii. 267; its English translations, i. 16; translations into other languages, ii. 274; testimonies to its excellence and preciousness, i. 16, 17
Bible Society, i. 34, 36
Birthright, ii. 22, 23
Bishops, ii. 173, 178; originally equivalent to presbyters or elders, ii. 176-178; traditional list of those ordained by the apostles or their coadjutors, ii. 277
Blessing, the duty of, ii. 186; the effect of the Gospel, ii. 305
"Blessed for ever," ii. 12, 13
Blessedness, i. 247
Blinded, ii. 110, 119
Blindness, Jewish, ii. 115, 135, 136
Blood of Christ, its significance, i. 228, 288
Boasting, a true and false, i. 165, 232
Body, the, wonderful construction of, i. 80; to be presented to God as a living sacrifice, ii. 154; a figure of the church, ii. 165; the special sphere of sin, i. 341; mortal, i. 341, 342, 442; dead in a believer, i. 439; quickened by the Spirit, i. 442, 443; its deeds, i. 446, 447; its redemption, i. 479, 480
Body of sin, i. 333, 334, 446, 447; of death, i. 406
Bolsec, i. 501
Bonaventura, i. 327
Bones, the, i. 81
Boniface, i. 33
Boniface II., i. 500
Boniface III., ii. 313
Books, the, Scriptures so called, ii. 267
Books of Moses, their history, i. 151

Boyle, Hon. Robert, his views of the Scriptures, i. 17
Bozrah, ii. 25
Bradford, John, saying of, i. 125
Brainerd, i. 34
Branches, as applied to the Jews, ii. 123, 124, 129, 130, 133
Brethren, use and application of the term, i. 52, 497, ii. 329, 330
Brotherly love, ii. 180
Bricks of Nineveh and Babylon, ii. 345
Bucer, i. 327; his views of Christ's death, ii. 251
Buildings, when first erected for Christian worship, ii. 320; how named, ii. 322
Bull of Boniface III., ii. 313
Bullinger, his views of Christ's death, ii. 251
Bunyan, John, his views of the millennium, ii. 220
Burial, spiritual, in baptism, i. 327, 328
Business, worldly, ii. 315, 346
Byblos, ii. 267, 345
Byron, Lord, his view of innate depravity, i. 307

C.

Caaba, at Mecca, i. 94
Cabbala, Jewish, ii. 335
Cadmus, the Phenician, i. 56, ii. 344
Cæsar of Arelata, i. 500, ii. 75
Cæsaro-papacy, ii. 314
Caius of Rome, i. 465
Caligula, i. 60, 116, 120, ii. 309
Call, i. 262, ii. 47, 49
Called, meaning and use of the term, i. 8, 10, 37, 491, 493, 498, 499, ii. 46, 47
Calling of God, ii. 21, 22, 142, 143
Calling upon Christ, ii. 83, 84
Calvin, ii. 251; his views of the fall, i. 299; of baptism, i. 326; of the Lord's Supper, i. 327; of predestination, i. 501; of Christ's death, ii. 251; of church discipline, ii. 314
Calvinists, i. 501; their views of Christ's person, ii. 14
Canaan, i. 255, 256
Canon of Old Testament, i. 14, 15; of New Testament, i. 15, 16

Canute, i. 95
Captives after the Jewish war, ii. 131
Captivity, the Great, ii. 51, 131
Carey, ii. 292
Carlstadt, i. 327
Carnal mind, i. 429, 432
Carpocrates, i. 18
Carthage, ii. 298
Carthaginians, ii. 298
Cassian, John, i. 500; his statement regarding the Sabbath, ii. 237; regarding Lent, ii. 238
Castellio, i. 501
Catacombs at Rome, i. 46, ii. 321, 322
Catechising among the Jews, i. 168
Cathari, ii. 75
Catholic Church, ii. 313
Cato, i. 99, 114
Celestine, bishop of Rome, ii. 14
Celestius, i. 298
Celsus, i. 18
Celtic nations, their views of God, i. 95
Cemeteria, ii. 322
Cemeteries, i. 210, ii. 322
Cenchreæ, ii. 312, 314
Censor, Roman, ii. 202, 209
Census, Roman, i. 117, ii. 202, 209; time and mode of taking it, ii. 209
Ceremonial law, i. 219
Corinthians, i. 465
Cerinthus, i. 18, 23, ii. 13, 335
Chaldean Christians, ii. 14
Chalmers, Dr, his view of a first and second resurrection, ii. 220
Chambering, ii. 222
Chamberlain, ii. 346
Chapters, when divided in the Bible, i. 19
Character of the Epistle to the Romans, i. 2
Children exposed by their parents, i. 120; offered in sacrifice, *ib.*
Children of God, i. 456, ii. 17, 50; of Abraham, ii. 16; of the flesh, ii. 17; of the promise, *ib.*
China, the religion of, i. 91
Chnouphis, i. 179
Chons, i. 178
Chosen, ii. 329
CHRIST, meaning, origin, and use of the name, i. 8, 11, 225; His twofold nature, i. 22, 225, ii. 11; His office as Judge, i. 158, ii. 244; as Mediator, i. 43, 44, ii. 352; our clothing, ii. 224–226; a founda-

tion-stone, ii. 60, 61 ; a stone of stumbling, ii. 61, 62, 82, 83 ; sprung from Israel, ii. 11 ; expressly called God, ii. 11, 13; divine attributes ascribed to Him, ii. 11, 12 ; called Lord or Jehovah, ii. 84 ; a King and Prince, ii. 276 ; High Priest and Chief Minister, ii. 283, 284 ; our Captain, ii. 321 ; to be served as God, ii. 336
Christianity, evidences of, i. 28
Christians of St Thomas, ii. 14
Christmas, its origin and time of observance, ii. 239
Chrysostom, his use of the Epistle to the Romans, i. 3 ; his view of the Bible, i. 17 ; of the fall, i. 298; of infant baptism, i. 325; of the Lord's Supper, i. 326 ; of predestination, i. 500; of Christ's death, ii. 251
Church, meaning and use of the term, ii. 165, 312, 313, 320 ; its origin, ii. 312, 322 ; distinguished as visible and invisible, ii. 312, 313; in the house, ii. 312, 321 ; its value as an institution, ii. 330
Churches, when first consecrated, ii. 322
Church members, ii. 165
Cicero, his views of God and the popular deities, i. 193 ; his practice, *ib.*
Circumcision, i. 182-185, 250, 251
Citizenship, Roman, rights of, ii. 209
Civil year of the Jews, ii. 296
Clement, bishop of Rome, ii. 176, 277
Clement of Alexandria, his views of the fall, i. 298; of man, *ib.* ; of the Lord's Supper, i. 326 ; of predestination, i. 500 ; of Christ's body, ii. 13 ; of His death, ii. 251 ; of His descent into Hades, ii. 75 ; of the church, ii. 313
Clement V., bishop of Rome, i. 327
Clothing of a believer, ii. 225, 226
Cneph, i. 96
Coals of fire, ii. 196, 197
Cock, killed by the Jews as an atonement, i. 128
Codrus, king of Athens, i. 56, ii. 7
Colleges, Jewish, ii. 168
Comfort, i. 51 ; designed by the Scriptures, ii. 266
Coming of Christ, ii. 137, 138

Commandments, the, i. 382, 386, ii. 211 ; order of, ii. 211, 212
Commendation, letters of, ii. 311
Communication of the properties in Christ's person, ii. 14
Communion of saints, i. 51, 297
Community of goods, ii. 300
Condemnation, freedom from, in Christ, i. 411, 506
Condescension, Christian, ii. 190
Confess, meaning and use of the term, ii. 78, 245, 246, 273
Confession, made over the sacrifices, i. 229 ; of Christ, ii. 78-81
Confession of Basle on the Lord's Supper, i. 327 ; on election, i. 501
Confucius, i. 91
Congregations, various, at Rome, ii. 330
Conquerors, as applied to believers, i. 513, 514
Conscience, what it is, i. 154, 157, ii. 2, 206 ; meaning and use of the term, i. 157 : may be improved or injured, i. 154 ; various qualities ascribed to it, i. 155 ; a Christian conscience, ii. 2
Consecration of church, earliest date of, ii. 322
Constantine the Great, his edict regarding the Lord's day, ii. 237 ; builds a church on the supposed site of the Holy Sepulchre, ii. 289
Consubstantiation, i. 327
Consul, Roman, ii. 202
Contents of the Epistle to the Romans, i. 2
Contribution to the saints, ii. 300, 302
Conventicle, a name given to churches, ii. 322
Conversion, ii. 287 ; of Israel, ii. 136, 139
Coracion, i. 465
Corinth, ii. 300, 314, 321, 346 ; the source of its riches, i. 107 ; its fall, i. 56, ii. 314 ; its restoration, ii. 314 ; its church, ii. 346
Corinthianise, to, ii. 314
Corinthians, Paul's Epistles to the, i. 4, ii. 346
Cornelius, successor of Zaccheus as bishop of Cæsarea, ii. 277
Corpus Christi day, i. 327
Council of Jerusalem, i. 4 ; of Nice, i. 23, ii. 13, 239 ; of Constantinople,

i. 23, ii. 13, 14. 312: of Ephesus, i. 23, ii. 14; of Chalcedon, i. 23, ii. 14; of Laodicea, ii. 237; of Trent, ii. 176; of Worms, i. 325; of the Lateran, i. 327; of Valence, i. 500; of Antioch, ii. 312; of Basle, ii. 313; fifth and sixth general councils, ii. 14
Covenants made with Israel, ii. 9, 10, 139, 140
Creation, a witness for God, i. 83, 84; His instrument, ii. 152; its distress and abuse, i. 466–469; groaning and waiting for deliverance, i. 464, 465, 467, 473–476; view of the Persians in regard to it, ii. 221
Creationism, i. 297
Creature, the, i. 463, 465
Creed, the Apostles', ii. 170; sung in some churches, ii. 274
Crescens, bishop of Galatia, ii. 277
Crispus, bishop of Ægina, ii. 277
Critias, i. 112
Crosses, want of, at the siege of Jerusalem, ii. 114
Crucifixion, i. 332
Crusades, i. 512
Cumæan sybil, i. 18
Cup, claimed exclusively for the clergy, i. 327
Cupai, i. 95
Cursing, i. 209, ii. 186
Curtius, ii. 7
Customs, ii. 208, 209; to be duly paid, ii. 208
Cynics, i. 98
Cyprian, bishop of Carthage, i. 325; his views of baptism, i. 325, 326; of the Lord's Supper, i. 324, 326; of an intermediate state, ii. 75; of the millennium, i. 465; of Christ's death, ii. 251; of the church, ii. 313
Cyril, bishop of Alexandria, i. 23, 283, ii. 14
Cyril, bishop of Jerusalem, i. 298; his views of the Lord's Supper, i. 326; of the person of Christ, ii. 13
Cyrus, patriarch of Alexandria, ii. 14

D.

Dagon, i. 96, 102, 178
Dalmatia, ii. 290

Darkness, its figurative meaning, ii. 218; works of, *ib.*
Date of Epistle to the Romans, i. 1
Date wine, ii. 223
David, his life and character, i. 21; his tomb, ii. 63; son of, a title of the Messiah, i. 23; Messiah called by his name, ii. 273
Day, how reckoned and divided, ii. 219, 220; how named, ii. 220; length of, in Palestine, *ib.*; figurative meaning of, ii. 217, 219–221
Day of atonement, i. 127, 128
Day of judgment, i. 158
Day of wrath, i. 134
Days, observance of, ii. 235, 237
Deacons, ii. 170, 171, 173, 175, 176
Deaconesses, ii. 311–313
Dead to sin, i. 320, 339; to the law, i. 369, 375; with Christ, i. 336; applied to the body, i. 441; to sin, i. 381
Death, meaning and use of the term, i. 295, 297, 308, 349, 361, 363, 373, 374, 384, 388, 429, 432, 515
Death of Christ, i. 226, 270, 271, 285, 417; its particular and general reference, ii. 250, 251
Death of believers, i. 439, 440
Debs, ii. 223
Debtor, as applied to Paul and believers in general, i. 54, 444; to Gentile Christians in particular, ii. 302
Decalogue, ii. 235
Decemviri, Roman, i. 365
Deceivers, ii. 337
Deeds, i. 135
Deep, the, ii. 74
Degrees, of excommunication, ii. 7; in merit and honour, ii. 324; in labour and activity, ii. 328; in holiness, ii. 330
Deism, systems of, i. 92
Deities of Greece, i. 90; of Egypt, i. 91, 178; of the heathen in the Old Testament, i. 177; in the New, i. 178
Delai Lama, i. 91
Deliverance, temporal, to be prayed for, ii. 308
Deliverer, the, ii. 137, 138
Delphi, oracle at, ii. 105
Demetrius, bishop of Philadelphia, ii. 277

INDEX. 361

Demons, i. 96
Demon-worship, i. 91
Demoniacal possessions, i. 516
Depravity of human nature, i. 115–122, 203–215
Deputy, ii. 201
Derceto, i. 178
Descent of Christ into Hades, ii. 75
Destruction, ii. 43; of Antichrist, ii. 121
Devil, his personal existence denied, i. 516
Devil-worship, i. 91, 95
Devoted, ii. 7
De Wette, i. 226, ii. 291
Dials, ii. 220
Diana, i. 94, 178; her worship, i. 95, 178; her image and temple at Ephesus, i. 103, 178
Die to sin, i. 337
Diodore of Tarsus, ii. 14
Dionysius, bishop of Alexandria, i. 465
Dionysius the Areopagite, ii. 298; bishop of Athens, ii. 277
Dioscurus, bishop of Alexandria, ii. 14
Discipline, church, ii. 313, 314
Disputations, ii. 228, 229
Distinction of animals and meats, ii. 248
Distress, i. 509, 510
Divinity, of Christ, i. 23, 24, ii. 11–13; ascribed by the Jews to the Messiah, i. 29
Divisions, ii. 332–335
Docetæ, i. 18, 23, ii. 13
Docetism, i. 423, ii. 335
Doctrine, of the Gospel, i. 353
Dodona, oracle at, ii. 105
Donatists, ii. 313
Donative, i. 364
Doubts, ii. 228, 229, 261–263
Doxology, ii. 274
Draco, his penal code, i. 123
Dress of a believer, ii. 225
Drink, strong, ii. 223
Drinks, various kinds of, ii. 223
Druids, i. 97
Druidical worship, i. 95
Drunkenness, ii. 222, 223
Duns Scotus, i. 298; his views of the sacraments, i. 324
Durando, i. 327

E.

Early Christians, views of, concerning Christ's divinity, ii. 12, 13, 322; concerning His second coming, i. 465; their care of their poor and suffering brethren, ii. 178; their worldly avocations, ii. 183, 184; family devotions, ii. 186; hospitality, ib.; conduct under persecution, ii. 188; their morals, ii. 193; their sufferings, ii. 198; their conscientiousness in paying taxes, ii. 207; their observance of the weekly Sabbath, ii. 236, 237; of festivals, ii. 238, 239; their thanksgivings at meals, ii. 240; their preaching, ii. 86; singing, ii. 273; practice at the Lord's Supper, ii. 332; time of observing Easter and Christmas, ii. 238, 239; miraculous gifts, ii. 291
Easter, ii. 238; dispute as to the time of celebrating it, ii. 335
Eastern churches, present condition of, ii. 131
Eastern and Western churches, disruption of, i. 283
Ebionites, i. 18, 23, ii. 335; their celebration of the Lord's Supper, i. 326; views of the millennium, i. 465; of the person of Christ, i. 23, ii. 13
Ecclesiastical year of the Jews, ii. 296
Economy of the Godhead, ii. 280
Edification, mutual, ii. 256; of others, ii. 264
Edom, ii. 25, 26
Edomites, ii. 23, 25, 26
Effectual calling, i. 491, 492, 498, 499. *See* Called.
Egyptians, i. 89, 90, 97, 110; their deities, i. 178; their priests, ii. 231
Elders, ii. 172, 173, 175; supported by the church, ii. 173; originally equivalent to bishops, ii. 176, 177; plurality in a church, ii. 177
Elect, i. 505, 506
Election, i. 505; in the family of Abraham and Isaac, ii. 19; in a general sense, ii. 21, 22; by grace, ii. 107, 109. *See also under* Predestination.
Elias, or Elijah, ii. 100
Elipand, bishop of Toledo, ii. 14

Elliott, the apostle of the Indians, i. 34
Emanations, divine, i. 95, ii. 335
Emmanuel, ii. 311
Empedocles, his views of God, i. 99
Emulation, ii. 117, 120
Ensign, ii. 276, 277
Epenetus, ii. 321, 322
Ephesus, ii. 131
Ephraim, the Syrian, i. 298; a composer of hymns, ii. 274
Epictetus, i. 99
Epicurus, i. 98, 399
Epicureans, i. 98
Epicurism, i. 98
Epiphanius, i. 283
Episcopius, i. 500
Epistle to the Romans, its authenticity, i. 1; object, *ib.*; contents, i. 2; language and style, *ib.*; general character, i. 2, 3
Erastianism, ii. 314
Erastus, chamberlain of Corinth, ii. 345, 346
Erastus, Thomas, of Heidelberg, ii. 314
Esaias, his time and prophecies, ii. 50
Esau, ii. 22, 23; his history. ii. 25
Essenes, i. 163, 165, ii. 157, 231, 259
Establishment in grace, i. 50, ii. 347-349
Eugenius, bishop of Toledo, ii. 298
Eunomius of Cyzicum, ii. 14
Euodius, bishop of Antioch, ii. 277
Eusebius of Cæsarea, his views regarding the Lord's Supper, i. 326; regarding Christ's person, ii. 13; regarding His death, ii. 251; his testimony as to His divinity, ii. 14
Eusebius of Nicomedia, ii. 13
Eutychus, i. 23, ii. 14
Evidences of Christianity, i. 28. See Proofs.
Evil, ii. 339
Excommunication, ii. 7
Exhortation, ii. 172, 174, 175
Exhorters, ii. 174
Expectation of the creature, i. 463-465
Experience, i. 280
Eye, wonderful construction of the, i. 80

F.

Faith, meaning and use of the term, i. 32, 36, 41, 51, 195, 196, 274, 276, ii. 163-165, 169, 227, 229, 260, 351; its nature, excellence, and use, i. 70, 72, 220, 221, 227, 231, 233, 235, 238, 243, 244, 246, 254, 259. ii. 69, 71; different kinds of, i. 71; degrees of, i. 264; capable of growth, i. 264; imputed for righteousness, i. 268; views of it in the early church, i. 274; among the schoolmen, *ib.*; the Roman Catholics, *ib.*; the Protestants, *ib.*; subjective and objective, *ib.*; its relation to hope, i. 481, 482; to joy and peace, i. 273, 276, ii. 279, 280
Fall of man, i. 294-299, 303, 304; different views of it, i. 298
False teachers, ii. 332-336, 341
Family religion, ii. 321
Family worship of early Christians, ii. 186
Families, converted, ii. 327
Famine, i. 510, 511
Father, as applied to God, i. 41, 453; to Abraham, i. 240, 250, 253, 261-263, ii. 20
Fathers of Israel, ii. 11
Faustus of Rhegium, i. 500
Fear, different kinds of, ii. 129; of God, i. 213; due to magistrates and others, ii. 208
Felix of Urzella, ii. 14
Fellow-prisoners of Paul, ii. 323, 324
Fellowship of believers, ii. 310; threefold, ii. 324
Female agency in the church, ii. 312, 319; devotedness, ii. 318, 328
Festivals, Jewish, ii. 235, 237; Christian, ii. 237-239
Fetishism, i. 90, 93
Fire-worship, i. 94
First day of the week, ii. 235-237
First resurrection, ii. 121, 220
First-born, i. 496-498; privileges of, ii. 22
First-fruits, i. 476, 480, ii. 122, 123, 321, 322; of the Spirit, i. 476, 480
Fish-god, i. 96, 102, 177
Flatterers, ii. 339
Flavian, bishop of Antioch, ii. 274
Flesh, meaning and use of the term, i. 22, 216, 240, 241, 372, 409, 419, 420, 434, 444, ii. 11, 13, 120, 226;

INDEX.   363

believers no longer walk according to it, i. 411, 425; and are not in it, i. 435
Forbearance of God, i. 129, 228
Foreknowledge of God, i. 494, ii. 99, 101
Forgiveness, i. 248, 249
Form, mould, or type, i. 353, 354
Frictrices, i. 111
Friedolin, i. 33
Fringes on the garment, i. 188, 189
Frontlets, i. 188, 189
Fruit, meaning and use of the term, i. 53, 359, 361, ii. 304
Fulgentius of Ruspe, i. 500
Fulness of the Gentiles, ii. 135, 136; of the Jews, ii. 280, 281; of blessing, ii. 305
Functions, ii. 165
Future punishment, views of ancient heathens regarding it, i. 123

G.

Gaius, Paul's host at Corinth, ii. 345, 346; bishop of Pergamus, ii. 277
Galatians, Epistle to the, i. 2, 4
Galen, i. 110
Gallus, i. 33
Gamaliel, i. 173, 180
Gelasius, bishop of Rome, his views of the Lord's Supper, i. 327
Gemara, the, i. 18
Gentiles, i. 53, 54, 144, 152, 153, 253, ii. 47–50, 277; their calling, ii. 273, 275; admission into the church, ii. 50, 274, 276; their salvation, ii. 117; fulness, ii. 135; duty, ii. 274
Genuineness of Epistle to the Romans, i. 1; of Old Testament Scriptures, i. 194; of New Testament Scriptures, i. 16
Geology, discoveries of, evidences of God's eternal power, i. 85
Georgius of Laodicea, ii. 13
Germans, ancient worship of, i. 95
Gessius Florus, ii. 130
Gifts, spiritual, i. 50; various kinds of, ii. 166–169
Giving of the law, ii. 9, 10
Glad tidings of the Gospel, ii. 87, 88
Gladiators, i. 116, 118
Glorification, i. 499
Glorified with Christ, i. 460

Glorious liberty, i. 469, 472
Glory, meaning and use of the term, i. 138, 145, 462, 463, 469, 472, ii. 8, 10, 45, 46; glory of God, i. 223, 277, 278, ii. 10; glory belonging to Israel, ii. 8, 10
Gnosticism, ii. 333–335
Gnostics, i. 95, ii. 333–335; their views of evil, i. 298; of baptism, i. 326; of the millennium, i. 465; of angels, i. 516
God, i. 432, 433; evidences of His existence and character, i. 79–87; wisdom and knowledge of, ii. 147; the true God, i. 88, 432; His relations and character, i. 433; everlasting and unchangeable, ii. 351; only wise, ii. 352, 353; the Judge, i. 215; God of peace, ii. 310, 311, 339, 340
Godhead, i. 85, 86; economy of, in redemption, ii. 280
Golden Age, i. 476, ii. 221
Gomarists, i. 501
Gomarus, i. 501
Gomorrha, ii. 56
Good, ii. 339; good works, i. 137; good words, ii. 336, 337
Goodness, ii. 281; of God, ii. 130
Gortho, the ancient Corinth, ii. 346
Gospel, meaning, origin, and use of the term, i. 9, 10, 61, ii. 87; how characterised, i. 9, 10; to be gloried in, i. 60; what it had to oppose it, i. 61; Gospel of peace, ii. 87; the true Gospel, ii. 348; the word of God, ii. 91; by whom received, ii. 89
Gospels, how received, i. 18; different names of, i. 19
Gotteschalk, i. 500
Governments, ii. 200, 203
Governors, ii. 200; of provinces, ii. 201
Grace, meaning and use of the term, i. 31, 40, 224, 245, 276, 304–306, 308, ii. 107, 282, 341; believers under it, i. 347, 348
Grafting, ii. 125, 126; allusion to, i. 330–333
Graves, i. 207
Greece, sketch of its history, i. 56; character of its people, i. 57, 114; its language and civilisation, ib.; its religion and morals, i. 57, 58, 114; its deities, i. 90

Greek Church, its views in regard to the sacraments, i. 324; to the Lord's Supper, i. 327; to purgatory and an intermediate state, ii. 75; to indulgences and masses for the dead, ib.; its practice in baptism, i. 325
Geeek Empire, i. 56; language, i. 57, 66; art and civilisation, i. 57, 114
Greeks, i. 54-56, 66; their character, i 57, 114
Greek translations of the Old Testament, i. 151
Greeting, ii. 316. *See* Salutation.
Gregory of Nazianzum, i. 283; his views of sin, i. 298; of the Lord's Supper, i. 326, 327; of angels, i. 516; of Christ's death, ii. 251; of purgatory, ii. 75; a composer of hymns, ii. 274
Gregory of Nyssa, his views of Christ's death, i. 226, ii. 251; of the Holy Spirit, i. 283; of man by nature, i. 298; of angels, i. 517; his language in regard to the Lord's Supper, i. 326
Gregory the Great, his views of predestination, i. 500; of angels, i. 516; of purgatory, ii. 75; his language in regard to the Lord's Supper, i. 327
Groans of creation, i. 477
Grotius, i. 501; his views of Christ's death, i. 226
Guebres, i. 94
Guides, Jewish, i. 170, 171
Guilt, i. 214

H.

Hades, ii. 74, 75
Hale, Sir Matthew, his views of the Scriptures, i. 17
Hales, i. 327
Hand, wonderful construction of the, i. 81
Hannibal, ii. 298
Haphtaroth, or sections of the prophets, ii. 267
Hardening, ii. 35, 36, 109, 110
Hardness of heart, i. 132
Hathor, an Egyptian deity, i. 179
Heart, construction and action of the, i. 80; its figurative meaning, i. 353

Heathen deities, i. 176-180; names, ii. 311
Heaven, blessedness of, i. 82
Heavenly bodies, the, i. 82
Hebron, i. 240
Heir, as applied to Abraham, i. 255; to Christ, ib.; to believers, i. 255, 257, 456
Heirs of God, i. 457
Hell, ii. 74; different apartments ascribed to it, ii. 75
Hellenists, i. 65
Helots, i. 56
Henry, Philip, his remark on his ordination, i. 31; in regard to a journey, i. 48
Heraclius, ii. 14
Herald, ii. 78, 86; how employed among Greeks and Romans, ii. 86
Herbert, Lord, his system of deism, i. 92
Herbs, why eaten by some, ii. 230, 231
Hercules, i. 18, 94, 95, ii. 106
Heresies, early, i. 23, 30; the effect of ignorance of the Scriptures, i. 17
Heretics, early, i. 18, 23, 30
Hermas, i. 500, ii. 330
Herod the Great, i. 64, 65, ii. 309
Herod Agrippa, ii. 309
Herodians, i. 165
Hero-worship, i. 91, 95
Hesiod, i. 15, 107; his account of man's fall and degeneracy, i. 476
Hetairia, i. 107
Hierarchy, ii. 313
High priest, applied to Christ, ii. 283
Hilary of Poictiers, i. 298; his views of Christ's death, ii. 251; a composer of hymns, ii. 274
Hildebert of Tours, i. 327
Hillel, i. 170, 173, ii. 335
Hincmar of Rheims, i. 500
Hindooism, i. 94
Hinds, Dr, his views of ministerial orders, ii. 177
History of English Bible, i. 16; of the books of Moses, i. 151; of missions, i. 33; of Greece, i. 56; of the Jews, i. 64; of the Ten Tribes, ii. 48; of Judæa, ii. 309; of Jerusalem, ii. 288, 289; of the Edomites, ii. 23; of Abraham, i. 239; of Jacob, ii. 24; of Esau, ii. 25; of Moses, ii. 28; of David, i. 21; of idolatry, i. 93; of Roman legis-

lation, i. 365; of the doctrine concerning the person of Christ, i. 23, ii. 13; concerning His death, i. 226, ii. 251; concerning sin and the fall, i. 298; faith and justification, i. 274; predestination, i. 500; the sacraments, i. 326; purgatory, ii. 75; miracles, ii. 291; the church, ii. 313; the millennium, i. 465

Holiness, i. 357, 362; different kinds of, ii. 123, 124

Holy City, ii. 290; sepulchre, ii. 289

Holy Spirit, the, i. 24, 30, 282, 283, 415, 416, ii. 2, 3; called the Spirit of Christ, i. 437, 438; and of the Father, i. 441; dwells in believers, i. 436, 443; is God's seal upon them, i. 443; His office, i. 448, 483, 484; His character, i. 450; the Author of Christian hope, ii. 279; operates as Christ's Agent, ii. 288

Homer, i. 15, 107; the influence of his writings on the Greeks, i. 57

Homoiousios, ii. 13

Homoousios, ii. 13

Honour, i. 138; to be rendered to magistrates and others, ii. 208

Hooker, his views as to church government, ii. 177

Hope, Christian, i. 263, 273, 280, 481, 482, ii. 184, 185, 267, 278; false hope, ii. 278; characteristics of the true, ii. 278; its origin, ii. 280; Christ our hope, ii. 277; God the God of hope, ii. 278; the Holy Spirit its Author, ii. 279; hope capable of increase, *ib.*; believers to abound in it, *ib.*; its value and importance, *ib.*

Hope, goddess of, ii. 278; her temple at Rome, ii. 280

Horace, i. 112

Horites, the, ii. 25

Hormisdas, bishop of Rome, ii. 14

Horpe-Khroti, an Egyptian deity, i. 179

Horus, i. 179

Hosea, his age and prophecies, ii. 47

Hospitality, ii. 186, 187; of early Christians, ii. 187

Hottentots, religion of, i. 95

Hours, where first mentioned, ii. 220; how counted and named, *ib.*

House-congregations, ii. 330, 331

Household, ii. 326, 327, 330

Hugo of St Victor, his views of the death of Christ, i. 226; of the sacraments, i. 324; of the church, ii. 313; claimed the cup for the laity, i. 327

Human instrumentality, ii. 287

Human nature, depravity of, i. 390, 391

Human sacrifices, i. 117

Humanity of Christ, early denied, i. 23

Hume, ii. 291

Hunger, i. 510

Huss, John, his views of the church and the Christian priesthood, ii. 313

Hussites, i. 327

Hymn-book of Jewish church, ii. 273

Hymns, their use in the early church, ii. 273, 274; by whom composed, *ib.*

Hypocrisy of Pharisees, i. 175

Hyrcanus, ii. 309

I.

Ichneumon, the, i. 179

Idols, i. 176-180

Idolatry, progressive steps of, i. 90, 93; productive of uncleanness, i. 105

Idumæa, ii. 26

Idumæans, ii. 25, 26; their hostility to Israel, ii. 26

Ignatius, ii. 176, 274, 277; his saying in regard to the church, ii. 313

Ignorance, ii. 66, 135

Illyricum, ii. 290, 292

Image of Christ, i. 495; of Jupiter, i. 101, 102, 103; of Diana, i. 103; of Isis, *ib.*

Image-worship, i. 100, 102

Images, i. 100, 101, 103; first made by the Egyptians, i. 97, 103

Immersion, i. 324

Immortality, i. 139

Imprisonments of Paul, ii. 323, 324

Imputation, i. 244, 247, 248, 268; familiar to the Jews, i. 245

"In Christ," i. 412-414, ii. 324-326

"In the Lord," ii. 325, 328, 329, 344, 345

Incas, the, of Peru, i. 95

Incense, spiritual, ii. 285

Indulgences, ii. 75
Indwelling sin, i. 394, 396, 397
Infallibility claimed by the Popes, ii. 313
Infant baptism, history of, i. 325; arguments in favour of, i. 326
Infirmities, of the weak, ii. 263
Ink, ancient, ii. 345
Inkhorn, ii. 345
Innate depravity, i. 307
Innocent III., i. 327
Inquisition, the, i. 510
Institutions of Justinian, i. 366
Instruments, i. 342, 344, 345
Instrumental music in churches, ii. 274, 275
Intercalary month, ii. 296
Intercession of the Spirit, i. 485, 487; of Christ, i. 507, 508; of believers, ii. 100
Intercessory prayer, i. 49, ii. 100, 306
Intermediate state of the dead, ii. 75
Intoxicating drink, ii. 223
Invocation of angels, i. 516
Inward man, i. 402
Iona, presbyters of, i. 33
Irenæus, ii. 288; his views of Christ, ii. 13; of His death, i. 226; of presbyters or elders, ii. 176; of the fall, i. 298; of the millennium, i. 465; of predestination. i. 500; of Christ's descent into Hades, ii. 75; his language in regard to the Lord's Supper, i. 326; censures the bishop of Rome for disturbing the church's peace, ii. 335
Isaac, i. 261, ii. 16, 17; a type of Christ, ii. 16, 18
Isidore of Pelusium, i. 500
Isis, i. 103, 178, 179
Israel, ii. 8, 51; application of the term, ii. 93; distinction between the true and nominal, ii. 15, 16; conversion of, ii. 135, 136, 139; enemies for our sakes, ii. 140, 141
Israelite, ii. 8, 15
Isthmian games, ii. 314
Isthmus of Corinth, ii. 314

J.

Jacob, ii. 23; his history, ii. 24, 25
Jacobellus of Misa, i. 327
James, the Lord's brother, ii. 231
Jansenists, i. 500, 501

Jason, ii. 343
Jealousy on the part of the Jews, ii. 117
Jebus, ii. 289
Jehovah, meaning of the name, i. 20, 29; not used by the Jews, i. 181
Jerome, his views as to bishops and presbyters, ii. 176; of Christ's death, ii. 251
Jerome of Prague, i. 327
Jerusalem, ii. 288; its other names, ib.; its history, ii. 288, 289; population, ii. 290; present condition, ib.; its early church, ii. 301; siege and destruction by the Romans, ii. 33, 130, 131; its wickedness the cause of it, i. 180; Paul's journey to, ii. 299
Jesse, ii. 276
Jesus, meaning and origin of the name, i. 7, 11, 225, 269
Jews, i. 188; different kinds of, i. 65; their history, i. 64; laws, i. 66; delusions, i. 127, 128, 150, 151; privileges, i. 146, 162, 193, 194; hopes of justification, i. 150, 151; character, i. 162, 180; sects, i. 163; sufferings, ii. 51, 130, 131; miserable condition, ii. 115, 116; our indebtedness to them, ii. 302
Jewel, bishop, his views of Christ's death, ii. 251
Jewish, Christians, ii. 231: priests at Rome, ii. 231; festivals, ii. 235, 237; Sabbath, ii. 237; form of thanksgiving at meals, ii. 240; war, ii. 53, 130, 131; zealots, ii. 335
John, bishop of Ephesus, ii. 277
—— bishop of Antioch, ii. 14
—— II., bishop of Rome, ii. 14
—— of Paris, i. 32
—— of Salisbury, ii. 313
Johnson, Dr, his advice in regard to the Scriptures, i. 17
Joint-heirs with Christ, i. 457, 458, 460
Joints, the, ii. 81
Jones, Sir William, his eulogium of the Scriptures, i. 17
Josephus, i. 195, ii. 130
Joshua, a type of Christ, i. 7
Joy, i. 292, ii. 184, 278; in the Holy Ghost, ii. 253, 254; its importance to believers, ii. 278; to ministers and preachers, ii. 309
Journey, Paul's, to Spain, ii. 297, 298; to Jerusalem, ii. 305, 306

Journeys, duty in regard to, i. 48
Judæa, ii. 308, 309; its former populousness. ii. 512; state after the war, ii. 53, 54, 131; its history, ii. 309
Judah, the kingdom of, ii. 55
Judaizers, ii. 332-335
Judas Gaulonitis, ii. 207
Jude, ii. 293
Judge, the, i. 158, 159, 186, 215
Judging others, i. 125, 126, ii. 232, 233; to be avoided, ii. 232, 247
Judgment, the, i. 200; public, i. 158, 159; the work of the Godhead, i. 158; ascribed to Christ, ii. 244
Judgment-seat of Christ, ii. 244
Judson, Dr, ii. 292
Julian the Apostate, i. 18
Julian, bishop of Eclanum, i. 298
Julianus, i. 366
Julius Cæsar, ii. 202, 309
Junia, ii. 223, 224
Jupiter, i. 178, ii. 106; his statue at Olympia, i. 101-103
Jupiter Capitolinus, ii. 289
Just, i. 72, 149, 230
Justification, way of, shown in the Gospel, i. 150, 231; various aspects of, i. 235; ground of it, i. 27, 272, 505; confounded with sanctification, i. 274; different views in regard to it, i. 274
Justify, meaning and use of the term, i. 150, 231; how justified, i. 216, 231, 505
Justin Martyr, i. 326; his views of the millennium, i. 465; of predestination, i. 500; of Hades, ii. 75; his language in regard to the Lord's Supper, i. 326; defence of the Christians, ii. 198; account of Christian worship, ii. 237; appeal to miracles as still wrought in the church, ii. 291
Justinian, i. 366, ii. 14, 202, 289; his code and institutions, i. 366

K.

Kalimiki, ii. 314
Kant, his views of Christ's death, i. 226; of miracles, ii. 291
Karaites, the, i. 66
Killing the prophets, ii. 101
"Killing times," i. 512

Kindred, ii. 323
"King of the Jews," ii. 276
Kingdom of Christ, ii. 122, 220, 276; of God, ii. 252-254; of Israel, ii. 48, 51; of Judah, ii. 55
Kinsman, ii. 323, 327, 343
Kirjath-sepher, ii. 344
Kirk, or church, ii. 322
Kiss, ii. 331, 332; its practice in the early church, ii. 332
Knowledge, i. 79, ii. 65, 66; of God, i. 78, 79, 83, 84, 92; of the law, i. 216; degrees and progress in it, ii. 281; different kinds of it, ii. 135; contents of spiritual knowledge, ii. 281
Krishna, i. 18

L.

Lactantius, i. 283; his views of the body, i. 298; of the millennium, i. 465
Land of Israel, ii. 50
Language of the Epistle to the Romans, i. 2
Laodicea, ii. 131
Lateran Council, i. 327
Latimer, bishop, his views of Christ's death, ii. 251
Lavater, his view of miracles, ii. 291
Law, meaning and use of the term, i. 147, 164, 168, 169, 219, 233, 234, 364; 400, 401, 415, 417, 418; believers not under it, i. 346, 348; its summary, ii. 211; its fulfilment, ii. 211-213; its end and object, ii. 68, 69
Law of God, i. 216, 418, 424, 433; established by the Gospel, i. 238, 402; its spirituality, i. 389
Law of Moses, i. 169, 173, 219, 315, ii. 9; read in the synagogue, i. 149; 150; its history, i. 150; why given, i. 378, ii. 9
Law of the mind, i. 404, 405; of sin, i. 404, 405, 409, 417, 418; of death, i. 417, 418; of righteousness, ii. 57, 58
Laws of Rome, i. 365, ii. 204; of the Twelve Tables, i. 123, 365, ii. 202
Lead, used in writing, ii. 345
Lechæum, ii. 314
Lent, its origin and history, ii. 238

Leo, the Emperor, his edict regarding the Lord's-day, ii. 237
Letter, as opposed to spirit, i. 187, 190, 376, 377
Letters of the alphabet, ii. 344
Letters of the apostle, ii. 288; of recommendation, ii. 311, 312
Libamen, ii. 285
Libation, ii. 240, 285
Liberty, true and false, i. 359; awaiting the sons of God, i. 469–472
Life, meaning and use of the term, i. 139, 310, 430, 440, 441; eternal, i. 139; from the dead, ii. 121, 122
Light, in a figurative sense, ii. 218, 219; armour of, ii. 218; of the world, i. 171
Limborch, Philip à, i. 501
Limbus, ii. 75
Linus, bishop of Rome, ii. 277
Literæ formatæ, ii. 186
Live, meaning of the term, i. 72; with Christ, i. 336
Living Christianity, ii. 312
Locke, John, his saying in regard to the New Testament, i. 17
Logos, the, or Word of God, i. 29, 307, ii. 13; sometimes identified with the Holy Spirit, i. 283
Lombard, Peter, his views of the death of Christ, i. 226; of faith, i. 274; of the Sacraments, i. 324; of the Lord's Supper, i. 327; of election, i. 500
Long-suffering of God, i. 129, ii. 42.
Lord, meaning and use of the term, i. 20, 22, 270, ii. 84; our Lord, i. 270
Lord Herbert, his system of deism, i. 92
Lord Rochester, i. 17
Lord Shaftesbury, i. 92
Lord's-day, the, ii. 337
Lord's Supper, i. 250, 326; different views of it, i. 326
Lordship of Christ over the world, i. 255, 256; over dead and living, ii. 243
Lothaire II., i. 366
Love of God, i. 281, 518; of Christ, i. 509; to one another, ii. 210; to all men, ii. 211, 212; a debt due to all, ii. 210; the fulfilment of the law, ii. 210, 211
Love-feast, primitive, ii. 182, 322
Lucina, i. 179

Lucius, one of Paul's companions, ii. 343; bishop of Cenchræa, ii. 277
Luther, his views of baptism, i. 325; of the Lord's Supper, i. 327; of the death of Christ, ii. 251
Lutherans, i. 501; their views regarding the person of Christ, ii. 14
Lycurgus, i. 56
Lying, i. 197

M.

Maccabees, the, i. 64, ii. 309
Macedonia, i. 56, ii. 290, 300; its ancient name, ii. 302; its inhabitants, ib.; its history, ib.; ancient churches, ii. 300
Macedonius, i. 30, 283.
Magi, i. 89, 97, 103, ii. 231
Magicians, Pharaoh's, ii. 287
Magistrates, ii. 200, 201, 207; duty in regard to them, ii. 200
Magnus, i. 33
Maimonides, i. 171
Man, wonderful constitution of his body, i. 80; his place as a creature, ii. 37, 38
Manes, i. 23; ii. 335
Manichæans, i. 18, 298: their practice in reference to the church, ii. 313
Manichæism, i. 423, ii. 335
Maranatha, ii. 7
Marathon, battle of, i. 56
Marcellus, bishop of Ancyra, i. 283, ii. 14
Marcion, i. 18, ii. 262
Marcionites, i. 326.
Marcus Aurelius, i. 99, ii. 198
Marinus Sanutus, first introduced instrumental music into churches, ii. 274
Marius, i. 117
Mark the Evangelist, ii. 293
Marones, bishop of Tripolis, ii. 277
Marriage, i. 366, 368; taken spiritually, i. 366–371; sanctified, ii. 319, 330; forbidden by early heretics, ii. 334
Martial, i. 112; his Epigrams, i. 114
Martyn, Henry, ii. 292
Martyr, Justin. *See* Justin.
Martyr, Peter, ii. 251,
Martyrs, i. 512–514
Martyria, ii. 322

INDEX.

Mary, daughter of Eliezer, ii. 131; of Rome, ii. 322
Marys, the, of the New Testament, ii. 322
Mass, sacrifice of the, i. 326, ii. 157; contrasted with the preaching of the Gospel, ii. 283
Masses for the dead, ii. 75
Massacres of Christians, i. 512
Matthew the Apostle, ii. 293
Matthias, ii. 293
Maut, an Egyptian deity, i. 178
Mayhew, i. 34
Meals, practice at, among the Romans, 224–240
Meat-offering, typical, ii. 283
Meats, distinction of, ii. 248, 249, 252, 230
Mede, his view of the millennium, ii. 220
Medicated wine, ii. 223
Melancthon, views of, regarding man's nature, i. 299; regarding Christ's death, ii. 251; Christ's kingdom, ii. 220
Members of the body, i. 342, 373, ii. 165; of the church, ii. 166
Menœceus, ii. 7
Menno, i. 325
Mennonites, views of, regarding justification, i. 274; the sacraments, i. 324; baptism, i. 325
Mercury, i. 178
Mercy, ii. 29, 30, 34, 272
Mercy-seat, i. 227, 229, 248
Messiah, meaning of the term, i. 8; His sufferings substitutional, i. 220; views of the Jews in regard to a Messiah and His sufferings, i. 220, 229, 232, 272; their figment of a twofold Messiah, i. 23; Messiah believed by the older Rabbies to be already come, i. 232; and to be the subject of the 53d chapter of Isaiah, ii. 90
Mezuzah, the, i. 188, 189
Midrashim, ii. 95, 96
Military life, Paul's frequent allusion to, ii. 214
Millennium, i. 465, ii. 220; seventh of the world, ii. 217
Miltiades, i. 56
Milton, his testimony to the Scriptures, i. 16
Mind, meaning and use of the term, i. 427–432

VOL. II.

Minister, meaning and application of the term, ii. 204, 205, 207, 208, 271, 272, 283, 284, 299, 303
Ministræ, ii. 312
Ministry, office and work of the, i. 31, ii. 283
Miracles, wrought by the apostle, ii. 287, 288; their use and importance, ii. 288; insufficiency for faith, ib.; in themselves no proof of truth, ii. 287; evidences of their reality, ii. 288; miracles probable, ib.; distinguished as "signs and wonders," ii. 290; views regarding them, ii. 291; appealed to by early Christians, ib.
Mishna, i. 18, 166
Missions, sketch of the history of, i. 33
Mission-societies, ii. 330
Missionary journeys of the apostle, i. 4
Missionary societies, i. 34, 35
Mithra, i. 94
Mnephis, i. 179
Moffat, Robert, ii. 292
Molina, i. 501
Moloch, i. 177, ii. 106
Monophysites, i. 23, ii. 14
Monotheism, i. 92
Month, an Egyptian deity, i. 179
Months, when and how distinguished, ii. 296
Moon, the great divinity of the Arabians and others, i. 94
Moral depravity, i. 298, 307
Moral law, i. 216, 378
Morrison, Robert, ii. 292
Mortification of sin, i. 446, 447
Moses, his history, ii. 28; a type of Christ, ii. 29; his prophetic song ii. 274
Mother, twofold sense of, ii. 329
Mother of God, title given to Mary, i. 23; how brought into use, ii. 14; by whom opposed or disapproved, ib.
Mother-night, ii. 239
Mount Zion, ii. 61, 62, 289
Murder, prevalence of, i. 180, 211
Muscles, the, i. 81
Music in the church, ii. 274
Myconius, Oswald, i. 327
Mystery, meaning and application of the term, ii. 134, 135, 348, 349; name given to the sacraments, i. 324

2 A

Mysteries, Pagan, i. 67; of Eleusis, *ib.*
Myths, ii. 291

N.

Nakedness, i. 510
Narcissus, ii. 327
Natural depravity, i. 390, 398
Natural functions, ii. 165
Natural relationships, ii. 323
Natural religion, i. 78–86; insufficiency of, i. 87
Nazarenes, ii. 357
Nazarites, ii. 259
Neith, an Egyptian deity, i. 179
Nepos, i. 465; a composer of hymns, ii. 274.
Nero, i. 60, 120; his cruelty to the Christians, i. 510, ii. 198
Nerves, the, i. 82
Nestorians, the, i. 34, ii. 14, 48
Nestorius, bishop of Constantinople, i. 23, ii. 14
New Testament Scriptures, i. 15, 16, 19
Newness of spirit, i. 376, 377
Newton, Sir Isaac, his views of the Scriptures, i. 17; his humility, i. 55, ii. 147
Nicetes, ii. 277
Nicetius, author of the Te Deum, ii. 274
Nicholas I., bishop of Rome, i. 283
Night, how divided, ii. 220; taken figuratively, ii. 216, 217, 219; now far spent, ii. 217, 219
Nineveh, its ancient monuments, ii. 344, 345
Nitzsch, his views of Christ's obedience, i. 226
Noum, an Egyptian deity, i. 179
Novatian, his views of the church, ii. 313
Novum Testamentum, or New Testament, when first applied to the evangelical Scriptures, ii. 267
Numa, i. 102

O.

Obedience to the Gospel, i. 32, ii. 351; to God's Word, ii. 338; of Christ, i. 313

Object of Epistle to the Romans, i. 1
Œcolampadius, i. 327, ii. 314
Offence, occasions of it in Jesus, ii. 61, 257; caused by false teachers, ii. 334, 335
Offended, ii. 259
Office, ii. 165
Okkam, i. 327
Old man, meaning of the term, i. 332
Old serpent, ii. 340, 342
Old Testament Scriptures, i. 14, 15, 151, 169, 173; how given, i. 193, 194; how called, ii. 267
Olive-tree, ii. 124–126; symbol of the church, ii. 126, 133
Olympiads, ii. 296
One God, i. 237
Onesimus, slave and successor of Philemon, ii. 277
Ophel, a part of Jerusalem, ii. 289
Optatus, of Mileve, ii. 313
Oracles of God, i. 193, 194; of the heathen, i. 194, ii. 105
Oral law, i. 176, 181
Oratory, or house of prayer, ii. 322
Order of service in early church, ii. 322
Organs, used in Christian worship, ii. 274
Organism of sin, i. 334, 407
Origen, his views regarding Christ's body, ii. 13; regarding His death, i. 226, ii. 251.; His descent into Hades, ii. 75; the Holy Spirit, i. 283; moral evil, ii. 298; the fall, *ib.*; the Lord's Supper, i. 326; the millennium, i. 465; predestination, i. 500; angels, i. 517; miracles, ii. 291
Original sin, i. 294, 297; the author of the term (vitium originis), i. 298
Ormuzd, i. 95, 476, ii. 342.
Osiander, his views of justification, i. 275
Osiris, i. 95, 96, 178, 179

P.

Pachacamac, i. 95
Pagans, origin of the term, ii. 296
Palamedes, ii. 344
Pan, i. 94, 96; his image, i. 103
Pangs of Messiah, i. 476
Pantheism, i. 90, 94, 98
Papias, bishop of Hierapolis, i. 465

Papyrus, ii. 267, 345
Parabolani, ii. 178
Parashioth, or sections of the law, ii. 267
Parchment, ii. 345.
Pareus, his views of Christ's death, ii. 251
Parsees, i. 90, 94
Parthenon, the, i. 93
Parvati, i. 178
Pascal, i. 500
Pasch, ii. 238, 239
Paschal feast, ii. 238
Paschasius, Radbert, i. 327
Pasht, an Egyptian deity, i. 179
Passion-week, ii. 238
Passover, ii. 238; section read on the eighth day of the, ii. 277
Patience, i. 279, 483, ii. 185, 266
Patriarchs, ii. 11, 123, 124
Patrick, the Apostle of Ireland, i. 33
Paul, meaning and use of the name, i. 3, 10; his life and labours, i. 3, 4, 10; his education, i. 10, 11; character, i. 5, 6; physical appearance, i. 6; fellow-prisoners, ii. 323, 324; relatives, *ib.*; converts, ii. 321, 325, 326; defective sight, ii. 344
Paul of Samosata, i. 23
Paulinus, a composer of hymns, ii. 274
Peace, meaning and use of the term, i. 41, 145, 212, 273, 431, 432, ii. 253, 254, 256, 279, 340; its origin, ii. 279; how given, ii. 310; peace with God, i. 273; Jesus our peace, i. 273, ii. 279; God the God of peace, ii. 310, 340
Peaceableness ii. 194
Pelagius, i. 297, 298; his views on the fall and original sin, i. 298; on predestination, i. 500; on the church, ii. 313
Pelagianism, i. 274, 297, 298
Pelagians, i. 56
Pelican, his views of Christ's death, ii. 251
Pens, different kinds of, ii. 345
Pentateuch, i. 15; the Samaritan, i. 151
Peor, i. 106
Perdition, i. 148
Pericles, i. 115.
Peril, i. 510
Persecution, i. 509-511, ii. 186
Persian Magi, i. 89, ii. 231

Persians, ancient, worship of the, i. 94, 95; their views of the present and future state of the world, i. 476
Persis, ii. 328
Peruvians, worship of the, i. 94, 95
Peschito Version, the, i. 195
Pesukim, or verses, when first used, ii. 267
Peter, whether the founder of the church of Rome, i. 42; the reputed sphere of his labours, ii. 293
Peter Fullo, ii. 14
Peter Lombard, his views regarding Christ's death, i. 226
Peter Martyr, ii. 251
Peter of Bruis, i. 325
Petra, ii. 25
Pfaff, Councillor, ii. 314
Phallus, the, i. 67, 96, 106
Pharaoh, meaning of the title, ii. 32, 34; the Pharaohs of Scripture, *ib.*
Pharisees, i. 163, 165; their hypocrisy, i. 175
Phebe, ii. 311-313
Phigaleia, gratitude of its inhabitants, i. 93
Philemon, bishop of Colosse, ii. 277
Philip the Apostle, ii. 293
Philip à Limborch, i. 500
Philip of Macedon, i. 56
Philo, i. 29, 65, 195, 307
Philologus, ii. 330
Philosophers, ancient, i. 89; of Greece, i. 98; their views of God, i. 92, 99; their practice, i. 102, 112
Phœnicians, ii. 297, 298; the reputed inventors of letters, ii. 344
Photius, bishop of Sirmium, ii. 14
Photius, patriarch of Constantinople, i. 283
Phtah, an Egyptian deity, i. 179
Phylacteries, i. 188, 189
Pilgrim fathers, i. 34
Pilgrims to the Holy City, ii. 290
Plan of labour, ii. 294, 295
Plants, construction and economy of, i. 82
Plato, i. 98; his views of God, i. 92, 99; of nature, i. 99; of future punishment, i. 123; of man's moral nature, i. 410; his practice, i. 93
Platonics, their views of God, i. 92, 96, 110
Plebiscita, Roman, i. 365

Pliny, his letter to Trajan, i. 30; ii. 84, 193, 198, 273, 312, 313; his views of God and nature, i. 94, 99
Ploughing on the Sabbath, ii. 262
Poets, their influence in favour of idolatry, i. 92, 107
Polycarp, ii. 13, 176
Polycrates, ii. 335
Polytheism, i. 95
Pompey, i. 64, ii. 309
Pope, the, viewed as Antichrist, i. 465
Porphyry, i. 18
Postscripts to the Epistle to the Romans, ii. 343
Potter, God compared to a, ii. 39-41
Potter's Field, ii. 41
Pottery among the Jews, ii. 41
Power, divine, indications of, i. 85; ii. 42
Powers, civil, ii. 200, 202; angelic, i. 515, 517
Prætor, Roman, ii. 202
Praise, what is implied in it, ii. 275; a part of public worship, ii. 273-275
Praxiteles, i. 107
Prayer, i. 47, 48, ii. 63, 185, 306-310; how to be made, ii. 306; to whom to be addressed, ii. 307; to be asked for, ii. 305-307; help in offering, i. 484, 486; when first made for the dead, ii. 75
Preacher, the, ii. 85, 86; his mission, ii. 86; his ministry, ii. 283
Preaching, i. 175, ii. 85
Precentor, ii. 274
Predestination, meaning and use of the term, i. 494, 497; history of the doctrine of, i. 500
Presbyters, ii. 173, 175, 177; equivalent to bishops, ii. 176, 177
Pretermission, i. 228, 229
Priapus, i. 96, 106
Priest, the true evangelical, ii. 283, 284, 287; the spiritual, ii. 284, 285
Priesthood, ii. 284, 287; universal, ii. 313
Priestly service, ii. 283, 284
Principalities, i. 514, 517
Printing, invention of, i. 149
Prisca, ii. 318, 319
Priscilla, ii. 318, 319
Private houses used for Christian worship, ii. 320
Proclus, his views of God, i. 92

Proconsul, Roman, ii. 201, 202; of Achaia, ii. 362
Prometheus, i. 18, ii. 39
Promise of the Gospel and a Saviour, i. 12, 18; traces of it among the heathen, i. 18; promise made to Abraham, i. 253
Promises made to Israel, ii. 9, 10
Proprætors, Roman, ii. 202
Proofs' of authenticity and genuineness of the Epistle to the Romans, i. 1; of genuineness and divine authority of the New Testament, i. 16; of the Old Testament, i. 194; of Jesus's Messiahship, i. 25; of His resurrection, i. 26; of the truth of Christianity, i. 28; of God's existence and character, i. 79, 84-86
Prophecy, meaning and use of the term, ii. 168, 169; gift of, ib.
Prophecies concerning Christ, i. 13
Prophets, i. 13, 219, ii. 168, 169, 350; of Antichrist, ii. 287
Propitiation, meaning and use of the term, i. 227, 229
Propitiatory sacrifice, ii. 7
Proportion of faith, ii. 168, 169
Proselytes, Jewish, i. 323, ii. 230
Prosper of Aquitaine, i. 500
Προστατης, ii. 316
Prostitution, i. 106, 107
Protagoras, his views of God, i. 99
Protestant doctrine concerning the church, ii. 313
Providence of God, ii. 149, 151
Province of Judæa, ii. 309
Provinces of the Roman Empire, ii. 201
Prudentius of Troyes, i. 500; a composer of hymns, ii. 274
Psalms of David, ii. 273; sung in the Synagogue and the Christian church, ib.
Psalter, ii. 273
Pseudo-Dionysius, i. 516
Publicani, ii. 208
Publicans, ii. 208, 209
Pulleyn, Robert, claimed the cup exclusively for the clergy, i. 327
Purgatory, history of the doctrine of, ii. 75
Purifying fire, doctrine of a, ii. 75
Purim, feast of, ii. 224
Puritans, their persecution, ii. 34
Purpose of God, i. 492, 493, ii. 20-22

Pydna, battle of, i. 56
Pyramid, the great, of Ghizeh, i. 92
Pythagoras, i. 97, 98, ii. 157; his views of God, i. 92, 96, 102; of nature, i. 99; his practice, i. 93
Pythagoræans, ii. 231
Pythian Apollo, ii. 105
Python, ii. 105.

Q.

Quæstors, Roman, ii. 202, 347
Quakers, their views of justification, i. 274
Quartus, ii. 346
Quesnel, i. 500

R.

Ra, the sun, i. 179
Rabanus Maurus, i. 500
Rabbi, title of, i. 172; their ordination, i. 173; office and duties, i. 174
Rabbies, i. 168, 172, 175; their character, i. 180, 181
Radbert Paschasius, his views of the Lord's Supper, i. 327
Rameses I., i. 96; the Great, ii. 34
Ransom, Christ's death a, i. 226
Rationalists, their views of Christ's death, i. 226; of the sacraments, i. 324; of miracles, ii. 291
Ratramnus, i. 500
Real presence, doctrine of, i. 327
Rebecca, ii. 19
Rechabites, ii. 259
Reconciliation, i. 290, 293
Redeemer, i. 225, 226, ii. 137-139
Redemption, meaning and use of the term, i. 224, 479; of the body, i. 479
Reformed Church, their view of Christ's death, i. 226
Refreshment, spiritual, ii. 274
Reign of death, i. 309; of sin, i. 317, 340; of grace, i. 317, 318; of believers, i. 310; of Christ on earth, ii. 220
Rejoicing, the duty of believers, ii. 274
Remission of sin, i. 228, ii. 189
Remnant, ii. 51, 52, 106, 107
Renovation of the earth, i. 476, ii. 122, 221

Repentance, i. 130-132; applied to God, ii. 142, 143
Reprobate, i. 113
Responsive singing in churches, ii. 274
Restoration of creation, i. 475, 476, ii. 121, 221; of Israel, ii. 121, 122, 132, 133, 136
Resurrection, i. 25, 30, ii. 121, 122; different kinds of, i. 272; first and second, ii. 220; of Christ, i. 25, &c., 269, 271, 272, 329, 370, 506, 507, ii. 74, 79; the proofs of it, i. 26-28; that of His members included in it, i. 28
Retribution on the Jews, ii. 114
Revelling, ii. 223
Revenues of Roman Empire, ii. 207
Riches, meaning and use of the term, i. 128, 129; of God's glory, ii. 45, 46; of the world, ii. 118; of the Gentiles, ib.
Right hand of God, i. 507, 508
Rights of Roman citizenship, i. 39, ii. 209
Righteousness, meaning and use of the term, i. 68, 73, 244, 247, 310, 350, ii. 56, 253, 254; of God, i. 69, 73, 217-219, 220, 221, 228, 440, 441, ii. 66, 68; of faith, i. 251, 256, ii. 57; of the law, ii. 70; of Christ, i. 310, 312, 313; our own, ii. 67; of life, ii. 253
Rioting, ii. 222, 223
Rochester, Lord, his remark in regard to the Bible, i. 17
Rock of offence, ii. 61
Roman Empire, i. 56, 116, ii. 200, 201; its revenues, ii. 207
Roman legislature, i. 365; laws, ii. 204; administration, ii. 204; government, ii. 200, 205; villas, ii. 327; establishments, ib.
Roman Catholic doctrine of the church, ii. 313
Romans, Epistle to the, proofs of its authenticity and genuineness, i. 1; its date, ib.; object, ib.; contents, i. 2; language, ib.; style, ib.; general character, ib.; why placed first in the Canon, i. 3; its peculiar excellence, ib.
Romans, ancient, religion of the, i. 102, 114; their character, i. 114, 116, 117, 121, 123; wars, i. 116; laws, i. 123, 365; customs in regard to meals, ii. 224, 240

Rome, i. 38, 45; its extent, i. 38; public buildings, *ib.*; citizenship, i. 39; ancient and modern population, i. 39, 59 ; influence, i. 45, 59 ; moral and social character, i. 59, 60 ; slaves, i. 59 ; early church, i. 38, 42, 44, 45, ii. 318, 330, 336 ; church of, ii. 129, 132, 307
Root, applied to Abraham, ii. 123–127 ; to Christ, ii. 276, 277
Rufus, ii. 328, 329
Rule in the church, ii. 173, 176
Rulers of the synagogue, ii. 175 ; of the church, ii. 176 ; in the state, ii. 200, 201, 204
Ruling elders, ii. 176, 177
Rupert, i. 327
Rutherford, Samuel, i. 511, 514

S.

Sabaoth, ii. 55, 56
Sabæism, i. 90, 94
Sabbath, its institution and observance, ii. 235
Sabbaths, Jewish, ii. 235
Sabellianism, ii. 14
Sabinus, i. 366
Sacraments, meaning and use of the term, i. 324 ; different views regarding them, i. 324, 325 ; number of them, i. 324
Sacrifice in the Lord's Supper, i. 326
Sacrifice of the Mass, i. 326, ii. 157
Sacrifices, their origin, object, and universality, ii. 154, 155, 157; their character, ii. 284 ; those under the law typical, ii. 283 ; spiritual, ii. 284 ; human, i. 117
Sacrilege, i. 176, 180
Sadducees, i. 163, 165
Saints, meaning and use of the term, i. 39, ii. 186, 309, 315, 330; how made, ii. 330
Salt, its use among the Romans, ii. 240 ; with the sacrifices, ii. 284
Salutations, ii. 332, 343 ; their significance in the epistle, ii. 317, 343 ; how classified, ii. 343 ; how accounted for, *ib.*
Salvation, meaning and use of the term, i. 62, ii. 81, 214, 216, 219 ; its means, i. 291 ; stages of development, ii. 215 ; constant approach, *ib.* ; completion, ii. 214,

216 ; importance, ii. 64 ; relation to reconciliation, i. 291 ; to justification, ii. 81
Samaritan Pentateuch, i. 151
Sanctification, not to be confounded with justification, i. 274
Sarah, i. 265, ii. 18, 19
Sardis, ii. 131
Satan, ii. 340–342
Saturn, i. 177
Saturnalia, ii. 239
Saul, meaning and use of the name, i. 3, 10
Savanarola, i. 274, ii. 313
Scandals, ii. 335, 336
Scandinavians, ancient, their views of God, i. 95
Scape-goat, i. 219, 232, 243, 271
Schleiermacher, his views of the sufferings of Christ, i. 226 ; of miracles, ii. 291
Schœnus, ii. 314
Schools, Jewish, i. 168–170, 174, ii. 95
Scipio, Publius Cornelius, ii. 298
Scriptures, meaning and use of the term, i. 14, 18 ; of the Old Testament, i. 14, ii. 350 ; of the New, i. 15 ; their preciousness, i. 16 ; teaching, i. 168, 172 ; written for patience and comfort, ii. 266; testimonies borne to their excellence, i. 16, 17
Scruples, ii. 227, 230
Seal, to, meaning and use of the term, ii. 303, 304
Seals, their use in common life, i. 250, 252, ii. 304 ; in a religious sense, i. 250–252
Second coming of Christ, i. 465, 475, ii. 121, 217, 219, 220 ; viewed as near, ii. 215, 216
Second imprisonment of Paul at Rome, ii. 298
Seducers, ii. 337
Sedulius, a composer of hymns, ii. 274
Seed of Abraham, i. 255, 259, ii. 16, 17, 98
Seeds, their constitution and development, protection and dissemination, i. 82
Seir, Mount, ii. 25
Sejanus, i. 120
Self-exaltation, ii. 190
Semi-arians, ii. 13
Semi-pelagians, i. 298, 500

Seneca, i. 98, 99; his view of God and the heathen deities, i. 92, 110; of the soul, i. 98; of natural depravity, i. 394, 397, 399; of man's fall, i. 476; of the destruction and renovation of the world, ii. 221
Seniores plebis, ii. 177
Separation from false teachers, ii. 334
Septuagint, the, i. 15, 18, 151, 195
Serpent, the, traditions regarding it, i. 18, ii. 221; old serpent, ii. 340–342
Serpents, i. 210
Servant, meaning and use of the term, i. 6, 7, 10, ii. 311
Servetus, ii. 14
Service, ii. 308; of God, ii. 9, 10
Set, an Egyptian deity, i. 179
Sethi I., i. 96
Seven, a symbolical number, ii. 103
Seven churches of Asia, ii. 129, 131
Seven wise men of Greece, i. 98
Seventh day of the week, ii. 236
Severity, ii. 130, 132; of God, ii. 130
Severus, ii. 193
Sexual worship, i. 96
Shaftesbury, Lord, his system of deism, i. 92
Shame, a holy and sinful, i. 60, 360
Shammai, i. 173, ii. 335
Shekinah, the, i. 102, ii. 8, 10
Shepherd, the, of Hermas, ii. 330
Sigæan inscription, the, ii. 345
Sign, i. 250–252; a species of miracles, ii. 290, 291
Signet, i. 252
Silas, ii. 344
Simon the Canaanite, ii. 293; the Cyrenian, ii. 328, 329
Simonides, ii. 344
Simple, the, ii. 337, 339
Sin, meaning and use of the term, i. 217, 294–296, 363, 380, 387, 421, 423, 441; dead, i. 380; its revival, i. 383; its indwelling, i. 396, 417; condemned in Christ, i. 421; the cause of death, i. 349, 363, 440
Sing, to, meaning of the term, ii. 273
Singing, a part of Christian worship, ii. 273; early modes of, ii. 274
Sion, ii. 137. *See* Zion.

Sister, ii. 311
Skins, used for writing, ii. 345
Slaves, their number at Rome, i. 59, 351; and in Italy, ii. 327; their treatment at Rome, i. 116, 120, 121, 351; in Sparta, i. 120, 351; in Athens and Corinth, i. 351; among the Israelites, i. 351, 352; how made, i. 351; how freed, *ib.*; how named, ii. 328; made Christians, ii. 326, 328; slaves of sin, i. 352, 356, 358; of righteousness, i. 357, 358
Slavery, i. 351
Sleep, the character of man's present natural condition, ii. 214
Slumber, spirit of, ii. 111, 112
Smyrna, i. 56; view of the church there in regard to Christ, ii. 13
Socinus, Lelius, and his nephew Faustus, ii. 14
Socinians, ii. 14; their views regarding Christ's person, ii. 14; His death, i. 226; justification, i. 274; original sin, i. 299; the sacraments, i. 324; baptism, i. 325; predestination, i. 501
Socrates, i. 98, 112; his views of God, i. 92; his practice, i. 93
Sodom, ii. 55, 56; the occasion of its destruction, ii. 56
Sold, as slaves, i. 390; to or under sin, i. 390–392
Soldiers, Roman, their pay, i. 363, 364; customs, ii. 214
Solon, i. 56, 58, 112, 115
Son of God, applications of the term, i. 19, 28; how belonging to Christ, i. 19, 23, 420, 496, 503, 504, ii. 269
Sons of God, applied to believers, i. 448, 464
Song of Solomon, ii. 48
Sopater, ii. 343
Sophronius, patriarch of Jerusalem, ii. 14
Sosipater, ii. 343
Soul, animal, i. 410
Souvan, an Egyptian deity, i. 179
Sovereignty of God, ii. 17, 29, 30, 36
Spain, ii. 297; its ancient names, ii. 297, 298; its history, ii. 298
Spanish Armada, ii. 34
Sparta, i. 56, 57, 120
Sphinx, the, i. 103
Spiced wine, ii. 223

Spine, wonderful construction of the, i. 81
Spinoza, ii. 291
Spirit, application of the term, i. 24, 413, 440, 441, 446; of bondage, i. 450, 451, 453, 454; of adoption, i. 452–454
Spirit-world, the, ii. 73, 74
Sponsors in baptism, i. 325
Spouse of Jehovah, ii. 18
St Thomas, Christians of, ii. 14
Stachys, ii. 326
Standard, ii. 277
Stephanas, ii. 321, 322
Stephen, bishop of Rome, i. 326
Stoics, i. 97, 98
Stoicism, i. 98
Strangers, custom of accompanying, ii. 298
Strataeus, bishop of Smyrna, ii. 277
Stumble, ii. 59, 60, 259
Stumbling-block, ii. 113, 114, 247, 248
Stumbling-stone, ii. 59, 60, 61
Style, used for writing, ii. 345
Style of Epistle to the Romans, i. 2; of the apostle, *ib.*
Subjection to magistrates, ii. 199, 206
Sublapsarianism, i. 500
Subscription of the epistle, ii. 354
Substitution, doctrine of, taught in the law, i. 219; acknowledged by the Jews, i. 210
Suffering with Christ, i. 459; for God and Christ, i. 511
Sufferings of the Messiah, i. 220, 229; of believers, i. 461; of early Christians, ii. 198
Sunday, i. 95, ii. 337
Supralapsarianism, i. 501
Supranaturalists, i. 516
Swedenborg, i. 516
Sword, i. 510, 511, ii. 205, 206
Sybil, Cumaean, prophecy of, i. 18
Symbol, i. 252
Symmachus, his translation of the Old Testament into Greek, i. 151, 195
Sympathy, the duty of, ii. 189
Synagogues, i. 151; service of, i. 150, 151, ii. 176; minister of, ii. 171; ruler of, *ib.*
Synod of Carthage, i. 298; of Constance, i. 327; of Ephesus, i. 500,
ii. 335; of Valencia, i. 500; of Mayence, *ib.*; of Savonieres, *ib.*; of Dort, i. 501; of Laodicea, i. 516; of Frankfort, ii. 14

T.

Table, ii. 113, 114
Tablets, used for writing, ii. 345
Talith, i. 187
Talmud, i. 18, 65, 166; its stories, i. 180
Tammuz, i. 106, 178, ii. 238
Taoer, an Egyptian deity, i. 179
Targums, i. 13, 195
Tarshish, ii. 297, 298
Tarsus, i. 10
Tatian, i. 18
Taxes, ii. 207, 208; different kinds of, ii. 209
Tax-gatherers, ii. 209
Te Deum, author of the, ii. 274
Teacher, ii. 169, 171, 172
Teaching, gift of, ii. 169, 171, 172; right of, ii. 172
Temple, ii. 322; of Diana, i. 103; of Jerusalem, ii. 53, 131
Temples, of Greece and Egypt, i. 103; first built by Egyptians, *ib.*
Temple-furniture, ii. 53
Ten persecutions, the, i. 510
Ten tribes, the, ii. 48, 49, 51; various opinions regarding them, ii. 99
Tephillim, i. 189
Territorial system, the, ii. 314
Tertius, ii. 344
Tertullian, his views regarding the human soul, i. 298; original sin, *ib.*; infant baptism, i. 325; the Lord's Supper, i. 326; the millennium, i. 465; predestination, i. 500; the death of Christ, ii. 251; His descent into Hades, ii. 75; an intermediate state, *ib.*; the church, ii. 313, 321; the power of the keys, *ib.*; his defence of the Christians, ii. 198
Testimonies borne to the Scriptures, i. 16
Thales, i. 98; his views of God, i. 92
Thammuz. *See* Tammuz.
Thankfulness, i. 43
Thanksgiving at meals, Jewish and Christian forms of, ii. 240
Themistocles, i. 118

Theodore of Mopsuestia, i. 283, 500, ii. 14, 291
Theodoret, i. 283; his views of the Lord's Supper, i. 326; of predestination, i. 500; of the worship of angels, i. 516
Theodosius the Younger, i. 366
Theodotion, his translation of the Old Testament into Greek, i. 151, 195
Theodotus, i. 23
Theophilus, bishop of Antioch, his views of man, i. 298
Theophilus, third bishop of Cæsarea, ii. 277
Therapeutæ, i. 165
Thomas the Apostle, ii. 293
Thomasius, ii. 314
Thor, i. 18
Thoth, an Egyptian deity, i. 178
Thothmes I., probably the Pharaoh from whom Moses fled, ii. 32
Thothmes II., perhaps the Pharaoh of the Exodus, ii. 32, 34
Thothmes III., probably the Pharaoh of the Exodus, ii. 34
Thousand years' period, ii. 221
Time, of Christ's appearing and death, i. 230, 232, 284; character of the present, ii. 213-217; to be understood by believers, ii. 213
Timotheus, ii. 342
Tithes, ii. 208; for the poor, ii. 302
Titus, ii. 51, 53
Tombs, i. 210
Tongues, gift of, ii. 169
Tradition, i. 15; Jewish, i. 16, 18, 166; Christian, i. 16
Traducianism, i. 297
Translations, of the Old Testament, i. 15; of the New, i. 16; of the whole Bible, ib.
Transubstantiation, ii. 157; first use of the term, i. 327; progressive development of the doctrine, i. 326, 327; its establishment in the Romish Church, i. 327
Trap, ii. 113, 114
Treasure, i. 133
Trebonius, i. 366
Tribades, i. 111
Tribes of Israel, ii. 98, 99
Tribulation, meaning and use of the term, i. 143, 145, 509, 510, ii. 185; distinguished from anguish, i. 145; 278; awaits believers, i. 509

Tribunal, ii. 244, 245; different kinds of, among the Romans, ii. 245
Tribute, ii. 207
Tried Christians, ii. 326, 327
Trinity of persons in the Godhead, i. 29
Troglodytes, ii. 25
Truth, meaning and use of the term, i. 76, 78, 141. 172
Tryphena and Tryphosa, ii. 327, 328
Tuscans, ancient, their view of the creation, ii. 221
Twelve Tables, laws of, ii. 220. See Laws.
Twiss. Dr, his views of the millennium, ii. 220; of Christ's death, ii. 251
Two natures of a believer, i. 392-410
Two principles, worship of, i. 91, 95, in man, i. 394, 410
Two Resurrections, the, ii. 220
Two souls in man, i. 394
Two swords, the, ii. 313
Types under the law, i. 219
Typhon, i. 95, 179

U.

Ulphilas, the Apostle of the Goths, i. 33
Ulysses, i. 120
Unbelief, ii. 89, 144
Uncircumcision, i. 184, 189
Unclean meats, ii. 248, 249
Uncleanness, i. 104; promoted by ancient idolatry, i. 105, 106
Ungodliness, meaning of the term, i. 76, 77
Union in prayer, ii. 307
Unity of God, i. 237
Universe, proofs of its being under a Divine Ruler, i. 85
Universal church, ii. 313; priesthood, ib.
Universalism, i. 500, 501
Unknown God, i. 57, 92, 110
Unnatural lust, i. 111, 112, 114
Unrighteousness, i. 76, 77
Upper room at Jerusalem, ii. 320
Urban IV., i. 327
Urbane, ii. 325

V.

Valentinus, i. 18, ii. 13, 335
Valentinians, i. 326

Value of the soul, ii. 64
Vengeance, ii. 195
Venus, worship of, i. 106, 107
Verses, when first used in the Scriptures, i. 19; ii. 267
Vessels of wrath, ii. 43, 44; of mercy, ii. 45, 46
Victor, bishop of Rome, ii. 335
Victoria, Queen, her remark in regard to the Bible, i. 17
Vine, its cultivation, ii. 223; its juice before fermentation, *ib.*
Vinegar used as a beverage, ii. 258
Vishnu, i. 94
Voltaire, i. 476

W.

Waddington, Dean, his views of ministerial orders, ii. 177
Wages, i. 363, 364
Waiting of the creation, i. 464, 465; of believers, i. 478
Waldenses, i. 510, 512; opposed to the doctrine of purgatory, ii. 75
Walk of a believer, i. 411, 414, ii. 221
Wantonness, ii. 220
Warfare, inward, i. 403
Watches of the night, ii. 220
Water as a beverage, ii. 258
Waterclocks, ii. 220
Weak brethren, ii. 227, 229, 330; how to be treated, ii. 228, 229
Wedlock, sanctified, ii. 319, 330
Weeks, first trace of, ii. 237, 296
Weekly division of time, ii. 235, 237 296
Well-doing. i. 137
Wessel, John, i. 274; his views of Christ's death, i. 226; of the sacraments, i. 324; of the Lord's Supper, i. 327; of the church and the priesthood, ii. 313
Wild olive-tree, ii. 124, 125, 133, 134
Will of God, i. 48, ii. 309
Williams, John, ii. 292
Willibrod, i. 33
Wine, different kinds of, ii. 223; its preparation, preservation, and use, *ib.*; fermented and unfermented, *ib.*; when drunk by the Romans and others, ii. 224, 258; lawful or unlawful in its use, ii. 258
Wisdom, ii. 338; of God, ii. 352
Wise, i. 55

Wise men, i. 97
Witness of the Spirit, i. 455, 456
Women, their relation to Christ and the Gospel, ii. 312, 318, 322, 323, 328; in the East, ii. 311
Wonders, a species of miracles, ii. 290-291
Word, the, or Logos, i. 29
Word of God. *See* Scriptures and Bible.
Works, our own, no ground of justification, i. 247
Works of the law, ii. 59
Workfellows, ii. 343
World, meaning and use of the term, i. 256, ii. 158; world to come, i. 472, 473
Worship, i. 46; Romish distinction in regard to it, i. 48; worship of angels, i. 516
Wrath, meaning of the term, i. 74, 77, 133, 258, ii. 205; of God, i. 74, 77, 133, 289, ii. 42; how manifested, i. 74; distinguished from indignation, i. 142, 143
Wretched, i. 405
Writing, its origin and history, ii. 344, 345
Writings, name given to the sacred books, i. 14, 18, ii. 266, 267
Wycliffe, John, his views of Christ's death, i. 226; of the sacraments, i. 324; of the Lord's Supper, i. 327; of Antichrist and the end of the world, i. 465; of predestination, i. 500; of the church and the priesthood, ii. 313; opposed to the doctrine of purgatory, ii. 75

X.

Xenocrates, his views of God, i. 99
Xenophanes, his views of God, i. 92
Xenophon, his views of God, i. 92, 99; his practice, i. 93; his experience, i. 394

Y.

Years, how regarded and reckoned, ii. 296; two kinds of, among the Jews, *ib.*
Yezidis, or devil-worshippers, ii. 238
Yule, ii. 239

Z.

Zacchæus, ii. 277
Zanchius, his views of Christ's death, ii. 251
Zeal, religious, ii. 65, 66
Zeuxis, ii. 183
Zinzendorf, his views of Christ's death, i. 226

Zion, Mount, ii. 61, 62, 137, 138, 289
Zuinglius, his views of the fall, i. 299; of the sacraments, i. 324; of baptism, i. 325, 326; of the Lord's Supper, i. 327; of election, i. 501; of church discipline, ii. 314
Zythos, ii. 223

THE END.

www.ingramcontent.com/pod-product-compliance
Lightning Source LLC
Chambersburg PA
CBHW032034220426
43664CB00006B/470